Neuropsychology of Alcoholism

NEUROPSYCHOLOGY OF ALCOHOLISM

Implications for Diagnosis and Treatment

Edited by

OSCAR A. PARSONS
University of Oklahoma Health Sciences Center

NELSON BUTTERS
San Diego Veterans Administration Medical Center
University of California at San Diego School of Medicine

PETER E. NATHAN
Rutgers—The State University of New Jersey

THE GUILFORD PRESS
New York London

A Division of Guilford Publications, Inc.
200 Park Avenue South, New York, N.Y. 10003

Printed in the United States of America

Last digit is print number: 9 8 7 6 5 4 3 2 1

LIBRARY OF CONGRESS CATALOGING-IN-PUBLICATION DATA

Neuropsychology of alcoholism.

Consists mainly of updated and revised versions of papers presented at a conference, held in Boston in 1984, as well as additional contributions.

Includes bibliographies and index.

1. Alcoholism—Congresses. 2. Neuropsychology—Congresses. 3. Alcohol—Physiological effect—Congresses. 4. Physiology, Pathological—Congresses. I. Parsons, Oscar A. II. Butters, Nelson. III. Nathan, Peter E. [DNLM: 1. Alcoholism—diagnosis—congresses. 2. Alcoholism—therapy—congresses. 3. Neuropsychology—congresses. WM 274 N4945]

RC565.N387 1987 616.86′1 86-29583

ISBN 0-89862-696-X

CONTRIBUTORS

Henri Begleiter, MD, PhD, Department of Psychiatry, State University of New York, Health Science Center at Brooklyn, Brooklyn, New York.

Mats Berglund, MD, Department of Psychiatry I, University Hospital, Lund, Sweden.

Hans Bergman, PhD, Department of Clinical Alcohol and Drug Research, Karolinska Institute, Karolinska Hospital, Stockholm, Sweden.

Nelson Butters, PhD, Psychology Service, San Diego Veterans Administration Medical Center, San Diego, California; Department of Psychiatry, University of California at San Diego School of Medicine, La Jolla, California.

Laird S. Cermak, PhD, Psychology Research, Boston Veterans Administration Medical Center, Boston, Massachusetts; Neurology Department, Boston University School of Medicine, Boston, Massachusetts.

Dennis M. Donovan, PhD, Alcohol and Drug Dependence Treatment Programs, Veterans Administration Medical Center, Seattle, Washington; Department of Psychiatry and Behavioral Sciences, University of Washington School of Medicine, Seattle, Washington.

Mark S. Goldman, PhD, Department of Psychology, University of South Florida, Tampa, Florida. (Formerly, Department of Psychology, Wayne State University, Detroit, Michigan.)

Gerald Goldstein, PhD, Neuropsychology Research Program, Veterans Administration Medical Center, Pittsburgh, Pennsylvania; Departments of Psychiatry and Psychology, University of Pittsburgh, Pittsburgh, Pennsylvania.

Eric Granholm, BS, Psychology Service, San Diego Veterans Administration Medical Center, San Diego, California; Department of Psychiatry, University of California at San Diego School of Medicine, La Jolla, California.

Daniel R. Kivlahan, PhD, Alcohol and Drug Dependence Treatment Programs, Veterans Administration Medical Center, Seattle, Washington; Department of Psychiatry and Behavioral Sciences, University of Washington School of Medicine, Seattle, Washington.

Barbara S. McCrady, PhD, Rutgers Center of Alcohol Studies, Rutgers—The State University of New Jersey, Piscataway, New Jersey.

Nancy K. Mello, PhD, Alcohol and Drug Abuse Research Center, Harvard Medical School–McLean Hospital, Belmont, Massachusetts.

Peter E. Nathan, PhD, Rutgers Center of Alcohol Studies, Rutgers—The State University of New Jersey, Piscataway, New Jersey; Graduate School of

Applied and Professional Psychology, Rutgers—The State University of New Jersey, New Brunswick, New Jersey.

Marlene Oscar-Berman, PhD, Departments of Psychiatry and Neurology, Boston University School of Medicine, Boston, Massachusetts; Aphasia Research Center, Veterans Administration Medical Center, Boston, Massachusetts.

Oscar A. Parsons, PhD, Oklahoma Center for Alcohol and Drug-Related Studies, Department of Psychiatry and Behavioral Sciences, University of Oklahoma Health Sciences Center, Oklahoma City, Oklahoma.

Bernice Porjesz, PhD, Department of Psychiatry, State University of New York, Health Science Center at Brooklyn, Brooklyn, New York.

Jarl Risberg, PhD, Department of Psychiatry I, University Hospital, Lund, Sweden.

Maria A. Ron, MPhil, PhD, MRCPsych, Consultant Psychiatrist, The National Hospitals for Nervous Diseases, London, England.

Terry G. Shaw, PhD, Private Practice, McAlester, Oklahoma. (Formerly, Cerebrovascular Research Program, Veterans Administration Medical Center, Houston, Texas; Baylor Stroke Center, Baylor College of Medicine, Houston, Texas.)

R. Dale Walker, MD, Alcohol and Drug Dependence Treatment Programs, Veterans Administration Medical Center, Seattle, Washington; Department of Psychiatry and Behavioral Sciences, University of Washington School of Medicine, Seattle, Washington.

D. Adrian Wilkinson, PhD, Addiction Research Foundation, Toronto, Ontario, Canada; Hjellestad Clinic, Hjellestad, Norway; Institute of Psychology, University of Bergen, Bergen, Norway.

Harold L. Williams, PhD, Oklahoma Center for Alcohol and Drug-Related Studies, Department of Psychiatry and Behavioral Sciences, University of Oklahoma Health Sciences Center, Oklahoma City, Oklahoma.

Barbara Wilson, PhD, Department of Psychology, Charing Cross Hospital, London, England. (Formerly, Department of Clinical Psychology, Rivermead Rehabilitation Centre, Oxford, England.)

PREFACE

This book, as well as the conference that gave birth to it, are products of the fertile mind of Dr. Nathan Rosenberg. Nathan Rosenberg, a psychologist, has been an integral part of the Extramural Research Branch of the National Institute on Alcohol Abuse and Alcoholism (NIAAA) since the NIAAA's founding in the early 1970s. It was Dr. Rosenberg who had the idea, a few years ago, to bring together a diverse group of scientists and clinicians—including neuropsychologists, neurophysiologists, clinical psychologists, behavioral pharmacologists, and psychiatrists—to review and evaluate recent findings on neuropsychological deficits in alcoholics, in order to determine the implications (if any) of these findings for the improved diagnosis and treatment of alcoholism. The conference, subsequently funded by the NIAAA and held in Boston in May 1984, brought together a distinguished international group of scientists and clinicians for 3 stimulating and exciting days of review, discussion, and debate.

The intellectual fervor of that meeting was so memorable that the three editors of this volume, who joined Nathan Rosenberg as organizers of that meeting, decided to try to put together a book that would not only recreate the excitement and promise of the Boston meeting, but also present the latest research findings. Because the conference format did not permit as full an exploration of some key issues as would a book, other contributors have been added to the group of conference participants to create this volume.

The book begins, as did the meeting, with a detailed summary of current research findings on central nervous system (CNS) deficits associated with chronic alcoholism. Both the meeting and the volume then proceed to a searching consideration of the significance of the current findings on CNS deficits for possible improvements in both the reliability and utility of alcoholism diagnoses and the efficacy of treatment for alcoholism.

For his vision in serving as the moving force behind the conference and this book, as well as for his long and valued service to colleagues in alcoholism research, the editors of this book fondly dedicate it to Nathan Rosenberg.

Peter E. Nathan

CONTENTS

Neuropsychology of Alcoholism

Introduction

OSCAR A. PARSONS

Alcoholism and alcohol abuse constitute a major problem for Western civilization. The medical, social, economic, legal, interpersonal, marital, and familial consequences of protracted alcohol ingestion have been detailed in countless scientific and lay publications. While a number of genetic, biological, psychological, and sociocultural variables have been found to be relevant to the disorder, a definitive etiology, diagnosis, and treatment have yet to be established.

In the last several decades, two pertinent lines of research have had vigorous development: the biomedical measurements of brain structure and function (e.g., computerized tomography [CT], evoked potentials, and cerebral blood flow), and the neuropsychological (cognitive, perceptual, and perceptual–motor) changes accompanying brain alterations. With the discovery that alcoholics manifest altered brain structures and functions, and that they also have impaired neuropsychological functioning similar to that of other brain-damaged persons, the stage was set for an intensive examination of the contributions that the two research areas and their interrelationships could make to our scientific and clinical understanding of alcoholism.

In this volume on the implications of neuropsychological deficits for diagnosis and treatment of alcoholics, our contributors summarize the current state of knowledge; critically evaluate the methods; identify the relevant variables that should be considered in conducting this type of research; consider the implications for diagnosis, recovery, and treatment; and suggest future research directions. The book is divided into four sections. Each of the first three sections has a similar organization: The initial chapters are reports of research by individuals who have received international recognition for their work on alcoholism. These are followed by discussions, also written by internationally recognized individuals, who not only critically evaluate the previous presentations but, as requested by the editors, also contribute data from their own research.

Section I is titled "Changes in Brain Structure and Function in Alco-

Oscar A. Parsons. Oklahoma Center for Alcohol and Drug-Related Studies, Department of Psychiatry and Behavioral Sciences, University of Oklahoma Health Sciences Center, Oklahoma City, Oklahoma.

holics." The focus is upon the biomedical methods of measurement and their relationship to neuropsychological functioning. In the first chapter of this section, Ron, of the National Hospitals for Nervous Diseases in London, presents an overview of the neuropathological findings in alcoholics. She then describes the abnormalities found in British alcoholics and their relationship to neuropsychological functioning as measured by a variety of cognitive, perceptual, and perceptual–motor tests. Ron's data suggest that CT density measurements give rise to higher relationships with neuropsychological test performance than the more traditional clinical measurements of ventricular and sulcal widening.

Bergman, of the Karolinska Institute, follows with a report of a study from the Stockholm KARTAD Project. This massive project is one of the best-designed and most comprehensive series of studies of CT abnormalities and performance on neuropsychological tests in alcoholics and nonalcoholics that has been initiated. Bergman arrives at a number of important conclusions: for example, that there are at least two types of morphological changes in the brains of alcoholics, accompanied by different neuropsychological deficits; and that a genetically based threshold model of vulnerability to alcoholism effects is the preferred working model.

In Chapter 3, Porjesz and Begleiter, of the Downstate Medical Center, Brooklyn, New York, cover the evoked brain potential changes in sober chronic alcoholics. Both brain stem potentials and event-related potentials (the P300 wave) have been shown to be altered in alcoholics. The former recover with abstinence, but the P300 wave does not. The fact that these experimenters have found that preadolescent sons of alcoholics also exhibit the altered P300 wave suggests the presence of a possible biological marker for alcoholism.

Cerebral blood flow studies in alcoholics are summarized by Risberg and Berglund in Chapter 4, with special emphasis on the pioneering studies from their laboratory in Lund, Sweden. Among their interesting findings, they report that alcoholics who continue to drink after the age of 45 to 50 are likely to have progressively lower blood flow rates, particularly in the frontal region. They also find that the right-hemisphere flow may be more disturbed than that of the left hemisphere—an asymmetry that needs further study.

The first discussant in Section I, Wilkinson, of the Toronto Addiction Research Foundation, provides a penetrating critique and integrative analysis of the relationships reported by Ron and Bergman. Reviewing the findings from his own research, Wilkinson agrees with Ron and Bergman's conclusions that there are two major kinds of brain impairment in alcoholics. He argues that recent refined methods of CT abnormality measurement and neuropsychological test performance provide evidence for convergent validity—that is, that both reflect a common underlying neuropathological process in alcoholic but nonamnesic patients.

Williams, of the Oklahoma Center for Alcohol and Drug-Related Studies, evaluates the studies of evoked brain potentials in alcoholics and suggests important problem areas to be resolved. In addition to methodological suggestions for improving both the brain stem and event-related potential recordings and their interpretation, Williams calls for greater efforts to relate the abnormalities in these brain potentials to information processing and other cognitive behaviors. He is also concerned that lowered motivation or levels of arousal have not been considered as possible contributing factors in the altered brain potentials. Finally, he recommends that experimental designs in this area pay particular attention to genetic–environmental interactions as they may relate to brain potentials.

The final contribution to this section, by Shaw, currently in private practice and formerly of the Houston Veterans Administration (VA) Medical Center and Baylor College of Medicine, first considers the biomedical approaches to alcoholics' brain changes in the context of the aging brain and then specifically focuses on measurement of cerebral blood flow. Shaw sees the spatial and temporal problems in the measurement of cerebral blood flow in relation to neuropsychological test performance as limitations that must be surmounted if the promise of the blood flow studies is to be realized. One of the more interesting findings from his own research is that social drinking is related to reduced cerebral blood flow; that is, the typical number of drinks per month is significantly correlated (negatively) with resting levels of hemisphere blood flow. These findings suggest that cerebral blood flow studies in alcoholics should continue to be fruitful.

Section II is titled "Neuropsychological Consequences of Alcohol Abuse." In the first chapter of this section, I list the major questions that have been addressed in neuropsychological research on alcoholics and indicate the status of answers to these questions. Among the "answers" reported are the following: The presence of neuropsychological deficits in alcoholics has been repeatedly confirmed in various countries; alcoholics subjectively see themselves as impaired; measures of alcohol consumption are inconsistently related to neuropsychological deficits but are related to their subjective impairment; certain subtypes of alcoholics show more deficits than others; and a generalized/diffuse model of brain impairment seems to account for most of the data.

In Chapter 9, Butters, of the San Diego VA Medical Center and the University of California at San Diego School of Medicine, and his colleague Granholm suggest that the Korsakoff patient suffers from the impact of two factors: long-term alcoholism and malnutrition. Furthermore, they hypothesize that the memory disturbances in Korsakoff's syndrome may be due to neuronal loss in basal forebrain structures rather than to diencephalic changes. Butters and Granholm's summary of the series of experiments that Butters and his colleagues have conducted over the years on the Korsakoff disorder, together with his more recent comparisons of the neuropsychological functioning of these patients and long-term alcoholics, Alzheimer's disease, and Huntington's patients, is a fascinating scientific exercise.

Cermak, of the Boston VA Medical Center and Boston University School of Medicine, reviews models of memory loss in Korsakoff's syndrome in Chapter 10. He concludes that the popular hypothesis of a continuum of deficits from normal social drinking through alcoholism to Korsakoff's syndrome cannot be supported; rather, the data support the premature-aging hypothesis of alcoholism's effects. Cermak's attention to theoretical measures that have experimental implications, and his design of specific experiments that support one of several alternative theories, contribute to both theoretical and empirical knowledge in this area.

The first of the discussants in this section, Goldstein, of the Pittsburgh VA Medical Center and the University of Pittsburgh, emphasizes that the time has arrived to focus upon the etiological factors in the neuropsychological and biomedical consequences of alcoholism. Factors such as malnutrition, head trauma, systemic illness, liver disease, and possible interaction with other forms of psychopathology must be thoroughly explored. He also notes that, while the premature-aging and continuity models have not fared well scientifically, the preferred generalized/diffuse model also needs specification.

Mello, of Harvard Medical School–McLean Hospital, calls attention to an important but neglected variable in measuring deficits on neuropsychological tests: the subjects' attitude and motivation. More specifically, she emphasizes the critical role of attention and task-specific reinforcement on both behavioral measures and metabolic responses. Thus, interpretations of alcoholics' biobehavioral impairment should consider the possibility of altered motivation as a contributing factor.

Using the list in Chapter 8 of questions concerning neuropsychological deficits, Oscar-Berman, of the Boston VA Medical Center and Boston University School of Medicine, provides an illuminating comparison of the contributions of Chapters 8, 9, and 10. She also cites much of her own recent work of relevance to these areas. Interestingly, she reports the only study, to my knowledge, in which a task specific reward research (using money as an incentive) was used to motivate sober alcoholics and Korsakoff patients. This study shows that Korsakoff and alcoholic patients are less responsive to monetary incentives than controls; if confirmed, this finding indicates that the concerns about alcoholics' motivation expressed by Mello and Williams are well founded. She also proposes the very interesting hypothesis that there is a subgroup of alcoholics whose right hemispheres have developed slowly, leaving them with behavioral symptoms of hyperkinesis, minimal brain damage, and/or learning disabilities.

Section III is titled "Recovery and Remediation of Neuropsychological Functions." In the first chapter of this section, I discuss four major issues in this area of research. The conclusions reached are as follows: Recovery of neuropsychological functions in sober alcoholics does occur, but is variable (some functions appear to recover in weeks or months, while others may take several years); neuropsychological test performance predicts therapists' ratings of alcoholics' cognitive behavior and improvement during therapy; alcoholics who resume drinking are more impaired at a retesting 1 year later than those who remain sober; and cognitive retraining of alcoholics for their deficits may be a fruitful area for future research.

In Chapter 15, Goldman, of the University of South Florida (formerly of Wayne State University), reports an innovative series of studies on the role of time and practice in recovery of alcoholics' functions. As regards time, Goldman concludes that verbal abilities recover rapidly but that visual–spatial abilities, abstraction and problem solving, and short-term memory may show persisting impairment, especially in patients over 40. Goldman's review of animal experiments in recovery of function, together with his human studies of the role of practice in recovery, leads him to conclude that practice may play a critically facilitating role in alcoholics' regaining of cognitive competence, at least as measured by neuropsychological tests.

The chapter by Wilson, of Charing Cross Hospital, London (formerly of the Rivermead Rehabilitation Centre, Oxford), describes techniques for identifying and remediating everyday problems in memory-impaired patients. One of the common complaints of alcoholics is impaired memory. While many of the patients Wilson has studied are more impaired than the typical alcoholic patient, her methods and techniques serve as a paradigm for the burgeoning work in cognitive retraining. Her exemplification and discussion of individual and group methods for memory training are of particular interest to both clinicians and researchers.

The first discussion chapter in this section is by Donovan, Walker, and Kivlahan, of the Seattle VA Medical Center and the University of Washington School of Medicine. These authors integrate their own studies on the relationship of neuropsychological measures to treatment outcome with the findings reported in the earlier chapters of Section III. They conclude that while neuropsychological impairment influences the rehabilitative process and outcome, the neuropsychological measures must be coupled with other pertinent variables in order to be effective in a predictive sense. They advocate and demonstrate the use of a multiple-domain analysis approach that leads to the identification of clusters of alcoholics, each defined by a different pattern on a broad array of variables. Their message is clear: To predict treatment outcome and recovery, neuropsychological measures must be embedded in a matrix of other treatment-related variables.

In his second contribution to this volume, Goldstein places the incipient efforts at cognitive retraining described in Chapters 14, 15, and 16 on recovery in perspective with other approaches to treatment of alcoholics. He believes that Goldman's emphasis on practice may be useful with some patients, while strategy training may be more productive with others. Goldstein, like Mello, Oscar-Berman, and Williams, also raises the issue of altered motivation of alcoholics. He points out that some alcoholics may have limited arousal levels associated with brain dysfunction. Such alcoholics are likely to need special attention in the cognitive retraining work. Goldstein suggests that neuropsychologists could benefit from greater interdisciplinary contacts—indeed, the complexity of the disease almost demands it. Finally he recommends that alcoholic patients be carefully examined to determine the degree of cognitive deficit, psychopathology, and concurrent medical problems; the patients could then be assigned to the most appropriate treatment program.

The final section is titled "Implications for Treatment and Future Directions." The implications of neuropsychological research for the clinician are considered in a perceptive chapter by McCrady of Rutgers University. After reviewing the salient features of the neuropsychological deficits described in earlier chapters and the structure of most alcoholic treatment programs, she makes a series of recommendations. These include programmatic changes, such as making a thorough screening of alcoholics (especially patients over 40 years of age) to evaluate the status of their cognitive functioning, and having a "preprogram" program for the more impaired alcoholics whose recovery of cognitive functions after detoxification has been slow. For facilitating individual treatment of patients, McCrady lists a number of recovery-related skills that, in her clinical experience, pose difficulties for the neuropsychologically impaired patient. Skills training then could become a focus for treatment, with each individual being trained to minimally acceptable levels. Finally, ethical and treatment research issues attendant on the presence of neuropsychological deficits are considered.

In the final chapter, Butters, Nathan, and I present our suggestions as to the directions that research on the neuropsychology of alcoholism will take in the next decade. Improved biomedical techniques such as magnetic resonance imaging and the positron emission tomography scan will give researchers improved methods for detecting subtle structural and metabolic changes in the brains of alcoholics. The relationship between these changes and measures of neuropsychological functioning in alcoholics will be a major research area. The continued investigation of Korsakoff's syndrome should provide new insights into the ongoing debate about the continuum of alcohol effects, as well as contribute to our basic understanding of brain–behavior relationships. Detailed investigations of the neuropsychological characteristics of subtypes of alcoholics clearly will be a dominant research area. Two subtypes in particular will receive attention: The first is characterized by type of brain changes (i.e., subcortical vs. cortical) and the accompanying patterns of neuropsychological deficits, and the second by presence or absence of family history of alcoholism. The effects of altered motivational states in alcoholics, whether of organic or functional origin, is a research area that urgently needs exploration. The use of neuropsychological deficits in the diagnosis of alcoholism, especially to distinguish alcohol abuse from alcohol dependence, may help resolve what is currently a thorny diagnostic problem. Continued research on the recovery process in sober alcoholics will be a major emphasis. The relationship between subjective reports of cognitive functioning by recovering alcoholics and objective measurement of these functions is a critically important issue. Finally, in view of the fact that the characteristics of treatment programs are generally unrelated to outcome of treatment, a concerted effort is needed on identifying those processes that contribute to the "natural healing process" in alcoholism. The conditions under which these processes are affected by the deficits in the neuropsychological functioning of alcoholics remain to be explored.

SECTION ONE

CHANGES IN BRAIN STRUCTURE AND FUNCTION IN ALCOHOLICS

1

The Brain of Alcoholics: An Overview

MARIA A. RON

Introduction

There is no doubt that alcohol abuse can cause brain damage. However, few studies have looked at the prevalence of organic psychosyndromes in the alcoholic population. Horvath (1975) claimed that in an Australian university center for the treatment of alcoholism, 100 out of 1100 patients seen in the course of 5 years had chronic organic syndromes as defined by progressive failure of memory, loss of intellectual ability, and personality deterioration. Out of these 100 patients, only 20 presented the typical picture of the Wernicke–Korsakoff psychosis; the rest presented with a combination of apathy, depression, lack of motivation, and, in some cases, neurological deficits such as dysphasia and dyspraxia. Lesser degrees of brain damage received little attention, and it was commonly believed that most alcoholics, once the period of detoxification was over, escaped without detectable impairment.

In recent years the advent of computerized tomography (CT) has challenged this belief, and a great deal of attention has been focused on chronic alcoholics with less severe deficits but in whom brain damage may nevertheless play an important role in potentiating and perpetuating addiction. The aim of this chapter is to review the salient research findings in this group of subjects and to discuss their implications.

Neuropathological Lesions in Chronic Alcoholics

Courville (1955) described in his well-known monograph the neuropathological changes in chronic alcoholics who did not exhibit the clinical picture of the Wernicke–Korsakoff syndrome. The main lesions were widespread cortical atrophy preferentially affecting the frontal lobes, together with ventricular enlargement and meningeal thickening. Microscopically, neuronal loss, disruption of cortical laminae, pigmentary degeneration, and glial

Maria A. Ron. Consultant Psychiatrist, The National Hospitals for Nervous Diseases, London, England.

proliferation were the main findings. He also stated that alcoholism was the commonest cause of brain atrophy in the fifth and sixth decades of life, and believed that these lesions were due to the direct effect of alcohol rather than to thiamine deficiency. Similar lesions were reported by others at the time (Lynch, 1960; Mancall, 1961; Neuberger, 1957), but the topic was soon forgotten; the Wernicke–Korsakoff syndrome was receiving increasing attention.

There is little doubt that the neuropathological changes described by Courville coexist in some cases with the lesions surrounding the third and fourth ventricles and aqueduct found in the Wernicke–Korsakoff syndrome. Werner (1934) found them together in three out of seven alcoholics, and more recently Victor, Adams, and Collins (1971) described cortical atrophy and ventricular enlargement in a quarter of their Wernicke–Korsakoff patients. Furthermore, Cravioto, Korein, and Silverman (1961) and Harper (1979) found a high prevalence of lesions of the Wernicke–Korsakoff type in unselected postmortems (1.7% in both series), often in subjects who had not experienced the typical amnesic syndrome.

The mechanism of production of these lesions is uncertain. Alcohol can cause neuronal death in experimental animals (Riley & Walker, 1978), and it seems likely that similar mechanisms operate in humans. In a given patient, other factors—dietary deficiencies, metabolic changes that take place during acute intoxication and withdrawal, head injury, and liver disease—are also likely to play a part.

Radiological Findings in Chronic Alcoholics

Studies using pneumoencephalography demonstrated long ago the presence of enlarged ventricles and widened sulci in chronic alcoholics in whom brain damage was clinically suspected. The limitations of this technique precluded its use in subjects in whom impairment was less evident. Nevertheless, the studies of Tumarkin, Wilson, and Snyder (1955) and Brewer and Perrett (1971) suggested that these abnormalities might be present in young alcoholics in whom other causes of brain damage had been excluded.

Studies using CT have been reported in the last few years (Bergman, Borg, Hindmarsh, Idestrom, & Mutzell, 1980; Cala, Jones, Wiley, & Mastaglia, 1980; Ishii, 1983; Wilkinson & Carlen, 1980), and for the first time it has been possible to examine carefully selected populations and normal controls. The London Institute of Psychiatry study (Ron, 1983; Ron, Acker, Shaw, & Lishman, 1982) is one of these, and much of what follows is based on its findings.

A total of 100 male alcoholics admitted to the Alcoholic Unit at the Bexley Hospital in greater London were included in the study. The mean age of the patients was 43, and they had been abstinent for at least 2 weeks when scanned. Fifty age-matched volunteers who were either lifelong abstainers or light, sporadic drinkers were used for comparison.

The methods used to quantify CT scan abnormalities have been described elsewhere (Ron *et al.*, 1982). Suffice it to say that the ventricle–brain ratio (VBR) was used as an index of ventricular size and that the width of sulci, sylvian, and interhemispheric fissures was assessed using scales with operationally defined grades. Both types of measurements had a high interrater reliability (intraclass correlation coefficient = .90). In addition, the density of the frontal white matter (Hounsfield numbers), caudate nucleus, and medial thalamus was measured using a computerized procedure that allowed the display of a slice and the selection of a region of interest. This procedure also had a high interrater reliability (intraclass correlation coefficient = .90). Density measurements are of considerable interest, in that they are likely to reflect changes in brain tissue more directly than the size of the ventricular system or sulci. However, their interpretation is not without problems, and allowances have to be made for potential sources of error, such as artifacts due to beam hardening, software changes, cranial size, and so on.

All the radiological measurements were significantly different in alcoholics when compared with controls (see Table 1-1). The size of the ventricular system and that of the sulci, sylvian, and interhemispheric fissures were significantly greater in the alcoholic group. Cerebellar sulci were only visible in the alcoholics. When the mean VBR of the control group plus one standard deviation was taken as a cutoff point, 64% of alcoholics and only 12% of controls exceeded this value.

Table 1-1. Mean CT Scan Measurements in Alcoholics and Controls

Measurement	Alcoholics (n = 100)	Controls (n = 50)	Significance
VBR	9.6 (SD = 3.0)	6.2 (SD = 2.0)	$t = 7.2, p < .01$
Sulcal width			
Grade 0	32	37	$\chi^2 = 29.8, df = 3, p < .001$
1	24	11	
2	29	2	
3	14	0	
Sylvian fissure width			
Grade 0	51	44	$\chi^2 = 20.7, df = 2, p < .001$
1	35	6	
2	14	0	
Interhemispheric fissure			
Grade 0	71	46	$\chi^2 = 7.4, df = 1, p < .01$
1	29	4	

Clinical Counterparts of Radiological Abnormalities

It could be argued that the radiological abnormalities antedate the onset of alcoholism, and that if this was the case their presence would be coincidental or causally related to the development of the addiction. However, the presence of CT scan abnormalities in a large proportion of alcoholics makes this unlikely. Moreover, the strong correlation between age and their severity argues against this possibility (see Table 1-2).

By far the strongest evidence in favor of radiological changes resulting from alcohol abuse derives from the twin studies of Gurling and colleagues (Gurling, Murray, & Ron, 1986; Gurling, Reveley, & Murray, 1984), who found significantly higher VBRs in the alcoholic cotwins of 11 monozygotic pairs discordant for the alcohol dependence syndrome (mean VBRs for normal and alcoholic cotwins, 6.7 and 9.7, respectively; $p = .003$). The alcoholic cotwins also had significantly higher frontal densities than the nonalcoholic cotwins.

The duration of the drinking history, on the other hand, does not appear to be significantly related to the severity of the radiological abnormalities. Thus, when two subgroups of subjects of the same age but different duration of alcohol abuse were compared, no significant CT scan differences could be found. This finding could be interpreted as indicating a greater vulnerability of the "older" brain when exposed *de novo* to the effect of alcohol at a comparatively late age.

The relationship among structural changes, drinking pattern, and other alcohol-related disabilities is even more difficult to unravel. In the London Institute of Psychiatry study, a simple "social decline" scale was constructed to incorporate items such as marital problems, financial and employment difficulties, and convictions related to alcohol abuse. High scores on this scale were significantly related to parameters indicative of an irregular

Table 1-2. CT Scan Indices in Relation to the Drinking History

	Sulcal width	Sylvian fissure width	VBR
Age	.42[a]**	.46[a]**	.28[a]**
Duration of history	.06	.12	.14
Peak amount (g/day)	−.10	−.15*	−.12
Days of abstinence before scanning	−.14[b]**	−.20[b]**	−.13
Total life consumption	.10	.13	.08

[a]Significant when corrected for duration of abstinence.

[b]Significant when corrected for age.

*$p < .05$.

**$p < .01$.

drinking pattern in which high alcohol consumption was interspersed with periods of total or relative withdrawal. On the other hand, the radiological abnormalities did not correlate significantly with the degree of social disruption as measured by the scale. This seems to indicate that a distinction can be made between structural brain changes and other alcohol-related disabilities, which could follow divergent paths in the course of alcoholism.

Women alcoholics have received comparatively little attention, and large studies of women comparable to the one just mentioned, which examined only men, are not available. Preliminary findings from a parallel study in progress at the London Institute of Psychiatry suggest that radiological changes are also detectable in women alcoholics when compared with controls. One striking finding, in need of confirmation from larger samples, is that CT scan abnormalities seem to be confined to the ventricular system, while cortical indices do not differ significantly from those of age-matched controls.

Psychometric Testing in Chronic Alcoholics

As a group, alcoholics have been found to have normal IQs, although in abstinent alcoholics an increase in IQ has been documented in serial testing (Boeke, 1970). When tests designed to detect the presence of brain damage were used in detoxified alcoholics, poor performance was documented in tests of psychomotor speed, problem-solving ability, and abstract thinking (Fitzhugh, Fitzhugh, & Reitan, 1965; Jones & Parsons, 1971; Long & McLachlan, 1974; Smith, Burt, & Chapman, 1973) and in memory (Ryan, Butters, Montgomery, Adinolfi, & Didario, 1979).

The correlation between radiological findings and cognitive impairment is not always a close one. In heterogeneous samples in which alcoholics with amnesic syndromes were included (Wilkinson & Carlen, 1980), those with poor memory had more severe radiological abnormalities. In more homogeneous populations, Bergman *et al.* (1980) found ventricular enlargement to be correlated with poor performance on tests of general intelligence and memory, while sulcal widening was significantly correlated with the Performance Index of the Halstead–Reitan Neuropsychological Test Battery.

The findings of the London Institute of Psychiatry study (Acker, Ron, Lishman, & Shaw, 1984) are less clear-cut. The alcoholic and control groups differed significantly when tests of perceptual–motor speed, logical memory, and abstracting ability were administered. However, the relationship between perceptual tests and size of the sylvian fissure was the only correlation between radiological and psychometric variables to reach statistical significance. Thus, the presence of a normal CT scan appears to have little or no bearing on the cognitive status of the alcoholic.

More interesting correlations accrued from comparisons between density measurements and psychometric testing. Thus, when a subgroup of alcoholics with poor memory was compared to another subgroup with preserved memory functions, the caudate and thalamic densities were significantly lower in the former group. These differences continued to be significant when age, IQ, duration of abstinence, and VBR were controlled for. By contrast, the frontal density was negatively but significantly correlated with a test of verbal fluency, even after the effects of age and IQ were accounted for. The significance of these findings is unclear; the fact that white-matter and central gray-matter densities appear to change in opposite directions in the course of alcoholism suggests that we may be in the presence of two different types of alcohol-related pathologies. The changes in the central grey matter are likely to be due to the effects of thiamine deficiency, while those in the frontal white matter could be due to the direct effect of alcohol. However, only carefully designed experimental animal studies could confirm or refute this hypothesis.

What Is the Natural History of the Radiological Abnormalities?

The subjects who took part in the London Institute of Psychiatry study were scanned after variable periods of abstinence ranging from 2 weeks to 3 months. The duration of abstinence was found to be significantly and negatively correlated with the width of the sulci and sylvian fissures. This suggests that some changes in the radiological appearances of brain take place with abstinence. When the patients were divided into "younger" and "older" groups according to the mean age for the whole group, a significant correlation between the duration of abstinence and radiological measurements was only present in the "older" group (see Table 1-3). This may reflect the more severe and persistent effects of alcohol in older individuals. Lesser, short-lived abnormalities may have been missed in younger subjects, due to the design of the study, which required a minimum of 2 weeks of abstinence before scanning. The density measurements in the caudate and thalamus were also significantly correlated with the duration of abstinence prior to scanning, with higher densities observed in those who had abstained longer.

The follow-up studies so far available cover a maximum of 3 years; longer-term changes remain uncharted at this writing. Carlen and Wilkinson (1980) were the first to point out the reversibility of the CT scan abnormalities, and the results of the London Institute of Psychiatry study have confirmed their findings. Of the 56 patients who were scanned at follow-up, 14 had less severe radiological abnormalities than in the initial examination. The CT scan appearances had remained unchanged in 34 and were worse in 8. The only significant differences among the three groups

Table 1-3. CT Scan Indices in Relation to Duration of Abstinence in "Younger" and "Older" Alcoholics

	Sulcal width[a]	Sylvian fissure width[a]	VBR[b]
"Younger" (age < 43) ($n = 48$)			
Days of abstinence before scanning	.02	−.06	.15
Weeks of abstinence previous year	.07	−.02	.06
"Older" (age > 43) ($n = 52$)			
Days of abstinence before scanning	−.17	−.27**	−.29
Weeks of abstinence previous year	−.02	−.25**	−.31*

[a]Kendall correlation coefficient.
[b]Pearson correlation coefficient.
*$p < .05$.
**$p < .01$.

were the duration of abstinence prior to the second CT scan and the proportion of the follow-up period spent without drinking (see Table 1-4). The initial scans of these three groups did not differ significantly in the severity of the abnormalities, and this would suggest that it is abstinence that determines reversibility, rather than that abstinence is easier to achieve for those with comparatively less severe radiological abnormalities. Nevertheless, the radiological appearances remained unchanged in a large proportion of subjects despite continuous drinking, and the presence of individual protective factors needs to be explored.

Summary and Conclusions

1. Brain damage of varying severity is a common consequence of alcohol abuse. Radiological and cognitive changes have been demonstrated in a large proportion of male subjects. These abnormalities are age-related and are, at least in part, reversible with abstinence. Evidence of brain damage has also been detected in women alcoholics. Whether women are more vulnerable to the effects of alcohol and whether the pattern of brain damage is different from that observed in men remain to be determined.

2. The mechanisms that determine cognitive and radiological abnormalities are little understood. Neuropathological studies suggest the presence of two different types of lesions, of different location and possibly different etiologies. Density measurements add some support to this hypothesis. It seems, therefore, increasingly artificial to separate the organic

Table 1-4. Changes in Cortex and/or Ventricles on Rescanning at Follow-Up in Relation to Drinking History

	Improved ($n = 14$)		Unchanged ($n = 34$)		Worse ($n = 8$)		
	Mean	(*SD*)	Mean	(*SD*)	Mean	(*SD*)	F (2, 52)
Age	40.4	(6.3)	44.2	(9.5)	47.1	(6.3)	1.599
Days abstinence prior to initial scanning	40.1	(24.9)	34.4	(19.6)	32.7	(20.2)	0.439
Days abstinence prior to follow-up scanning	262.0	(211.6)	70.8	(113.3)	51.2	(126.0)	9.381**
Weeks per year abstinence during follow-up period	42.5	(13.9)	29.5	(21.2)	20.9	(13.3)	3.693*

*$p < .05$.

**$p < .001$.

syndromes related to alcohol into discrete categories, and it would appear more appropriate to consider them as part of a continuum.

3. The available evidence does not allow us to draw firm conclusions about the mechansims and extent of the reversibility of the radiological abnormalities. The improvement that has been observed seems to take place over prolonged periods of time, and it is unlikely to be due solely to changes in water and electrolytes; more complex processes such as protein regeneration or regrowth of dendritic arborization may be at play.

4. These findings have some practical implications. If abstinence is the key to the resolution of radiological and psychological abnormalities, then all efforts should be made to insure it, although this may place an impossible burden on already overstretched services. The current practice of admitting people to hospitals for brief periods of detoxification seems painfully inadequate, as does enrolling them in rehabilitation programs that require well-preserved intellectual functions during the early withdrawal period.

References

Acker, W., Ron, M. A., Lishman, W. A., & Shaw, G. K. (1984). A multivariate analysis of psychological, clinical and CT scanning measures in detoxified chronic alcoholics. *British Journal of Addiction, 79*, 293–301.

Bergman, H., Borg, S., Hindmarsh, T., Idestrom, C. M., & Mutzell, S. (1980). Computed tomography of the brain and neuropsychological assessment of male alcoholic patients and a random sample from the general male population. *Acta Psychiatrica Scandinavica, 62*(Suppl. 286), 47–56.

Boeke, P. E. (1970). Some remarks about alcohol—dementia in clinically treated alcoholics. *British Journal of Addiction, 65*, 173–180.

Brewer, C., & Perrett, L. (1971). Brain damage due to alcohol consumption: An air-encephalographic, psychometric and electroencephalographic study. *British Journal of Addiction, 66*, 170–182.

Cala, L. A., Jones, B., Wiley, B., & Mastaglia, F. L. (1980). A computerized axial tomography (CAT) study of alcohol induced cerebral atrophy, in conjunction with other correlates. *Acta Psychiatrica Scandinavica, 62*(Suppl. 286), 31–40.

Carlen, P. L., & Wilkinson, D. A. (1980). Alcoholic brain damage and reversible deficits. *Acta Psychiatrica Scandinavica, 62*(Suppl. 286), 103–118.

Courville, C. B. (1955). *Effects of alcohol in the nervous system of man.* Los Angeles: San Lucas Press.

Cravioto, H., Korein, J., & Silverman, J. (1961). Wernicke's encephalopathy: A clinical and pathological study of 28 autopsied cases. *Archives of Neurology, 4*, 510–519.

Fitzhugh, L. C., Fitzhugh, K. B. and Reitan, R. M. (1965). Adaptive abilities and intellectual functioning of hospitalized chronic alcoholics: Further considerations. *Quarterly Journal of Studies on Alcohol, 26*, 402–411.

Gurling, H. M. D., Murray, R. M., & Ron, M. A. (1986). Detection of increased brain radiodensity in alcoholism using the cotwin control method. *Archives of General Psychiatry, 43*, 764–767.

Gurling, H. M. D., Reveley, M. A., & Murray, R. M. (1984). Increased cerebral ventricular volume in monozygotic twins discordant for alcoholism. *Lancet, i*, 986–988.

Harper, C. (1979). Wernicke's encephalopathy: A more common disease than realised. A neuropathological study of 51 cases. *Journal of Neurology, Neurosurgery and Psychiatry, 42*, 226–231.
Horvath, T. B. (1975). Clinical spectrum and epidemiological features of alcoholic dementia. In J. G. Rankin (Ed.), *Alcohol, drugs and brain damage* (pp. 1–16). Toronto: Addiction Research Foundation.
Ishii, T. (1983). A comparison of cerebral atrophy in CT scan findings among alcoholic groups. *Acta Psychiatrica Scandinavica, 68*(Suppl. 309).
Jones, B. M., & Parsons, O. A. (1971). Impaired abstracting ability in chronic alcoholics. *Archives of General Psychiatry, 24*, 171–175.
Long, J. A., & McLachlan, J. F. (1974). Abstract reasoning and perceptual motor efficiency in alcoholics: Impairment and reversibility. *Quarterly Journal of Studies on Alcohol, 35*, 1220–1229.
Lynch, M. J. G. (1960). Brain lesions in chronic alcoholics. *Archives of Pathology, 69*, 342–353.
Mancall, E. C. (1961). Some unusual neurological diseases complicating chronic alcoholism. *American Journal of Clinical Nutrition, 9*, 404–413.
Neuberger, K. T. (1957). The changing neuropathological picture of chronic alcoholism. *Archives of Pathology, 63*, 1–6.
Riley, J. N., & Walker, D. W. (1978). Morphological alterations in hippocampus after long-term alcohol consumption in mice. *Science, 201*, 646–648.
Ron, M. A. (1983). The alcoholic brain: CT scan and psychological findings. *Psychological Medicine* (Monograph Suppl. 3).
Ron, M. A., Acker, W., Shaw, G. K., & Lishman, W. A. (1982). Computerised tomography of the brain in chronic alcoholism: A survey and follow-up study. *Brain*, 105, 497–514.
Ryan, C., Butters, N., Montgomery, K., Adinolfi, A., & Didario, B. (1979). Memory deficits in chronic alcoholics: Continuities between the "intact" alcoholic and the alcoholic Korsakoff patient. *Advances in Experimental Medicine and Biology, 126*, 701–718.
Smith, J. W., Burt, D. W., & Chapman, R. F. (1973). Intelligence and brain damage in alcoholics. A study of patients of middle and upper social class. *Quarterly Journal of Studies on Alcohol, 34*, 414–422.
Tumarkin, B., Wilson, J. D., & Snyder, G. (1955). Cerebral atrophy due to alcoholism in young adults. *U.S. Armed Forces Medical Journal, 6*, 57–74.
Victor, M., Adams, R. D., & Collins, G. H. (1971). *The Wernicke–Korsakoff syndrome.* Oxford: Blackwell.
Werner, F. J. (1934). The brain changes in chronic alcoholism and Korsakoff's psychosis. *Journal of Nervous and Mental Disease, 80*, 629–644.
Wilkinson, D. A., & Carlen, P. L. (1980). Relationship of neuropsychological test performance to brain morphology in amnesic and non-amnesic chronic alcoholics. *Acta Psychiatrica Scandinavica, 62*(Suppl. 286), 89–102.

2

Brain Dysfunction Related to Alcoholism: Some Results from the KARTAD Project

HANS BERGMAN

Introduction

Clinical experience and results from many studies of male alcoholic patients published during the last few years indicate a relationship between alcoholism and brain damage. When the morphological cerebral state is assessed by computerized tomography (CT) scan, the damage can be recognized by one or more of the following criteria: dilation of the ventricular system, visible widening of cerebral fissures or cortical sulci, and enlargement of cerebellar cisterns and sulci. Although the etiology behind these changes is not yet fully understood, they have been interpreted as signs of central, cortical, and cerebellar atrophy, respectively. Recent research has indicated that such changes can often be detected not only in alcoholic patients with clinical symptoms of brain damage, but also in alcoholic patients without these symptoms. In such patients, varying degrees of neuropsychological impairment are also often found, most often mild to moderate. On the basis of results from many studies on male alcoholic patients, particularly using the Halstead–Reitan Neuropsychological Test Battery, the impairment can be characterized as cognitive rather than sensory or motor. General intelligence as conventionally assessed by the Wechsler Adult Intelligence Scale (WAIS) or the Wechsler–Bellevue Scale is most often spared and reported to be average or even slightly above. However, visual–spatial functions involving abstracting and problem solving, and information handling requiring complex sensory–motor coordination, are vulnerable. Less complex sensory or motor functions, and functions that are mainly dependent on long-term memory (e.g., vocabulary), are generally less sensitive. With regard to learning and memory, again, visual–spatial functions seem to be more vulnerable than verbal. However, the pattern of neuropsychological deficits

Hans Bergman. Department of Clinical Alcohol and Drug Research, Karolinska Institute, Karolinska Hospital, Stockholm, Sweden.

found in alcoholism is dependent on the type of test methods used. Thus, the results from studies using more demanding information-processing methods than are commonly used in clinical practice indicate that verbal learning might be impaired in alcoholic patients without clinical symptoms of brain damage (Ryan & Butters, 1983). Very few studies on brain damage in female alcoholics have been published, particularly studies using CT scans, but it has been suggested that female alcoholics have the same cognitive deficits as the males (Parsons & Leber, 1982).

Despite the progress in knowledge on brain damage in alcoholism, particularly during recent years, we still have rather few hard facts. This is probably due to small sample size and comparatively few clinical variables simultaneously assessed, by contrast with the great complexity of the subject area in terms of the large number of important and interacting factors (e.g., drinking-pattern variables, withdrawal reactions, and complicating diseases). Important drinking-pattern variables include age of onset, duration of heavy drinking, continuous versus periodic drinking, preferred type of beverage, typical amount of alcohol consumed per drinking occasion, the evolution of the drinking pattern during the whole "alcoholic career," and the time interval between the last drink and examination. Serious withdrawal reactions are also important to consider—for example, a history of repeated delirious episodes and/or epileptic fits. Other important factors to consider are current heavy medication, abuse of hypnotics/sedatives or of narcotic drugs, previous brain injury, peripheral neuropathy, serious liver disease, poor nutritional status, and other relevant neurological and medical complications. Furthermore, effects of age, sex, education, socioeconomic status, cultural deprivation, premorbid cerebral state, psychopathology (e.g., depression or anxiety), and the motivational state of the patient are also essential to consider. (For recent reviews on alcoholism and brain damage, see Parsons & Leber, 1982; Porjesz & Begleiter, 1983; Ryan & Butters, 1983; Wilkinson & Carlen, 1981.)

In a series of studies (Bergman, 1981, 1983, 1985; Bergman, Axelsson, *et al.*, 1983; Bergman, Borg, Hindmarsh, Ideström, & Mützell, 1980a, 1980b, 1980c, 1980d), we have reported on brain damage in male alcoholic patients and in a male random control sample taken from the general population. On CT scan, symmetrical dilation of the cerebral ventricles, a visible widening of cortical sulci, and cerebellar changes were more often observed in the patients than in the random control sample. However, the cortical and central changes seemed to follow different courses in many alcoholics: Cortical changes were often observed already in young alcoholic patients with a relatively short duration of heavy drinking, while central changes were more often observed in older alcoholics with a longer duration of heavy drinking. Furthermore, there was a positive correlation between cortical and central changes in young to middle-aged alcoholics that dropped with advancing age. Thus, the hypothesis of a generalized overall effect of long-term heavy drinking on the brains of alcoholics was not supported in these studies. Instead, two different morphological syndromes seemed to develop—a cortical and a central. Cognitive deficits like those reported in other studies were also often observed in the patient group. However, there was a difference in the pattern of cognitive deficits between the young and old alcoholic patients. Thus, a deficit in abstracting ability was already often found in young patients and was relatively constant over age groups. Conversely, memory deficits and generalized intellectual impairment were not evident in the young patients, but appeared successively in increasing age groups.

The relationship between morphological cerebral changes and neuropsychological deficits is important for an understanding of the relation between brain and behavior in alcoholism and has practical implications for diagnostic routines. In previous studies, including our own, the relationship between morphological changes and neuropsychological performance was found to be low to moderate and tended to disappear when age was partialed out. However, the partialing out of age might have led to an underestimation of the true relationship between brain morphology and neuropsychological deficits, since that part of the covariance that was due to duration of heavy drinking per se was also taken away. The relationship between morphological changes and neuropsychological deficits in alcoholics should also be considered in the light of the corresponding relationship in the general population.

In our previous studies on male alcoholic patients, we could not show any significant correlations between selected clinical drinking-related variables on the one hand and CT scan and neuropsychological test results on the other when age was partialed out. An exception to this was a small but significant correlation between history of delirious episodes and dilated ventricles. With better control of age than is possible when using partial correlation, the hypothesized relationships between crucial drinking-habit variables and signs of brain damage may become evident. With the exception of a handful of neuropsychological studies, the prognostic significance of signs of brain damage for the outcome of alcoholics after treatment has not been reported. The few results are not encouraging, despite the fact that neuropsychological assessment of the single patient on a routine clinical basis is considered to provide valuable information for treatment planning.

In our most recent study (Bergman, 1985), correlations between some drinking-pattern variables and signs of brain damage, as assessed by neuropsychological tests and CT scan of the brain, were observed in the random control sample from the general population. In male social drinkers, mild cognitive deficits and morphological cerebral changes as a result of high recent alcohol intake were observed. After the effects of recent alcohol intake were excluded, mild cognitive deficits could still be detected in the males, but no morphological changes. The cognitive deficits were correlated with long-term excessive social drinking. In the females, there was no association between the drinking variables and cognitive deficits or morphological changes, probably due to the less advanced drinking habits of the females. From the results of the study, it can be concluded that mild signs of brain damage can appear not only in alcoholic patients, but also in advanced male social drinkers randomly taken from the general population.

The purpose of the present study was to investigate the relationship between alcoholism and brain damage, as assessed by CT scan and neuropsychological tests, in a large and representative sample of male and female inpatients and in male and female random control persons from the general population, particularly with regard to possible sex differences. This relationship was to be studied with more adequate control of age and education differences than in previous studies. A second purpose was to examine the relationship between CT scan findings and age- and education-scaled neuropsychological test results in both the alcoholic patients and the random control sample. A third purpose was to investigate the relationship between some crucial clinical drinking-related variables, including outcome at 6 months and 2½ years after treatment, and CT scan and neuropsychological test results in the male alcoholic patients.

Method

Subjects

The alcoholic patient sample consisted of 161 male and 35 female inpatients at the Magnus Huss Clinic of the Karolinska Hospital in Stockholm, who fulfilled the following criteria: (1) They were admitted to the KARTAD Project (*KA*rolinska Project for *R*esearch and *T*reatment of *A*lcohol *D*ependence; Ideström, 1977) during the 2-year period February 1977–January 1979; (2) they were 20–65 years of age; (3) they were born on an uneven date of the month; (4) they had no clinical symptoms of intoxication or withdrawal; and (5) their withdrawal medication had been discontinued. According to the intake criteria of the clinic, narcotic drug addicts, patients with severe neuropsychiatric complications (e.g., the Wernicke–Korsakoff syndrome), and those in need of intense medical care were not admitted.

In the KARTAD Project, a consecutive series of more than 700 patients living in a defined geographical sector of Stockholm containing about 80,000 people admitted for voluntary inpatient treatment of alcoholism during the 4-year period 1976–1980 has been systematically investigated to create a vast data bank on alcoholism. Large subsamples have also been reinvestigated at repeated follow-ups at various times after discharge from the clinic. Medical and social case history data were collected by means of a standardized procedure of questionnaires with predefined response alternatives, combined with a checkup interview carried out by a physician and a social worker according to the routines of the KARTAD Project. The methodology has been found to have satisfactory test–retest reliability (Mützell, Bergman, Borg, Lindberg, & Olsson, 1978).

As a control group for the KARTAD patients, and in order to get general reference values, an age-stratified random sample of 200 men and 200 women taken from the same geographical area as the KARTAD patients was also investigated. The random control sample was drawn from a national register covering all inhabitants of Sweden. According to a two-stage sampling plan, 228 men and 240 women were picked out in order to finally obtain 200 investigated persons of each sex. The subjects were collected so as to achieve a rectangular age distribution ranging from 20 to 65 years. Thus, in comparison with the distribution of the alcoholic patients, persons aged 20–29 and 60–65 were oversampled. This was done in order to be able to estimate different parameters in the general population with the same precision, regardless of age (see Table 2-1). The mean age of the four alcoholic patient and random control groups varied between 43.8 ± 9.9 years and 44.8 ± 13.5 years.

The random control subjects were investigated by methods identical to those used in the alcoholic patients, with the exception that some questions related to particularly advanced drinking habits were dropped. The loss of subjects when collecting the random control sample was less than 10% among the males and about 15% among the females. This low dropout rate was due to repeated home visits, payment for participation in the study, and a health control. Subgroups of 31 men and 17 women defined as "excessive alcohol consumers" were detected and included among the random control sample. The criteria for "excessiveness" were reported subjective relative loss of control over drinking and an above-average quantity of alcohol consumed per drinking occasion.

Some social and medical case history data of the investigated groups are shown in Table 2-2. The maximum quantity of alcohol consumed per drinking occasion was reported to be about 1½ times greater in the male than in the female patients (299.1 ± 161.8 g vs. 189.3 ± 133.2 g). Duration of

Table 2-1. Age Distributions of 196 Alcoholic Inpatients and 400 Random Controls from the General Population by Sex

	20–29	30–39	40–49	50–59	60–65	*M* ± *SD*
Men						
Patients	16	47	35	48	15	44.7 ± 11.7
Controls	40	40	40	40	40	44.4 ± 13.8
Women						
Patients	4	8	10	11	2	43.8 ± 9.9
Controls	35	43	44	32	46	44.8 ± 13.5

Table 2-2. Social and Medical Case History Data (% or $M \pm SD$) for 196 Alcoholic Patients and 400 Random Controls from the General Population by Sex

	Male		Female	
	Alcoholic patients ($n = 161$)	Random controls ($n = 200$)	Alcoholic patients ($n = 35$)	Random controls ($n = 200$)
Secondary school or higher completed	21%	46%	24%	40%
Employed at least 16 hours/week	62%	83%	68%	78%
Living with a partner	29%	71%	45%	69%
Maximum alcohol per drinking occasion	299.1 ± 161.8 g	32.6 ± 58.2 g	189.3 ± 133.2 g	23.8 ± 29.0 g
Drinking every day	28%	—[a]	31%	—[a]
Mainly drinking hard liquor	75%	—[a]	65%	—[a]
Duration of subjective loss of control over drinking	12.4 ± 8.1 years	17.6 ± 11.5 years[b]	6.7 ± 5.6 years	7.0 ± 5.6 years[b]
Age at onset of subjective loss of control	32.4 ± 11.5 years	25.9 ± 10.1 years[b]	38.4 ± 10.1 years	30.2 ± 10.6 years[b]
Regular use of hypnotics or sedatives	8%	4%	11%	8%
Felt much depressed previous 12 months	13%	1%	25%	3%
Regular memory lapses after drinking	15%	2%	11%	2%
History of hallucinations or of predelirious or delirious states	36%	1%	25%	1%
History of epileptic fits	22%	1%	21%	0%
History of hospital treatment for head trauma	18%	5%	0%	2%
Actions from the Temperance Board[c]	64%	13%	57%	2%

Note. Data were not complete for 31 patients and 7 control persons.

[a]Question excluded for the random controls.

[b]Subjective loss of control over drinking was only reported by 57 men and 25 women in the random control sample.

[c]Data from Swedish Temperance Board register.

subjective loss of control was also much longer in the male group as compared to the female group (12.4 ± 8.1 years vs. 6.7 ± 5.6 years). All patients were screened with electroneurography of peripheral nerves of the upper and lower limbs. With regard to the upper limbs, only one patient showed neuropathy of the median nerve of the dominant arm on the screening. Thus, polyneuropathy should not confound the neuropsychological test results of the present study. Only 14 patients reported a history of liver disease. Hospital treatment for head trauma was reported by 18% of the male alcoholic patients, but not by any of the female patients. However, no significant correlation between liver disease or hospital treatment for head trauma and the assessments of the cerebral state was found.

Investigation Methods

The average interval between admission and psychological examination was 10.5 ± 4.3 days for the male patients and 11.2 ± 5.6 days for the female patients on the average. Only two neuropsychological tests in the male group (Finger Tapping and Synonyms, $p < .05$) and none in the female group were associated with interval length. The examination included some personality questionnaires and a comprehensive neuropsychological test battery. The SRB tests (the Synonyms, Reasoning [i.e., Thurstone's Figure Classifications], and Block Design tests) of general intelligence were given in order to assess vocabulary, logical reasoning, and visual–spatial pattern reproduction. The Halstead–Reitan Neuropsychological Test Battery was also given. Included here were the Category Test of nonverbal abstracting ability; the Tactual Performance Test (TPT) of tactual–motor coordination and problem solving (TPT Time, TPT Memory, and TPT Localization); the Trail Making Test (TMT) of visual–spatial scanning and visual–motor coordination (TMT A) and flexibility (TMT B); the Rhythm Test of sustained attention and auditory discrimination; and the Finger Tapping Test of motor speed. Three memory tests, the Claeson–Dahl Verbal Learning and 30-Minute Retention tests and the Memory for Designs Test of visual–graphic short-term memory, were also given. Raw scores were transformed to non-normalized T scores ($M = 50$, $SD = 10$), based on the results of the subjects in the random control sample from each combination of three age intervals and two levels of school education. In the random control sample, the neuropsychological performance profiles of the two sexes were the same, except that men were slightly superior in Reasoning, Block Design, TPT Memory, Finger Tapping, and Memory for Designs, and women in Claeson–Dahl Verbal Learning.

An overall assessment of intellectual impairment was also carried out by the psychologists using a 3-point rating scale (1 = no signs of impairment, 2 = slight signs of impairment, and 3 = definite signs of impairment). The ratings were not made blindly. The methods used in the impairment rating were as follows: (1) level of performance in relation to normative data and educational and occupational background; (2) the differential score approach; (3) qualitative deficiencies and pathognomonic signs during performance. The interrater reliability of the 3-point scale has been found to be .68 and .72 (Bergman & Ågren, 1974). The premorbid intellectual competence and the age of the subject were taken into consideration in the rating. This was not the case for the Impairment Index of the Halstead–Reitan Battery. The neuropsychological investigation was carried out in 142 male and 32 female patients and in 195 men and 192 women of the random control sample. (For more information about the psychological examination, see Bergman, Bergman, *et al.*, 1983.)

The morphological cerebral state was assessed by CT scan in 134 male and 32 female alcoholic patients and in 193 men and 188 women in the random control sample. On average, it was carried out 2 days after the psychological examination for the patients (i.e., 12.5 days after admission for the males and 13.2 days for the females) and on the same day for the control sample. There was a moderate but significant positive ($p < .05$) correlation between the interval between admission and examination and cortical changes. No relationship was observed for central changes. Central changes were assessed by calculating an index of the width of the lateral ventricles divided by the maximum inner skull diameter (anterior horn index) and by measuring the maximum transverse diameter of the third ventricle. An anterior horn index greater than 0.31 and a third ventricle more than 6 mm in natural size were considered pathological. Cerebellar changes were not analyzed in the present study but are reported elsewhere (Hillbom, Muuronen, Holm, & Hindmarsh, 1986).

Cortical changes were assessed by an overall evaluation of the width of cortical sulci, using a 4-point rating scale. On this scale, a rating of 1 was "normal" (i.e., no sulci visible or only sulci of natural size [<3 mm]); a rating of 2 indicated suspected degenerative changes (i.e., up to five sulci exceeding 3 mm in diameter); a rating of 3 indicated clear-cut changes (i.e., more than five sulci exceeding 3 mm in diameter); and a rating of 4 signified high-grade changes (i.e., a marked widening of a great number of sulci). A rating of 3 or 4 (i.e., more than five sulci exceeding 3 mm in diameter) was considered pathological. The interrater reliability of the scale has been found to be .81 (Elofsson *et al.*, 1980).

Results

Prevalence and Pattern of Morphological Changes and Neuropsychological Deficits

On CT scan, both cortical (particularly high-grade) and central symmetrical changes were observed much more often in the male alcoholic patients than in the male random controls ($p < .001$). The differences were most pronounced for cortical changes and least for dilated lateral ventricles (see Table 2-3). Corresponding changes were also detected more often in the female alcoholic patients than in the female random controls ($p < .001$ for cortical changes and dilated third ventricles, and $p < .01$ for dilated lateral ventricles). There were no significant differences between male and female patients in the prevalence of cortical changes, but a trend toward less central changes was observed in the females. The significantly lower prevalence of a dilated third ventricle in the female group than in the male group ($p < .05$) should, however, partly be due to a basic cerebral sex difference, as we have

Table 2-3. CT Scan and Neuropsychological Findings in 196 Alcoholic Patients and 400 Random Controls from the General Population by Sex

	Men		Women	
	Patients (%)	Controls (%)	Patients (%)	Controls (%)
Cortical changes				
None	12	57	19	50
Suspected	27	27	29	28
Clear-cut	40	15	23	20
High-grade	21	1	29	3
Patients vs. controls	$p < .001$		$p < .001$	
Men vs. women patients	n.s.			
Dilated lateral ventricles				
No	66	89	81	97
Yes	34	11	19	3
Patients vs. controls	$p < .001$		$p < .01$	
Men vs. women patients	n.s.			
Third ventricle dilated				
No	45	87	69	92
Yes	55	13	31	8
Patients vs. controls	$p < .001$		$p < .001$	
Men vs. women patients	$p < .05$			
Halstead–Reitan Impairment Index				
0.0–0.4	49	71	37	61
0.5–0.8	32	16	23	22
0.9–1.0	19	13	40	17
Patients vs. controls	$p < .001$		$p < .01$	
Men vs. women patients	n.s.			
Signs of intellectual impairment				
None	43	71	29	68
Slight	34	20	32	20
Clear	23	9	39	12
Patients vs. controls	$p < .001$		$p < .001$	
Men vs. women patients	n.s.			

Note. CT scans were only carried out on 166 patients and 381 random controls; neuropsychological examinations were only performed on 174 patients and 387 controls.

previously reported (3.9 ± 1.4 mm in the women vs. 4.7 ± 1.2 mm in the men of the random control sample).

In the male patients, neuropsychological deficits as assessed by high scores on the Halstead–Reitan Impairment Index were also more prevalent than in the male random controls ($p < .001$), particularly mild to moderate impairment (.05–0.8). The average Impairment Index was 0.50 ± 0.31 in the male patients and 0.36 ± 0.31 in the male random controls. Signs of intellectual impairment according to the psychologists' overall assessment were also more prevalent ($p < .001$). More than one-third of the female patients were rated to show clear signs of intellectual impairment, compared to about one-tenth of the female random controls ($p < .001$). There was also a higher prevalence of neuropsychological deficits according to the Impairment Index ($p < .01$), particularly with regard to profound impairment (0.9–1.0). The average Impairment Index was 0.65 ± 0.31 in the female patients and 0.43 ± 0.31 in the female controls.

There was a consistent trend toward higher prevalence of neuropsychological impairment among the female patients than among the male patients. This was observed despite only half as long duration of heavy drinking (6.7 ± 5.6 years vs. 12.4 ± 8.1 years of subjective loss of control) and much less alcohol reported per drinking occasion (189.3 ± 133.2 g vs. 299.1 ± 161.8).

There were no significant deficits in either the male or the female patients in comparison with the male and female random controls (Student's t test) on TPT localization, Finger Tapping (dominant hand), Rhythm (men only), or Claeson–Dahl Verbal Learning and 30-Minute Retention. In vocabulary (Synonyms) the deficit was quite small and only significant ($p < .05$) in the male patients. In TPT Memory the deficit was also small, at least in the male patients, but it was significant ($p < .05$) in both groups. In all other tests the deficits were more pronounced ($p < .01$ or $p < .001$) in both male and female patients. Nearly identical results were achieved when data was analyzed by a two-way analysis of variance (ANOVA) controlling for the differences in age distribution. From most to least neuropsychological deficit, the male rank order was as follows: TMT B, Block Design, Category, Reasoning, Memory for Designs, TMT A, and TPT Time. The corresponding female rank order was as follows: Reasoning, TMT B, Memory for Designs, Block Design, Category, TMT A, and TPT Time. On most tests the female alcoholics scored lower than the male alcoholics, particularly in Reasoning ($p < .001$) and Memory for Designs ($p < .05$). (See Figure 2-1.)

There was no association between high scores on the Anxiety, Psychasthenia, or Sociopathy personality scales of the Karolinska Scales of Personality (Schalling, Edman, & Åsberg, 1983) and neuropsychological impairment in the male patients. In the female patients, with the exception of Sociopathy scale scores, a trend in this direction was observed, particularly for the Psychasthenia scale. Reported depression during the last 12 months

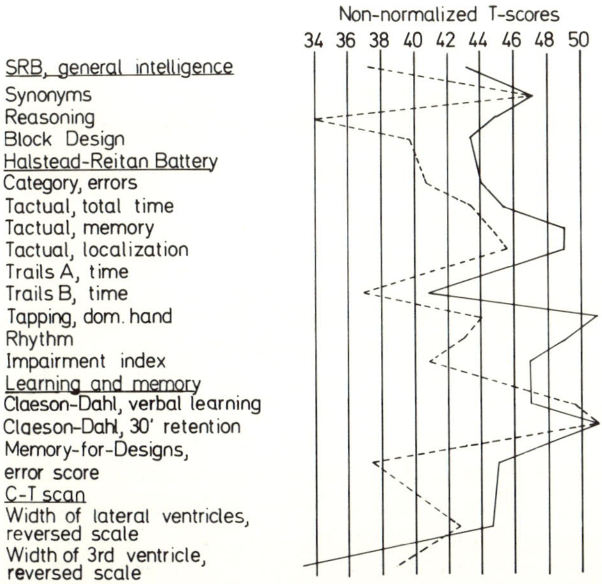

Figure 2-1. Neuropsychological and CT findings in 142 male (—) and 32 female (----) alcoholic inpatients, in comparison with 387 randomly selected men and women from the general population, in age- and education-scaled scores (mean *T* score = 50). (*Note.* CT scan was only carried out in 166 patients and 381 random controls.)

was not associated with impaired neuropsychological performance in either patient group. When Psychasthenia was partialed out in the two-way ANOVA for females, the results were essentially the same as before. Thus, a high anxiety level, lack of psychic energy, sociopathic tendencies, or reported depression could not explain the neuropsychological deficits observed in the alcoholic patients.

For comparison, the CT scan results for central changes are also plotted in Figure 2-1 in terms of age-scaled *T* scores for each sex. In both the male and female patients, the ventricles (in particular, the third ventricle in the male patients) were considerably wider than in the men and women of the random control sample ($p < .001$).

One can therefore conclude that both morphological cerebral changes and intellectual impairment were more prevalent in the alcoholic patients than in the random control sample from the general population. Central changes were observed relatively more often in the male than in the female patients, partly due to a basic difference between the sexes. On the contrary, intellectual impairment was more common in the female than in the male patients. The pattern of neuropsychological deficits was also somewhat different between the two sexes. Anxiety, reported depression, psychasthenia, or sociopathic tendencies could not explain the neuropsychological deficits in the alcoholic patients.

The Relationship between CT Scan and Neuropsychological Findings

Apart from the relatively small female patient sample, the correlations between age and the morphological changes were significant in both alcoholics and random controls ($p < .001$) (see Table 2-4). Age explained 13% of the CT scan variance. The average product–moment correlations in the male and female patients and controls were .36, .35, .37, and .35. Thus, there was no trend indicative of higher correlations in the patients than in the random controls. This might have been expected on the basis of the "premature-aging hypothesis"—that is, the suggestion that the brain gets prematurely old because of exposure to long-term heavy drinking, or simply because of the correlation between age and duration of heavy drinking (which is hypothesized to cause brain damage).

The product–moment correlations between cortical changes and the width of the lateral ventricles and between cortical changes and width of the third ventricle were averaged in the patient sample and in the random control sample. This was done separately for the two age intervals of 20–44 years and 45–65 years. In the random controls, there was no correlation in the young group ($r = .08$, n.s.) and a low but statistically significant correlation in the old group ($r = .18, p < .05$). The reverse of this trend was observed in the alcoholic patients: There was a significant correlation in the young group ($r = .27, p < .05$) but not in the old ($r = .09$, n.s.).

The correlations between neuropsychological *T* scores and CT scan (raw scores) in the patient group, separated into the age intervals of 20–44 years and 45–65 years, are shown in Table 2-5. The corresponding correlation matrix for the random control persons is shown in Table 2-6. In the 20- to 44-year-old patients ($n = 70$), but not in the 20- to 44-year-old controls ($n = 183$), there was a consistent trend toward more neuropsychological

Table 2-4. Product–Moment Correlations between CT Scan Findings (Raw Scores) and Age in 166 Alcoholic Patients and 387 Random Controls by Sex

	Men		Women	
	Patients ($n = 134$)	Controls ($n = 193$)	Patients ($n = 32$)	Controls ($n = 188$)
Width of lateral ventricles	.43**	.36**	.26	.33**
Width of third ventricle	.36**	.26**	.52*	.34**
Cortical changes	.28**	.44**	.32	.38**
Averaged correlation	.36	.35	.37	.35

*$p < .01$.
**$p < .001$.

Table 2-5. Product–Moment Correlations between Age- and Education-Scaled Neuropsychological Test Results and CT Scan Findings (Raw Scores) in 144 Alcoholic Patients by Age Group

	Width of lateral ventricles		Width of third ventricle		Cortical changes	
	20–44 years	45–65 years	20–44 years	45–65 years	20–44 years	45–65 years
SRB (general intelligence)	−.32**	−.34**	.05	−.37**	−.03	−.13
Synonyms	−.28*	−.32**	−.11	−.27*	−.08	−.03
Reasoning	−.19	−.22	.16	−.33**	.10	−.17
Block Design	−.32**	−.31**	.06	−.34**	−.08	−.12
Halstead–Reitan Battery						
Category (errors)	−.21	−.21	.02	−.37**	.00	−.05
TPT Time	−.14	−.23	.01	−.38**	.01	−.03
TPT Memory	−.07	.07	.03	−.11	−.11	−.05
TPT Localization	−.06	.02	.06	−.24	−.11	−.21
TMT A (time)	−.13	−.44***	−.02	−.37**	.00	−.01
TMT B (time)	−.21	−.33**	.07	−.33**	−.07	.00
Finger Tapping (dominant hand	−.05	−.01	−.05	−.38**	−.08	−.27*
Rhythm	−.21	−.01	.24	−.01	−.18	.11
Impairment Index	−.06	−.13	.08	−.31*	−.14	−.23
Learning and memory						
Claeson–Dahl Verbal Learning	−.29*	−.36**	−.02	−.31**	.02	.04
Claeson–Dahl 30-Minute Retention	−.30*	−.05	−.13	.00	−.02	.00
Memory for Designs (errors)	−.35**	−.29*	.06	−.30*	−.20	−.00
Overall assessment of intellectual impairment (reversed scale)	−.27*	−.10	−.02	−.23	−.23	−.18

Note. Correlations in expected direction are negative. Data were not complete for 26 patients (Impairment Index).

*$p < .05$.

**$p < .01$.

***$p < .001$.

deficits for those with wider lateral ventricles. This trend was significant ($p < .05$ or $p < .01$) for general intelligence (due to Synonyms and Block Design), verbal learning and retention (the Claeson–Dahl tests), visual–graphic short-term memory (Memory for Designs), and the overall assessment of intellectual impairment. In the 45- to 65-year-old patients ($n = 74$), but to a much lesser extent in the 45- to 65-year-old controls ($n = 191$), the same consistent trend was observed. Neither in the 20- to 44-year-old patients nor in any of the control groups was a correlation between neuropsychological performance and the width of the third ventricle observed. However, a consistent relationship between a dilated third ventricle and neuropsychological impairment was observed in the 45- to 65-year-old

Table 2-6. Product–Moment Correlations between Age- and Education-Scaled Neuropsychological Test Results and CT Scan Findings (Raw Scores) in 374 Random Controls by Age Group

	Width of lateral ventricles		Width of third ventricle		Cortical changes	
	20–44 years	45–65 years	20–44 years	45–65 years	20–44 years	45–65 years
SRB (general intelligence)	.05	−.12	.06	−.08	−.11	.08
Synonyms	−.04	−.10	−.01	.02	−.02	.09
Reasoning	.04	−.07	.05	−.07	−.08	.01
Block Design	.11	−.11	.11	−.12	−.09	.08
Halstead–Reitan Battery						
Category (errors)	−.01	−.08	−.05	−.06	−.08	.05
TPT Time	.03	−.11	.00	−.07	−.20**	.11
TPT Memory	−.06	−.07	.02	.00	−.09	.16*
TPT Localization	−.02	−.13	.01	−.08	−.11	.07
TMT A (time)	−.01	−.06	−.10	−.12	−.19*	−.09
TMT B (time)	.00	−.18*	−.05	−.12	−.14	.01
Finger Tapping (dominant hand)	.05	.05	−.02	.05	−.05	−.07
Rhythm	−.07	−.15*	−.10	−.09	−.14	.08
Impairment Index	.00	−.10	−.09	−.08	−.20**	.11
Learning and memory						
Claeson–Dahl Verbal Learning	−.07	−.19**	−.19*	.00	−.02	−.04
Claeson–Dahl 30-Minute Retention	−.13	−.18*	−.05	−.04	.01	−.05
Memory for Designs (errors)	−.06	−.06	−.05	−.10	−.02	.08
Overall assessment of intellectual impairment (reversed scale)	−.01	−.15*	−.11	−.07	−.20**	.02

Note. Correlations in expected direction are negative. Data were not complete for 32 controls (Impairment Index).

$^{*}p < .05$.

$^{**}p < .01$.

$^{***}p < .001$.

patients ($p < .05$ or $p < .01$). Cortical changes in the 20- to 44-year-old alcoholic patients were not correlated to neuropsychological deficits, but such a correlation was suggested in the 20- to 44-year-old controls, where four of the correlations were significant ($p < .05$ or $p < .01$). There was essentially no relationship between cortical changes and neuropsychological test performance in the 45- to 65-year-old alcoholics or controls.

Thus, central morphological changes in alcoholic patients (particularly in middle-aged or older patients with a dilated third ventricle), but not in the general population, seem to be associated with neuropsychological deficits. On the contrary, cortical changes do not seem to be associated with neuropsychological deficits in alcoholic patients. However, despite statistical significance, the correlations between central changes and neuropsychological deficits in the alcoholic patients were modest, never explaining more than 20% of the common variance.

The Correlation between Clinical Drinking-Related Variables and Cerebral State in the Male Alcoholic Patients

Duration of subjective loss of control (dichotomized at the median) was not associated with any of the other drinking-related variables in the male patient sample. A high quantity of alcohol consumed per drinking occasion (dichotomized) was associated with a low age of onset of subjective loss of control (dichotomized) ($p < .01$). A high quantity of alcohol consumed was also correlated with such medical complications as regularly having had blackouts ($p < .01$) , reporting previous hallucinations or delirious episodes ($p < .01$), or reporting epileptic fits ($p < .05$). An early onset was associated with regular blackouts and reported depression for the last year ($p < .01$ or $p < .001$). Depression was also associated with preference for relatively weak beverages (i.e., wine or beer; $p < .001$) and regular consumption of hypnotics or sedatives ($p < .01$).

A multiple-regression analysis was then performed using the age- and education-scaled neuropsychological test results and age-scaled CT scan findings as dependent variables in the male patient sample. Duration and onset of subjective loss of control, quantity of alcohol consumed per drinking occasion, periodic versus continuous drinking, preference for weak versus strong beverages, and regular use of hypnotics or sedatives were independent variables (dichotomized at the medians).

Only vocabulary (Synonyms) and verbal retention scores (Claeson–Dahl 30-Minute Retention) could be predicted from the drinking-pattern variables to a significant degree ($p < .01$). However, these functions were not vulnerable in our alcoholic patients as compared to the random controls (see Table 2-7). Somewhat unexpectedly, an early onset and a long duration of subjective loss of control were associated with superior vocabulary ($p < .05$), while, less surprisingly, regular consumption of hypnotics or sedatives (including benzodiazepines) was associated with low verbal retention. There was an unexpected trend indicative of superior neuropsychological performance in patients reporting an early subjective loss of control (before 30 years of age). The trend was fairly consistent but only significant ($p < .05$) in three tests. Neither duration of subjective loss of control nor amount of alcohol consumed per drinking occasion showed any predictive power. The morphological cerebral state could not be predicted from any of the drinking-related variables.

It can therefore be concluded that the duration of subjective loss of control, amount of alcohol consumed per drinking occasion, preference for weak versus strong beverages, periodic versus continuous drinking, and

Table 2-7. Standardized Beta Weights and Multiple Correlations (*R*) between Some Drinking-Related Variables and Age- and Education-Scaled Neuropsychological and CT Scan Results in 142 Male Alcoholic Patients

	Duration of subjective loss of control	Age of onset of loss of control	Maximum alcohol per drinking occasion	Periodic versus continuous drinking	Weak versus strong beverages	Regular hypnotic/sedative consumption	*R*
SRB (general intelligence)	.09	−.19	.14	.04	.01	.00	.29
Synonyms	.18*	−.20*	.13	.11	−.08	.05	.37**
Reasoning	.05	−.18	.06	−.03	.18	−.01	.27
Block Design	−.02	−.15	.13	.00	−.09	−.08	.24
Halstead–Reitan Battery							
Category	.06	−.10	.13	.04	.02	−.03	.20
TPT Time	.04	−.11	.10	−.01	−.11	−.04	.21
TPT Memory	−.07	−.05	−.02	−.02	−.13	−.05	.16
TPT Localization	.01	−.03	.06	.09	−.07	−.14	.18
TMT A	.15	−.08	.16	.05	−.14	.02	.29
TMT B	.12	−.12	.12	.09	−.03	.03	.26
Finger Tapping (dominant hand)	.00	.02	.09	.00	.02	.02	.10
Rhythm	.10	−.10	−.07	−.04	−.11	−.18	.25
Impairment Index	−.02	−.08	.03	.03	−.06	−.24*	.25
Learning and memory							
Claeson–Dahl Verbal Learning	.03	−.24*	.02	.06	−.04	−.07	.27
Claeson–Dahl 30-Minute Retention	−.15	−.17	−.07	−.06	.18*	−.27**	−.37**
Memory for Designs	.06	−.18	.05	.03	−.13	.00	.26
Overall assessment of intellectual impairment (reversed scale)	−.17	−.19*	.05	.03	−.15	−.04	.32
CT scan							
Width of lateral ventricles (reversed scale)	−.15	−.15	.03	−.01	.07	.09	.23
Width of third ventricle (reversed scale)	.01	.02	−.05	.10	.09	−.06	.16
Cortical changes (reversed scale)	−.04	−.06	−.03	.09	.14	.02	.17

Note. CT scans were only carried out on 134 male patients. Expected correlations are negative with the exception of age of onset of loss of control. Intellectual impairment and cortical changes were not age- and education-scaled.

$^{*}p < .05$.

$^{**}p < .01$.

regular consumption of hypnotics or sedatives as assessed here do not predict morphological changes or neuropsychological deficits in male alcoholic patients. The proportion of explained variance among our patients never exceeded 15%! An unexpected trend of late onset of subjective loss of control was observed in patients with neuropsychological deficits.

The neuropsychological and CT scan results were then correlated with a criterion measure of the severity of alcohol problems at a 6-month and a 2½-year follow-up. This criterion measure was based on reports of amount of alcohol consumed, drinking pattern, signs of dependence on alcohol, and time sober during the preceding 6 months. The measure satisfied conventional psychometric criteria (Sandahl, Lindberg, & Bergman, 1985). In only one of the neuropsychological tests (Finger Tapping) was a positive and significant correlation observed between high scores and favorable outcome. Thus, we were not able to demonstrate that the cerebral state as assessed by CT scan and a comprehensive neuropsychological test battery during treatment had any prognostic value for drinking status after treatment.

Summary and Discussion

In the present study, 196 male and female alcoholic patients of a consecutive and representative series of inpatients without neuropsychiatric diagnoses were investigated on a routine basis. For comparison purposes, a random control sample of 200 men and 200 women, stratified with regard to age, from the general population of the same geographical sector as the alcoholic patients was also investigated. On CT scan of the brain, clear-cut or high-grade visible symmetric widening of cortical sulci was observed in 61% of the male alcoholic patients and in 16% of the male random controls. The corresponding prevalence in the women was 52% among the patients and 23% among the random controls. Central changes indicated by pathologically and symmetrically dilated lateral ventricles were observed in 34% of the male patients and in 11% of the control men. The corresponding prevalence among females was 19% versus 3%. A pathologically dilated third ventricle was observed in 55% of the male patients versus 13% of the male controls, and in 31% of the female patients versus 8% of the female controls.

On neuropsychological testing, modest to profound neuropsychological impairment according to the Halstead–Reitan Impairment Index was observed in 51% of the male patients versus 29% of the male controls, and in 63% of the female patients versus 39% of the female controls. According to the psychologists' overall assessment of test results in the light of relevant anamnestic data, clear signs of intellectual impairment in comparison with premorbid level was observed in 23% of the male patients versus 9% of the male controls, and in 39% of the female patients versus 12% of the female controls.

Thus, a significantly higher prevalence of both morphological and behavioral indications of brain damage was found in the alcoholic patients as compared to the random controls, particularly with regard to morphological signs in the male patients and neuropsychological signs in the female patients. This higher prevalence was not due to different age distributions, since essentially identical results were obtained when differences in age distribution were controlled for. Furthermore, the higher prevalence was not due to liver disease, head trauma, polyneuropathy, narcotic drug abuse, anxiety, psychasthenia, sociopathy, or reported depression. Moreover, the higher prevalence could not have been due to clinically manifest withdrawal states, since the CT scan and neuropsychological assessment were not performed until signs of (or medication for) withdrawal reactions were no longer at hand. Of course, the possible influence of subclinical withdrawal states cannot be ruled out, and the patients might rightly be called "intermediate-stage alcoholics." Neuropsychological performance was negatively correlated with age and positively correlated with education. Widened cortical sulci and dilation of the ventricular system were positively correlated with age.

In our previous studies (Bergman, Axelsson, *et al.*, 1983) we have found that the sex of a person is important for ventricular size, but not for cortical changes. Age, sex, and (to a certain extent) education are also correlated with important drinking-pattern variables (e.g., duration of heavy drinking). They are generally controlled for by partial correlation or through careful pairwise matching of subjects. In the present study, the control was achieved by using age- and education-scaled neuropsychological test scores and age- and sex-scaled CT scan scores (except for the cortical changes variable, which was left untransformed). The double scaling was based on the results of the 400 randomly drawn control persons from the general population. Since the sample loss was less than 10% in the males and about 15% in the females, the control sample should be representative for the corresponding age strata of the general population.

The neuropsychological deficit pattern of the male alcoholic patients was in agreement with that generally reported in male alcoholics. Thus, visual–spatial functions involving abstracting and problem solving, and information handling requiring complex sensory–motor coordination, were found to be impaired (e.g., TMT B, Block Design, Category, and Reasoning). On the contrary, vocabulary, which is mainly dependent on long-term memory and not on current problem-solving ability, was found to be comparatively unaffected. With regard to learning and memory, deficits were found in visual–spatial–motor abilities (e.g., Memory for Designs), and to a certain extent tactual–motor abilities (TPT Memory), but not auditory–verbal functions (the Claeson–Dahl tests). When the neuropsychological tests were rank-ordered in terms of magnitude of deficit, the same seven tests appeared first in the male and female alcoholic patients. Despite this, there were sex differences in both the level and the pattern of deficits. Thus, the female patients showed more deficits than the male patients, and the rank order of the most vulnerable cognitive functions was somewhat different. In comparison with the many American studies (e.g., those reviewed by Parsons & Leber, 1982), there were some differences in the rank order of deficits (e.g., TMT B was relatively more sensitive and TPT Time and TPT Localization were relatively less sensitive in our patients).

During recent years, the permanence of cerebral changes observed on CT scan in alcoholic patients during treatment has been called into question. Observations in small reinvestigated samples suggest that the damage might regress after a long period of abstinence from alcohol (see Porjesz & Begleiter, 1983, for a review). Such a regression of cortical changes was observed in a 5-year follow-up of the alcoholic patients in the present study (Muuronen, Bergman, & Hindmarsh, 1984). Central changes seemed to be somewhat more permanent. The "brain morphology regression" issue has considerable theoretical and clinical implications with regard to the exact nature of the morphological cerebral changes in alcoholic patients and the prognosis for these patients after treatment. Until we have better knowledge about the nature of these changes, it might be wise to use the term "volume reduction" instead of "brain atrophy." With regard to the permanence of the neuropsychological deficits observed in the present study, both the level and the pattern of these deficits (controlling for effects of training) have been found to be quite stable over time, despite greatly decreased drinking (Bergman, 1983). One exception to this was significantly improved visual–spatial pattern reproduction (Block Design) as revealed in a combined independent-groups and test–retest design. When neuropsychological improvement did occur, it was observed during the first 6 months after treatment and was not associated with low age, short duration of heavy drinking, or a high previous consumption level; nor was it associated with unaffected brain morphology, according to CT scan. After 6 months, no further improvement in Block Design performance occurred.

Age was found to explain 13% of the variance of the separate CT scan parameters in the present study, and the relationship between age and cerebral state was practically identical in the male and female patients and controls. Thus, the relationship was not greater in the alcoholics, which might be expected on the basis of the premature-aging hypothesis. When the relationship between cortical and central morphological changes was analyzed as a function of age, there was no correlation in the young to middle-aged persons and a low but statistically significant correlation in the older persons of the random control sample. The reverse of this finding was observed in the patients: The correlation between cortical and central changes that was found in the young to middle-aged group was *not* present in the older age group. Nor does this finding support the premature-aging hypothesis. Furthermore, our suggestion made previously—that cortical and central changes often follow different courses in alcoholism—is again supported. The results indicate that two different pathological CNS processes or syndromes (an early, more acute, and less permanent cortical process versus a later, more insidious, and longer-lasting central process) are involved in alcoholism and cannot be observed in the general population as the result of the more or less "normal" aging process.

In general, a correlation between neuropsychological deficits and morphological cerebral changes is not a necessity, since even dementia may occur without clear radiological signs of brain atrophy. However, such a correlation has both theoretical and practical implications. When age (and education) was controlled for in the present study, central changes in the patients, particularly in middle-aged or older patients with a dilated third ventricle, were found to be associated with neuropsychological deficits. This result was not found in the random controls. Conversely, cortical changes were not associated with such deficits in the patients, but was suggested in the young to middle-aged random controls. Although statistically significant, the relationship between central morphological changes and neuropsychological deficits in the patients was modest and explained no more than 20% of the common variance. The clinical implication of this finding is that CT scan signs of *cortical* brain atrophy do not provide any information about the neuropsychological state in alcoholic patients. Conversely, if an alcoholic patient has *central* changes, as indicated by a dilated ventricular system on the CT scan, the probability of neuropsychological deficits is increased, particularly in middle-aged or older patients with a dilated 3rd ventricle (and a reported history of delirious episodes). The moderate correlation with neuropsychological deficits for central changes and the nonexistent correlation for cortical changes clearly indicate that CT scan and neuropsychological testing cannot replace each other in the routine clinical diagnostic assessment of alcoholic patients. Thus, they seem to reflect disparate aspects of cerebral function in alcoholism. For this reason, CT scan should not be used to confirm the validity of neuropsychological tests in alcoholics, and vice versa, although both types of assessment provide useful information about certain aspects of CNS integrity in their own right. Since cortical changes were not associated with neuropsychological deficits and were found to be less pronounced when drinking decreased significantly during a 5-year follow-up period, the relevance of cortical changes as indicators of *permanent* brain damage in alcoholism might be questioned.

If alcohol abuse causes brain damage, it is reasonable to expect an association between pertinent drinking-habit variables and signs of brain damage in alcoholic patients. It might not be a simple, continuous dose–response relationship, since there are complex interactions between drinking habits and between those habits and many other patient characteristics. In many alcoholics, a threshold model instead of a dose–response model is probably more appropriate; that is, there might be no relationship up to a threshold level of exposure, but above that level the expected relationship between drinking habits and signs of brain damage might occur. This hypothetical threshold level is probably very different in different individuals, due to constitutional characteristics. In the present study, onset and duration of subjective loss of control, amount of alcohol consumed per drinking occasion, type of alcoholic beverage used, drinking pattern, and consumption of sedatives or hypnotics were together found to explain less than 15% of the variance of the separate neuropsychological tests or CT scan parameters in the male alcoholic patients. The clinical implication of this finding is that in alcoholic patients without clinically manifest symptoms of brain damage, it is generally unwise to draw conclusions about the cerebral state on the basis of drinking habits alone. The lack of predictive power of the drinking-habit variables for signs of brain damage is unlikely to have been caused by lack of reliability, since the variables were found to have satisfactory test–retest reliability, were not correlated to a measure of social desirability, and showed a meaningful and consistent pattern of intercorrelations.

The lack of correlations between drinking-habit variables and signs of brain damage, and the relative permanence of neuropsychological deficits and ventricular dilation over different phases of the drinking cycle observed in the present study, have implications for the etiology of brain damage in alcoholism. Thus, our results are in agreement with the view that brain damage in many alcoholics might be more dependent upon a genetically based vulnerability than upon long-term excessive alcohol consumption per se. Such a conclusion was drawn by Kaij (1960) from the results of a study of monozygotic and dizygotic twins. The findings of the present study—together with our previously reported finding that deficits in abstracting ability were relatively constant, while memory deficits and generalized intellectual impairment appeared increasingly in advancing age groups—also support the view of Parsons and Leber (1982) that many alcoholics might be recruited from a pool of persons with inferior abstracting and current problem-solving abilities. This view seems particularly relevant for the female alcoholic patients, since more neuropsychological deficits were observed in the female than in the male patients, despite much less exposure to alcohol and fewer morphological cerebral changes.

Practically no significant correlations were found between CT scan and neuropsychological findings on the one hand, and the outcome after treatment (as assessed by a comprehensive measure of drinking status at a 6-month and a 2½-year follow-up) on the other. Thus, we could not predict outcome with regard to drinking status from a knowledge of the cerebral state. We are currently investigating the potential relationship of cerebral state during treatment to mental health and social functioning at follow-up in the alcoholic patients.

From the results of the present study, the following conclusions can be drawn:

1. Morphological and neuropsychological signs of brain damage are more prevalent in alcoholic patients, unselected with regard to suspected brain damage, than in the general population.
2. Morphological signs are more prevalent than neuropsychological signs, at least in male alcoholic patients.
3. Morphological changes of the central parts of the brain of alcoholics are associated with neuropsychological deficits of a cognitive nature, particularly in middle-aged or older alcoholics.
4. Cortical changes as indicators of permanent brain damage in alcoholics are of questionable clinical and neuropsychological relevance.
5. A threshold model and a genetically based vulnerability model of the etiology of brain damage in alcoholism might be valid alternatives to a dose–response model.
6. Many alcoholics seem to come from a pool of persons with poor abstracting and problem-solving abilities, particularly female alcoholic patients.

Acknowledgments

I am grateful to Stefan Borg, Tomas Hindmarsh, and Carl-Magnus Ideström, who have taken part in the KARTAD Project. Special thanks go to Göran Axelsson and Sture Mützell for the medical examination of the random control sample. I am also grateful to Inger Bergman, Karin Engelbrektson, Kerstin Johannesson, Lena Holm, and Staffan Lindberg for making the psychological assessments; to Torsten Kullman and Staffan Lindberg for the computer work; to Matti Hillbom for valuable comments; to Kenneth Hodson for checking the language of the manuscript; and to Carina Aronsson and Birgitta Strimme for typing it. The KARTAD Project was supported by grants from the Swedish Welfare Department and the Bank of Sweden Tercentenary Foundation.

References

Bergman, H. (1981). Sambandet mellan neuropsykologiska och datortomografiska fynd hos alkoholpatienter [The relationship between neuropsychological and computer-tomographic findings in alcohol patients]. In J. Wadstein & B. Sternebring (Eds.), *Proceedings of the First Malmö Symposium of Alcohol 1980* (pp. 101–113). Malmö: Alkoholkliniken, Allmänna Sjukhuset, & Ferrosan.

Bergman, H. (1983, June–July). *Neuropsychological recovery in alcoholics after treatment.* Paper presented at the 29th International Institute on the Prevention and Treatment of Alcoholism, Zagreb, Yugoslavia.

Bergman, H. (1985). Cognitive deficits and morphological cerebral changes in a random sample of social drinkers. In M. Galanter (Ed.), *Recent developments in alcoholism* (Vol. 3, pp. 265–276). New York: Plenum Press.

Bergman, H., & Ågren, G. (1974). Cognitive style and intellectual performance in relation to the progress of alcoholism. *Quarterly Journal of Studies on Alcohol, 35*, 1242–1255.

Bergman, H., Axelsson, G., Ideström, C.-M., Borg, S., Hindmarsh, T., Mackower, J., & Mützell, S. (1983). Alcohol consumption, neuropsychological status and computer tomographic findings in a random sample of men and women from the general population. *Pharmacology, Biochemistry and Behavior, 18* (Suppl. 1), 501–505.

Bergman, H., Bergman, I., Engelbrektson, K., Holm, L., Johannesson, K., & Lindberg, S. (1983). *Psykologhandboken* [*Manual for psychologists*]. Stockholm: Magnus Huss Klinik, Karolinska Sjukhuset.

Bergman, H., Borg, S., Hindmarsh, T., Ideström, C.-M., & Mützell, S. (1980a). Computed tomography of the brain and neuropsychological assessment of alcoholic patients. In H. Begleiter (Ed.), *Biological effects of alcohol* (pp. 771–786). New York: Plenum Press.

Bergman, H., Borg, S., Hindmarsh, T., Ideström, C.-M., & Mützell, S. (1980b). Computed tomography of the brain and neuropsychological assessment of male alcoholic patients. In D. Richter (Ed.), *Addiction and brain damage: Biochemical aspects of dependence and brain damage. Proceedings of the Symposium on Addiction, Oxford 1979* (pp. 201–214). London: Croom Helm.

Bergman, H., Borg, S., Hindmarsh, T., Ideström, C.-M., & Mützell, S. (1980c). Computed tomography of the brain and neuropsychological assessment of male alcoholic patients and a random sample from the general male population. *Acta Psychiatrica Scandinavica, 62* (Suppl. 286), 77–88.

Bergman, H., Borg, S., Hindmarsh, T., Ideström, C.-M., & Mützell, S. (1980d). Computed tomography of the brain, clinical examination and neuropsychological assessment of a random sample of men from the general population. *Acta Psychiatrica Scandinavica, 62* (Suppl. 286), 47–56.

Elofsson, S. A., Gamberale, F., Hindmarsh, T., Iregren, A., Isaksson, A., Johnsson, J., Knave, B., Lydahl, E., Mindus, P., Persson, H. E., Philipson, B., Steby, M., Struwe, G., Söderman, E., Wennberg, A., & Widén, L. (1980). Exposure to organic solvents: A cross-sectional epidemiologic investigation on occupationally exposed car and industrial spray painters with special reference to the nervous system. *Scandinavian Journal of Work, Environment and Health, 6*, 239–273.

Hillbom, M., Muuronen, A., Holm, L., & Hindmarsh, T. (1986). The clinical versus radiological diagnosis of alcoholic cerebellar degeneration. *Journal of the Neurological Sciences, 73*, 45–53.

Ideström, C.-M. (Ed.). (1977). *Recent advances in the study of alcoholism: Proceedings of the First International Magnus Huss Symposium, Stockholm 1976* (Excerpta Medica International Congress Series 407). Amsterdam: Excerpta Medica.

Kaij, L. (1960). *Alcoholism in twins.* Stockholm, Almqvist & Wiksell.

Mützell, S., Bergman, H., Borg, S., Lindberg, S., & Olsson, L. (1978). Reliabiliteten hos anamnestiska enkätmetoder för inneliggande alkoholpatienter [The reliability of anamnestic questionnaires for alcoholic inpatients]. *Acta Societatis Medicorum Suecanae, 87*, 310.

Muuronen, A., Bergman, H., & Hindmarsh, T. (1984). Recovery from structural and functional brain damage in abstinent alcoholics. *Alcoholism: Clinical and Experimental Research, 8*, 109.

Parsons, O. A., & Leber, W. R. (1982). Alcohol, cognitive dysfunction and brain damage. In National Institute on Alcohol Abuse and Alcoholism (Ed.), *Biomedical processes and consequences of alcohol use* (Alcohol and Health Monograph No. 2, DHHS Publication No. ADM 82-1191, pp. 213–253). Washington, DC: U. S. Government Printing Office.

Porjesz, B., & Begleiter, H. (1983). Brain dysfunction and alcohol. In B. Kissin & H. Begleiter

(Eds.), *The biology of alcoholism: Vol. 7. The pathogenesis of alcoholism: Biological factors* (pp. 415–484). New York: Plenum Press.

Ryan, C., & Butters, N. (1983). Cognitive deficits in alcoholics. In B. Kissin & H. Begleiter (Eds.), *The biology of alcoholism: Vol. 7. The pathogenesis of alcoholism: Biological factors* (pp. 485–538). New York: Plenum Press.

Sandahl, C., Lindberg, S., & Bergman, H. (1985). Severity of alcohol problems at follow-up—an outcome measure. *Acta Psychiatrica Scandinavica, 71*, 458–467.

Schalling, D., Edman, G., & Åsberg, M. (1983). Impulsive cognitive style and inability to tolerate boredom: Psychobiological studies of temperamental vulnerability. In M. Zuckerman (Ed.), *Biological bases of sensation seeking, impulsivity, and anxiety* (pp. 123–145). Hillsdale, NJ: Erlbaum.

Wilkinson, D. A., & Carlen, P. L. (1981). Chronic organic brain syndromes associated with alcoholism: Neuropsychological and other aspects. In Y. Israel, F. B. Glaser, H. Kalant, R. E. Popham, W. Schmidt, & R. G. Smart (Eds.), *Research advances in alcohol and drug problems* (Vol. 6, pp. 107–145). New York: Plenum Press.

3

Evoked Brain Potentials and Alcoholism

BERNICE PORJESZ
HENRI BEGLEITER

Introduction

The relative inaccessibility of the living human brain to direct neurobiological scrutiny has made it difficult to examine brain dysfunction in alcoholism. While it has long been apparent that the human brain is very susceptible to both the acute and chronic effects of alcohol, it is only recently, with the development of sophisticated technology, that these effects have been studied *in vivo*. The development of advanced computer technology has made it possible to investigate functional brain deficits in alcoholics with noninvasive evoked brain potential (EP) techniques. These EP techniques permit an examination of more subtle forms of brain damage and/or dysfunction that was heretofore not possible. The event-related potential (ERP) techniques offer a unique approach for assessing level of brain functioning, as they permit the simultaneous observation of electrophysiology and cognition.

An ERP is obtained by recording the time-locked brain electrical activity with a noninvasive scalp electrode following the delivery of a discrete stimulus to any sensory modality (e.g., auditory, visual). Signal-averaging techniques make it possible to extract these time-locked neuroelectric signals (ERPs) from the background random "noise," which is canceled out with these procedures. Depending on stimulation properties and recording sites, these time-locked signals represent activity at neural generators from the peripheral end organ to higher integrative centers of the brain. The quantitative measurement of salient features extracted from ERP recordings provide objective neurophysiological data reflecting various aspects of brain function related to integrative processes, as well as the functional integrity of different neuroanatomical systems. Thus, with the use of these sophisticated neurophysiological techniques, the functional integrity of various systems of the brain (from peripheral end organs to the neocortex) can be assessed.

Bernice Porjesz and Henri Begleiter. Department of Psychiatry, State University of New York, Health Science Center at Brooklyn, Brooklyn, New York.

ERP techniques have proven to be very useful in indexing electrophysiological concomitants of complex cognitive tasks (Donchin, 1979; Donchin, Ritter, & McCallum, 1978; Hillyard, Picton, & Regan, 1978). They can be recorded in conjunction with behavior, or even when no behavioral response is required, to both attended and unattended stimuli. Thus the ERP techniques are very sensitive indices of the functional integrity of the brain. They differ from the computerized tomography (CT) scan in that they reflect subtle, dynamic, moment-to-moment changes in brain functioning that are elicited while the brain is being challenged, rather than the static, gross brain damage that is apparent on the CT scan. ERP aberrations are often observed in the absence of brain damage as visualized on CT scan.

Evoked Brain Potentials and Alcoholism

EP techniques have provided indices sensitive to the various alcohol effects—namely, alcoholization, tolerance, withdrawal, and long-term brain dysfunction. Alcoholization is characterized by marked depressions in EP amplitude (Bierley, Cannon, Wehl, & Dustman, 1980) and by prolongations in conduction velocities of the brain stem potential (BSP) (Chu, Squires, & Starr, 1978; Squires, Chu, & Starr, 1978a, 1978b). Chronic alcohol intake is accompanied by EP amplitude reductions (Begleiter & Porjesz, 1977; Porjesz, Begleiter, & Hurowitz, 1976) and by BSP delays that are less pronounced when tolerance develops (Chu *et al.*, 1978; Squires *et al.*, 1978a, 1978b; Zilm, Kaplan, & Capell, 1981). These techniques are also very sensitive to withdrawal phenomena, which are characterized by increased EP voltages and extremely shortened BSP latencies, indicative of underlying CNS hyperexcitability (Begleiter & Porjesz, 1977, 1979; Begleiter, DeNoble, & Porjesz, 1980; Chu *et al.*, 1978; Hunter & Walker, 1980; Squires *et al.*, 1978a, 1978b). Finally, long-term abstinence is marked by decreased EP amplitudes (hyporeactivity) and by prolonged BSP latencies and slower conduction velocities (Begleiter, Porjesz, & Chou, 1981; Porjesz & Begleiter, 1983). The duration of these prolonged CNS disturbances and their potential recovery are not yet known. For the last several years in our laboratory, we have undertaken a systematic program of research to assess brain dysfunction in alcoholics with the use of these sensitive EP techniques.

Auditory Brain Stem Potentials

We have recently recorded auditory BSPs from hospitalized alcoholics who were abstinent from alcohol for 1 month (Begleiter *et al.*, 1981). With this technique, it is now possible to investigate subcortical brain functioning with a noninvasive scalp electrode (Jewett, 1970; Jewett & Williston, 1971; Sohmer & Feinmesser, 1967). These "far-field" potentials consist of time-locked positive waves, each presumed to reflect activity at different sites along the auditory pathway from the auditory nerve through the brain stem (Buchwald & Huang, 1975; Jewett, 1970; Lev & Sohmer, 1972; Starr & Achor, 1975; Starr & Hamilton, 1976; Stockard & Rossiter, 1977). The latencies of each of these peaks, as well as "central conduction time" (the latency of each peak with respect to peak I), are accurate in localizing sites of pathology from the peripheral end organ to the brain stem; the time interval between the peak I and peak V of the inferior colliculus is most often taken as a measure of brain stem transmission time (Fabiani, Sohmer, Tait, Gafni, & Kirati, 1979).

In our study, we found that alcoholic patients manifested significant delays in latencies and central conduction velocities of peaks II–V. These findings are remarkably similar to those reported with acute doses of alcohol in animals (Squires *et al.*, 1978b) and humans (Squires *et al.*, 1978a). Our study provides the first systematic electrophysiological evidence of brain dysfunction at levels other than neocortex in alcoholics without overt clinical signs of neurological damage. The increase in neural transmission time may reflect the process of demyelination, which has long been suspected in alcoholics (Adams, Victor, & Mancall, 1959) and has been observed in rats chronically exposed to alcohol (Moscatelli & Demediuk, 1980). Similar results have recently been reported in neurologically impaired alcoholics (Chu & Squires, 1980; Chu, Squires, & Starr, 1982; Haas & Nickel, 1981; Nickel & Ludewig, 1981; Rosenhamer & Silfverskiold, 1980) and in neurologically intact alcoholics (Cassvan, Rosenberg, & Caliguiri, 1984). The etiology of these auditory BSP delays, and the drinking-history factor(s) (e.g., length of drinking history, amount consumed per sitting, number of withdrawals, nutritional factors, etc.) that result in brain stem aberrations, have not yet been definitively determined. It is even possible that nutritional deficiencies alone produce demyelination and hence the BSP delays. Nutritional deficits are known to lead to demyelinating diseases such as polyneuropathy (Hillman, 1974). At present, we are investigating the relationship between drinking-history and nutritional factors and the magnitude of BSP aberration. Our preliminary data suggest that alcoholics with signs of nutritional deficits and/or polyneuropathy display BSP waveforms that are different from those of other alcoholics. Furthermore, length of drinking history does not seem to correlate with BSP delay; in fact, alcoholics with relatively short histories of heavy drinking (less than 8 years) but evidence of nutritional deficits manifested greater BSP aberrations than alcoholics with long drinking histories (more than 20 years) and no signs of nutritional deficits.

Taken together, these findings suggest that BSP aberrations in alcoholics may be the result of alcohol and/or nutritional factors. The results of animal data (Chu *et al.*, 1978) suggest that other factors besides chronic alcohol exposure are necessary to produce BSP abnormalities, as chronic alcohol ingestion in the absence of nutritional deficits in laboratory animals is not sufficient to cause BSP delays after withdrawal.

Event-Related Potentials

As noted earlier, another promising neurophysiological approach in assessing brain functioning is the ERP technique. For the past several years, we have systematically examined ERPs in medication-free alcoholics who have been abstinent for approximately 1 month. These ERP techniques require the subject to be engaged in a task (usually information processing). Each task is designed to examine deficits of a particular ERP component. In the ERP literature, these components have been well documented to vary predictably under specific conditions in normal subjects (Donchin *et al.*, 1978; Hillyard *et al.*, 1978).

In one bimodal (visual and auditory) study, we investigated the ability of alcoholics to focus on a relevant stimulus modality and inhibit responding to an irrelevant modality, by examining the N100 component of the ERP (Porjesz & Begleiter, 1979), a component that occurs at a latency of about 100 msec. The N100 component is sensitive to the selection of a relevant or irrelevant stimulus modality in healthy subjects; it is enhanced to all stimuli in a relevant stimulus modality, and reduced to stimuli in irrelevant modalities (Hillyard, Hink, Schwent, & Price, 1973; Hillyard *et al.*, 1978; Picton & Hillyard, 1974). The patients were presented with a sequence of randomized single flashes and clicks, with rarely occurring double flashes and clicks interspersed among them. They were required to "shift attentional sets" by counting either the double flashes or double clicks, or ignoring all stimuli, in an otherwise identical stimulus sequence. ERPs were obtained only to the irrelevant single flashes, which were either in the relevant or irrelevant stimulus modality in a given condition; such frequent single flashes elicit N100 components that are differentially enhanced in the relevant channel (stimulus modality).

The results indicated that abstinent alcoholics manifested abnormally reduced late-component amplitudes (less than 100 msec), but not early-component amplitudes. These findings in abstinent alcoholics are remarkably similar to results obtained when healthy subjects ingested single doses of alcohol (E. G. Lewis, Dustman, & Beck, 1969; Porjesz & Begleiter, 1975; Rhodes, Obitz, & Creel, 1975). This suggests that the neurophysiological brain dysfunction observed in abstinent alcoholics may resemble brain functioning detected in normal persons under the influence of alcohol. Often it is the differential voltage between ERPs obtained to stimuli in relevant and irrelevant channels that is more revealing about the nature of brain functioning than absolute voltages to either relevant or irrelevant stimuli. Consistent with the ERP literature (Hillyard *et al.*, 1973, 1978), control subjects in our study manifested significantly enhanced N100 components to stimuli in the relevant as compared to the irrelevant modality; however, alcoholics maintained the same low amplitude of N100, regardless of degree of task relevance. These results suggest that alcoholics may be incapable of appropriate "sensory filtering," as they do not neurophysiologically differentiate between relevant and irrelevant channels.

We have also used the P300 component of the ERP to examine brain dysfunction in alcoholics, with many different experimental paradigms. The P300 component is a large positive deflection that occurs approximately 300–500 msec after the stimulus. It can only be elicited under certain rather specific conditions related to the "subjective significance" of a stimulus—namely, task relevance (Sutton, Tueting, Zubin, & John, 1967), unpredictability (Donchin *et al.*, 1978), and infrequency (Tueting, Sutton, & Zubin, 1971)—as well as by motivational factors (Begleiter, Porjesz, Chou, & Aunon, 1983). The characteristics of P300 are unrelated to stimulus parameters, and can even be elicited in the absence of an expected stimulus (emitted potentials) (Klinke, Fruhstorfer, & Finkenzeller, 1968). In terms of scalp topography, P300 has been found to be maximum over parietal areas; it is bilaterally distributed without apparent hemispheric asymmetry, with similar distributions regardless of the sensory modality of the stimulus (Simson, Vaughan, & Ritter, 1976, 1977a, 1977b).

In one study in our laboratory, we investigated the P300 component with a visual target-selection paradigm (Porjesz, Begleiter, & Garozzo, 1980). The target selection paradigm is most frequently used to elicit a P300 component; it requires the subject to detect a designated rarely occurring target stimulus embedded in a series of frequently occurring nontarget stimuli. ERPs recorded to frequently occurring nontarget stimuli elicit N100 components, but no P300, while rare target stimuli elicit both N100 and P300 components. In our study (Porjesz *et al.*, 1980), the stimuli were geometric shapes. One rare geometric shape (e.g., a triangle) was designated target, and the subject was required to press a button only to that stimulus. Target and nontarget stimuli were alternated every other block, enabling the recording of ERPs to the same stimulus when it was target or nontarget. ERPs were recorded to target (rarely occurring, task-relevant geometric shapes), nontarget (frequently occurring, task-relevant geometric shapes), and novel (rarely occurring, task-irrelevant random shapes) stimuli.

Despite the fact that all stimuli were in the relevant channel, we found that the N100 amplitudes were significantly depressed in alcoholics to all stimuli, to levels comparable to an irrelevant stimulus modality. As in our bimodal study (Porjesz & Begleiter, 1979), this suggests that "sensory-filtering" mechanisms are impaired in chronic alcoholics. Furthermore, we found that P300 amplitudes were significantly reduced or absent in alcoholic patients to rare target stimuli under conditions optimal for eliciting large P300s (Donchin *et al.*, 1978). This finding was most pronounced over parietal areas, where P300 amplitude is maximal at scalp (Ritter, Vaughan,

& Costa, 1968; Simson *et al.*, 1977a, 1977b). Furthermore, while controls manifested differentially enhanced late P300 components to target stimuli, alcoholics manifested identical low-amplitude P300 waves with the same P300 latencies, regardless of whether a stimulus was target or nontarget. Thus, the major ERP aberrations manifested by alcoholics are the lack of differentiation between their responses to relevant and irrelevant inputs, and the low voltages of their event-related activity. This seems to suggest underlying brain dysfunction that impairs "sensory-filtering" and "probability-matching" processes.

Despite its maximal amplitude over parietal areas at the scalp, recent evidence suggests that the neural origins of P300 may be subcortical and may implicate the amygdala and hippocampus. One recent study investigating the neural origins of P300 with implanted electrodes in humans reported that P300 was maximum at subcortical loci (Wood, Allison, Goff, Williamson, & Spencer, 1980). Similarly, Halgren *et al.* (1980) have recently recorded large late potentials from the limbic system with implanted electrodes in humans. They postulate that P300 may be generated in the hippocampus or the amygdala.

Thus, our findings that alcoholics manifest low-voltage or even absent P300 components under conditions designed to elicit maximum P300 component amplitudes may be indicative of hippocampal deficits. While these results do not rule out the contributions of cortical sites, they emphasize the important role of limbic structures in generating the P300 component. The involvement of the hippocampus in chronic alcohol intake in the absence of malnutrition has been recently demonstrated in neuropathological and neurophysiological studies in animals (Begleiter, DeNoble, & Porjesz, 1980; Riley & Walker, 1978; Walker, Barnes, Zornetzer, Hunter, & Kubanis, 1980; Walker, Hunter, & Abraham, 1981). Long-term ethanol consumption has been found to result in the loss of dendritic spines in mouse (Riley & Walker, 1978) and rat (Walker *et al.*, 1980) hippocampus. In our laboratory, we have also demonstrated a hippocampal susceptibility to both acute and chronic alcohol effects with evoked potentials recorded from monkey hippocampus (Begleiter, DeNoble, & Porjesz, 1980).

We were interested in determining the relationship between electrophysiological deficits and structural deficits assessed with CT scan in alcoholics (Begleiter, Porjesz, & Tenner, 1980). We selected two groups of alcoholics who had been subjected to CT scans following 1 month of abstinence: namely, those manifesting a high degree of widened cortical sulci (Pos-CT) and those without any evidence of widened cortical sulci (Neg-CT). Patients in the two groups did not differ with regard to age, education, and drinking history (duration and amount). ERPs were recorded on the same day as the CT scan and involved the same P300 paradigm previously described (Porjesz *et al.*, 1980). Alcoholics with enlarged cortical sulci (Pos-CT) had significantly reduced (or absent) P300 amplitudes to target stimuli as compared to alcoholics without signs of enlarged cortical sulci (Neg-CT); however, both groups manifested smaller P300s to targets than did control subjects. Furthermore, both groups of alcoholics displayed similar P300 components to all categories of stimuli, regardless of task relevance.

As alcoholics without signs of widened cortical sulci also manifested diminished P300 amplitudes when compared to healthy nonalcoholics, neocortical shrinkage alone cannot explain these P300 reductions. These findings suggest that chronic alcohol abuse not only results in changes in the neocortex, but may also involve electrophysiological aberrations indicative of other brain (e.g., limbic system) deficits. Often the neocortical deficits in chronic alcoholics are emphasized while subcortical aberrations are overlooked. Our results suggest that alcoholics manifesting observable widened cortical sulci on CT scan are more likely to manifest hippocampal deficits as well. This perhaps lends support to the hypothesis that alcohol produces diffuse brain damage that is not solely circumscribed in neocortical areas.

We have recently completed a study examining the N200 component of the ERP in abstinent alcoholics (Porjesz & Begleiter, 1981a, 1981b; Porjesz, Begleiter, Bihari, & Kissin, 1987). The N200 component is a modality-specific negative deflection with a maximum amplitude at occipito-parietal scalp for the visual modality, and at central regions for the auditory modality. Recent evidence suggests that the latency of N200 can be taken as an early index of stimulus evaluation time (Renault & Lesevre, 1979); the more difficult the discrimination, the longer the latency of N200 (Gaillard & Lawson, 1980; Ritter, Simson, Vaughan, & Friedman, 1979; Towey, Rist, Hakerem, Ruchkin, & Sutton, 1980). The N200 component is a better index of stimulus evaluation time than is reaction time (RT), because it is not confounded by the motor response. RT is a complex measure of speed of information processing, as it depends on the end product of stimulus evaluation, response selection and organization, and the motor response. Therefore, although there are some reports of delayed RTs in chronic alcoholics (Bertera & Parsons, 1973; Talland, 1963; Vivian, Goldstein, & Shelly, 1973), these studies cannot determine which aspect or aspects of information processing are slower in alcoholics.

We were interested in specifically examining the speed of stimulus evaluation in chronic alcoholics, using the N200 component of the ERP as an index. Therefore, we designed an RT study involving easy and difficult line-orientation discriminations. This visuospatial RT design enabled us to investigate the relationship among difficulty of discrimination, N200 latency, P300 characteristics, and RT in abstinent chronic alcoholics. ERPs were obtained to frequent nontargets (vertical line), and infrequent easy (90° deviant from vertical) and difficult (3° deviant) line orientations.

Our results indicated that the latency of N200 reflected difficulty of discrimination in the control subjects, being significantly delayed for the difficult as compared to the easy discrimination. However, it failed to do so in the alcoholics, where N200 latencies were similar regardless of difficulty of discrimination. Furthermore, the N200 latency occurred significantly later in the alcoholic group than in the control group for both easy and difficult discriminations, suggesting that the alcoholics found the discrimination task more difficult, and hence needed more time for stimulus evaluation. The latency difference between groups was even more apparent for the easy discrimination than for the difficult discrimination. This suggests that the alcoholics needed proportionately more time to make an easy discrimination (vertical from horizontal) when compared to the controls (who could process this information more quickly) than to make a difficult discrimination (which both groups presumably found difficult).

In addition, alcoholics manifested delayed P300 latencies to easy discriminations when compared to controls; these P300 latencies were comparable to those expected for a difficult task. These results suggest that the alcoholics, finding all tasks difficult, adopted an undifferentiated mode of responding regardless of task requirements. While the amplitude of N200 was larger for easy discriminations than difficult discriminations in the control group, the amplitude of N200 was the same in the alcoholics regardless of task difficulty. The amplitude of N200 has been shown to be related to degree of stimulus deviance in normal subjects (Näätänen, Hukkanen, & Järvilehto, 1980).

There were no significant differences in RTs between the two groups of subjects, although the alcoholics tended to have somewhat faster RTs than controls. However, the alcoholics tended to make more errors, both in terms of false alarms and in terms of missing target stimuli, although these results were not significant. This response pattern indicates that speed was stressed over accuracy (Kutas, McCarthy, & Donchin, 1977), implying that the alcoholics adopted different response strategies from the controls. These results suggest a lack of inhibition in the chronic alcoholics, reflected by their apparent inability to withhold responding until certainty of accuracy or correctness was established.

In addition to these latency results, we found that alcoholics had significantly depressed P300 amplitudes. This low-amplitude P300 was even more apparent for the easy discrimination, where controls exhibited very high P300 voltages. The P300 voltage was significantly larger for the 90° target as compared to the 3° target in the control but not the alcoholic subjects. This result is predicted by many ERP studies, which have demonstrated that the more deviant a rare stimulus is from the background (the more easily discriminable it is), the larger the P300 amplitude (Ford *et al.*, 1979; Johnson & Donchin, 1978; Ritter, Simson, & Vaughan, 1972; Ruchkin & Sutton, 1978; Towey *et al.*, 1980). Perhaps the lack of P300 amplitude difference in the alcoholic group indicates that they were more uncertain of the correctness of their decision than were the controls, as they stressed speed over accuracy. Furthermore, while controls manifested significant target–nontarget P300 measures, alcoholics did not.

Thus on the basis of both the N200 and P300 ERP components, it was concluded that alcoholics have difficulty evaluating the potential significance of a stimulus. The alcoholic subjects did not electrophysiologically differentiate between relevant and irrelevant, or easy and difficult discriminations but rather maintained the same ERP characteristics (both amplitude and latency), regardless of the task requirements. This perhaps indicates that alcoholics' template for match–mismatch decisions is lost or not readily available. In either case, it suggests a memory deficit in which each incoming stimulus must be evaluated anew. Our data suggests that alcoholics manifest both types of brain dysfunction: The delay in N200 latency suggests that the template for comparison is not as readily accessible in alcoholics, while the low P300 voltages suggest that once retrieved, the match–mismatch processes themselves are impaired in alcoholics.

Recovery of Evoked Brain Potentials with Abstinence

We are currently examining the reversibility of the BSP and ERP deficits observed at 1 month of abstinence and following 4 months of continued abstinence in the same hospitalized alcoholics (Porjesz, 1983; Porjesz & Begleiter, 1987). Preliminary data following 4 months of abstinence indicate improved morphology of BSP waveforms, shortening of latencies, and improved conduction times. However, group data indicate that these peaks are still occurring somewhat later than those of control subjects.

The relative roles of abstinence from alcohol and nutritional factors in so-called "recovery" still remain to be determined. Throughout the long-term abstinence program in our hospital, patients receive extensive vitamin therapy and may be manifesting improvements in nutritional status. Furthermore, the role of withdrawal cannot be overlooked; CNS hyperexcitability may be followed by a period of subacute hypoexcitability. We might speculate that this hypoexcitability may be manifested by a prolongation of brain stem latencies caused by aberrant fluidizing effects on the membranes, which may result in edema. It should be noted that edema resulting from osmotic stress can lead to demyelination (Feigen & Budzilovich, 1978, 1980; Kleinschmidt-DeMasters & Norenberg, 1981; V. Lewis, 1976; Yates, 1976).

However, it should be noted that those alcoholics who remain in treatment for the full 4 months have less impaired BSPs at initial testing (3–4 weeks) when the data are analyzed retrospectively. As we are only able to examine reversibility in alcoholics who remain in long-term treatment, and these alcoholics tend to be less impaired initially, we cannot be certain that recovery occurs in all alcoholics regardless of degree of impairment. It remains to be determined whether recovery occurs as a function of the initial degree of impairment, whether greater impairment requires longer time periods for reversibility, or whether recovery ceases beyond a certain critical level of impairment.

While the BSP delays seem to improve with prolonged abstinence, the decreased voltages in the P300 component of the ERP do not seem to change with prolonged abstinence (Porjesz, 1983; Porjesz & Begleiter, 1987). We examined the possibility of reversibility of late-component P300 deficits in abstinent alcoholics following 3 weeks and 4 months of abstinence. Interestingly, no improvement in ERP morphology or late-component amplitude was noted following 4 months of abstinence in the same alcoholics; in fact, the waveforms were strikingly similar at initial test and retest. Furthermore, there was no improvement in the differential enhancement of P300 amplitudes on the basis of task relevance to target stimuli in these abstinent alcoholics. Thus, even following 4 months of abstinence, these alcoholics manifested abnormally low P300 amplitudes. We have observed these P300 decrements in response to both auditory and visual target stimuli following 3 weeks and 4 months of abstinence in a bimodal target-selection study. These results suggest that the P300 deficits may not be reversible, or may perhaps reverse much more slowly following very long abstinence periods. It is even possible that these P300 deficits may precede alcoholism, and may represent a predisposing factor differentiating those individuals with a susceptibility to alcoholism.

We are currently investigating electrophysiological aberrations in another group of nonhospitalized alcoholics sober for 3–10 years, and have found that they manifest normal BSPs. This suggests that perhaps 4 months is not a long enough time interval to investigate reversibility of brain dysfunction following years of heavy drinking. However, it should be noted that these long-term abstinent alcoholics were not tested initially, and therefore the extent of BSP aberration they may have manifested immediately following alcohol abuse is not known. It is possible that these alcoholics never exhibited BSP delays, as we do not see BSP delays in all alcoholics tested. While the issue of reversibility is still unresolved, the data seem to indicate slow reversibility of BSP deficits with prolonged abstinence. However, as P300 deficits were still observed following the same prolonged sobriety period (more than 3 years), the data suggest no recovery of P300 deficits following long-term abstinence. This it seems that some electrophysiological aberrations observed in chronic alcoholics improve with prolonged abstinence, while other electrophysiological aberrations do not change with prolonged sobriety. Caution is suggested in interpreting the results, as they are based on small samples. We are currently continuing to examine this issue with larger sample sizes in an effort to determine the important factors of susceptibility and reversibility of brain dysfunction in alcoholism.

Possible Evoked Brain Potential Markers for Alcoholism

It has generally been assumed that the brain abnormalities observed in alcoholics are due to the toxic effects of alcohol on the brain, nutritional deficits, or an interaction of alcohol and nutrition-related factors. The possibility that these brain deficits may in fact precede alcohol abuse has only been suggested recently. There is increasing evidence that certain individuals are at high risk for developing alcoholism. Specifically, sons of alcoholic fathers are four times more likely to develop alcoholism than sons of nonalcoholics (Goodwin, 1979; Goodwin, Schulsinger, Hermansen, Guze, & Winokur, 1973), even when they are separated from their biological parents soon after birth. Studies of male adoptees indicate that the biological rather than the adoptive parent is predictive of later drinking problems (Bohman, 1978; Cadoret & Gath, 1978; Cadoret, Cain, & Grove, 1980; Goodwin & Guze, 1974; Goodwin *et al.*, 1973; Schuckit, Goodwin, & Winokur, 1972). Furthermore, the concordance rate for alcohol abuse among identical twins is almost double the rate for fraternal twins (Kaij, 1960); patterns of alcohol consumption have also been found to be highly concordant among identical twins (Jonsson & Nilsson, 1968; Loehlin, 1972; Partanen, Brun, & Markkamen, 1966). Taken together, these studies suggest that a genetic factor predisposing sons of alcoholics to alcoholism may be involved.

The identification of a suitable biological marker or markers that is genetically transmitted would provide more definitive evidence that the etiology of alcoholism involves genetic factors. It is very likely that brain function is involved in the genetic predisposition for alcoholism. There is good evidence to indicate that brain EP waveforms are genetically determined. Monozygotic twins manifest EP waveforms that are as concordant with each other as EPs obtained from the same individual tested twice (Dustman & Beck, 1965).

We have recently undertaken a major project to investigate the possibility that sons of male alcoholics manifest differences in EPs that antedate any exposure to alcohol. In order to study this problem, we are recording EPs and ERPs in boys between the ages of 6 and 18 and comparing electrophysiological responses from sons of alcoholics (high-risk) and age- and education-matched sons of nonalcoholics (low-risk). Children whose mothers abused alcohol are excluded in order to rule out the contribution of the fetal alcohol syndrome.

In one ERP study (Begleiter, Porjesz, Bihari, & Kissin, 1984) we examined the P300 component in boys between the ages of 7 and 13 who had no prior experience with alcohol. The high-risk group consisted of 25 sons of alcoholic fathers with a mean age of 11.9 ($SD = 2.1$). In each case, the father had received the exclusive diagnosis of alcoholism (DSM-III) and had been in treatment for alcoholism at some time. Boys whose mothers had ingested alcohol during pregnancy or who drank excessively after giving birth were excluded. Only boys without medical problems and without exposure to alcohol or other substances of abuse were included in this study. The 25 normal control subjects were boys who were matched for socioeconomic status and age to the high-risk subjects. The control group had a mean age of 12.5 years ($SD = 2.4$). They were included only if they had no exposure to alcohol or other substances of abuse, and had no history of alcoholism or other psychiatric disorder in first- or second-degree relatives. Except for alcohol history, the same exclusion criteria were used as for the high-risk group.

The experimental design consisted of a visual head-orientation task. The nontarget stimulus was a frequently occurring oval presented in the center of a computer-generated display. The target stimulus was a rarely occurring aerial view of the head with the nose and one ear drawn in, rotated in four possible positions: nose up and right ear, nose up and left ear, nose down and right ear, nose down and left ear. Subjects pressed one of two microswitches as quickly and accurately as possible (RT) with either the right or left index finger to indicate whether the right or left ear was present on the display, respectively. In the "easy" condition, the head was facing forward (nose up on the screen) and the left or right ear appeared on the same side that corresponded to the appropriate button; in the "difficult" condition, the head was facing back (nose down on the screen) and the left or right ear appeared on the side opposite the corresponding button.

RTs for easy stimuli were significantly shorter than for difficult stimuli ($p < .0001$); there were no significant RT differences between groups. However, the number of correct behavioral responses was significantly less for the high-risk group for easy ($p < .001$) and difficult stimuli ($p < .001$). The entire raw data set was subjected to a principal-components analysis with varimax rotation using the covariance matrix. Basis waveforms were extracted, and the component scores for each of the four factors were then subjected to an analysis of variance. Our results indicated that only the factor representing the P300 component was significantly different between the high- and low-risk groups; the P300 amplitudes were found to be significantly smaller in the high-risk group as compared to the control group. This group difference was found to be significant at the parietal electrode (where P300 is maximum) for both the easy condition ($p < .01$) and the difficult condition ($p < .002$). These findings are the first to indicate a significant difference in P300 amplitude between boys at high risk for alcoholism and normal control boys, without exposure to alcohol.

Differences in electrophysiological recordings in response to challenge doses of alcohol have recently been reported between males with some family history of alcoholism and control subjects. This has been reported for EEG (Pollock *et al.*, 1983) and ERP (Elmasian, Neville, Woods, Schuckit, & Bloom, 1982) recordings. In a study conducted at the Salk Institute, Elmasian *et al.* (1982) found that male college students with family historics of alcoholism manifested different ERPs to challenge doses of both placebo and alcohol, when compared to matched controls without a family history of alcoholism; these differences between the two groups were apparent in the P300 component.

Our findings are particularly interesting, as they were obtained without the use of alcohol. We found that approximately 36% of the sons of alcoholics manifested this P300 difference. However, whether these low-amplitude ERPs are in fact markers for a predisposition to alcoholism remains to be tested. Studies are under way in our laboratory to retest these children each year to determine whether those manifesting ERP differences are in fact those who go on to develop problems with alcohol.

It is interesting to note that the P300 deficits we have observed in abstinent alcoholic patients are also present in some boys at high risk for alcoholism. We were interested in determining whether other electrophysiological deficits observed in alcoholic patients would be apparent in boys at risk for alcoholism. As we have observed brain stem abnormalities in abstinent alcoholics (Begleiter *et al.*, 1981), we decided to record BSPs in high-risk boys.

In this study (Begleiter, Porjesz, & Bihari, in press) we examined another sample of 23 sons of alcoholic fathers between the ages of 7 and 13 with a mean age of 12.2 ($SD = 2.1$). The 23 normal control subjects were boys who were matched for socioeconomic status, age, and education to the high-risk boys. The control group had a mean age of 12.4 ($SD = 2.3$). The inclusion and exclusion criteria were identical to those previously described for the P300 study. Again, we only included boys without prior exposure to alcohol or other illicit drugs. As in our study with alcoholics, the latency of the first five positive peaks and the interpeak latencies between peak 1 and each successive peak were measured.

We did not find any differences in the auditory BSPs obtained from sons of alcoholic fathers and those obtained from matched control subjects. The individual peak latencies and the brain stem transmission times were found to be similar in the two groups. The lack of significant differences in BSPs between high-risk and control subjects is interesting in light of our observed difference in P300 between high-risk and control subjects. These findings indicate that while P300 deficits may be antecedents of the development of alcoholism in some high-risk individuals, the brain stem deficits that we have observed in abstinent alcoholics are most probably alcohol-related changes. Further evidence for this hypothesis is provided by our findings that the BSP abnormalities observed in abstinent alcoholics seem to "recover" with prolonged abstinence, while the P300 deficits do not.

Conclusion

It remains for future research to separate those brain aberrations that are antecedents of alcohol abuse from those that are the consequences of years of heavy drinking. It is not known at the present time which innate differences determine responsiveness to alcohol, including predisposition to alcohol abuse. Genetic differences in strains of animals have been found to determine whether they are predisposed to drink alcohol or find it to be aversive (Rogers, 1972). Furthermore, differences in neurophysiological responses to alcohol have been reported in different genetic rat strains (Sorenson, Palmer, Dunwiddie, & Hoffer, 1980). Humans have also been found to differ in their responsiveness to alcohol—for example, in augmenting–reducing (Buchsbaum & Ludwig, 1980; Spilker & Callaway, 1969), in family history of alcoholism (Elmasian *et al.*, 1982; Pollock *et al.*, 1983), and in flushing–nonflushing (Fukui *et al.*, 1981). For example, recent findings in Japan indicate that "flushers" (those who manifest an adverse flushing reaction to alcohol) are more susceptible to delayed BSPs than "nonflushers" when ingesting a challenge dose of alcohol (Fukui *et al.*, 1981). It is possible that the low P300 amplitudes we have observed in young sons of alcoholics represent a vulnerability marker that may only become apparent in response to alcohol. For example, it is possible that although we did not observe BSP differences between boys at high and low risk for alcoholism without the ingestion of alcohol, BSP differences may become apparent once alcohol is introduced. It may in fact be those boys who manifest P300 decrements without alcohol who will respond differently to alcohol on other EP measures (e.g., BSPs). Studies are under way in our laboratory to test adolescents with family histories of alcoholism under the influence of challenge doses of alcohol with a full battery of EP tests.

The ability to utilize sophisticated neurophysiological tools to assess brain dysfunction in abstinent alcoholics and individuals at risk for alcoholism may prove most valuable in separating the deleterious effects of alcoholism on the CNS from the brain deficits that may be antecedents of the development of alcoholism. The delineation of similar neurophysiological deficits in abstinent alcoholics and children at high risk for alcoholism may be of fundamental importance in the identification of possible genetic marker(s). The search for a possible cluster of neurophysiological deficits in children at high risk for alcoholism is presently under way in our laboratory.

References

Adams, R. D., Victor, M., & Mancall, E. (1959). Central pontine myelinolysis: A hitherto undescribed disease occurring in alcoholic and malnourished patients. *Archives of Neurology and Psychiatry*, *81*, 136.

Begleiter, H., DeNoble, V., & Porjesz, B. (1980). Protracted brain dysfunction after alcohol withdrawal in monkeys. In H. Begleiter (Ed.), *Biological effects of alcohol* (pp. 231–250). New York: Plenum Press.

Begleiter, H., & Porjesz, B. (1977). Persistence of brain hyperexcitability following chronic alcohol exposure in rats. *Advances in Experimental Medicine and Biology*, *85B*, 209–222.

Begleiter, H., & Porjesz, B. (1979). Persistence of a "subacute withdrawal syndrome" following chronic ethanol intake. *Drug and Alcohol Dependence*, *4*, 353–357.

Begleiter, H., Porjesz, B., & Bihari (in press). Auditory brainstem potentials in sons of alcoholic fathers. *Alcoholism: Clinical and Experimental Research.*

Begleiter, H., Porjesz, B., Bihari, B., & Kissin, B. (1984). Event-related potentials in boys at high risk for alcoholism. *Science*, *225*, 1493–1496.

Begleiter, H., Porjesz, B., & Chou, C. L. (1981). Auditory brainstem potentials in chronic alcoholics. *Science*, *211*, 1064–1066.

Begleiter, H., Porjesz, B., Chou, C. L., & Aunon, J. (1983). P3 and stimulus incentive value. *Psychophysiology*, *20*, 95–101.

Begleiter, H., Porjesz, B., & Tenner, M. (1980). Neuroradiological and neurophysiological evidence of brain deficits in chronic alcoholics. *Acta Psychiatrica Scandinavica*, *62*(Suppl. 286), 3–13.

Bertera, J. H., & Parsons, O. A. (1973). Reaction time and S-R compatibility effects in detoxified alcoholics. *Alcohol Technical Reports*, *1*, 15–22.

Bierley, R. A., Cannon, D. S., Wehl, C. K., & Dustman, R. E. (1980). Effects of alcohol, on visually evoked responses in rats during addiction and withdrawal. *Pharmacology, Biochemistry and Behavior*, *12*, 909–915.

Bohman, M. (1978). Some genetic aspects of alcoholism and criminality: A population of adoptees. *Archives of General Psychiatry*, *35*, 269–276.

Buchsbaum, M. S., & Ludwig, A. M. (1980). Effects of sensory input and alcohol administration on visual evoked potentials in normal subjects and alcoholics. In H. Begleiter (Ed.), *Biological effects of alcohol* (pp. 561–572). New York: Plenum Press.

Buchwald, J. S., & Huang, C. M. (1975). Far field acoustic response: Origins in the cat. *Science*, *189*, 382–384.

Cadoret, R. J., Cain, C., & Grove, W. M. (1980). Development of alcoholism in adoptees raised apart from alcoholic biologic relatives. *Archives of General Psychiatry*, *37*, 561–563.

Cadoret, R. J., & Gath, A. (1978). Inheritance of alcoholism in adoptees. *British Journal of Psychiatry*, *132*, 252–258.

Cassvan, A., Rosenberg, A., & Caliguiri, M. (1984). Brainstem auditory evoked potentials in chronic alcoholic patients. *American Society for Clinical Evoked Potentials Bulletin*, *3*, 10–11.

Chu, N. S., & Squires, K. C. (1980). Auditory brain stem response study in alcoholic patients. *Pharmacology, Biochemistry and Behavior*, *13*, 241–244.

Chu, N. S., Squires, K. C., & Starr, A. (1978). Auditory brain stem potentials in chronic alcohol intoxication and alcohol withdrawal. *Archives of Neurology*, *35*, 596.

Chu, N. S., Squires, K. C., & Starr, A. (1982). Auditory brainstem responses in chronic alcoholic patients. *Electroencephalography and Clinical Neurophysiology*, *54*, 418–425.

Donchin, E. (1979). Event-related brain potentials: A tool in the study of human information processing. In H. Begleiter (Ed.), *Evoked brain potentials and behavior* (pp. 13–88). New York: Plenum Press.

Donchin, E., Ritter, W., & McCallum, W. C. (1978). Cognitive psychophysiology: The endogenous components of the ERP. In E. Callaway, P. Tueting, & S. H. Koslow (Eds.), *Event-related brain potentials in man* (pp. 349–411). New York: Academic Press.

Dustman, R. E., & Beck, E. C. (1965). The visually evoked potentials in twins. *Electroencephalography and Clinical Neurophysiology*, *19*, 541–638.

Elmasian, R., Neville, H., Woods, D., Shuckit, M., & Bloom, F. (1982). Event-related potentials are different in individuals at high risk for developing alcoholism. *Proceedings of the National Academy of Sciences USA*, *79*, 7900–7903.

Fabiani, M., Sohmer, H., Tait, C., Gafni, M., & Kirati, R. (1979). A functional measure of brain activity: Brain stem transmission time. *Electroencephalography and Clinical Neurophysiology*, *47*, 483–492.

Feigen, I., & Budzilovich, G. N. (1978). The role of edema in diffuse sclerosis and other leukencephalopathies. *Journal of Neuropathology and Experimental Neurology*, *37*, 326–362.

Feigen, I., & Budzilovich, G. N. (1980). The influence of ground substance on the extracellular water of normal and edematous human brain: Focal edema and the demyelinating diseases including multiple sclerosis. *Journal of Neuropathology and Experimental Neurology*, *39*, 13–29.

Ford, J. M., Hink, R. F., Hopkins, W. F., Roth, W. T., Pfefferbaum, A., & Kopell, B. S. (1979). Age effects on event related potentials in a selective attention task. *Journal of Gerontology*, *34*, 388–395.

Fukui, Y., Mori, M., Kohga,M., Tadai, T., Tanaka, K., & Katoh, N. (1981). Reassessment of CNS effects of acute ethanol administration with auditory evoked response: A comparative study of brain stem auditory evoked response, middle latency response and slow vertex response. *Japanese Journal of Alcohol and Drug Dependence*, *16*, 9–32.

Gaillard, A. W. K., & Lawson, E. A. (1980). Mismatch negativity (N2) following the discrimination of consonant vowel stimuli. *Psychophysiology*, *18*, 172–173.

Goodwin, D. W. (1979). Alcoholism and heredity: A review and hypothesis. *Archives of General Psychiatry*, *36*, 57–61.

Goodwin, D. W., & Guze, S. B. (1974). Heredity and alcoholism. In B. Kissin & H. Begleiter (Eds.), *The biology of alcoholism: Vol. 3. Clinical pathology* (pp. 37–52). New York: Plenum Press.

Goodwin, D. W., Schulsinger, F., Hermansen, L., Guze, S. B., & Winokur, G. (1973). Alcohol problems in adopteees raised apart from alcoholic biological parents. *Archives of General Psychiatry*, *28*, 238–243.

Haas, W., & Nickel, B. (1981). Differenzierung zwischen Delirium tremens und Wernicke-Enzephalopathie durch die Untersuchung der akustisch evozierten Hirnstammpotentiale. *Schweizer Archiv für Neurologie, Neurochirurgie und Psychiatrie*, *129*, 315–323.

Halgren, E., Squires, N. K., Wilson, C. L., Rohrbaugh, J. W., Babb, T. L., & Crandall, P. H. (1980). Endogenous potentials generated in the human hippocampal formation and amygdala by infrequent events. *Science*, *210*, 803–805.

Hillman, R. W. (1974). Alcoholism and malnutrition. In B. Kissin & H. Begleiter (Eds.), *The biology of alcoholism: Vol. 3. Clinical pathology* (pp. 513–586). New York: Plenum Press.

Hillyard, S. A., Hink, R. F., Schwent, U. L., & Picton, T. W. (1973). Electrical signs of selective attention in the human brain. *Science*, 182, 177–180.

Hillyard, S. A., Picton, T. W., & Regan, D. (1978). Sensation, perception and attention: Analysis using ERP's. In E. Callaway, P. Tueting, & S. H. Koslow (Eds.), *Event-related brain potentials in man* (pp. 223–321). New York: Academic Press.

Hunter, B. E., & Walker, D. W. (1980). The neural basis of ethanol dependence. In H. Begleiter (Ed.), *Biological effects of alcohol* (pp. 251–270). New York: Plenum Press.

Jewett, D. L. (1970). Volume conducted potentials in response to auditory stimuli as detected by averaging in the cat. *Electroencephalography and Clinical Neurophysiology*, *28*, 609–618.

Jewett, D. L., & Williston, J. S. (1971). Auditory evoked far field averaged from the scalp of humans. *Brain*, *94*, 681–696.

Johnson, R., & Donchin, E. (1978). On how P300 amplitude varies with the utility of the eliciting stimuli. *Electroencephalography and Clinical Neurophysiology*, *44*, 424–437.

Jonsson, E., & Nilsson, T. (1968). Alkohol Konsumtion hos monorygota och dizygota tuillingpar. *Nordisk Hygiensik Tidskrift*, *49*, 21–25.

Kaij, L. (1960). *Alcoholism in twins: Studies on the etiology and sequels of abuse of alcohol.* Stockholm: Almqvist & Wiksell.

Kleinschmidt-DeMasters, B. K., & Norenberg, M. D. (1981). Rapid correction of hyponatremia causes demyelination: Relation to central pontine myelinolysis. *Science, 211*, 1068–1070.

Klinke, R., Fruhstorfer, H., & Finkenzeller, P. (1968). Evoked responses as a function of external and stored information. *Electroencephalography and Clinical Neurophysiology, 25*, 119–122.

Kutas, M., McCarthy, G., & Donchin, E. (1977). Augmenting mental chronometry: The P300 as a measure of stimulus evaluation. *Science, 197*, 792–795.

Lev, A., & Sohmer, H. (1972). Sources of averaged neural responses recorded in animal and human subjects during cochlear audiometry (electrocochleogram). *Archiv für Klinische Experimentale Ohren-Nasen Kehlkopfheildiagnostik, 201*, 79.

Lewis, E. G., Dustman, R. E., & Beck, E. C. (1969). The effect of alcohol on sensory phenomena and cognitive motor tasks. *Quarterly Journal of Studies on Alcohol, 30*, 618–633.

Lewis, V. (1976). *Cerebral edema: Mechanisms of neurologic disease.* Boston: Little, Brown.

Loehlin, J. C. (1972). Analysis of alcohol-related questionnaire items from the National Merit Twin Study. *Annals of the New York Academy of Sciences, 197*, 117–120.

Moscatelli, E. A., & Demediuk, P. (1980). Effects of chronic consumption of ethanol and low protein diets on the lipid composition of rat whole brain and brain membranes. *Biochimica et Biophysica Acta*, 596, 331–337.

Näätänen, R., Hukkanen, S., & Järvilehto, T. (1980). Magnitude of stimulus deviance and brain potentials. In H. H. Kornhuber & L. Deeke (Eds.), *Motivation, motor and sensory processes of the brain: Electrical potentials, behaviour and clinical use* (pp. 337–342). Amsterdam: Elsevier/North-Holland Biomedical Press.

Nickel, B., & Ludewig, L. (1981). Die Bedeutung der fruhen akustisch evozierten Potentiale für die klinische Diagnose der alkoholischen Wernicke-Enzephalopathie. *Psychiatrie, Neurologie und Medizinische Psychologie, 33*, 193–198.

Partanen, J., Brun, K., & Markkamen, T. (1966). *Inheritance of drinking behavior: A study on intelligence, personality, and use of alcohol of adult twins.* Helsinki: Finnish Foundation for Alcohol Studies.

Picton, T. W., & Hillyard, S. A. (1974). Human auditory evoked potentials: II. Effects of attention. *Electroencephalography and Clinical Neurophysiology, 36*, 191–200.

Pollock, V. E., Volavka, J., Goodwin, D. W., Mednick, S. A., Gabrielli, W. F., Knop, J., & Schulsinger, F. (1983). The EEG after alcohol administration in men at risk for alcoholism. *Archives of General Psychiatry, 40*, 857–861.

Porjesz, B. (1983). *Neurophysiological brain dysfunction in alcoholics.* Paper presented at the 14th Annual National Council of Alcoholism/American Medical Society on Alcoholism/Research Society on Alcoholism Conference, Houston.

Porjesz, B., & Begleiter, H. (1975). Alcohol and bilateral evoked brain potentials. *Advances in Experimental Medicine and Biology, 59*, 553–567.

Porjesz, B., & Begleiter, H. (1979). Visual evoked potentials and brain dysfunction in chronic alcoholics. In H. Begleiter (Ed.), *Evoked brain potentials and behavior* (pp. 277–302). New York: Plenum Press.

Porjesz, B., & Begleiter, H. (1981a). *Event related potentials and decision time in chronic alcoholics.* Paper presented at the International Council on Alcohol Abuse, Vienna.

Porjesz, B., & Begleiter, H. (1981b). *Event related potentials in chronic alcoholics.* Paper presented at the 134th Annual Meeting of the American Psychiatric Association, New Orleans.

Porjesz, B., & Begleiter, H. (1983). Brain dysfunction and alcohol. In B. Kissin & H. Begleiter (Eds.), *The biology of alcoholism: Vol. 7. The pathogenesis of alcoholism: Biological factors* (pp. 415–483). New York: Plenum Press.

Porjesz, B., & Begleiter, H. (1987). *Reversibility of electrophysiological deficits following prolonged abstinence in chronic alcoholics.* Manuscript in preparation.

Porjesz, B., Begleiter, H., Bihari, B., & Kissin, B. (1987). The N2 component of the event related brain potential in abstinent alcoholics. *Electroencephalography and Clinical Neurophysiology, 66*, 121–131.

Porjesz, B., Begleiter, H., & Garozzo, R. (1980). Visual evoked potential correlates of information processing deficits in chronic alcoholics. In H. Begleiter (Ed.), *Biological effects of alcohol* (pp. 603–623). New York: Plenum Press.

Porjesz, B., Begleiter, H., & Hurowitz, S. (1976). Brain excitability subsequent to alcohol withdrawal in rats. In D. H. Ford & D. H. Clouet (Eds.), *Tissue responses to addictive substances* (pp. 461–469). New York: Spectrum.

Renault, B., & Lesevre, N. (1979). A trial by trial study of the visual omission response in reaction time situations. In D. Lehmann & E. Callaway (Eds.), *Human evoked potentials: Applications and problems* (pp. 317–329). New York: Plenum Press.

Rhodes, L. E., Obitz, F. W., & Creel, D. (1975). Effect of alcohol and task on hemispheric asymmetry of visually evoked potentials on man. *Electroencephalography and Clinical Neurophysiology, 38*, 561–568.

Riley, J. N., & Walker, D. W. (1978). Morphological alterations in hippocampus after long-term alcohol consumption in mice. *Science, 201*, 646–648.

Ritter, W., Simson, R., & Vaughan, H. G., Jr. (1972). Association cortex potentials and reaction time in auditory discrimination. *Electroencephalography and Clinical Neurophysiology, 33*, 547–555.

Ritter, W., Simson, R., Vaughan, H. G., Jr., & Friedman, D. (1979). A brain event related to the making of a sensory discrimination. *Science, 203*, 1358–1361.

Ritter, W., Vaughan, H. G., Jr., & Costa, L. D. (1968). Orienting and habituation to auditory stimuli: A study of short-term changes in average evoked response. *Electroencephalography and Clinical Neurophysiology, 25*, 550–556.

Rogers, D. A. (1972). Factors underlying differences in alcohol preference of inbred strains of mice. In B. Kissin & H. Begleiter (Eds.), *The biology of alcoholism: Vol. 2. Physiology and behavior* (pp. 107–130). New York: Plenum Press.

Rosenhamer, H. J., & Silfverskiold, B. I. (1980). Slow tremor and delayed brainstem auditory evoked responses in alcoholics. *Archives of Neurology, 37*, 293–296.

Ruchkin, D. S., & Sutton, S. (1978). Equivocation and P300 amplitude. In D. A. Otto (Ed.), *Multidisciplinary perspectives in event-related brain potential research: Proceedings of the Fourth International Congress on Event-Related Slow Potentials of the Brain, Hendersonville, North Carolina* (pp. 175–177). Washington, DC: U.S. Environmental Protection Agency. (EPA-600/9-77-043).

Schuckit, M. A., Goodwin, D. A., & Winokur, G. (1972). A study of alcoholism in half siblings. *American Journal of Psychiatry, 128*, 1132–1136.

Simson, R., Vaughan, H. G., Jr., & Ritter, W. (1976). The scalp topography of potentials associated with missing visual or auditory stimuli. *Electroencephalography and Clinical Neurophysiology, 40*, 33–42.

Simson, R., Vaughan, H. G., Jr., & Ritter, W. (1977a). The scalp topography of potentials in auditory and visual discrimination tasks. *Electroencephalography and Clinical Neurophysiology, 42*, 528–535.

Simson, R., Vaughan, H. G., Jr., & Ritter, W. (1977b). The scalp topography of potentials in auditory and visual go/no go tasks. *Electroencephalography and Clinical Neurophysiology, 43*, 864–875.

Sohmer, H., & Feinmesser, M. (1967). Cochlear action potentials recorded from external ear in man. *Annals of Otology, Rhinology, and Laryngology, 76*, 427–435.

Sorenson, S., Palmer, M., Dunwiddie, T., & Hoffer, B. (1980). Electrophysiological correlates of ethanol-induced sedation in differentially sensitive lines of mice. *Science, 210*, 1143–1144.

Spilker, B., & Callaway, E. (1969). Effects of drugs on "augmenting/reducing" in averaged visual evoked response in man. *Psychopharmacology*, *15*, 116–124.

Squires, K. C., Chu, N. S., & Starr, A. (1978a). Acute effects of alcohol on auditory brainstem potentials in humans. *Science*, *201*, 174–176.

Squires, K. C., Chu, N. S., & Starr, A. (1978b). Auditory brain stem potentials with alcohol. *Electroencephalography and Clinical Neurophysiology*, *45*, 577–584.

Starr, A., & Achor, L. J. (1975). Auditory brainstem response in neurological disease. *Archives of Neurology*, *32*, 161–168.

Starr, A., & Hamilton, A. E. (1976). Correlation between confirmed sites of neurological lesions and far-field auditory brainstem responses. *Electroencephalography and Clinical Neurophysiology*, *41*, 595–608.

Stockard, J. J., & Rossiter, U. S. (1977). Clinical and pathological correlates of brainstem auditory response abnormalities. *Neurology*, *27*, 316–325.

Sutton, S., Tueting, P., Zubin, J., & John, E. R. (1967). Information delivery and the sensory evoked potential. *Science, 155*, 1436–1439.

Talland, G. A. (1963). Alcoholism and reaction time. *Quarterly Journal of Studies on Alcohol*, *24*, 610.

Towey, J., Rist, F., Hakerem, G., Ruchkin, D., & Sutton, S. (1980). N250 latency and decision time. *Bulletin of the Psychonomic Society*, *15*, 365–368.

Tueting, P., Sutton, S., & Zubin, J. (1971). Quantitative evoked potential correlates of the probability of events. *Psychophysiology*, *7*, 385–394.

Vivian, T. N., Goldstein, G., & Shelly, C. (1973). Reaction time and motor speed in chronic alcoholics. *Perceptual and Motor Skills*, *36*, 136–138.

Walker, D. W., Barnes, D. E., Zornetzer, S. F., Hunter, B. E., & Kubanis, P. (1980). Neuronal loss in hippocampus induced by prolonged ethanol consumption in rat. *Science*, *209*, 711–713.

Walker, D. W., Hunter, B. E., & Abraham, W. C. (1981). Neuroanatomical and functional deficits subsequent to chronic ethanol administration in animals. *Alcoholism: Clinical and Experimental Research*, *5*, 267–282.

Wood, C. G., Allison, T., Goff, W. B., Williamson, P. D., & Spencer, D. B. (1980). On the neural origins of P300 in man. In H. H. Kornhuber, & L. Deeke (Eds.), *Motivation, motor and sensory processes of the brain: Electrical potentials, behaviour and clinical use* (pp. 51–56). Amsterdam: Elsevier/North-Holland Biomedical Press.

Yates, P. O. (1976). Vascular disease in the central nervous system: In W. Blackwood & J. A. N. Corsellis (Eds.), *Greenfield's neuropathology* (pp. 86–147). London: Arnold Press.

Zilm, D., Kaplan, H. L., & Capell, H. (1981). Electroencephalographic tolerance and abstinence phenomena during repeated alcohol ingestion by nonalcoholics. *Science*, *212*, 1175–1177.

4

Cerebral Blood Flow and Metabolism in Alcoholics

JARL RISBERG
MATS BERGLUND

There is little evidence indicating that cerebrovascular disturbances are the primary cause of alcohol-related conditions and disorders. However, abnormal cerebral blood flow (CBF) is a common finding in alcoholism, as will be evident from this review. The reason for this relationship is the now very well-documented coupling between cerebral function and metabolism and CBF (Frackowiak *et al.*, 1981; Raichle, Grubb, Gado, Eichling, & Ter-Pogossian, 1976). This coupling makes the regional CBF (rCBF) an indicator of neuronal function. The changes of rCBF seen in alcoholism are thus caused by the adaptation of the flow to the changed demand for oxygen and glucose by the cerebral tissue.

Until recently, only a few rCBF laboratories have focused upon alcoholism and alcohol-related disorders. Such studies seem to evoke less interest than studies of cerebrovascular disorders, organic dementia, schizophrenia, and so on. Thus, the number of investigations to be reviewed is small, and the area is, as a matter of fact, dominated by work from our group. In an earlier review of CBF in chronic alcoholics (Berglund, 1981), studies up to 1980 were discussed. In the present review, we emphasize four main topics: intoxication, withdrawal, the Wernicke–Korsakoff syndrome, and alcohol dementia. We also discuss some recent findings of reversibility of rCBF disturbances during abstinence, and also address the problem of an increased vulnerability of the right hemisphere to the effects of alcohol. We commence, however, with a short description of the methods used for measurement of CBF and metabolism.

Jarl Risberg and Mats Berglund. Department of Psychiatry I, University Hospital, Lund, Sweden.

Methods for Measurement of Cerebral Blood Flow and Metabolism

Global Techniques

The first quantitative technique for measurement of CBF and cerebral metabolic rate for oxygen ($CMRO_2$) was developed by Kety and Schmidt (1948). The technique was based on inhalation of N_2O and determination of tracer concentrations in serial blood samples drawn from an artery and from the jugular sinus. An important feature of the tracer was that it was diffusible; that is, it passed the blood–brain barrier easily. Flow calculations were made from arterial and venous saturation curves using equations based on the Fick principle. The difference in oxygen saturation between arterial and venous blood could easily be obtained from the blood samples, and $CMRO_2$ was then calculated by multiplying this difference by CBF. The Kety–Schmidt technique was the standard method for several years, but its use has diminished during the last two decades, due to the availability of regional and noninvasive methods.

Regional Techniques

The first method for determination of rCBF was developed in the early 1960s by Lassen and Ingvar (1961). It was based on a rapid injection into the internal carotid artery of a diffusible gamma-emitting tracer (^{85}Kr or ^{133}Xe). The arrival and clearance of the tracer was recorded by multiple scintillation detectors covering the injected hemisphere. The intra-arterial injection technique was the dominant method for about 10 years. The applicability of the technique in clinical research was, however, severely limited by medical and ethical problems in conjunction with the arterial puncture. During the last 10 years, the use of this technique has almost ceased, and the field is now dominated by the noninvasive methods. Thus, the arterial injection has been replaced by inhalation or intravenous injection of ^{133}Xe. The inhalation technique had been proposed in the 1960s (Mallett & Veall, 1965), but was criticized for measurement errors caused by extracranial contamination and recirculation of the tracer. The technique was, however, further refined during the late 1960s and early 1970s (Obrist, Thompson, King, & Wang, 1967; Obrist, Thompson, Wang, & Wilkinson, 1975; Risberg, Ali, Wilson, Wills, & Halsey, 1975). Today the inhalation technique and the intravenous injection technique are generally recognized as valid and reliable methods. In addition to the advantage of safety and noninvasiveness, the possibility of simultaneous bilateral recordings is of great clinical and scientific importance. Further development of the measurement technique has involved improving the spatial resolution by increasing the number of detectors and adding three-dimensional resolution (tomography). These newer techniques have, however, not yet been used in the study of alcoholism.

Intoxication

The effects of acute alcohol intoxication on CBF and $CMRO_2$ were studied by Battey, Heyman, and Patterson (1953), using the Kety–Schmidt technique. They found that lower doses of alcohol administered intravenously to normal subjects did not change the parameters measured. Larger doses of alcohol (resulting in a blood alcohol level [BAL] of about 0.3%) administered to alcoholics were, however, associated with elevated CBF values and a decrease of $CMRO_2$. In a more recent study, Newlin, Golden, Quaife, and Graber (1982) used the ^{133}Xe inhalation technique to study rCBF in 10 social drinkers. The first measurement was made while the subjects were sober, and the second study when the subjects had a BAL of about 0.05%. The results showed a significant increase of the gray-matter blood flow after drinking. The increase was seen in all areas except frontal parts of the left hemisphere. The mean hemisphere flow increased more on the right side than on the left side.

We have studied one alcoholic in a state of blackout (Berglund, Prohovnik, & Risberg, 1987). At a BAL of 0.41%, the mean blood flow was 30–50% above the level recorded at an earlier occasion, when the patient was sober. The rCBF pattern in the blackout state was characterized by relatively low values in parieto-occipital regions and somewhat elevated values in frontal and fronto-temporal regions.

Most of the limited evidence available on the effects of acute alcohol intoxication on CBF thus point to an elevation as being the main change also at fairly high alcohol concentrations. The finding of a decrease of $CMRO_2$ by Battey *et al.* (1953) might, however, indicate an uncoupling between CBF and metabolism at higher alcohol concentrations. It is possible that alcohol may interfere with the mechanisms that couple CBF to cerebral metabolism and function. In this situation, a functional depression might thus be paralleled by a paradoxical elevation of the CBF level. Because of the few data available, this possibility remains speculative.

Withdrawal

Six patients with delirium tremens (DT) were studied by Eisenberg (1968) using the Kety–Schmidt technique. The results showed slightly subnormal rCBF levels. Marx, Neundörfer, Potz, and Hoyer (1975) used the same measurement technique in a study of three groups of alcoholics. One group was studied before DT, one during DT, and one after DT. No significant differences between the groups were found regarding CBF and $CMRO_2$. A tendency for the before-DT group to show lower values than the other two groups was, however, noted. A trend toward subnormal values of $CMRO_2$ was also noted in the alcoholics who were studied before DT. Dobrzanski

(1975) used a semiquantitative rCBF method in his study of alcoholics during withdrawal. He found significant correlations between decreases of a flow index and the severity of withdrawal symptoms, especially the presence of symptoms of clouding of the sensorium.

We (Berglund & Risberg, 1981) studied rCBF during 13 withdrawal periods in 12 severely dependent alcoholics by means of the ^{133}Xe inhalation technique. A global reduction of rCBF (19%, $p < .001$) was seen during the first 2 days of withdrawal (Figure 4-1). Significant correlations were seen between the amplitude of the flow decrease and symptoms of clouding of the sensorium ($r = .62, p < .05$), as well as between this amplitude and length of the preceding drinking episode ($r = .70, p < .01$). The patients were treated with chlomethiazol and dixyrazine, but a lack of relationship between amount and type of medication and the flow decrease seemed to indicate that the treatment had no significant effects on the main results of the study. A special relationship between rCBF and symptoms was seen in two patients with auditory and visual hallucinations during measurement. Flow increases that were related to the modality of the hallucinations. Thus in one case, involving continuous auditory hallucinations, elevated flow was seen primarily in left temporal regions (Figure 4-2); occipital increases dominated in the other case, where visual hallucinations were present.

Available information about rCBF during withdrawal thus indicate that low values are seen in its early phase, with the extent of the decrease being linked to such symptoms of brain dysfunction as clouding of the sensorium. Further research in this area is needed, with minimal and care-

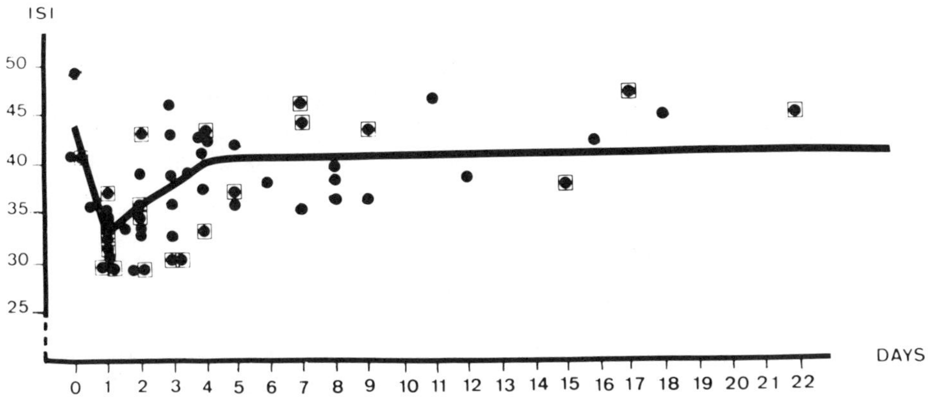

Figure 4-1. Mean hemispheric blood flow values (initial slope index [ISI] parameter) during 13 periods of alcohol withdrawal in 12 male alcoholics. Squares around circles indicate patients with longer previous bender (median cut). Note the low values during the first 2 days, followed by normalization. (Adapted from Berglund & Risberg, 1981.)

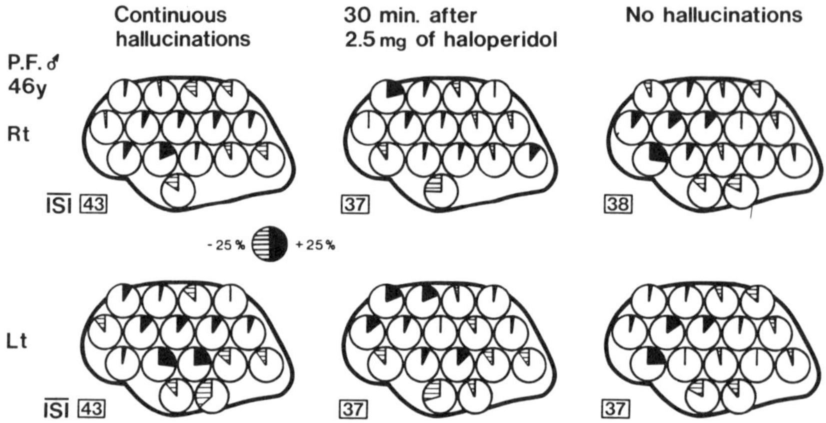

Figure 4-2. A series of rCBF measurements (ISI parameter) in a 46-year-old chronic alcoholic with continuous auditory hallucinations during alcohol withdrawal. The hemispheric mean values are indicated in the boxes. The regional values are shown as clock symbols. A black area indicates a value above the hemispheric mean (180° = 25%), and a hatched area indicates a value below the mean. At the first measurement, the patient reported hearing his brother singing very loudly and his sister singing very weakly in the background. He identified the proper text and melody of several religious hymns throughout the measurement. Note the left temporal increases of rCBF. At the second study, which was made 30 minutes after intramuscular injection of 2.5 mg of haloperidol, the brother stopped singing, while the patient still could hear his sister's voice. He could no longer identify the lyrics. Note the fading flow elevation temporally and the difference in the flow pattern recorded when no hallucinations were reported. (Adapted from Berglund & Risberg, 1981.)

fully controlled administration of drugs, and if possible some control of the alcohol consumption during the preceding drinking episode. Further studies of patients with signs of confusion during withdrawal would also be of special interest.

The Wernicke–Korsakoff Syndrome

Shimojyo, Scheinberg, and Reinmuth (1967) studied 11 patients in the acute phase of Wernicke's encephalopathy. They found a reduction of CBF and $CMRO_2$ of about 35%. No relation was found, however, between the severity of the symptoms and the amplitude of the decrease of flow and metabolism. Studies of the chronic stage of Korsakoff's psychosis have found a marked variance of the flow level, with reports of subnormal as well as supernormal values (Berglund & Ingvar, 1976; Simard, Olesen, Paulson,

Lassen, & Skinhøj, 1971). One patient has been investigated in the acute as well as the chronic phase of the Wernicke–Korsakoff syndrome, and the result indicated a reduced flow at the first occasion, followed by a normalization of the flow level (Berglund, 1981). No systematic CBF abnormalities have been found in this group of patients.

Alcohol Dementia

Most studies of cerebral circulation and metabolism in alcoholism have concerned the rather unspecific "alcohol dementia" state. Four studies using the Kety–Schmidt technique have been published (Battey *et al.*, 1953; Hine, Shick, Margolis, Burbridge, & Simon, 1952; Krüger & Hoyer, 1979; Sutherland, Burbridge, Adams, & Simon, 1960). Normal values were reported in three of these studies, while Krüger and Hoyer (1979) reported a pronounced decrease of CBF and $CMRO_2$ in three cases of severe alcohol dementia. Three studies with the intra-arterial ^{133}Xe technique have been published (Berglund & Ingvar, 1976; Heiss, Küfferle, & Demel, 1974; Heiss, Küfferle, Demel, Reisner, & Roszucrky, 1976). Heiss and coworkers studied 35 alcoholics, 20 of whom had been admitted in a state of DT. They were examined 1–4 days after the acute symptoms had disappeared. The mean cortical flow level in the alcoholics was significantly lower than in a control group. The most marked decrease (about 25%) was seen in the most delirious group. Nineteen of the patients showed focal accentuations of the flow decrease, mainly in frontal and parietal regions. Berglund and Ingvar (1976) found subnormal gray-matter blood flow in 53 alcoholics. The amplitude of the decrease was found to be related to the age of the patients. In the younger group, the flow values were generally within the normal range, with markedly subnormal values in alcoholics over 50 years of age. The older alcoholics also had an accentuation of the reduction in lower frontal and anterior temporal regions, compared to the younger group.

More recent studies using the ^{133}Xe inhalation technique have given similar results. In a study of 22 severely dependent alcoholics treated at an institution for alcoholics, the mean CBF was significantly reduced even after 7 weeks of abstinence in subjects above the age of 45 (Berglund, Hagstadius, *et al.*, 1987). The younger alcoholics had a normal CBF level. Regionally, the flow of the right frontal lobe showed the largest decrease. Finally, some unpublished data from our laboratory have shown a normal flow level in abstinent outpatient alcoholics 30–50 years of age.

On the basis of the studies cited, it can be concluded that the "average" 30- to 40-year-old alcoholic has a relatively normal cortical perfusion. However, alcoholics who continue drinking after the age of 45–50 are likely to have progressive subnormal flow values. The age-related reduction of the rCBF level found in most studies of normal aging thus seems to be accelerated by alcohol abuse (Melamed, Lavy, Bentin, Cooper & Rinot, 1980; Risberg & Hagstadius, 1983; and others). This reduction seems to be somewhat more pronounced in frontal regions than in other parts of the brain. Some recent results seem to indicate that social drinking also might be of importance for the reduction of the rCBF level. Rogers, Meyer, Shaw, and Mortel (1983) have reported a significant negative relationship between the CBF level and the amount of alcohol consumed by social drinkers.

Most of the studies have only reported on blood flow in grey matter. This is unfortunate, because white-matter changes in alcoholics are well known (Alling & Boström, 1980; Lesch, Schmidt, & Schmidt, 1972; Lynch, 1960). Two studies using the ^{133}Xe injection technique (Berglund & Ingvar, 1976; Johannesson, Berglund, & Ingvar, 1982) have reported a reduction of white-matter blood flow in alcoholics, which was not related to age. These findings do not agree with the results of the previously cited studies by Heiss *et al.* (1974, 1976), who reported normal values. Of special interest is the observation by Johannesson *et al.* (1982) that the reduction of white-matter blood flow correlated strongly with the degree of abnormality on the liver function tests. It was assumed that the underlying factor was the intensity of drinking prior to admission.

Reversibility

The reversibility of cerebral disturbances in abstinent alcoholics has been much discussed during recent years. Moderate degrees of normalization have been reported for mental functions (Parsons & Leber, 1981), for cerebral atrophy as determined by computerized tomography (Artmann, Hacker, & Herrlick, 1981; Carlen, Wortzman, Holgate, Wilkinson, & Rankin, 1978), and for electrophysiological changes (Begleiter & Porjesz, 1979). Available CBF data also suggest recovery during abstinence. The rapid normalization of flow during the initial phase of withdrawal has already been cited (Berglund & Risberg, 1981).

In a more recent study in our laboratory (Berglund, Hagstadius, *et al.*, 1987), 22 abstinent alcoholics were studied with repeated measurements of rCBF and mental functions during 7 weeks of abstinence. During this period, alcoholics older than 45 showed an increase of the rCBF level of 8% ($p < .05$). In contrast, unchanged rCBF levels were recorded in the younger group throughout the period. In the older group, a significant correlation was found between the improvement of the rCBF level and less pronounced symptoms of low vitality and emotional deficiency. The alcoholics who had inferior scores on a mental test (the Trail Making Test, Part B) showed improvement of the rCBF level (Figure 4-3); this finding suggests that long-term reversibility is most prominent in alcoholics with the severest cognitive deficits.

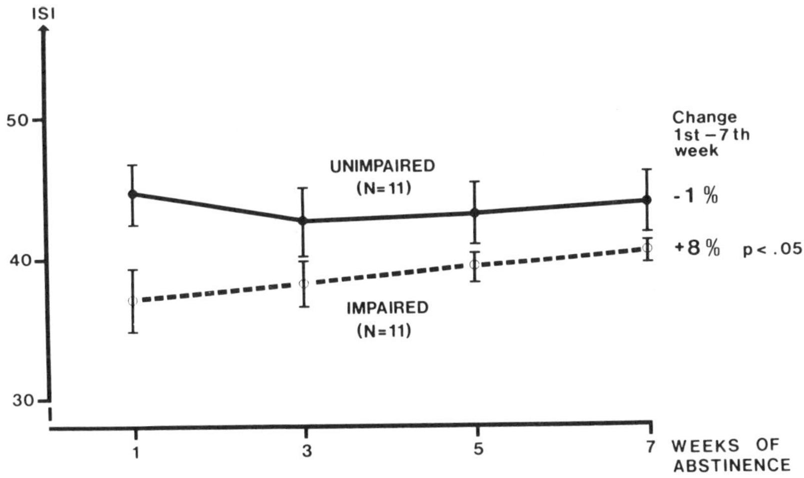

Figure 4-3. Mean (± *SEM*) hemispheric blood flow (ISI parameter) in 22 alcoholics during 7 weeks of abstinence. Based on the performance on the Trail Making Test, Part B, the group was divided by median cut in one impaired and one unimpaired group. Measurements of rCBF were made after 1, 3, 5 and 7 weeks of abstinence. Note the significant increase of the flow level in the impaired group only.

Right-Hemisphere Vulnerability

One of the most controversial issues regarding brain dysfunction in alcoholics is the possibility of a special vulnerability of the right hemisphere to the toxic effects of alcohol. In Tarter's (1975) review, this hypothesis was supported primarily by psychometric data indicating impairment of such right-hemisphere functions as spatial and visuoconceptual abilities. Conclusive evidence is still lacking, but some studies based on bilateral rCBF recordings have provided supporting results. Newlin *et al.* (1982) reported more pronounced increases in the right than in the left hemisphere during alcohol intoxication. Our recent study of 22 abstinent alcoholics (Berglund, Hagstadius, *et al.*, 1987) showed that the frontal distribution flow values were significantly lower than control values on the right side only. Although this asymmetric change was most marked after 1 week of abstinence, it was still evident after 7 weeks. The previously described recovery of flow in the older alcoholics during the abstinence period was also somewhat more pronounced on the right than on the left side.

Changes of Regional Cerebral Blood Flow during Mental Activation

The studies cited so far have been based on measurements of rCBF during a basic resting condition. As already stated, the rCBF measure is an indicator of cortical function. It is very well documented that a flow study during an activated state (e.g., solving of mental problems) will show an elevated flow level and a changed distribution of flow compared to the resting measurement (Ingvar & Risberg, 1967; Risberg & Ingvar, 1973). Such activation responses of rCBF have been studied extensively in normal subjects, and also to some extent in clinical conditions. We have made some efforts to study rCBF during mental activation in alcoholics, with the aim of getting better prognostic information from the rCBF study. Such a prognosis of future functional gain in an alcoholic would be of great value for planning of inpatient treatment. It is our impression that flow changes during activation have better prognostic power than the standard resting flow measurements. Preliminary results from our previously cited study of 22 abstinent alcoholics (Berglund, Hagstadius, *et al.*, 1987) indicate that a large increase of rCBF during activation at the first examination is coupled to a more marked recovery of the resting flow level from 1 week to 7 weeks of abstinence. The results thus indicated that the brains with the largest potential for recovery also showed the largest flow increase during activation. Further work is in progress regarding this possibility of obtaining additional information from the rCBF measurements.

Summary

Although cerebrovascular disturbances are not the primary cause of brain dysfunction in alcoholism, changes of CBF are commonly found in this patient group. This is due to the coupling between CBF and cerebral function and metabolism. In this chapter, some recent findings regarding global and regional CBF in alcohol-related conditions are reviewed. The limited data available regarding acute effects of alcohol intoxication indicate an elevation of CBF at moderate as well as high alcohol concentrations. Results from studies of withdrawal from alcohol abuse show subnormal CBF levels during the first couple of days, followed by a normalization. Studies of patients with the Wernicke–Korsakoff syndrome have reported subnormal as well as elevated flow values, while more consistent results have been obtained in alcohol dementia. Younger alcoholics have been found to have relatively normal cortical perfusion, while alcoholics who continue drinking after the age of 45–50 are likely to have progressively lower values, especially in frontal regions. The decreases found in older alcoholics show some reversibility during extended periods of abstinence. Some recent data indicate that the right hemisphere has a more pronounced flow disturbance than the left. Measurements of CBF are thus useful for elucidating some of the effects of alcohol on global and regional brain function.

Acknowledgments

The writing of this chapter was supported by the Swedish Medical Research Council (Project No. 4969). Special thanks to Helena Fernö, BA, for aid with the illustrations, and to Eva Skagert and Maria Regnér for secretarial aid.

References

Alling, C., & Boström, K. (1980). Demyelination of the mamillary bodies in alcoholism: A combined morphological and biochemical study. *Acta Neuropathologica, 50*, 77–80.

Artman, H., Hacker, H., & Herrlick, J. (1981). Reversible enlargement of cerebral spinal fluid spaces in chronic alcoholics. *American Journal of Neuroradiology, 2*, 23–27.

Battey, L. L., Heyman, A., & Patterson, J. L., Jr. (1953). Effects of ethyl alcohol on cerebral blood flow and metabolism. *Journal of the American Medical Association, 152*, 6–10.

Begleiter, H., & Porjesz, B. (1979). Persistence of a "subacute withdrawal syndrome" following chronic ethanol intake. *Drug and Alcohol Dependence, 10*, 327–368.

Berglund, M. (1981). Cerebral blood flow in chronic alcoholics. *Alcoholism: Clinical and Experimental Research, 5*, 295–303.

Berglund, M., Hagstadius, S., Risberg, J., Johanson, A., Bliding, Å., & Mubrin, Z. (1987). Normalization of regional cerebral blood flow in alcoholics during the first 7 weeks of abstinence. *Acta Psychiatrica Scandinavica, 75*, 202–208.

Berglund, M., & Ingvar, D. H. (1976). Cerebral blood flow and its regional distribution in alcoholism and in Korsakoff's psychosis. *Journal of Studies on Alcohol, 37*, 586–597.

Berglund, M., Prohovnik, I., & Risberg, J. (1987). *Regional cerebral blood flow in a case of alcohol black-out.* Manuscript submitted for publication.

Berglund, M., & Risberg, J. (1981). Regional cerebral blood flow during alcohol withdrawal. *Archives of General Psychiatry, 38*, 351–357.

Carlen, P. L., Wortzman, G., Holgate, R. C., Wilkinson, D. A., & Rankin, J. G. (1978). Reversible cerebral atrophy in recently abstinent chronic alcoholics measured by computed tomography scans. *Science, 200*, 1076–1078.

Dobrzanski, T. (1975). Radiotracer transit measurements as an index of regional cerebral blood flow: II. Results in acute alcohol withdrawal syndromes. *Polski Przeglad Radiologi, 39*, 201–213.

Eisenberg, S. (1968). Cerebral blood flow and metabolism in patients with delirium tremens. *Clinical Research, 16*, 71.

Frackowiak, R. S. J., Pozzilli, C., Legg, N. J., du Boulay, G. H., Marshall, J., Lenzi, G. L., & Jones, T. (1981). Regional cerebral oxygen supply and utilization in dementia: A clinical and physiological study with oxygen-15 and positron tomography. *Brain, 104*, 753–778.

Heiss, W. D., Küfferle, B., & Demel, I. (1974). Störungen der Hirndurschblutung bei chronischen Alkoholikern in Abhängigkeit vom klinischen Bild. *Psychiatria Clinica* (Basel), *7*, 181–191.

Heiss, W. D., Küfferle, B., Demel, I., Reisner, T., & Roszucrky, A. (1976). Cerebral blood flow and severity of mental dysfunction in chronic alcoholism. In J. S. Meyer, H. Lechner,

& M. Reivich (Eds.), *Cerebral vascular disease* (pp. 89–93). Stuttgart, West Germany: Georg Thieme.

Hine, C. H., Shick, A. F., Margolis, L., Burbridge, N., & Simon, A. (1952). Effects of alcohol in small doses and tetraethylthiuramdisulphide (Antabuse) on the cerebral blood flow and cerebral metabolism. *Journal of Pharmacology and Experimental Therapeutics, 106*, 253–260.

Ingvar, D. H., & Risberg, J. (1967). Increase of regional cerebral blood flow during mental effort in normals and in patients with focal brain disorders. *Experimental Brain Research, 3*, 195–211.

Johannesson, G., Berglund, M., & Ingvar, D. H. (1982). Reduction of blood flow in cerebral white matter in alcoholics related to hepatic function: A CBF and EEG study. *Acta Neurologica Scandinavica, 65*, 190–202.

Kety, S. S., & Schmidt, C. F. (1948). The nitrous oxide method for the quantitative determination of cerebral blood flow in man: Theory, procedure, and normal values. *Journal of Clinical Investigation, 27*, 476–483.

Krüger, G., & Hoyer, S. (1979). Brain blood flow and metabolism related to psychiatric syndromes in alcoholism. *Acta Neurologica Scandinavia, 60* (Suppl. 72), 570–571.

Lassen, N. A., & Ingvar, D. H. (1961). The blood flow of the cerebral cortex determined by radioactive krypton-85. *Experimentia, 17*, 42–50.

Lesch, P., Schmidt, E., & Schmidt, F. W. (1972). Effects on chronic alcohol abuse on the structural lipids in the human brain. *Zeitschrift für Klinische Chemie und Klinische Biochemie, 10*, 410–415.

Lynch, M. J. G. (1960). Brain lesions in chronic alcoholism. *Archives of Pathology, 69*, 342–353.

Mallett, B. L., & Veall, N. (1965). The measurement of regional cerebral clearance rates in man using xenon-133 inhalation and extracranial recording. *Journal of Clinical Sciences, 29*, 179–191.

Marx, P., Neundörfer, B., Potz, G., & Hoyer, S. (1975). Cerebral blood flow and amino-acid metabolism in chronic alcoholism. In A. M. Harper, W. B. Jennett, J. D. Miller, & J. O. Rowan (Eds.), *Blood flow and metabolism in the brain* (pp. 11.31–11.35). Edinburgh: Churchill Livingstone.

Melamed, E., Lavy, S., Bentin, S., Cooper, G., & Rinot, Y. (1980). Reduction in regional cerebral blood flow during normal aging in man. *Stroke, 11*, 31–34.

Newlin, D. B., Golden, C. J., Quaife, M., & Graber, B. (1982). Effect of alcohol ingestion on regional cerebral blood flow. *International Journal of Neuroscience, 17*, 145–150.

Obrist, W. D., Thompson, H. K., King, C. H., & Wang, H. S. (1967). Determination of regional cerebral blood flow by inhalation of 133-xenon. *Circulation Research, 20*, 124–135.

Obrist, W. D., Thompson, H. K., Wang, H. S., & Wilkinson, W. E. (1975). Regional cerebral blood flow estimated by 133-xenon inhalation. *Stroke, 6*, 245–256.

Parsons, O. A., & Leber, W. R. (1981). The relationship between cognitive dysfunction and brain damage in alcoholics: Casual, interactive or epiphenomenal. *Alcoholism: Clinical and Experimental Research, 5*, 326–343.

Raichle, M. E., Grubb, R. L., Gado, M. H., Eichling, J. O., & Ter-Pogossian, M. M. (1976). Correlation between regional cerebral blood flow and oxidative metabolism. *Archives of Neurology, 33*, 523–526.

Risberg, J., Ali, Z., Wilson, E. M., Wills, E. L., & Halsey, J. H. (1975). Regional cerebral blood flow by ^{133}xenon inhalation: Preliminary evaluation of an initial slope index in patients with unstable flow compartments. *Stroke, 6*, 142–148.

Risberg, J., & Hagstadius, S. (1983). Effects on the regional cerebral blood flow of long-term exposure to organic solvents. *Acta Psychiatrica Scandinavica, 67* (Suppl. 303), 92–99.

Risberg, J., & Ingvar, D. H. (1973). Patterns of activation in the grey matter of the dominant hemisphere during memorization and reasoning. *Brain, 96*, 737–756.

Rogers, R. L., Meyer, J. S., Shaw, T. G., & Mortel, K. F. (1983). Reductions in regional cerebral blood flow associated with chronic consumption of alcohol. *Journal of the American Geriatrics Society, 31*, 540–543.

Shimojyo, S., Scheinberg, P., & Reinmuth, O. (1967). Cerebral blood flow and metabolism in the Wernicke–Korsakoff syndrome. *Journal of Clinical Investigation, 46*, 849–854.

Simard, D., Olesen, J., Paulson, O. B., Lassen, N. A., & Skinhøj, E. (1971). Regional cerebral blood flow and its regulation in dementia. *Brain, 94*, 273–288.

Sutherland, V. C., Burbridge, T. N., Adams, J. E., & Simon, A. (1960). Cerebral metabolism in problem drinkers under the influence of alcohol and chlorpromazine hydrochloride. *Journal of Applied Physiology, 15*, 189–196.

Tarter, R. E. (1975). Psychological deficit in chronic alcoholics: A review. *International Journal of the Addictions, 10*, 327–368.

5

Discussion

CT Scan and Neuropsychological Assessments of Alcoholism

D. ADRIAN WILKINSON

Introduction

"There is no doubt that alcohol abuse can cause brain damage." The opening sentence of Ron's contribution to this volume has a confident ring, and certainly no reasonable person would dispute it. Any reasonable person might, however, ask for more specific definitions of the terms "alcohol abuse" and "brain damage," and might also wonder why the word "cause" in the confident assertion has to be preceded by the qualification "can." In this discussion, I suggest that considerable progress has been made toward the operational definition of the neuropsychological (NP) and neuroradiological (CT scan) abnormalities that are common concomitants of alcoholism, and the studies reviewed by Ron and Bergman have contributed significantly to that process. However, progress in isolating a cause of these abnormalities has been slow. This is probably because the impairments seen in alcoholism have more than one cause; indeed, the hypothesis that some of these abnormalities are antecedents of alcoholism is seriously entertained and empirically confirmed (see Parsons, Chapter 8, this volume).

Chapters 1 and 2 of this volume represent reviews of two of the best-controlled and most comprehensive studies of CT scan and NP abnormalities in alcoholics. In these two chapters, the previous work of the authors has been importantly extended, both methodologically and empirically. Among the most salient of these advances are the inclusion of samples of female alcoholics, and a very good random age-stratified sample of women drawn from the same population as the alcoholics. In addition, Ron has begun to investigate the neuroradiological characteristics of brain tissue in neuroanatomically specified regions of interest, instead of relying as most of

D. Adrian Wilkinson. Addiction Research Foundation, Toronto, Ontario, Canada; Hjellestad Clinic, Hjellestad, Norway; Institute of Neuropsychology, University of Bergen, Bergen, Norway.

us have in the past upon indirect measures of brain integrity via cerebrospinal fluid (CSF). Bergman has been able to scale the measures he uses according to subject age, education, and gender. This would have been impossible but for the very large random samples collected during the KARTAD Project, from whom NP and CT scan results were obtained. The availability of such data permits much more confident assertions about the nature and extent of brain abnormalities observed in alcoholics.

Issues in the Interpretation of CT Scans

The Use of Cerebrospinal Fluid Parameters

The majority of CT scan studies of alcoholism have involved measurement of CSF parameters as indirect evidence of decreased brain mass. The measurements have ranged from dichotomous clinical evaluations to planimetric measures on the "hard copy" computer printout (for reviews, see Cala & Mastaglia, 1981; Wilkinson, 1982b, 1985). This procedure has a long history in the neuroradiological assessment of cortical atrophy, but it has also recently been likened by Jacoby to "assessing the size of a doughnut by measuring the hole in the middle. Not only are assumptions made about the size of the doughnut, but also about the consistency of the dough" (quoted in Bird, 1982, p. 112). This observation is clearly apt if one is attempting to make predictions about function in the individual case, but it does not invalidate the approach when trying to demonstrate differences in gross brain morphology between groups.

In addition to raising questions of validity, the use of CSF indices creates a number of formidable measurement problems. The most common procedures for evaluating the output of the CT scanner involve the use of subjective clinical assessment or linear measurements on the photographic output from the machine (Wilkinson, 1982b, 1985). Since the object is to use these procedures to represent CSF volume, the process constitutes indirect measurement of an indirect assessment of cerebral morphology. Thus, it is not clear that high correlations between CT scores and other indirect evaluations of brain damage should be expected, particularly when such evaluations (e.g., NP, evoked response) do not indicate the integrity of the brain considered as an organic whole.

The CT scanner is intrinsically inconsistent in its sensitivity to distributed, as opposed to local, changes in CSF volume. Thus a change in total volume in the cortical sulci might not be visible (being distributed), but the same change might be detected if it occurred in the third ventricle. Relative sensitivity to local and distributed CSF changes is a potential problem for the human operator as well as the scanner. With one notable exception (Jernigan *et al.*, 1982), all published studies of CT scans in alcoholics have involved some sort of psychological judgments by the investigators. There have been no studies of this subject, and we do not know, for example, whether the psychophysical judgments used in assessing changes in cortical sulci are more or less sensitive than those for detecting ventricular change, particularly when clinical ratings are used. Thus, assertions about differential vulnerability to change of structures have to be evaluated with this qualification in mind.

The Use of Criterion Scores or Cutoffs

A final measurement problem with the output from CT scans derives from the use of categorical or ordinal ratings, without correction for between-subject variables, such as gender or age. This problem causes an interaction between the uncontrolled variable and the criterion level in determining the sensitivity of the test, as illustrated in idealized form in Figure 5-1. Presented in this hypothetical example are the best-fitting (linear) functions relating age to some measure of CSF volume for a group of alcoholics and nonalcoholic controls. The two age distributions are rectangular, with 30 subjects per condition in each decade of age. Within-group variance does not change with age, and is the same for the two groups. The criterion score has been set at 1.5 standard deviations above the mean for a control subject of average

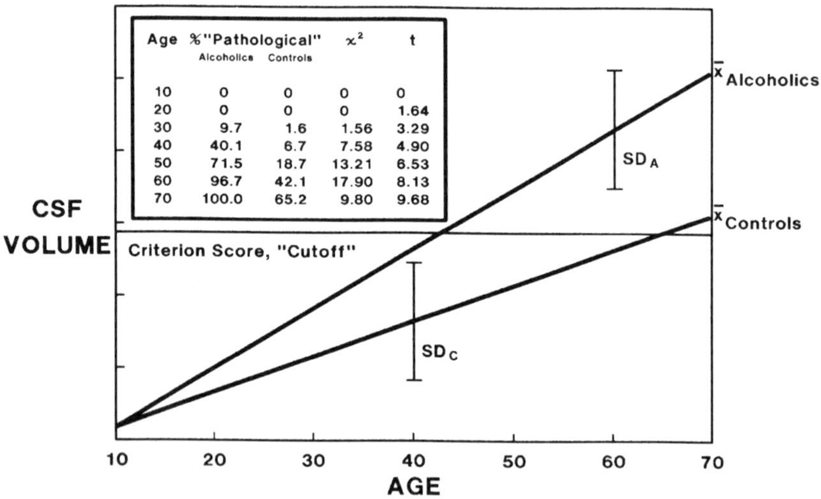

Figure 5-1. Hypothetical functions relating age to CSF volume in alcoholics and control subjects. If a cutoff score is used to categorize subjects as "pathological" or "normal," the point of maximum discriminability of the groups is not the point of maximum separation of the scores.

age. The table of areas under the normal curve is used to estimate the number of subjects categorized as "normal" or "pathological" in each decade. These values are presented in the upper left quadrant of the figure. The chi-square values associated with these results, and the *t*-test values for the difference between the means in each age decade, are also presented. As one would expect, the chi-square is less sensitive than the *t*-test, even when the criterion is optimally placed.

The major problem with the categorical scale is that as the hit rate in the abnormal group becomes asymptotic, the sensitivity of the test declines, although the separation between the means of the groups is at its maximum. This type of problem can also arise when more extended ordinal scales of clinical ratings are used, such as ratings of the degree of sulcal expansion. This analysis indicates that caution should be exercised when one attempts to estimate the *relative* frequency with which abnormalities are observed. However, it does not raise any questions about between-group differences, indicated on the basis of a particular criterion. In the present context, this type of analysis might call into question, for example, assertions about the relative frequency of ventricular and cerebellar abnormalities in alcoholics, but not assertions that such abnormalities are more frequently observed in alcoholics than in control groups.

Sampling Problems in Neuroradiological Studies of Alcoholism

Exclusion Criteria

Neuroradiological and NP studies of alcoholics have varied greatly in the criteria by which potential alcoholic subjects have been excluded from the study (Parsons, 1977; Wilkinson & Carlen, 1981; Wilkinson, 1982b). Some investigators have attempted to exclude subjects in whom a variable other than excessive alcohol consumption itself might reasonably be considered to have caused any observed brain abnormalities. Thus, criteria such as positive history of head trauma; neurological disease not related to alcohol consumption; addiction to drugs other than alcohol; presence of alcoholism-related liver disease; the presence of the Wernicke–Korsakoff syndrome; epilepsy and seizures other than withdrawal seizures; and old age have been employed to exclude potential alcoholics from the studied group. A slightly different approach has been employed where the investigators have apparently been seeking a "subclinical" level of impairment in alcoholics, and therefore have excluded all subjects with clinically apparent brain disorders (whether produced by alcohol consumption or not), as well as subjects with a history of other potential causes of brain damage. These approaches are effective if one wishes to be able to argue that brain damage may be a consequence of excessive alcohol consumption per se, rather than one of the many other risks (e.g., head injury, malnutrition) that are frequently a part of the alcoholic lifestyle. In addition, such studies have provided considerable information about the types of tests that are most sensitive in separating alcoholic from nonalcoholic groups (Parsons & Farr, 1981). Such studies are much less helpful in indicating the variety and severity of impairments seen in clinically treated alcoholics. To accomplish that task, the investigator has to be much less exclusive, and must include subjects whose impairment is very probably related (at least in part) to head injury, malnutrition, and liver disease—conditions to which alcoholics are disproportionately prone.

There are several reasons why the exclusion criteria have left many issues in this field problematic. One of the most important relates to the effectiveness with which the criteria have been applied. Few investigators have used biopsy data to exclude subjects with active liver disease, despite the prevalence of this condition in hospitalized alcoholics having normal clinical and laboratory tests (Rankin, Orrego-Matte, & Deschenes, 1978). Similarly, alcoholics in treatment have a high incidence of rib fractures and other signs of trauma that have healed without treatment (Israel, Orrego, Holt, MacDonald, & Meema, 1980). There is no reason to believe that the heads of alcoholics should be any less prone to such unidentified injuries than their ribs, and therefore successful exclusion of alcoholics with a history of significant head trauma is unlikely. Finally, several neuropathological studies have shown that the characteristic brain lesions of the Wernicke–Korsakoff syndrome are much more prevalent at autopsy than the clinical literature would suggest (Cravioto, Korein, & Silverman, 1961; Harper, 1979; Torvik, Lindbøe, & Rogde, 1982). In short, it is likely that there are "subclinical" forms of head injury, thiamine deficiency or malabsorption, and liver disease. Hence, these conditions have probably been well represented in samples that have excluded those with frank clinical signs. Thus, when the interpretation of such studies depends upon the effectiveness of the exclusion procedures, those interpretations are compromised. Methodological problems such as this may account in part for the problems in identifying etiological factors in the CT scan and NP attributes of alcoholism.

Inclusion Criteria

Almost all studies of alcoholism involve subjects who are in the treatment system. Hence, questions are correctly raised concerning the legitimacy of generalizing from such samples to the population of alcoholics at large. In the present context, it is plausible to suggest that alcoholics with cerebral deficits are less likely to be able to cope in the natural environment than their unimpaired counterparts, and may thus be overrepresented in the population of alcoholics in treatment. The most powerful way to test this idea would be to sample at random from the population, to identify a subgroup of the heaviest drinkers, and to examine the pattern and prevalence of cerebral deficits in this group. If these were to be consistent with the findings in groups of treated alcoholics, one could conclude that alcoholics with brain damage are not overrepresented among alcoholics in treatment. This, of course, describes the design of the study by Bergman and his colleagues at the Karolinska Hospital. They found that the prevalence of heavy or problem drinking in the random sample was quite consistent with the frequency one might expect on the basis of epidemiological and survey data (Cahalan & Room, 1974; Hauge & Irgens-Jensen, 1984). Furthermore, the nature and frequency of NP and CT scan abnormalities in the randomly selected heavy-drinking males and females were very consistent with the findings from groups of treated alcoholics, including the Swedish group with which they were directly compared. Thus, this study does not suggest that brain-damaged alcoholics make excessive use of treatment facilities. The KARTAD Project clearly demonstrates that the brain dysfunction common in clinic alcoholics is indicative of a large pool of brain-injured persons at large in the community, and this should constitute a serious issue for those concerned with the public health.

Recent studies have raised the possibility that there is a dose–response relationship between alcohol consumption and cognitive performance in social drinkers (Bergman, 1985; MacVane, Butters, Montgomery, & Farber, 1982; Parker & Parker, 1982). Such studies generate serious questions concerning safe levels of consumption for social drinkers, and this in turn raises the issue of the proper definition of "alcoholism." Clearly there are considerable cultural differences in the way in which the term applies. Of the social drinkers in Cala, Jones, Mastaglia, and Wiley's (1978) study, about 20% would have been categorized as "amnesic" on the psychometric criteria used in our group (Wilkinson & Carlen, 1980b). Similarly, a Norwegian colleague (F. Duckert, personal communication, February 1985) reports the confusion that arose at an international conference when she described the number of subjects, in her study of treatment of alcoholism, who had reported hallucinosis or delirium tremens. An Italian colleague was confused because, according to his training, these symptoms were necessary precursors to a diagnosis of alcoholism. It is a commonplace observation that the operational definition of "alcoholism" is moot, and as long as clinical researchers were concerned principally with the precise description of the CNS complications in their patients, this was a rather academic matter. However, once it is asserted that measurable cognitive impairment can be associated with nonalcoholic patterns of alcohol consumption, this definitional issue attains greater importance (MacVane *et al.*, 1982; Parker, 1982). It is not clear that the poor definition of "alcoholism" in studies of CNS abnormalities in "clinic alcoholics" is relevant to the debate on the correlates of heavy drinking, since an etiological role of alcohol consumption has not been demonstrated in alcoholics (Tarter & Alterman, 1984; Wilkinson & Carlen, 1981).

Selection of Control Groups

The most appropriate control group for studies of the CNS consequences of alcohol abuse is a group of healthy subjects drawn from the same population as the alcoholics (e.g., Bergman, Chapter 2, this volume; Cala, Jones, Wiley, & Mastaglia, 1980; Ron, Chapter 1, this volume). A less desirable alternative is to select persons referred for evaluation of CNS function and found to be normal (e.g., von Gall, Becker, Artmann, & Hacker, 1978; Wilkinson & Carlen, 1980b). In either of these cases, it is important that the control group be comparable in age to the alcoholic group. This end can be achieved either by using age-matched controls (see Ron, Chapter 1, this volume) or by taking a stratified, rectangular sample with the same mean and range as the alcoholic group (see Bergman, Chapter 2, this volume; Carlen & Wilkinson, 1980). The latter strategy has the advantage that age-matched controls can be selected post hoc. However, its disadvantage is that when cutoff or criterion scores are used the problems associated with such procedures can be amplified, particularly if age effects in the control group are positively accelerated, as some seem to be (Bergman, Chapter 2, this volume; Carlen *et al.*, 1981). A major advantage of having a stratified sample of control subjects is that their results can be used to generate age-scaled *T* scores, provided that the original data are on an interval scale. This is the method that Bergman has begun to apply to the KARTAD data, and it clearly increases the confidence one can have in the interpretation of certain results. For example, the gender difference in scores on third-ventricle width (see Bergman, Figure 2-1, this volume) clearly represents an alcoholism-related gender difference. Such a conclusion could not have been reached without the use of age- and gender-scaled *T* scores, given the sex difference on this variable in the general population.

CT Scan Findings in Alcoholics

Recent reviews of the general literature on CT scan assessments of alcoholics have yielded conclusions very consistent with those presented in this volume (Cala & Mastaglia, 1981; Wilkinson, 1982b, 1985). However, the procedural and methodological advances described by Bergman and Ron significantly enhance the confidence with which some earlier findings can be interpreted, and raise important questions concerning other earlier interpretations.

Local Vulnerability to CT Scan Changes

It has consistently been found that expansion of the cortical sulci is a more prominent and earlier CT abnormality in alcoholics than dilation of the lateral ventricles (Wilkinson, 1982b, 1985). (No such statement can be made with regard to the third ventricle, since this anatomical feature has been much less frequently reported on. The work of Bergman and his colleagues indicates that this was an important oversight in other studies.) Evidence of cerebellar degeneration is less common in CT studies of alcoholics than are either cortical or ventricular changes (Bergman, Borg, Hindmarsh, Idestrøm, & Mützell, 1980a; von Gall *et al.*, 1978). These findings suggest differential vulnerability to damage in cortex, midbrain, and cerebellum, but should be interpreted with caution. As indicated above, they may instead reflect differential sensitivity of CT scan to changes of equal functional and morphological significance. This alternate interpretation is consistent with the observation that cortical and ventricular abnormalities were frequently seen in a randomly selected control sample (Bergman, Borg, Hindmarsh, Idestrøm, & Mützell, 1980b). Furthermore, neuropathological studies (to which the same caution applies) indicate that cerebellar changes are more frequent than cortical or midbrain changes (Martin & Eckardt, 1985).

Among cortical changes, there is evidence of a graded vulnerability from anterior to posterior. In the two studies that have included analysis of this regional distribution (von Gall *et al.*, 1978; Cala *et al.*, 1980), local vulnerability has been ranked frontal–temporal–parietal–occipital (Wilkinson, 1985). These results are consistent with the nature of functional impairments seen in alcoholics (e.g., see Parsons & Farr, 1981; Wilkinson & Carlen, 1981). Nonetheless, the psychophysical problems of rating the degree of frontal versus parietal sulcal expansion are very complex, given the differences in morphology and probable differences in the depth represented in a single CT slice. Hence, it is quite possible that equal structural changes could consistently give rise to slight differences in neuroradiological judgments of sulcal expansion (see "The Use of CSF Parameters," above).

Effects of Age on CT Scan Results

Many reports indicate that scores on CT measures of CSF parameters are related to subject age, both in nonalcoholic controls and in alcoholics (Bergman *et al.*, 1980b; Cala *et al.*, 1980; Carlen *et al.*, 1981; Ron, Acker, & Lishman, 1980; von Gall *et al.*, 1978). The age-relatedness of cerebellar scores is moot (Wilkinson, 1985). The relative sensitivity of CSF measures to age varies among studies. Thus, Bergman (Chapter 2, this volume) has found the correlations of age with the ventricular and cortical measures to be very similar between groups and between measures. In apparent contrast, we (Carlen *et al.*, 1981) obtained higher correlations between age and CT scores on cortical than on ventricular indices, in both the alcoholic group and the control group. This discrepancy is most parsimoniously explained by procedural differences. We scored sulcal expansion in a manner that approximated interval scaling, whereas Bergman and his colleagues used a 4-point rating scale. Thus, the issue of the relative sensitivity of brain structures to age effects is unresolved, as is the issue of the sensitivity of various CT measures. However, it is clear that when the scores of alcoholics and control groups are compared, the selected measures should be age-scaled, or age-matching of subjects should be employed. The use of criterion scores that are not age-scaled makes a study particularly prone to the types of problems outlined in "The Use of CSF Parameters," above.

Description of the age-relatedness of CT scores has usually been on the basis of the correlation of age with the selected CT index. This method is, of course, a test of the fit of the data to a linear model. However, this assumption of linearity is apparently unwarranted, both for nonalcoholics and for alcoholics. We (Carlen *et al.*, 1981) found that our measure of sulcal expansion was correlated to subject age our younger alcoholic subjects, but not in the older group. In contrast, for the control group, sulcal score was correlated significantly to age in the older but not in the younger subjects. On the ventricular measure (intercaudate width), the age changes in both the groups were fitted by a simple linear function. These results are entirely consistent with the findings reported by Bergman of correlation of ventricular and cortical scores only in the younger alcoholics and the older control subjects. In short, on the measures of sulcal expansion, the scores of alcoholics appear to fit a negatively accelerated function of age, whereas the curve for control subjects seems positively accelerated. Two such "mirror-image" curves could be approximated by the same best-fit linear solution. The simplest solution to this problem is to generate age-scaled *T*-scores for a normative group, using raw scores or several class intervals (e.g., decades).

In commenting on the correlations found in the KARTAD study, Bergman concludes that they are not consistent with the "premature-aging hypothesis." This assertion is difficult to defend, since the hypothesis in question has been proposed in various forms (Ryan & Butters, 1984), but has consisted mainly of rather casual observations of similarities between the characteristics of alcoholics and older persons (Ryan & Butters, 1984; Wilkinson, 1982a; Wilkinson & Carlen, 1982). In the present context, Bergman interprets the hypothesis to predict that the correlation between age and the CT scores should be higher in the alcoholics than in the controls. (For a contrasting position, see Ryan & Butters, 1984.) Furthermore, he states that the different patterns of intercorrelation of cortical and ventricular scores in the old and the young alcoholics and controls are inconsistent with the premature-aging hypothesis. This indicates that assumptions are being made about the aging process—specifically, that "aging" is a linear function of chronological age, and that the variability of points about the line relative to total variability is equal in alcoholics and controls. Since the first of these assumptions seems untenable, it might be better to defer tests of the hypothesis until the notion of "aging" has been more adequately defined.

Stability of CT Abnormalities

There have now been at least eight independent confirmations of the finding that CT abnormalities in some alcoholics normalize after periods of abstinence, or greatly reduced drinking (for reviews, see Porjesz & Begleiter, 1983; Wilkinson, 1982b, 1985). Of the CSF parameters, it has consistently been found that decreased sulcal volume is the most prominent of these changes. However, reductions in the apparent volume of the lateral ventricles have also been observed (Carlen, Wilkinson, Wortzman, & Holgate, 1979). The finding of reversible cortical abnormalities is reported in both Chapter 1 and Chapter 2 of this volume. Ron reports that the previously noted negative correlation of duration of abstinence with sulcal expansion (e.g., Ron, 1980, 1983) is paralleled by increased tissue density in the caudate and thalamus. This is consistent with previous reports of increases in tissue density in abstinent alcoholics (Cala, Jones, & Burns, 1983; Carlen *et al.*, 1979), and suggests that the observed changes are not simply the result of a reabsorption of displaced water and electrolytes from extracellular space (Carlen, 1982). Ron also reports that alcoholics have elevated tissue density in frontal white matter. This is a novel finding. If this abnormality turns out to be reversible, the hypothesis of fluid reabsorption may need to be revived as part of the explanation of morphological plasticity in the brains of recently abstinent alcoholics.

Findings on Tissue Density

In assessing possible brain damage with the CT scan, it is clearly preferable to use direct measures of tissue characteristics, rather than relying on indirect CSF scores. With the development of CT technology, such studies are appearing (Cala *et al.*, 1983; Carlen *et al.*, 1979; Gebhardt, Naeser, & Butters, 1984; Golden *et al.*, 1981; Ron, Chapter 1, this volume). The simpler of these studies have measured the CT characteristics of large areas of brain, but the more sophisticated (Gebhardt *et al.*, 1984; Ron, Chapter 1, this volume) have involved examination of neuronanatomically defined regions of interest, and have attempted to relate the CT characteristics of those regions to specific functions. This approach permits the testing of much more precise NP hypotheses than before, and is clearly the optimum use of CT scanning for research on alcoholism.

All the studies of tissue density have given some indication that this parameter tends to be reduced in recently abstinent alcoholics. Thus, Cala *et al.* (1983) and Golden *et al.* (1981) found lower density figures in the alcoholic subjects. In Golden *et al.*'s subjects, this attribute was found in the left hemisphere particularly. Cala *et al.* found that the reduced densities normalized significantly with abstinence. We (Carlen *et al.*, 1979) and Ron (Chapter 1, this volume) have also reported decreased density scores in abstinent subjects, though in Ron's subjects this was restricted in central gray matter (caudate and thalamus), whereas in frontal white matter the scores of the alcoholics were elevated relative to controls. This last finding is apparently inconsistent with the elegant results of Gebhardt *et al.* (1984), who found that lower frontal and parietal density scores were correlated with deficient visuospatial problem-solving ability, whereas reduced thalamic density was associated with impairment of memory. The discrepancy of their findings with Ron's may result from the differences in the cortical areas measured, and from differences in the inclusion of gray matter in those samples.

Etiology of CT Abnormalities in Alcoholics

The studies by Gurling and colleagues (cited by Ron) clearly indicate that at least some of the radiological abnormalities of alcoholics do not antecede the alcoholism as a result of genetic factors. The mean ventricle–brain ratio (VBR) scores of the alcoholic and nonalcoholic cotwins (9.7 and 6.7) were very similar to the mean VBRs of the larger alcoholic and control groups previously described by Ron (9.6 and 6.2). Hence, there is no indication that the nonalcoholic cotwins were different from the general nonalcoholic population on this measure.

Bergman has suggested that there are two etiological processes involved in the CSF abnormalities of alcoholics, one of which expresses itself in abstracting deficits, is related to the cortical abnormalities, and is possibly antecedent to alcoholism. The second process is related to alcohol consumption exceeding some genetically determined threshold, and is expressed ventricular dilation and deficits in memory and general intellectual abilities. The twin studies of Gurling and colleagues are consistent with the latter hypothesis; the alcoholism-related CSF abnormalities involved ventricular enlargement. However, it is not clear how the finding of higher densities in the frontal white matter of the alcoholic cotwins would be accommodated in the formulation that Bergman proposes.

Profile of Neuropsychological Deficits in Alcoholics

The frequent use of standardized psychological test batteries, such as the Wechsler Adult Intelligence Scale (WAIS), the Halstead–Reitan Neuropsychological Test Battery, and the Wechsler Memory Scale (WMS), for assessing the cognitive status of groups of alcoholics, has led to a considerable literature on the transcultural stability of the cognitive profile of alcoholics (Løberg & Miller, 1986). A very consistent pattern has emerged, involving poor performance on tests of immediate adaptive ability such as abstraction, visuospatial problem solving, and formation of novel associations (see Parsons, Chapter 8, this volume).

Among the tests of the WAIS and the Halstead–Reitan, the performance of alcoholics is consistently impaired on tests such as the Category Test, Block Design, Tactual Performance Test (TPT) Time, Digit Symbol, and Part B of the Trail Making Test (TMT B). On the other hand, Vocabulary, Information, Rhythm Test, and Digit Span tend to be performed normally (for reviews, see Løberg & Miller, 1986; Miller & Saucedo, 1983; Parsons & Farr, 1981).

Since the KARTAD subjects were tested with the Halstead–Reitan Battery and the Block Design test, their results can be compared to the profile just described. By and large, the findings are consistent with the expected pattern, though the rank ordering of the most sensitive tests is slightly different, with TMT B ranked higher than expected, and TPT Time somewhat lower. The rank ordering of the sensitivity of the tests for women is quite consistent with that for men. Thus, despite any culturally based differences in pattern and quantity of alcohol consumption, the Swedish sample seems representative of alcoholics in treatment generally. In this regard, it is worth noting that Løberg (1980) has indicated that the NP profile of Norwegian alcoholics is almost identical to that seen in the predominantly North American groups that have been assessed with the WAIS and the Halstead–Reitan.

The subjects in the London Institute of Psychiatry study were tested with a battery that overlapped less with those most commonly used, but the results seem consistent with those usually observed (Ron, 1983).

Two Neuropsychological Syndromes in Alcoholism?

As Ron points out, neuropathological studies indicate that there are at least two types of alcoholism-related cerebral disorders: the thiamine deficiency syndrome associated with the Wernicke–Korsakoff syndrome (Victor, Adams, & Collins, 1971), with characteristic lesions in the mamillary bodies and the medial thalamus; and the neuropathic profile described by Courville (1955), with changes most prominent in the cerebral cortex. The relation of other common neuropathological changes (in cerebellum and brain stem) to these other conditions is uncertain.

NP studies of alcoholism have frequently involved the tacit acknowledgment of this dichotomy, in that malnourished alcoholics, and those with the diagnosis of Korsakoff's disease, have either been excluded from such studies or evaluated as a distinct group (Wilkinson & Carlen, 1981). In fact, in studies of Korsakoff's amnesia, it has been common practice to include a group of nonamnesic alcoholics as a control group (Butters & Cermak, 1980). Recently, however, continuities in the impairment of memory in social drinkers, alcoholics, and amnesic alcoholics have suggested a continuum of impairment (Butters & Granholm, Chapter 9, this volume; Ryan & Butters, 1980; Ryback, 1971).

In Chapters 1 and 2 of this volume, several strands of evidence are presented that suggest two etiologically, functionally, and neuroradiologically distinct types of brain abnormality in alcoholics. These findings are consistent with those from our laboratory (Wilkinson & Carlen, 1980a, 1980b). In the London Institute of Psychiatry study, it was found that thalamic and caudate densities were depressed in the alcoholics, whereas the density of frontal white matter was elevated. In addition, the degree of memory impairment within the alcoholic group was related to the lower thalamic and caudate densities, and to the value of VBR. Cortical density was related to a measure of verbal fluency, but not memory function. Ron suggests in Chapter 1 that thiamine deficiency causes the subcortical changes and alcohol the cortical ones. Having proposed "the presence of two different types of lesions, of different location and possibly different etiologies" (p. 17), she draws this puzzling conclusion: "It seems, therefore, increasingly artificial to separate the organic syndromes related to alcohol into discrete categories, and it would appear more appropriate to consider them as part of a continuum" (pp. 18–19). Clearly, it would be artificial to separate the syndromes as if they were mutually exclusive; however, considering the evidence presented in Ron's chapter, separation with regard to etiological processes and NP descriptions seems both valid and useful.

Bergman and colleagues have also found evidence for at least two NP and CT scan syndromes of impairment in alcoholism. They have noted that the time courses of cortical and ventricular abnormalities in their alcoholic subjects vary, and that statistical correction for the effects of age eliminates the significance of the correlations between cortical scores and task performance on abstracting and visuospatial problem solving. In contrast, age correction does not destroy the significance of the correlations of ventricular scores with tests of memory and general intellectual ability. The dissociation of cortically mediated visuospatial ability from memory related to thalamic integrity was recently demonstrated by Gebhardt *et al.* (1984), using CT density scores as the predictor of test performance. Their findings are quite consistent with those of Bergman and colleagues, and the correlation of decreased memory with lowered thalamic density has been replicated by Ron and her colleagues.

Several findings in our studies have suggested that two distinct NP and CT scan syndromes can be observed in chronic alcoholics. In brief, after our subjects were separated into two groups (those with Wernicke's encephalopathy and/or psychometrically defined amnesia [WA], and those with neither of these syndromes [OA]), the following differences between the groups were observed:

1. In the OA group, CT sulcal and ventricular scores were correlated to subject age, but neither measure was age-related in the WA group.
2. The test scores that best correlated with the CT scores were different for the two groups (Wilkinson & Carlen, 1980a, 1980b).
3. The WA group has the same Average Impairment Rating on the Halstead–Reitan as the OA group, despite great differences in performance on the WMS.
4. There was a strong correlation between the sensitivity of a test (as a discriminator of alcoholics from nonalcoholics) and the CT scores for the OA group, but no such relationship was found for the WA group (Wilkinson, 1985).
5. At retest, change in performance on the Visual Reproduction test of the WMS was the best discriminator of WA and OA subjects, whereas change in Block Design performance best separated abstinent from drinking subjects (Wilkinson & Carlen, 1983).

These results are not consistent with the hypothesis that alcoholism-related cognitive deficits represent a single continuum of impairment. They are consistent with Bergman's finding that the more common deficits of abstracting and visuospatial abilities can be dissociated from the problems of memory that tend to be identified in older alcoholics. It should be noted, however, that in the KARTAD Project subjects with clinically apparent memory deficit were excluded. This suggests that impairment of memory in alcoholics does not occur as a "quantum jump" to amnesia, but may be represented as a gradual erosion of memorial ability that culminates in the catastrophic end point of Korsakoff's amnesia. Thus, in alcoholism, two NP syndromes of different etiology may tend to develop in parallel. (See Butters & Granholm, Chapter 9, this volume for a similar view of alcohol-related NP syndromes.)

Alcoholic Dementia

Some alcoholics with profound amnesia do not fit the clinical or psychometric definitions of Korsakoff's amnesia, since they do not have preserved intelligence. In fact, they have a global loss of cognitive ability, or a dementia. In the Clinical Institute of the Addiction Research Foundation, we see about one case of alcoholic dementia to every two cases of Korsakoff's amnesia. When such clear general loss of cognitive capacity is observed, the use of the descriptive term "alcoholic dementia" is quite justified. However, it is not so obvious that it is justified to view such persons as representing the end stage of the deficiency in abstraction and problem-solving ability often seen in alcoholics, since this deficiency clearly does not involve a global loss of cognitive ability. Hence, to refer to persons with such circumscribed functional deficits as having a "dementia" (Lishman, 1981; Martin & Eckardt, 1985) is to make unjustified etiological assumptions, and involves somewhat unorthodox use of the term "dementia."

Convergent Validation of CT Scan and Neuropsychological Findings

In the concluding section of his chapter, Bergman makes a thought-provoking and important statement with which I am obliged to take some issue. He states:

> The moderate correlation with neuropsychological deficits for central changes and the nonexistent correlation for cortical changes clearly indicate that CT scan and neuropsychological testing cannot replace each other in the routine clinical diagnostic assessment of alcoholic patients. Thus, they seem to reflect disparate aspects of cerebral function in alcoholism. For this reason, CT scan should not be used to confirm the validity of neuropsychological tests in alcoholics, and vice versa . . . (p. 40)

This statement includes two assertions—the first concerning the advisability of predicting CT scores from NP test scores in the individual case, and the second about methods of convergently validating the two types of assessment. Since the proportion of common variance in CT and NP test scores, even without statistical correction for age, is at most about 30% (Bergman *et al.*, 1980a; Wilkinson & Carlen, 1980b), it is clearly unwise to make individual predictions from one type of measure to the other. The same qualification may not, however, apply to the issue of convergent validation of the measures.

One approach to the convergent validation of CT scan and NP assessment of alcoholics is to test whether the sensitivity of a test, as a discriminator of alcoholics from nonalcoholics, predicts the strength of the correlation of NP test score with CT scan score (Wilkinson, 1985). The sensitivity of WAIS and Halstead–Reitan tests has recently been reviewed by Parsons and Farr (1981) and by Miller and Saucedo (1983), with very similar results (Wilkinson, 1985). For present purposes, the results of Parsons and Farr are used, since they confined their analysis to studies using complete test batteries, thus providing more control for possible effects of subject age on the estimates of test sensitivity. The measures of sensitivity are plotted on a scattergram (Figure 5-2) against the values of the correlations between test performance and an index of CSF volume (Wilkinson, 1985) for the OA group from our study (Wilkinson & Carlen, 1980b). More than 30% of the

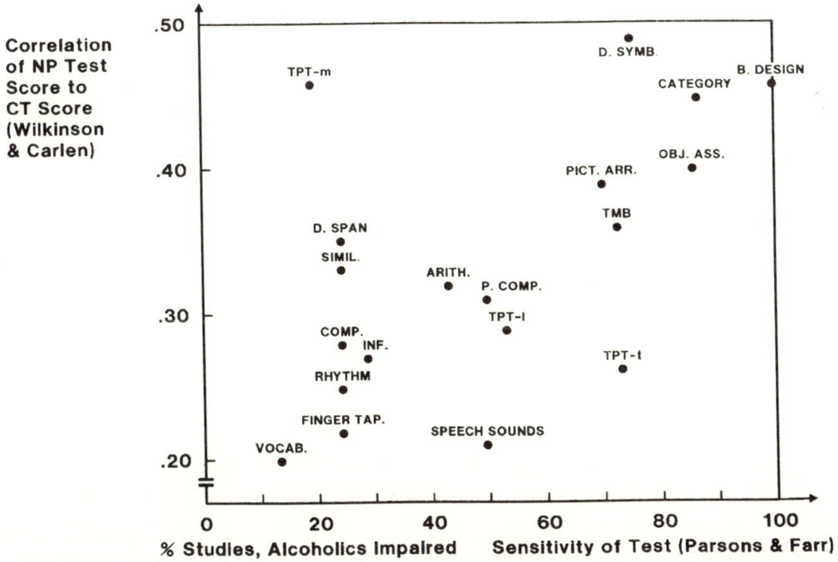

Figure 5-2. Scatterplot of the sensitivity of subtests of the WAIS and the Halstead–Reitan Battery (after Parsons & Farr, 1981) against degree of correlation of NP test scores with CT scan scores (Wilkinson & Carlen, 1980b). Data for nonamnesic subjects only.

variance in the measures is shared, convergently validating the two procedures, and suggesting that a common neuropathic process underlies both the CSF expansion and the cognitive impairment that are often found in nonamnesic alcoholics.

Why the discrepancy with Bergman's interpretation? It is probably illusory. In the analyses reported in his chapter, Bergman introduces sophisticated statistical controls for the contribution of age to the variance of the data. If there were a common neuropathic process, accounting both for much of the variance in CT scores and in the results of the more sensitive tests, and if this process were also strongly age-related, then the statistical procedures used by Bergman would reveal statistically significant common variance only in the residual unexplained variance in the data, representing a second neuropathic process that is independent of age. As previously indicated, several independent lines of research suggest that there are two syndromes of impairment in alcoholics, the less common of which seems to be of subcortical origin, to consist mainly of impairment of memory, and to be independent of age. Thus, an alternate description of Bergman's results is that they represent the statistical isolation of a subcortical alcohol amnesic syndrome, and the convergent validation of its NP and CT scan manifestations.

Etiological Factors

The research for solid clues to the etiology of alcoholism-related brain dysfunction has been largely unsuccessful, except for the role of thiamine in Wernicke's encephalopathy (Victor *et al.*, 1971). It is very likely that aspects of alcohol consumption per se, or in interaction with other variables, are of etiological importance, but there are many potential relevant measures of drinking, and the science of quantifying them is still early in its development.

Antecedents to Alcoholism

It is possible that some of the cognitive abnormalities of alcoholics are antecedents of heavy drinking (Parsons, Chapter 8, this volume; Tarter & Alterman, 1984). Ron considers this an unlikely hypothesis to account for the CT abnormalities seen in alcoholics. She bases her position on three points. The sheer prevalence of CT signs in treated alcoholics suggests that antecedent brain anomalies are unlikely to prove more than a small part of their explanation. The anomalies are related to age and duration of the alcoholism, and, most persuasively, genetically based accounts of antecedent abnormalities are excluded by Gurling and colleagues' studies of monozygotic twins discordant for alcoholism.

According to Bergman, his data suggest that the deficit in abstracting and current problem-solving abilities is antecedent to alcoholism, and is also more common in women. However, if this antecedent abnormality is presumed to be genetically based, it would need to be distinct from the proposed genetic basis for predisposition to alcoholism, since this is found to be more common in males (Murray, Clifford, & Gurling, 1983).

Alcohol Consumption Variables

There are many plausible candidates among consumption variables for an etiological role in cognitive and CT findings from alcoholics. These would include average dose per drinking occasion, maximum dose per drinking occasion, chronicity of heavy alcohol consumption, drinking pattern, and duration of abstinence before assessment. In collecting such information, arbitrary decisions must be made about how the data are scored. For example, the average dose can be expressed in absolute quantities, or in dose per unit mass of subject. Thus, though Bergman found that the male alcoholics consumed a higher mean maximum quantity per drinking occasion, they may have been exposed to very similar circulating levels of alcohol. Given these sorts of problems, it is perhaps not surprising that, with the notable exception of recency of drinking, consumption variables have yielded so little in the prediction of brain disorders in alcoholism. Because so many potential predictors and criterion variables are available, it would be unwise to give weight to unreplicated findings.

Ron reports that subjects of the London Institute of Psychiatry study who scored high on an index of "social decline" did not have worse CT results than less deteriorated patients. She also notes that such persons tended to drink in an episodic pattern. Haug (1968) has previously noted that episodic drinkers have less severe neuroradiological abnormalities than daily drinkers, and Sanchez-Craig (1980) and Tarbox, Wiegel, and Biggs (1984) have found the same with a behavioral test (TMT B). Thus, the possible effects of severe alcohol involvement may be offset by a change over time to a more benign drinking pattern.

An alternative to the assessment of consumption variables is to measure consequences of drinking, such as blackouts and delirious episodes. Bergman has found that such symptoms are related to central CT changes, which may indicate that reports of such symptoms are a more valid indicator of severity of alcohol involvement than is recall of typical drinking practices.

Reversibility of Changes

It is now clear that the neuroradiographic abnormalities observed in alcoholics are in some cases at least partly reversible (Artmann, von Gall, Hacker, & Herrlick, 1981; Bergman, Chapter 2, this volume; Cala *et al.*, 1983; Carlen, Wortzman, Holgate, Wilkinson, & Rankin, 1978; Ledesma, 1958; Porjesz & Begleiter, 1983; Ron, Chapter 1, this volume; Sarabia, Bowden, & Tex, 1980). These changes are most prominent in the size of cortical sulci, but changes in ventricular measures have also been observed (Carlen *et al.*, 1978, 1979). The report of Ron that densities of thalamic and caudate grey matter are higher in patients who have abstained for longer periods is consistent with the notion that reversible CT scan findings are not confined to the cortex in abstinent subjects.

The time course of some of the reversible changes appears to be rapid. For example, Bergman (1985) found that drinking in the past week was related to CT scan measures in his group of randomly selected "excessive drinkers." Similarly, we (Carlen, Wilkinson, Wortzman, & Holgate, 1984) found that CT changes were significantly related to the interval between drinking and the first scan, in a group of subjects whose initial scan took place, on average, in the fourth week of abstinence. Studies of CSF volume in the early stages of abstinence may reveal much more extensive and frequent morphological changes than were indicated by earlier studies. Earlier scanning for the first scan will also reveal whether the younger brain is more plastic in this regard, as Ron has hypothesized in her chapter.

The mechanism, time course, etiology, and functional significance of these reversible changes are unknown. Carlen (1982) has proposed that such changes are of functional significance, and may involve structural changes such as axonal sprouting, dendritic arborization, and revascularization of tissue. The overall increases in tissue density that seem to occur in abstinent alcoholics makes reabsorption of displaced fluid improbable. We (Carlen *et al.*, 1984) found that change scores on repeated neurological examinations were correlated with CT change scores, suggesting functional significance. As Ron and Bergman show, the changes are clearly related to reduced alcohol consumption; however, this is not necessarily the cause, because with reduced drinking must come changes in a number of other aspects of the alcoholic lifestyle. We (Carlen *et al.*, 1980) found that there is a severe but reversible CSF acidosis in many alcoholics. This abnormality may indicate the neurochemical substrate of the reversible CT changes.

A number of controlled studies have demonstrated functional improvement in abstinent alcoholics (Goldman, 1982; Parsons & Farr, 1981; Wilkinson & Carlen, 1981). The Block Design test has consistently been among the most sensitive in identifying this improvement (Kish, Hagen, Woody, & Harvey, 1980; McLachlan & Levinson, 1974; Schau, O'Leary, & Chaney, 1980). In his test battery, Bergman (1983) has also found Block Design to be the most sensitive measure of NP improvement. We (Wilkinson & Carlen, 1983) found that Block Design was the test most sensitive in discriminating between groups of nonamnesic alcoholics who had been either abstinent or drinking between the first and the second testing. In contrast, abstinent amnesics improved significantly more on the Visual Reproduction test of the WMS than both abstinent and nonabstinent nonamnesics. In a discriminant analysis, change scores on this test were the best discriminator of amnesics from nonamnesics. Taken together, these results confirm the hypothesis that there are two alcoholism-related NP disorders, with separate courses of recovery. One of these involves abstraction and visuospatial problem solving, and the second is a disorder of memory. Brandt, Butters, Ryan, and Bayog (1983) reached essentially the same conclusion, using a battery of sensitive tests and between-groups control of the duration of abstinence. In Bergman's subjects, recovery from the memory impairment may not have been detected, because patients with the greatest potential for recovery on this dimension (Korsakoff amnesics) were excluded from the study.

Gender and Brain Dysfunction in Alcoholics

The chapters by Bergman and Ron indicate a number of sex differences, in CT scan results and NP test scores, both in alcoholics and in controls. Among the findings showing differences are these: (1) Alcoholic women were less vulnerable to cortical abnormalities than men (Ron); (2) male alcoholics had more dilation of the third ventricle than their female counterparts (Bergman); (3) nonalcoholic males had larger third ventricles than nonalcoholic women (Bergman); (4) overall, women performed worse than men on the KARTAD neuropsychological test battery (Bergman); and (5) alcoholic women tended to have greater neuropsychological impairment than alcoholic men, despite shorter histories of "loss of control" drinking and lower mean maximum dose per occasion (Bergman).

Ron's preliminary finding that CT abnormalities are confined to the ventricular system is not consistent with the results of the KARTAD Project, or with the data of Cala *et al.* (1980). It is probably the result of sampling error. The larger third ventricles of the control males in Bergman's study seem clearly to indicate a gender-related morphological difference. This does not, however, account for all the difference observed in the alcoholic groups. Since this gender difference was based upon age- and gender-corrected *T* scores, it represents a true sex difference in alcoholism-related CT findings.

The sex difference in severity of alcohol-related NP impairment is not so firmly based. Bergman found that the female controls did not do as well as the male controls on a number of the psychological tests, and performed better on one. The tests on which the control women did significantly worse than the men were Reasoning, Block Design, TPT Memory, Finger Tapping, and Memory for Designs. The women were superior on Claeson–Dahl Verbal Learning. Three of the tests on which the control women did worse than the control men are among the seven most sensitive tests in the battery (Reasoning, Block Design, and Memory for Designs). The women alcoholics were particularly impaired relative to the males on Reasoning, Memory for Designs, and Finger Tapping, and outperformed the males only on Claeson–Dahl Verbal Learning. Since the *T* scores for the psychological tests were not corrected for gender differences, this pattern of findings in the alcoholics may well have been the result of gender differences that are independent of alcoholism.

Thus the gender difference that emerges securely from Bergman's study is the CT difference, which is readily interpretable in terms of the more chronic and severe alcoholism of the men. The hypothesis of greater NP vulnerability of alcoholic women could be tested if gender-corrected *T* scores were used. Such a study could be strengthened by the use of a matched-subjects design (Sanchez-Craig & Wilkinson, 1982), which should be quite possible, given the large sample of male alcoholics in the KARTAD study.

Clinical Relevance of Alcohol-Related Brain Dysfunction

NP impairment of alcoholics may have clinical relevance in determining who receives treatment, in selecting the appropriate treatment, in motivating patients for treatment, and in evaluating the outcome of treatment.

Whether a person presents for treatment or does not might be influenced by the presence of cognitive impairment. As previously indicated, the results of the KARTAD Project indicate that NP impairment is not more prevalent among alcoholics in treatment than among excessive drinkers outside the treatment system (Bergman, Chapter 2, this volume; Bergman *et al.*, 1980b). Cala *et al.* (1978, 1980) have found cognitive and CT abnormalities in heavy drinkers not diagnosed as alcoholics, though their data did not permit conclusions about prevalence. Although the presence of brain dysfunction does not appear to influence the chances of an alcoholic's entering treatment, there is mounting evidence that cognitive and brain anomalies are associated with an elevated risk of alcoholism (Tarter & Alterman, 1984).

Since treatment of alcohol problems often consists of teaching new ways of coping with the tendency to drink, it seems clear that impairment in the acquisition of new information may be relevant to treatment (Wilkinson & Sanchez-Craig, 1981). The degree of cognitive impairment should influence decisions about the cognitive complexity of the treatment, the duration of training in treatment, and the interval from the beginning of abstinence to the start of the more cognitive aspects of the treatment (Goldman & Rosenbaum, 1977; Wilkinson & Sanchez-Craig, 1981). Since abstinence is sufficient to ensure some recovery, Ron has suggested that keeping patients in an environment that precludes relapses may be a legitimate end in itself. Such advice may be more easily justified to those concerned with health costs if cognitive retraining procedures (Goldman, 1982 and Chapter 15, this volume; Wilson, Chapter 16, this volume) are found to accelerate or enhance the recovery process.

The studies reviewed in this chapter suggest that there may be two ways in which the cognitive abilities of alcoholics in treatment should be tuned to the capabilities of the clients. The deficit in abstracting and current problem-solving abilities suggests that treatments demanding such skills—either during therapy, or subsequently as an aspect of coping—may not be advisable in cases where impairment is apparent. In addition, many alcoholics, particularly the older patients, have impaired memory (Ryan & Butters, 1980); this may reflect a continuum of impairment culminating in Korsakoff's amnesia. In theory, such deficits would be likely to retard the acquisition of new skills during treatment, and hence the pacing of treatment should reflect this fact (O'Leary & Donovan, 1979). It may be useful to assess retention as part of the treatment process. Of course, this is based on the premise that information learned in treatment is important to treatment outcome. Few have tried to measure learning in treatment. Sanchez-Craig and Walker (1982) found that alcoholics who were trained in goal setting and problem solving to a criterion of performance had forgotten much of what was taught 1 month later. Since the majority of these patients were cognitively impaired, it is possible that the forgetting was a consequence of the deficits. Chaney, O'Leary, and Marlatt (1978) found that a measure of speed of problem solution was predictive of outcome. Since the nature of the test was determined by the content of one of the treatments being evaluated, this result may indicate the importance of experiences in treatment to outcome, but the results can also be interpreted as indicating that pretreatment cognitive ability is predictive of status at follow-up (Wilkinson & Sanchez-Craig, 1981).

Information about the risks and the extent of NP impairment may be useful in motivating alcoholics to change their drinking habits; and since the deficits are, in many cases, reversible, feedback about cognitive or CT scan normalization may be effective ways of consolidating the decisions of patients to maintain the initial gains of abstinence (Wilkinson & Sanchez-Craig, 1981). It may be worth noting that, even in patients with no sign of impairment, the ability to benefit from practice on a test can apparently be compromised by continuing to drink, even at significantly reduced levels (Wilkinson & Sanchez-Craig, 1981).

Finally, NP data may be useful in evaluating alcoholism treatment. A variety of subject characteristics have been found to be predictive of outcome status in treated alcoholics (Ogborne, 1978), and it may be that pretreatment cognitive status is such a predictor, though initial studies (Bergman, Chapter 2, this volume; O'Leary, Donovan, Chaney, & Walker, 1979; Walker, Sanchez-Craig, & Bornet, 1982) have failed to confirm this hypothesis. In addition, results of repeated testing may be used to corroborate levels of posttreatment drinking in groups of alcoholics, since improvement with repeated testing is affected by consumption levels between tests (Wilkinson & Carlen, 1983; Wilkinson & Sanchez-Craig, 1981).

Summary

Large-scale NP and CT studies of alcoholism indicate that there are two major kinds of brain impairment in alcoholics—one involving current problem-solving ability, and the other involving memory. These behavioral deficits are related to different CT abnormalities, and appear to be of different etiology. Attempts at convergent validation of the CT and NP findings from alcoholics have been variously interpreted as unsuccessful (and possibly irrelevant) or as successful. The latter view is advanced in this chapter.

The research discussed in this chapter includes important advances over previous work. In particular, the use of direct assessment of brain tissue, the use of CT density measures, and the collection of good control values (for both males and females, and for both CT and NP test scores) constitute significant improvements on other comparable studies. Despite these advances, the issues of etiology and possible differences in vulnerability of males and females remain moot, though the twin studies discussed by

Ron exclude genetic differences as the sole etiological factor. Despite cultural variations, there is remarkable international congruence on the CT and NP profiles of alcoholics.

Acknowledgments

The writing of this chapter was supported in part by a grant from the National Institute on Alcohol Abuse and Alcoholism. Thanks to Martha Sanchez-Craig for criticism of an initial draft, and for assistance in the preparation of the manuscript.

References

Artmann, H., von Gall, M., Hacker, H., & Herrlick, J. (1981). Reversible enlargement of cerebral spinal fluid spaces in chronic alcoholics. *American Journal of Neuroradiology, 2*, 23–27.

Bergman, H. (1983, June). *Neuropsychological recovery in alcoholics after treatment.* Paper presented at the 29th International Institute on the Prevention and Treatment of Alcoholism, Zagreb, Yugoslavia.

Bergman, H. (1985). Cognitive deficits and morphological cerebral changes in a random sample of social drinkers. In M. Galanter (Ed.), *Recent developments in alcoholism* (Vol. 3, pp. 265–276). New York: Plenum Press.

Bergman, H., Borg, S., Hindmarsh, T., Idestrom, C.-M., & Mutzell, S. (1980a). Computed tomography of the brain and neuropsychological assessment of male alcoholic patients and a random sample from the general male population. *Acta Psychiatrica Scandinavica, 62*(Suppl. 286), 47–56.

Bergman, H., Borg, S., Hindmarsh, T., Idestrom, C.-M., & Mutzell, S. (1980b). Computed tomography of the brain, clinical examination and neuropsychological assessment of a random sample of men from the general population. *Acta Psychiatrica Scandinavica, 62*(Suppl. 286), 77–88.

Bird, J. M. (1982). Computerized tomography, atrophy and dementia: A review. *Progress in Neurobiology, 19*, 91–115.

Brandt, J., Butters, N., Ryan, C., & Bayog, R. (1983). Cognitive loss and recovery in long-term alcohol abusers. *Archives of General Psychiatry, 40*, 435–442.

Butters, N., & Cermak, L. S. (1980). *Alcoholic Korsakoff's syndrome: An information-processing approach to amnesia.* New York: Academic Press.

Cahalan, D., & Room, R. (1974). *Problem drinkers among American men.* New Brunswick, NJ: Rutgers Center for Alcohol Studies.

Cala, L. A., Jones, B., & Burns, P. (1983). Results of computerized tomography, psychometric testing and dietary studies in social drinkers, with emphasis on reversibility after abstinence. *Medical Journal of Australia, 70*, 264–269.

Cala, L. A., Jones, B., Mastaglia, F. L., & Wiley, B. (1978). Brain atrophy and intellectual impairment in heavy drinkers—a clinical psychometric and computed tomography study. *Australian and New Zealand Journal of Medicine, 8*, 147–153.

Cala, L. A., Jones, B., Wiley, B., & Mastaglia, F. L. (1980). A computerized axial tomography (C.A.T.) study of alcohol induced cerebral atrophy, in conjunction with other correlates. *Acta Psychiatrica Scandinavica, 62*(Suppl. 286), 31–40.

Cala, L. A., & Mastaglia, F. L. (1981). Computerized tomography in chronic alcoholics. *Alcoholism: Clinical and Experimental Research, 5*, 283–294.

Carlen, P. L. (1982). Reversible effects of chronic alcoholism on the human central nervous system: Possible biological mechanisms. In D. A. Wilkinson (Ed.), *Cerebral deficits in alcoholism* (pp. 107–123). Toronto: Addiction Research Foundation.

Carlen, P. L., Kapur, B., Huszar, L. A., Lee, M. A., Moddel, G., Singh, R., & Wilkinson, D. A. (1980). Prolonged cerebrospinal fluid acidosis in recently abstinent chronic alcoholics. *Neurology, 30*, 956–962.

Carlen, P. L., & Wilkinson, D. A. (1980). Alcoholic brain damage and reversible deficits. *Acta Psychiatrica Scandinavica,* 1980, *62*(Suppl. 286), 103–118.

Carlen, P. L., Wilkinson, D. A., Wortzman, G., Holgate, R. C., Cordingley, J., Lee, M. A., Huszar, L., Moddel, G., Singh, R., Kiraly, L., & Rankin, J. G. (1981). Cerebral atrophy and functional deficits in alcoholics without clinically apparent liver disease. *Neurology, 31*, 377–385.

Carlen, P. L., Wilkinson, D. A., Holgate, R. C., & Wortzman, G. (1979). Computed tomography scans of alcoholics: Cerebral atrophy? [Letter to the editor]. *Science, 204*, 1238.

Carlen, P. L., Wilkinson, D. A., Wortzman, G., & Holgate, R. C. (1984). Partially reversible cerebral atrophy and functional improvements in recently abstinent alcoholics. *Canadian Journal of Neurological Science, 11*, 441–446.

Carlen, P. L., Wortzman, G., Holgate, R. C., Wilkinson, D. A., & Rankin, J. G. (1978). Reversible cerebral atrophy in recently abstinent chronic alcoholics measured by computed tomography scans. *Science, 200*, 1076–1078.

Chaney, E. F., O'Leary, M. R., & Marlatt, G. A. (1978). Skill training with alcoholics. *Journal of Clinical and Consulting Psychology, 46*, 1092–1104.

Courville, C. B. (1955). *Effects of alcohol on the nervous system of man.* Los Angeles: San Lucas Press.

Cravioto, H., Korein, J., & Silverman, J. (1961). Wernicke's encephalopathy: A clinical and pathological study of 28 autopsied cases. *Archives of Neurology, 4*, 510–519.

Gebhardt, C. A., Naeser, M. A., & Butters, N. (1984). Computerized measures of CT scans of alcoholics: Thalamic region related to memory. *Alcohol, 1*, 133–140.

Golden, C. J., Graber, B., Blose, I., Berg, R., Coffman, J., & Bloch, S. (1981). Difference in brain densities between chronic alcoholic and normal control patients. *Science, 211*, 508–510.

Goldman, M. S. (1982). Reversibility of psychological deficits in alcoholics: The interaction of aging with alcohol. In D. A. Wilkinson (Ed.), *Cerebral deficits in alcoholism* (pp. 79–107). Toronto: Addiction Research Foundation.

Goldman, M. S., & Rosenbaum, G. (1977). Psychological recoverability following chronic alcohol abuse. In F. A. Seixas (Ed.), *Currents in alcoholism* (Vol. 2, pp. 187–196). New York: Grune & Stratton.

Harper, C. (1979). Wernicke's encephalopathy: A more common disease than realised. A neuropathological study of 51 cases. *Journal of Neurology, Neurosurgery and Psychiatry, 42*, 226–231.

Haug, J. O. (1968). Pneumoencephalographic evidence of brain damage in chronic alcoholics. *Acta Psychiatrica Scandinavica, 203*, 135–143.

Hauge, R., & Irgens-Jensen, O. (1984). *Use of alcohol and the negative consequences of such use among men and women in four Nordic countries* (SIFA Report no. 88). Oslo: National Institute for Alcohol Research.

Israel, Y., Orrego, H., Holt, S., Macdonald, D. W., & Meema, H. E. (1980). Identification of alcohol abuse: Thoracic fractures on routine chest x-rays as indicators of alcoholism. *Alcoholism: Clinical and Experimental Research, 4* 420–422.

Jernigan, T. L., Zafz, L. M., Ahumada, A. J., Pfefferbaum, A., Tinklenberg, J. R., & Moses, J. A. (1982). CT measures of cerebrospinal fluid volume in alcoholics and normal volunteers. *Psychiatry Research, 7*, 9–17.

Kish, G. B., Hagen, J. M., Woody, M. M., & Harvey, H. L. (1980). Alcoholics' recovery from cerebral impairment as a function of duration of abstinence. *Journal of Clinical Psychology, 36*, 584–589.

Ledesma, J. A. (1958). Estudios pneumoencefalograficos en el alcoholismo. *Revista Clínica España, 68*, 161–171.

Lishman, W. A. (1981). Cerebral disorder in alcoholism: Syndromes of impairment. *Brain, 104*, 1–20.

Løberg, T. (1980). Alcohol misuse and neuropsychological deficits in men. *Journal of Studies on Alcohol, 41*, 119–128.

Løberg, T., & Miller, W. R. (1986). Personality, cognitive, and neuropsychological correlates of harmful alcohol consumption: A cross-national comparison of clinical samples. *Annals of the New York Academy of Sciences, 472*, 75–97.

MacVane, J., Butters, N., Montgomery, K., & Farber, J. (1982). Cognitive functioning in men social drinkers: A replication study. *Journal of Studies on Alcohol, 43*, 81–95.

Martin, P. R., & Eckardt, M. J. (1985). Pharmacological interventions in chronic organic brain syndromes associated with alcoholism. In C. A. Naranjo & E. M. Sellers (Eds.), *Research advances in new psychopharmacological treatments for alcoholism*. Amsterdam: Elsevier.

McLachlan, J. F. C., & Levinson, T. (1974). Improvement on WAIS Block Design performance as a function of recovery from alcoholism. *Journal of Clinical Psychology, 30*, 65–66.

Miller, W. R., & Saucedo, C. F. (1983). Assessment of neuropsychological impairment and brain damage in problem drinkers. In C. J. Golden, J. A. Moses, J. A. Coffman, W. R. Miller, & F. D. Strider (Eds.), *Clinical neuropsychology: Interface with neurologic and psychiatric disorders* (pp. 141–271). New York: Grune & Stratton.

Murray, R. M., Clifford, C. A., & Gurling, H. M. D. (1983). Twin adoption studies: How good is the evidence for a genetic role? In M. Galanter (Ed.), *Recent developments in alcoholism* (Vol. 1, pp. 25–48). New York: Plenum Press.

Ogborne, A. C. (1978). Patient characteristics as predictors of treatment outcome for alcohol and drug abusers. In Y. Israel, H. Kalant, R. E. Popham, W. Schmidt, & R. G. Smart (Eds.), *Research advances in alcohol and drug problems* (Vol. 4, pp. 177–223). New York: Plenum Press.

O'Leary, M. R., & Donovan, D. M. (1979). Male alcoholics. Treatment outcome as a function of length of treatment and level of current adaptive abilities. *Evaluation and the Health Professions, 2*, 373–384.

O'Leary, M. R., Donovan, D. M., Chaney, E. F., & Walker, R. D. (1979). Cognitive impairment and treatment outcome with alcoholics: Preliminary findings. *Journal of Clinical Psychiatry, 40*, 397–398.

Parker, E. S. (1982). Comments on "Cognitive functioning in men social drinkers: A replication study." *Journal of Studies on Alcohol, 43*, 170–177.

Parker, E. S., & Parker, D. (1982). Towards an epidemiology of cognitive deficits among alcohol consumers. In D. A. Wilkinson (Ed.), *Cerebral deficits in alcoholism* (pp. 21–47). Toronto: Addiction Research Foundation.

Parsons, O. A. (1977). Neuropsychological deficits in alcoholics: Facts and fancies. *Alcoholism: Clinical and Experimental Research, 1*, 51–56.

Parsons, O. A., & Farr, S. P. (1981). The neuropsychology of alcohol and drug use. In S. Filskov & T. Boll (Eds.), *Handbook of clinical neuropsychology* (pp. 320–365). New York: Wiley.

Porjesz, B., & Begleiter, H. (1983). Brain dysfunction and alcohol. In B. Kissin & H. Begleiter (Eds.), *The biology of alcoholism: Vol. 7. The pathogenesis of alcoholism: Biological factors* (pp. 415–484). New York: Plenum Press.

Rankin, J. G. D., Orrego-Matte, H., & Deschenes, J. (1978). Alcoholic liver disease: The problem of diagnosis. *Alcoholism: Clinical and Experimental Research, 2*, 327–338.

Ron, M. A. (1983). The alcoholic brain: CT scan and psychological findings. *Psychological Medicine*, (Monograph Suppl. 3).

Ron, M. A., Acker, W., & Lishman, W. A. (1980). Morphological abnormalities in the brains of chronic alcoholics—a clinical, psychological and computerized axial tomographic study. *Acta Psychiatrica Scandinavica, 62*(Suppl. 286), 41–46.

Ryan, C., & Butters, N. (1980). Further evidence for a continuum of impairment encompassing male alcoholic Korsakoff patients and chronic alcoholics. *Alcoholism: Clinical and Experimental Research, 4*, 190–198.

Ryan, C., & Butters, N. (1984). Alcohol consumption and premature aging: A critical review. In M. Galanter (Ed.), *Recent developments in alcoholism* (Vol. 2, pp. 223–250). New York: Plenum Press.

Ryback, R. S. (1971). The continuum and specificity of the effects of alcohol on memory: A review. *Quarterly Journal of Studies on Alcohol, 32*, 995–1016.

Sanchez-Craig, M. (1980). Drinking pattern as a determinant of alcoholics' performance on the Trail Making Test. *Journal of Studies on Alcohol, 41*, 1082–1090.

Sanchez-Craig, M., & Walker, K. (1982). Teaching coping skills to chronic alcoholics in a coeducational halfway house: I. Assessment of programme effects. *British Journal of Addiction, 77*, 35–50.

Sanchez-Craig, M., & Wilkinson, D. A. (1982). Investigations of brain function in alcoholics: A methodological critique. In D. A. Wilkinson (Ed.), *Cerebral deficits in alcoholism* (pp. 1–20). Toronto: Addiction Research Foundation.

Sarabia, F., Bowden, C. L., & Tex, S. A. (1980). Computerized tomographic evidence of cerebral atrophy in heavy drinkers. *Southern Medical Journal, 73*, 716–718.

Schau, E. J., O'Leary, M. R., & Chaney, E. F. (1980). Reversibility of cognitive deficit in alcoholics. *Journal of Studies on Alcohol, 41*, 733–740.

Tarbox, A. J., Wiegel, J., & Biggs, J. T. (1984, August). *A cognitive typology of alcohol abuse: Implications for treatment outcome.* Poster presentation given at the Third International Conference on the Treatment of Addictive Behaviours, North Berwick, Scotland.

Tarter, R. E., & Alterman, A. (1984). Neuropsychological deficits in alcoholics: Etiological considerations. *Journal of Studies on Alcohol, 45*, 1–9.

Torvik, A., Lindbøe, C. F., & Rogde, S. (1982). Brain lesions in alcoholics: A neuropathological study with clinical correlations. *Journal of Neurological Science, 56*, 233–248.

Victor, M., Adams, R. D., & Collins, G. H. (1971). *The Wernicke-Korsakoff syndrome.* Philadelphia: F. A. Davis.

von Gall, M., Becker, H., Artmann, H., & Hacker, H. (1978). Results of computer tomography on chronic alcoholics.*Neuroradiology, 16*, 329–331.

Walker, K., Sanchez-Craig, M., & Bornet, A. R. (1982). Teaching coping skills to chronic alcoholics in a coeducational halfway house: II. Assessment of outcome and identification of outcome predictors. *British Journal of Addiction, 77*, 185–196.

Wilkinson, D. A. (1982a). Accelerated mental aging in alcoholism: Working hypothesis or uncontrolled variable? In D. A. Wilkinson (Ed.), *Cerebral deficits in alcoholism* (pp. 61–79). Toronto: Addiction Research Foundation.

Wilkinson, D. A. (1982b). Examination of alcoholics by computed tomographic (CT) scans: A critical review. *Alcoholism: Clinical and Experimental Research, 6*, 31–45.

Wilkinson, D. A. (1985). Neuroradiological investigations of alcoholism. In R. E. Tarter & D. Van Thiel (Eds.), *Alcohol and the brain: Chronic effects* (pp. 183–215). New York: Plenum Press.

Wilkinson, D. A., & Carlen, P. L. (1980a). Relation of neuropsychological test performance in alcoholics to brain morphology measured by computed tomography. In M. Begleiter (Ed.), *Biological effects of alcohol* (pp. 683–700). New York: Plenum Press.

Wilkinson, D. A., & Carlen, P. L. (1980b). Relationship of neuropsychological test performance to brain morphology in amnesic and non-amnesic chronic alcoholics. *Acta Psychiatrica Scandinavica, 62*(Suppl. 286), 89–101.

Wilkinson, D. A., & Carlen, P. L. (1981). Chronic organic brain syndromes associated with alcoholism: Neuropsychological and other aspects. In Y. Israel, F. Glaser, H. Kalant, R. E. Popham, W. Schmidt, & R. G. Smart (Eds.), *Research advances in alcohol and drug problems* (Vol. 6, pp. 107–145). New York: Plenum Press.

Wilkinson, D. A., & Carlen, P. L. (1982). Morphological abnormalities in the brain of alcoholics. Relationship to age, psychological test scores and patient type. In W. G. Wood & M. F. Elias (Eds.), *Alcoholism and aging: Advances in research* (pp. 61–77). Boca Raton, FL: CRC Press.

Wilkinson, D. A., & Carlen, P. L. (1983, February). *Recoverability in recently abstinent alcoholics: Results of repeated neuropsychological, EEG, CT scan, and neurological examinations.* Paper presented at the Eleventh Annual Meeting of the International Neuropsychological Society, Mexico City.

Wilkinson, D. A., & Sanchez-Craig, M. (1981). Relevance of brain dysfunction to treatment objectives: Should alcohol-related cognitive deficits influence the way we think about treatment? *Addictive Behaviors, 6*, 253–260.

6

Discussion

Evoked Brain Potentials and Alcoholism: Questions, Hypotheses, New Approaches

HAROLD L. WILLIAMS

Introduction

In a systematic sequence of evoked potential (EP) studies, Begleiter and his colleague, Porjesz, have obtained tentative answers to a considerable number of important questions about the effects of chronic alcohol abuse on the functional integrity of the central nervous system (CNS). Because their methods can examine neuroelectric signals from the peripheral end organ to the higher integrative centers of the brain, their studies and findings encompass a broad range of brain functions and structures. Yet, as should be anticipated from this excellent work in a relatively young field, their data evoke more questions than they answer. It is, of course, this aspect that imbues their research with high heuristic power. Employing their research and their chapter in this volume as a framework, my discussion focuses on several questions raised by their data, points out other interpretations where such alternatives seem to have any merit, and suggests some additional methods and concepts that might shed further light on the antecedents and functional consequences of alcohol use and abuse. More specifically, the discussion focuses on two major topics: short-latency EPs and long-latency event-related potentials (ERPs). In the discussion of short-latency EPs, I refer to several additional physiological and behavioral techniques and concepts that might profitably be applied to alcohol-related problems. For long-latency ERPs, I discuss some of the complexities that have developed recently in this area and their implications for the study of alcoholics.

Harold L. Williams. Oklahoma Center for Alcohol and Drug-Related Studies, Department of Psychiatry and Behavioral Sciences, University of Oklahoma Health Sciences Center, Oklahoma City, Oklahoma.

After these sections, there follows a brief discussion of some relevant individual-difference variables, a rather neglected area in the field of alcohol studies.

A major aim of the first series of studies by Begleiter and colleagues was to examine the extent of brain dysfunction consequent to persistent alcohol abuse. They found that the range of functional impairments in alcoholics was extensive, indeed, implicating both cortical and subcortical systems. It had been well understood that both acute and chronic alcohol ingestion can impair cortical, cerebellar, and hippocampal functions, but the effects of alcohol on subcortical sensory pathways were less well known. Although depressive effects of acute alcohol intake had been found in vestibular neurons (Eidelberg, Bond, & Kelter, 1971), trigeminal cutaneous afferent fibers (Sauerland, Mizuno, & Harper, 1970), the inferior colliculus (DiPerri, Dravid, Schweigerdt, & Himwich, 1968), the superior colliculus, and the lateral and medial geniculate bodies (Klemm *et al.*, 1976), as well as in the vestibular (Money, Johnson, & Corlett, 1965) and cochlear (Gieldanowski, 1965) end organs, Begleiter and his colleagues were the first to report electrophysiological evidence of subcortical brain dysfunction in alcoholics who had no overt clinical signs of neurological damage.

Short-Latency Evoked Potentials

Auditory Brain Stem Potential

Using the far-field auditory brain stem potential (BSP), Begleiter, Porjesz, and Chou (1981) found significant delays in peak latencies as well as slowed central conduction velocities from waves II to V in detoxified alcoholics whose wave I latencies were normal. Porjesz and Begleiter suggest that this central slowing might be the result of demyelination in the brain stem, and they cite evidence from an animal investigation that favors this hypothesis. There are, of course, other possible neuropharmacological effects of alcohol that might account for these findings. For example, slowing of central conduction velocity could be synaptic in origin (e.g., Kalant, 1970), or due to neuronal loss in the brain stem, or both, or could even be due to lowered brain temperature.

As Porjesz and Begleiter point out, their BSP findings are remarkably similar to those reported with acute doses of alcohol in both animals and humans. One unresolved issue concerning the acute effects of alcohol on BSP latencies involves the extent to which alcohol-induced hypothermia, rather than alcohol per se, may be the proximate cause of slowing in brain stem transmission time. It has been found that a decrease in body temperature of about 0.5°C (Jones, Stockard, & Weidner, 1980) can cause significant prolongation of BSP latencies. Alcohol, like other anesthetics, does reduce body (and brain) temperature. To test the possibility that these BSP changes are mediated by hypothermia, Jones *et al.* (1980) maintained their animals' midesophageal temperatures at prealcohol baseline levels. Finding no significant changes in BSP latencies at about 2 hours after dose, they concluded that the alcohol effects previously reported by other investigators were mediated entirely by alcohol-induced hypothermia.

We investigated dose- and time-dependent effects of alcohol on both BSP latencies and tympanic (brain) temperature in healthy young men (Church & Williams, 1982). As in earlier studies, the chief effect of alcohol was to cause a cumulative increase in the latencies of successive BSP waves while failing to cause any change in their amplitudes. The earliest wave to show significant latency shifts was wave II. Since this wave apparently reflects neural activity in the cochlear nucleus, it appears that a single dose of ethanol can significantly influence neural activity as far caudally as the medulla. Porjesz and Begleiter's data indicate that chronic alcohol abuse and/or associated nutritional deficiencies can have the same result. In general, we observed very little change in tympanic temperature with alcohol, and our results were not very consistent with the temperature-dependence hypothesis. However, our subjects were kept fully alert in a thermoregulated room, performing postural equilibrium–ataxia tests at regular intervals. These exercises may have prevented any notable decline in brain temperature. Although we were unable to draw a firm conclusion about temperature-dependent versus temperature-independent effects of alcohol on BSP latencies, we suspect that central slowing will eventually turn out to be a combination of the two.

Do recently abstinent alcoholics have lowered brain temperatures? Possibly. As Begleiter and colleagues have reported, alcoholics in early detoxification tend toward CNS hyperexcitability, with increased EP amplitudes and sharply reduced central conduction times. However, with a longer period of abstinence (e.g., a month), there is evidence of hypoexcitability—that is, decreased EP amplitudes and slowed conduction velocities. (See, e.g., Chu, Squires, & Starr, 1982; Porjesz & Begleiter, 1981c, 1983.) Perhaps these latter phenomena signify reduced levels of CNS arousal after a month or so of sobriety. A notion that the underaroused detoxified alcoholic might have reduced brain temperature and that this might be one mediator of increased BSP latencies certainly lacks the pizazz of hypotheses that invoke demyelination or neuronal loss. Yet perhaps the notion is worth refuting. Tympanic thermometry, which provides a relatively noninvasive index of brain temperature, should be included as an adjunct in future BSP research with chronic alcoholics.

PREVALENCE

What is the prevalence of slowed auditory conduction velocities among alcoholics? Begleiter and colleagues typically report the results of analyses of variance or *t* tests applied to grouped data. For clinical applications, prevalence data would also be helpful. Both between and within healthy adults, the means and variances of BSP latencies are extremely stable. Thus, for individual cases, abnormal slowing can be detected with considerable confidence. For example, Chu *et al.* (1982) classified the BSP as abnormal when either the wave I–V, I–III, or III–V intervals were 2.5 to 3.0 standard deviations greater than the normal mean. Among the alcoholic subgroup in their sample who manifested no neurological complications, only 12% had abnormal BSPs. The incidence of abnormal BSPs in their patients increased systematically with chronological age, with numbers of neurological complications, and with computerized tomographic (CT) evidence of cerebral atrophy. All of the patients with evidence of both cerebral and cerebellar atrophy in CT scans had abnormal BSP latencies. Begleiter, Porjesz, and Tenner (1980) had earlier found that alcoholics with enlarged cortical sulci had smaller late positive (P300) waves than alcoholics without signs of cortical atrophy. It would be interesting to know whether Begleiter's group also finds greater slowing of BSP conduction velocities in alcoholics with enlarged cortical sulci. As Chu *et al.* (1982) point out, the high correlation found in their studies between abnormal BSPs and signs of cerebral atrophy in CT scans suggests that the pathological processes responsible for diffuse cerebral atrophy are widespread, possibly involving the brain stem as well.

Chu *et al.* (1982) showed the utility of examining not only the wave I–V interval in the BSP, but also the I–III and III–V intervals. Among the 25 patients in their sample who had abnormal wave I–V intervals, some had prolonged I–III intervals and others had prolonged III–V intervals, but few showed prolongation of both intervals. Although Chu *et al.* did not speculate about possible differences between these subgroups, it is tempting to do so. Perhaps those patients with specific slowing of I–III conduction will be found to have impairments associated with functions of the cochlear nucleus and/or superior olivary complex, whereas patients with slowed III–V conduction will have impairments associated with functions of higher brain stem structures (e.g., the inferior colliculus).

REPETITION RATE

In future studies of the BSP in alcoholics, the effects of stimulus repetition rate should be investigated. Although there has been some controversy about the diagnostic utility of high repetition rates (e.g., Chiappa, Gladstone, & Young, 1979), there is now considerable evidence that this otoneurological stressor can exacerbate subtle brain stem abnormalities in both humans and animals (Daly, Roeser, Aung, & Daly, 1977; Fujikawa & Weber, 1977; Robinson & Rudge, 1975; Stockard & Rossiter, 1977; Yagi & Kaga, 1979). Thus, Gerling and Finitzo-Hieber (1982) found that high stimulus rate was often the only parameter that signaled brain stem involvement in patients with documented CNS pathology.

OTHER PHYSIOLOGICAL METHODS

I now mention briefly two other methods that could be useful adjuncts to the BSP, in that they might help to increase our understanding of the locus and nature of the brain stem dysfunctions found among alcoholics. The first of these is the acoustic reflex. This event involves contraction of the intra-aural muscles (the stapedius and the tensor tympani), which causes damping of loud sounds passing through the middle ear. The reflex is mediated by a neuronal arc through several stations in the brain stem auditory pathway, including the ventral cochlear nucleus, the trapezoid body, and the medial superior olive. From there, the signal is delivered to both the ipsilateral and contralateral motor nuclei of the 7th nerve and on to the stapedius muscles of both ears. (See Spitzer, 1981, for an excellent review.) The acoustic reflex is sensitive to alcohol dose effects in that alcohol raises the threshold for its elicitation (Borg & Moller, 1967; Cohill & Greenburg, 1977), and reduces the magnitude of stapedius contraction (Robinette & Brey, 1978).

Among chronic alcoholics, Spitzer and Ventry (1980) found absent acoustic reflexes in 5 of 15 gamma alcoholics who were in their second week of detoxification. All of these subjects had normal audiometric thresholds for their age. Integrating these data with those from other tests in their diagnostic battery, Spitzer and Ventry (1980) concluded that brain stem dysfunction was present in about half of their alcoholics. Obviously, it would be useful to know the degree of concordance between BSP and acoustic reflex findings in alcoholics. The two methods could provide converging evidence of local brain stem dysfunction, particularly for those alcoholics with specific prolongation of the I–III BSP intervals.

The second physiological method examines binaural interaction in the BSP (Levine, 1981). This is assessed with the so-called "binaural-difference waveform." The latter is derived by computing the difference between the BSP evoked by simultaneous, in-phase (diotic) clicks from both earphones and the sum of two other monotic BSPs—one evoked by clicks from the left and one by clicks from the right earphone. If no interaction occurs between inputs from the two ears, then the diotic potential equals the sum of the monotic potentials. (See Levine, 1981, for a detailed presentation.) In normal subjects, Levine found that for waves I, II, and III of the BSP, the sums of the monotic traces were essentially identical to the diotic trace. After wave III, however, two positive peaks appeared in the difference trace. The first of these occurred consistently on the descending limb of wave V. The second positive peak, which appeared only with high click intensities, had a peak latency of about 10 msec. This difference waveform was found to be quite reproducible, both within and between sessions. As Levine (1981) points out, a nonzero difference waveform could result from such nonneural factors as acoustic crosstalk or the middle-ear reflex. However, he offers methods for eliminating the contributions of these variables. He shows also that in normal subjects the second positive component in the binaural-difference waveform, found at high click intensities, is probably due to acoustic crosstalk. The first positive peak in the difference trace is almost certainly a signal of binaural interaction. Levine (1981) suggests that the binaural-difference waveform may have greater localizing value than the BSP alone, because it probably represents a subpopulation of neural generators of the BSP that show binaural interaction at the single-unit level.

BEHAVIORAL IMPLICATIONS

Could a small decrease in central conduction velocity or an impairment of binaural interaction have significant consequences for information processing? Probably. Candidate tasks would be ones that require analysis of temporal aspects of acoustic information. The remarkable constancy of peak latencies across trials and sessions strongly suggests that the BSP is generated by the so-called "fast time-constant" neural units found throughout the auditory pathway (Gersuni, 1971; Huang & Buchwald, 1977). N. Squires (1984a) and others (e.g., Gersuni, 1971) cite evidence favoring the notion that the fast time-constant neural system subserves functions related to the precise analysis of temporal aspects of acoustic information. The second and parallel auditory neural system, composed of "slow time-constant" units, probably subserves other acoustic functions such as pitch perception (Gersuni, 1971; N. Squires, 1984a). As N. Squires (1984a) has pointed out, if the fast and slow time-constant systems can be differentially affected by neurological disorders, then functions dependent on the analysis of temporal information may be disturbed, while pitch perception and other functions are preserved. Such differential neural effects might account for data reported by Worthington and Peters (1980) and by Ochs, Markand, and DeMyer (1979), in which BSPs were apparently absent in some neurological patients who had normal audiometric thresholds.

What information processing tasks require precise analysis of temporal aspects of acoustic information? One example is speech perception. Jerger, Neely, and Jerger (1980) observed that certain brain stem tumors affected both BSPs and speech perception in patients who had normal pure-tone thresholds. (See N. Squires, 1984a and 1984b, for discussions of this and her own observations in Down's syndrome.)

Spatial localization of a source of sound also depends in part upon precise analysis of temporal information. The two binaural cues important for sound localization are the difference in time of arrival and the difference in intensity of sounds at the two ears. Humans with total loss of hearing in one ear show considerable impairment of the capacity to localize sounds, particularly when head position is fixed (Mountcastle, 1974). These phenomena suggest that the CNS loci needed for sound localization are those that receive convergent inputs from the two ears. As auditory signals ascend the auditory pathways, the first locus to mediate binaural interactions is the medial superior olive. Differential signals based on such interactions in the superior olive are transmitted to the nucleus of the lateral lemniscus, the inferior colliculi, and the auditory cortex. Lesions in any of those areas produce severe deficits in the ability to localize sound (Mountcastle, 1974). Although the loci of the generators of the several waves of the BSP are not firmly established, the working hypothesis has assigned wave III to the superior olivary complex and wave V either to the lateral lemniscus or the inferior colliculus.

It is reasonable to predict that slowed conduction in this olivary–lemniscal–collicular–cortical complex will result in impairment of interaural time discrimination. Hausler and Levine (1980) found this to be true for patients with multiple sclerosis (MS). In normal subjects aged 21 to 39, the just-noticeable difference (JND) for interaural discrimination of time of stimulus arrival ranged from 10 to 30 μsec. The JND for MS patients with notable BSP abnormalities ranged up to 280 μsec. Presumably, such patients would show great impairment in the localization of sound sources. Clearly, interaural time discrimination should be studied in alcoholics.

One of the more striking behavioral measures of binaural interaction in the auditory system is the masking-level difference (MLD) effect (Jerger, Hannley, & Rivera, 1982). When a binaural noise is used to mask a binaural tone, the degree of masking is a function of the interaural phase relations of the noise and the tone. If both the tone and masking noise are either in phase or out of phase at the two ears, masking of tone by noise is greater than if, say, the tone is in phase at both ears and the noise is 180° out of phase for the two ears. The difference in masking effects for these two conditions is called the binaural MLD. It has been suggested that, like interaural time discrimination, the MLD effect is a behavioral correlate of binaural interaction at the brain stem level (Robinson & Rudge, 1977). Jerger *et al.* (1982) compared the BSP and MLD in patients with MS. In separate studies, MS had earlier been shown to affect both the BSP and the MLD. Since wave III of the BSP is putatively linked to activity in the superior olivary complex, Jerger and colleagues wanted to determine whether delay or loss of wave III was related to impairment of the MLD effect. As predicted, they found a strong and specific relationship between abnormality of BSP wave III (delay or absence) and reduction of the MLD effect.

Application of these physiological and behavioral methods to the study of alcoholics could enhance our understanding of the CNS dysfunctions associated with alcoholism by providing at least tentative answers to such questions as the following: (1) Given BSP abnormality, where is the brain stem dysfunction most probably located? (2) Do abnormal BSPs signal impairment of binaural interaction processes? (3) Do abnormal BSPs signal deficits in information processing?

Somatosensory Evoked Potential and the Pattern-Shift Visual Evoked Potential

The finding of abnormal BSPs among alcoholics leads naturally to speculation about specific impairments of auditory information processing. Yet the anatomical distribution of alcohol effects undoubtedly extends beyond the auditory pathways. If other sensory systems are abnormal in alcoholics, then behavioral tests for functional impairment should include challenges both to other sensory systems and to multimodal sensory–perceptual integration.

Along with the BSP, two other EP tests, the short-latency somatosensory EP (SEP) and the pattern-shift visual EP (PSVEP), are now commonly used in the clinical EP laboratory. Taken together, the three tests provide sensitive quantitative extensions of the clinical neurological examination. (See Chiappa's [1985] text for description and detailed analysis of these applications.)

With upper-limb stimulation—say, of the median nerve at the wrist—the first recorded SEP event is usually derived from Erb's point in the supraclavicular fossa. There, a diphasic positive–negative component with a normal latency of about 9.7 msec signals approach and passage of the action–potential volley through the brachial plexus. This provides a measure of peripheral conduction velocity, rather like wave I of the BSP. Following this, a negative potential appearing at 11–12 msec over the neck and lower back of the head appears to be generated in the cervical cord root entry zone or in nearby posterior columns. The next event, which shows relative positivity at about 13–15 msec at scalp derivations (e.g., either frontal or parietal sensory), is probably generated in the dorsal column nucleus (cuneatus) and medial lemnicus of the lower medulla (Chiappa, 1985). There has been considerable controversy about the loci of sources of the following negative activity, appearing in scalp electrodes between 16 and 19 msec after median nerve stimulation. Several investigators have concluded that these components are generated in the parietal sensory cortex (e.g., Allison, Goff, Williamson, & Van Gilder, 1980). However, Chiappa (1985) cites considerable evidence in support of his view that the thalamus contains the sources of this activity. More specifically, the generators may be located in the primary receiving station of the thalamus, the ventroposterolateral nucleus. Finally, most investigators agree that the subsequent positivity (P22) is generated in the parietal sensory cortex.

Abnormal latencies in SEP waves occur with disorders of touch, vibration, stereognosis, and perception of joint position, but not with disorders affecting only pain and temperature perception (Chiappa, 1985). The significance of SEP studies for alcohol research lies in the fact that the several early components from N11 to P22 can be related to specific anatomic structures along the somatosensory pathway from the brachial plexus to (mainly) the contralateral cortical receiving area. Furthermore, the SEP should be a useful measure in tests of the hypothesis that right-hemisphere functions are particularly vulnerable to chronic alcohol abuse (e.g., Parsons, Chapter 8, this volume). The somatosensory system crosses to the contralateral side of the brain stem in the lower medulla just above the dorsal column nuclei. Thus, if right-hemisphere dysfunction were rather general among alcoholics, then with stimuli to the left wrist, one might anticipate a specific increase in the relative latency of SEP component P22 recorded from a parietal sensory lead on the right side.

Although the potentials of the PSVEP are long-latency components, they are employed clinically much like those of the SEP and the BSP. The stimulus for the PSVEP usually consists of a black-and-white checkerboard pattern in which adjacent squares shift from black to white and white to black without any change in overall luminance. Compared to the visual EP to flash stimuli, the PSVEP is less complex and shows less variability within and between subjects. Also, the PSVEP has proved to be more sensitive than the flash-induced EP to conduction defects in the visual pathways. The most prominent component of the PSVEP is a positive wave usually recorded at the occipital scalp, with an average latency of about 100 msec (P100). In normal subjects, variability of P100 latencies is relatively small. P100 is generated somewhere in striate and prestriate occipital cortex, but the precise location of generator sources is not yet known.

When P100 latency is employed as a criterion, the PSVEP is extremely sensitive to any disorder that causes a conduction defect in the optic pathway. For example, Chiappa's (1985) review of the literature indicates that about 90% of patients with a history of optic neuritis have abnormal PSVEPs. Further, in a series of studies of MS reviewed by Chiappa (1985), where patients were classified as possible, probable, and definite cases of MS, the average abnormality rates for PSVEP were 37%, 58%, and 85%, respectively. Thus, the likelihood of optic nerve pathophysiology increased with the certainty of diagnosis.

One might reasonably predict that diminished visual acuity due to peripheral changes in the eye would be associated with increased P100 latencies, and this appears to be true, but only when small checks are employed as stimuli (Collins, Carroll, Black, & Walsh, 1979; Halliday, McDonald, & Mushin, 1973). If large enough check sizes are used (e.g., visual angle greater than 35′), no latency shifts are found even with 20/200 visual acuity (Chiappa, 1985). There is evidence, though, that when diminished visual acuity is associated with toxic optic neuropathies such as alcohol–tobacco amblyopia, P100 latencies are likely to be increased even with larger check sizes (e.g., Kriss, Carroll, Blumhardt, & Halliday, 1982). However, there are also reports of negative PSVEP findings in this disorder (Kupersmith, Weiss, & Carr, 1983). Demyelination of the optic nerves has been noted in some cases of alcohol–tobacco amblyopia (Victor, Mancall, &

Dreyfus, 1960), and this has been suggested as the cause of the visual loss. Porjesz and Begleiter (1981c) reported that P100 of the PSVEP was abnormally delayed in chronic alcoholics abstinent for 1 month. Similar results were reported by Posthuma and Visser (1982) in alcoholics with normal (or corrected) vision. Preliminary results from our laboratory suggest that interocular latency differences may be a sensitive indicator of optic tract dysfunction among alcoholics. Nonalcoholic control subjects with normal visual acuity (Snellen chart) show nearly identical P100 latencies for the two eyes. On the other hand, a proportion of our alcoholics show large interocular latency differences, despite normal visual acuity. These qualitative observations do not permit any firm conclusions, but if they are confirmed by quantitative analysis, we will conclude that a subgroup of our alcoholic patients have monocular abnormalities. As Chiappa (1985) makes clear, if the PSVEP abnormality is monocular, the pathophysiological locus must be anterior to the chiasm.

Long-Latency Evoked Potentials

The Processing Negativities

Employing bimodal information-processing tasks with simultaneous ERP recording, Porjesz and Begleiter (1979) investigated the ability of alcoholics to focus attention on relevent stimuli in a designated sensory modality, visual or auditory, and to inhibit responding to stimuli in the irrelevant modality. Among healthy subjects, selective attention to an information channel is signaled by amplitude enhancement of a negative ERP component with a latency of about 100 msec (N100) (Hillyard, Hink, Schwent, & Picton, 1973). As expected, Porjesz and Begleiter's normal controls showed significant N100 amplitude enhancement to both target and nontarget stimuli in the attended modality. However, their alcoholics maintained the same low-amplitude N100 for stimuli in both the attended and unattended modality. Porjesz and Begleiter concluded that alcoholics may be incapable of appropriate "sensory filtering."

In early reports of N100 enhancement to stimuli presented in the attended channel, Hillyard and colleagues referred to this attention effect as "N1 enhancement" (Hillyard *et al.*, 1973). We now know that this so-called N1 (here, N100) effect is at least partly composed of a broad endogenous negativity that can begin as early as 30 msec poststimulus and last for several hundred milliseconds (Hansen & Hillyard, 1980; Hillyard, 1984; Näätänen & Michie, 1979).

Several negative components have now been identified in ERPs, and each of these seems to be related to different aspects of information processing. These waves are elicited by different instructional and stimulus conditions; they have different topographic distributions on the scalp, as well as different latencies. In terms of latency, the first of these processing negativities is Hillyard's "N1 effect," now often called the "Nd wave" (Ritter *et al.*, 1984). This wave occurs when two or more sets of stimuli are randomly interspersed, and the subject's attention is directed to designated target stimuli in one of the sets. In most such tasks, the set of stimuli containing the target can be distinguished from the nontarget set on the basis of simple characteristics such as pitch or location (Hillyard, 1984). The N100 amplitude effects found by Porjesz and Begleiter (1979) should probably be considered Nd effects. Porjesz and Begleiter found no differences in N100 peak latency between alcoholics and controls. However, realizing that Nd onset can occur as early as 30 msec after the stimulus and that the onset latency increases as separation between channels decreases, the question of Nd latency in alcoholics merits a closer look. Hansen and Hillyard (1980) now suggest that the onset latency of Nd is related to the duration of processing required to decide to which channel a given stimulus belongs. Porjesz and Begleiter's results with later ERP components (e.g., N200) suggest that alcoholics may have difficulty making such decisions.

Nd latency is apparently not affected by stimulus complexity, but Ritter, Simson, and Vaughan (1983) have identified a second processing negativity (NA), which is present during choice reaction-time tasks. NA has a constant onset latency of about 150 msec, but its peak latency increases both with stimulus complexity and with low stimulus quality.

Porjesz and Begleiter (1981a, 1981b, and Chapter 3, this volume), employing a visual-discrimination task, reported that a negative component peaking at about 200 msec had longer latencies in alcoholics than in healthy controls. Furthermore, in control subjects, but not in alcoholics, N200 latency increased with discrimination difficulty. Thus, in normals, N200 latency might index stimulus evaluation time.

As is true for other long-latency ERP components such as P300, the functional significance of N200 is not easily conceptualized. First, there are considerable data to suggest that N200 signals the activity of an automatic mismatch detector. Thus, the N200 event often described is modality-specific and is elicited by low-probability stimuli, whether or not they are in the attended channel. N200 can occur to target stimuli that subjects fail to detect, and in some experiments it appears not to be under voluntary control. Such findings do not seem consistent with the notion that N200 latency is an index of stimulus evaluation time. However, there is another body of data that is consistent with this hypothesis. Ritter *et al.* (1983) found evidence that N200 might reflect automatic cognitive processes in some circumstances but voluntary intentional processes in others. Furthermore, as Porjesz and Begleiter point out, there is convincing evidence that in normal subjects, N200 latency increases as a function of discrimination difficulty. Finally, increases in peak latency of Ritter *et al.*'s (1983) NA are accompanied by delays of N200, and the peak latencies of both events covary with choice reaction time.

Could there be more than one N200—one signaling automatic cognitive processes and the other controlled processes? Renault, Ragot, Lesevre, and Remond (1982) have described two N200 waves. The first is modality-specific (as above) and correlates in latency both with the duration of perceptual processing and with reaction time. The second negative event (N250) is modality-nonspecific (i.e., maximum at the vertex), constant in latency, and probably associated with orienting. Renault *et al.* (1982) suggest that the modality-specific N200 signals a process of stimulus identification, whereas the modality-nonspecific N250 signals a postidentification (automatic?) orienting response.

Whatever the case, it should be informative to measure both NA and N200 in alcoholics. Ritter *et al.* (1984) suspect that NA and their N200 are associated with two different kinds of perceptual processes. Their data suggest that NA peak latency is affected both by stimulus complexity and stimulus quality, while N200 peak latency is related specifically to the processes of stimulus identification and mismatch detection.

Where more complex verbal materials are employed, another negative component can be observed, peaking at about 400 msec (N400). One way to elicit this event is to present sentence stems that are followed by pictures of contextually anomalous objects (e.g., "I planted string beans in my . . . , followed by a line drawing of a car) (Kutas & Hillyard, 1980, discussed by Ritter *et al.*, 1984). Such data suggest that, like N200, N400 may also signal the detection of a mismatch. In fact, N400 and N200 may be the same event. As Ritter *et al.* (1984) point out, since N200 latency varies with discrimination difficulty, it is not unreasonable that N200 could have much longer latencies in tasks requiring semantic discrimination. It will be informative to learn whether alcoholics show delayed N200 peaks to anomalous completion of sentences. Generally speaking, alcoholics have shown less impairment of verbal than of visual–spatial abilities.

The Long-Latency Positive Complex

The late positive event P300, discovered in 1965 by Sutton, Braren, Zubin, and John, is typically elicited in the task called "oddball target selection." The subject is instructed to detect a rarely occurring target stimulus embedded in a series of frequently occurring nontarget stimuli. In healthy subjects, the P300 event is evoked by the target stimuli and not by the nontarget stimuli.

Begleiter and his colleagues have usually found reduced amplitudes but not increased latencies of P300 in chronic alcoholics. Alcholics have manifested low-amplitude P300 waves to both target and nontarget stimuli. Patients with enlarged cortical sulci (CT scans) had lower P300 amplitudes than patients with normal cortical sulci. After 4 months of abstinence, hospitalized alcoholics showed no recovery of P300 amplitudes and no differential enhancement of P300 to target stimuli. In fact, a group of alcoholics who had been sober for 3–10 years also showed P300 amplitude deficits, as did about 36% of 7- to 13-year-old nondrinking sons of male alcoholics (Porjesz & Begleiter, Chapter 3, this volume). The apparent lack of reversal of P300 deficits with more than 3 years of abstinence and the finding of reduced P300 amplitudes in high-risk boys suggest that P300 impairment may have preceded the onset of alcoholism and that low-amplitude ERPs might be biological markers of risk for alcoholism.

While Begleiter and Porjesz's alcoholics have usually shown reduced P300 amplitudes but normal latencies, Pfefferbaum's alcoholics have usually shown increased P300 latencies but normal amplitudes (Johnson, Pfefferbaum, Hart, & Kopell, 1984; Pfefferbaum, Horvath, Roth, & Kopell, 1979). Skerchock and Cohen (1984) also report longer P300 latencies in alcoholics. Pfefferbaum and colleagues suggest that alcoholics require more time than healthy controls to evaluate the stimuli. Interestingly, as discussed above, Porjesz and Begleiter offer the same hypothesis for their finding of increased N200 latencies in alcoholics. In that single N200 study, Porjesz and Begleiter's alcoholics did show increased P300 latencies, but for easy rather than difficult discriminations. Presently, the reasons for these differences between laboratories are not known. The studies of Begleiter's group and Pfefferbaum's group differ in terms of the characteristics of patient populations sampled, measurement techniques, experimental designs, and experimental tasks. (See Porjesz and Begleiter, 1983, for a discussion of these issues.)

As with the processing negativities, it now appears possible that more than one late positive component can be evoked in the ERP. For example, N. Squires and her collaborators (N. Squires, Squires, & Hillyard, 1975) isolated the late positive slow wave (SW), which overlaps P300 but is longer-lasting. Later, she and other investigators suggested that there is a family of P300 components (the late positive complex), with at least two or three members. Besides Sutton *et al.*'s (1965) P300 (sometimes now called P3b), there is P3a and Sutton's P300E (Sutton & Ruchkin, 1984), each of which has a different scalp topography and may have different functional significance. Finally, the positive SW described by N. Squires *et al.* (1975) may be composed of at least two functionally different components, a tonic SW and a phasic SW.

The validity of the late positive complex as a conceptual model depends partly on whether the several positive components do indeed indicate different functional states of the brain. Some of these components can be differentially affected by experimental variables. For example, in the oddball paradigm, where Sutton's P3b is evoked by target stimuli in an attended channel, P3a can be evoked by all low-probability stimuli in that channel, whether or not they are designated targets. Thus, P3a may be part of the mismatch detector system represented by N200. In another example, Ruchkin, Sutton, Kietzman, and Silver (1980) showed that while P3b increased in amplitude with increasing detection accuracy, tonic SW increased in amplitude with decreasing detection accuracy. Distinguishing P3b from positive SW can be difficult. Thus, Ruchkin, Sutton, and Stega (1980) first noted that a difference between the effects of two instructional sets on two tasks with identical stimuli appeared to occur primarily in P3b. However, principal-components analysis showed that the instruction effect was actually on tonic SW (Sutton & Ruchkin, 1984).

As Sutton and Ruchkin (1984) point out, an unfortunate consequence of this complex state of affairs may be that for many experiments reported in the literature, we cannot be certain whether the late positivity under study is Sutton's P3b, tonic or phasic SW, or possibly one of the earlier-occurring members of the late positive complex.

Begleiter and his colleagues, and Pfefferbaum *et al.* (1979), each identify their late positive events as P300. Are they actually studying the same event? First, in their early studies of alcoholics, Pfefferbaum's group employed a three-tone version of the auditory oddball task, whereas Begleiter *et al.* typically use visual stimuli in somewhat more complex paradigms. Although most investigators assume that, functionally speaking, auditory and visual P300 signal the same processing functions, their identity is not a certainty. More recently, Pfefferbaum's group (Johnson *et al.*, 1984) presented a preliminary report based on ongoing research in alcoholics, in which visually presented semantic stimuli were used. In that study, "P300" latencies ranged from about 550 to 800 msec, depending on task difficulty. Is this late positivity Sutton's P3b or a later SW component?

For future research with alcoholics, we should specify scalp distributions of the long-latency components, and we should consider using some appropriate form of multivariate analysis of ERP wave forms, such as principal-components analysis. Note that Porjesz and Begleiter now employ principal-components analysis, but note also Hunt's (1985) critique of this type of analysis in EP research. In addition, we should exercise considerable caution in relating P300 findings to cognitive functions. No single psychological concept so far suggested is capable of handling all of the concepts and data putatively asociated with P300. P300 has been related to uncertainty reduction, memory scanning, orienting, salience of stimuli, value and reward, a limited-capacity attentional resource, and updating of recent memory, among other ideas. A general conceptual framework capable of integrating all of these ideas may eventually be found, but it is not yet in the literature. The possibility that each of the several late positive components signals a different processing function complicates integrative efforts (Rösler, 1983).

A final caveat with regard to interpretation of the EP data on alcoholics concerns the question of arousal and motivation. As summarized earlier, Begleiter, Porjesz, and Yerre-Grubstein (1974), Porjesz and Begleiter (1979), Coger, Dymond, Serafetinedes, Lowenstein, and Pearson (1976), Wagman, Allen, Funderbuck, and Upright (1978), and others find evidence for enhanced CNS excitability during the early stages of withdrawal from alcohol. That is, EP amplitudes are increased, amplitude–intensity slopes are steeper, and peak latencies are shorter than in controls or in alcoholics who have been abstinent for a month or more. As reported above, longer-term abstinence is associated with longer peak latencies and lower EP amplitudes. Suppose the alcoholic at 3 or 4 weeks of abstinence is physiologically depressed, in a low state of CNS excitability, and, moreover, unmotivated for these boring laboratory tasks. Might such a person have low N100 and P300 amplitudes and fail to show physiological differentiation between stimuli designated arbitrarily as relevant or irrelevant? Moreover, could CNS hypoexcitability cause slowed conduction in the auditory brain stem pathways?

For the question of motivation and ERP component amplitudes, Begleiter, Porjesz, Chou, and Aunon (1983) found that P300 in normal subjects was larger to stimuli linked to financial reward than to stimuli with no payoff. Interpretation of the ERP findings in the studies of alcoholics depends on the assumption that alcoholics and controls are complying fully with task instructions. If the same group differences were to be found with contingent financial reward, the interpretations of these differences offered by Porjesz and Begleiter would be strengthened. For the question of CNS depression and increased BSP latencies, investigators often cite Amadeo and Shagass (1973) for evidence that BSP latencies do not change in low arousal states even during sleep. It should be noted that Amadeo and Shagass's significance tests were based on four subjects and that the subjects' wave IV latency did, in fact, increase during sleep by a noteworthy 50–190 μsec. Another argument that might be leveled against the notion of low-arousal, slowed BSP is that some anesthetics, such as pentobarbital and ketamine, reportedly have no effects on BSP latencies. Yet recent investigations by Henry (1979), Jewett and Romano (1972), and Stockard, Stockard, and Sharbrough (1978) do show that acutely administered anesthetics cause significant increases in brain stem conduction times. Thus, the low-motivation, low-arousal hypothesis may merit some attention. Admittedly, it is altogether unlikely that this hypothesis could account for all of the Porjesz–Begleiter data. For example, the P300 findings in long-abstinent alcoholics and in the 7- to 13-year-old nondrinking sons of alcoholics are very likely due to other causes. But, for the active alcoholics tested at 1 month of abstinence, the low-arousal, and low-motivation hypothesis should be tested by appropriate experimental manipulations.

Individual Differences: Age, Gender, Cognitive Deficit, and Family History

Where data are available, chronological age, gender, cognitive deficit, and familial factors have been shown to account for substantial inter- and intrasubject variability in EPs. Since alcoholics vary in age, gender, cognitive impairment, and family history of alcoholism, it is important in EP work to measure or control for these effects. This brief review points out some new information and some gaps in our knowledge that indicate a need for more study of these variables and their relationships to the EP deficits associated with chronic alcohol abuse.

Chronological Age

AUDITORY BRAIN STEM POTENTIAL

There is controversy about whether normal aging in adults is associated with any change in central auditory conduction velocities. If there are increased interpeak latencies in the elderly (e.g., at age 60–70), the increase is on the order of 0.1 msec. This is not in the abnormal range for young adults. It should be noted that age-related changes found in the BSP could be due to either cochlear (e.g., presbycusis), conductive, or central impairment. There seems to be a consensus that the increased wave V latencies sometimes observed in the healthy elderly are due to cochlear dysfunction (with prolongation of wave I latency) rather than to central slowing (Harkins & Lenhardt, 1980).

However, as reviewed earlier, Chu *et al.* (1982) did find age-related increases in central conduction time in their chronic alcoholics. Considered as a whole, the available data suggest that aging may increase CNS vulnerability to alcohol abuse.

PATTERN-SHIFT VISUAL EVOKED POTENTIAL

As is true for the BSP, investigations of the effects of chronological age on components of the PSVEP have produced somewhat inconsistent results. However, it now appears that most of those discrepancies can be resolved by consideration of stimulus variables. Small checks (e.g., visual angle 30′ or less) and relatively low luminance of the checkerboard display are associated with a monotonic increase in both P100 and N70 latencies in healthy adults from the second decade on up (Celesia & Daly, 1977; Sokol, Moskowitz, & Towle, 1981).

There is very little information in the literature about the combined effects of aging and alcohol abuse on PSVEP latencies. Kelley, Pena, Reilly, Overall, and Colton (1984) reported systematic increases in both P100 and

N70 peak latencies as functions of age in detoxified alcoholics and normal controls, but P100 differences between the two groups were not significant. Conversely, N70 latencies were significantly lengthened among alcoholics, especially during early withdrawal. After 3 weeks of sobriety, older alcoholics showed a persistent trend toward increased N70 latencies, whereas latencies for the younger alcoholics were in the normal range. Again, the data suggest a possible interaction between the effects of aging and alcohol abuse.

SHORT-LATENCY SOMATOSENSORY EVOKED POTENTIAL

For the SEP, age changes in healthy adults have received very little attention. However, most of the data currently available suggest significant slowing of conduction velocity with advancing age. The increase in peak latencies is believed to occur in both peripheral and central segments of the somatosensory pathway (e.g., Chiappa, 1985; Desmedt & Cheron, 1980; Dorfman & Bosley, 1979). I was unable to locate a study of the combined effects of age and alcoholism on SEP latencies.

EVENT-RELATED POTENTIALS

In an auditory selective-attention task, Ford *et al.* (1979) found no effects of normal aging on N100 (i.e., Nd) amplitudes or latencies. Furthermore, in the elderly, N100 amplitudes were enhanced in the attended channel and attenuated in the unattended channel, as they are in young adults. Porjesz, Begleiter, and Samuelly (1980), employing a visual target-selection task, obtained similar effects of normal aging on N100 latencies but reported a nonsignificant trend for overall N100 amplitudes to be attenuated in their elderly subjects. Nevertheless, Porjesz *et al.* (1980) agree with Ford *et al.* (1979) that the healthy elderly manifest enhanced N100 amplitudes to stimuli in an attended channel. Since N100 amplitude (i.e., the elicitation of Nd) increases with concentration of attention, these findings suggest that healthy elderly persons can muster the attentional resources necessary to attend to the relevant channel in both auditory and visual selective-attention tasks.

For P300, Ford *et al.* (1979) and Porjesz *et al.* (1980) agree that the normal elderly have longer peak latencies than younger adults. Brown, Marsh, and La Rue (1983), among others, confirm these results but show that P300 latency probably increases exponentially with age. All three groups of investigators conclude that healthy elderly persons can use probability information as well as young adults (i.e., that they show no significant decline in P300 amplitude), but that they require more time to make decisions about stimulus identity. Note here that decision time, which many investigators believe occurs at P300 latency, may in fact occur at N200 latency (Sutton & Ruchkin, 1984). (See Porjesz & Begleiter, 1982, for an excellent review of the EP literature on aging.)

The relationship between age and P300 latency has clinical significance. Linear regression functions of P300 on age have been proposed as baseline criteria for the presence of CNS dysfunction (e.g., Goodin, Squires, Henderson, & Starr, 1978; K. C. Squires, Chippendale, Wrege, Goodin, & Starr, 1980). Several investigators have reported that P300 latencies in the demented elderly fall beyond 2 standard deviations of the mean for their age. If the normal age–latency function for P300 is in fact nonlinear, then reliance on the linear hypothesis will result in overestimation of deviance among the elderly.

Since both aging and chronic abuse of alcohol can alter ERPs, it is reasonable to inquire whether the patterns of deficit are similar for alcoholics and elderly persons. As summarized earlier, N100 amplitude effects are approximately normal in healthy old people (Ford *et al.*, 1979; Porjesz *et al.*, 1980). Also, as noted earlier, although Begleiter's and Pfefferbaum's findings agree that normal aging is accompanied by increasing P300 latencies and that P300 is altered in chronic alcoholics, they disagree as to whether P300 amplitude (Porjesz & Begleiter, 1982) or P300 latency (Pfefferbaum *et al.*, 1979) is the valid discriminator between alcoholics and controls. If P300 latency is involved, then one might anticipate an interaction between the effects of aging and alcoholism. I was unable to locate any investigations of ERPs that included both aging normals and aging alcoholics.

To summarize, I found only one BSP and one PSVEP study that compared younger and older alcoholics. No relevant SEP studies were found, nor were any identified in the ERP literature. Several significant questions come to mind that could be answered by research on alcohol abuse and aging: (1) Are older alcoholics relatively more impaired than younger alcoholics? (2) Are older persons more vulnerable to alcohol toxicity than younger persons? (3) Are alcohol dependence and/or tolerance effects different for the late-onset alcoholic than for the early-onset alcoholic? (4) To what extent do such background variables as amount of alcohol consumed, duration of abstinence, typical drinking patterns, or family history influence relationships of age and alcohol abuse?

Gender

A general finding for the BSP, the PSVEP, and the SEP is that women have shorter central conduction times than men. These gender differences are usually attributed to differences in head, brain, and body size, but there is no systematic evidence to support or refute such hypotheses. Stockard, Hughes, and Sharbrough (1979) reported that females have slightly higher core body temperatures than males, and that this might account for their faster central conduction velocities. (Recall a suggestion earlier in this chapter that typmanic temperature should be investigated in sober alcoholics.)

Possible gender differences in the long-latency components of the ERP have been ignored by investigators in this field. Yet reports of gender differences in cognitive performance (Maccoby & Jacklin, 1974) and in functional hemispheric laterality (Levy & Reid, 1978) suggest that studies of gender effects may be informative. Again, there are no systematic studies comparing EPs in alcoholic men and women.

Cognitive Deficit

The neuropsychological literature indicates that chronic alcoholics tend to be deficient in their ability to abstract, to perform visual–spatial tasks, and to shift flexibly from one perspective to another in problem-solving tasks. If, as is suggested by the EP literature, they also suffer from various sensory and perceptual deficits, then it is of interest to know whether their EP-defined deficits covary systematically with their more globally defined neuropsychological deficits. Only one published study (Skerchock & Cohen, 1984) has examined that question. These investigators defined three groups of alcoholic patients in terms of degree of neuropsychological deficit. They reported that P300 latencies increased with cognitive deficit.

Our research team is engaged presently in longitudinal studies of alcoholics and matched controls stratified on gender and on history versus no history of alcoholism in first-degree relatives. Each subject undertakes a battery of sensitive neuropsychological tests and an EP battery composed of the BSP (with varied rates of stimulus repetition), the PSVEP, and a dual-modality visual–auditory ERP task modeled after one of the Porjesz–Begleiter tasks. Among other issues, we will inquire into the relationship between neuropsychological and EP deficits in male and female alcoholics.

Family History and Biological Markers

Susceptibility to alcoholism is familial, and well-designed studies of adoptees and twins implicate genetic factors in both male and female alcoholics (Bohman, Sigvardsson, & Cloninger, 1981; Cloninger, Bohman, & Sigvardsson, 1981; Goodwin, Schulsinger, Hermansen, Guze, & Winokur, 1973). Such findings encourage a search for biological markers of alcoholism. However, as Cloninger (1983) cautions, such research should take account of the great heterogeneity among alcoholics at every level of analysis. Furthermore, recent evidence from the Stockholm Adoption Study identifies two genetically distinct forms of alcoholism for which biological mediators may differ. One type affects both men and women, but is expressed only in particular postnatal environments. The second, less common type is highly heritable from father to son, but mothers and daughters in such families are seldom affected (Cloninger, 1983). Current literature recently reviewed by Cloninger (1983) identifies several variables that may underlie vulnerability to alcoholism, and thus may qualify as biological or behavioral markers in young men with a family history of alcoholism. Among these are the following: fewer signs of intoxication after ingestion of a standard dose of alcohol, rapid development of tolerance to alcohol, childhood hyperkinesis, poor performance on certain neuropsychological tests, low platelet monoamine oxidase activity, and alpha wave desynchronization in the resting EEG.

Until recently, the EP abnormalities found among alcoholics have been presumed to reflect the neurophysiological consequences of chronic alcohol abuse (and/or nutritional deficits). However, Begleiter and his colleagues have recently reported a cluster of findings that suggest that among persons at high risk for alcoholism, P300 amplitude deficits may antedate the onset of alcohol abuse. As reported earlier, deficits in P300 amplitude were found in two groups of abstinent chronic alcoholics (4 months to 10 years), and, most importantly, in 7- to 13-year-old healthy, nondrinking sons of alcoholic fathers. Thus, P300 amplitude is a possible biological marker of vulnerability to alcoholism.

Employing similar research designs, Begleiter and his colleagues also investigated slowed BSP conduction velocity as a possible biological marker. In those studies, BSP latencies approached normal values in alcoholics abstinent for 4 months, and were quite normal in the adolescent sons of alcoholic fathers. These results imply that the brain stem deficits found among recently abstinent alcoholics are due either to alcohol abuse or to some associated factor such as nutritional deficits.

New research designs planned in this area, either cross-sectional or prospective, should assess simultaneously all of the putative biological markers so far identified and should respond to Cloninger's (1983) evidence for genetic heterogeneity and gene–environment interactions in the etiology of alcoholism.

Summary

This commentary on alcoholism and EPs has raised some questions about interpretation of recent results, has offered some alternative hypotheses, and has reviewed some curent concepts and techniques that might profitably be applied in alcohol-related studies.

Employing diverse EP methods, Porjesz and Begleiter, along with other investigators, find that both acute and chronic alcohol ingestion influence numerous brain structures and functions, ranging from the sensory end organs to higher integrative systems. For example, both auditory and visual conduction times can be prolonged in detoxified male alcoholics. The data on short-latency auditory EPs suggest that among alcoholics who manifest no overt symptoms of brain damage, brain stem dysfunction can often be demonstrated as far caudally as the medulla. The incidence of significant slowing of central conduction in alcoholics increases with age, with number of neurological complications, and wth CT evidence of cerebral atrophy.

The endogenous long-latency ERPs that can be evoked or modified in information-processing contexts are also altered in alcoholics. The deviations found in the N100, N200, and P300 components are consistent with impairment of brain functions that support selective attention to relevant information sources and that mediate perceptual discrimination and signal analysis.

Porjesz and Begleiter hypothesize that the slowing of central auditory conduction velocity observed in their alcoholics may be due to demyelination in the brain stem. There are, of course, other pathological processes that could cause such slowing, such as neuronal loss. Moreover, one nonpathological condition that merits some consideration is reduced brain temperature. Tympanic thermometry might prove to be a useful adjunct in future BSP studies with alcoholics. Two additional methods from auditory physiology are likely to prove useful for more precise localization of dysfunction along the auditory pathway. These are the acoustic reflex for which the brain stem neuronal arc is well documented, and the binaural-difference waveform, which indexes binaural interaction in the brain stem. Localization of dysfunction could be further enhanced by employment of the short-latency SEP. Taken together, the BSP, PSVEP, and SEP would provide sensitive, quantitative extensions of the clinical neurological examination.

One issue not yet explored in alcohol-related studies is whether the small decreases in central conduction velocity found in alcoholics have any consequences for information processing. Candidate tasks for such investigations are sound localization and speech perception, which require precise analysis of temporal aspects of acoustic information.

For the longer-latency task-related ERP components, we need more precise definition and measurement. Some investigators now identify several endogenous negativities and positivities that were not recognized a few years back, each of which may relate to a different functional state of the brain. These potentials are elicited by different instructional and stimulus conditions; they have different latencies and different scalp topographies. An unfortunate consequence of this state of affairs is that for many research reports we cannot be certain whether the late components investigated in one laboratory are the same ones studied in another. Whatever the case, the data currently available do imply that the abstinent alcoholic often fails to show physiological differentiation between stimuli designated as relevant or irrelevant, and/or as signals or nonsignals. However, before accepting these EP alterations as evidence of impaired ability, we should evaluate low motivation and low arousal as possible mediators of the findings. Finally, we need more data on alcohol-related EP alterations as functions of age, gender, cognitive deficits, and familial factors. Future research designs should take account of recent evidence for genetic heterogeneity and gene–environment interactions in the etiology of alcoholism.

Acknowledgment

The writing of this chapter was supported in part by Grant No. AA06135 from the National Institute on Alcohol Abuse and Alcoholism.

References

Allison, T., Goff, W. R., Williamson, P. D., & Van Gilder, J. C. (1980). On the neural origin of early components of the human somatosensory evoked potential. *Progress in Clinical Neurophysiology, 7*, 56–68.

Amadeo, M., & Shagass, C. (1973). Brief latency click-evoked potentials during waking and sleeping in man. *Psychophysiology, 10*, 244–250.

Begleiter, H., Porjesz, B., & Chou, C. L. (1981). Auditory brainstem potentials in chronic alcoholics. *Science, 211*, 1064–1066.

Begleiter, H., Porjesz, B., Chou, C. L., & Aunon, J. (1983). P_3 and stimulus incentive value. *Psychophysiology, 20*, 95–101.

Begleiter, H., Porjesz, B., & Tenner, M. (1980). Neuroradiological and neurophysiological evidence of brain deficits in chronic alcoholics. *Acta Psychiatrica Scandinavica, 62*(Suppl. 286), 3–13.

Begleiter, H., Porjesz, B., & Yerre-Grubstein, C. (1974). Excitability of somatosensory evoked potentials during experimental alcoholization and withdrawal. *Psychopharmacology, 37*, 15–21.

Bohman, M., Sigvardsson, S., & Cloninger, C. R. (1981). Maternal inheritance of alcohol abuse: Cross-fostering analysis of adopted women. *Archives of General Psychiatry, 38*, 965–969.

Borg, E., & Moller, A. (1967). Effect of ethyl alcohol and phenobarbital sodium on the acoustic middle ear reflex in man. *Acta Oto-Laryngologica, 64*, 415–426.

Brown, W. S., Marsh, J. T., & La Rue, A. (1983). Exponential electrophysiological aging: P3 latency. *Electroencephalography and Clinical Neurophysiology, 55*, 277–285.

Celesia, C. G., & Daly, R. F. (1977). Visual electroencephalographic computer analysis (VECA). *Neurology, 27*, 637–641.

Chiappa, K. H. (1985). *Evoked potentials in clinical medicine*. New York: Raven Press.

Chiappa, K. H., Gladstone, K. J., & Young, R. R. (1979). Brainstem auditory evoked responses: Studies of wave form variations in 50 normal human subjects. *Archives of Neurology, 36*, 81–87.

Chu, N. S., Squires, K. C., & Starr, A. (1982). Auditory brainstem responses in chronic alcoholic patients. *Electroencephalography and Clinical Neurophysiology, 54*, 418–425.

Church, M. W., & Williams, H. L. (1982). Dose- and time-dependent effects of ethanol on brainstem auditory evoked responses in young adult males. *Electroencephalography and Clinical Neurophysiology, 54*, 161–174.

Cloninger, C. R. (1983). Genetic and environmental factors in the development of alcoholism. *Journal of Psychiatric Treatment and Evaluation, 5*, 487–496.

Cloninger, C. R., Bohman, M., & Sigvardsson, S. (1981). Inheritance of alcohol abuse: Cross-fostering analysis of adopted men. *Archives of General Psychiatry, 38*, 861–868.

Coger, R. W., Dymond, A. M., Serafetinedes, E. A., Lowenstein, I., & Pearson, D. (1976). Alcoholism: Averaged visual evoked response amplitude–intensity slope and symmetry in withdrawal. *Biological Psychiatry, 11*(4), 435–443.

Cohill, E. N., & Greenberg, H. J. (1977). Effects of ethyl alcohol on the acoustic reflex threshold. *Journal of the American Audiological Society, 2*, 121–123.

Collins, D. W. K., Carroll, W. M., Black, J. L., & Walsh, M. (1979). Effect of refractive error on the visual evoked response. *British Medical Journal, i*, 121–123.

Daly, D. M., Roeser, R. J., Aung, M. H., & Daly, D. D. (1977). Early evoked potentials in patients with acoustic neuroma. *Electroencephalography and Clinical Neurophysiology, 43*, 151–159.

Desmedt, J. E., & Cheron, G. (1980). Somatonsensory evoked potentials to finger stimulation in healthy octogenarians and in young adults: Wave forms, scalp topography and transit times of parietal and frontal components. *Electroencephalography and Clinical Neurophysiology, 50*, 404–425.

DiPerri, R., Dravid, A. R., Schweigerdt, A. K., & Himwich, H. E. (1968). Effect of alcohol on evoked potentials of various parts of the central nervous system in cat. *Quarterly Journal of Studies on Alcohol, 29*, 20–37.

Dorfman, L. J., & Bosley, T. M. (1979). Age-related changes in peripheral and central nerve conduction in man. *Neurology, 29*, 38–44.

Eidelberg, E., Bond, M. L., & Kelter, A. (1971). Effects of alcohol on cerebellar and vestibular neurones. *Archives Internationales de Pharmacodynamie et Therapie, 192*, 213–219.

Ford, J. M., Hink, R. F., Hopkins, W. F., Roth, W. T., Pfefferbaum, A., & Kopell, B. S. (1979). Age effects on event related potentials in a selective attention task. *Journal of Gerontology, 34*, 388–395.

Fujikawa, S. M., & Weber, B. A. (1977). Effects of increased stimulus rate on brainstem electric response (BER) audiometry as a function of age. *Journal of the American Audiological Society, 3*, 147–150.

Gerling, I. J., & Finitzo-Hieber, T. (1982, October). Repetition rate effects with the auditory brainstem response. *Hearing Aid Journal*, pp. 29–32.

Gersuni, G. V. (1971). Temporal organization of the auditory function. In G. V. Gersuni (Ed.), *Sensory processes at the neuronal and behavioral levels.* New York: Academic Press.

Gieldanowski, J. (1965). Studies on the toxic action of some alcohols upon the organ of Corti. *Medycyna Pracy, 16*, 448–452.

Goodin, D. S., Squires, K. C., Henderson, B., & Starr, A. (1978). Age-related variations in evoked potentials to auditory stimuli in normal human subjects. *Electroencephalography and Clinical Neurophysiology, 44*, 447–458.

Goodwin, D. W., Schulsinger, F., Hermansen, L., Guze, S. B., & Winokur, G. (1973). Alcohol problems in adoptees raised apart from biological parents. *Archives of General Psychiatry, 28*, 238–243.

Halliday, A. M., McDonald, W. I., & Mushin, J. (1973). Delayed pattern evoked responses in optic neuritis in relation to visual acuity. *Transactions of the Ophthalmological Society of the United Kingdom, 93*, 315–324.

Hansen, J. C., & Hillyard, S. A. (1980). Endogenous brain potentials associated with selective auditory attention. *Electroencephalography and Clinical Neurophysiology, 49*, 277–290.

Harkins, S. W., & Lenhardt, M. (1980). Brainstem auditory evoked potentials in the elderly. In L. W. Poon (Ed.), *Aging in the 1980s: Psychological issues* (pp. 101–114). Washington, DC: American Psychological Association.

Hausler, R., & Levine, R. A. (1980). Brain stem auditory evoked potentials are related to interaural time discrimination in patients with multiple sclerosis. *Brain Research, 191*, 589–594.

Henry, K. R. (1979). Differential changes of auditory nerve and brain stem short latency evoked potentials in the laboratory mouse. *Electroencephalography and Clinical Neurophysiology, 45*, 452–459.

Hillyard, S. A. (1984). Event-related potentials and selective attention. In E. Donchin (Ed.), *Cognitive psychophysiology: Event-related potentials and the study of cognition* (pp. 51–72). Hillsdale, NJ: Erlbaum.

Hillyard, S. A., Hink, R. F., Schwent, U. L., & Picton, T. W. (1973). Electrical signs of selective attention in the human brain. *Science, 182*, 177–180.

Huang, C. M., & Buchwald, J. S. (1977). Interpretation of the vertex short-latency response: A study of single neurons in the brainstem. *Brain Research, 137*, 291–303.

Hunt, E. (1985). Mathematical models of the event-related potential. *Psychophysiology, 22*, 4, 395–402.

Jerger, J., Hannley, M., & Rivera, V. (1982). Auditory brainstem response and the masking level difference. *Annals of the New York Academy of Sciences, 388*, 466–470.

Jerger, J., Neely, J. G., & Jerger, S. (1980). Speech impedance and auditory brainstem response audiometry in brainstem tumors. *Archives of Otolaryngology, 106*, 218–223.

Jewett, D. L., & Romano, M. N. (1972). Neonatal development of auditory system potential averaged from the scalp of rat and cat. *Brain Research, 36*, 101–115.

Johnson, R., Jr., Pfefferbaum, A., Hart, T., & Kopell, B. S. (1984). P300 latency in chronic alcoholics and depressed patients: A preliminary report. *Annals of the New York Academy of Sciences, 425*, 585–591.

Jones, T. A., Stockard, J. J., & Weidner, W. J. (1980). The effects of temperature and acute alcohol intoxication on brain stem auditory evoked potentials in the cat. *Electroencephalography and Clinical Neurophysiology, 49*, 23–30.

Kalant, H. (1970). Effects of ethanol on the nervous system. In J. Tremolieres (Ed.), *International encyclopedia of pharmacological therapeutics: Section 20, Vol. 1. Alcohols and derivatives* (pp. 189–230). New York: Pergamon Press.

Kelley, J. T., Pena, Y., Reilly, E. L., Overall, J. E., & Colton, G. S. (1984). Effects of age and alcohol abuse on pattern reversal evoked potentials. *Clinical Electroencephalography, 15*(2), 102–109.

Klemm, W. R., Mallari, C. G., Dreyfus, L. R., Fiske, J. C., Forney, E., & Mikeska, J. A. (1976). Ethanol-induced regional and dose–response differences in multiple-unit activity in rabbits. *Psychopharmacology, 46*, 235–244.

Kriss, A., Carroll, W. M., Blumhardt, L. D., & Halliday, A. M. (1982). Pattern- and flash-evoked potential changes in toxic (nutritional) optic neuropathy. In J. Courjon, F. Manguiere, & M. Revol (Eds.), *Clinical applications of evoked potentials in neurology* (pp. 11–19). New York: Raven Press.

Kupersmith, M. J., Weiss, P. A., & Carr, R. E. (1983). The visual-evoked potential in tobacco–alcohol and nutritional amblyopia. *American Journal of Ophthalmology, 95*, 307–314.

Kutas, M., & Hillyard, S. A. (1980). Reading senseless sentences: Brain potentials reflect semantic incongruity. *Science, 207*, 203–205.

Levine, R. A. (1981). Binaural interaction in brainstem potentials of human subjects. *Annals of Neurology, 9*(4), 384–393.

Levy, J., & Reid, M. (1978). Variations in cerebral organization as a function of handedness, hand posture in writing and sex. *Journal of Experimental Psychology: General, 107*, 119–144.

Maccoby, E. E., & Jacklin, C. N. (1974). *The psychology of sex differences.* Stanford, CA: Stanford University Press.

Money, K. E., Johnson, W. H., & Corlett, B. M. A. (1965). Role of semicircular canals in positional alcohol nystagmus. *American Journal of Physiology, 208*, 1065–1070.

Mountcastle, V. B. (1974). Central neural mechanisms in hearing. In V. B. Mountcastle (Ed.), *Medical physiology* (13th ed., Vol. 1, pp. 412–439). St. Louis: C. V. Mosby.

Näätänen, R., & Michie, P. T. (1979). Early selective attention effects on the evoked potential: A critical review and reinterpretation. *Biological Psychology, 8*, 81–136.

Ochs, R., Markand, O. N., & DeMyer, W. E. (1979). Brainstem and auditory evoked responses in leukodystrophies. *Neurology, 29*, 1089–1093.

Pfefferbaum, A., Horvath, T. B., Roth, W. T., & Kopell, B. S. (1979). Event-related potential changes in chronic alcoholics. *Electroencephalography and Clinical Neurophysiology, 47*, 637–647.

Porjesz, B., & Begleiter, H. (1979). Visual evoked potentials and brain dysfunction in chronic alcoholics. In H. Begleiter (Ed.), *Evoked brain potentials and behavior* (pp. 277–302). New York: Plenum Press.

Porjesz, B., & Begleiter, H. (1981a). *Event-related potentials and decision time in chronic alcoholics.* Paper presented at the International Council on Alcohol Abuse, Vienna.

Porjesz, B., & Begleiter, H. (1981b). *Event-related potentials in chronic alcoholics.* Paper presented at the 134th Annual Meeting of the American Psychiatric Association, New Orleans.

Porjesz, B., & Begleiter, H. (1981c). Human evoked brain potentials and alcohol. *Alcoholism: Clinical and Experimental Research, 5*(2), 304–317.

Porjesz, B., & Begleiter, H. (1982). Evoked brain potential deficits in alcoholism and aging. *Alcoholism: Clinical and Experimental Research, 6*(1), 53–63.

Porjesz, B., & Begleiter, H. (1983). Brain dysfunction and alcohol. In B. Kissin & H. Begleiter (Eds.), *The biology of alcoholism: Vol. 7. The pathogenesis of alcoholism: Biological factors* (pp. 415–483). New York: Plenum Press.

Porjesz, B., Begleiter, H., & Samuelly, I. (1980). Cognitive deficits in chronic alcoholics and elderly subjects assessed by evoked brain potentials. *Acta Psychiatrica Scandinavica, 62*(Suppl. 286), 15–29.

Posthuma, J., & Visser, S. L. (1982). Visual evoked potentials and alcohol-induced brain damage. In J. Courjon, F. Maugiere, & M. Revol (Eds.), *Clinical applications of evoked potentials in neurology* (pp. 149–155). New York: Raven Press.

Renault, B., Ragot, R., Lesevre, N., & Remond, A. (1982). Brain events: Their onset and offset as indices of mental chronometry. *Science, 215*, 1413–1415.

Ritter, W., Ford, J. M., Gaillard, A. W. K., Harter, M. R., Kutas, M., Näätänen, R., Polich, J., Renault, B., & Rohrbaugh, J. (1984). Cognition and event-related potentials: I. The relation of negative potentials to cognitive processes. *Annals of the New York Academy of Sciences, 425*, 24–38.

Ritter, W., Simson, R., & Vaughan, H., Jr. (1983). Event-related potentials and two sequential stages of information processing in physical and semantic discrimination. *Psychophysiology, 20*, 168–179.

Robinette, M., & Brey, R. H. (1978). Influence of alcohol on the acoustic reflex and temporary threshold shift. *Archives of Otolaryngology, 104*, 31–37.

Robinson, K., & Rudge, P. (1975). Auditory evoked responses in multiple sclerosis. *Lancet, i*, 1164–1166.

Robinson, K., & Rudge, P. (1977). The early components of the auditory evoked potential in multiple sclerosis. In J. Desmedt (Ed.), *Auditory evoked potentials in man.* Basel: Karger.

Rösler, F. (1983). Endogenous ER "Ps" and cognition: Probes, prospects and pitfalls in matching pieces of the mind–body puzzle. In A. W. K. Gaillard & W. Ritter (Eds.), *Tutorials in event-related potential research: Endogenous components* (pp. 9–35). Amsterdam: North-Holland.

Ruchkin, D. S., Sutton, S., Kietzman, M. L., & Silver, K. (1980). Slow wave and P300 in signal detection. *Electroencephalography and Clinical Neurophysiology, 50*, 35–47.

Ruchkin, D. S., Sutton, S., & Stega, M. (1980). Emitted P300 and slow wave event-related potentials in guessing and detection tasks. *Electroencephalography and Clinical Neurophysiology, 49*, 1–14.

Sauerland, E. K., Mizuno, N., & Harper, R. M. (1970). Presynaptic depolarization of trigeminal cutaneous afferent fibers induced by ethanol. *Experimental Neurology, 27*, 476–489.

Skerchock, S. A., & Cohen, J. (1984). Alcoholism, organicity and event-related potentials. *Annals of the New York Academy of Sciences, 425*, 623–628.

Sokol, S., Moskowitz, A., & Towle, V. L. (1981). Age-related change in the latency of the visual evoked potential: Influence of check size. *Electroencephalography and Clinical Neurophysiology, 51*, 559–562.

Spitzer, J. (1981). Auditory effects of chronic alcoholism. *Drug and Alcohol Dependence, 8*, 317–335.

Spitzer, J. B., & Ventry, I. M . (1980). Central auditory dysfunction among chronic alcoholics. *Archives of Otolaryngology, 106*, 224–229.

Squires, K. C., Chippendale, T. J., Wrege, K. S., Goodin, D. S., & Starr, A. (1980). Electrophysiological assessment of mental function in aging and dementia. In L. W. Poon (Ed.), *Aging in the 1980s: Psychological issues* (pp. 125–134). Washington, DC: American Psychological Association.

Squires, N. (1984a). Auditory brainstem responses in aberrant development: The case for a different approach to ERP research. *Annals of the New York Academy of Sciences, 425*, 324–337.

Squires, N. (1984b). ERPs and diminished mental functioning. In E. Donchin (Ed.), *Cognitive psychophysiology: Event-related potentials and the study of cognition. The Carmel Conferences* (Vol. 1, pp. 343–353). Hillsdale, NJ: Erlbaum.

Squires, N., Squires, K., & Hillyard, S. A. (1975). Two varieties of long-latency positive waves evoked by unpredictable auditory stimuli in man. *Electroencephalography and Clinical Neurophysiology, 38*, 387–401.

Stockard, J. J., Hughes, J. F., & Sharbrough, F. W. (1979). Visually evoked potentials to electronic pattern reversal: Latency variations with gender, age and technical factors. *American Journal of EEG Technology, 19*, 171–204.

Stockard, J. J., & Rossiter, V. S. (1977). Clinical and pathologic correlates of brainstem auditory response abnormalities. *Neurology, 27*, 316–325.

Stockard, J. J., Stockard, J. E., & Sharbrough, F. W. (1978). Non-pathologic factors influencing brainstem auditory evoked potentials. *American Journal of EEG Technology, 18*, 177–209.

Sutton, S., Braren, M., Zubin, J., & John, E. R. (1965). Evoked potential correlates of stimulus uncertainty. *Science, 150*, 1187–1188.

Sutton, S., & Ruchkin, D. S. (1984). The late positive complex: Advances and new problems. *Annals of the New York Academy of Sciences, 425*, 1–23.

Victor, M., Mancall, E. L., & Dreyfus, P. M. (1960). Deficiency amblyopia in the alcoholic patient. *Archives of Ophthalmology, 64*(1), 307–313.

Wagman, A. M. I., Allen, R. P., Funderbuck, F., & Upright, D. (1978). EEG measures of functional tolerance to alcohol. *Biological Psychiatry, 13*, 719–728.

Worthington, D. W., & Peters, J. F. (1980). Quantifiable hearing and no ABR: Paradox or error? *Ear and Hearing, 1*, 281–285.

Yagi, T., & Kaga, K. (1979). The effect of click repetition rate on the latency of evoked brainstem response and its clinical use for a neurological diagnosis. *Archives of Oto-Rhino-Laryngology, 222*, 91–97.

7

Discussion

Alcohol and Brain Function: An Appraisal of Cerebral Blood Flow Data

TERRY G. SHAW

Introduction

As one of the original anesthetics, alcohol was used in the late 19th century to induce a state of insensibility of sufficient depth to permit surgery. Unfortunately, acute alcohol administration in a large enough dose often brought about the demise of the patient. The deleterious effects associated with alcoholization have thus been acknowledged for close to a century. Within the past few decades, however, concern has focused more on the potential hazard associated with long-term social alcoholization.

The appearance of alcoholic dementia as an end-stage disease confirms our suspicion of a relationship between chronic consumption of alcohol and eventual brain damage. The question has less to do with the existence of such a relationship; more pragmatically, the issue is in what manner and under what range of conditions this influence occurs. It is only in the process of extrapolating backward toward normality that we encounter the myriad of causal factors that force us to qualify our pronouncements about the effects of alcohol.

Clearly, there are many variables at play in the evolution of brain damage secondary to alcoholism. This relationship is particularly confounded by the fact that the brain is already in a constant state of flux, whether one imbibes or abstains. Cells within the CNS are near maximum number at birth, and after CNS maturation (i.e., arborization, dendritic branching), abiotrophic processes become apparent whereby a progressive decline in cell numbers is evident with each passing decade of life. This

Terry G. Shaw. Private Practice, McAlester, Oklahoma. (Formerly, Cerebrovascular Research Program, Veterans Administration Medical Center, Houston, Texas; Baylor Stroke Center, Baylor College of Medicine, Houston, Texas.)

"inherent" change associated with merely growing older is apparent in CT studies of gross brain morphology (Barron, Jacobs, & Kinkel, 1976; Gyldensted, 1977; Yamagura, Ito, Kubota, & Matsuzawa, 1980) as well as actual cell counts and dendritic architecture (Brody, 1978; Henderson, Tomlinson, & Gibson, 1980; Scheibel & Scheibel, 1975). Unfortunately, the effects of long-term alcoholization of CNS tissue parallel this aging process. As a result, many alcoholic-dependent relationships are minimized when age is statistically partialed out (see Bergman, Chapter 2, this volume). Nevertheless, any description of "change" associated with chronic alcoholization must be viewed against a backdrop of this pre-eminent event.

Despite evidence of an innate abiotrophic process, aging is not a disease (Portnoi, 1980). Aging merely renders the CNS more susceptible to the effects of disease (including alcoholism), whereby inherent change presumably accelerates. Bergman's inability to document morphological evidence of a "premature-aging hypothesis" in alcoholics would seem to argue against the notion of accelerated change. However, Bergman's argument is not without flaws (see Wilkinson, Chapter 5, this volume) or contradictory results (Blusewicz, Schenkenberg, Dustman, & Beck, 1977; Hochla & Parsons, 1982).

In addition to aging, other antecedent factors such as gender and concomitant disease must be accounted for in any proposed relationship between alcoholism and brain damage. For the most part, the effects of these otherwise extraneous influences can be addressed by using appropriate sampling strategies and inclusion–exclusion criteria. Wilkinson (Chapter 5, this volume) has already provided a cogent discussion of these methodological considerations, and there is little need to belabor the issue here. There are, however, other points to be made.

First, the majority of results presented in this volume have been derived by comparing alcoholics with "normal controls." Unfortunately, what constitutes "normal" depends largely on one's definition and/or willingness to bend that definition to fit whoever is readily available to participate in an ongoing study. With respect to alcoholism, "normal" could be defined as someone who does not consume or has not consumed alcohol on a regular basis. However, some measurable effects on cognitive function (MacVane, Butters, Montgomery, & Farber, 1982; Parker & Noble, 1977) and cerebral blood flow (CBF) (Rogers, Meyer, Shaw, & Mortel, 1983) have been demonstrated with social, nonalcoholic patterns of drinking. "Normal" in the present context would, therefore, seemingly have to satisfy a more stringent criterion to avoid problems with subliminal or subclinical effects of alcohol.

Second, the sampling techniques (i.e., matched, stratified, "captive" inpatient populations, etc.) used in the research reported in the present volume are useful in identifying nomethetic hallmarks of alcoholism. They are, however, subject to a number of methodological errors, such as selection bias, survivor effects, generalizability, and so on (Schaie, 1968). These errors are acceptable only if the investigator is aware of and can tolerate their presence. Since the purpose of research such as that reported here is to eventually describe the effects of alcoholism on the brain over an extended period of time (Birren, 1959), longitudinal studies or cohort survival methods will ultimately be required to validate the results gathered on cross-sections of alcoholics. By these means, the parallelism between aging and long-term consumption may be teased apart.

Finally, on gross inspection, the brain appears as an amorphous gruel, of which one of the few distinguishing features is that it has cavities. On closer inspection, though, the composition of the brain becomes polymorphous and lends itself to being probed and analyzed with a variety of technologies. There are morphological, hemodynamic, metabolic, neuroelectric, and neurobehavioral domains of function, to name a few. While these substrates of function are symbiotically connected, our eyesight for their interrelationships is often too myopic, being generally focused on one domain at a time. In reviewing the proceeding chapters, I am reminded of Lillian F. Quigley's children's book, *The Blind Men and the Elephant* (1959). Each blind man was more than able to describe the part of the elephant he had in hand; it was the gestalt that could not be perceived.

> The Rajah spoke in a kind voice. "The elephant is a big animal. Each man touched only one part. You must put all the parts together to find out what an elephant is like." (p. 7)

Probably one of the most gratifying aspects of this volume is its attempt to push beyond complementarity in an effort to achieve convergent understanding about "what an alcoholic is like." Prior to appraising the contribution of CBF data to the emerging picture of what an alcoholic's brain is like, a brief review of the studied effects of alcohol on other domains of brain function seems in order.

Neuroelectric Findings

Porjesz and Begleiter (Chapter 3, this volume) have accumulated considerable evidence regarding the effects of alcohol on time-locked neuroelectric signals. In acute alcoholization as well as chronic alcoholism, there is a dampening of the amplitude of certain event-related potentials (ERPs), accompanied by an increased latency for other components. With long-term abstinence, the latency of the brain stem potential (BSP) appears to recover. However, aberrations in other ERP waveforms, particularly the P300 component, appear to be resistant to recovery.

Since ERPs are elicited by repetitive presentations of discrete sensory stimuli, cross-correlations with traditional neuropsychological results are not easily obtained. Nevertheless, on a more qualitative level of analysis, these unremitting neuroelectric changes associated with alcoholism appear to reflect rather specific information-processing deficits. Stated simply, alcoholics display increased difficulty in filtering sensory input, require more time for stimulus evaluation, and lack the normal differential responsivity to relevant versus irrelevant input. In somewhat compensatory fashion, alcoholics also appear to adopt a behavioral response pattern that stresses speed over accuracy of response. In the absence of definitive cross-correlations, these information-processing problems would presumably be a precipitating factor in subpar levels of performance on any standard neuropsychological assessment.

Most of Porjesz and Begleiter's ERP findings have centered around identification of P300 aberrations in alcoholics, which are maximally recorded over the parietal lobes. Given some of the typical neuropsychological impairments evident in chronic alcoholics in the absence of thiamine deficiency (i.e., visual–spatial functions of a complex, cognitive nature, rather than sensory–motor tasks; see Parsons, Chapter 8, this volume) the territorial overlap with ERP findings may be more than mere coincidence. Yet convergences in neuroelectric and neurocognitive data remain elusive, due to limitations in matching the two technologies.

The relationship between documented neuroelectric and morphological change is unclear. P300 irregularities in alcoholics are observed in the presence as well as the absence of sulcal widening (determined by CT parameters). The absence of a relationship between this waveform and *cortical* morphological change is not surprising, as sulcal widening seems to be a poor indicator of brain damage (see Bergman, Chapter 2, this volume). Whether or not the P300 waveform is influenced by *central* morphological change is, at present, undetermined. Yet evidence of P300 deficits in high-risk sons of alcoholics (who have not yet begun to consume alcohol) argues against any relationship between alcohol-induced brain damage (cortical or central) and P300 neuroelectric change. A predisposing, genetic etiology for the appearance of this aberration, independent of brain damage, seems more likely. Alcoholics may therefore be recruited from a pool of inferior problem solvers, and the P300 ERP deficit may be a marker for this vulnerability rather than an indicator of any sustained damage. Similar hypotheses are emerging with regard to antecedent neuropsychological factors (see Parsons, Chapter 8, this volume).

Anecdotally, we are once again confronted with the possibility of convergent data for neuroelectric and neuropsychological domains.

Morphological Findings

The issue of alcohol-induced brain damage, irrespective of any antecedent factors, persists. In that regard, the results of the KARTAD Project clearly demonstrate significant morphological permutations secondary to chronic alcohol consumption. *Central* (ventricular) CT changes are more evident in older alcoholics, compared to age-matched controls, while *cortical* (sulcal) CT changes are more prevalent in younger alcoholics. Cortical CT changes also appear to remit with abstinence (i.e., reabsorption rather than atrophy) and are poorly correlated with evidence of neuropsychological impairment. On the basis of these cumulative findings, the validity and diagnostic utility of cortical CT changes is brought into question. Evidence of ventricular or central widening appears to be more permanent in abstinent alcoholics and more strongly correlated with observed neuropsychological deficits. Thus, central changes appear to be a better indicator of brain damage secondary to chronic alcohol consumption.

Somewhat surprisingly, gender interacts with these noted changes, such that alcoholic men are more likely to demonstrate morphological attenuation while alcoholic women are more likely to display neuropsychological impairment. The basis for this interaction is unclear, given the limited number of gender studies in the literature devoted to the effects of alcohol. Developmentally, males have consistently demonstrated a relative superiority for visual–spatial skills, while females appear to be intrinsically better at language skills (Maccoby & Jacklin, 1974). If the effects of alcoholism preferentially impair complex, abstract, visual–spatial functions (as has been suggested in the literature), perhaps females are already at a decided disadvantage and simply have a lower threshold prior to the onset of objective neuropsychological deficits.

A similar genetic disadvantage for sex-linked central morphological susceptibility strains the law of parsimony. Nevertheless, gender differences in brain morphology have been documented and may have relevance to the preferential appearance of central changes in men (Conel, 1963; Taylor, 1969). At the same time, this finding may simply represent differences in the social acceptance and subsequent rate of alcohol consumption between the sexes. Women tend to use other prescribed drugs with alcohol more often than men and frequently become polyaddicted. While other plausible (but equally unfounded) explanations are possible, little is to be gained by blind speculation. The absence of further gender studies precludes a more cogent understanding for the time being.

Alcoholic Effects: Continuum or Threshold?

The disappointing absence of a convincing relationship between drinking-pattern variables and signs of brain damage or dysfunction (i.e., neuroelectric, neuropsychological, or morphological) seems to argue against adoption of a dose–response model to describe the continuum of alcohol effects. Although consumption appears necessary for “damage” to become apparent, it may not be sufficient. Accumulated brain damage in alcoholics might evolve as a result of an interaction between consumption and pre-eminent vulnerability to "damage." Consistent with previous interpretations, a genetic predisposition toward initially becoming dependent on alcohol *and* subsequently evidencing accelerated morphological change seems likely. Perhaps violation of some intrinsic, genetically based threshold with sustained consumption ultimately gives rise to true alcoholic encephalopathy.

As alcoholism is a generational disease, children raised in alcoholic families often lack the emotional nurturance necessary for appropriate psychological development. The words that best describe living in an alcoholic family are "inconsistency" and "unpredictability." As a result of instability, children of alcoholics seldom learn the combinations of roles that mold healthy personalities, and instead become locked into roles based upon their perception of what they need to survive. Given a genetic predisposition, the actual evolution of alcoholic behavior may arise as a result of the psychological problems encountered while growing up in an alcoholic family (Black, 1981), and alcoholism may become generational by virtue of the interaction between genetically predetermined vulnerability and disturbed psychological development (i.e., unmet dependency needs, low self-esteem, etc.). Alcoholism and subsequent brain damage would not be the first problems that have been found to emerge via nature–nurture interactions.

Cerebral Blood Flow

To examine the extent to which CBF patterns contribute to this picture, we must now turn to the data provided by Risberg and Berglund (see Chapter 4, this volume). However, before this information can be adequately integrated with the existing knowledge, several methodological issues must be addressed. First, CBF research in alcoholic states is admittedly in its infancy, compared to progress in other areas. While volumes have been accumulated regarding the influence of other neurological conditions on CBF and cerebral metabolic rate (CMR), there is a comparative dearth of information about the effects of alcohol on CBF. As indicated by Risberg and Berglund, the small amount of information accumulated to date has been dominated by the Lund group.

Second, a number of different technologies for measuring CBF have evolved over the past 30 years. Since the results summarized by Risberg and Berglund span those three decades, clear understanding of their relative contributions is dependent on assessing the limitations and capabilities of these various methodologies.

All CBF methods share a common interest: indirect estimation of dynamic brain function. On the one hand, CBF is intimately susceptible to ischemic disease and other altered states of perfusion. This is why much of the CBF literature has been dominated by studies of vascular disorders (transient stroke, ischemic attacks, migraine, etc.). Yet, because of the normally tight coupling that exists between CBF and CMR, estimates of more dynamic brain function are possible in a range of conditions by mere examination of CBF.

The mutual reciprocity between CBF and CMR is depicted in Figure 7-1. In "normal," nonpathological states, CMR dictates CBF, whereby flow adjusts to demand. In instances of functional brain activity, regionally increased CMR gives rise to increased blood carbon dioxide levels, which in turn induce relative vasodilation, resulting in increased CBF. In periods of relative inactivity, decreased regional CMR effectively lowers the level of blood carbon dioxide, which allows for relative vasoconstriction and subsequent lowering of CBF. To reiterate, in most instances, CMR dictates CBF. Yet there are at least two major processes that modulate this reciprocity: abiotrophy and cerebrovascular disease.

Antecedent decrements in cell numbers related to aging (Brody, 1978) are thought to be the basis for normal abiotrophic processes. Normal, age-related declines in neuronal populations will necessarily give rise to decrements in CMR, with subsequent but "normal" lowering or adjustment of CBF. The toxicity of alcohol on neuronal populations has been well established in animal models (Freund, 1973). Thus, some pathological states such as alcoholism are theoretically capable of accelerating this otherwise normal reduction in CMR (and CBF) by virtue of increasing the rate of cell loss secondary to toxicity.

However, CMR does not always pace CBF. In pathological vascular states (i.e., atherosclerotic disease), progressive, age-related CMR decrements become exaggerated by virtue of diminished nutritional flow, further reducing cell populations through ischemic tissue loss. In cerebrovascular disease, the availability of CBF limits CMR. Whether or not normal vascular processes, such as loss of vascular reserve, exert any significant influence on CMR is at present unclear.

As a result of these interactions, it is often difficult to understand the etiology underlying any measured change in CBF. If the schematic diagram in Figure 7-1 is a fairly accurate reflection of the situation, CBF and CMR can be expected to decline with aging irrespective of the state of the brain. In this view, pathology (alcohol-related or other) simply enhances, accelerates, and compounds the inherent processes of change (i.e., the premature-aging hypothesis).

It must be reiterated that the existence of a tight coupling with CMR is a basis by which CBF takes on functional meaning. Unfortunately, the reciprocal connection between CBF and CMR is known to break down in some pathological conditions (Lassen, 1966; Obrist, Langfitt, Jaggi, Cruz, & Gennarelli, 1984). Risberg and Berglund acknowledge this problem in discussing some of the early results on the effects of acute alcohol intoxication. While the problem of uncoupling may be addressed by including simultane-

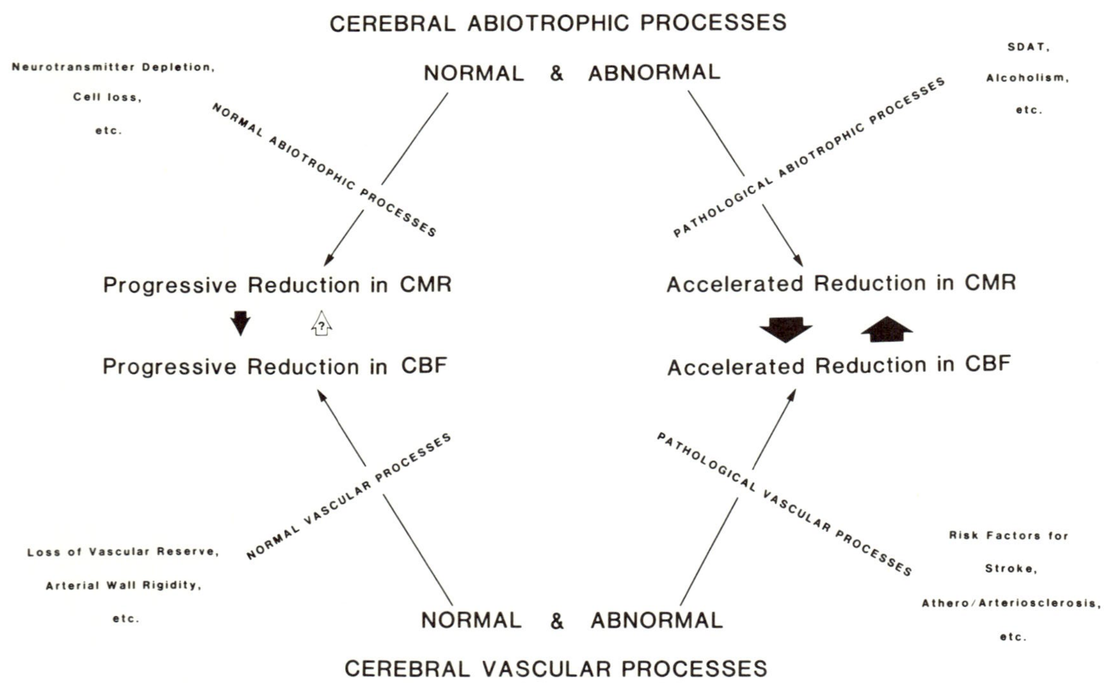

Figure 7-1. Schematic diagram demonstrating the "coupling" relationship between cerebral blood flow (CBF) and cerebral metabolic rate (CMR). This mutual reciprocity is thought to be modulated by at least two known processes—abiotrophy and cerebrovascular processes, each of which has normal and pathological rates of expression.

ous measures of CMR, the majority of contemporary studies have focused solely on CBF for ethical reasons and have simply assumed that their measurements accurately reflect CMR. To what extent chronic alcoholism interferes with the mechanism that couples CBF and CMR is unknown, but the functional validity of contemporary CBF data hinges on that very issue.

There are still other important methodological problems that must be taken into account. The pioneering work of Kety and Schmidt (1948) with the nitrous oxide method provided the technique used to establish the early data base. Unfortunately, this method only yielded estimates of CBF and CMR for the brain taken as a whole. The lack of any regional differentiation of brain function and CBF prompted the development of additional techniques that made it possible to simultaneously study CBF in multiple regions of the same hemisphere. While this increased spatial resolution significantly enhanced the applicability and regional sensitivity of the method, it should be borne in mind that most of these earlier technologies were invasive and required carotid puncture. This procedure was mainly limited to patients undergoing angiographic examinations and was hardly suitable for studying "normals." The generalizability of early studies on alcoholics without concomitant disease is therefore suspect.

For ethical reasons, invasive techniques were discontinued, and simultaneous measurement of CMR fell by the wayside in favor of less traumatic methods of simply ascertaining CBF. The introduction of the ^{133}Xe inhalation technique (Mallet & Veall, 1963), with subsequent modifications for clinical application (Meyer, Ishihara, & Deshmukh, 1978; Obrist, Thompson, & Wang, 1975) provided a safe alternative means of measuring CBF on a regional basis that yielded results comparable to the Kety and Schmidt method (Reivich, Obrist, Slater, Greenberg, & Goldberg, 1975). Today, the ^{133}Xe technique (inhalation or intravenous injection) is the most widely used noninvasive method of measuring regional CBF (Meyer & Shaw, 1984).

In this technique, ^{133}Xe gas is administered as an inert radioactive indicator. The tracer gas diffuses rapidly into brain tissue, and after peak saturation is reached, administration of the isotope is eliminated. Desaturation or "washout" curves are then recorded from external collimators mounted over multiple preselected regions of the scalp. Regional flows are then calculated using standard computer algorithms. Gray-matter tissue has a higher perfusion rate than white matter, and the regional washout curves are subjected to analysis via a two-compartmental model that yields flow estimates of average CBF, gray-matter flow, and white-matter flow. Additional flow indices have been developed with subsequent mathematical derivations and manipulations of regional washout curves, but these are not as universally accepted or used as frequently.

Some of the problems previously encountered in earlier techniques, such as Compton scatter, slippage, temporal resolution, and possible uncoupling of CBF and CMR, are still inherent with the ^{133}Xe inhalation method (Meyer & Shaw, 1984). Nevertheless, the technique is atraumatic and can be applied safely to subjects of any age and physical status. It also has suitable test–retest reliability coefficients (Blauenstein, Halsey, Wilson, Willis, & Risberg, 1975; McHenry, Merory, & Bass, 1978).

In the present context, spatial resolution constitutes a fairly significant limitation of the method. The majority of "counts" picked up by a detector are derived from the clearance of tracer material from tissue nearest the probe. As shown in Figure 7-2, with increasing distance from the collimator, effective count rates decline quite rapidly, and laminal tissue volume increases exponentially. CBF estimates are therefore largely a reflection of

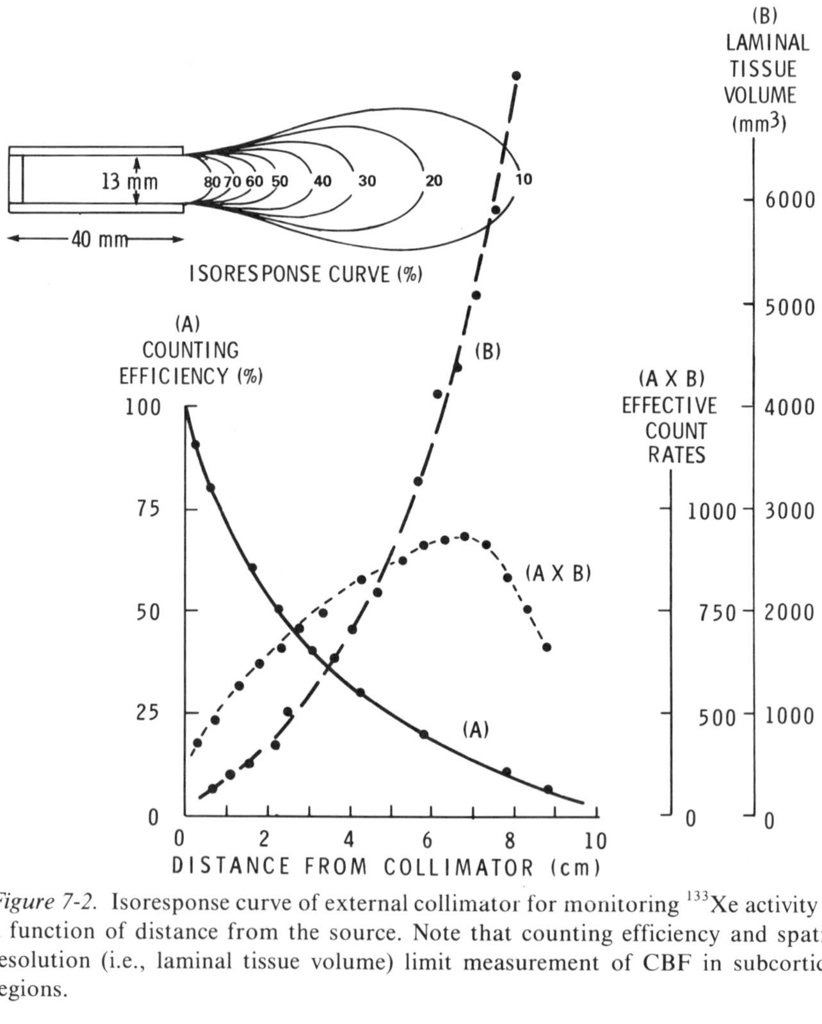

Figure 7-2. Isoresponse curve of external collimator for monitoring ^{133}Xe activity as a function of distance from the source. Note that counting efficiency and spatial resolution (i.e., laminal tissue volume) limit measurement of CBF in subcortical regions.

cortical gray-matter flow and white-matter flow (i.e., corona radiata). Subcortical gray-matter estimates are largely masked. If, as Bergman points out, *central* morphology seems to be more vulnerable to the long-term effects of alcohol, the poor spatial resolution inherent in the ^{133}Xe CBF method may be self-limiting, and the data may be intrinsically less applicable to studying the effects of alcohol-induced brain damage.

The Effects of Age and Disease on Cerebral Blood Flow

As with other measurement techniques presented in this volume, the effects of alcohol on hemodynamic patterns must be considered against the backdrop of those factors believed to have pre-eminent effects. In that regard, the effects of age, gender, and cerebrovascular disease on CBF have been fairly well documented. As shown in Figure 7-3, progressive declines in resting grey-matter CBF were observed in 130 healthy volunteers between the ages of 40 and 100 years. As also shown in Figure 7-3, significantly higher CBF values were generally observed in younger women. Theoretically, this CBF advantage occurs in accord with early gender differences in progesterone levels, oxygen-carrying capacity, and blood viscosity factors associated with menstruation. This male–female differential also corresponds well with the morbidity and mortality data on stroke incidence

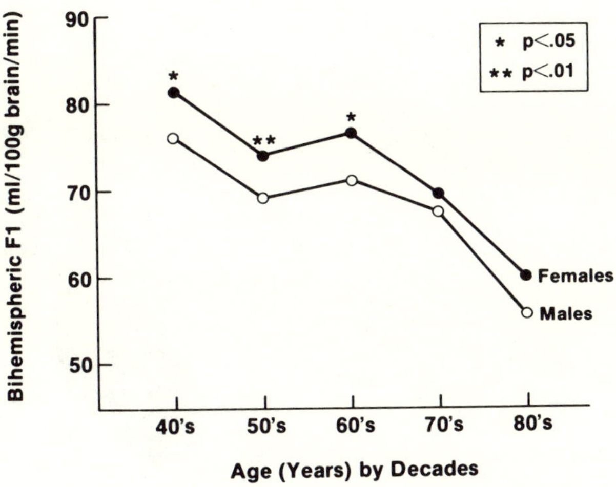

Figure 7-3. Cross-sectional analysis of benign age-related declines in resting, bihemispheric gray-matter CBF (here designated as F1) measured among 130 healthy volunteers. Younger females had significantly higher CBF values than their age-matched counterparts.

(McDowell, Guth, Posner, Ransohoff, & Toole, 1979; Wolf & Kannel, 1982) and has been confirmed by other investigators (Davis *et al.*, 1983). Unfortunately, Risberg and Berglund have failed to qualify their findings in alcoholics by providing control data on nonalcoholics matched for age and (as necessary) gender.

In Figure 7-4, CBF data obtained on a sample of 701 carefully screened patients and volunteers are rendered in a three-dimensional topography map in an attempt to portray the joint effects of age and progressive cerebrovascular disease. Subjects ranged in age from 40 to over 80 years and were subdivided into categories based on a "degree of disease" gradient; these groups ranged from healthy volunteers to patients with multi-infarct dementia. A small group of patients with senile dementia of the Alzheimer's type (SDAT) was included for comparison.

Examination of the results depicted in Figure 7-4 yields the following conclusions: First, CBF declines as a function of age as well as a function of degree of cerebrovascular disease. Second, reductions in CBF are more readily apparent with progressive cerebrovascular disease than with age. For example, age had little to do with CBF values measured in patients with multi-infarct dementia in this study. Third, the influences of advancing age and of progressive cerebrovascular disease appear to converge in the elderly; intergroup differences between the volunteers and the patients aged 70 and

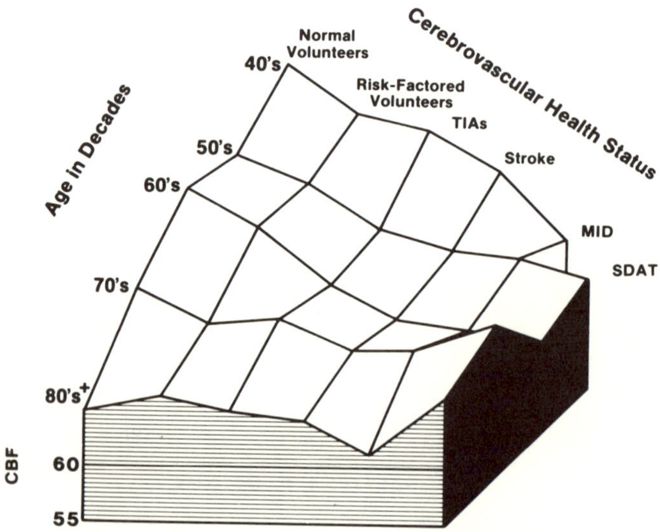

Figure 7-4. Three-dimensional topography map derived from cross-sectional analysis of resting CBF, showing interrelationship among aging, CBF, and cerebrovascular health status (i.e., degree of disease).

above in this study were virtually nonexistent. Given this interaction, the prognostic utility of resting, bihemispheric gray-matter flow values tends to be primarily limited to younger individuals, in whom the ravages of cerebrovascular disease are comparatively more pronounced than the aging effect. This finding is analogous to the problem encountered in using CT data as a basis of differentiating normal aging and dementia, in that ventricular enlargement and sulcal widening among the aged become diagnostically equivocal (Barron *et al.*, 1976; Hubbard & Anderson, 1981a, 1981b; Wilson, Fox, Huckman, Bacon, & Lobick, 1982). In large part, these results based on cross-sectional data have now been confirmed with 5-year longitudinal follow-up data (Shaw *et al.*, 1984).

Alcohol and Cerebral Blood Flow

While Risberg and Berglund indicate that there is no firm evidence of any kind of cerebrovascular disturbance arising in connection with alcohol-related conditions or disorders, this assertion is far from absolute. Negative associations between alcohol intake and coronary heart disease have been found in a number of epidemiological studies; however, increased risk of coronary heart disease has also been noted with alcohol abuse. A possible explanation for the beneficial effect of moderate alcohol intake is the existence of a strong positive association with high-density lipid cholesterol and a negative association with athrogenic low-density lipid cholesterol.

The Honolulu Heart Study and the Hishayama Study in Japan have shown a positive association of hemorrhagic strokes with alcohol intake (Kagen, Popper, & Rhoads, 1980; Marshall, 1971). A positive association between alcohol consumption and stroke mortality in the Honolulu Heart Study was attributed to the coexisting hypertension with which alcohol intake is associated. The Framingham data also suggests an association for men between alcohol intake and stroke incidence in general (Wolf & Kannel, 1982). Thus, equivocal data regarding the effects of alcohol on the vascular system, independent of any direct neuronal effect, are apparent in the literature. In many clinics, alcohol consumption is often considered a non-specific risk factor for cerebrovascular disease, albeit a minor one. Thus, while Risberg and Berglund appropriately point out that the relatively lower CBF values evidenced in alcoholics are primarily thought to be attributable to reduced demand (decreased CMR, secondary to decreased cell populations, secondary to toxicity), some direct effect of alcohol on the vasculature is implicit in the data, if only by virtue of coexisting hypertension.

During my tenure at Baylor, initial interest in the potential effects of alcohol on CBF came about quite serendipitously. In trying to ascertain the relative influence of known cerebrovascular risk factors on CBF (e.g., hypertension, heart disease, diabetes, hyperlipidemia, etc.), we examined

CBF values among a group of otherwise healthy volunteers. The need was also envisioned to control for the possible effects of various lifestyle factors (e.g., alcohol history, smoking, etc.). As a result of that analysis, it soon became apparent that alcohol exerted an influence on CBF, independent of other known risk factors (Rogers *et al.*, 1983). As shown in Figure 7-5, there was a small but significant negative correlation between the amount of alcohol consumed and resting level of CBF in otherwise healthy volunteers. Furthermore, the relative effect of alcohol appeared to be more pronounced in volunteers with one or more "other" risk factors for cerebrovascular disease; this was suggestive of an additive effect for alcohol. The small group of patients with alcoholic dementia depicted in Figure 7-5 was included for comparison only and was not used in deriving the statistical results. By virtue of these findings, it seems apparent that social, nonalcoholic patterns of drinking are clearly related to decreases in average hemispheric CBF. Whether this effect primarily represents a vascular or an abiotrophic process is unclear, but the net effect for social consumption of alcohol is nonetheless evident.

From all of the foregoing, a few assumptions appear to be in order if any meaningful relationship between CBF and alcoholism is to be extracted from the current database. First and foremost, we must necessarily assume that chronic alcoholism does not significantly impair the mechanism that couples CBF and CMR, if we are to use CBF data to indirectly address

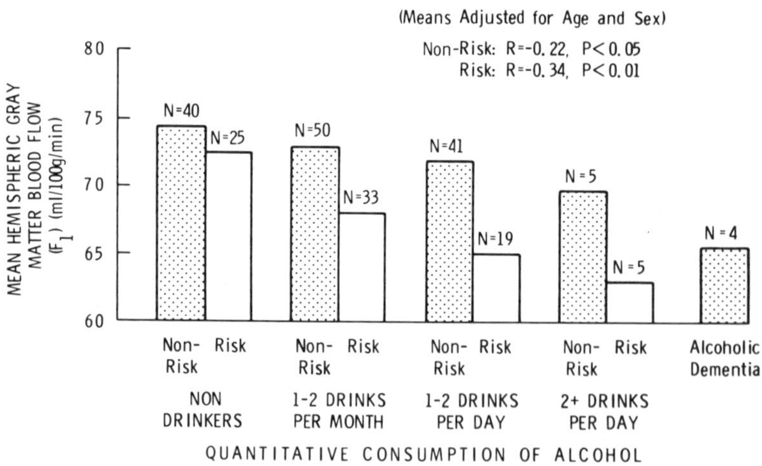

Figure 7-5. Histographic representation of the relationship between resting CBF in healthy volunteers and volunteers with known risk factors for stroke as a function of average amount of alcohol consumed on a social basis. Note that alcohol consumption appears to have had an independent effect, as well as an additive effect in combination with other risk factors.

functional activity of the brain. Second, due to limitations of the method, we must also assume that estimates of cortical flow are inherently valuable in understanding the alcoholic brain, irrespective of Bergman's conclusions on the validity of cortical CT changes. Third, we must also assume that the effects of alcohol on brain vasculature are minimal in comparison to induced abiotrophic changes in brain cell populations. With these "assumptions" in hand, we may now turn to Risberg and Berglund's data.

To judge by the results of early investigations with the nitrous oxide method, the effects of acute alcoholization (in sufficiently large quantities) appear to uncouple CBF and CMR. Thus while Risberg and Berglund report regional CBF trends with intoxication, the validity and utility of these findings as they relate to functional brain activity (i.e., CMR) are questionable. In the absence of metabolic "matching," these results would appear to suggest an initial intravascular effect for alcoholization (i.e., hemodilution, viscosity, etc.), followed by or in conjunction with depressed CMR due to impaired neuronal function. This also seems to be a likely explanation for the large CBF increases evident in Risberg and Berglund's patient during blackout.

If, however, widespread increases in CBF during alcoholization are to be accounted for via a generalized intravascular effect, explanation of a lateralized intravascular response consistent with regional trends would strain the law of parsimony. For the time being, the absence of concomitant metabolic data to accompany the recent CBF studies precludes a more cogent understanding of these relationships.

The effects of long-term alcoholism on CBF appear to yield a different scenario. Although the results are somewhat contradictory, patients with alcoholic dementia and/or the Wernicke–Korsakoff syndrome generally display subnormal CBF and CMR, consistent with advanced neuronal depletion (see also Figure 7-5). In these conditions, CBF and CMR appear to be in sync.

According to Risberg and Berglund, subnormal CBF emerges only after many years of consumption as younger and middle-aged alcoholics display normal perfusion values. This conclusion at first appears to be at odds with the results from our laboratory at Baylor (Figure 7-5). Much of the confusion, however, stems from the broad range of accepted "normal" perfusion rates. In point of fact, the social drinkers in our study maintained CBF values within normal limits (albeit low-normal for some). They simply displayed lower CBF values than their counterparts who drank less or none at all. With continued consumption (and aging), abstinent alcoholics over age 45 were likely to display progressively subnormal CBF.

Compilation of these results appears to support a dose–response model for the effects of alcohol. Healthy individuals who do not drink seem to have the highest CBF values; social drinkers display low-normal values in conjunction with amount consumed; older abstinent alcoholics present with progressively subnormal values; and patients with alcohol dementia have significantly impaired CBF and CMR. Despite this apparent continuum of hemodynamic effects secondary to alcohol, drinking-history variables have typically not been well controlled in these studies. Thus, the possibility of an intrinsic, genetically based threshold model alluded to by Risberg and Berglund in their discussion of an accelerated aging effect (i.e., the premature-aging hypothesis revisited) cannot be ruled out completely. In the absence of appropriate control groups, this issue remains moot and an accelerated aging effect remains unsubstantiated.

Finally, as regards the process of recovery, withdrawal is initially occasioned by a global reduction in CBF; the amount of decrease is qualitatively related to the degree of "clouding of consciousness." This process is short-lived, however, and within a matter of a few days some normalization (or at least a rebound to prewithdrawal levels) occurs for older, more impaired alcoholics. Concomitant decreases in some psychological symptoms are also noted with this recovery process. Nevertheless, the absence of long-term recovery data prohibits an understanding of extent of recovery. While a relative rebound may occur, the overall effect of alcohol on CBF seems to suggest some permanence of reduced flows.

Neuropsychology, Alcoholism, and Cerebral Blood Flow

Derivations of regional CBF flow patterns would seem to offer an excellent opportunity to cross-correlate neuropsychology and CBF changes. There is, however, one minor limitation of the CBF method that limits this marriage: the temporal resolution of the technique. Although the initial 3-minute period of recording is most crucial for determining gray-matter flow, it takes approximately 10–15 minutes of total "washout" time to provide stable estimates of CBF parameters. A lot of regional variation in function can occur during that time frame. Many neuropsychological tests require only seconds of sustained regional activity, while others require tens of minutes with multiple repetitions. Thus, the establishment of relationships between cognitive function and CBF patterns will necessarily be limited, due to a mismatch in methodologies. Nevertheless, some qualitative matching of regional function and CBF is possible, given our knowledge of brain specialization and localization.

Risberg and Berglund whet our appetite for concomitance by anecdotally relating regional CBF increases (consistent with known localization of functions) to the appearance of auditory and visual hallucinations secondary to withdrawal (i.e., delirium tremens). In addition, they report a qualitative correlation between "degree of clouding of consciousness" and the amount of CBF reduction following withdrawal from alcohol. These anecdotes are, however, only first approximations of the relationship between neuropsychology and CBF.

As a secondary approximation, Risberg and Berglund further note the selective vulnerability and responsivity of the right hemisphere to CBF changes during acute alcoholization, withdrawal, and recovery. During acute intoxication, irrespective of a possible uncoupling of CBF and CMR, increases in flow are more evident in the right hemisphere. Furthermore, withdrawal from chronic consumption is occasioned by initially lower right-hemisphere values, particularly right frontal CBF. Finally, right-hemisphere CBF appears to demonstrate a "more pronounced" hemodynamic recovery, consistent with Risberg and Berglund's "law of initial values" concept.

In general, the average CBF value of the left hemisphere is slightly higher than that measured on the right in healthy volunteers (Shaw *et al.*, 1984), such that some of the aforementioned flow asymmetries may be intrinsic to everybody, not just alcoholics. This could be attributable to known morphological asymmetries (Geschwind & Levitsky, 1968). Nevertheless, the implication is well taken, given the typical neuropsychological deficits seen in alcoholics without thiamine deficiency (i.e., visual–spatial deficits usually ascribed to right-hemisphere function). Unfortunately, a more exact relationship between CBF and CMR on the one hand and neuropsychological performance on the other is not possible, given the limited data base. For the time being, anecdotal relationships based on territorial overlap must suffice.

Finally, many of the CBF data gathered to date reflect static flow patterns obtained in states of cognitive inactivity (i.e., steady-state, resting conditions). Unfortunately, the dynamic qualities of a responsive, active brain remain largely untapped, due to this standardization process. While "resting" CBF seems to be negatively influenced by long-term alcohol consumption, impaired CBF patterns in alcoholics might be more easily identified in instances where the brain is challenged with some cognitive task. In fact, Risberg and Berglund point out the diagnostic significance of functional CBF gains in abstinent alcoholics under states of brain work. In their study, large CBF increases evident during an undefined problem-solving task seem to be associated with a better potential for recovery.

This concept of a hemodynamic functional reserve (i.e., the ability to augment CBF and presumably CMR on demand) has previously been examined under such "challenge" conditions as hyperoxia, hypercapnia, and selected cognitive tasks, and has been demonstrated to be negatively influenced by aging, cerebrovascular disease, and dementia (Shaw & Meyer, 1982). Consensus of the data suggests that pathology in general lowers both resting CBF *and* its functional reserve (Rogers, Meyer, Mortel, Mahurin, & Thornby, 1985). Yet, in Risberg and Berglund's results, abstinent alcoholics with initially lower CBF values are more likely to display the larger functional gains during activation (i.e., the law of initial values). Either the lower resting CBF values apparent in abstinent alcoholics only represent somewhat of a suppression effect, or a paradox has emerged regarding the influence of alcohol on hemodynamic reserve. The availability of concomitant CMR data would perhaps shed more light on this subject.

Summing Up

I have begun this discussion by acknowledging that studies of the effects of alcohol on CBF are in their infancy, compared to progress in other fields of study. While information concerning the pre-eminent effects of age and cerebrovascular disease on demodynamic function has been well developed, these factors have yet to be successfully incorporated into the studying of the effects of alcoholism on CBF. Experimental methods for teasing apart the intricacies of cause and effect have improved (e.g., knowing which extraneous variables to control), as has the ability to select an appropriate control group to avoid subliminal or subclinical effects associated with social drinking.

As the methods for measuring CBF have radically changed over the past three decades, so too has our understanding of what constitutes "normal" hemodynamics. With this retooling process, we have abandoned the invasive methods in favor of the atraumatic techniques. But we have consequently lost the ability to simultaneously measure CMR, thereby limiting our ability to address brain function, due to the possibility of an uncoupling of CBF and CMR. Current CBF methods are also inherently limited by problems of spatial and temporal resolution. Nevertheless, the data presented by Risberg and Berglund are not without merit; they are simply limited in interpretability.

Due to the possibility of intravascular effects associated with alcohol intoxication and "known" uncoupling, the CBF data on acute alcoholization are moot and of only passing interest. Nevertheless, the long-term effects of chronic alcohol consumption appear consistent across many research laboratories; resting levels of CBF appear to decline with continued consumption in a dose–response fashion, from social drinking to alcoholic dementia. The known toxicity of alcohol on CNS tissue appears to accelerate cell loss, which in turn limits CMR, thereby giving rise to accelerated reductions in CBF. Whether or not an inherent, genetically determined threshold exists, these changes are clearly accelerated beyond what is expected through normal abiotrophy.

Initial recovery of CBF following abstinence is apparent but seems limited by cumulative effects (i.e., damage). This rebound is probably attributable to release from a suppressive effect of alcohol on brain tissue, rather than to any real recovery of already impaired tissue. The absence of long-term follow-up data, however, prevents any conclusions as to the full extent of the recovery process.

Neuropsychologically, anecdotal relationships abound, and many of the regional CBF permutations appear to overlap theoretically with areas that are presumed to be involved by alcoholism, based upon neuropsychological profiles. It is, however, doubtful that a resting CBF pattern will be defined for those who may have a genetic predisposition for alcoholism, due to the inherent variability in hemodynamics secondary to problems in spatial resolution. If the problem of the temporal resolution of CBF measurement can be successfully circumvented, activation studies may eventually help by augmenting the "signal-to-noise" ratio inherent in hemodynamics.

Although there are a number of advantages to the current CBF methodology as compared to previous techniques, several significant limitations remain. New technologies that circumvent these problems have recently been developed and will soon be applied to the many remaining questions. Noninvasive, positron-emitting analogues of the autoradiographic deoxyglucose method (i.e., PET scanning) have recently been developed and will permit more direct investigation of CMR in the conscious human brain. Although PET scanning will, in future, provide greater insight into the study of brain function (in both health and disease, including alcoholism), the availability and cost of a cyclotron or linear accelerator will be self-limiting. Nuclear magnetic resonance scanning has also come of age. But for now, we must wait until future investigators take up the standard.

Acknowledgments

This work was supported in part by the Veterans Administration, Washington, D.C., and by U.S. Public Health Service Grant No. NS09287.

References

Barron, S. A., Jacobs, L., & Kinkel, W. R. (1976). Changes in size of normal lateral ventricles during aging determined by computerized tomography. *Neurology, 26*, 1011–1013.

Birren, J. E. (1959). Principles of research on aging. In J. E. Birren (Ed.), *Handbook of aging and the individual* (pp. 545–551). Chicago: University of Chicago Press.

Black, C. (1981). *It will never happen to me.* Denver, CO: MCA.

Blauenstein, U. W., Halsey, H. J., Wilson, E. M., Willis, E. L., & Risberg, J. (1975). The ^{133}Xe inhalation method: Analysis of reproducibility. In A. M. Harper, W. B. Jennett, J. D. Miller, & R. O. Rowan (Eds.), *Blood flow and metabolism in the brain* (pp. 819–821). New York: Churchill Livingstone.

Blusewicz, M. J., Schenkenberg, T., Dustman, R. E., & Beck, E. C. (1977). WAIS performance in young normal, young alcoholic, and elder normal groups: An evaluation of organicity and mental aging indices. *Journal of Clinical Psychology, 33*, 1149–1153.

Brody, H. (1978). Cell counts in cerebral cortex and brainstem. In R. Katzman, R. D. Terry, &

K. L. Bick (Eds.), *Aging: Vol. 7. Alzheimer's disease: Senile dementia and related disorders* (pp. 345–350). New York: Raven Press.

Conel, J. L. R. (1963). *The postnatal development of the human cerebral cortex* (Vol. 7). Cambridge, MA: Harvard University Press.

Davis, S. M., Ackerman, R. H., Correia, J. A., Alpert, N. M., Chang, J., Buonanno, F., Kelley, R. E., Rosner, B., & Taveras, J. M. (1983). Cerebral blood flow and cerebrovascular CO^2 reactivity in stroke-age normal controls. *Neurology, 33*, 391–399.

Freund, G. (1973). Chronic central nervous system toxicity of alcohol. *Annual Review of Pharmacology, 13*, 217–277.

Geschwind, N., & Levitsky, W. (1968). Human brain: Left–right asymmetries in temporal speech region. *Science, 161*, 186–189.

Gyldensted, C. (1977). Measurements of normal ventricular system and hemispheric sulci of 100 adults with computed tomography. *Neuroradiology, 14*, 183–192.

Henderson, G., Tomlinson, B. E., & Gibson, P. H. (1980). Cell counts in human cerebral cortex in normal adults throughout life using an image analyzing computer. *Journal of Neurological Sciences, 46*, 113–136.

Hochla, N. A. N., & Parsons, O. A. (1982). Premature aging in female alcoholics: A neuropsychological study. *Journal of Nervous and Mental Disease, 170*, 241–245.

Hubbard, B. M., & Anderson, J. M. (1981a). Age, senile dementia and ventricular enlargement. *Journal of Neurology, Neurosurgery and Psychiatry, 44*, 631–635.

Hubbard, B. M., & Anderson, J. M. (1981b). A quantitative study of cerebral atrophy in old age and senile dementia. *Journal of Neurological Sciences, 50*, 135–145.

Kagan, A., Popper, J. S., & Rhoads, G. G. (1980). Factors related to stroke incidence in Hawaii on Japanese men: The Honolulu Heart Study. *Stroke, 11*, 14–21.

Kety, S. S., & Schmidt, C. F. (1948). Nitrous oxide method for the quantitative determination of cerebral blood flow in man: Theory, procedure and normal values. *Journal of Clinical Investigation, 27*, 476.

Lassen, N. A. (1966). The luxury–perfusion syndrome and its possible relation to acute metabolic acidosis localized within the brain. *Lancet, ii*, 1113–1115.

Maccoby, E. E., & Jacklin, C. (1974). *The psychology of sex differences*. Stanford, CA: Stanford University Press.

MacVane, J., Butters, N., Montgomery, K., & Farber, J. (1982). Cognitive functioning in men social drinkers: A replication study. *Journal of Studies on Alcohol, 43*, 81–95.

Mallet, B. L., & Veall, N. (1963). Investigation of cerebral blood flow determination by 133 Xe inhalation and external recording. *Lancet, i*, 1080–1082.

Marshall, J. (1971). Familial incidence of cerebrovascular disease. *Journal of Medical Genetics, 8*, 84–89.

McDowell, F., Guth, L., Posner, J. B., Ransohoff, J., & Toole, J. F. (Eds.). (1979). *Report of the Panel on Stroke, Trauma, Regeneration and Neoplasm* (DHEW Publ. No. NIH 79-1915) (pp. 3–58). Washington, DC: U.S. Government Printing Office.

McHenry, L. C., Merory, J., & Bass, E. (1978). Xenon-133 inhalation method for regional cerebral blood flow measurements: Normal values and test–retest results. *Stroke, 9*, 195–205.

Meyer, J. S., Ishihara, N., & Deshmukh, V. D. (1978). An improved method for non-invasive measurement of regional cerebral blood flow by 133 Xe inhalation. *Stroke, 9*, 195–210.

Meyer, J. S., & Shaw, T. G. (1984). Cerebral blood flow and aging. In M. L. Albert (Ed.), *Clinical neurology of aging* (pp. 178–196). New York: Oxford University Press.

Obrist, W. D., Langfitt, T. W., Jaggi, J. L., Cruz, J., & Gennarelli, T. A. (1984). Cerebral blood flow and metabolism in comatose patients with acute head injury. *Journal of Neurosurgery, 61*, 241–253.

Obrist, W. D., Thompson, H. K., Jr., & Wang, H. S. (1975). Regional cerebral blood flow estimated by 133 Xe inhalation. *Stroke, 6*, 245–256.

Parker, E. S., & Noble, E. P. (1977). Alcohol consumption and cognitive functioning in social drinkers. *Journal of Studies on Alcohol, 38*, 1224–1232.

Portnoi, V. (1980). Aging, natural death, and the compression of morbidity. *New England Journal of Medicine, 303*, 1369.

Quigley, L. F. (1959). *The blind men and the elephant.* New York: Scribner's.

Reivich, M., Obrist, W. D., Slater, R., Greenberg, J., & Goldberg, H. I. (1975). A comparison of the Xe 133 intracarotid injection and inhalation techniques for measuring regional cerebral blood flow. In A. M. Harper, W. B. Jennett, J. D. Miller, & R. O. Rowan (Eds.), *Blood flow and metabolism in the brain* (pp. 8.3–8.6). New York: Churchill Livingstone.

Rogers, R. L., Meyer, J. S., Mortel, K. F., Mahurin, R. K., & Thornby, J. (1985). Age-related reductions in cerebral vasomotor reactivity and the law of initial values: A 4-year prospective longitudinal study. *Journal of Cerebral Blood Flow and Metabolism, 5*, 79–85.

Rogers, R. L., Meyer, J. S., Shaw, T. G., & Mortel, K. F. (1983). Reductions in regional cerebral blood flow associated with chronic consumption of alcohol. *Journal of the American Geriatrics Society, 31*, 540–543.

Schaie, K. W. (1968). Age changes and age differences. In B. L. Neugarten (Ed.), *Middle age and aging* (pp. 558–562). Chicago: University of Chicago Press.

Scheibel, M. D., & Scheibel, A. B. (1975). Structural changes in the aging brain. In H. Brody, D. Harmann, & J. M. Ordy (Eds.), *Clinical morphological and neurochemical aspects of the aging nervous system* (pp. 11–37). New York: Raven Press.

Shaw, T. G., & Meyer, J. S. (1982). Aging and cerebrovascular disease. In J. S. Meyer & T. G. Shaw (Eds.), *Diagnosis and management of stroke and TIA's* (pp. 1–24). Menlo Park, CA: Addison-Wesley.

Shaw, T. G., Mortel, K. F., Meyer, J. S., Rogers, R. L., Hardenberg, J., & Cutaia, M. M. (1984). Cerebral blood flow changes in benign aging and cerebrovascular disease. *Neurology, 34*, 855–862.

Taylor, D. C. (1969). Differential rates of cerebral maturation between hemispheres. *Lancet, ii*, 140–142.

Wilson, R. S., Fox, J. H., Huckman, M. S., Bacon, L. D., & Lobick, J. J. (1982). Computed tomography in dementia. *Neurology, 32*, 1054–1057.

Wolf, P. A., & Kannel, W. A. (1982). Controllable risk factors for stroke: Preventive implications of trends in stroke mortality. In J. S. Meyer & T. G. Shaw (Eds.), *Diagnosis and management of stroke and TIA's* (pp. 25–61). Menlo Park, CA: Addison-Wesley.

Yamagura, H., Ito, M., Kubota, K., & Matsuzawa, T. (1980). Brain atrophy during aging: A quantitative study with computed tomography. *Journal of Gerontology, 35*, 492–498.

SECTION TWO

NEUROPSYCHOLOGICAL CONSEQUENCES OF ALCOHOL ABUSE

8

Neuropsychological Consequences of Alcohol Abuse: Many Questions—Some Answers

OSCAR A. PARSONS

Introduction

After a decade or more of accelerated research on the neuropsychological consequences of alcohol abuse, it is time to take stock. We should assess what has been established, consider what is currently being fleshed out, and identify those areas that might be most fruitfully explored in the future. With these objectives in mind, I have formulated 10 questions, the answers to which are critical to an understanding of this important health problem area:

1. What are the neuropsychological deficits that accompany alcohol abuse?
2. What is the relationship among alcohol intake, duration of alcoholism, and neuropsychological deficits?
3. Do alcoholics perceive impairment in their everyday cognitive and perceptual–motor functioning?
4. Are there differences in degree of impairment manifested by subgroups of alcoholics?
5. What is the likelihood that at least some of the deficits in alcoholics may be present premorbidly?
6. Which neuropsychological models best account for the findings?
7. What is the posttreatment course of recovery of cognitive and perceptual–motor functions for treated alcoholics?
8. Do neuropsychological tests predict treatment benefits, recidivism, and recovery?

Oscar A. Parsons. Oklahoma Center for Alcohol and Drug-Related Studies, Department of Psychiatry and Behavioral Sciences, University of Oklahoma Health Sciences Center, Oklahoma City, Oklahoma.

9. If sober alcoholics resume drinking, does it affect their neuropsychological test performance and life adaptation?
10. Will cognitive retraining speed the course of recovery?

The first six of these questions are considered in this chapter; the remaining four questions are dealt with in Chapter 14.

Neuropsychological Deficits Accompanying Alcohol Abuse

Starting with the review by Kleinknecht and Goldstein (1972), there has been a recognition that alcoholics perform more poorly than nonalcoholics on a variety of neuropsychological tests. Kleinknecht and Goldstein (1972) concluded that alcoholics manifested deficits in abstraction, problem solving, and tasks involving speed and complex perceptual–motor performance, but "performed at or above average standard intelligence tests with the exception of some Wechsler Performance Subtests" (p. 1008). These conclusions have been largely reaffirmed by subsequent reviewers (Chelune & Parker, 1981; Goldstein, 1976; Goodwin & Hill, 1975; Miller & Saucedo, 1983; Parsons & Leber, 1981, 1982; Tarter & Ryan, 1983). In our recent reviews of the area (Parsons & Leber, 1981, 1982), we concluded that there exists firm evidence that alcoholics perform more poorly than appropriate nonalcoholic controls in problem solving, nonverbal abstracting, and perceptual–spatial motor performance. There is also evidence that memory and new learning skills are depressed. Finally, while tests of general verbal intelligence such as the Wechsler Adult Intelligence Scale (WAIS) often show no impairment, other verbal–linguistic skills of a more demanding nature may be impaired in alcoholics (Parsons & Leber, 1981; Ryan & Butters, 1980).

It is important to note that the neuropsychological deficits described above are typically found in samples of alcoholics that fall into the "intermediate stage of alcoholism." As described by Smith (1977), the intermediate-stage alcoholic is one who may manifest cognitive and behavioral inefficiencies, but does not have a clinically diagnosable organic brain syndrome. However, it is clear that the pattern of deficits found in the neuropsychological studies of such intermediate-stage alcoholics resemble those found in patients with known brain damage who exhibit mild to moderate cognitive and perceptual–motor impairment. Heaton and Pendleton (1981) have pointed out the implications of such impairment for lessened effective functioning in everyday life. The presence of similar deficits in alcoholics suggests that the treatment plan for them should employ some of the approaches that have been found useful with other brain-damaged patients (Caster, 1977).

Quantity and Frequency of Alcohol Intake, Duration of Alcoholism, and Neuropsychological Deficits

While the deficits described above are sound and repeatable in laboratories throughout the world, and appear to hold for both male and female alcoholics (Parsons & Leber, 1981), a number of problems remain in interpreting the results. One vexing problem is that measures of alcohol intake such as duration, quantity, and frequency of drinking are inconsistently related to neuropsychological impairment. Given the plausible assumption by most clinicians and experimenters that the deficits in cognitive performances in alcoholics are a consequence of alcohol abuse, the diverse and scattered findings are a challenge.

Let us consider several examples from our laboratories. In our initial studies of alcoholics in a Veterans Administration (VA) treatment program, we found that duration of alcoholism (years of alcohol abuse) was significantly and inversely correlated with quality of performance on the Halstead Category Test (Jones & Parsons, 1971) and with performance on the Wisconsin Card Sorting Test (Tarter & Parsons, 1971). Several years later, using alcoholics from the same VA treatment program, we found no significant effects of duration of alcohol abuse upon Wisconsin Card Sorting Test performance (Klisz & Parsons, 1979) or upon performances on a concept-identification problem (Klisz & Parsons, 1977). In another study, involving female alcoholics, we found highly significant differences between alcoholics and nonalcoholic controls on neuropsychological tests drawn largely from the Halstead–Reitan Battery, but performance was uncorrelated with duration (Fabian, Parsons, & Silberstein, 1981). It would appear that duration of alcoholism has an unpredictable relationship with neuropsychological test performance.

Given that duration estimates involve recall over a number of years, perhaps recent quantity–frequency measures would be more appropriate variables to relate to test performance. If these are recalled for the last 6 months or 1 year before the detoxified alcoholic is tested, such information is likely to be more accurate. Indeed, Eckardt, Parker, Noble, Fieldman, and Gottschalk (1978), using multiple-regression techniques, demonstrated that various measures of recent drinking behavior correlated significantly with performance on cognitive and perceptual–motor tests once age and education were partialed out. Different drinking measures were correlated with different cognitive and perceptual–motor performances, suggesting that the relationship may be quite complex. Unfortunately, Eckardt *et al.*'s study, comprehensive as it is, has several problems that limit interpretation. First, their alcoholics were tested after a mean abstinence of 5 days (none after more than 7 days). Many alcoholics may be suffering from the withdrawal syndrome, at least in its subclinical form, at that time. Second, they correlated numerous test variables with many different drinking-practice measures, including interaction terms among these variables; such procedures demand replication before their results can be generalized. Finally, they did not consider the possible complicating role of affective disturbances such as anxiety and depression, in their results.

We recently conducted a study of drinking practices and neuropsychological deficits in 1-month-sober alcoholics that attempts to correct for some of the limitations noted above (Schaeffer & Parsons, 1985). Sixty male middle-aged alcoholics from our VA medical center treatment program had undergone an extensive interview concerning their drinking practices. We selected the following drinking variables (measured over the last 6 months before treatment) to relate to performance on neuropsychological tests: typical quantity of alcohol consumed per occasion (TQ); frequency of typical drinking (TF); typical quantity × frequency (TQF); maximal quantity drunk per occasion (MQ); the frequency of maximal amount drunk (MF); maximal quantity × frequency (MQF); and chronicity (duration) of alcoholism. These variables were then correlated with the following clusters of neuropsychological variables: Verbal, Learning/Memory, Abstracting/Problem Solving, Perceptual–Motor, and General Impairment (see Table 8-8, below, for complete listing). None of the typical quantity–frequency measures correlated significantly with the neuropsychological clusters. However, MF, MQ, and MQF all correlated significantly with performance on most of the clusters and tests.

Using the best predictive measure of drinking practices (MQF), together with age, education, state anxiety (Spielberger, Gorsuch, & Lushene, 1970), depression (Beck, 1967) and chronicity, we then performed stepwise multiple-regression analyses of the relationship of these variables to the neuropsychological test clusters. The results are presented in Table 8-1. With the exception of the Perceptual–Motor cluster, MQF added significantly to the variance in each of the clusters. Chronicity or duration of alcoholism entered significantly only on one cluster (Perceptual–Motor). Depression and anxiety measures were significantly higher in alcoholics than controls (but mean scores were not in a clinically significant range for either variable). Neither depression nor anxiety entered significantly into any of the predictive equations. By way of contrast, the same analyses were performed for age- and education-equated social drinkers who served as controls ($n = 43$). Neither MQF nor TQF predicted performance, but anxiety was significant and was the highest predictor on every cluster except Verbal (Table 8-1).

These results have some important implications. First, they indicate rather clearly that it is the maximal quantity and the frequency of drinking that quantity that relate to neuropsychological test performance in alcoholics. The typical quantity–frequency measures did not predict performance, despite being correlated +.68 ($p < .001$) with MQF. This suggests that it is

Table 8-1. Significant Predictors of Neuropsychological Performance by Stepwise Multiple-Regression Analysis

	Significant predictors (cumulative R^2)[a]	
Cluster	Alcoholics ($n = 60$)	Social drinkers ($n = 43$)
Verbal	Education (.15), MQF (.23)	Education (.26)
Learning/Memory	MQF (.13), education (.23), age (.32)	Anxiety (.13), education (.20), age (.32)
Abstracting/Problem Solving	Education (.18), MQF (.26), age (.33)	Anxiety (.16), years drinking (.23), education (.33)
Perceptual–Motor	Age (.21), education (.35), chronicity (.40)	Anxiety (.27), education (.38), age (.44)
General Impairment	Education (.14), age (.27), MQF (.36)	Anxiety (.26), age (.33), education (.42)

[a]All R^2 values are significant at $p < .05$ or better; all variables that added a significant increment to the R^2 are presented.

the toxic effect of frequent high levels of alcohol intake that may result in neuropsychological deficits. If these results are replicated in other alcoholic samples, the assumption that excessive alcohol ingestion leads to impairment in neuropsychological function has a firmer base. The second implication of the results is that depression and anxiety (i.e., psychological distress) have little or no apparent effect upon the neuropsychological functioning of alcoholics. However, in view of the relationship between anxiety and performance in the controls, the lack of such relationships in the alcoholics may have been due to the overriding effect of the alcohol condition. To put it somewhat differently, alcoholism may either obscure or alter the typical relationship between anxiety and performance found in nonalcoholics.

Alcoholics' Perceived Impairment

Do alcoholics perceive impairment in their cognitive and perceptual–motor functions? Or does the "denial" that characterizes many alcoholics in regard to their pretreatment problems with alcohol abuse extend to the appraisal of its impact on their mental functioning? While there is anecdotal evidence suggesting that alcoholics presenting for treatment do perceive themselves as having problems with certain areas of cognitive functioning, there is no published report of systematic research that directly addresses this issue, although the question could have profound implications for treatment and recovery.

In order to study this problem, we (Shelton & Parsons, in press) selected a questionnaire, the Patient's Assessment of Own Functioning Inventory (PAOFI) developed by Heaton and Pendleton (1981). This questionnaire was constructed to assess the perceptions of respondents with suspected or diagnosed brain dysfunctions as to their effectiveness in cognitive, intellectual, and psychomotor functioning in their everyday lives. The questionnaire has four subscales: Memory (e.g., "How often do you lose things or have trouble remembering where they are?"), Language and Communication (e.g., "How often do you have difficulties in understanding what is said to you?"), Perceptual–Motor (e.g., "How often do you have difficulties in performing tasks with your hands?"), and Higher Cognitive Functions (e.g., "How often do you have more difficulty now than you used to in solving problems that come up around the house?"). A fifth score representing total impairment is also obtained. As might be expected, Heaton and Pendleton (1981) found that brain-damaged patients had much higher scores (i.e., more self-assessed impairment) than non-brain-damaged patients. Given the evidence from neuropsychological tests for alcoholics' impairment on the dimensions covered by the PAOFI, it seemed to be a most appropriate instrument for our purposes.

We administered the PAOFI to a pilot group of 54 male adult middle-aged alcoholics in our VA medical center treatment unit. The alcoholics reported intermittent difficulties on all four of the PAOFI scales. On the basis of these data, we then conducted a study in which PAOFI scores for 60 different alcoholics (days abstinent, $M = 31$) from the same treatment unit were compared with 60 nonalcoholic community controls, who were matched for age, education, and Shipley Vocabulary Age. These data and the pilot data are presented in Table 8-2. The pilot alcoholics and experi-

Table 8-2. Means and Standard Deviations on Relevant Variables for Pilot Alcoholics ($n = 54$), Experimental Alcoholics ($n = 60$), and Controls ($n = 60$)

Variable	Pilot alcoholics	Experimental alcoholics	Controls
PAOFI			
Memory	18.0 ± 10.0	17.5 ± 8.7	11.3 ± 5.5
Language and Communication	15.2 ± 8.0	12.6 ± 7.1	8.8 ± 4.9
Perceptual–Motor	6.1 ± 1.8	4.9 ± 4.0	2.4 ± 2.7
Cognitive	15.3 ± 9.0	11.7 ± 7.8	4.5 ± 4.8
Total	55.0 ± 28.8	46.6 ± 23.8	27.1 ± 14.4
BDI	—	9.9 ± 5.9	3.0 ± 3.1
AI	—	53.9 ± 10.3	43.6 ± 7.2
Chronicity	—	11.3 ± 7.4	—
QFI	—	10.0 ± 5.9	0.2 ± 0.3

Note. Experimental alcoholics did not differ from pilot alcoholics on any measure; they differed from controls on all PAOFI subscales (t tests) at $p < .001$.

mental alcoholics did not differ in their mean scores on any PAOFI subscale; the experimental alcoholics differed highly significantly from the nonalcoholic controls on all subscales ($p < .001$). Control subjects rated themselves as experiencing lessened effectiveness "very infrequently" on Memory and on Language and Communication items, and "almost never" on Perceptual–Motor and Higher Cognitive Functions items. Alcoholics generally claimed lessened effectiveness "once in a while" for all items except those on the Perceptual–Motor subscale, which they rated as "very infrequently."

In order to determine whether claims of lessened effectiveness were related to drinking variables and measures of affective distress, we conducted a series of stepwise multiple-regression analyses on the 60 experimental alcoholics and 60 controls. The predictor variables were the Quantity Frequency Index (QFI; Cahalan, Cissin, & Crossley, 1969), based on drinking behavior over the last 6 months; the duration of alcohol abuse, or chronicity; the Beck Depression Inventory (BDI; Beck, 1967) and the Spielberger State Anxiety Inventory (AI; Spielberger *et al.*, 1970).

In Table 8-3, it is evident for the alcoholics, that the higher the QFI, BDI, and AI scores, the more impairment was claimed. The QFI was either the first predictor variable or the second, in terms of amount of variance accounted for on all PAOFI subscales. With one exception, the BDI was of similar importance. Interestingly, chronicity did not add significantly to the predictive variance on any scale. In the controls, on the other hand, the BDI accounted for a significant amount of the variance (although at a much lower level than in the alcoholics). The AI appeared to play a significant role on the Higher Cognitive Functions subscale in both groups, but had less of an effect than the BDI and, in the alcoholics, the QFI.

Table 8-3. Order and R^2 Values for Forward Stepwise Multiple-Regression Loadings of PAOFI Subscales on QFI, Chronicity, BDI, and AI Scores

PAOFI Memory	PAOFI Language and Communication	PAOFI Perceptual–Motor	PAOFI Cognitive	PAOFI total
		Alcoholics		
BDI .27	QFI .15	QFI .24	BDI .38	BDI .30
QFI .38	AI .28	BDI .25	QFI .50	QFI .46
			AI .54	
		Controls		
BDI .10	BDI .06	BDI .06	AI .15	BDI .14
			BDI .20	

Note. All correlations listed contributed significantly to the variance.

What do we conclude from these data? These alcoholics certainly saw themselves as less effective in their cognitive and perceptual–motor functioning than did the nonalcoholics. Furthermore, while degree of depression and anxiety contributed significantly to the reported impairment, drinking behavior as measured by the QFI accounted for a significant amount of the variance, independent of the measures of affective distress. Zero-order correlations between QFI and the subscales indicated correlations between +.39 and +.52: the higher the QFI, the greater the reported impairment. In summary, alcoholics' claimed impairment in cognitive and perceptual–motor functioning in everyday life is positively related to reported alcohol intake. However, unlike the lack of relationship between measures of affective distress and neuropsychological test performance in alcoholics reported in the previous section, depression and anxiety play a significant role in subjective complaints and should be considered in making clinical inferences as to probable behavioral deficits.

In our next study, we (Parsons, Tassey, & Schaeffer, 1985) used a somewhat different way of approaching alcoholics' perceived impairment. The Neuropsychological Impairment Scale (NIS) was developed by O'Donnell and Reynolds (1983) "to identify neuropsychological symptoms and deficiency" (p. 549). It is a 50-item screening instrument that has had extensive normative development (O'Donnell & Reynolds, 1983; O'Donnell, DeSoto, & Reynolds, 1984; O'Donnell, Reynolds, & DeSoto, 1984). The NIS has been validated with a group of patients with neurological disorders and test–retest reliability is approximately .84 to .86. There are eight subscales, described in Table 8-4. In these scales, the Pathognomic Scale (PAT) is of particular interest, as it is comprised of those items that best discriminate neurological from non-neurological populations. On the other hand, the Global Measure of Impairment (GMI) and the Symptom Intensity Measure (SIM) correlate more consistently with the Halstead–Reitan Battery (measures such as the Impairment Index, Category Test, Part B of the

Table 8-4. The Neuropsychological Impairment Scale (NIS) Scores

1. Global Measure of Impairment (GMI): Total raw score sum of 45 items (LIE scale not included).
2. Total Items Checked (TIC): Total number of the 45 items with an intensity score of 0.
3. Symptom Intensity Measure (SIM): The average intensity rating (4-point scale).
4. LIE Scale (LIE): Measures test-taking attitude.
5. General Scale (GEN): Measures mental efficiency, alertness, endurance, etc.
6. Pathognomic Scale (PAT): Items that best discriminate brain-damaged from non-brain-damaged persons.
7. The Learning–Verbal Scale (L-V): Reflects problems with verbal communication and learning.
8. Frustration Scale (FRU): Reflects affective and motivational problems.

Note. The NIS is a screening test that consists of a total of 50 items, each rated by the respondent on a scale of 0 ("not at all present") to 3 ("very much so") (O'Donnell & Reynolds, 1983).

Trail Making Test, and Tactual Performance Test Localization) than other NIS subscales (O'Donnell & Reynolds, 1983).

Our first analyses compared 99 alcoholics from our VA medical center treatment program to the normative samples. In Figure 8-1, two curves of *T* scores are presented. The first is based on the normative data for subjects in the same age and education range as our alcoholics, compared to the total normative sample. The latter, by definition, has a mean *T* score of 50 on each subscale. The second curve is for our alcoholics compared to the total normative sample. Tests of significance (*t* tests) between the two groups' means on each of the NIS subscales resulted in quite significant differences ($p < .001$) on seven of the eight subscales, with the alcoholics reporting more symptomatic behaviors. Thus, alcoholics claimed far more symptoms or behaviors characteristic of the neurologically impaired than did the controls.

Again, the question arises: To what extent are the symptoms related to depression and anxiety as opposed to alcohol-drinking behavior? We entered five predictor variables into our multiple regression analyses: age, chronicity, AI, BDI, and average ethanol consumed daily over the last 6 months (ETOH). The BDI contributed significantly to the variance on six of the eight scales; the AI contributed significantly on five. Age effects were significant on only one scale (the General Scale, or GEN). Chronicity was a significant predictor in two analyses: GMI and PAT; ETOH was a significant predictor in one analysis, the SIM score. Thus the self-reported GMI

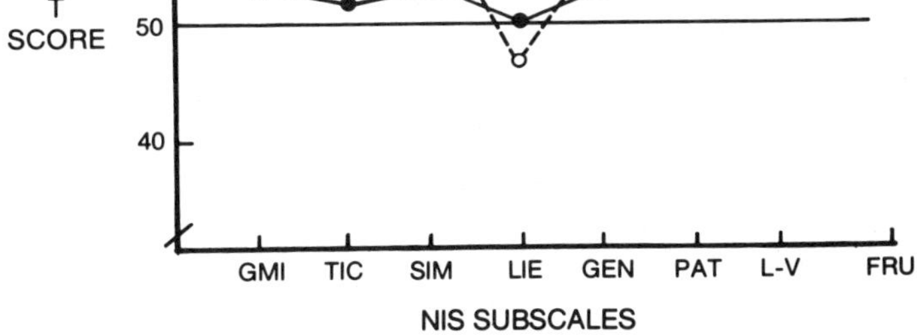

Figure 8-1. Alcoholics compared to same-age normative sample on the Neuropsychological Impairment Scale (NIS). Alcoholics reported significantly more impairment on all NIS subscales except LIE.

and the PAT subscale items were related to the duration of alcohol abuse even after the effects of age, anxiety, and depression were removed. In contrast, ETOH (based on drinking behavior of the last 6 months of drinking) predicted symptom intensity (i.e., the degree to which the alcoholic experienced the symptoms or behaviors indicative of impairment).

In summary, sober alcoholics do claim impairment of behaviors that are important to adapting to everyday life demands. The perceived lessened effectiveness in memory, cognitive/intellectual, language and communication, and perceptual–motor behavior is related to drinking behavior; the higher the amount of alcohol consumed, the greater the perceived impairment. Furthermore, alcoholics report symptoms that are similar to those reported by patients with neurological disorders; the more chronic the abuse, the greater the similarity to neurological patients. The higher the alcohol consumption in the 6 months preceding treatment, the more intensely these symptoms are experienced by the alcoholics. However, our data also suggest a caution to clinicians and researchers. The reported impairments in both studies were associated with the affective variables of depression and anxiety. In most analyses, these variables accounted for more variance than the drinking-behavior variables. The fact that the BDI and, to some extent, the AI were predictive of PAOFI reports of lessened effectiveness in the controls suggests that there is an independent contribution, regardless of drinking behavior, of such variables to claimed impairment. As suggested earlier, the role of these affective reactions should be considered when making judgments about impairment in alcoholics' functioning based on their self-reports.

Obviously, the next step in this research would be to compare alcoholics' perceived impairment in everyday-life adaptation to ratings of their actual lessened effectiveness by significant others who know the patients well enough to rate them. Furthermore, claimed neurological impairment on the NIS could be related to performance on neuropsychological tests (currently under way in our laboratory) and to a thorough neurological examination, including "soft signs."

Differences in Impairment in Subgroups of Alcoholics

Alcoholics are diverse with respect to many parameters; age, sex, socioeconomic level, race, culture, severity, presence of other disorders, and so forth. Does the neuropsychological impairment evidenced by alcoholics vary as a function of these variables? With respect to age, there certainly seems to be evidence that the effects of alcohol abuse are greater in older than in younger alcoholics (Klisz & Parsons, 1977; Ryan & Butters, 1980). As regards sex, we have reported a large-scale study in which female alcoholics exhibited essentially the same type of deficits as reported for male alcoholics (Fabian *et al.*, 1981). Other variables, such as socioeconomic level, race, and culture, have been shown to be related to drinking practices and alcohol abuse (Vaillant, 1983), but have not been investigated systematically as regards differences in neuropsychological impairment. Similarly, the presence of other psychiatric syndromes in alcoholics, such as depression, mania, and antisocial personality, has been shown to affect the onset course and outcome of treatment (Penick *et al.*, 1985); however, again, these multidiagnosed alcoholics have not been investigated as to differential neuropsychological impairment.

The importance of investigating subtypes of alcoholics is emphasized by our studies of "Primary" and "Secondary" alcoholics. For these investigations, we followed the definition of alcoholism given in the Primary–Secondary Scale used by Tarter, McBride, Buopane, and Schneider (1977). This scale defines Primary alcoholics as those who cannot identify any precipitating or specific cause for their excessive drinking and have any six of the eight characteristics listed in Item 2 of Table 8-5. The classification appears to be similar to that of the "essential" versus "reactive" dimension proposed by Rudie and McGaughran (1961), but is more behaviorally oriented. Both we (DeObaldia & Parsons, 1983) and Tarter *et al.* (1977) have found that Primaries claim more symptoms of childhood hyperkinesis and/or minimal brain damage (Hk/MBD) than Secondaries. In addition, we (DeObaldia & Parsons, 1983) found that Primaries performed more poorly on the Shipley Abstracting Age and Raven's Progressive Matrices (Form I) than did Secondaries. These results suggested that the Primary–Secondary Scale classification could result in differential neuropsychological impairment. We undertook a much larger study to test this notion (DeObaldia & Parsons, 1984).

Using the Primary–Secondary Scale we classified 28 alcoholics as Primaries and 32 alcoholics as Secondaries. These 60 subjects were then compared with 60 nonalcoholic community controls on a broad battery of neuropsychological tests. These data are presented in Table 8-6. Before the

Table 8-5. Primary–Secondary Scale

1. Absence of stressful life events in the initiation of heavy drinking.
2. Six of the eight following characteristics.
   - 2.1. Withdrawal symptoms in absence of drinking.
   - 2.2. Increased tolerance with alcohol intakes.
   - 2.3. Positive psychic experience with first alcohol drink.
   - 2.4. Positive psychic experience with first alcohol drink after period of abstinence.
   - 2.5. Loss of control after first drink.
   - 2.6. Absence of history of social drinking.
   - 2.7. Excessive drinking prior to age 40.
   - 2.8. Personal and/or interpersonal problems from alcohol prior to age 40.

Note. A positive score on each item is in the Primary direction. Criteria for Primary designation are a positive response to Item 1 *and* six of the eight Item 2 characteristics. Patients not meeting these criteria are called Secondary.

Table 8-6. Comparisons among Primary and Secondary Alcoholics and Nonalcoholic Controls on Relevant Variables

	Controls ($n = 60$)		Secondary alcoholics ($n = 32$)		Primary alcoholics ($n = 28$)		
Test variables	*M*	(*SD*)	*M*	(*SD*)	*M*	(*SD*)	*F*
Age	40.2[a]	(11.45)	40.5[a]	(9.75)	39.2[a]	(11.63)	0.11
Education	12.7[ab]	(1.92)	13.3[a]	(1.90)	11.8[b]	(2.13)	4.38**
Hk/MBD (positive)	9.3[b]	(7.34)	11.8[b]	(6.16)	17.9[a]	(6.67)	14.81***
Hk/MBD (not sure)	2.2[a]	(3.69)	2.4[a]	(3.05)	3.4[a]	(3.87)	1.07
BDI	3.0[b]	(3.14)	10.4[a]	(6.69)	9.3[a]	(6.65)	26.51**
AI	43.6[b]	(7.18)	52.3[a]	(10.07)	55.7[a]	(10.48)	21.47***
QFI	0.2[b]	(0.28)	9.7[a]	(6.99)	10.3[a]	(4.50)	80.88***
			Verbal tests				
Word Finding	37.9[a]	(7.28)	37.8[a]	(9.92)	32.6[b]	(9.74)	4.08*
Rattan & Chapman Vocabulary	48.3[a]	(11.04)	49.3[a]	(10.99)	43.0[b]	(10.12)	2.95*
Shipley Vocabulary Age	17.0[a]	(1.44)	17.4[a]	(1.34)	16.3[b]	(1.68)	4.49**

Perceptual–Motor tests							
WAIS Block Design	9.8^a	(2.75)	9.1^a	(2.38)	8.8^a	(2.39)	1.92
Trail Making Test, Part B	79.3^b	(33.54)	80.3^b	(25.69)	99.4^a	(44.86)	3.50*
Grooved Pegboard	70.8^a	(10.56)	73.6^a	(10.25)	74.3^a	(20.25)	0.84
WAIS Digit Symbol	7.9^a	(2.05)	7.7^a	(1.97)	7.6^a	(2.18)	0.17
Sentence Writing	8.9^a	(2.40)	9.0^a	(2.32)	8.8^a	(1.85)	0.06
Learning/Memory tests							
WMS Semantic Memory—Immediate	24.1^a	(5.14)	23.2^a	(6.76)	19.9^b	(5.99)	5.09**
WMS Figural Memory—Immediate	10.2^a	(2.47)	9.0^{ab}	(2.66)	8.4^b	(3.15)	5.04**
WMS Semantic Memory—Delayed	21.6^a	(5.60)	20.9^a	(7.00)	16.7^b	(5.07)	6.77***
WMS Figural Memory—Delayed	9.5^a	(2.67)	8.1^b	(2.76)	7.0^b	(3.31)	7.84***
Symbol–Digit Paired-Associate Learning	19.7^a	(6.21)	19.8^a	(6.09)	15.8^b	(6.73)	4.15**
Abstracting/Problem Solving							
Booklet Category	47.2^b	(28.19)	49.6^b	(31.03)	68.3^a	(29.48)	5.22**
Shipley Abstracting Age	15.1^a	(2.75)	15.1^a	(2.87)	13.6^b	(3.03)	3.10*
Test of attention							
Digit Vigilance	409.3^a	(69.30)	402.5^a	(71.86)	405.2^a	(89.28)	0.09

Note. Means with the same superscript were not significantly different at $\alpha = .05$; all others were significantly different (Duncan's multiple-range test).

$^{*}p < .05$.

$^{**}p < .01$.

$^{***}p < .001$.

results are discussed, however, it should be noted that Primaries and Secondaries were not significantly different on duration, QFI, or days abstinent before testing.

The data in the upper part of the table lead to several important conclusions. First, we replicated our finding with a questionnaire assessing Hk/MBD; Primary alcoholics claimed significantly more such childhood symptoms than Secondaries. The latter did not differ from controls. Second, Primary alcoholics did not differ on age, BDI, or AI from Secondaries, although both alcoholic groups had significantly higher BDI and AI scores than controls. Thus, any differences between Primaries and Secondaries could not be ascribed to differences in affective distress. The groups did differ on education: Primary alcoholics had significantly lower educational levels than Secondaries, a not surprising finding in light of their self-reports of greater childhood Hk/MBD symptomatology. We analyzed the groups of tests (Verbal, Abstracting/Problem Solving, Learning/Memory, and Perceptual–Motor) listed in Table 8-6 by first doing multivariate analyses with Hotelling's T^2 test. Primaries were found to differ significantly from controls on each cluster, with the exception of the Perceptual–Motor cluster. There were no significant differences between Secondaries and controls. Primaries differed significantly from Secondaries on the Verbal and Abstracting/Problem Solving clusters, with trends toward significance on the Perceptual–Motor ($p < .06$) and Learning/Memory tests ($p < .10$). Finally, the groups did not differ on a measure of attention (a cancellation task).

Separate one-way analyses of variance (ANOVAs) for each variable for the three groups were run, and F's are listed in the right-hand portion of Table 8-6. Duncan multiple-range t tests were conducted to determine between-group differences. The subscripts following the mean scores indicate group similarity or difference: Means with the same subscript did not differ significantly; those with different letters, of course, did differ significantly. It can be readily observed that the Secondaries differed from the other two groups on each test for which there was an overall significant F, with the exception of Wechsler Memory Scale (WMS) Figural Memory, both Immediate and Delayed. Secondaries differed from controls only on the WMS Figural Memory—Delayed; otherwise, the two groups' scores were remarkably similar. As educational levels were significantly different between Primaries and Secondaries, we did analyses of covariance on all individual tests. The differences between the two groups on the Verbal tests were no longer significant, nor were those for Part B of the Trail Making Test and Shipley Abstracting Age, although all showed a trend for poorer performance by Primaries. However for the remainder of the tests (i.e., the Learning/Memory tests and the Booklet Category Test), the groups remained significantly different.

These results emphasize an important point. Neuropsychological test results, and therefore inferences about the brain–behavior effects of alcoholism, will vary as a function of the particular sample of alcoholics. According to our results, the Secondaries (53% of our alcoholic sample) were virtually indistinguishable from the controls, while the Primaries (47%) of our alcoholic sample differed from both. Granted, the criteria for acceptance into our study were strict: Alcoholics could not have a history of other neurological disorders or severe psychiatric diagnosis (schizophrenia or major depressive disorder), or medical conditions such as chronic obstructive pulmonary disease that would affect the brain. The point is that generalizations about neuropsychological functioning in alcoholics should be limited to populations that have characteristics similar to the samples studied. Furthermore, the results suggest that grouping alcoholics into subtypes such as Primaries and Secondaries may lead to different treatment approaches and different outcomes.

Finally, a word of caution: Our results with the Primary–Secondary dimension in VA male patients obviously need to be replicated in other laboratories, using samples that may vary with respect to sex, race, and socioeconomic level, before generalizations can be made.

Premorbid Neuropsychological Deficits in Alcoholics

The important question of possible premorbid neuropsychological deficits in alcoholics was first addressed, to my knowledge, by Goodwin and Hill (1975). In their review of alcohol effects on intellect, learning and memory, they stated:

> The difficulty of alcoholics in "adapting" after they have stopped drinking is often attributed to permanent effects on brain function from years of heavy drinking. Longitudinal studies are needed to show whether adaptive difficulties precede, as well as follow, the drinking history. The psychological tests which are most sensitive to organicity in alcoholics, namely, the Halstead Category Test and the Wisconsin Card Sorting Test, have not been administered to alcoholics before they became alcoholic. Since the children of alcoholics are particularly high risk for developing alcoholism themselves, a worthwhile study would be to administer these tests to offspring of alcoholics and determine whether they would perform more poorly than a matched control group. Perhaps poor "conceptual shifting" is a cause rather than a result of heavy drinking. (p. 63)

In the last several years, Goodwin and Hill's prescient recommendation concerning testing offspring of alcoholics has been pursued. Goodwin (1983) has reported that nonalcoholic sons of alcoholics had poorer performance on the Halstead Category Test than nonalcoholic sons of nonalcoholics. Tarter, Hegedus, Goldstein, Shelly, and Alterman (1984) have found that male delinquents with a positive family history for alcoholism (FH+), compared to male delinquents with a negative familial history of alcoholism

(FH−), performed more poorly on Part B of the Trail Making Test, as well as on the Semantic Memory and Figural Memory subtests of the WMS and the Peabody Picture Vocabulary Test.

In our laboratories, we have studied 41 FH+ and 27 FH− alcoholics and 19 FH+ and 43 FH− nonalcoholic community controls (Schaeffer, Parsons, & Yohman, 1984). Most of these subjects were the same as reported in the preceding discussion of the Primary–Secondary dimension, but additional subjects were added. The four groups did not differ on age or education. FH+ and FH− alcoholics did not differ on days abstinent before testing or on the QFI. However, they did differ on duration (years) of alcohol abuse: FH+, $M = 12.83 \pm 7.90$; FH−, $M = 9.19 \pm 5.78$ ($t = 2.06$, $p < .05$).

For the first analysis, we transformed all of the data to a common metric, *T* scores, derived from the overall control group's performance. We then performed 2 × 2 ANOVAs on the mean scores for each of the four groups on each of our four clusters of tests: Verbal (three measures), Learning/Memory (six measures), Abstracting/Problem Solving (six measures), and Perceptual–Motor (four tests). In addition, we derived a General Impairment index based on the 11 tests that best discriminated alcoholics from controls. In Table 8-7, the first column shows that the four groups differed overall on Learning/Memory, Abstracting/Problem Solving, and General Impairment. As regards the group main effects, the alcoholics differed significantly from the controls ($p < .01$) on the same three clusters. The family history differences were that FH+ differed significantly from FH− on the General Impairment cluster ($p < .05$) and tended to differ on Learning/Memory, Abstracting/Problem Solving, and Perceptual–Motor performance ($p < .10$). Most importantly, there were *no* significant interactions between alcoholics versus controls and FH+ versus FH− in the test performance. These two major variables are thus independent of each other as regards relationship to neuropsychological functioning.

The second way we analyzed our data was to use Hotelling's T^2 multivariate analyses to compare FH+ alcoholics and FH− controls, and to compare FH− alcoholics and FH+ controls. The former comparison should give rise to maximal differences, the latter to minimal differences. In Table 8-8, this effect is rather strikingly illustrated. As indicated in the right-hand portion of the table, there were no cluster differences for the FH− alcoholics and the FH+ controls, and only 3 of the 19 individual tests showed significant differences. For the FH+ alcoholics and the FH− controls, the Learning/Memory, Abstracting/Problem Solving, and Perceptual–Motor clusters were significantly different. On the individual tests, FH+ alcoholics were significantly poorer than FH− controls on 15 out of 19 comparisons; most differences were at the .01 level of significance or better.

These data deserve two comments. The first is that subgrouping within

Table 8-7. Means (Standard Deviations) and Analyses of Variance for FH+ and FH− Alcoholics and Controls

Test cluster[a]	Overall		Group			Family History			Interaction
	F	p	Alcoholics ($n = 68$)	Controls ($n = 63$)	p	FH+ ($n = 60$)	FH− ($n = 70$)	p	p
Verbal (3)	1.64	.18	46.9 (10.1)	49.8 (9.3)	.21	46.6 (10.6)	49.7 (8.9)	.19	.69
Learning/Memory (6)	5.19	.002	44.7 (9.7)	49.9 (7.1)	.007	44.9 (9.8)	49.1 (7.6)	.07	.98
Abstracting/Problem Solving (6)	4.89	.003	45.1 (7.9)	49.7 (7.8)	.01	45.4 (7.9)	49.0 (8.0)	.08	.59
Perceptual–Motor (4)	2.21	.09	46.6 (9.2)	49.2 (8.3)	.31	46.2 (10.1)	49.2 (7.4)	.09	.24
General Impairment (11)	5.57	.001	45.0 (7.9)	49.6 (6.9)	.006	45.1 (8.1)	48.9 (7.1)	.05	.63

[a]The number of tests in each cluster is given in parentheses.

Table 8-8. Means and Significant Probability Levels for Differences between FH+ Alcoholics and FH− Controls, and between FH− Alcoholics and FH+ Controls

Neuropsychological test	FH+ Alcoholics	FH− Controls	*p*	FH− Alcoholics	FH+ Controls	*p*
Verbal						
Shipley Vocabulary Age	16.47	16.97	—	16.97	17.08	—
Rattan & Chapman Vocabulary						
With associative distractors	16.61	19.93	.03	20.04	18.21	—
Without associative distractors	18.71	21.26	.03	19.93	19.74	—
Learning/Memory			.001			—
Wechsler Memory Scale						
Semantic Memory—Immediate	20.28	24.35	.001	22.81	23.34	—
Semantic Memory—Delayed	17.27	21.99	.001	20.52	20.39	—
Figural Memory—Immediate	8.15	10.28	.001	8.52	9.95	—
Figural Memory—Delayed	7.05	9.60	.001	7.37	9.32	.03
Verbal Paired-Associate Learning[a]	82.34	75.72	—	78.63	84.68	—
Symbol–Digit Paired-Associate Learning	16.76	20.51	.01	18.33	16.84	—
Abstracting/Problem Solving			.02			—
Shipley Abstracting Age	13.85	15.65	.01	14.07	13.51	—
Levine Hypothesis Testing	2.73	3.91	.001	2.96	3.84	.05
Conceptual Level Analogies	15.41	22.00	.001	20.04	17.47	—
Word Finding	34.85	37.65	—	33.70	39.00	.03
WAIS Block Design	26.20	31.93	.01	26.74	27.84	—
Booklet Category[a]	65.95	44.88	.001	54.63	56.42	—
Perceptual–Motor			.04			—
Trail Making Test, Part B[a]	98.10	73.44	.001	83.33	101.53	—
Grooved Pegboard (nondominant hand)[a]	82.23	78.05	—	84.19	77.89	—
Sentence Writing[a]	9.40	8.88	—	9.43	10.17	—
WAIS Digit Symbol	45.66	50.36	.03	46.78	45.79	—

Note. Hotelling's T^2 was used to calculate p's for cluster areas, and Student's t (two-tailed p's) was used for individual test comparisons.

[a]Scored in terms of errors or time; higher scores indicate worse performance. For all other measures, higher scores indicate better performance.

the alcoholics, and this time also within the controls, gave rise to marked differences in the results. In this context, it should be noted that family history in the alcoholics was related to the Primary–Secondary dimension although not identical to it: 63% of our FH+ alcoholics, but only 33% of the FH− alcoholics, were Primaries, a significant difference ($\chi^2 = 5.90$, $p < .02$). This certainly seems to be an important area for future research. What factors helped the remaining 37% FH+ alcoholics to avoid the Primary designation, and thus the more impaired neuropsychological functioning? Conversely, the same question can be raised as to why the other 33% of the FH− alcoholics fell into the Primary rather than the Secondary group. Obviously, there are other important variables yet to be identified in predicting alcoholics' neuropsychological deficits.

A second comment is that while our results, together with those of Tarter *et al.* (1984) and Goodwin (1983), form a rather consistent picture, at least one other investigator (Hesselbrock, 1983) has not found differences between progeny of alcoholics and controls on neuropsychological tests. While there were differences of several decades in the ages of the subjects in our study and Hesselbrock's (Hesselbrock's progeny were about 20 years younger), and in other aspects of the methodology, his data certainly indicate that more research is needed before definite conclusions concerning family history and neuropsychological functioning are possible.

Which Neuropsychological Models Best Account for the Data?

In our last two reviews (Parsons & Leber, 1981, 1982), we have examined the evidence for and against three different neuropsychological models of alcoholism effects on brain–behavior relationships: frontolimbic dysfunction, right-hemisphere differential sensitivity, and generalized/diffuse dysfunction. Our conclusion was that the data best fit the generalized/diffuse model. Our reasons for this conclusion are detailed in those articles; space constraints prevent reiteration here.

In addition, we considered two other neurobehavioral explanations of the neuropsychological deficits in alcoholics. These two lie on opposite ends of the continuum of development. On the one hand, there is the hypothesis that childhood Hk/MBD is predisposing for alcoholics; on the other hand, there is the "premature-aging hypothesis" of alcoholism effects. While the latter has much support, our review of the studies (Parsons & Leber, 1982) suggests that the effects of aging and alcohol abuse on the brain are different processes—a conclusion reached by other investigators in a recent volume on alcoholism and aging (Hartford & Samorajski, 1983).

The childhood Hk/MBD hypothesis has been suggested by a number of authors (Goodwin & Hill, 1975; Tarter & Ryan, 1983; Tarter *et al.*, 1977;

Wood, Reimherr, Wender, & Johnson, 1976). In brief, this hypothesis suggests that many alcoholics are "MBD children grown up." The supposition is that children with the Hk/MBD syndrome are children at risk for developing various disorders, such as alcoholism, sociopathy, or hysteria (Wood *et al.*, 1976). We have presented data earlier that would support such a hypothesis; that is, alcoholics do claim more symptoms of childhood Hk/MBD than nonalcoholics, and Primary alcoholics do claim more of such childhood behaviors than do Secondaries. But it should be made clear that this hypothesis was never meant to account for the full range of alcoholism; it has been concerned with a subgroup of alcoholics. For example, in our studies, only approximately one-third of our alcoholics have significantly elevated scores on the Hk/MBD symptoms checklist (DeObaldia & Parsons, 1983). Furthermore, Vaillant (1983) found in his prospective study that hyperactivity in childhood was minimally correlated with subsequent alcohol abuse.

The search for satisfactory neuropsychological models continues. My prediction is that the "generalized/diffuse" model will become increasingly refined, perhaps along lines suggested by Butters and Granholm in Chapter 9 (i.e., alcohol abuse results in cortical and subcortical changes that give rise to different impairments, which may have different courses of recovery). Furthermore, it would appear that the developmental model of children at risk—whether that risk comes from a genetic or familial loading (as in a positive family history), or from the presence of childhood Hk/MBD syndrome in Primary alcoholics—certainly should be pursued. These factors seem to be relevant to understanding the presence of neuropsychological deficits in a substantial minority of alcoholics.

Summary and Implications

A substantial number of sober alcoholics manifest deficits in abstracting, problem solving, learning, memory, and complex perceptual–motor functioning. While the causal role played by duration of alcohol abuse and current drinking practices in these deficits has not been clearly established, recent evidence suggests that maximal quantity drunk per occasion and the frequency of those occasions are predictive of neuropsychological deficits. Alcoholics rate themselves as less efficient on everyday tasks involving memory, problem solving, language and communication, and perceptual–motor functioning. The more they have drunk in the past 6 months, the greater their reported impairment. They also report more symptoms than nonalcoholics on a neuropsychological impairment scale. The longer the duration of their drinking, the closer their scores are to other types of brain-damaged patients; the more thay have drunk in the last 6 months, the higher the intensity of symptom complaint. In contrast to subjective claims of impairment, neither depression nor anxiety is related to neuropsychological deficits in alcoholics. The relationship between subjective claims of impairment and actual impairment in life situations or on neuropsychological tests remains to be investigated.

Differences in degree of impairment of subtypes of alcoholics need to be explored further. Primary versus Secondary alcoholism appears to result in differential impairment, but this finding needs replication in other laboratories. There is a strong likelihood that *some* neuropsychological deficits are present in *some* alcoholics premorbidly. Family history of alcoholism and presence of childhood Hk/MBD symptoms need to be further explored as possible factors of relevance here. The generalized/diffuse model of the effects of alcohol abuse on the brain appears to account for more of the data than other models, although it needs to be specified in more detail for any theoretical or practical utility.

What do these conclusions imply for diagnosis and treatment? It seems rather clear that the diagnosis of "alcoholism" covers a broad spectrum. As pointed out by Jellinek (1960) many years ago, there are many types of alcoholics as defined by life history and drinking variables. Tarter *et al.*'s (1977) Primary–Secondary dimension separates alcoholics with impaired neuropsychological functioning from those who are not impaired. As such, it would appear to be a potentially useful augmentation to current diagnostic practices. Furthermore, treatment programs for the Primary alcoholics could be tailored in recognition of the subclinical, mild to moderate brain dysfunctional state that is present. The manifestations of such a state (i.e., impaired problem solving, abstracting, memory, and new learning) suggest that a treatment strategy modeled after the approaches used with other brain-damaged patients may be effective.

Acknowledgments

The research from my laboratory cited herein was supported in part by U.S. Public Health Service (National Institute on Alcohol Abuse and Alcoholism) Grant Nos. AA1434, AA01464, and AA06135. Thanks are due to the following persons from our research team: Janice Boon, PhD; Ricardo DeObaldia, PhD; Nancy Nichols, MA; Kim Walter Schaeffer, PhD; Melvin D. Shelton, PhD; and J. Robert Yohman, PhD. Without their individual and collective contributions, this chapter could not have been written.

References

Beck, A. T. (1967). *Depression: Clinical, experimental and theoretical aspects.* New York: Harper & Row.

Cahalan, O., Cissin, I., & Crossley, H. (1969). *American drinking practices.* New Brunswick, NJ: Rutgers Center for Alcohol Studies.

Caster, D. U. (1977). Treatment of the recidivist alcoholics. *Alcoholism: Clinical and Experimental Research, 1*, 87–90.

Chelune, G. J., & Parker, J. B. (1981). Neuropsychological deficits associated with chronic alcohol abuse. *Clinical Psychology Review, 1*, 181–195.

DeObaldia, R., & Parsons, O. A. (1983). Minimal brain dysfunction symptoms claimed by primary and secondary alcoholics: Relation to cognitive functioning. *International Journal of Neuroscience, 20*, 173–181.

DeObaldia, R., & Parsons, O. A. (1984). Neuropsychological performance related to primary alcoholism and self-reported symptoms of childhood MBD. *Journal of Studies on Alcohol, 45*, 386–392.

Eckardt, M. J., Parker, E. S., Noble, E. P., Fieldman, D. J., & Gottschalk, L. A. (1978). Relationship between neuropsychological performance and alcoholic consumption in alcoholics. *Biological Psychiatry, 13*, 551–565.

Fabian, M. S., Parsons, O. A., & Silberstein, J. A. (1981). Impaired perceptual–cognitive functioning in alcoholic women: Cross-validated findings. *Journal of Studies on Alcohol, 42*, 217–229.

Goldstein, G. (1976). Perceptual and cognitive deficit in alcoholics. In G. Goldstein & C. Neuringer (Eds.). *Empirical studies of alcoholism* (pp. 115–151). Cambridge, MA: Ballinger.

Goodwin, D. W. (1983). Familial alcoholism: A separate entity? *Substance and Alcohol Actions/Misuse, 4*, 129–136.

Goodwin, D. W., & Hill, S. Y. (1975). Chronic effects of alcohol and other psychoactive drugs on intellect, learning and memory. In G. Rankin (Ed.), *Alcohol, drugs and brain damage* (pp. 55–69). Toronto: Addiction Research Foundation.

Hartford, J. T., & Samorajski, T. (1983). *Alcoholism in the elderly*. New York: Raven Press.

Heaton, R. F., & Pendleton, M. D. (1981). Use of neuropsychological tests to predict adult patients' everyday functioning. *Journal of Consulting and Clinical Psychology, 99*, 807–821.

Hesselbrock, V. (1983, April). Neuropsychological functioning in offspring of alcoholics. In H. Begleiter (Chair), *Subjects at risk for alcoholism: Recent findings*. Symposium conducted at the National Alcoholism Forum, Houston.

Jellinek, E. M. (1960). *The disease concept of alcohol*. New Haven, CT: College and University Press.

Jones, B., & Parsons, O. A. (1971). Impairment of abstracting ability in chronic alcoholics. *Archives of General Psychiatry, 24*, 71–75.

Kleinknecht, R. A., & Goldstein, S. G. (1972). Neuropsychological deficits associated with alcoholism: A review and discussion. *Quarterly Journal of Studies on Alcohol, 33*, 999–1019.

Klisz, D. K., & Parsons, O. A. (1977). Hypothesis testing in chronic alcoholics. *Journal of Studies on Alcohol, 38*, 1718–1729.

Klisz, D. K., & Parsons, O. A. (1979). Cognitive dysfunction in alcoholics and social drinkers: Problems in assessment and remediation. *Journal of Studies on Alcohol, 88*, 268–276.

Miller, W. R., & Saucedo, C. F. (1983). Assessment of neuropsychological impairment and brain damage in problem drinkers. In C. J. Golden, J. A. Moses, J. A. Coffman, W. R. Miller, & F. D. Strider (Eds.), *Clinical neuropsychology: Interface with neurological and psychiatric disorders* (pp. 141–196). New York: Grune & Stratton.

O'Donnell, W. E., De Soto, C. B., & Reynolds, D. M. (1984). Sensitivity and specificity of the Neuropsychological Impairment Scale (NIS). *Journal of Clinical Psychology, 40*, 553–555.

O'Donnell, W. E., & Reynolds, D. M. (1983). *Neuropsychological Impairment Scale manual*. Annapolis, MD: Annapolis Psychological Service.

O'Donnell, W. E., Reynolds, D. M., & De Soto, C. B. (1984). Validity and reliability of the

Neuropsychological Impairment Scale (NIS). *Journal of Clinical Psychology, 40*, 549–552.

Parsons, O. A., & Leber, W. R. (1981). The relationship between cognitive dysfunction and brain damage in alcoholics: Causal, interactive or epiphenomenal? *Alcoholism: Clinical and Experimental Research, 5*, 326–343.

Parsons, O. A., & Leber, W. R. (1982). Alcohol, cognitive dysfunction and brain damage. In National Institute on Alcohol Abuse and Alcoholism (Ed.), *Biomedical processes and consequences of alcohol use* (Alcohol and Health Monograph 2, DHHS Publication. No. ADM 82-1191, pp. 213–253). Washington, DC: U. S. Government Printing Office.

Parsons, O. A., Tassey, J., & Schaeffer, K. W. (1985). Unpublished study.

Penick, E. C., Powell, B. J., Othmer, E., Bingham, S. F., Rice, A. S., & Liese, B. S. (1985). Subtyping alcoholics by coexisting psychiatric syndromes: Course, family history, outcome. In D. W. Goodwin, R. T. Van Dusen, & S. A. Mednick (Eds.), *Longitudinal research in alcoholism* (pp. 449–469). Boston: Kluwer-Nijoff.

Rudie, R. R., & McGaughran, L. A. (1961). Differences in developmental experience, defensiveness and personality organization between two classes of problem drinkers. *Journal of Abnormal and Social Psychology, 62*, 659–665.

Ryan, C., & Butters, N. (1980). Learning and memory impairments in young and old alcoholics: Evidence for the premature-aging hypothesis. *Alcoholism: Clinical and Experimental Research, 4*, 288–293.

Schaeffer, K. W., Parsons, O. A., & Yohman, J. R. (1984). Neuropsychological differences between male familial and nonfamilial alcoholics and nonalcoholics. *Alcoholism: Clinical and Experimental Research, 8*, 347–351.

Shelton, M. D., & Parsons, O. A. (in press). Neuropsychological performance in alcoholics: I. Self-assessment of everyday functioning. *Journal of Clinical Psychology.*

Smith, J. W. (1977). Neurological disorders in alcoholism. In N. J. Estes & M. E. Heineman (Eds.), *Alcoholism* (pp. 109–128). St. Louis: C. V. Mosby.

Spielberger, C. D., Gorsuch, R. L., & Lushene, R. E. (1970). *Test manual for the State–Trait Anxiety Inventory.* Palo Alto, CA: Consulting Psychologists Press.

Tarter, R. E., Hegedus, A. M., Goldstein, G., Shelly, C., & Alterman, A. I. (1984). Adolescent sons of alcoholics: Neuropsychological and personality characteristics. *Alcoholism: Clinical and Experimental Research, 8*, 216–221.

Tarter, R. E., McBride, H., Buopane, N., & Schneider, D. U. (1977). Differentiation of alcoholics. *Archives of General Psychiatry, 34*, 761–768.

Tarter, R. E., & Parsons, O. A. (1971). Conceptual shifting in chronic alcoholics. *Journal of Abnormal Psychology, 77*, 71–75.

Tarter, R. E., & Ryan, C. M. (1983). Neuropsychology of alcoholism: Etiology, phenomenology, process and outcome. In M. Galanter (Ed.), *Recent developments in alcoholism* (Vol. 1). New York: Plenum Press.

Vaillant, G. E. (1983). *The natural history of alcoholism.* Cambridge, MA: Harvard University Press.

Wood, D. R., Reimherr, F. W., Wender, P. H., & Johnson, G. E. (1976). Diagnosis and treatment of minimal brain dysfunction in adults. *Archives of General Psychiatry, 33*, 1453–1460.

9

The Continuity Hypothesis: Some Conclusions and Their Implications for the Etiology and Neuropathology of Alcoholic Korsakoff's Syndrome

NELSON BUTTERS
ERIC GRANHOLM

Introduction

In 1970, when Butters and his colleague Laird Cermak began their assessment of the memory and cognitive disorders of alcoholic Korsakoff patients, their main focus was on the role of various information-processing factors (e.g., storage, retrieval, encoding, attention) in these patients' dense amnesia. Since the "conventional wisdom" of the early 1970s was that the Wernicke–Korsakoff syndrome developed acutely as the result of a thiamine deficiency, and that ethanol had no direct deleterious effects upon the brain, there seemed little rationale for evaluating memory dysfunctions in detoxified long-term alcoholics. Alcoholism and Korsakoff's syndrome were viewed as two distinct disorders, and the average alcoholic did not have to be concerned with significant brain dysfunction from extensive alcohol intake if he or she simply maintained a normal nutritional status.

The *Zeitgeist*, and our research group's focus, quickly changed when the results of animal and neuroradiological investigations and the demonstration of cognitive disorders in social drinkers forced us to re-evaluate our conception of the relationship between Korsakoff's syndrome and long-term alcohol abuse (for review, see Butters & Brandt, 1985). Since the results of these studies suggested that ethanol has a direct toxic effect on cortical and subcortical brain structures, regardless of the nutritional status of the organism, it seemed reasonable to assume that the memory and cognitive disorders that characterize Korsakoff's syndrome may not appear acutely, but

Nelson Butters and Eric Granholm. Psychology Service, San Diego Veterans Administration Medical Center, San Diego, California; Department of Psychiatry, University of California at San Diego School of Medicine, La Jolla, California.

rather may develop slowly over decades of severe alcoholism (i.e., the continuity hypothesis). Given this possibility, much of our research effort since 1975 has been concerned with the presence, severity, and recovery of "Korsakoff-like" memory deficits in detoxified alcoholics. That is, we wished to determine whether, as Ryback (1971) had suggested many years ago, there is a continuum of cognitive impairment, with the alcoholic Korsakoff patient occupying one end of this spectrum and the heavy social drinker occupying the other end. As seen in Figure 9-1, the continuity hypothesis predicts that a given individual's degree of cognitive deficit is determined by his or her drinking history as measured by indices of quantity, frequency, and duration.

Our major intention in this chapter is to present some new notions about the neuropathology of alcoholic Korsakoff's syndrome. To develop a behavioral background for this anatomical hypothesis, we first quickly review the major cognitive deficits of alcoholic Korsakoff patients, and then discuss some evidence demonstrating the limitations of the continuity hypothesis as an etiological explanation of the Korsakoff patients' amnesic syndrome. Following this discourse on the continuity hypothesis, we describe the findings of a recent neuropathological paper that serves as the basis of our anatomical speculations. Finally, some initial neuropsychological data supportive of the anatomical notion being advanced are presented. These latter findings involve a comparison of the memory disorders of alcoholic Korsakoff patients, patients with Alzheimer's disease (AD), and patients with Huntington's disease (HD).

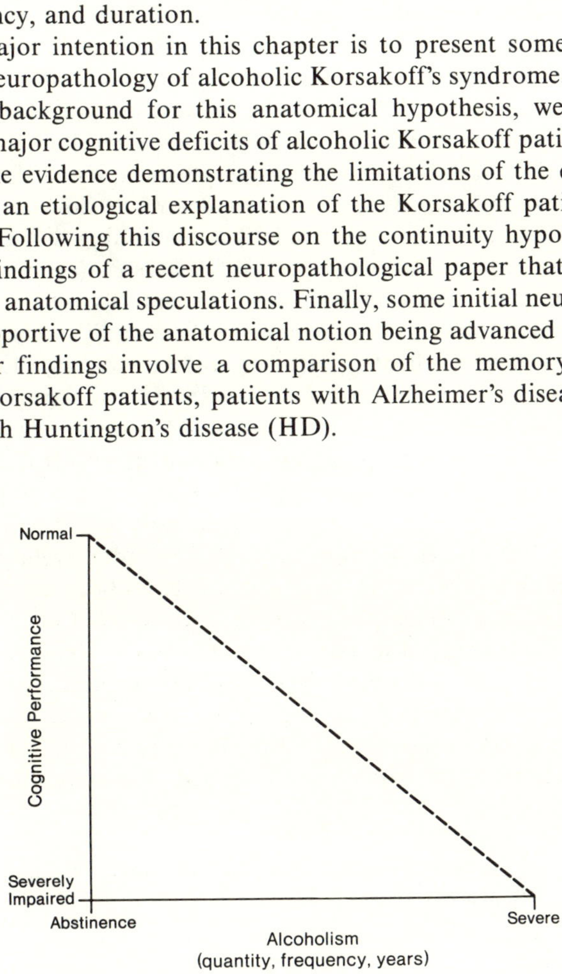

Figure 9-1. Diagrammatic presentation of Ryback's (1971) continuity hypothesis. Degree of cognitive dysfunction is based upon frequency, quantity, and temporal (years) indices of alcohol consumption.

Cognitive Symptoms of Alcoholic Korsakoff's Syndrome

Table 9-1 lists the major cognitive disorders of alcoholic Korsakoff patients and the neuroanatomical structures often assumed to be responsible for the deficits. The patients' anterograde amnesia is the most striking feature of their neuropsychological deficits. They are unable to learn new verbal and nonverbal information from the time of onset of the illness. Learning the names of their physicians and nurses, and even the location of their beds, may require weeks or months of constant repetition and rehearsal. In addition to failing to learn the names of important individuals, they will often not remember previous encounters with these individuals. If the patients spend 3 hours completing a number of psychometric tasks, they may fail to recall the entire test session 2 hours after it has ended. Experimentally, this severe anterograde amnesia has been exemplified by the severe difficulty Korsakoff patients have had in learning even short lists of five or six verbal paired associates (Ryan & Butters, 1980a; Winocur & Weiskrantz, 1976) and in retaining three words or consonants in working (i.e., short-term) memory for more than 9 seconds if a demanding distractor activity intervenes between presentation and recall (Butters & Cermak, 1980).

The inability of alcoholic Korsakoff patients to retain information when distractors are used to prevent rehearsal exemplifies one of the most prominent features of their anterograde amnesia—that is, their increased sensitivity to interference. Numerous investigations have reported that alcoholics with Korsakoff's syndrome are unable to acquire new information because of interference from previously learned materials (i.e., proactive interference). These patients have tended to perseverate responses (i.e., intralist intrusions) on tests of short-term memory and free recall (Fuld, 1976; Meudell, Butters, & Montgomery, 1978), and they have evidenced improved learning and retention when learning conditions are structured to reduce proactive interference (for review, see Butters & Cermak, 1980).

Retrograde amnesia is also a distinct and consistent feature of alcoholic Korsakoff's syndrome. Korsakoff patients have trouble retrieving from long-term memory events that occurred prior to the onset of their illness. When asked who was President of the United States before Ronald Reagan, a Korsakoff patient might answer "Johnson" or "Kennedy." This difficulty

Table 9-1. Cognitive Disorders Associated with Alcoholic Korsakoff's Syndrome

Disorder	Presumed neuropathological basis
Anterograde amnesia	Medial diencephalon
Retrograde amnesia	Medial diencephalon
Visuoperceptive deficits	Association cortex
Problem-solving deficits	Association cortex

in retrieving old memories is usually temporally graded, with events from the 20-year period immediately preceding the illness most adversely affected. Surprisingly, remote events from the patients' childhood and early adulthood are reasonably well recalled. This temporal "gradient" is not only evident during mental status examinations, but also has been demonstrated in numerous experimental studies using public events recall questionnaires, photographs of famous people, voices of famous people, and questionnaires concerned with television programs (Albert, Butters, & Levin, 1979; Butters & Albert, 1982; Cohen & Squire, 1981; Meudell, Northern, Snowden, & Neary, 1980; Squire & Cohen, 1982). Figure 9-2 (from Albert *et al.*, 1979) shows the Korsakoffs' extensive, but graded, retrograde-memory loss for "easy" and "hard" items from a public events questionnaire and photographs of famous people.

Both the anterograde and retrograde components of the amnesic syndrome have been attributed to the development of small hemorrhagic lesions in the region of the dorsomedial nucleus of the thalamus. In their postmortem study of 82 alcoholic Korsakoff brains, Victor, Adams, and Collins (1971) carefully examined the medial diencephalic region in 43 cases. In 38 of the 43 brains, extensive atrophy of the dorsomedial nucleus was noted. Since the 5 brains without atrophy of the dorsomedial nucleus represented cases without lasting memory impairments, Victor *et al.* con-

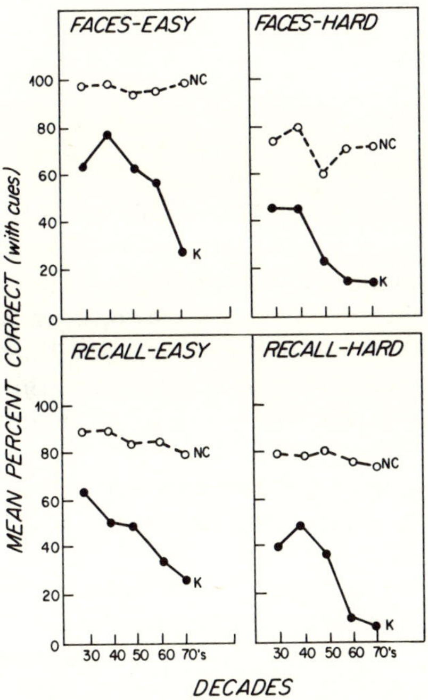

Figure 9-2. Mean percentage of easy and hard items correctly recalled by alcoholic Korsakoff (K) and normal control (NC) subjects on Albert *et al.*'s (1979) famous persons test (top) and public events questionnaire (bottom). (From "Temporal Gradients in the Retrograde Amnesia of Patients with Alcoholic Korsakoff's Disease" by M. S. Albert, N. Butters, and J. Levin, 1979, *Archives of Neurology*, *36*, 211–216. Reprinted by permission.)

cluded that the dorsomedial nucleus of the thalamus is the critical structure for the amnesic syndrome. Reports of anterograde- and retrograde-memory deficits in patients with traumatic, vascular, or space-occupying lesions of the midline thalamus support the notion that the medial diencephalic region plays a vital role in learning and memory (e.g., Butters, 1984; Guberman & Stuss, 1983; Speedie & Heilman, 1982, 1983; Squire & Moore, 1979; Squire & Slater, 1978).

Although the amnesic syndrome is the Korsakoff patients' most obvious cognitive deficit, impairments on visuoperceptual and problem-solving tasks should not be ignored. Despite attaining IQ scores well within the normal range, alcoholic Korsakoff patients are dramatically impaired on digit–symbol substitution tasks (Glosser, Butters, & Kaplan, 1977; Kapur & Butters, 1977; Talland, 1965), on embedded-figures tests (Glosser *et al.*, 1977; Kapur & Butters, 1977; Talland, 1965), and on various concept-formation tests that require the learning and shifting of problem-solving strategies (Oscar-Berman, 1973; Talland, 1965). Although there are some indications that these visuoperceptual and conceptual deficits, like the patients' memory disorders, may be due to damage to diencephalic structures surrounding the third ventricle (Jarho, 1973), some investigators have attributed these disorders to atrophy of association cortex (Moscovitch, 1982; Squire, 1982).

Similarities and Differences between Long-Term Alcoholics and Alcoholics with Korsakoff's Syndrome

Visuoperceptive and Problem-Solving Impairments

The most impressive evidence favoring Ryback's (1971) continuity hypothesis emanates from comparisons of the visuoperceptive and problem-solving deficits (i.e., cortical dysfunctions) of alcoholic Korsakoff patients and long-term alcoholics. For example, both alcoholic populations are consistently impaired on digit–symbol and symbol–digit substitution tasks, and these deficits appear to be related to deficiencies in analyzing geometrical forms, as well as to some retardation in learning specific digit–symbol associations (Glosser *et al.*, 1977; Kapur & Butters, 1977). For both Korsakoff patients and long-term alcoholics, degree of impairment on these substitution tasks correlates very highly with their capacity to locate embedded figures and to conduct a rapid visual search.

Although there are numerous demonstrations that detoxified long-term alcoholics are impaired on problem-solving tasks such as the Wisconsin Card Sorting Test and the Halstead–Reitan Category Test (for reviews, see Goldman, 1983; Parsons, 1975; Parsons & Farr, 1981; Parsons & Leber,

1981; Ryan & Butters, 1983), only a few studies have directly compared the problem-solving strategies of alcoholic Korsakoff patients and long-term alcoholics with those of appropriate control populations. Oscar-Berman (1973) administered a series of two-choice visual discriminations to alcoholic Korsakoff patients, long-term alcoholics, aphasics, and normal control subjects. This task, designed to evaluate hypothesis formation and focusing behavior, required the subjects to discover the particular stimulus dimension (color, size, form, position) the examiner had chosen to reinforce. The results indicated that alcoholic Korsakoff patients could formulate and use hypotheses, but that their strategies were inefficient and insensitive to feedback provided by the examiner. The performance of the long-term alcoholics fell between those of the Korsakoff patients and the two control groups. Like the alcoholic Korsakoff patients, the alcoholics did not fully use the examiner's feedback to guide their problem-solving strategies.

A recently completed study from our laboratory (Becker, Rivoira, Butters, & Ciraulo, 1984) confirms these similarities in the problem-solving ability of alcoholic Korsakoff patients and long-term alcoholics. The task used was a modification of the old parlor game "20 Questions" (Laine & Butters, 1982). The subjects were shown a presentation card with 42 stimuli (e.g, outlined drawings of objects) arranged in a 6 × 7 matrix, and were asked to "figure out" which object the examiner was thinking of at that time. The subjects could ask any question as long as the examiner could answer it with a "yes" or "no" response. The subjects' goal was to identify the preselected object in as few questions as possible. Figure 9-3 shows the results for three trials with this identification task. Nonalcoholic control subjects adopted the efficient strategy of first asking "constraint-seeking" questions, which reduced by as much as 50% the number of possible alternatives (objects), regardless of a "yes" or "no" answer (e.g., "Is it a tool?" "Is it in the first three columns?"). Only when two or three alternative objects remained did a nonalcoholic subject ask a "hypothesis-scanning" question, which referred to a single object (e.g., "Is it the saw?" "Is it the scissors?"). In contrast, both the alcoholic Korsakoff patients and detoxified long-term alcoholics quickly abandoned the efficient use of constraint-seeking questions and shifted to hypothesis-scanning and even "pseudoconstraint" questions, which superficially seemed to be general questions but actually referred to only one object on the card (e.g., the question "Is it something to tell time with?" was only relevant to the drawing of a clock and not to any other alternative).

The important point about these findings, like those of Oscar-Berman (1973), is that the alcoholics demonstrated not only a quantitatively significant impairment, but also an approach to problem solving that was qualitatively similar to that of alcoholic Korsakoff patients. Both alcoholic groups seemed unable to initiate and maintain an optimal strategy for identifying the chosen objects. Such deficiencies in planning and problem solving have

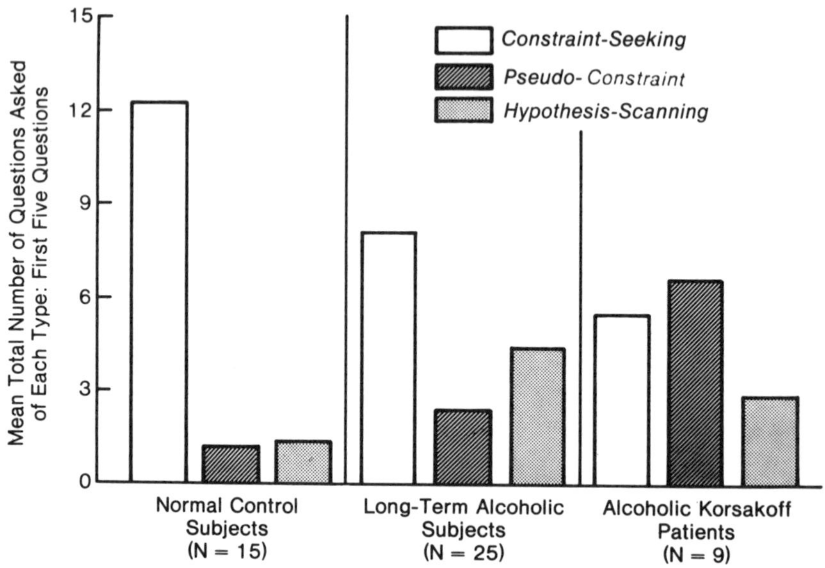

Figure 9-3. Performance of long-term alcoholics, alcoholic Korsakoff patients, and nonalcoholic (i.e., normal) control subjects on Becker *et al.*'s (1984) object identification task. Mean number of constraint-seeking, pseudoconstraint, and hypothesis-scanning questions asked by each group on the first five questions is shown. (From *Asking the Right Questions: Problem Solving Skills in Alcoholics and Alcoholics with Korsakoff's Syndrome* by J. Becker, P. Rivoira, N. Butters, and D. Ciraulo, 1984, paper presented at the annual meeting of the Research Society on Alcoholism, San Antonio, TX.)

often been associated with damage to the frontal association cortex (Damasio, 1979; Luria, 1966; Milner, 1964).

On the basis of these findings for visuoperceptual and problem-solving functions, it would seem that the cortical dysfunctions of alcoholic Korsakoff patients may develop slowly during many years of alcohol abuse and do not appear suddenly with the onset of Wernicke's encephalopathy. The severity of visuoperceptual and problem-solving deficits evidenced by a given detoxified alcoholic may be more a function of how much, how often, and how long the individual has abused alcohol than of an acute thiamine deficiency. This latter statement is not meant to deny that the chronic nutritional problems that plague many alcoholics may also contribute to the gradual development of the alcoholics' perceptual and conceptual problems, especially those apparent at the beginning of the detoxification period (Albert, Butters, Rogers, Pressman, & Geller, 1982).

Anterograde-Memory Deficits

While the data reviewed concerning visuoperceptual and problem-solving functions suggest that the cortical dysfunctions of alcoholic Korsakoff patients may develop slowly over a period of time, the available evidence concerning deficits in anterograde (and retrograde) memory does not strongly support the continuity hypothesis. There is little doubt that some statistically significant memory dysfunctions can be shown in non-Korsakoff alcoholics, but these deficits are relatively mild, are often material-specific, and do not seem to involve the same processes characteristic of Korsakoff patients.

Between 1977 and 1983, Christopher Ryan, James Becker, Jason Brandt, and Butters published several papers assessing the severity of anterograde-memory impairments in detoxified alcoholics with more than 20-year histories of heavy drinking. Having heeded Parsons and Prigatano's (1977) conclusion that research findings provide little evidence that detoxified alcoholics have a permanent memory impairment, the group began by assuming that there were two possible explanations for the failure of previous studies to demonstrate significant learning and retention problems. One was that, unlike the visuoperceptual and problem-solving deficits apparent in both the alcoholic and the alcoholic Korsakoff patient, a significant memory loss emerges only when diencephalic lesions are present. Since these lesions have been linked to a chronic deficiency in thiamine, it is possible that most chronic alcoholics consume sufficient thiamine to prevent significant atrophy of the midline diencephalic region, and thereby escape significant memory impairments. A second possibility was that these early studies, which relied primarily on standard clinical tests such as the Wechsler Memory Scale, were simply too easy to detect a subtle but real memory problem. If the chronic alcoholic does, in fact, have a mild to moderate defect in the ability to store, process, and retrieve new information, this impairment may be evident only with highly sensitive psychometric instruments.

To evaluate this latter possibility, Ryan, Butters, Montgomery, Adinolfi, and Didario (1980) developed a battery of neuropsychological tests specifically designed to uncover subtle memory deficits. Among the tests used were the Verbal Paired-Associate Learning Test, the Symbol–Digit Paired-Associate Learning Test, and a four-word short-term memory task with a distractor procedure (i.e., counting backward) to prevent rehearsal. When Ryan *et al.* administered this battery of memory tests to alcoholic Korsakoff patients, thoroughly detoxified long-term alcoholics (with at least 10-year histories of alcoholism), and age- and education-matched nonalcoholic controls, the two alcoholic groups demonstrated significant deficits on all memory tasks. The performance of the detoxified alcoholics fell between the scores of the normal controls and the amnesic Korsakoff patients.

In a second study, Ryan and Butters (1980a) again assessed the performance of alcoholic Korsakoff patients, long-term alcoholics, and nonalcoholic controls on the same battery of memory tasks. However, on this occasion the long-term alcoholics were divided into two subgroups: One group consisted of alcoholics who complained about deficiencies in their everyday memory; the other group was made up of alcoholics who claimed to have encountered no memory difficulties in their day-to-day existence. The findings of this study seemed to provide further evidence for Ryback's continuity hypothesis. The Korsakoff patients and the alcoholics with memory complaints were severely and equally impaired on all memory tasks. Although the alcoholics without memory complaints had significant deficits compared to nonalcoholic controls, their performance on the memory test was superior to those of the other two alcoholic groups. Unfortunately, the results of this study were flawed by the existence of floor effects, which may have diminished significant differences between the Korsakoff patients and the long-term alcoholics with memory complaints, and by a failure to separate the nonalcoholic controls into two subgroups based upon their judgment of their memory capacities.

A third investigation in this series (Ryan & Butters, 1980b) compared the memory capacities of young (mean age = 42 years) and old (mean age = 54 years) alcoholics with equivalent long-term drinking histories. The results showed that both young and old alcoholics had poorer memory capacities than did nonalcoholics of the same age. More recently, Brandt and his colleagues (Brandt, Butters, Ryan, & Bayog, 1983) replicated most of Ryan *et al.*'s results with a relatively large population of alcoholics ($n = 134$) and nonalcoholic controls ($n = 76$). Figure 9-4 shows Brandt *et al.*'s results for the Symbol–Digit Paired-Associate Learning Test. Although the difference between the alcoholics and their age-matched controls were statistically significant, the clinical relevance of the results is questionable. When alcoholic Korsakoff patients were administered this task, they averaged less than one correct response on each of the four learning trials. Thus, unlike the results on the visuoperceptual and problem-solving tasks discussed previously, there was a vast difference in the severity of anterograde-memory impairments demonstrated by alcoholic Korsakoff patients and long-term alcoholics. If, as suggested by the continuity hypothesis, the severity of patients' memory disorders is a function of drinking history, the long-term alcoholics, whose duration of alcohol abuse was similar (approximately 20–25 years) to that of the Korsakoff patients, should have had more pronounced memory deficits.

Memory impairments in young and old alcoholics with matched drinking histories have also been reported by Becker and his colleagues (Becker, Butters, Hermann, & D'Angelo, 1983b) on the Face–Name Paired-Associate

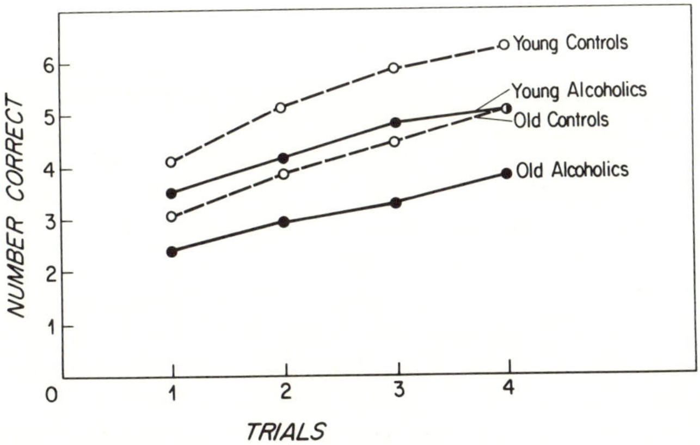

Figure 9-4. Learning curves of "young" and "old" alcoholics and nonalcoholics on the Symbol–Digit Paired-Associate Learning Test. (From "Cognitive Loss and Recovery in Long-Term Alcohol Abusers" by J. Brandt, N. Butters, C. Ryan, and R. Bayog, 1983, *Archives of General Psychiatry, 40,* 435–442. Reprinted by permission.)

Learning Test. This task requires subjects to associate 12 photographs of middle-aged men with 12 surnames (e.g., "Mr. Baker"). The alcoholics were significantly retarded in their acquisition of the face–name associations over nine learning trials, but their learning impairment seemed mild when compared to the amnesic condition of Korsakoff patients. In addition, when Becker *et al.* (1983b) assessed the types of errors (omission errors, perseverative errors) produced by the two groups, no significant differences were found. This lack of evidence that the alcoholics' errors were related to an increased sensitivity to proactive interference provided no support for the contention that similar information-processing problems underlie the impairments of both Korsakoff and non-Korsakoff alcoholic patients.

Further evidence that increased sensitivity to proactive interference is *not* a major contributor to the moderate memory deficits of long-term alcoholics has been found in their performance on the four-word short-term memory task developed by Ryan and his colleagues (Brandt *et al.*, 1983; Ryan *et al.*, 1980). On each trial of this task, subjects are read four words and then asked to count backward from 100 by 3's (i.e., a distractor task to prevent rehearsal) for 15 or 30 seconds before attempting recall of the verbal stimuli. As noted previously, when alcoholic Korsakoff patients were evaluated on a simpler version (three words presented on each trial) of this test, their severely impaired recall was usually characterized by numerous intralist intrusions. For example, a Korsakoff patient who correctly recalled "ship" as a word presented on the first trial of the test might recall this word on the second and third trials, even though it had not been presented again.

As seen in Figures 9-5 and 9-6, alcoholics were impaired on the four-word short-term memory task, but their errors were not perseverative (i.e., intralist intrusions). Like nonalcoholic controls, alcoholics made primarily errors of omission.

When these findings are considered in conjunction with other data showing that alcoholic Korsakoff patients and long-term alcoholics have different patterns of encoding problems (Cermak & Peck, 1982), little evidence supporting the continuity hypothesis can be found. Without some demonstrations that factors such as increased sensitivity to proactive interference and deficiencies in encoding are as prominent in the retention difficulties of long-term alcoholics as they are in the anterograde amnesia of alcoholic Korsakoff patients, the alcoholics' moderately poor performances on short-term memory and paired-associate learning tasks remain ambiguous. If long-term alcoholics and alcoholic Korsakoff patients are encountering problems with a given memory task for different underlying reasons, then it is difficult to maintain that they represent two points along a single continuum of cognitive dysfunction.

Another factor questioning the validity of the continuity hypothesis concerns the material-specific nature of the long-term alcoholics' memory deficits. Almost all reviews of the neuropsychology of alcoholism have

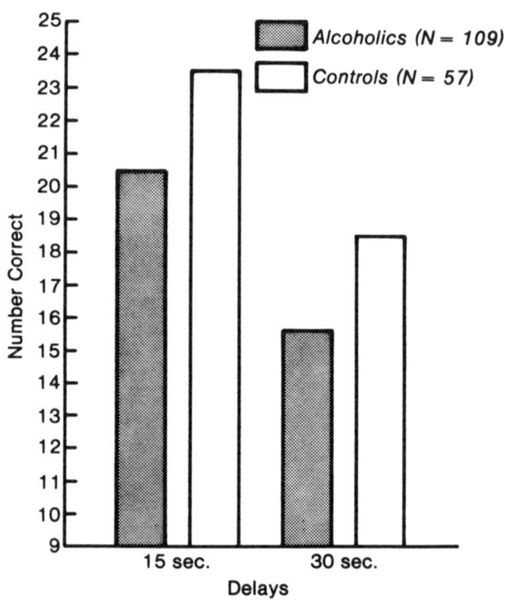

Figure 9-5. Performance of long-term alcoholics and nonalcoholic control subjects on Ryan *et al.*'s (1980) four-word short-term memory task. Number of words correctly recalled by each group after 15-second and 30-second delays is shown.

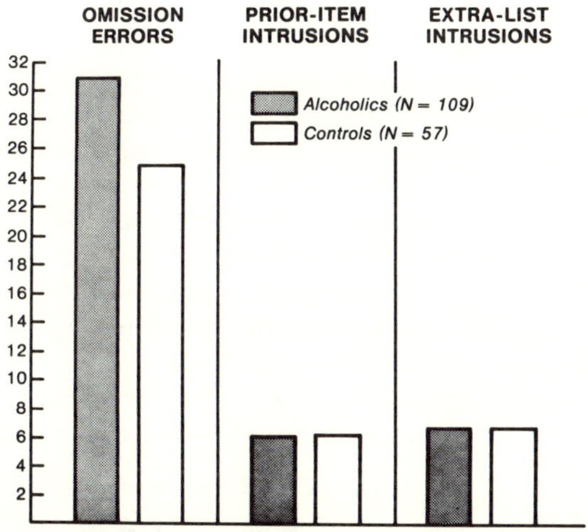

Figure 9-6. Types of errors made by long-term alcoholics and nonalcoholic control subjects on Ryan *et al.*'s (1980) four-word short-term memory task.

noted that alcoholics have more difficulty retaining patterned visual materials (e.g., geometric forms, faces) than verbal information (for reviews, see Parsons & Prigatano, 1977; Ryan & Butters, 1983), whereas alcoholic Korsakoff patients are severely impaired in acquiring both verbal and nonverbal materials, regardless of the sensory modality employed (Butters & Cermak, 1980; Talland, 1965). Our experiences with long-term alcoholics are consistent with this conclusion. Although we have found alcoholics to have significant and repeatable impairments on paired-associate tasks involving geometric patterns (Brandt *et al.*, 1983) and faces (Becker *et al.*, 1983b), deficits on verbal paired-associate tasks have been statistically marginal (Ryan & Butters, 1980a, 1980b; Ryan *et al.*, 1980) and difficult to replicate. In a recent study with relevance to this issue, Becker, Butters, Hermann, and D'Angelo (1983a) assessed the performance of long-term alcoholics and nonalcoholic controls on three divided-attention tasks requiring the retention of two series of stimuli simultaneously. One of the divided-attention tasks employed common words as the stimuli to be remembered; a second used single-digit numbers; and a third used photographs of faces. The results showed that only two of the three tests were influenced by long-term alcohol abuse. Both young and old alcoholics were impaired when faces had to be remembered, but neither group of alcoholics was impaired when words were used. On the numerical divided-attention task, only the old alcoholics encountered significant difficulty.

In conclusion, despite numerous demonstrations of anterograde-memory problems in detoxified long-term alcoholics, Ryback's (1971) continuity hypothesis is difficult to defend, for three reasons. First, long-term alcoholics with drinking histories similar to those of alcoholic Korsakoff patients have learning impairments that are far less severe than those of their amnesic counterparts. Second, there is little, if any, evidence that similar processes underlie the memory disorders of Korsakoff and alcoholic patients. Although the alcoholic Korsakoff patients' inability to acquire new information involves an increased sensitivity to interference, no evidence has been provided that the moderate learning deficits of long-term alcoholics reflect this process. Third, while the anterograde amnesia of Korsakoff patients is not limited by modality or material, the alcoholics' memory deficits are most pronounced and reliable when visual patterned materials serve as the stimuli to be remembered. There is very little evidence that the "typical" long-term alcoholic has a consistent problem in learning and remembering verbal information.

Retrograde Amnesia

The question of whether the temporally graded, extensive retrograde amnesia of alcoholic Korsakoff patients develops slowly during years of alcohol abuse has been addressed both by Squire and Cohen (1982) and by Butters and Albert (1982). Both sets of investigators have suggested that the alcoholic Korsakoff patients' extensive inability to retrieve remote memories may be secondary to a primary defect in establishing new memories (i.e., anterograde amnesia) during the 20 or more years of alcohol abuse that have preceded the diagnosis of the amnesic syndrome. If chronic alcoholics acquire less information each year, due to a progressive anterograde-memory deficit, then at the time an alcoholic patient is diagnosed as having Korsakoff's syndrome, one would expect to find a retrograde amnesia with a temporal gradient. From this viewpoint, the Korsakoff patients' loss of remote memories would be considered an artifact related to a primary defect in establishing new memories. A corollary of this hypothesis is that true retrograde amnesias, uncontaminated by deficiencies in original learning, are temporally limited and are far less severe and devastating than the alcoholic Korsakoff patients' anterograde-memory problems (Squire & Cohen, 1982).

To evaluate this "chronic" (i.e., continuity) explanation of the alcoholic Korsakoff's retrograde amnesia, Albert, Butters, and Brandt (1980) administered their battery of tests of remote memory to detoxified long-term (non-Korsakoff) alcoholics and nonalcoholic control subjects. They proposed that if the learning deficit related to alcoholism is responsible for alcoholic Korsakoff patients' difficulties in recalling past events, two predictions could be made: First, the alcoholics should be impaired in their identification of photographs of famous people and public events; and second, since the detrimental effects of alcohol on the learning of new materials are probably related to years of alcohol abuse, the alcoholics' deficits in recalling past events should be most apparent for the years immediately preceding testing. Their results did not provide strong support for these expectations. Although the alcoholics' mean identification scores for photographs of famous people from the 1960s and 1970s were poorer than the scores of the nonalcoholics controls, these differences did not attain statistical significance. However, on the recall questionnaire, the alcoholics had a significant but mild impairment in their recall of "hard" public events from the 1960s and 1970s. It should be stressed that for no decade did the recall performance of these long-term alcoholics approach the amnesic scores of alcoholic Korsakoff patients.

The findings of Albert *et al.*'s (1980) study are not especially supportive of the notion that the alcoholic Korsakoff patients' retrograde amnesia can be reduced to a failure to learn public events during their prolonged histories of alcohol abuse. While a mild deficiency in the original learning of public events may make a secondary contribution, the major factor in the development of the Korsakoff patients' retrograde amnesia must involve an acute loss of memories that occurred before the onset of their illness.

The most convincing evidence for this acute onset of the Korsakoff patients' problems with remote memory comes from a single-case study of autobiographical memory (Butters, 1984; Butters & Cermak, 1986). This patient (with the fictitious initials P. Z.), an eminent scientist and university professor who developed alcoholic Korsakoff's syndrome at the age of 65, had written several hundred research papers and numerous books and book chapters, including an extensive autobiography 2 years prior to the acute onset of his amnesic condition in 1981. Like all alcoholics with Korsakoff's syndrome, patient P. Z. had severe anterograde and retrograde amnesia as judged by both clinical and formal psychometric techniques. He was totally unable to learn verbal paired associates and was severly impaired in his identification of famous people and events from the past 50 years. To determine whether patient P. Z. had also lost access to autobiographical material familiar to him before his illness, a retrograde-amnesia test based upon his written autobiography was constructed. The test consisted of questions about relatives, colleagues, collaborators, conferences, research assistants, research reports, and books mentioned prominently in his autobiography.

Patient P. Z.'s recall of these autobiographical facts is shown in Figure 9-7. It is evident that patient P. Z. had a very severe retrograde amnesia for autobiographical events, with some sparing of information only from the very remote past. What is crucial for our present concerns is that patient P. Z.'s retrograde amnesia for autobiographical material could not have been secondary to a deficiency in original learning. Since all questions were drawn from his own autobiography, the possibility that patient P. Z. had never acquired the information was eliminated. Just 3 years prior to the

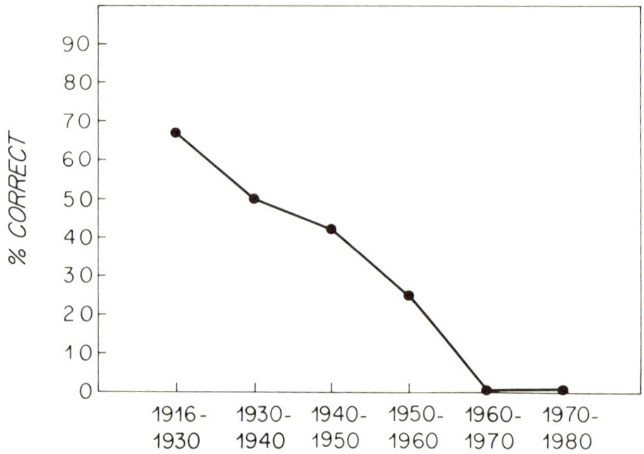

Figure 9-7. Patient P. Z.'s retrograde amnesia for information from his published autobiography. (From "Alcoholic Korsakoff's Syndrome: An Update" by N. Butters, 1984, *Seminars in Neurology*, *4*(2), 229–247. Reprinted by permission.)

onset of his Korsakoff's syndrome, patient P. Z. could retrieve this information that he considered most important in his professional and personal life. Clearly, patient P. Z.'s illness marked the acute onset of his inability to access information that was once readily available to him.

It is also pertinent that patient P. Z.'s loss of remote memories involved knowledge of his area of scientific expertise. Since our group had access to patient P. Z.'s numerous books and journal publications, it was possible to construct a vocabulary test consisting of 35 terms from patient P. Z.'s area of specialization. All of the scientific terms on this test appeared in one or more of P. Z.'s written works, and thus were part of his store of remote memories. To provide a standard for evaluating P. Z.'s scientific knowledge, another 65-year-old, highly prominent scholar in the same specialty area was administered this test of scientific definitions.

The results are shown in Figure 9-8. An ordinal rating of "0" indicates a total unawareness of the meaning of a term, whereas an ordinal score of "2" refers to a full and accurate definition of the term. A score of "1" is used when an incomplete partial definition was given. In comparison to his control subject, patient P. Z. was impaired in his ability to define scientific terms that were once well known to him. This lack of scientific knowledge not only is consistent with the previous evidence of an acute loss of remote autobiographical memories, but also demonstrates that *semantic* memory is not completely intact in alcoholic Korsakoff patients. If, as Tulving (1983) has suggested, the learning and retention of definitions can be used to evaluate the status of semantic memory, it is difficult to characterize P. Z.'s retrograde amnesia as a pure deficit in *episodic* memory (i.e., memory for

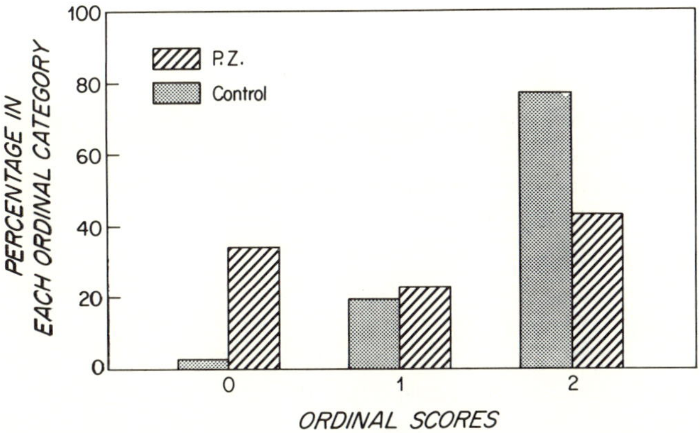

Figure 9-8. Performance of patient P. Z. and his matched control subject on the definition of scientific terms. Scores 0, 1, and 2 represent an ordinal scaling of the two subjects' responses. (From "A Case Study of the Forgetting of Autobiographical Knowledge: Implications for the Study of Retrograde Amnesia" by N. Butters and L. S. Cermak, 1986, in D. Rubin [Ed.], *Autobiographical Memory* [pp. 253–272]. New York: Cambridge University Press. Reprinted by permission.)

data or events associated with a specific temporal and/or spatial context). We shall return to this distinction between episodic and semantic memory when comparisons of the memory disorders of Korsakoff patients and of patients with AD are considered later in this presentation.

Etiological and Neuropathological Considerations in Alcoholic Korsakoff's Syndrome

Our review of the cognitive deficits of alcoholic Korsakoff patients and long-term alcoholics suggests that the continuity hypothesis has quite different merits when applied to cortical and subcortical dysfunctions. There is substantial evidence that visuoperceptual and problem-solving deficits, which presumably reflect the cortical abnormalities (e.g., widening of cortical sulci) frequently seen on CT scans of the brains of Korsakoff and alcoholic patients (e.g., Jernigan *et al.*, 1982; Ron, Acker, & Lishman, 1980; Wilkinson & Carlen, 1981), develop slowly during the Korsakoff patients' 20- to 30-year history of alcohol abuse. Alcohol may have a direct neurotoxic effect on association cortex, and a normal nutritional status may not protect the alcoholic patient from eventual visuoconceptual and analytical deficiencies. If Ryback's (1971) continuity model (see Figure 9-1) represents a good approximation of the relationship between alcohol abuse and higher cortical functions, then the daily consumption of a large quantity of alcohol for a sufficiently prolonged period may result in the "alcohol dementia" described by Cutting (1978) and Lishman (1981).

When we turn to alcoholic Korsakoff patients' memory deficits, which have been associated with medial diencephalic lesions (Victor *et al.*, 1971), the continuity model appears to have little applicability. Despite more than 20 years of severe alcoholism, non-Korsakoff alcoholics have relatively mild anterograde- and retrograde-memory deficits, which do not reflect the same information-processing impairments as those of alcoholic Korsakoff patients. As shown diagrammatically in Figure 9-9, the memory processes of alcoholics may evidence some moderate decline with continued alcohol abuse, but the truly amnesic performance of alcoholic Korsakoff patients cannot be achieved without some acute trauma combining with the chronic detrimental effects of ethanol. According to all published clinical histories of this disorder, the most likely precipitating process is a severe thiamine deficiency (i.e., malnutrition). The well-documented role of thiamine deficiency in the onset of the Wernicke–Korsakoff syndrome (for review, see Victor *et al.*, 1971) does not negate the possibility that the adverse effects of the combination of thiamine deficiency and alcoholism are exponentially worse than the effect of either factor alone. Freund's (1973) conclusion that only in alcoholics is Wernicke's encephalopathy followed by Korsakoff's syndrome remains a clinically valid observation.

Given that the Korsakoff patients' amnesic syndrome does develop

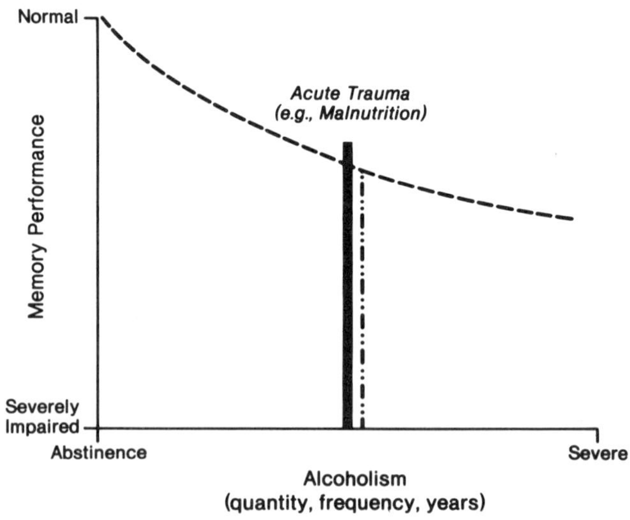

Figure 9-9. Proposed relationship between severity of alcoholism and memory performance. Without an acute trauma (e.g., malnutrition), severe alcoholism results in only mild to moderate memory deficits.

acutely as a result of the combination of thiamine deficiency and prolonged alcohol abuse, what neuropathological assumptions can be made? If one accepts the role of the medial diencephalic region (especially the dorsomedial nucleus of the thalamus) in the memory disorders of alcoholic Korsakoff patients (Victor *et al.,* 1971), two conclusions follow. First, long-term alcoholism may result in some minor damage to the medial diencephalic region, as evidenced by the findings of numerous neuroradiological studies. Some studies with CT scans have reported marked dilation of the third ventricle of long-term alcoholics (for reviews, see Cala & Mastaglia, 1981; Wilkinson, 1982; Wilkinson & Carlen, 1981), while other studies using computerized analyses of the CT scans of alcoholics have reported that the density of brain tissue surrounding the third ventricle is highly correlated with performance on paired-associate learning tasks (Gebhardt, Naeser, & Butters, 1984; Jernigan; 1982). Second, severe thiamine deficiency is followed by a marked acceleration in the development of hemorrhagic lesions in the medial diencephalic region. The Korsakoff patients' precipitous decline in memory performance would then represent the exceeding of a critical threshold of diencephalic damage for the maintenance of relatively intact memory functions. The numerous neuropsychological papers referring to alcoholic Korsakoff's syndrome as a "diencephalic amnesia" reflect the popularity of this neuropathological assumption (e.g., Butters & Cermak, 1980; Huppert & Piercy, 1978, 1979; Squire, 1981; Squire & Cohen, 1984).

Despite the evidence linking Korsakoff's syndrome to the medial diencephalic region, a recent neuropathological investigation by Arendt, Bigl, Arendt, and Tennstedt (1983) suggests that the critical area affected in alcoholic Korsakoff patients may be the basal forebrain—the major source of cholinergic input to the cerebral cortex and hippocampus. These investigators, using cresyl violet stains and light microscopy, derived total neuron counts and indices of maximum neuronal population density in the three subdivisions of the basal forebrain and in portions of the globus pallidus (Figure 9-10). Of the 72 cases studied, 14 were control cases, 3 were cases of alcoholic Korsakoff's syndrome, 5 were cases of chronic alcoholism without dementia, 14 were cases of AD, 9 were cases of HD, and 3 were cases of schizophrenia.

The major findings of this study are shown in Figure 9-11. In the AD and Korsakoff cases, the number of neurons in the basal forebrain was reduced by 70% and 47%, respectively. No significant loss of neurons in the basal forebrain was noted for the chronic alcoholics, schizophrenics, and HD cases. Of the five groups, only the AD group had a significant decrement (54%) in maximum population density in the basal forebrain. Scrutiny of the globus pallidus showed that only the HD brains had significant reductions in total neurons (40%) and maximum population density (29%).

Although Arendt *et al.*'s (1983) findings are based on few brains and

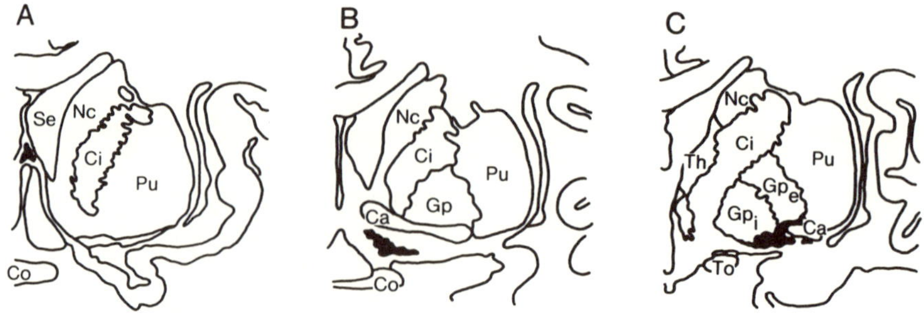

Figure 9-10. Schematic frontal sections through the human forebrain. Three subdivisions of the basal forebrain are shown in black. (A) Section through junction of the caudate and lenticular nuclei containing the medial septal nuclei. (B) Section through the anterior commissure containing the nucleus of the diagonal band of Broca. (C) Section through the diencephalon containing neurons in the substantia innominata. Ca, anterior commissure; Ci, internal capsule; Co, optic chiasm; Gp, globus pallidus; Gpe, external pallidum; Gpi, internal pallidum; Nc, caudate nucleus; Pu, putamen; Se, septum; Th, thalamus; To, optic tract. (Adapted from "Loss of Neurons in the Nucleus Basalis of Meynert in Alzheimer's Disease, Paralysis Agitans and Korsakoff's Disease" by T. Arendt, V. Bigl, A. Arendt, and A. Tennstedt, 1983, *Acta Neuropathologica, 61*, 101–108. Used by permission.)

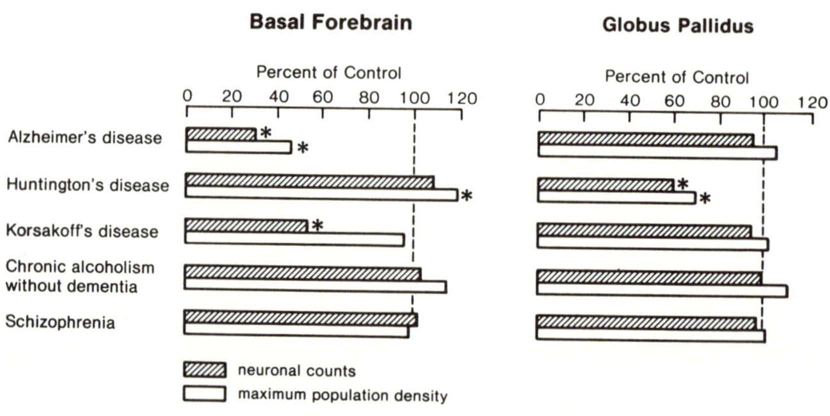

Figure 9-11. Neuronal counts (hatched bars) and maximum population density (white bars) in the basal forebrain and in the globus pallidus in five patient populations. Cell counts and maximum density for the five patient groups are expressed as percentages of such measures in 14 control brains. Bars with an asterisk indicate statistically significant deviations from the control indices. (Adapted from "Loss of Neurons in the Nucleus Basalis of Meynert in Alzheimer's Disease, Paralysis Agitans and Korsakoff's Disease" by T. Arendt, V. Bigl, A. Arendt, and A. Tennstedt, 1983, *Acta Neuropathologica, 61*, 101–108. Used by permission.)

need to be confirmed by other laboratories, their implications for our understanding of the neuropathology and neuropsychology of Korsakoff's syndrome are obvious. From a neuropathological perspective, alcoholic Korsakoff's syndrome may be more accurately viewed as a "cholinergic" than as a "diencephalic" amnesia. That is, the critical structures responsible for the Korsakoff patients' amnesic syndrome (and possibly for other cognitive deficits as well) may lie in the basal forebrain instead of the medial diencephalon. The onset of a severe thiamine deficiency combined with heavy alcohol consumption may result in the acute death of cells in the basal forebrain, and, consequently, in a sudden and marked reduction of cholinergic input to those cortical and limbic structures involved with memory. If this is the case, hemorrhagic lesions in the diencephalon may be as common in long-term alcoholics as in alcoholics with Korsakoff's syndrome, and may be responsible only for long-term alcoholics' mild to moderate memory deficits.

This emphasis upon the association between thiamine deficiency and the basal forebrain rather than the diencephalon receives some indirect support from animal studies concerned with the neuropathological effects of thiamine deficiency. As Irle and Markowitsch (1982) noted in their careful review of this literature, there is little evidence that prolonged thiamine deficiency will result in consistent damage to the dorsomedial nucleus of the thalamus. Witt and Goldman-Rakic (1983a, 1983b) observed that multiple bouts of thiamine deficiency in monkeys were followed by lesions in the basal ganglia, cerebellum, and discrete brain stem nuclei. Most surprising, however, was the lack of necrosis in either the mammillary bodies or the dorsomedial nucleus of the thalamus.

Arendt *et al.*'s (1983) failure to locate any cell loss in the basal forebrain of chronic alcoholics without dementia is very consistent with our reservations concerning the application of Ryback's (1971) continuity hypothesis to the memory disorders of alcoholics. If it is assumed that cholinergic activity is vital for the processing and storage of information, the intactness of the basal forebrain of chronic alcoholics without dementia makes it difficult to place long-term alcoholics and alcoholic Korsakoff patients on the same continuum of memory disorders.

It is important to stress that Arendt *et al.*'s (1983) findings and our extrapolations to the Korsakoff patients' amnesic syndrome are not intended to deny the existence of "diencephalic" amnesia. There are too many reports of amnesia following traumatic, vascular, and neoplastic lesions of the medial diencephalon to permit us to do so, although Markowitsch's (1982) reluctance to attribute memory functions specifically to the dorsomedial nucleus of the thalamus should be heeded. In essence, our only goal is to provide a neuropathological basis for separating the memory disorders of non-Korsakoff and Korsakoff alcoholics. The mild learning deficits of the former may be due to some limited damage to the diencephalon, whereas the severe amnesia of the latter may reflect the interaction of this limited diencephalic damage with a large decrement in cholinergic innervation of the cerebral cortex.

Neuropsychological Comparisons of Alcoholic Korsakoff's, Alzheimer's, and Huntington's Disease Patients

In addition to providing neuropathological data to help account for the cognitive differences between alcoholic Korsakoff patients and long-term alcoholics, Arendt *et al.*'s (1983) findings have substantial theoretical and heuristic value for neuropsychologists interested in cognitive similarities and differences among various demented and amnesic populations. If disruption of the cholinergic innervation of higher cortical areas is a common factor underlying Korsakoff's syndrome and AD, these two disorders should evidence similar patterns of memory deficits. In contrast, patients with HD, whose neuropathology is known to initially involve the basal ganglia (Kuhl *et al.*, 1982; Sandberg & Coyle, 1984) should perform quite differently from the other two patient groups. Since both HD and AD are progressive disorders in which memory deficits are often the first cognitive symptom (Butters, Sax, Montgomery, & Tarlow, 1978; Josiassen, Curry, & Mancall, 1983; Miller, 1977), such group comparisons should be most productive when they involve patients in the earliest detectable stages of the diseases.

While a number of studies have shown significant differences in the memory disorders of Korsakoff and HD patients (e.g., Butters, 1984; Oscar-Berman & Zola-Morgan, 1980a, 1980b), only recently have such comparative investigations included patients with AD. It is of some interest that the results of these initial neuropsychological comparisons are consistent with the expectations derived from Arendt *et al.*'s (1983) neuropathology paper. In a study concerned with the patients' pictorial memories, HD patients, but not AD and alcoholic Korsakoff patients, could use language to improve their picture–context recognition memory (Butters *et al.*, 1983). Furthermore, an analysis of the types of errors committed by three patient groups on the picture–context recognition task indicated that both the AD and Korsakoff patients made many more perseveration (i.e., intrusion) errors than did the HD patients and intact control subjects.

Moss, Albert, Butters, and Payne (1986) compared alcoholic Korsakoff, AD, and HD patients on a delayed non-matching-to-sample task designed to assess recognition memory for different classes of stimulus material (verbal, spatial, colors, geometric patterns, and faces). For each type of stimulus material, a "recognition span" was derived. The results showed that the Korsakoff and AD patients were equally impaired in each of the five stimulus conditions. However, the HD patients, though impaired in four of the recognition conditions, were unimpaired in their recognition of verbal stimuli. When the subjects were asked to recall after a 15-second delay the words used on the recognition test, the three patient groups were equally impaired. Martone and her collaborators (Martone, Butters, Payne, Becker, & Sax, 1984) have also noted that HD, but not Korsakoff, patients can perform normally on tests of verbal recognition and have suggested that the HD patients' problems with verbal memory represent an inability to initiate retrieval processes.

In addition to these studies, some data recently collected in our laboratory on retrieval from semantic memory and on the immediate recall of meaningful verbal passages also demonstrate similarities in the types of errors produced by alcoholic Korsakoff and AD patients. In one study, a letter-fluency task developed by Benton and his colleagues (Benton, 1968; Borkowski, Benton, & Spreen, 1967) was administered to alcoholic Korsakoff, HD, and early AD patients, and to groups of young (45-year-old) and old (65-year-old) normal control subjects. The subjects were shown the letters "F," "A," and "S" successively, and were asked to produce "all the words you can think of" that begin with these letters. The subjects were allowed 60 seconds to generate words for each letter. Although this task has often been used to assess verbal fluency, Martin and Fedio (1983) and Ober and her colleagues (Ober, Donkers, Koss, Delis, & Friedland, 1986) have accurately observed that the test involves the retrieval of information from *semantic* memory (Tulving, 1983). It has already been reported that patients in the early stages of AD (Martin & Fedio, 1983; Ober *et al.*, 1986; Rosen, 1980) and early and advanced HD patients (Butters *et al.*, 1978) are severely impaired on this letter-category and/or similar fluency tasks, but direct comparisons of overall performance and error types among these two demented patient populations and patients with alcoholic Korsakoff's syndrome have not been attempted.

Figure 9-12 shows our findings for the "F-A-S" test. The three patient groups all generated fewer total correct responses than did the two control groups, with the performance of the HD patients being the poorest. The major difference in the performances of the three patient groups was seen in the number of perseverations produced on the test. A "perseveration error" was defined as the repetition of a correct word within a given category. For example, if a subject gave "fork" as the 3rd and 12th responses to the letter "F," the latter response was counted as a perseveration error. To analyze the subjects' tendency to produce perseveration errors, the proportion of total responses that were perseverations was calculated. Although all three patient groups had a higher percentage of perseveration responses than did the two groups of control subjects (young = 1.9%; old = 2.4%), the alcoholic Korsakoff (11.3%) and AD (10.2%) patients had significantly higher percentages of perseverations than did the HD (5.8%) patients. As with the

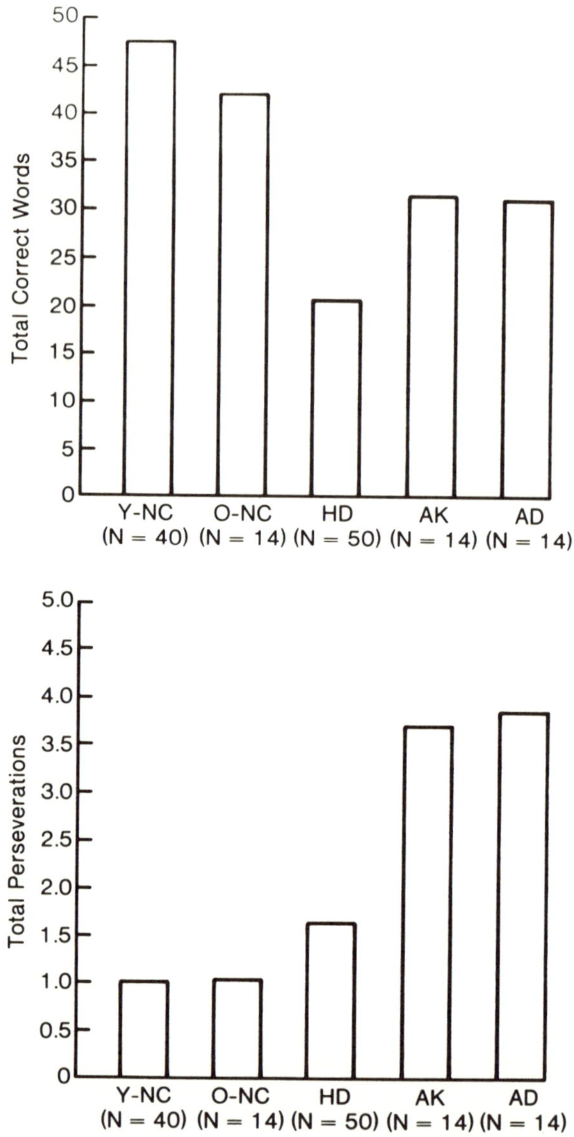

Figure 9-12. Performance of alcoholic Korsakoff (AK), Huntington's disease (HD), and Alzheimer's disease (AD) patients and of "young" and "old" normal control (Y-NC, O-NC) subjects on a letter-fluency ("F-A-S") task. Total number of correct words (top) and number of perseveration errors (bottom) are shown for each group.

picture–context recognition task employed by Butters *et al.* (1983), the Korsakoff and AD patients, but not the HD patients, appeared highly sensitive to interference from previously emitted responses.

The investigation concerned with the recall of meaningful verbal passages also demonstrated that the alcoholic Korsakoff and early AD patients could be differentiated from the HD patients on the basis of their sensitivity to interference (Figure 9-13). In this study subjects were read a series of four short stories, similar to those employed on the Logical Memories test of the Wechsler Memory Scale. Each paragraph consisted of 23 ideas or details concerning a specific incident. Thirty seconds after each paragraph had been read aloud by the examiner, the subject was asked to recall as much of the information as possible. Although the alcoholic Korsakoff, AD, and HD patients were equally impaired in their recall of the details of these passages, the groups differed in the number of intrusion errors they produced. An "intrusion error" refers to the inclusion of an idea from a preceding story in the attempted recall of a subsequent passage. For example, if the idea "Tim had a brown dog" was mentioned in the first story read to a subject and later was recalled by the subject as an idea from the third story, an intrusion error was scored. As shown in Figure 9-13, both the alcoholic Korsakoff and AD patients made many more intrusion errors than did the HD patients and the normal control subjects.

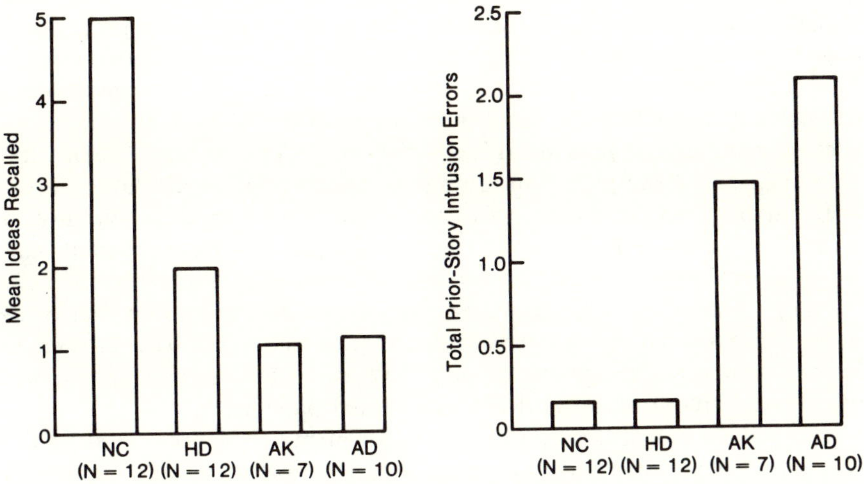

Figure 9-13. Performance of alcoholic Korsakoff (AK), Huntington's disease (HD), and Alzheimer's disease (AD) patients and of normal control (NC) subjects on recall of short passages. The mean number of ideas recalled by each group is presented on the left; the total number of prior-story intrusion errors made by each group is shown on the right.

These initial comparisons of alcoholic Korsakoff, AD, and HD patients are tantalizing, given Arendt *et al.*'s (1983) neuropathological findings. In all four studies, the early AD and alcoholic Korsakoff patients showed similar patterns of memory impairments, which, in turn, could be differentiated from the memory problems of HD patients. Although all three groups were severely impaired when asked to retrieve recently presented verbal materials and information from *semantic* memory, the HD patients proved to be superior to the alcoholic Korsakoff and AD patients on tests employing recognition measures of verbal learning. Close attention to the qualitative nature of the patients' errors on both recall and recognition tests revealed that the alcoholic Korsakoff and AD patients were more prone to perseveration and intrusion errors than were the HD patients.

Finally, we wish to emphasize that our brief review of the comparisons of the memory deficits of alcoholic Korsakoff and AD patients has been at least partially a heuristic exercise. It is obvious to any student of dementia that there are as many differences between alcoholic Korsakoff and AD patients as there are similarities. Beyond the very early stages of their disorders, AD patients often develop dysnomia and severe constructional apraxia. In contrast, alcoholic Korsakoff patients show little evidence of a general language dysfunction, and their constructional difficulties are usually mild to moderate in severity. Even when we limit our comparisons to memory dysfunctions, there are indications that the previously described parallels may be misleading. For example, Weingartner and his associates (Weingartner, Grafman, Boutelle, Kaye, & Martin, 1983) have suggested that while both alcoholic Korsakoff patients and patients with progressive degenerative dementia (probably AD) are severely impaired in the acquisition of *episodic* memories (e.g., the learning of a list of 12 unrelated words) the demented patients are more impaired than the Korsakoff patients in accessing and utilizing previously acquired general knowledge (i.e., *semantic* memory). This assumption concerning the intactness of the alcoholic Korsakoff patients' *semantic* memories can be questioned by their inability to recall overlearned remote public events (e.g., the Watergate scandal), and especially by patient P. Z.'s severe loss of knowledge about his scientific specialty (see Figure 9-8). However, the clinical demonstration that alcoholic Korsakoff patients retain the rules of grammar and of basic arithmetic is consistent with Weingartner *et al.*'s conclusion that *semantic* memory is more presevered in amnesic than in demented patients.

Given the convincing clinical and experimental evidence that alcoholic Korsakoff's syndrome and AD are not identical in terms of their pattern of cognitive impairments, are additional comparative studies justified? In our opinion, there are at least two compelling reasons for an affirmative answer to this question. First, the noted differences between alcoholic Korsakoff and AD patients may represent differences in the amount of damage to the basal forebrain. If, as in Arendt *et al.*'s (1983) study, AD patients generally have more neuronal loss in the basal forebrain than do the Korsakoff patients, the additional disruption of language and constructional abilities in AD may reflect a more drastic decrement of cholinergic innervation of the association cortices. If such is the case, further comparisons of alcoholic Korsakoff patients and AD patients in the earliest detectable stages of the disease would appear worthwhile. Second, comparative studies of various neurological populations have provided us with new insights into brain–behavior relationships. It was not long ago that all amnesic disorders, regardless of etiology and lesion site, were considered a unitary dysfunction. However, because of the numerous neuropsychological investigations comparing the cognitive processes underlying the memory disorders of patients with diencephalic, hippocampal, basal ganglial, and cortical lesions, the heterogeneity of memory failures has come to be appreciated. Such revelations should provide sufficient encouragement for the continuation of comparative studies aimed at uncovering the qualitative features of severe memory disorders.

Conclusions

We have attempted to emphasize the complexity of the etiological and neuropathological basis of alcoholic Korsakoff's syndrome and to suggest some new directions in which to search. The continuity hypothesis, which derives support from the evidence that ethanol is neurotoxic, may have some applicability to cortically mediated cognitive functions, but it seems inadequate in accounting for the severe anterograde and retrograde amnesias of Korsakoff patients. Although it is apparent that these amnesic problems develop acutely when severe malnutrition is combined with chronic alcoholism, the assumption that these memory dysfunctions can be attributed totally to hemorrhagic lesions of the medial diencephalic region can be questioned. On the basis of the recent neuropathological evidence that alcoholic Korsakoff patients, like patients with AD, have endured a significant loss of neurons in various structures comprising the basal forebrain, the possibility arises that alcoholic Korsakoff's syndrome might best be viewed as a "basal forebrain" rather than a "diencephalic" amnesia. The few neuropsychological studies that have compared the memory disorders of AD and Korsakoff patients provide some preliminary support for this notion that the memory disorders of these two patient populations share some common underlying features. Whether future neuropathological investigations of the brains of Korsakoff and AD patients do or do not confirm a common involvement of basal forebrain structures in these disorders, comparisons of the memory disorders of these and other neurological populations are still likely to produce new understandings of the processes underlying amnesic symptoms.

Acknowledgments

Some of the research cited in this chapter was supported by funds from the Medical Research Service of the Veterans Administration; by Grant No. AA-00187 from the National Institute on Alcohol Abuse and Alcoholism to Boston University; by Grant No. NS-16367 from the National Institute of Neurological and Communicative Disorders and Stroke to Massachusetts General Hospital; and by Grant No. AG-05131 from the National Institute on Aging to the University of California at San Diego. We wish to acknowledge the assistance of Drs. Jessica Wolfe and David Salmon in the preparation of this manuscript. This chapter is based upon Nelson Butters's Presidential Address presented at the International Neuropsychological Society's Annual Meeting on February 8, 1985, in San Diego. Portions of this chapter were published in the *Journal of Clinical and Experimental Neuropsychology*, 1985, *7*, 181–210. Copyright 1985 by Swets Publishing Co. Adapted by permission.

References

Albert, M. S., Butters, N., & Brandt, J. (1980). Memory for remote events in alcoholics. *Journal of Studies on Alcohol*, *41*, 1071–1081.

Albert, M. S., Butters, N., & Levin, J. (1979). Temporal gradients in the retrograde amnesia of patients with alcoholic Korsakoff's disease. *Archives of Neurology*, *36*, 211–216.

Albert, M. S., Butters, N., Rogers, S., Pressman, J., & Geller, A. (1982). A preliminary report: Nutritional levels and cognitive performance in chronic alcohol abusers. *Drug and Alcohol Dependence*, *9*, 131–142.

Arendt, T., Bigl, V., Arendt, A., & Tennstedt, A. (1983). Loss of neurons in the nucleus basalis of Meynert in Alzheimer's disease, paralysis agitans and Korsakoff's disease. *Acta Neuropathologica*, *61*, 101–108.

Becker, J., Butters, N., Hermann, A., & D'Angelo, N. (1983a). A comparison of the effects of long-term alcohol abuse and aging on the performance of verbal and nonverbal divided attention tasks. *Alcoholism: Clinical and Experimental Research*, *7*, 213–219.

Becker, J., Butters, N., Hermann, A., & D'Angelo, N. (1983b). Learning to associate names and faces: Impaired acquisition on an ecologically relevant memory task by male alcoholics. *Journal of Nervous and Mental Disease*, *171*, 617–623.

Becker, J., Rivoira, P., Butters, N., & Ciraulo, D. (1984). *Asking the right questions: Problem solving skills in alcoholics and alcoholics with Korsakoff's syndrome.* Paper presented at the annual meeting of the Research Society on Alcoholism, San Antonio, TX.

Benton, A. L. (1968). Differential behavioral effects in frontal lobe disease. *Neuropsychologia*, *6*, 53–60.

Borkowski, J. G., Benton, A. L., & Spreen, O. (1967). Word fluency and brain damage. *Neuropsychologia*, *5*, 135–140.

Brandt, J., Butters, N., Ryan, C., & Bayog, R. (1983). Cognitive loss and recovery in long-term alcohol abusers. *Archives of General Psychiatry*, *40*, 435–442.

Butters, N. (1984). Alcoholic Korsakoff's syndrome: An update. *Seminars in Neurology*, *4*(2), 229–247.

Butters, N., & Albert, M. S. (19822). Processes underlying failures to recall remote events. In L. S. Cermak (Ed.), *Human memory and amnesia* (pp. 257–274). Hillsdale, NJ: Erlbaum.

Butters, N., Albert, M., Sax, D., Miliotis, P., Nagode, J., & Sterste, A. (1983). Effect of verbal mediators on the pictorial memory of brain-damaged patients. *Neuropsychologia*, *21*, 307–323.

Butters, N., & Brandt, J. (1985). The continuity hypothesis: The relationship of long-term alcoholism to the Wernicke-Korsakoff syndrome. In M. Galanter (Ed.), *Recent developments in alcoholism* (Vol. 3, pp. 207–226). New York: Plenum Press.

Butters, N., & Cermak, L. S. (1980). *Alcoholic Korsakoff's syndrome: An information processing approach to amnesia.* New York: Academic Press.

Butters, N., & Cermak, L. S. (1986). A case study of the forgetting of autobiographical knowledge: Implications for the study of retrograde amnesia. In D. Rubin (Ed.), *Autobiographical memory* (pp. 253–272). New York: Cambridge University Press.

Butters, N., Sax, D., Montgomery, K., & Tarlow, S. (1978). Comparisons of the neuropsychological deficits associated with early and advanced Huntington's Disease. *Archives of Neurology, 35*, 585–589.

Cala, L. A., & Mastaglia, F. L. (1981). Computerized tomography in chronic alcoholics. *Alcoholism: Clinical and Experimental Research, 5*, 283–294.

Cermak, L. S., & Peck, E. (1982). Continuum versus premature aging theories of chronic alcoholism. *Alcoholism: Clinical and Experimental Research, 6*(1), 89–95.

Cohen, N. J., & Squire, L. R. (1981). Retrograde amnesia and remote memory impairment. *Neuropsychologia, 19*, 337–356.

Cutting, J. A. (1978). Relationship between Korsakoff's syndrome and alcoholic dementia. *British Journal of Psychiatry, 132*, 240–251.

Damasio, A. (1979). The frontal lobes. In K. M. Heilman & E. Valenstein (Eds.), *Clinical neuropsychology* (pp. 360–404). New York: Oxford University Press.

Freund, G. (1973). Chronic central nervous system toxicity of alcohol. *Annual Review of Pharmacology, 13*, 217–227.

Fuld, P. (1976). Storage, retention, and retrieval in Korsakoff's syndrome. *Neuropsychologia, 14*, 225–236.

Gebhardt, G., Naeser, M. A., & Butters, N. (1984). Computerized measures of CT scans of alcoholics. Thalamic region related to memory. *Alcohol, 1*, 133–140.

Glosser, G., Butters, N., & Kaplan, E. (1977). Visuoperceptual processes in brain-damaged patients on the digit-symbol substitution test. *International Journal of Neuroscience, 7*, 59–66.

Goldman, M. S. (1983). Cognitive impairment in chronic alcoholics. *American Psychologist, 38*, 1045–1054.

Guberman, A., & Stuss, D. (1983). The syndrome of bilateral paramedian thalamic infarction. *Neurology, 33*, 540–546.

Huppert, F. A., & Piercy, M. (1978). Dissociation between learning and remembering in organic amnesia. *Nature, 275*, 317–318.

Huppert, F. A., & Piercy, M. (1979). Normal and abnormal forgetting in organic amnesia: Effect of locus of lesion. *Cortex, 15*, 385–390.

Irle, E., & Markowitsch, H. J. (1982). Thiamine deficiency in the cat leads to severe learning deficits and to widespread neuroanatomical damage. *Experimental Brain Research, 48*, 199–208.

Jarho, L. (1973). *Korsakoff-like amnesic syndrome in penetrating brain injury.* Helsinki: Rehabilitation Institute for Brain Injured Veterans in Finland.

Jernigan, T. L. (1982). *Computed tomographic findings in alcoholic versus nonalcoholic dementia.* Paper presented at the Tenth Annual Meeting of the International Neuropsychological Society, Pittsburgh.

Jernigan, T. L., Zatz, L. M., Ahumada, A. J., Pfefferbaum, A., Moses, J. A., & Tinklenberg, J. (1982). CT measures of cerebrospinal fluid volume in alcoholics and normal volunteers. *Psychiatry Research, 7*, 9–17.

Josiassen, R. C., Curry, L. M., & Mancall, E. L. (1983). Development of neuropsychological deficits in Huntington's disease. *Archives of Neurology, 40*, 791–796.

Kapur, N., & Butters, N. (1977). Visuoperceptive deficits in long-term alcoholics with Korsakoff's psychosis. *Journal of Studies on Alcohol, 38*, 2025–2035.

Kuhl, D., Phelps, M., Markham, C., Metter, J., Riege, W., & Winters, J. (1982). Cerebral metabolism and atrophy in Huntington's Disease determined by 18 FDG and computed tomographic scan. *Annals of Neurology*, *12*, 425–434.

Laine, M., & Butters, N. (1982). A preliminary study of the problem solving strategies of detoxified long-term alcoholics. *Drug and Alcohol Dependence*, *10*, 235–242.

Lishman, W. A. (1981). Cerebral disorder in alcoholism: Syndromes of impairment. *Brain*, *104*, 1–20.

Luria, A. R. (1966). Two kinds of motor perservation in massive injury of the frontal lobes. *Brain*, *88*, 1–10.

Markowitsch, H. J. (1982). Thalamic mediodorsal nucleus and memory: A critical evaluation of studies in animals and man. *Neuroscience and Biobehavioral Reviews*, *6*, 351–380.

Martin, A., & Fedio, P. (1983). Word production and comprehension in Alzheimer's disease: The breakdown of semantic knowledge. *Brain and Language*, *19*, 124–141.

Martone, M., Butters, N., Payne, M., Becker, J., & Sax, D. (1984). Dissociations between skill learning and verbal recognition in amnesia and dementia. *Archives of Neurology*, *41*, 965–970.

Meudell, P. R., Butters, N., & Montgomery, K. (1978). Role of rehearsal in the short-term memory performance of patients with Korsakoff's and Huntington's disease. *Neuropsychologia*, *16*, 507–510.

Meudell, P. R., Northern, B., Snowden, J. S., & Neary, D. (1980). Long-term memory for famous voices in amnesic and normal subjects. *Neuropsychologia*, *18*, 133–139.

Miller, E. (1977). *Abnormal aging: The psychology of senile and presenile dementia.* London: Wiley.

Milner, B. (1964). Some effects of frontal lobectomy in man. In J. M. Warren & K. Akert (Eds.), *The frontal granular cortex and behavior* (pp. 313–334). New York: McGraw-Hill.

Moscovitch, M. (1982). Multiple dissociations of functions in amnesia. In L. S. Cermak (Ed.), *Human memory and amnesia* (pp. 337–370). Hillsdale, NJ: Erlbaum.

Moss, M., Albert, M. S., Butters, N., & Payne, M. (1986). Differential patterns of memory loss among patients with Alzheimer's disease, Huntington's disease and alcoholic Korsakoff's syndrome. *Archives of Neurology*, *43*, 239–246.

Ober, B. A., Donkers, N. F., Koss, E., Delis, D. C., & Friedland, R. P. (1986). Retrieval from semantic memory in Alzheimer-type dementia. *Journal of Clinical and Experimental Neuropsychology*, *8*, 75–92.

Oscar-Berman, M. (1973). Hypothesis testing and focusing behavior during concept formation by amnesic Korsakoff patients. *Neuropsychologia*, *11*, 191–198.

Oscar-Berman, M. & Zola-Morgan, S. M. (1980a). Comparative neuropsychology and Korsakoff's syndrome: I. Spatial and visual reversal learning. *Neuropsychologia*, *18*, 499–512.

Oscar-Berman, M., & Zola-Morgan, S. M. (1980b). Comparative neuropsychology and Korsakoff's syndrome: II. Two-choice visual discrimination learning. *Neuropsychologia*, *18*, 513–525.

Parsons, O. A. (1975). Brain damage in alcoholics. Altered states of unconsciousness. In M. Gross (Ed.), *Alcohol intoxication and withdrawal* (Vol. 2, pp. 564–584). New York: Plenum Press.

Parsons, O. A., & Farr, S. P. (1981). The neuropsychology of alcohol and drug abuse. In S. B. Filskov & T. J. Boll (Eds.), *Handbook of clinical neuropsychology* (pp. 320–365). New York: Wiley.

Parsons, O. A., & Leber, W. R. (1981). The relationship between cognitive dysfunction and brain damage in alcoholics: Causal, interactive, or epiphenomenal? *Alcoholism: Clinical and Experimental Research*, *5*, 326–343.

Parsons, O. A., & Prigatano, G. P. (1977). Memory functioning in alcoholics. In I. M. Birnham

& E. S. Parker (Eds.), *Alcohol and human memory* (pp. 185–194). Hillsdale, NJ: Erlbaum.

Ron, M., Acker, W., & Lishman, W. A. (1980). Morphological abnormalities in the brains of chronic alcoholics. *Acta Psychiatrica Scandinavica, 62*(Suppl. 286), 41–46.

Rosen, W. G. (1980). Verbal fluency in aging and dementia. *Journal of Clinical Neuropsychology, 2*, 135–146.

Ryan, C., & Butters, N. (1980a). Further evidence for a continuum-of-impairment encompassing male alcoholic Korsakoff patients and chronic alcoholic men. *Alcoholism: Clinical and Experimental Research, 4*, 190–198.

Ryan, C., & Butters, N. (1980b). Learning and memory impairments in young and old alcoholics: Evidence for the premature-aging hypothesis. *Alcoholism: Clinical and Experimental Research, 4*, 288–293.

Ryan, C., & Butters, N. (1983). Cognitive deficits in alcoholics. In B. Kissin & H. Begleiter (Eds.), *The biology of alcoholism: Vol. 7. The pathogenesis of alcoholism: Biological factors* (pp. 485–538). New York: Plenum Press.

Ryan, C., Butters, N., Montgomery, K., Adinolfi, A., & Didario, B. (1980). Memory deficits in chronic alcoholics: Continuities between the "intact" alcoholic and the alcoholic Korsakoff patient. In H. Begleiter (Ed.), *Biological effects of alcoholism* (pp. 701–718). New York: Plenum Press.

Ryback, R. (1971). The continuum and specificity of the effects of alcohol on memory: A review. *Quarterly Journal of Studies on Alcohol, 32*, 995–1016.

Sandberg, P., & Coyle, J. (1984). Scientific approaches to Huntington's disease. *Critical Reviews in Clinical Neurobiology, 1*, 1–44.

Speedie, L., & Heilman, K. (1982). Amnesic disturbance following infarction of the left dorsomedial nucleus of the thalamus. *Neuropsychologia, 20*, 597–604.

Speedie, L., & Heilman, K. (1983). Anterograde memory deficits for visuospatial material after infarction of the right thalamus. *Archives of Neurology, 40*, 183–186.

Squire, L. R. (1981). Two forms of human amnesia: An analysis of forgetting. *Journal of Neuroscience, 1*, 635–640.

Squire, L. R. (1982). Comparisons between forms of amnesia: Some deficits are unique to Korsakoff's syndrome. *Journal of Experimental Psychology: Learning, Memory and Cognition, 8*, 560–571.

Squire, L. R., & Cohen, N. J. (1982). Remote memory, retrograde amnesia, and the neuropsychology of memory. In L. S. Cermak (Ed.), *Human memory and amnesia* (pp. 275–303). Hillsdale, NJ: Erlbaum.

Squire, L. R., & Cohen, N. J. (1984). Human memory and amnesia. In G. Lynch, J. L. McGaugh, & N. Weinberger (Eds.), *Neurobiology of learning and memory* (pp. 3–64). New York: Guilford Press.

Squire, L. R., & Moore, R. Y. (1979). Dorsal thalamic lesion in a noted case of chronic memory dysfunction. *Annals of Neurology, 6*, 503–506.

Squire, L. R., & Slater, P. C. (1978). Anterograde and retrograde memory impairment in chronic amnesia. *Neuropsychologia, 16*, 313–322.

Talland, G. A. (1965). *Deranged memory*. New York: Academic Press.

Tulving, E. (1983). *Elements of episodic memory*. New York: Oxford University Press.

Victor, M., Adams, R. D., & Collins, G. H. (1971). *The Wernicke–Korsakoff syndrome*. Philadelphia: F. A. Davis.

Weingartner, H., Grafman, J., Boutelle, W., Kaye, W., & Martin, P. R. (1983). Forms of memory failure. *Science, 221*, 380–382.

Wilkinson, D. A. (1982). Examination of alcoholics by computed tomographic (CT) scans: A critical review. *Alcoholism: Clinical and Experimental Research, 6*, 31–45.

Wilkinson, D. A., & Carlen, P. L. (1981). Chronic organic brain syndromes associated with alcoholism: Neuropsychological and other aspects. In Y. Israel, F. Glaser, H. Kalant,

R. Popham, W. Schmidt, & R. Smart (Eds.), *Research advances in alcohol and drug problems* (Vol. 6, pp. 107–145). New York: Plenum Press.

Winocur, G., & Weiskrantz, L. (1976). An investigation of paired-associate learning in amnesic patients. *Neuropsychologia, 14*, 97–110.

Witt, E. D., & Goldman-Rakic, P. S. (1983a). Intermittent thiamine deficiency in the rhesus monkey: I. Progression of neurological signs and neuroanatomical lesions. *Annals of Neurology, 13*, 376–395.

Witt, E. D., & Goldman-Rakic, P. S. (1983b). Intermittent thiamine deficiency in the rhesus monkey: II. Evidence for memory loss. *Annals of Neurology, 13*, 396–401.

10

Models of Memory Loss in Korsakoff and Alcoholic Patients

LAIRD S. CERMAK

Introduction: Models of Memory Loss in Amnesic Patients

The amnesic syndrome has lately received a great deal of interest from cognitive, memory, and information-processing theorists, as well as from investigators concerned with the effects of alcohol on the aging brain. As a consequence, a tremendous influx of models have been introduced to explain or describe what amnesic patients can and cannot do. By dichotomizing between these groups of tasks, theorists have suggested that normal memory can also be divided into two components, which correspond to these abilities and disabilities of amnesic patients. What this means to the investigator of the effects of alcohol on the central nervous system (CNS) is that one type of memory ability might be more susceptible to the detrimental effects of long-term chronic consumption than the other might be.

One such major attempt to differentiate ability from disability in amnesia has been provided by Cohen and Squire (1980), who have divided memory tasks into those that involve "procedural" learning and those that involve "declarative" learning. They define "procedural" tasks as those that involve the learning and retention of a process of performance rather than a recitation of recent learning. Such tasks as maze learning, mirror writing, and mirror reading have been used as examples of this type of acquisition, and learning to ride a bicycle or to ski might also be good exemplars. "Declarative" tasks have been described as those in which subjects must in some manner demonstrate that they know that a particular stimulus or set of stimuli has been presented in a particular context. Recall, recognition, relearning, or other such tasks would fall under this rubric, regardless of the nature of the material to be retained. Cohen and Squire feel that amnesic patients perform procedural tasks normally, but fail on all types of declarative tasks. They describe the amnesic patients as "knowing how" to perform a particular task, but not "knowing that" they have learned it.

Laird S. Cermak. Psychology Research, Boston Veterans Administration Medical Center, Boston, Massachusetts; Neurology Department, Boston University School of Medicine, Boston, Massachusetts.

Perhaps the most impressive demonstration of the procedural–declarative distinction has been the reported performance of the amnesic patient H. M. on the Tower of Hanoi task. This task involves learning how to move doughnut-shaped disks from one peg to another following a particular set of rules. The disks themselves are arranged in a pyramid configuration on one of the three pegs when the task begins. The subject's task is to move the five disks one at a time from peg to peg until he or she is able to reproduce the pyramid on another peg. The only restriction is that a larger disk may not be put on a smaller one. Cohen (1984) has reported that H. M. not only learns this task at a normal rate, but retains it as well as normals do.

A second theoretical division of amnesia into abilities and disabilities has been based upon the distinction between "episodic" and "semantic" memory, introduced by Tulving (1972, 1983). He has defined "episodic" memory as memory for specific, personally experienced events, and "semantic" memory as memory for general principles, associations, rules, and so on. Because episodic memory includes information learned in laboratory situations, it has traditionally received more interest than semantic memory from experimental psychologists; moreover, because it is most affected in amnesia, it has also received the most attention from investigators of the amnesic syndrome. Differentiation of episodic from semantic memory by investigators of the amnesic syndrome was first attempted by Kinsbourne and Wood (1975), who suggested that amnesics might have an intact semantic memory in the presence of impairments in episodic memory. Kinsbourne and Wood's evidence was based on clinical observation, coupled with a rather informal experiment in which patients were asked to describe an object such as a railroad ticket (felt to be evidence of semantic memory), then asked to describe an instance in which they had used that object (an index of episodic memory). Since amnesic patients could do the former but not the latter, Kinsbourne and Wood felt that their theoretical distinction had been demonstrated.

We (Cermak, Reale, & Baker, 1978) made a somewhat more traditional assessment of the organization of semantic memory in amnesia, using a search-time paradigm. We found that amnesic patients evidenced little to no impairment in lexical search rate (finding an animal beginning with the letter "S"), but did demonstrate an impaired rate of search through conceptual semantic memory (finding an animal with stripes). It must be emphasized that it was rate of search that was impaired, and not the final selection of an answer, for on this latter measure amnesics were completely normal. Apparently, when amnesics' search depends upon the utilization of knowledge stored in semantic memory, the speed with which conceptual decisions can be made is radically reduced. This slower search rate implies that even though semantic memory retains its normal organization, the ease with which it can be accessed is affected by the brain injury suffered by the amnesics.

This impaired speed of access of conceptual semantic memory might actually help to explain why analysis of incoming episodic information is so deficient for amnesic Korsakoff patients (Butters & Cermak, 1980). Since semantic memory must be searched in order to compare and contrast each new bit of incoming information with what is already known, analysis may be delayed or even terminated prematurely when such comparison is slow. On the other hand, when retrieval from semantic memory is relatively easy and automatic, as when primary associations or initial letters are involved, the intact organization of semantic memory may actually appear to facilitate episodic retention, as in the case of cueing following a learning task (Warrington & Weiskrantz, 1978, 1982), or as in encoding-specificity tasks (Cermak & Stiassny, 1982).

The procedural–declarative and episodic–semantic models should not be viewed as being in opposition to each other, nor should they necessarily be seen as representing totally independent points of view. The episodic–semantic distinction might actually represent a subdivision of the procedural–declarative distinction (see a diagrammatic representation of this in Figure 10-1), since both episodic- and semantic-memory tasks generally require that patients "declare" that they "know that" certain information exists. In neither case is a procedural variable involved; instead, retrieval is required from either contextual material or general knowledge. Arguments between the two models should not center about which is the only explanation of amnesia, but rather around which is the correct location to place specific phenomena of amnesia.

An example of one such phenomenon has recently been introduced by Jacoby and Witherspoon (1982) under the rubric of "memory with awareness" and "memory without awareness." Jacoby and Witherspoon have suggested that amnesic patients can perform tasks in which the demand does not require that the patients identify when or where they have experienced information, but rather requires that the patients use this information in the completion of a different task. To demonstrate their belief, they developed a technique showing that amnesics could be biased toward a particular spelling of an ambiguous homonym when it was presented in the context of a particular biasing sentence. Despite this normal spelling bias, amnesics still were unable to recognize any of the words toward which they had been biased. In a similar vein, we (Cermak, Talbot, Chandler, & Wolbarst, 1985), using a modification of a perceptual-identification task introduced by Jacoby and Dallas (1981), found that the prior exposure of a word influenced amnesic patients' ability to identify that word when it was presented at an extremely short duration on a subsequent task. However, this ability occurred even though the patients could not recognize that word as having appeared on the prior list.

Jacoby (1984) has suggested that his distinction represents yet another subdivision of the diagram depicted in Figure 10-1. He views memory with

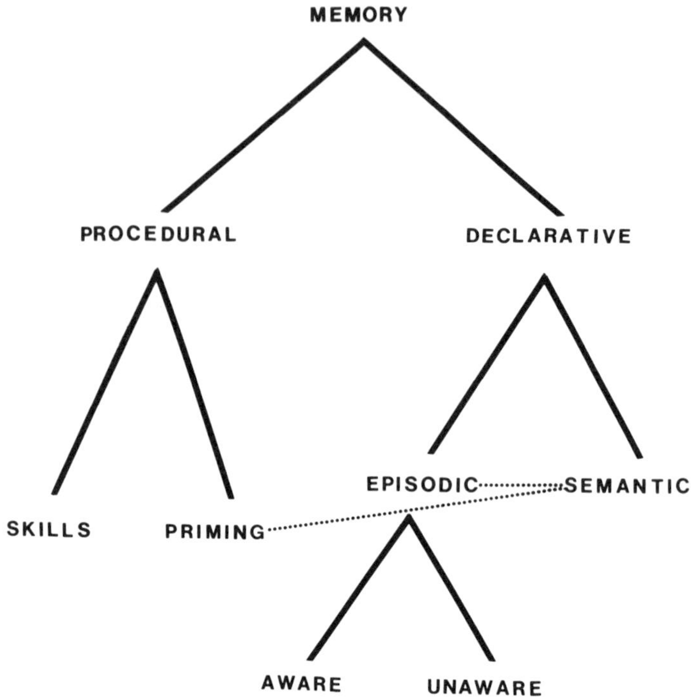

Figure 10-1. Diagrammatic representation of the relationship of existing models of amnesia to one another. All models represented tend to dichotomize memory into those tasks amnesics can perform and those they cannot.

awareness as being involved in the recognition of an episode such as the prior presentation of a word, event, or the like, and memory without awareness as being involved with the demonstration of the effects of that same specific episode on subsequent behavior such as perceptual identification. In other words, Jacoby feels that the distinction between what amnesics can and cannot do falls within the level of episodic memory and probably represents a difference in the type of processing required during performance of the retention task. To illustrate his reasoning, another subdivision has been added to the diagram shown in Figure 10-1.

Interestingly, each of the three dichotomies of amnesic abilities that have been described relies to some extent upon the same set of results for support. All tend to view the amnesics' ability to be influenced by prior exposure, despite an inability to describe that exposure, as representative evidence for their particular formulation. What Cohen and Squire term a form of procedural learning, I have called semantic-memory activation and Jacoby has determined to be memory without awareness. Obviously, all agree on the nature of the basic phenomenon. What is a matter for disagreement is the level of the diagram that best represents this phenomenon.

In addition, two other theories have added to the confusion surrounding the best diagrammatic representation of this distinction in amnesic abilities and disabilities. First, Warrington and Weiskrantz (1982) have suggested that the amnesic dissociation in abilities ought not to be interpreted in terms of an impaired episodic memory in the context of a normal semantic memory, but rather in terms of the disconnection of these two fairly intact systems. They propose that recognition depends upon the joint operation of the two systems (which they call semantic and "mediational"), while tasks such as perceptual identification, semantic biasing, and even cueing depend solely on the normal operation and activation of semantic memory. Their proposed interaction between semantic and episodic/mediational memory has been depicted in Figure 10-1 by a dotted line. The disconnection of these two systems in amnesia leaves identification intact while recognition becomes impaired.

Even more recently, Graf, Squire, and Mandler (1984) have suggested yet another connectionist model—one that depicts an interaction between procedural learning and semantic memory (see Figure 10-1). These authors propose that perceptual identification occurs as a result of "activation" of pre-existing traces in a semantic network via the procedural division of this diagram. Their proposal clarifies Cohen's (1984) depiction of procedural memory, in that Graf *et al.* state that semantic activation is similar to, but not synonymous with, procedural skill learning. Semantic activation and skill learning are similar in that both operate on pre-existing representations and both change these representations. However, they differ in that activation operates on a single representation and its effect is fleeting, while skill learning necessitates a recombination of a sequence of prior learning (usually motor) representations. This interaction is depicted in Figure 10-1 by a dotted line running from the priming component of procedural memory to semantic memory. According to this new model, the dissociation between recognition and identification seen in amnesia involves a distinction between declarative learning and procedural, semantic, activation.

Since all of these models of amnesia tend to rely upon Jacoby's basic recognition–identification distinction, it was felt that a disentanglement had to begin with one of his paradigms. The one we chose (Cermak *et al.*, 1985) was originally introduced for use with normals by Jacoby and Dallas (1981). In this procedure, the influence of a prior exposure of a word on the patient's ability to identify that word when it was presented at extremely short durations was contrasted with the ability to recognize that word among a series of other alternatives. We utilized three variants of the basic procedure with amnesic Korsakoff patients. In the first, a short list of words (10 items) was presented to the patients, who were then immediately asked either to recognize 5 of the items from among a series or to try to identify words presented at short (35-millisecond) intervals. If a word could not be identified, it was presented again and again at successively longer increments until identification was possible. In a second task, the same procedure was followed except that the recognition and identification tasks were delayed 1 minute prior to their introduction. It was proposed that such a delay might affect amnesics' identification more than that of normals. The third experiment substituted pseudowords in place of real words as stimuli to be retained in the task. It was felt that if activation alone produced the priming phenomenon for amnesics, then the presentation of pseudowords might not enhance their perceptual identification. It might very well produce priming for normals, since they could retain the pseudowords at some level; however, it should not produce priming for amnesics, both because they would not be able to retain the pseudowords and because these stimuli could not be activated in semantic memory, since no pre-established representation for them would exist.

The results of the first two experiments demonstrated that the amnesics' recognition ability for real words indeed did decline rapidly across brief retention intervals, but that their identification ability for the same material remained stable and normal. The amnesics could demonstrate immediately after presentation that they realized a specific word had been presented, but 1 minute later they had lost this ability. Nevertheless, that word still retained an effect on identification, and thus some representation must have existed in memory. The question that remained was whether this representation was a product of low-level retention of the specific item presented (memory without awareness) or the residual effect of semantic activation. The outcome of the pseudoword experiment answered this question.

The only difference in design between the first two experiments and the third involved the presentation of pseudowords as stimuli in the third task. These pseudowords were created by changing one of the letters of the real words that had been presented in the experiment above. The identification task was given immediately after presentation of the critical list of stimuli in order to favor the probability of any episodic retention. The outcome was that the amnesic patients demonstrated absolutely no priming effect at all, while the alcoholic controls did. Recognition was also, of course, at chance level for the amnesics, while the controls' recognition performance was as high as it had been for the real words.

This last experiment demonstrates that in order for priming to occur for amnesics during an identification task for amnesics, the item of information must represent a previously learned bit of information. Our amnesic patients simply could not be primed for pseudowords, which clearly have no representation in semantic memory. This argues against Jacoby's (1984) theory that perceptual identification by amnesics relies upon some form of memory (without awareness) for the prior presentation of an item, and not upon activation of semantic memory. His theory may well be true for normal memory, because the identification of the pseudowords was primed for our alcoholic controls, but the theory is certainly not true for amnesics. Amnesics cannot profit from a prior presentation involving learning a new item of information; they can only profit when an old item is activated.

The specificity of semantic activation for amnesics clearly argues against the notion that this effect represents procedural learning in its pure form (Cohen, 1984), but it can be incorporated into Graf *et al.*'s (1984) proposal. These latter authors point out that activation has properties in common with procedural skill learning, but that there are some differences, such as specificity. Precisely why activation has to come from procedural learning rather than via the more direct declarative route is, however, still unclear. The more direct route seems able to describe the results, and perhaps ought to be favored simply because it is more parsimonious.

Warrington and Weiskrantz's (1982) theory incorporates these pseudoword results easily, and, solely on the basis of this paradigm, the differentiation between their theory and the semantic–episodic model cannot be made. But this is because the difference between the two models lies in the nature of the interaction of episodic and semantic memory, not in the role of semantic memory in an identification task.

I favor placing amnesics' dichotomous performance on recognition and identification tasks at the level of the episodic–semantic distinction in Figure 10-1. Acceptance of this placement does, however, necessitate a partial redefinition of declarative memory, because the episodic–semantic level falls entirely within the declarative domain. Under the usual definition, subjects must be able to declare that they "know that" something has been presented. When primed for identification, the subjects do not have to declare, but they do have to demonstrate, that they "know that" something has occurred.

Retrograde Amnesia

Even since Seltzer and Benson (1974) and Marslen-Wilson and Teuber (1975) discovered that amnesic patients' retrieval of remote memories is much better than their retrieval of more recent memories, there has been controversy about the nature of the factors contributing to this phenomenon. This is largely because this so-called "shrinking retrograde amnesia" is in precisely the opposite direction from that normally expected (Bahrick, Bahrick, & Wittlinger, 1975; Sanders & Warrington, 1971). Normally, retention of remote events tends to decline with the age of the event. One must assume that such a decline exists for amnesics as well; thus, their improvement in performance as a function of age of the event must be viewed as being due more to the demise of recent memories than to the abnormal preservation of old memories (Albert, Butters, & Levin, 1979).

While most of the data seem to favor this proposal, an alternative theory has always also existed. This theory, forwarded by Sanders and Warrington (1971), stems from the notion that amnesic patients' entire memory disorder represents solely a difficulty in retrieval. Sanders and Warrington suggest that all memories are normally represented for amnesics but are nearly impossible to reproduce. Such a strict retrieval-deficit theory would have to predict that amnesics should have equal amounts of difficulty in answering questions involving retrograde memory across all decades. Sanders and Warrington (1973) have data to support their theory, and, since their baseline is more in line with that reported for normals (i.e., a progressive decline), it is surprising that their results have not been more generally accepted.

I (Cermak, 1982, 1984) have suggested that the retrieval-deficit theory of retrograde amnesia may actually be stronger than previously suggested. I have found that when a test of remote memories is repeated with the same patients as subjects, what is recalled one day may vary considerably from what is recalled the next day. In fact, we (Cermak & O'Connor, 1983) found that a postencephalitic patient's day-to-day performance on a battery of remote-memory tests varied as much as 50%. The patient recalled many items on a second testing that he had failed to retrieve on initial testing, and he seemed to "forget" others. Overall, his retrieval probability remained the same, even when assessed across decades, but the specific items that he recalled varied considerably. It seemed as if his limitation was more on the number he could recall at any one sitting than on the total number of items he had in memory. If this is true, then it argues that if the patient were tested often enough he might be able to demonstrate knowledge of as many facts as normals, but not at any one particular time. Comparable outcomes in performance protocols have been reported for Korsakoff patients as well (Cermak, 1982).

The distinction between episodic and semantic memory described earlier in this chapter could be invoked to explain why the various "slopes" of retrograde amnesia and the concomitant theories to explain each have been produced in the testing of amnesics. Many investigators of the amnesic process feel that the episodic–semantic distinction is removed from the controversy over retrograde amnesia, but this may be because they have not looked at the distinction in the same way as has been presented in this chapter. It has to be realized first that normal individuals remember fewer episodes from their youth and childhood than they do from more recent years, and when one analyzes even the most vivid episodic memories from distant childhood, one has to admit to the inflexibility of these memories. Indeed, through constant retelling, many of these supposed episodes become more like family folklore (or personal semantic memories) than truly retained episodes (see Loftus, 1980, for more on this possibility). As a consequence, normals tend to answer more distant remote-memory questions from their semantic memory and more of the recent questions from their episodic memory. While this is not an either–or situation, the relative reliance upon one type of memory over the other probably shifts as a function of the decade from which the question has been selected. An event from the 1950s might be remembered more as a matter of general or personal knowledge, while an event from the 1970s might still retain a personal episodic component to it. Individuals might recall where they were when President Nixon resigned, but not know where they were when President Eisenhower had a heart attack. Nevertheless, both "Who resigned as President?" and "Which President of the 1950s had a heart attack in office?" could be answered correctly, even though the relative reliance upon semantic memory as opposed to episodic memory might have shifted from the first to the second question.

Thus, "normal" retrograde retrieval probably changes from being dependent upon retrieval from semantic memory to being more dependent upon episodic memory as a function of the recency of acquisition. Consequently, tests of remote memory that are standardized on normals might be biased first toward retrieval from semantic memory (for more distant decades), then toward episodic memory (for recent decades). Even attempting to make all test items equally retrievable by a group of normal individuals does not change or reduce this bias. It simply makes the probability of producing the correct answer equal across decades; it does not control the mode of retrieval. Taking into account that Korsakoff patients have normal semantic memory in the presence of impaired episodic memory, it can be seen that this shifting bias might underlie their remote-memory gradient. Korsakoff patients might simply appear to have better recall from distant decades than from recent decades because the questions from these distant decades can be answered from their unimpaired retrieval-processing mode (i.e., semantic memory). The more a question depends upon semantic knowledge, the better they perform; the more the question depends on retention of an episode (as recent events tend to do), the worse they perform.

Amnesic Korsakoff patients' highly variable performance on tasks involving remote memory can be explained if it is acknowledged that normal retrieval from semantic memory involves some form of organized search process and that this process is slow and quite random in Korsakoff patients (Cermak *et al.*, 1978). Their organization of semantic memory appears to be more or less normal; it is the search through this system that is impaired. Consequently, items found during one search process might very well not be the same as those found on a subsequent search. In addition, our postencephalitic patient described above truly seems to have lost some material from semantic memory. Unlike Korsakoff patients' remote-retrieval profile of a sloping retrograde-memory gradient, the postencephalitic patient's gradient of retrieval probability is remarkably flat across decades. He seems less capable of semantic-memory recall than do alcoholic Korsakoff patients. His retrieval is highly variable, indicating a disorder of the search process, but, in addition, he also seems to have lost some material. Perhaps this loss of semantic information is a consequence of the more cortical nature of his deficit, since he appears to have suffered dense cerebral cortex degeneration with little to no subcortical loss. In contrast, Korsakoff patients' primary loss has been described as being in the limbic system and in the communicating network connecting this system to the higher-order cortical locations. The validity of this assumption must await further testing, but for now we know that our postencephalitic patient has a more deficient semantic-memory retrieval ability than Korsakoff patients, which supports the relative normality of these latter patients' semantic memory in a reverse sort of manner, by showing that it is not simply the simplicity of our test procedures that is making the alcoholic Korsakoff patients appear normal.

Anterograde Amnesia

The distinction between episodic and semantic memory can also be used to explain a number of other issues that exist in the field of human amnesia other than those involving priming and/or remote memory. Several of these issues have created heated controversies concerning the nature of the factors underlying alcoholic Korsakoff patients' total inability to learn and remember new information (i.e., their anterograde amnesia). Some theorists have placed these variables in the encoding (acquisition) stage of information processing, while others have emphasized the retrieval stage. Retrieval-stage models have primarily relied upon the influence of interference in determining the probability that an item will be recalled, while encoding models have proposed that the level at which items are processed by these patients precludes the possibility of retrieval.

The major proponents of the interference model of amnesia have been Warrington and Weiskrantz (1970, 1973), who have argued that amnesics have no trouble learning new material. They simply have trouble retrieving it because of an almost total inability to inhibit competing, previously learned material from intruding. Paradoxically, amnesics' problem is not that they forget too much, but that they forget too little. Warrington and Weiskrantz supported their thesis through studies (1968, 1970) that involved exposing patients to successively less fragmented words or pictures until identification was possible. The patients identified the information as quickly as normals, but, more importantly for the retrieval-deficit theories, they also showed normal savings when tested the next day. This lends credence to the notion that something had been learned by the patients, even though they could not recall ever having performed the task. Today this effect might be labeled "memory without awareness," but the point at the time was that material could get in but could not be freely recalled. It did not tell us why it could not be retrieved, but that became the focus for Warrington and Weiskrantz's research for the next decade.

To provide more direct evidence for their thesis that amnesic patients are unable to inhibit or reject incorrect responses during free recall, Warrington and Weiskrantz (1974) reported a series of cueing experiments designed either to limit or to increase the range of potentially interfering responses a patient carried into a recall task. They found that when the range of possible words was narrow (delimited by the use of unique first-three-letter cues to just two possible words), the amnesics demonstrated more susceptibility to interference than when the range of possible alternatives was wide. From this, Warrington and Weiskrantz (1974) concluded that, for single-list recall, reducing the number of alternative responses for amnesics creates fewer false-positive responses, while in two-list learning, reducing the number of potential alternatives allows items from the first list greater potential to intrude during recall of the second-list items without competition from the large class of alternative incorrect items. It was this latter point that later became the focus for a set of experiments designed to clarify the nature of this proactive interference (PI). At this point, however, Warrington and Weiskrantz concluded that cued recall bestows its benefit by eliminating false positives.

These authors' next set of experiments resulted in a modification of their interference hypothesis. They did not waver from their notion that interference during retrieval is the culprit in producing amnesics' memory disturbance, but they did change their opinion as to when and how this interference is produced. Rather than proposing that interference exerts its influence solely during the retrieval stage of information processing, Warrington and Weiskrantz (1978) came to realize that it probably creates the most disruption during acquisition. To demonstrate this point, they showed that the effects of learning a word list played an increasing role across trials in the inability of amnesics to learn a second list of highly similar words containing the same first three letters as recall cues. Although the normals improved performance across four learning–recall trials on a second list, the amnesics improved very little. When later asked to generate words from both lists to each three-letter cue, the amnesics still produced more List 1 responses than List 2 responses, while normals showed precisely the reverse outcome. Warrington and Weiskrantz took this to mean that the patients had difficulty rejecting List 1 responses, and that these responses were so domineering that they actually impeded "learning" of List 2 responses. A second task, using a recall procedure in which list inclusion did not have to be specified, produced the same results, indicating that not only were List 2 responses less well differentiated, but they were less available as well. Finally, Warrington and Weiskrantz showed that recall by amnesics of a list containing unique cues (three letters that only began one word in the dictionary) was actually superior to that of controls 24 hours after presentation. This, they felt, was yet further evidence that responses, once learned, actually extinguish more slowly for amnesics than for controls. This explains why these responses are more available to compete with retrieval of items learned subsequently, but, as Warrington and Weiskrantz now propose, this competition may initially have its effect on impeding learning of the new items, rather than just affecting retrieval.

The analytic, or encoding-deficit, theory has primarily been championed by me (1972, 1979) and by Butters (Butters & Cermak, 1974, 1975, 1980), but has also been acknowledged as a likely possibility by Baddeley (1975) and by Kinsbourne and Wood (1975). Basically, this view proposes that amnesic patients' memory disorder is related to an impairment in the extent to which they process information during presentation. Several experiments (Cermak & Butters, 1972; Cermak, Butters, & Gerrein, 1973; Cermak, Butters, & Moreines, 1974; Cermak, Naus, & Reale, 1976) have shown that these patients tend to spontaneously rehearse only the phonemic features of verbal information and to overlook analysis of the semantic features of the information. This puts the patient at a distinct disadvantage during retrieval of this material. Unlike even the most recent interference-deficit theory, this analytic model places the cause of the amnesic disorder (at least for alcoholic Korsakoffs) at the level of initial analysis—not in the difficulty of separating this word from others in memory, but in the very encoding and storing of the word itself. Therein lies the crux of the difference between the two theories.

All of the studies listed above were designed to assess the level at which alcoholic Korsakoff patients spontaneously process verbal information, but they did not develop the relationship between this difficulty and the patients' failures in retrieval. This did not transpire until the Wickens (1970) paradigm of release from PI was employed by Cermak *et al.* (1974). We felt that if Korsakoff patients' increased sensitivity to interference was related to their lack of semantic encoding, then a release from PI as a function of a change in category of material to be remembered ought not to occur for these patients. It was anticipated that Korsakoff patients might demonstrate normal PI release when the stimuli involved only rudimentary categorizations (e.g., letters vs. numbers), but not when the material involved more abstract semantic differences (e.g., taxonomic differences in classification, such as animals vs. vegetables). The results upheld these predictions, verifying the opinion that the Korsakoff patients could not immediately categorize material for future reference during storage and retrieval on the basis of semantic attributes of the verbal information.

Since Korsakoff patients did not appear capable of automatically detecting, analyzing, and storing on the basis of semantic features of a verbal item, the question was raised as to whether or not they could profit if they were instructed to analyze particular features of the information. The paradigm chosen for this investigation (Cermak & Reale, 1978) was one originally introduced by Craik and Tulving (1975), in which patients' analysis of incoming information was directed by asking them either an orthographic question (e.g., "Is the following word printed in capital letters?"), a phonemic question (e.g., "Does the next word rhyme with 'ring'?"), or a semantic question (e.g., "Does the following word fit into the sentence 'The man stooped and picked up the ______'?"). When these instructions were given to Korsakoff patients, it was discovered that very little improvement in retention occurred as a function of the level of analysis required during presentation. Only when very little material was presented for retention, and then only for a brief interval, was there any improvement at all.

Despite the presentation of a mechanism (semantic analysis) that normally promotes good retention, our amnesic patients still forgot the vast majority of the words that were presented to them. This was probably due to the patients' forgetting not only the specific word presented, but the manner in which they had been asked to analyze the word as well. In other words, the patients seemed to forget the "frame" into which the critical item had been analyzed, and, as a consequence, had neither the item nor its semantic referent available at retrieval. Thus, semantic analysis did not automatically produce improvements in retrieval ability. On the other hand, neither did the total elimination of otherwise competing, associatively related items during input. The phonemic cue should not have elicited inappropriate associates during learning and should therefore have provided good learning in the Warrington and Weiskrantz tradition. Thus, initial analysis of verbal material by amnesic patients, even when they performed it appropriately, did not produce a strengthening of the representation of the desired material in memory, nor did it insulate it from previously established interference. At least, it did not do so when retention of that analysis is necessary. However, the possibility still existed that some change might occur, but could only be demonstrated by the reintroduction of the encoding context—a reintroduction that normals could self-produce, but amnesics could not. Therefore, the next task introduced in this line of research utilized the same analysis paradigm, but added a cueing component to the retrieval portion of the task. The cueing component was simply a reintroduction of the encoding context of the specific word by the examiner.

We (Cermak, Uhly, & Reale, 1980) cued Korsakoff patients either with the same question used at input, or with a new, appropriate question from the same level of analysis, or with a new question from a different level of analysis. When this was done, it was discovered that the only beneficial condition for the Korsakoffs was the one that occurred when the same semantic set was provided at both input and output. The same precise operations performed on a word during its presentation had to be reproduced during retrieval in order for any improvement to occur. Next, and to follow this notion further, a procedure devised by Thompson and Tulving (1970) was adapted for use with amnesic patients.

In this task (Cermak *et al.*, 1980), patients were given a list of 12 word pairs consisting of a capitalized to-be-remembered (TBR) word and an associated word printed in lower-case letters above it. The patients were told to memorize each TBR word but to pay attention as well to the small related word, as it might help them to remember the TBR word. After the words were presented, each patient was given a sheet of paper with 12 cue words printed on it and told to write down the associated TBR words in the blank space next to each cue. This procedure was repeated five times so that five different input–output relationships could be investigated: (1) S-S, in which a strongly associated cue word occurred at input and again at output; (2) W-W, in which the same weakly associated cue word occurred at input and output; (3) S-W, in which a strong associate was presented at input, but a weak associate at output; (4) W-S, in which a weak associate was presented at input, but a strong one at output; and (5) 0-0, in which no cues were given.

The results (Table 10-1) demonstrated that, unlike normals, Korsakoff patients were not so much affected by encoding specificity (as evidenced by the poor W-W recall) as they were by the presence of a strong associate at retrieval. That this was most obvious in the S-S condition argues for some retention of the encoding operations, but apparently only when they reinforce something already existent in semantic memory, not when a new associate is formed. When the semantic context re-established previous learning, it seemed to be facilitating, but not when it required establishing a new connection.

The reader will probably appreciate that this conclusion is highly similar to that reached by Warrington and Weiskrantz in 1978, who contended that cues are only effective when they facilitate the "regeneration" of an appropriate response. When such regeneration does not lead directly to the appropriate response for amnesics, then either no response is given or the one that "appears" most appropriate to the cue is given. This led to the prediction that amnesic patients may be cued successfully under conditions that automatically regenerate a correct response, but then may fail to

Table 10-1. Percentage of Target Words Correctly Recalled in an Encoding-Specificity Experiment

	Condition				
Patient group	S-S	W-W	W-S	O-O	S-W
Korsakoff	57	14	33	29	7
Alcoholic	91	75	63	57	24
Normal	84	56	54	56	18

Note. See text for explanation of the abbreviations for the different conditions.

produce that same word immediately thereafter when given a cue that does not automatically generate the desired response.

To test this ultimate dependence on strong-associate cues, Korsakoff patients received three lists of TBR words, each paired with a corresponding weak associate (Cermak & Stiassny, 1982). Following the 12 words, the patients were given a recall form containing the weak-associate cue word and were asked to write the words they could recall beside the appropriate cue. After presentation of a third list in this manner, and before the third "recall," the task was changed. The patients were now given 12 "strong" associates of each TBR word, followed by four blank spaces into which they were told to write the first four words each cue brought to mind. After completing this generation task, the patients were asked to circle from among all the words those they remembered as being on the most recent list. Once this recognition task was over, the recall format using weak associates was completed.

As expected, the Korsakoffs' performance on recall using weak cues was very poor (never more than 8% correct), relative to normals, who averaged 50% correct. However, on the generation–recognition task, the patients' performance exceeded expectations in two ways: First, they generated as many of the critical TBR words as did normals, and second, they recognized as many of these critical words as having been presented on the prior list as did the controls. This generation–recognition performance was particularly striking when contrasted with the Korsakoff patients' inability to recall these same critical words in the presence of the very cues that existed at input. The Korsakoff patients could produce and recognize the critical words, but still failed to retrieve these words in the presence of weak cues.

Although this outcome is dramatic, it might simply have been due to the Korsakoffs' ability to utilize their intact semantic memory to answer questions. In other words, it was possible that the patients generated the critical words to the strong-associate cues, quite independently of the experimental events preceding such generation. Furthermore, the patients might have circled the strongest associate of each cue word simply on the basis of its apparent familiarity and not because they remembered that it had just been presented. They may have unintentionally equated familiarity with recency, and this may have produced their good performance. It became very easy to assess this possibility: We simply retested each patient 2 months later on only the generation–recognition portion of the task. We did not reintroduce the words; instead, the patients were asked to circle those words that they remembered seeing several months ago. No one working with amnesics would believe the patients could actually remember these words, let alone even remember being in an experiment. Nevertheless, the results described above were duplicated. Then, as new patients were discovered, they were given the generation–recognition task and told to circle words they had received in a "nonexistent" experiment, and they too produced the same apparently normal results. Obviously, the patients had operated on the basis of strength of association and used this as an index of recency.

Precisely why Korsakoff patients cannot utilize new associations to aid storage and retrieval is still a matter for debate, because it could be due to an inability to establish the connection during input, or it could be that they cannot reconstruct the association at retrieval. It is also possible that Korsakoff patients suffer from both difficulties: First, they cannot discriminate between frequency and recency during cued retrieval, and, in that respect, their retrieval (reconstructive) ability can be said to be impaired. Second, they cannot cognitively restructure their organization hierarchy at input, and, in that respect, their encoding ability can be said to be impaired. This combination of deficits would be most evident in the "acquisition" of new material, since both encoding and reconstructive deficits operate. It would be less evident in retrieval from remote long-term memory, since these items were encoded prior to injury, and thus only reconstructive deficits would be evident.

Premature-Aging versus Continuum Models of Alcohol's Effect on Memory

Having presented the current theories of alcoholic Korsakoff patients' memory difficulties, I believe it is important to try to contrast this theorizing with that prevalent in the field of memory disorders attributed to the effects of chronic misuse of alcohol. A good deal of evidence has been presented by Ryan and Butters (1980a, 1980b), and by several contributors to the present text, to support the notion that chronic alcoholics demonstrate deficits in verbal memory. From this evidence, two theories have emerged. One is that alcohol causes premature cognitive aging; the other is that a continuum of cognitive abilities exists between normals and alcoholic Korsakoffs, with chronic alcoholics' performance falling somewhere between these two groups.

We (Cermak & Peck, 1982) have pointed out that it is important to try to distinguish between these two theories, because each has differing implications for our understanding of the effect of alcohol on the CNS. The premature-aging theory presupposes that alcohol accelerates the "general" deterioration of the CNS, while the continuum theory suggests that alcohol affects the same "specific" midline diencephalic structures as seen in Korsakoff's syndrome. Behaviorally, the premature-aging hypothesis can easily be supported by consistent deficits in performance on any test in which alcoholics are compared to their contemporaries. However, for the continuum theory to be correct, the same specific "patterns" of performance seen in Korsakoff patients have to be approximated in alcoholics to a greater extent than that seen in the normally aging population. This means that performance on tasks that assess episodic memory ought to be relatively more affected by the chronic misuse of alcohol than would be the case for performance on semantic-memory tasks. Performance on retrograde tests ought to take the shape of performance by Korsakoff patients, and not the shape seen in the ordinary aging process. Performance on the tests of encoding and cueing described in the preceding section ought to mimic the performance of Korsakoff patients in the pattern of encoding and cueing abilities, and not the performance of the normal elderly.

Ryan and Butters, as well as most other investigators in this area, have provided ample evidence that chronic alcoholics' memory performance on a wide variety of tasks is depressed. However, these data support only the premature-aging hypothesis; they do not test the continuum-of-deficits theory. To support the latter theory, specific paradigms in which differential patterns of performance have been documented for Korsakoff patients have to be used. Then, if the alcoholics' performance parallels that of the Korsakoffs, a continuum model can be said to have received support. One such paradigm is the Thompson and Tulving (1970) cueing task described previously.

This task was one of those we gave to alcoholics (Cermak & Peck, 1982) to assess the effects of weak- and strong-associate cues given at input and output to two separate age ranges (one younger, one older) of chronic alcoholics and normal controls. The same conditions depicted in Table 10-1 were introduced to the patients, and it was discovered that the older alcoholics did perform below their contemporaries, but did so equally for all conditions. They were not differentially affected by the encoding–retrieval situations in the same manner as that seen for alcoholic Korsakoff patients; rather, they paralleled the performance of the controls. Thus, the premature-aging hypothesis received further support, while the continuum model failed to predict the results. As long as the performance of chronic alcoholics is simply depressed relative to normals and not differentially affected, the continuum model cannot be considered, and, to date, this has consistently been the reported result. A second experiment (Cermak & Peck, 1982) confirmed this outcome using a detection paradigm. Alcoholics' detection of repeated words or rhymes or category inclusion in a list of words was depressed but normal. Korsakoffs' performance was both depressed and different (Cermak & Moreines, 1976). From this, it has to be concluded that aging itself produces a debilitating effect on memory processing, and that this effect may be magnified by the effects of chronic alcohol consumption, but that it is not substantially altered by it.

In summary, since alcoholics do not show any difference in the pattern of their retrieval relative to nonalcoholics, support for a continuum of deficits between normal and Korsakoff patients has not been demonstrated. Instead, what has been shown is an accelerated depression of overall performance for some verbal-memory tasks. Consequently, a premature-aging theory can be proposed to account for those outcomes where older alcoholics' performance has been shown to be below that of their contemporaries, but the continuum model cannot be invoked. It might prove profitable to apply this differentiation (i.e., pattern changes vs. accelerated depression) as a test for any set of experimental outcomes (even those using nonverbal materials) that seek to support the continuum model. The research with Korsakoff patients can in this way continue to provide the cutting edge for information-processing research with chronic alcoholics, because it continues to supply the field with differential patterns of performance. These differential patterns can then be models for patterns that might imply differential brain degeneration in the chronic alcoholic relative to the normal aging individual.

Acknowledgments

My research reported herein was supported by Grant No. AA-00187 from the National Institute on Alcohol and Alcohol Abuse to Boston University School of Medicine, and by the Medical Research Service of the Veterans Administration.

References

Albert, M. S., Butters, N., & Levin, J. (1979). Retrograde amnesia in alcoholic Korsakoff patients. *Archives of Neurology, 36*, 211–216.

Baddeley, A. D. (1975). Theories of amnesia. In A. Kennedy & A. Wilkes (Eds.), *Studies in long term memory*. New York: Wiley.

Bahrick, H. P., Bahrick, P. D., & Wittlinger, R. P. (1975). Fifty years of memory for names and faces: A cross-sectional approach. *Journal of Experimental Psychology: General, 104*, 54–75.

Butters, N., & Cermak, L. S. (1974). The role of cognitive factors in the memory disorder of alcoholic patients with the Korsakoff syndrome. *Annals of the New York Academy of Sciences, 233*, 61–75.

Butters, N., & Cermak, L. S. (1975). Some analyses of amnesic syndromes in brain-damaged patients. In K. Pribram & R. Isaacson (Eds.), *The hippocampus* (pp. 377–409). New York: Plenum Press.

Butters, N., & Cermak, L. S. (1980). *Alcoholic Korsakoff's syndrome: An information processing approach to amnesia*. New York: Academic Press.

Cermak, L. S. (1972). *Human memory: Research and theory*. New York: Ronald Press.

Cermak, L. S. (1979). Amnesic patients' level of processing. In L. S. Cermak & F. I. M. Craik (Eds.), *Levels of processing in human memory*. Hillsdale, NJ: Erlbaum.

Cermak, L. S. (1982). The long and short of it in amnesia. In L. S. Cermak (Ed.), *Human memory and amnesia* (pp. 43–59). Hillsdale, NJ: Erlbaum.

Cermak, L. S. (1984). The episodic–semantic distinction in amnesia. In L. R. Squire & N. Butters (Eds.), *Neuropsychology of memory* (pp. 55–62). New York: Guilford Press.

Cermak, L. S., & Butters, N. (1972). The role of interference and encoding in the short-term memory deficits of Korsakoff patients. *Neuropsychologia, 10*, 89–96.

Cermak, L. S., Butters, N., & Gerrein, J. (1973). The extent of the verbal encoding ability of Korsakoff patients. *Neuropsychologia, 11*, 85–94.

Cermak, L. S., Butters, N., & Moreines, J. (1974). Some analyses of the verbal encoding deficit of alcoholic Korsakoff patients. *Brain and Language, 1*, 141–150.

Cermak, L. S., & Moreines, J. (1976). Verbal retention deficits in aphasic and amnesic patients. *Brain and Language, 3*, 16–27.

Cermak, L. S., Naus, M. J., & Reale, L. (1976). Rehearsal and organizational strategies of alcoholic Korsakoff patients. *Brain and Language, 3*, 375–385.

Cermak, L. S., & O'Connor, M. (1983). The anterograde and retrograde retrieval ability of a patient with amnesia due to encephalitis. *Neuropsychologia, 21*, 213–234.

Cermak, L. S., & Peck, E. (1982). Continuum versus premature aging theories of chronic alcoholism. *Alcoholism: Clinical and Experimental Research, 6*, 89–95.

Cermak, L. S., & Reale, L. (1978). Depth of processing and retention of words by alcoholic Korsakoff patients. *Journal of Experimental Psychology: Human Learning and Memory, 4*, 165–174.

Cermak, L. S., Reale, L., & Baker, E. (1978). Alcoholic Korsakoff patients' retrieval from semantic memory. *Brain and Language, 5*, 215–226.

Cermak, L. S., & Stiassny, D. (1982). Recall failure following successful generation and recognition of responses by alcoholic Korsakoff patients. *Brain and Cognition, 1*, 165–176.

Cermak, L. S., Talbot, N., Chandler, K., & Wolbarst, L. R. (1985). The perceptual priming phenomenon in amnesia. *Neuropsychologia, 23*, 615–622.

Cermak, L. S., Uhly, B., & Reale, L. (1980). Encoding specificity in the alcoholic Korsakoff patient. *Brain and Language, 11*, 119–127.

Cohen, N. J. (1984). Preserved learning capacity in amnesia: Evidence for multiple memory systems. In L. R. Squire & N. Butters (Eds.), *Neuropsychology of memory* (pp. 83–103). New York: Guilford Press.

Cohen, N. J., & Squire, L. R. (1980). Preserved learning and retention of pattern analyzing skill in amnesia: Dissociation of knowing how and knowing that. *Science, 210*, 207–209.

Craik, F. I. M., & Tulving, E. (1975). Depth of processing and retention of words in episodic memory. *Journal of Experimental Psychology: General, 104*, 268–294.

Graf, P., Squire, L. R., & Mandler, G. (1984). The information that amnesic patients do not forget. *Journal of Experimental Psychology: Learning, Memory and Cognition, 10*, 164–178.

Jacoby, L. L. (1984). Incidental versus intentional retrieval: Remembering and awareness as separate issues. In L. R. Squire & N. Butters (Eds.), *Neuropsychology of memory* (pp. 145–156). New York: Guilford Press.

Jacoby, L. L., & Dallas, M. (1981). On the relationship between autobiographical memory and perceptual learning. *Journal of Experimental Psychology: General, 3*, 306–340.

Jacoby, L. L., & Witherspoon, D. (1982). Remembering without awareness. *Canadian Journal of Psychology, 36*, 300–324.

Kinsbourne, M., & Wood, F. (1975). Short-term memory processes and the amnesic syndrome. In D. Deutsch & J. A. Deutsch (Eds.), *Short-term memory* (pp. 257–291). New York: Academic Press.

Loftus, E. F. (1980). *Memory: Surprising new insights into how we remember and why we forget*. Reading, MA: Addison-Wesley.

Marslen-Wilson, N. D., & Teuber, H.-L. (1975). Memory for remote events in anterograde amnesia: Recognition of public figures from news photographs. *Neuropsychologia, 13*, 347–352.

Ryan, C., & Butters, N. (1980a). Further evidence for a continuum-of-impairment encompassing male alcoholic Korsakoff patients and chronic alcoholic men. *Alcoholism: Clinical and Experimental Research, 4*, 190–198.

Ryan, C., & Butters, N. (1980b). Learning and memory impairments in young and old alcoholics: Evidence for the premature-aging hypothesis. *Alcoholism: Clinical and Experimental Research, 4*, 288–293.

Sanders, H. I., & Warrington, E. K. (1971). Memory for remote events in amnesic patients. *Brain, 94*, 661–668.

Seltzer, B., & Benson, D. F. (1974). The temporal pattern of retrograde amnesia in Korsakoff's disease. *Neurology, 24*, 527–530.

Thompson, D. M., & Tulving, E. (1970). Associative encoding and retrieval: Weak and strong cues. *Journal of Experimental Psychology: 86*, 255–262.

Tulving, E. (1972). Episodic and semantic memory. In E. Tulving & W. Donaldson (Eds.), *Organization of memory*. New York: Academic Press.

Tulving, E. (1983). *Elements of episodic memory*. Oxford: Clarendon Press.

Warrington, E. K., & Weiskrantz, L. (1968). A study of learning and retention in amnesic patients. *Neuropsychologia, 6*, 283–291.

Warrington, E. K., & Weiskrantz, L. (1970). Amnesic syndrome: Consolidation or retrieval? *Nature, 228*, 628–630.

Warrington, E. K., & Weiskrantz, L. (1973). An analysis of short-term and long-term memory deficits in man. In J. A. Deutsch (Ed.), *The physiological basis of memory* (pp. 395–396). New York: Academic Press.

Warrington, E. K., & Weiskrantz, L. (1974). The effect of prior learning on subsequent retention in amnesic patients. *Neuropsychologia, 12*, 419–428.

Warrington, E. K., & Weiskrantz, L. (1978). Further analysis of the prior learning effect in amnesic patients. *Neuropsychologia, 16*, 169–177.

Warrington, E. K., & Weiskrantz, L. (1982). Amnesia: A disconnection syndrome? *Neuropsychologia, 20*, 233–248.

Wickens, D. D. (1970). Encoding categories of words: An empirical approach to meaning. *Psychological Review, 77*, 1–15.

11

Discussion

Etiological Considerations Regarding the Neuropsychological Consequences of Alcoholism

GERALD GOLDSTEIN

A Perspective on Neuropsychological Research into Alcoholism

The three chapters I am discussing here can be viewed as dealing with what appear to be two different disorders. The chapters by Butters and Granholm, and by Cermak, deal largely with alcoholic Korsakoff's syndrome—a relatively rarely occurring but obviously interesting disorder in which impairment of memory is the outstanding characteristic. The chapter by Parsons has largely to do with the far more common condition of chronic alcoholism and with the cognitive deficits and personality changes that accompany it. The study of alcoholic Korsakoff's syndrome generally only involves chronic alcoholics as control subjects, while studies of chronic alcoholism have typically taken place in settings in which the probability of finding Korsakoff patients is low (i.e., Veterans Administration hospital short-term alcoholism treatment programs). My discussion has mainly to do with chronic alcoholism, an area in which I have slightly more experience and expertise, but the implications of the Korsakoff research for our general understanding of the neuropsychology of alcoholism are not neglected. Reflecting a personal bias, I initially express my regret that the research with Korsakoff patients has rarely involved administration of standard, comprehensive neuropsychological test procedures, while the careful and detailed measurement of specific information-processing skills and deficits that characterizes the Korsakoff research has not been widely ap-

Gerald Goldstein. Neuropsychology Research Program, Veterans Administration Medical Center, Pittsburgh, Pennsylvania; Departments of Psychiatry and Psychology, University of Pittsburgh, Pittsburgh, Pennsylvania.

plied to chronic alcoholic patients who have been studied with the standard comprehensive batteries. I admit to a great deal of curiosity concerning how the subjects in the studies described by Parsons would fare on some of the more detailed memory tests described by Butters and Granholm and by Cermak. On the other hand, I am equally curious about how the patients involved in these latter studies would do on some standard comprehensive procedure, such as the Halstead–Reitan Neuropsychological Test Battery (Reitan & Davison, 1974).

In the past years, alcoholism research was eschewed by many behavioral and biomedical scientists because of the complexity of the disorder. The complications imposed by the interaction between excessive use of alcoholic beverages and associated behaviors of alcoholics seemed to produce almost insurmountable obstacles to research. One need only mention the effects of malnutrition; systemic illnesses associated with combinations of alcohol abuse and vitamin deficiency; head trauma; and the interaction between alcoholism and other forms of psychopathology, notably the affective disorders (Goodwin & Erickson, 1979). Thus, alcoholism was not viewed, at least in the individual patient, as a single disease, but as a variety of disorders one or all of which may be present in the same person. The "pure alcoholic," when defined as an individual who only abuses or becomes dependent upon beverage alcohol and is free of other physical and mental disorders, appeared to be taking on unicorn-like characteristics. Nevertheless, alcoholism as a world-wide health problem of substantial magnitude needed to be studied, and so research was undertaken despite the complexities. However, that research and the forms of clinical practice associated with it produced a number of models (or, perhaps better put, images) of alcoholism, such that the term has come to mean very different things to different people. Thus, to some the term "alcoholic" conjures up the image of an individual who for reasons of some deficiency in character has taken on a lifestyle characterized by self-abuse, while to others an "alcoholic" is an individual with a form of possibly hereditary/familial medical illness.

These diverse images have had a major impact on scientific and professional activity within the alcoholism area, such that treatments and research programs being carried out in one setting may not resemble what is taking place elsewhere. Some years ago, Wallerstein and Chotlos (1957) wrote a book entitled *Hospital Treatment of Alcoholism* that already reflected the numerous treatment methods applied to alcoholic patients. By now, the number of attempted treatments has increased remarkably, ranging from the fellowship of Alcoholics Anonymous through psychotherapy, hypnosis, and various behavioral approaches (some involving controlled drinking) to pharmacological approaches involving long-term or single doses of some agent (the work with LSD being the primary example of the latter method; see Abramson, 1967). Historically, the work involving neuropsychological studies of alcoholics began within the context of inpatient treatment programs. I pursue the matter of the interface between neuropsychological research and treatment elsewhere in this volume (see Chapter 18). Here, I only wish to provide the setting in which these studies took place.

The work I am discussing now appears to represent a confluence of the research initiated by George Talland and the studies with standard, comprehensive neuropsychological test batteries that were done in the Midwest during the 1960s, particularly in Oklahoma City and Topeka, Kansas. Talland's early studies with Korsakoff patients, and the work done in the Midwest with chronic alcoholics, ushered in the modern era of neuropsychological research in the alcoholism area. During the early period, the basic outlines of the cognitive structure of the amnesic syndrome were drawn, and the characteristics of the cognitive deficits associated with chronic alcoholism were discovered and examined scientifically. While the term "confluence" used above may be something of an exaggeration, the studies of the premature-aging and continuity hypotheses in particular appear to have promoted a set of mutual interests between those involved primarily with Korsakoff patients and those mainly interested in chronic alcoholism. Thus, Butters and his colleagues are interested in and have studied problem-solving abilities in Korsakoff patients, while at the same time pointing out the deficiencies in memory assessment characteristic of many of the standard neuropsychological test batteries. Recent efforts have been made to correct these deficiencies through incorporation of formal memory testing into comprehensive neuropsychological assessment.

The early work in this area can perhaps be best described as "descriptive neuropsychology," in that it addressed itself almost entirely to Parsons's first question (see Chapter 8): "What are the neuropsychological deficits that accompany alcohol abuse?" Although we are continuing to refine the answer to that question, a great deal is already known. The findings regarding impairment of abstracting, problem-solving, and visual–spatial abilities, with well-preserved language skills and general psychometric intelligence, seem well confirmed and have been replicated in numerous laboratories (Parsons & Farr, 1981). In its extreme form, clinicians may apply the DSM-III (American Psychiatric Association, 1980) diagnosis of "dementia associated with alcoholism," but that term is not an uncontroversial one (Goldstein, 1985). The neuropsychological findings to a great extent reflect the clinical phenomenology of moderately advanced chronic alcoholism, which is described by Strub and Black (1981) with the following points: The condition occurs during middle age, following a 15- to 20-year drinking history. It takes a gradually deteriorating course, and the deterioration will persist as long as the individual is an active alcoholic. It is initially manifested by lack of concern and poor self-care, poor judgment and attention, and a generalized slowness. Later, formal cognitive processes begin to deteriorate, with the sparing of language.

It was always assumed, I think, that these research findings and clinical observations were associated with some form of progressive brain damage, although the specific neuropathology of that purported damage is only beginning to be understood. Nevertheless, there clearly has been an impact of these findings on health service providers, and it now appears to be a well-established belief that alcohol abuse and its characteristic concomitants put a person at risk for continuing deterioration of cerebral function and for the acquisition of those adaptive deficits associated with that deterioration. Thus, the descriptive neuropsychology of alcoholism has served at least two functions. First, it has documented and made more plausible the venerable belief that "alcoholism causes brain damage." Second, it has pointed out to those engaged in alcoholism treatment and management that a substantial number of alcoholic patients have significant intellectual impairment, and that somehow this impairment has to be taken into account in treatment planning and implementation.

Etiological Considerations

Having established all of this, we are left with Parsons's other nine questions and numerous others that could be added to the list. Several of these questions are treatment- or management-related, and are dealt with elsewhere. Others, however, deal in some way with etiology and have more to do with the present topic, involving neuropsychological correlates of alcohol abuse. The point to be elaborated on in the bulk of the remainder of this discussion is that now that a reasonable description has been obtained, we should begin looking at etiological considerations. This progression would appear to be very much in keeping with the nature of scientific inquiry in general, which typically begins with phenomenology and goes on to considerations related to causality.

Within the field of alcoholism neuropsychology, one might wish to make a distinction between the etiology of alcoholism per se and the etiology of the neuropsychological deficits associated with chronic alcoholism. Thus, for example, alcoholism may have a completely psychosocial etiology, but the neuropsychological deficits may be largely attributable to nutritional deficiencies acquired during the alcoholic history. However, that distinction may be a naive one. For example, the etiology of alcoholism may be an inborn metabolic disorder that, in addition to producing the clinical condition of alcohol addiction, also makes one more susceptible to purported neurotoxic effects of alcohol. Parsons's consideration of the distinction between "Primary" and "Secondary" alcoholism makes this latter consideration particularly poignant. Thus, there may be a group of individuals who, for some presently unknown reason, are born with a particular susceptibility to alcoholism and who are also more than typically susceptible to acquisition of neuropsychological deficits.

Some years ago, the common wisdom was that alcoholism was a psychosocially acquired disorder, but that the deteriorative lifestyle associated with it, including the combination of alcohol abuse, head trauma, and malnutrition, gradually produced increasing degrees of structural brain damage and the cognitive deficits associated with it. Some observers believed that the effects were those of the alcohol itself, while others believed that cognitive deterioration could be prevented by maintenance of adequate nutrition. The latter alternative has been posited most directly by Victor and Banker (1978), who make the following comment regarding the nature of alcoholic dementia: "In the genesis of these disorders, the role of alcohol is a secondary one, the adverse effects on the nervous system being the result of nutritional disease, liver deficiency or both, which are engendered by chronic abuse of alcohol" (p. 149). On the other side, Lieber (1982) has defended the view that there may be a direct chronic effect of alcohol on the brain. His review of studies of effects of alcohol on the brain contain the following comments. First, he says, "Chronic intake of substantial amounts of alcohol may lead to three, often related clinical abnormalities of the central nervous system: physical dependence and the alcohol withdrawal state, tolerance and organic brain disease" (p. 482). He continues, "As regards to organic brain disease, it seems fairly clear that such an entity exists independent of nutritional deficits that may accompany chronic alcoholism, but organic brain disease certainly is at times aggravated by them" (p. 511).

If alcohol itself is directly associated with the neuropathology, then common sense would dictate that the more one drinks and the longer the drinking history becomes, the more severe the brain damage and associated deficits. However, as Parsons points out in Chapter 8, it has been difficult to obtain consistent relationships between drinking-history parameters and neuropsychological test results. The newly reported finding that it is a history of frequent high levels of alcohol intake that seems to make the difference with regard to neuropsychological test results is obviously an important one, but I think that everyone would still agree that the drinking history does not tell the entire story. Indeed, Parsons goes on to report that there are neuropsychological differences between Primary and Secondary alcoholics who do not differ with regard to drinking-history parameters.

There has been some suggestion in the literature that the cognitive deficits documented by neuropsychological tests in adult alcoholics are not necessarily directly alcoholism-related, but may have antedated the acquisition of alcoholism; indeed, they may be associated with why these individuals have become alcoholics. While Parsons attributes the first formulation of this notion to Goodwin and Hill (1975), some of us may recall that several years previously, Herman Witkin and his collaborators (Karp, Poster, & Goodman, 1963; Karp, Witkin, & Goodenough, 1965a, 1965b; Witkin, Karp, & Goodenough, 1959) postulated that a particular cognitive characteristic, field dependence, was etiologically related to the acquisition of alcoholism; that is, people were field-dependent before they became alcoholics. The finding that alcoholics performed in the field-dependent range on the Witkin group's major tests (the Rod and Frame and Embedded Figures Tests) proved to be a very robust one and was replicated in several laboratories (Bailey, Hustmyer, & Kristofferson, 1961; Goldstein & Chotlos, 1965). However, the neuropsychologists tended to believe that the results on these tests were more the product of alcoholism than of an antecedent personality-related cognitive style. This argument was felt to be compelling, because individuals with structural brain damage unrelated to alcoholism were known to do poorly on tasks such as the Rod and Frame and Embedded Figures Tests (e.g., Teuber & Mishkin, 1954).

Viewing all of these old studies in the perspective of the antecedent-predisposition hypothesis, it is intriguing to speculate on the notion that field dependence is not, as Witkin's group thought, a psychosocially acquired personality characteristic, but rather is an antecedent neuropsychological deficit of the type found in several of the studies done with nonalcoholic sons of alcoholics and nonalcoholics. In other words, both Witkin's group and the neuropsychologists may have been wrong, in that field dependence may not be an antecedent personality disposition *or* a direct neuropsychological consequence of alcoholism; rather, it may be an antecedent neuropsychological deficit. The same phenomenon may be occurring in the case of the Static Ataxia Test (Lipscomb, Carpenter, & Nathan, 1979), particularly since Hegedus, Tarter, Hill, Jacob, and Winsten (1984) reported that nonalcoholic sons of alcoholic fathers were more ataxic than were sons of depressed and normal fathers. We would suggest that a promising area of future research might involve a determination of whether such procedures as the Rod and Frame and Static Ataxia Tests are really markers that may be predictive of risk of acquiring alcoholism later in life. While it is now not uncommon to see studies of familial and nonfamilial alcoholics, as reported by Parsons in Chapter 8, and of nonalcoholic sons of alcoholics, we still need the long-sought-after longitudinal study in order to really determine whether individuals having these alleged markers do in fact become alcoholic.

In summary, it would appear that the neuropsychological profiles found among chronic alcoholics are determined by numerous factors, many of which can be subsumed under the categories of the antecedent or premorbid cognitive profile, the consequences of the drinking history itself, and the consequences of a number of phenomena that are not directly alcohol-related but that are commonly associated with alcoholism. We can mention as examples the consequences of multiple head traumas and of the reduced oxygen supply to the brain produced by the chronic obstructive pulmonary disease frequently seen in alcoholics. Over and above these considerations, there would appear to be a variety of presently poorly or incompletely understood individual differences that make the individual more or less vulnerable to the consequences of an alcoholic history. It is probably fair to say that most clinicians have observed substantial variability with regard to cognitive status among their alcoholic patients, with no ready explanation for that variability in terms of the drinking history. We (Shelly & Goldstein, 1976), utilizing the Halstead–Reitan Battery, subtyped a sample of chronic alcoholics utilizing cluster analysis, and were able to provide an empirical demonstration of that variability. However, our attempts to anchor our subtypes to clinical and demographic variables was far from telling the whole story with regard to explaining the individual differences noted.

It has always been of particular interest to me that some long-term and very chronic alcoholics do not develop significant neuropsychological deficits. Surely an understanding of these cases would have major treatment implications. Perhaps they simply have the right genes, eat right, or avoid head trauma, or all or some crucial combination of these conditions prevail. In this respect, Parsons's finding that there were no neuropsychological differences between his nonfamilial alcoholics and his controls with positive family histories for alcoholism is of particular interest. Parenthetically, this discussion of research involving consideration of the family history suggests that the research with Korsakoff patients may be substantially enriched through obtaining the family histories of patients with this diagnosis and possibly studying memory function in unaffected relatives. The obstacles to doing such research are obviously formidable, but it might be worth the effort.

The Role of Medical Factors

I now turn to another aspect of the etiological question, the matter of the general medical correlates of alcoholism. It is no doubt completely clear to the internist and general practitioner that alcoholism is not only a disease of the central nervous system, but may also be a disease, in particular, of the liver, pancreas, and gastrointestinal system. Gastroenterologists are often as concerned with alcoholism as are psychologists, psychiatrists, and neurologists. Biological considerations in the etiology of alcoholism, and of the neuropsychological deficits associated with alcoholism, can be divided into several aspects. There is, first of all, the matter of constitution—the individual's genetic endowment and its implications for the acquisition of alcoholism. Perhaps the most popularized study is that of Blass and Gibson (1977), in which it was reported that a defect in the liver enzyme transketolase is associated with impaired efficiency in the metabolism of thiamine. Thus, individuals with this inborn metabolic defect who do not eat sufficient amounts of thiamine are at risk for the hemorrhagic lesions that give rise to Korsakoff's syndrome. While the details of this research may be subject to change, it nevertheless has substantial heuristic significance, in the sense that it demonstrates a clear interaction between a genetic predisposition (the enzyme defect) and an environmental contingency (insufficient ingestion of thiamine). Thiamine-deficient individuals without the genetic defect may never develop Korsakoff's syndrome, nor may individuals with the defect who eat enough thiamine. It apparently takes a combination of the two factors to produce the disorder. One might wonder about the extent to which this phenomenon provides a model for the etiology of alcoholism in general.

Recently, studies have been mounted aimed at eliciting the specific roles of organs other than the brain in producing neuropsychological deficit (e.g., McSweeny, Grant, Heaton, Prigatano, & Adams, 1985). In the case of alcoholism, the organ of particular interest would appear to be the liver. One important methodology has been that of assessing patients who have the kinds of liver disease commonly found among alcoholics, such as cirrhosis, who are not alcoholics. Cirrhosis can be produced by numerous disorders such as hepatitis and is not specifically tied to alcoholism. Indeed, it is estimated that only 10–30% of chronic alcoholics develop frank cirrhosis of the liver. In a series of studies, Tarter and collaborators (Tarter, Hegedus, *et al.*, 1983; Tarter, Hegedus, Van Thiel, Schade, & Starzl, 1984) have been able to demonstrate that nonalcoholic cirrhotics exhibit much the same pattern of neuropsychological deficits found among chronic alcoholics. Furthermore, investigators have reported highly significant correlations between measures of liver function, notably serum albumin and serum ammonia, and neuropsychological test performance (Gilberstadt *et al.*, 1980; Tarter, Hegedus, Van Thiel, Schade, Pollit-Heyl, & Gavaler, 1984). It is becoming increasingly clear that liver function may play a crucial role in accounting for the neuropsychological deficits found among chronic alcoholics. Even in cases where there is not frank cirrhosis, intactness of liver function may be a consideration. Another consideration is the status of the immune system, which may make an individual more or less susceptible to the liver disease that in turn is associated with encephalopathy.

In addition to the matter of liver dysfunction, Tarter and Alterman (1984) indicate that numerous brain mechanisms have been postulated to be associated with alcoholic encephalopathy. These include such considerations as neuron metabolic factors, membrane permeability, neurotransmitter status, and endocrinological disruption. With regard to neurotransmitter status, I was most interested in Butters's suggestion that Korsakoff's syndrome, like Alzheimer's disease, may be associated with a central cholinergic deficiency; this suggestion is based on a neuropsychological investigation conducted by Arendt, Bigl, Arendt, and Tennstedt (1983). While chronic alcoholics did not demonstrate neuronal loss in the nucleus basalis, the possibility may be raised that a different neurotransmitter source structure is involved in chronic alcoholism from the one that is involved in Korsakoff's syndrome. In any event, the finding is of interest, because it appears to constitute another line of evidence for the view that Korsakoff's syndrome and chronic alcoholism are different disorders.

This material on biological contributions to the neuropsychological deficits found in alcoholics can be summarized with the following somewhat speculative remarks. Individuals who become alcoholic and cognitively impaired in association with the alcoholism may be constitutionally predisposed to do so, possibly because of some inborn error of the immune system or some other factor that makes them particularly susceptible to liver disease or dysfunction. However, this postulated inborn metabolic error may be of no consequence in individuals who do not drink large quantities of alcohol for long periods of time and/or who eat enough food containing thiamine. There is some suggestion that the encephalopathy that occurs may be mediated via the liver, and it is not necessary for there to be frank liver disease for this to be the case. Even liver dysfunction (as measured by serum ammonia and albumin levels), without clear cirrhosis, appears to be associated with the extent of cognitive deficit. Thus, liver dysfunction severe enough to permit the entrance of toxic substances into the brain could be the major culprit. However, an individual need not be an alcoholic in order for this to happen, since Tarter and his colleagues have demonstrated "alcoholic-like" neuropsychological deficits in nonalcoholic cirrhotics.

These speculations receive some support from family studies, such as the one by Schaeffer, Parsons, and Yohman (1984), reviewed in Parsons's chapter, in which it was shown that nonalcoholic individuals with positive family histories for alcoholism did not differ substantially on a battery of neuropsychological tests from alcoholics with a negative family history. Similarly, Tarter and colleagues (Tarter, Hegedus, Goldstein, Shelly, & Alterman, 1984) found neuropsychological deficits in nonalcoholic sons of alcoholics. Thus far, this type of research has only come up with descriptive findings. However, there must be some reason for the phenomenon of deficit in individuals who do not have a disease, but only a positive family history for that disease. Obviously, further intensive research with "at-risk" populations, including nonalcoholic children and siblings of alcoholics, is much needed.

The point I am suggesting here is that the presence of an "alcoholic-like" neuropsychological profile in nonalcoholic individuals with liver disease, in combination with the presence of deficits in nonalcoholic "at-risk" populations, suggests some underlying biological dimension that is not directly related to alcohol abuse (since these individuals are not alcoholics) but that alters brain function adversely. I suspect that whatever this dimension is, it interacts with alcoholism but is not inextricably associated with it. As Parsons and Farr (1981) have pointed out, the alcoholic pattern of impairment is not specific. As they say, "the pattern of impairment in alcoholics is quite similar to that seen in most brain-damaged populations and in aging—namely less efficient nonverbal abstracting and problem solving, visual-spatial and tactual-spatial difficulties, and slowed visuomotor performance" (p. 355). Thus, the neuropsychological deficit pattern found among alcoholics does not appear to be exotic, but resembles what is seen in a wide variety of organic mental disorders. It is noteworthy that the authors of DSM-III (American Psychiatric Association, 1980), perhaps correctly, have made the criteria for dementia associated with alcoholism the same as the criteria for dementia in general, with the exception of the criteria having to do with the alcoholic history.

The Role of Psychopathological Factors

The final etiological consideration to be discussed here is psychopathology. What I really mean here is psychopathology other than alcoholism that exists concurrently in alcoholic patients. It is noteworthy that this dimension of alcoholism is only considered in the chapter by Parsons, and not in those written by Cermak and by Butters and Granholm. The psychopathology of Korsakoff's syndrome has not been systematically studied, to the best of my knowledge, although the clinical folklore typically describes these individuals as essentially pathologically passive, inert, and unmotivated. The confabulation noted in the older literature as a cardinal symptom of Korsakoff's syndrome does not seem to be present in many, if not most, well-diagnosed Korsakoff patients, but I have observed it in some patients. In these cases, it sometimes had delusional aspects, as in the case of a patient who believed (falsely) that the name used for him was not his real name. He consistently insisted that a particular different name was, in fact, his correct name. In any event, psychopathology of Korsakoff's syndrome is not well understood—primarily, I feel, because it has not been extensively studied. I hasten to add, however, that it is not being suggested that functional, psychosocial factors play any kind of major role in the etiology of Korsakoff's syndrome. It is possible, however, that psychosocial considerations such as motivation may play some role in determining performance levels on memory and other cognitive tasks at any particular time.

The case is quite different in regard to chronic alcoholism. There is an enormous literature concerning the psychopathology of alcoholism, and the interaction between alcoholism and other psychiatric disorders. With regard to the matter of neuropsychological deficits, however, the findings have been extremely minimal, in the sense that there does not appear to be any consistent relationships between psychopathological symptoms (e.g., depression and anxiety) and objective neuropsychological test results. As Parsons has suggested in his chapter, and as Heaton and Pendleton (1981) have pointed out in a more general way, anxiety and depression are more highly associated with claims of impairment than with objective neuropsychological test results. Similar findings have been reported in the case of depressive syndrome of dementia (pseudodementia) (Wells, 1979), in that more claimed impairment is commonly observed in patients with depressive pseudodementia than in patients with "actual" dementia (e.g., Alzheimer's disease). It seems clear that we can now essentially reject what now appears as the naive presumption that alcoholics perform poorly on neuropsychological tests because they are nervous and depressed. They may well be nervous and depressed, but that does not seem to account for their poor performance levels.

Can we provide a more sophisticated model describing the relationship between psychopathology and the neuropsychological aspects of alcoholism? Recently, Ralph Tarter and I have been discussing a scheme based on the following considerations. From observation of psychopathological characteristics in chronic alcoholics, and from the existing literature, it would appear that some alcoholics are clinically depressed when they appear for treatment and may have had recurrent depressive episodes; others are clearly sociopathic; and still others appear to have no identifiable psychopathology other than alcoholism. At a second level in this scheme, each individual in each of these cases may or may not have a family history of alcoholism. We have begun an exploration of this scheme in a study (Goldstein, Shelly, Mascia, & Tarter, 1985) in which a sample of chronic alcoholics were administered the Halstead–Reitan Battery and the Minnesota Multiphasic Personality Inventory (MMPI). This study did not involve family history considerations, but we attempted to classify the MMPIs in accordance with the types of psychopathology described above. Differing code types were the primary consideration in this classification process.

We were not entirely successful in our endeavor. There were very few subjects in the study who could reasonably be classed as sociopathic. Instead, there was a substantial number of profiles that could very reasonably be described as reflecting psychosis. However, there were several depressed-looking profiles and a substantial number of normal profiles. What we found, first of all, was no difference between alcoholics with normal profiles and profiles characteristic of depression. However, while only half of the subjects in both the "depressed" and "normal" groups had Average Impairment Ratings (AIRs; Russell, Neuringer, & Goldstein, 1970) in the impaired range (>1.55), 80% of the cases with "psychotic" profiles had impaired-range AIRs. More interestingly, perhaps, the "psychotic" profile cases were more impaired than the others on the Wechsler Adult Intelligence Scale (WAIS) Arithmetic and Vocabulary subtests, even when educational level was covaried out. The finding is of interest because deficient performance on these subtests is not a part of the typical Halstead–Reitan Battery "alcoholic impairment pattern."

It is therefore suggested that while (as others have found) depression does not appear to be causally related to the cognitive deficits found in chronic alcoholics, there does appear to be a subgroup of alcoholic patients characterized by manifestations of substantial disorganization, who show more severe and widespread neuropsychological impairment than do other alcoholic inpatients. The nature of this group has not yet been characterized, and we may be only dealing with individuals who are less completely detoxified than the others. Further studies should look at this group more closely, perhaps with more refined diagnostic instruments than the MMPI, and should also explore the family history dimension. In any event, if our data base is typical of what has been used for other neuropsychological studies of chronic alcoholics, it would be interesting to determine to what extent the burden of neuropsychological deficit is borne by alcoholics experiencing some kind of disorganizing process at the time of assessment. It may be noted that in our study, the Halstead–Reitan and the MMPI were administered at about the same time (i.e., about 2 weeks after admission to an inpatient alcoholism treatment program).

To summarize this aspect of the present discussion, the exploration of various aspects of psychopathology as an etiological factor for the neuropsychological deficit found in alcoholics has not been a particularly fruitful endeavor. The psychopathology of alcoholism is clearly a fascinating area, but as far as we can tell at present, it has little to do with the neuropsychology of alcoholism. We may recall seemingly endless attempts made during the 1960s to correlate some personality test score with some neuropsychological test score; for the most part, these attempts only led to impressively large matrices of nonsignificant correlation coefficients. However, more sophisticated approaches, including such considerations as reliable and valid diagnostic evaluations for psychopathology, acknowledgment of the family history as an interactive factor, evaluation of the purported relationship between individual-hemisphere function and psychopathology, and consideration of individual nosological groups when the conditions are compounded with alcoholism, may lead to more promising results. In regard to the last point, some progress has been made in reaching an understanding of the condition in which alcoholism and schizophrenia are compounded (Alterman, Ayre, & Williford, 1984).

Theoretical Models

Models for Korsakoff's Syndrome versus Chronic Alcoholism

My concluding remarks are concerned with the matter of models. First, it would appear that the models for Korsakoff's syndrome must be different from the ones used in the case of chronic alcoholism. In the case of Korsakoff's syndrome, I will not deal with the intricacies of Cermak's deliberations, leaving that to Oscar-Berman (see Chapter 13) and others with more expertise than I possess. I would only suggest, however, that the model Cermak proposes really is for amnesia rather than for Korsakoff's syndrome as an entity. Korsakoff's syndrome is, by definition, a syndrome—that is, a collection of symptoms that characteristically occur together and are indicative of a disease. In the case of alcoholic amnesic disorder (Korsakoff's syndrome), DSM-IIII makes reference to such matters as disorientation, confabulation, apathy, peripheral neuropathy, and cerebellar ataxia, in addition to the cardinal symptom of amnesia. These associated features of Korsakoff's syndrome do not necessarily appear in all cases, but they are all thought to be manifestations of the same underlying disease.

The point I am trying to make is that there is what I believe to be an important distinction between a model for a specific cognitive disorder (in this case, amnesia) and a model for a disease entity or syndrome. Cermak, and the neuropsychologically oriented Korsakoff researchers in general, have provided us with highly sophisticated and elegant models for amnesia, but not for Korsakoff's syndrome *as a syndrome*. Doing the latter would require consideration of all of the associated symptoms and their relationships with one another. For example, it might consider the role of presence or extent of peripheral neuropathy and its relationship to the severity of the amnesia. It would appear that the difficulty generated by this distinction is that while the Korsakoff researchers have historically been inclined to look largely at the amnesia aspect of Korsakoff's syndrome, the chronic alcoholism researchers have been more inclined to look at patterns of test performance that sample a wide range of behaviors. Some have even gone beyond the field of cognitive abilities and have examined personality and psychopathological aspects of alcoholism. There are of course numerous exceptions to this statement, and there is no implication that one course or the other is a correct one to pursue. However, I think that the distinction is generally true, and does create difficulties when one attempts to relate one body of research to the other.

Admittedly, some degree of scientific controversy has emerged from this distinction. The people who use standard, comprehensive test batteries may suggest that the Korsakoff researchers may know little more about their patients than that they have poor memories, and that such a limited body of knowledge is of little clinical value. The Korsakoff researchers may reply that the battery users know too little about any aspect of cognitive function they assess, since their instruments are only really screening tests, some of them screening in irrelevant areas and based on incomplete if not incorrect conceptualizations of the cognitive deficit associated with the disorder being considered. Such limited detail and possibly incorrect assumptions may provide major difficulties for clinical application.

In consideration of these difficulties, it would appear to be most pragmatic to view the neuropsychological literature on chronic alcoholism and on Korsakoff's syndrome as two distinct bodies of knowledge. Not only do the two disorders appear to be different from each other, but, as I have attempted to point out, the nature of the research typically done with chronic alcoholics has been substantially different from what has been the case for Korsakoff patients. I would simply suggest that the research with Korsakoff patients may benefit from the taking of a broader perspective through assessment of areas other than memory. Butters and his colleagues have already taken steps in that direction, through looking at problem solving, visual–spatial abilities, and even olfactory discrimination (Jones, Butters, Moskowitz, & Montgomery, 1978; Jones, Moskowitz, & Butters, 1975; Jones, Moskowitz, Butters, & Glosser, 1975) in Korsakoff patients. On the other hand, those investigators utilizing standard test batteries in their research with chronic alcohols may wish to learn more about the specific aspects of the deficits elicited through more detailed assessment. Steps in that direction have been taken by Parsons and his colleagues with regard to the nature of alcoholics' difficulty with card sorting (Jones & Parsons, 1971; Tarter, 1971), and by our research group in reference to the matter of field dependence in alcoholics (see Goldstein, 1976 for a review).

Premature-Aging and Continuity Models

Having deferred to Oscar-Berman with regard to discussion of the Korsakoff models, I now turn to the matter of models of chronic alcoholism. As pointed out by Parsons, the most current models revolve around the premature-aging hypothesis, the continuity hypothesis, and various hypotheses related to brain localization (fronto-basal, right-hemipshere, and generalized/diffuse). The chapter by Butters and Granholm addresses the continuity hypothesis directly, concluding that Ryback's (1971) theory that chronic alcoholism and Korsakoff's syndrome represent end points on a continuum of memory impairment does not comport well with recent findings. As indicated above, this conclusion is in essential agreement with what is contained in Cermak's chapter and with other lines of evidence, all of which suggest that Korsakoff's syndrome is the product of a different neuropathological process from that associated with chronic alcoholism.

The fate of the premature-aging hypothesis has been somewhat the same. The view that alcoholics, and inferentially the brains of alcoholics, become old before their time clearly is congruent with clinical impressions; therefore, it becomes easy to nod one's head when the hypothesis is stated and to agree that it is a good way of putting the matter. However, the scientific evidence for it has not fared well. It suggests that the resemblance between alcoholic deterioration and normal aging is superficial, and that probably quite different processes are involved. To begin with the neuropathology, the CT scans for elderly individuals may demonstrate some degree of cortical atrophy, but (as may be seen elsewhere in this volume), alcoholics with CT scan abnormalities frequently show them in both cortex and regions surrounding the third ventricle. Third-ventricle lesions are not typically seen in normal elderly individuals. With regard to course, alcohol deterioration appears to be associated with a continuous decrement in ability level. It is now felt that normal aging is characterized by relative stability of function until shortly before death. The year before death is generally marked by rapid decline (the "terminal-drop hypothesis") (Kleemeier, 1962; Siegler, 1975). Other considerations are that at least two studies (Noonberg, Goldstein, & Page, 1985; Ryan & Butters, 1980) have shown that 30- to 40-year-old alcoholics already perform significantly more poorly than controls. At that age range, it would be difficult to attribute this finding to aging, even premature aging. Furthermore, the literature alluded to above regarding antecedent neuropsychological impairment and the role of hepatic dysfunction would not be consistent with the premature-aging hypothesis, particularly if what is meant by "premature aging" is premature aging of the brain. In general, the premature-aging hypothesis would appear, in the light of current evidence, to be more of a descriptive analogy than a scientific conceptualization of alcoholic deterioration.

Brain Localization Models

With regard to the various brain localization hypotheses, Parsons favors the generalized/diffuse model. I am forced to agree with him, because our own work in this area also favors that model (Goldstein & Shelly, 1980, 1982). Basically, we found that the pattern of neuropsychological deficit found among alcoholics resembled what was found in patients with documented nonalcoholic diffuse brain damage more than it resembled what was found for patients with anterior, posterior, left-hemisphere, or right-hemisphere brain damage. As Parsons suggests, the model has to be refined, and the CT scan studies demonstrating both cortical and subcortical pathology are quite helpful in that regard. In connection with the generalized/diffuse model, I would like to clarify a misunderstanding that may have developed. The model does not imply that all higher brain functions are impaired, or that those affected are impaired to an equal extent. Diffuse brain damage is not necessarily synonymous with diffuse, unpatterned cognitive deficit. Even patients with known non-alcohol-related diffuse lesions, such as those sometimes associated with closed head injury or toxicity, do not typically have global impairment. Furthermore, different kinds of diffuse lesions are likely to be associated with different patterns of neuropsychological deficit. As suggested by Parsons, we need to know specifically how the "diffuse lesion of alcoholism" relates to the pattern of observed neuropsychological deficits.

Also implicit in Parsons's remarks is a belief, which I share, that ultimately a single model will not suffice. There appears to be a subgroup of alcoholics in whose disorder genetic and antecedent cognitive dysfunction plays a large role. While it is the general impression that this group only contains a minority of alcoholics, we really do not know its extent, and we will not know it until the appropiate genetic and epidemiological research has been conducted. There may also be another subgroup that is particularly susceptible to liver disease, and so may be more than normally vulnerable to neurological dysfunction. As I have indicated above, individuals who ultimately develop Korsakoff's syndrome, and possibly some of the other more exotic alcoholism-related disorders (e.g., Marchiafava–Bignami disease or central pontine myelinolysis), may be constitutionally different from chronic alcoholics and may have different historical antecedents. For example, the chemical composition of the beverages consumed may be a major consideration. On a more positive note, there appear to be some individuals who have long alcoholic histories but who do not undergo substantial cognitive deterioration.

As a final example of the complexities involved here, after having found no differences in neuropsychological test performance between alcoholics with and without histories of alcoholic withdrawal seizures (Tarter, Goldstein, Alterman, Petrarulo, & Elmore, 1983), we found that when subjects were divided by race, white alcoholics with and without seizure histories again showed no neuropsychological differences, but black alcoholics did (Goldstein, Tarter, Shelly, Alterman, & Petrarulo, 1983). In discussing this finding, we considered the alternative possibilities that (1) blacks who have withdrawal seizures have a greater vulnerability to the effects of alcohol than do whites; (2) blacks characteristically drink alcoholic beverages containing more toxic congeners than beverages drunk by whites contain; (3) there was more malnutrition and associated liver disease in the black patients we studied than there was among the whites. Thus, in the course of testing the rather straightforward hypothesis that individuals with alcoholism sufficiently severe to produce withdrawal seizures would do more poorly on standard neuropsychological tests than seizure-free alcoholics, these unexpectedly complicated and difficult-to-interpret results associated somehow with race differences were found. I suspect that our fate in this difficult area is to continue to find these complexities and conundrums as our research proceeds.

Summary

This discussion of the neuropsychological consequences of alcoholism has begun with a presentation of the view that chronic alcoholism and alcoholic Korsakoff's syndrome represent two different disorders. I have elected to focus primarily on chronic alcoholism, with an emphasis on the point that, following an active period of developing sophisticated descriptions of the consequences of alcoholism for brain function, it is now time to start examining etiological factors. With that in mind, I have briefly considered a number of possible influences on the development of brain dysfunction in alcoholic individuals, including malnutrition, head trauma, antecedent neuropsychological deficits, and general systemic illnesses that are frequently found among alcoholics.

The roles of medical factors and of psychopathology as etiological considerations have been briefly reviewed. It is suggested that some component of the deficits found among alcoholics may be mediated by liver disease or dysfunction. With regard to psychopathology, it is suggested that while there is no clear connection between affective state and degree of neuropsychological dysfunction, there may be complex interconnections among type of psychopathology, family history, and neuropsychological status. The discussion concludes with a consideration of a number of theoretical models, including the premature-aging hypothesis, the continuity hypothesis, and various brain localization models. It is indicated that while the premature-aging and continuity models have not fared well scientifically, the generalized/diffuse brain model continues to hold up well. However, it needs to be refined in the direction of further specification of the nature of the diffuse process, and its connection with the pattern of neuropsychological deficits typically found among alcoholics.

Acknowledgment

Indebtedness is expressed to the Veterans Administration for support of this work.

References

Abramson, H. A. (1967). *The use of LSD in psychotherapy and alcoholism.* Indianapolis: Bobbs-Merrill.

Alterman, A. I., Ayre, F., & Williford, W. (1984). Diagnostic validation of conjoint schizophrenia and alcoholism. *Journal of Clinical Psychiatry*, *45*, 300–303.

American Psychiatric Association. (1980). *Diagnostic and statistical manual of mental disorders* (3rd ed.). Washington, DC: Author.

Arendt, T., Bigl, V., Arendt, A., & Tennstedt, A. (1983). Loss of neurons in the nucleus basalis of Meynert in Alzheimer's disease, paralysis agitans and Korsakoff's disease. *Acta Neuropathologica*, *61*, 101–108.

Bailey, W., Hustmyer, F., & Kristofferson, A. (1961). Alcoholism, brain damage and perceptual dependence. *Quarterly Journal of Studies on Alcohol*, *22*, 387–393.

Blass, J. P., & Gibson, G. E. (1977). Abnormality of a thiamine-requiring enzyme in patients with Wernicke–Korsakoff syndrome. *New England Journal of Medicine*, *297*, 1367–1370.

Gilberstadt, S., Gilberstadt, H., Zieve, L., Buegel, B., Collier, R., & McClain, C. (1980). Psychomotor performance deficits in cirrhotic patients without overt encephalopathy. *Annals of Internal Medicine*, *140*, 519–521.

Goldstein, G. (1976). Perceptual and cognitive deficit in alcoholics. In G. Goldstein & C. Neuringer (Eds.), *Empirical studies of alcoholism* (pp. 115–151). Cambridge, MA: Ballinger.

Goldstein, G. (1985). Dementia associated with alcoholism. In R. E. Tarter & D. H. van Thiel (Eds.), *Alcohol and the brain: Chronic effects* (pp. 283–294). New York: Plenum.

Goldstein, G., & Chotlos, J. W. (1965). Dependency and brain damage in alcoholics. *Perceptual and Motor Skills, 21*, 135–150.

Goldstein, G., & Shelly, C. (1980). Neuropsychological investigation of brain lesion localization in alcoholism. In H. Begleiter (Ed.), *Biological effects of alcohol* (pp. 731–743). New York: Plenum Press.

Goldstein, G., & Shelly, C. (1982). A multivariate neuropsychological approach to brain lesion localization in alcoholism. *Addictive Behaviors, 7*, 165–175.

Goldstein, G., Shelly, C., Mascia, G. V., & Tarter, R. E. (1985). Relationships between neuropsychological and psychopathological dimensions in male alcoholics. *Addictive Behaviors, 10*, 365–372.

Goldstein, G., Tarter, R. E., Shelly, C., Alterman, A. I., & Petrarulo, E. (1983). Withdrawal seizures in black and white alcoholic patients: Intellectual and neuropsychological sequelae. *Drug and Alcohol Dependence, 12*, 349–354.

Goodwin, D. W., & Erickson, C. K. (1979). *Alcoholism and affective disorders: Clinical, genetic and biochemical studies.* New York: Spectrum.

Goodwin, D. W., & Hill, S. Y. (1975). Chronic effects of alcohol and other psychoactive drugs on intellect, learning and memory. In J. Rankin (Ed.), *Alcohol, drugs and brain damage* (pp. 55–69). Toronto: Addiction Research Foundation.

Heaton, R. K., & Pendleton, M. G. (1981). Use of neuropsychological tests to predict adult patients' everyday functioning. *Journal of Consulting and Clinical Psychology, 49*, 807–821.

Hegedus, A. M., Tarter, R. E., Hill, S. Y., Jacob, T., & Winsten, N. E. (1984). Static ataxia: A possible marker for alcoholism. *Alcoholism: Clinical and Experimental Research, 8*, 580–582.

Jones, B. P., Butters, N., Moskowitz, H. R., & Montgomery, K. (1978). Olfactory and gustatory capacities of alcoholic Korsakoff patients. *Neuropsychologia, 16*, 323–337.

Jones, B. P., Moskowitz, H. R., & Butters, N. (1975). Olfactory discrimination in alcoholic Korsakoff patients. *Neuropsychologia, 13*, 173–179.

Jones, B. P., Moskowitz, H., Butters, N., & Glosser, G. (1975). Psychophysical scaling of olfactory, visual, and auditory stimuli by alcoholic Korsakoff patients. *Neuropsychologia, 13*, 387–393.

Jones, B. P., & Parsons, O. A. (1971). Impaired abstracting ability in chronic alcoholics. *Archives of General Psychiatry, 24*, 71–75.

Karp, S. A., Poster, D., & Goodman, A. (1963). Differentiation in alcoholic women. *Journal of Personality, 31*, 386–393.

Karp, S. A., Witkin, H., & Goodenough, D. (1965a). Alcoholism and psychological differentiation: Effect of achievement of sobriety on field dependence. *Quarterly Journal of Studies on Alcohol, 26*, 580–585.

Karp, S. A., Witkin, H., & Goodenough, D. (1965b). Alcoholism and psychological differentiation: Effect of alcohol on field dependence. *Journal of Abnormal Psychology, 70*, 262–265.

Kleemeier, R. W. (1962). Intellectual changes in the senium. *Proceedings of the American Statistical Association, 1*, 290–295.

Lieber, C. S. (1982). *Medical disorders of alcoholism: Pathogenesis and treatment.* Philadelphia: W. B. Saunders.

Lipscomb, T., Carpenter, J., & Nathan, P. (1979). Static ataxia: A predictor of alcoholism. *British Journal of Addiction, 74*, 289–294.

McSweeny, A. J., Grant, I., Heaton, R. K., Prigatano, G. P., & Adams, K. M. (1985). Relationship of neuropsychological status to everyday functioning in healthy and chronically ill persons. *Journal of Clinical and Experimental Neuropsychology, 7,* 281–291.

Noonberg, A., Goldstein, G., & Page, H. A. (1985). Premature aging in male alcoholics: "accelerated aging" or "increased vulnerability"? *Alcoholism: Clinical and Experimental Research, 9,* 449–469.

Parsons, O. A., & Farr, S. P. (1981). The neuropsychology of alcohol and drug abuse. In S. B. Filskov & T. J. Boll (Eds.), *Handbook of clinical neuropsychology* (pp. 320–365). New York: Wiley-Interscience.

Reitan, R. M., & Davison, L. A. (Eds.). (1974). *Clinical neuropsychology: Current status and applications.* Washington, DC: Winston.

Russell, E. W., Neuringer, C., & Goldstein, G. (1970). *Assessment of brain damage: A neuropsychological key approach.* New York: Wiley-Interscience.

Ryan, C., & Butters, N. (1980). Learning and memory impairments in young and old alcoholics: Evidence for the premature aging hypothesis. *Alcoholism: Clinical and Experimental Research, 4,* 288–293.

Ryback, R. (1971). The continuum and specificity of the effects of alcohol on memory. *Quarterly Journal of Studies on Alcohol, 32,* 995–1016.

Schaeffer, K. W., Parsons, O. A., & Yohman, J. R. (1984). Neuropsychological differences between male familial and nonfamilial alcoholics and nonalcoholics. *Alcoholism: Clinical and Experimental Research, 8,* 347–351.

Shelly, C., & Goldstein, G. (1976). An empirically derived typology of hospitalized alcoholics. In G. Goldstein & C. Neuringer (Eds.), *Empirical studies of alcoholism* (pp. 195–229). Cambridge, MA: Ballinger.

Siegler, I. C. (1975). The terminal drop hypothesis: Fact or artifact. *Experimental Aging Research, 1,* 169–185.

Strub, R. L., & Black, F. W. (1981). *Organic brain syndrome.* Philadelphia: F. A. Davis.

Tarter, R. E. (1971). *A neuropsychological examination of cognition and perceptual capacities in chronic alcoholics.* Unpublished doctoral dissertation, University of Oklahoma.

Tarter, R. E., & Alterman, A. I. (1984). Neuropsychological deficits in alcoholics: Etiological considerations. *Journal of Studies on Alcohol, 45,* 1–9.

Tarter, R. E., Goldstein, G., Alterman, A., Petrarulo, E. W., & Elmore, S. L. (1983). Alcoholic seizures: Intellectual and neuropsychological sequelae. *Journal of Nervous and Mental Disease, 171,* 123–125.

Tarter, R. E., Hegedus, A. M., Goldstein, G., Shelly, C., & Alterman, A. I. (1984). Adolescent sons of alcoholics: Neuropsychological and personality characteristics: *Alcoholism: Clinical and Experimental Research, 8,* 216–222.

Tarter, R., Hegedus, A., Van Thiel, D., Schade, R., Iwatsuki, S., & Starzl, T. (1983). Neuropsychological capacity of alcoholic and nonalcoholic cirrhotics. *Alcoholism: Clinical and Experimental Research, 7,* 124.

Tarter, R., Hegedus, A., Van Thiel, D., Schade, R., Pollit-Heyl, A., & Gavaler, J. (1984). Association between hepatic dysfunction and neuropsychological capacity in cirrhotic alcoholics. *Alcoholism: Clinical and Experimental Research, 8,* 123.

Tarter, R., Hegedus, A., Van Thiel, D., Schade, R., & Starzl, T. (1984). Nonalcoholic cirrhosis associated with neuropsychological dysfunction in the absence of overt evidence of hepatic encephalopathy. *Gastroenterology, 86,* 1421–1427.

Teuber, H. L., & Mishkin, M. (1954). Judgment of visual and postural vertical after brain injury. *Journal of Psychology, 38,* 161–175.

Victor, M., & Banker, B. Q. (1978). Alcohol and dementia. In R. Katzman, R. D. Terry, & K. L. Bick (Eds.), *Aging: Vol. 7. Alzheimer's disease: Senile dementia and related disorders* (pp. 149–170). New York: Raven Press.

Wallerstein, R. S., & Chotlos, J. W. (1957). *Hospital treatment of alcoholism.* New York: Basic Books.

Wells, C. E. (1979). Pseudodementia. *American Journal of Psychiatry*, *136*, 895–900.

Witkin, H., Karp, S., & Goodenough, D. (1959). Dependence in alcoholics. *Quarterly Journal of Studies on Alcohol*, *20*, 493–504.

12

Discussion

Some Implications of Motivated Performance for Neuropsychological Assessments

NANCY K. MELLO

Introduction

Chronic alcohol abuse is associated with a variety of deficits in brain function, including disorders of memory, attention, cognitive processes, and sleep (Parsons, Chapter 8, this volume; Victor & Adams, 1953). Many of these disorders are reversible during sobriety (Parsons & Prigatano, 1977). However, repeated chronic alcohol intoxication may lead to permanent brain dysfunctions such as Wernicke's disease and Korsakoff's psychosis, which are characterized by profound impairment of memory and deranged thinking processes (Talland, 1965; Victor, Adams, & Collins, 1971). Chronic alcoholics often have a variety of neurological disorders now thought to result from a combination of the direct toxic effects of alcohol and nutritional deficiencies and malabsorption syndromes (Dreyfus, 1974; Victor, 1975). There is an extensive literature describing the clinical neurology and neuropathology associated with alcohol-related disorders of the central nervous system (CNS) (see Butters & Granholm, Chapter 9, this volume; Cermak, Chapter 10, this volume; Dreyfus, 1974; Victor, 1975; Victor *et al.*, 1971).

The degree of impairment appears to covary with duration and severity of alcoholism (Parsons, Chapter 8, this volume), but the mechanisms by which alcohol disrupts CNS processes during intoxication and permanently impairs brain function in some alcoholics are poorly understood. Although some disorders have been shown to be associated with discrete lesions of the CNS, as in the case of Wernicke–Korsakoff psychosis, a more diffuse

Nancy K. Mello. Alcohol and Drug Abuse Research Center, Harvard Medical School–McLean Hospital, Belmont, Massachusetts.

deterioration of brain tissue is also observed. Radiologists have been able to detect evidence of ventricular enlargement and diffuse cortical atrophy in alcoholics, using new imaging techniques (Wilkinson, 1982). Biological scientists have shown that alcohol can disrupt the nerve cell membrane (Chin & Goldstein, 1977).

Precise characterization of disordered brain function associated with alcohol provides a continuing challenge. There appears to be a continuum of alcohol-related memory deficits, ranging from transient memory problems during acute intoxication to the most profound and irreversible disorders associated with Wernicke–Korsakoff psychosis. Neuropsychologists interested in the effects of alcohol and other drugs on cognitive function have tended to use an acute-intoxication paradigm in normal volunteer subjects and to compare performance during intoxication with performance during sobriety (for reviews, see Biernbaum & Parker, 1977; Mello & Mendelson, 1978). Under conditions of acute alcohol intoxication, the degree of detectable cognitive impairment appears to be alcohol-dose-dependent. Interpretation of the existing data is complicated by factors such as behavioral tolerance and state-dependent effects (Mello & Mendelson, 1978). Alcohol intoxication appears to be consistently associated with a fragmentary dissociative memory loss, sometimes thought to reflect problems in information retrieval rather than problems in information acquisition or retention (Petersen, 1977).

Studying the most severely afflicted alcoholic Korsakoff patients during sobriety presents both special opportunities and limitations, since it is rarely possible to evaluate premorbid function. One of the first comprehensive efforts to characterize and analyze the complex disturbances afflicting patients with Korsakoff's psychosis was published by Talland in 1965. Twenty years later, Butters and Granholm (Chapter 9, this volume) have reviewed the current efforts to describe the memory dysfunctions in Korsakoff syndrome patients. Despite different theoretical emphases, these accounts separated by two decades are concordant in the basic clinical description of the disorder and the continuing enigma it presents.

In the chronic alcoholic, years of heavy drinking, age, and history of head injury are some of the factors that combine to exacerbate memory dysfunction; however, these disorders may spontaneously remit during sobriety (Parsons & Prigatano, 1977). Such data suggest the potential resiliency of the human brain to repeated episodes of inebriation. The lack of general memory impairment in some detoxified alcoholics (Parsons & Prigatano, 1977) may also be interpreted to suggest that evidence of impaired memory function during intoxication may reflect the subjects' uncooperativeness and indifference to the task, as well as the direct effects of alcohol. The conditions under which performance capacity is evaluated are one important dimension of the resulting diagnosis of impairment.

Concerning Motivated Performance

The central thesis of this essay is that any neuropsychological assessment is likely to be influenced by the subjects' attitude and motivation. Performance deficits may reflect real incapacity or indifference and inattention. Unless the experimental conditions are arranged to maximize the probability that the subjects will perform as well as possible, confidence in interpretation of the resulting data may be limited.

Motivation

Most studies of the behavioral effects of alcohol require the subjects' cooperation, and subjects are often paid for participation in the study. However, payment is rarely made contingent upon accurate performance. Most investigators appear to assume that their subjects will try to perform as well as possible. But there is no reason to assume that subjects will consistently do their best, unless they are specifically paid to do so. To the extent that the accuracy of performance results in a task-specific reinforcement, the investigator can be more confident that any alcohol-related performance decrement reflects an alcohol effect rather than boredom or fatigue. The considerable literature attesting to the powerful behavioral control exerted by contingent reinforcement is the cornerstone of the experimental analysis of behavior, but is often ignored in other areas of psychology (Skinner, 1953).

Attention

A related issue is whether or not the subject is in fact attending to the task. Some behavioral tasks are more vulnerable to distractibility than others, but most assessments of some aspects of cognitive function before and during alcohol intoxication require that the subject attend to, and perhaps learn, some verbal, visual, or auditory stimulus pattern. It is obvious that inattention and distractibility can defeat the goal of studies of memory function. Valid evaluation of the effects of intoxication on subsequent recall requires that the subject attend to the stimuli to be recalled, but this variable is seldom controlled. Inconsistencies in the literature on alcohol and memory function may reflect some investigators' inattention to the dimension of attention (Mello & Mendelson, 1978).

Behavioral science has devised reliable techniques for controlling attention that are independent of stimulus content. The most generally applicable of these is to require an observing response before performance. This standard technique can be used in both animal and human subjects to ensure that the subject does attend to the discriminative stimulus upon which subsequent performance is based (Mello, 1973). There are many variations on the basic procedure, but essentially, the subject is required to make a motor or verbal response to produce a stimulus. It is assumed that the subject is more likely to attend to a self-produced stimulus than to one which is introduced by the investigator or a programming apparatus.

Evidence That Motivated Performance Is Important

The notion that people will do well if they are motivated to do so has a simplistic common-sense appeal—an almost irrefutable face validity that may work against its being taken seriously. The importance of B. F. Skinner's contributions to behavioral science are generally recognized today, and the principle that behavior is maintained by its consequences is an accepted principle of behavioral science. The challenge in human studies is to find a meaningful consequence that will in fact maintain the behavior of interest. Pennies and candy may be effective reinforcements for small children, but are hardly adequate for college students. Alcohol-dependent subjects pose a special problem, since they have usually abandoned conventional reinforcers as alcoholism progresses. In our studies of alcoholic men, we have concluded that alcohol is the only reinforcer that will consistently maintain accurate performance during intoxication (for reviews, see Mello, 1972, 1973; Mello & Mendelson, 1978).

One example will suffice. In the early 1970s, there was considerable controversy over alcohol's effects on short-term memory and whether or not "blackouts" reported during alcohol intoxication could be attributed to an alcohol-induced short-term memory deficit (see Mello & Mendelson, 1978, for review). To evaluate this question, we studied memory function prior to and during acute and chronic alcohol intoxication (Mello, 1973). Twenty alcoholic men were studied, and 13 of these subjects reported a history of occasional blackouts during heavy intoxication that lasted several hours to several days. Subjects with and without a history of blackouts were compared on a delayed matching-to-sample procedure designed to examine short-term memory function. The subjects' task was to choose one of four visual comparison stimuli that was identical to a sample stimulus. The delay between sample stimulus offset and the onset of comparison stimuli defined the span of "short-term" memory. Since there were no spatial cues, correct matching after a delay interval necessarily required recall of the sample stimulus. The length of the delay interval increased with each correct match trial, and decreased with each incorrect trial in 4-second increments. The possible delay intervals ranged between 0 and 6 minutes.

Attention to the sample stimulus was ensured by requiring the subject to initiate each trial by making an observing response. Motivation to perform well was aided by requiring completion of four correct trials before four error trials to earn a single token.

Readily discriminable visual stimuli were selected to ensure that a poor performance could be interpreted in terms of memory function and would not be confounded by any difficulty in discriminating the sample stimuli from the comparison stimuli. The matching-to-sample stimuli consisted of a film of 120 stimulus sets. These included pictures of faces of research ward staff, movie stars, and political figures; familiar household objects; liquor and cigarette labels; nude figures; trigrams; and abstract geometric designs. These multiple stimulus categories were intended to increase subjects' interest in the task and to minimize predictability of stimulus occurrence.

Accurate performance was paid for in tokens. Each token was interchangeable for one cigarette or 15 minutes of television time during the prealcohol baseline and for 1 ounce of alcohol during the alcohol availability period.

In addition to overall accuracy of performance, evaluation of delayed matching-to-sample data requires consideration of the temporal distribution of errors. Demonstration of short-term memory impairment would require that error frequency increase at progressively longer delays between sample and match stimuli. The effects of a single acute dose of alcohol that produced peak blood alcohol levels above 200 mg/dl on matching-to-sample performance are shown in Figure 12-1. It is obvious that each subject maintained accurate performance during the 2½-hour matching-to-sample session. During acute alcohol intoxication, four of the five "blackout" subjects whose peak blood alcohol levels exceeded 200 mg/dl improved their performance over prealcohol baseline levels. We interpreted these data to indicate that alcoholic men with a history of blackouts did not differ from control subjects in accuracy of performance on a delayed matching-to-sample task at comparable blood alcohol levels (Mello, 1973).

The absence of an alcohol-induced impairment of matching-to-sample performance when blood alcohol levels exceeded 200 mg/dl was also observed during a 10- to 12-day period of chronic intoxication. Seven of the subjects with a history of blackouts and four control subjects actually improved matching-to-sample performance during chronic intoxication in comparison to the prealcohol baseline. These data are consistent with earlier studies of the effects of chronic intoxication in alcoholics (Talland, 1966; Talland, Mendelson, & Ryack, 1964). A parallel study of the effects of alcohol (1–3.5 g/kg) on matching-to-sample performance in male rhesus monkeys also failed to show an alcohol-induced impairment of short-term memory (Mello, 1971).

These data illustrate that chronic alcoholic men are able to perform accurately during intoxication when acquisition of a meaningful reinforcer, alcohol, is contingent upon performance accuracy (Mello, 1978). The degree of behavioral tolerance for alcohol that can develop in chronic alcoholic individuals is also shown by these data. The extent to which comparable excellent performance on complex tasks could be maintained in alcoholic

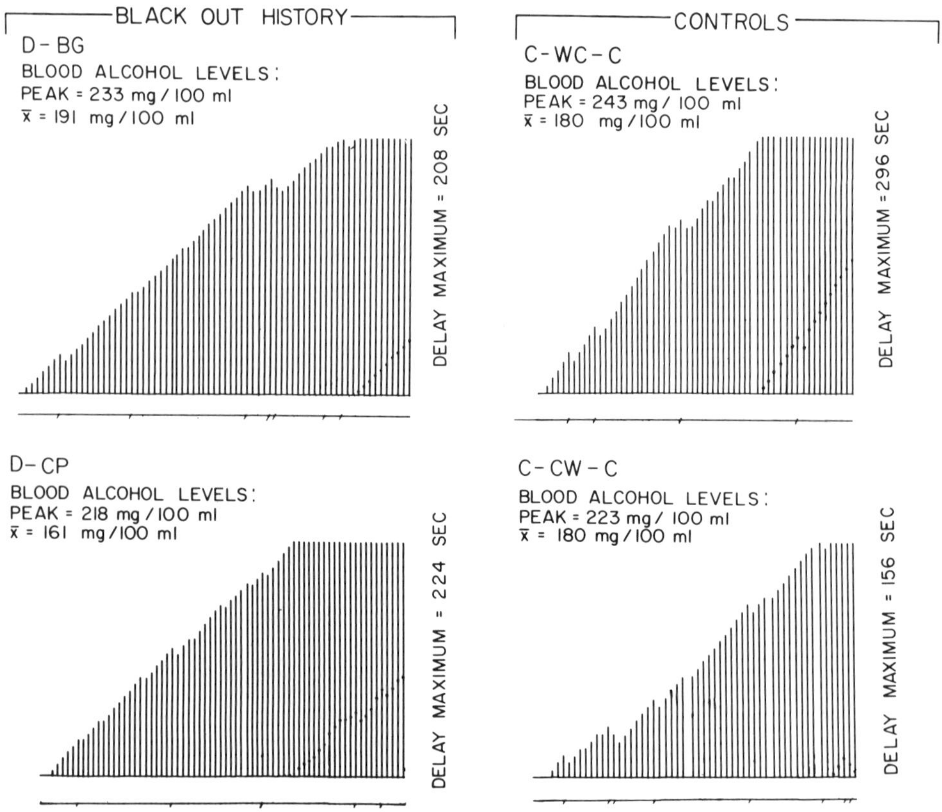

Figure 12-1. Effects of an acute alcohol dose (3.5 ml/kg) on delayed matching-to-sample performance in subjects with and without a history of alcohol-related blackouts. An analog readout of the delay intervals on successive matching-to-sample trials is shown for each of four representative subjects whose peak blood alcohol levels exceeded 200 mg/dl. The vertical bars represent the delay between the sample stimulus offset and the comparison stimulus onset of each successive trial. Once the recorder pen reached the limit of its excursion, it reset and continued up the same line until the delay interval terminated. This is indicated by the small dots superimposed on the vertical lines. The maximum delay interval reached by each subject during the 2½-hour session is shown at the right of each histogram; the maximum delays are a function of the amount of time that each subject spent working at the task. Errors are indicated by a downward deflection of the baseline pen. Each error was followed by a 4-second decrease in the sample-to-match delay interval. (From "Short-Term Memory Function in Alcohol Addicts during Intoxication" by N. K. Mello, 1973, in M. M. Gross [Ed.], *Alcohol Intoxication and Withdrawal: Experimental Studies. Proceedings of the 30th International Congress on Alcoholism and Drug Dependence* [pp. 333–344]. New York: Plenum Press. Reprinted by permission.)

individuals with adequate contingent reinforcement is an empirical question. However, it would be useful to include motivated performance measures in future assessments of alcohol-related impairments to ensure maximally accurate characterization of the extent of the deficit. If performance capability proved to be amenable to contingent reinforcement, this could also have important implications for rehabilitation strategies.

Motivated Performance: Applications in Brain-Imaging Studies

Although neuropsychologists have often neglected to arrange contingencies to ensure motivation and attention in research subjects, neurologists and neuroradiologists who use imaging techniques to study brain processes have recognized the importance of these issues. For example, positron computed tomography (PCT) can be used to visualize cerebral structures and to measure functional processes in the intact human brain (Phelps & Mazziotta, 1985; Phelps, Mazziotta, & Huang, 1982). The noninvasive quantitative measurement of radioactivity concentrations in human brain tissue is useful for diagnostic localization and functional analysis of a variety of CNS disorders, ranging from stroke to schizophrenia (Phelps *et al.*, 1982).

In one study designed to evaluate the feasibility of using PCT to study the cerebral processing of auditory stimuli, it was necessary to motivate the subjects to attend to both nonverbal (music, tone sequences, chord pairs) and verbal (a factual story) stimuli, presented both monaurally and binaurally (Mazziotta, Phelps, Carson, & Kuhl, 1982). Subjects were told that they would be paid in proportion to their accuracy in answering specific questions about the auditory stimuli in the nonverbal paradigm. Accuracy was monitored with a microswitch push-button system to signal the subjects' responses to test comparisons. In the verbal task, subjects were asked about auditory stimuli after stimulation. In control studies, where specific auditory stimuli were not presented, subjects were told that they would be paid only if they remained awake throughout the session. In fact, subjects were always paid the full amount for their efforts, but the instructional set was thought necessary for the accurate evaluation of metabolic responses to auditory stimuli (Mazziotta *et al.*, 1982). The investigators concluded that stimulus content and the analysis strategy of the subject were more important determinants of metabolic responses to auditory stimuli than the side of stimulation (Mazziotta *et al.*, 1982). In describing the methodological considerations affecting PCT tomographic studies, the investigators commented that

> because of the long duration of the stimulation period (30 to 40 minutes), the subjects must attend to the stimuli without habituation and with constant

> vigilance. Since electrical recordings of evoked brain potentials are typically measured in milliseconds, many stimuli must be provided to minimize the time for brain activity other than that related to the stimulus. Highly motivated subjects and monetary rewards can help. (Mazziotta *et al.*, 1982, p. 933)

Although imaging techniques are now in the early stages of development (Phelps *et al.*, 1982), it is reasonable to predict a closer integration between neuropsychology, neuroscience, and behavioral science in the future. The rapidly developing technology of imaging appears to hold special promise for the functional analysis of alcohol effects on many dimensions of cognitive processes. Eventually, the effects of alcohol and other drugs on motivated performance in attentive subjects may be studied with a combination of imaging procedures and the many sophisticated analytic techniques devised by neuropsychologists and described elsewhere in this volume. Resulting data should help us to better understand how alcohol affects brain function, and may also suggest testable hypotheses for clarifying the neural aspects of alcohol dependence.

Acknowledgments

Preparation of this chapter was supported in part by Grant No. DA 00101 from the National Institute on Drug Abuse and by Grant Nos. AA 04368 and AA 06252 from the National Institute on Alcohol Abuse and Alcoholism, Alcohol, Drug Abuse and Mental Health Administration.

References

Biernbaum, I. M., & Parker, E. S. (Eds.). (1977). *Alcohol and human memory*. Hillsdale, NJ: Erlbaum.

Chin, J. H., & Goldstein, D. B. (1977). Effects of low concentrations of ethanol on the fluidity of spin-labeled erythrocyte and brain membranes. *Molecular Pharmacology, 13*, 435–441.

Dreyfus, P. M. (1974). Diseases of the nervous system in chronic alcoholics. In B. Kissin & H. Begleiter (Eds.), *The biology of alcoholism: Vol. 3. Clinical pathology* (pp. 265–290). New York: Plenum Press.

Mazziotta, J. C., Phelps, M. E., Carson, R. E., & Kuhl, D. E. (1982). Tomographic mapping of human cerebral metabolism: Auditory stimulation. *Neurology, 32*(29), 921–937.

Mello, N. K. (1971). Alcohol effects on delayed matching to sample performance by rhesus monkey. *Physiology and Behavior, 7*, 77–101.

Mello, N. K. (1972). Behavioral studies of alcoholism. In B. Kissin & H. Begleiter (Eds.), *The biology of alcoholism: Vol. 2. Physiology and behavior* (pp. 219–291). New York: Plenum Press.

Mello, N. K. (1973). Short-term memory function in alcohol addicts during intoxication. In M. M. Gross (Ed.), *Alcohol intoxication and withdrawal: Experimental studies. Pro-*

ceedings of the 30th International Congress on Alcoholism and Drug Dependence (pp. 333–344). New York: Plenum Press.

Mello, N. K. (1978). Alcoholism and the behavioral pharmacology of alcohol: 1967–1977. In M. A. Lipton, A. DiMascio, & K. F. Killam (Eds.), *Psychopharmacology—a generation of progress* (pp. 1619–1637). New York: Raven Press.

Mello, N. K., & Mendelson, J. H. (1978). Alcohol and human behavior. In L. L. Iversen, S. D. Iversen, & S. H. Snyder (Eds.), *Handbook of psychopharmacology: Vol. 12. Drugs of abuse* (pp. 235–317). New York: Plenum Press.

Parsons, O. A., & Prigatano, G. P. (1977). Memory functioning in alcoholics. In I. M. Biernbaum & E. S. Parker (Eds.), *Alcohol and human memory* (pp. 185–194). New York: Plenum Press.

Petersen, R. C. (1977). Retrieval failures in alcohol state dependent learning. *Psychopharmacology, 55*(2), 141–146.

Phelps, M. E., & Mazziotta, J. C. (1985). Positron emission tomography: Human brain function and biochemistry. *Science, 228*, 799–909.

Phelps, M. E., Mazziotta, J. C., & Huang, S. C. (1982). Study of cerebral function with positron computed tomography. *Journal of Cerebral Blood Flow and Metabolism, 2*, 113–162.

Skinner, B. F. (1953). *Science and human behavior*. New York: Macmillan.

Talland, G. A. (1965). *Deranged memory*. New York: Academic Press.

Talland, G. A. (1966). Effects of alcohol on performance in continuous attention tasks. *Psychosomatic Medicine, 28*(2), 596–604.

Talland, G. A., Mendelson, J. H., & Ryack, P. (1964). Experimentally induced chronic intoxication and withdrawal in alcoholics: 5. Tests of attention. *Quarterly Journal of Studies on Alcohol* (Suppl. 1), 74–86.

Victor, M. (1975). Nutrition and diseases of the nervous system (including psychiatric disorders). *Progress in Food and Nutrition Science, 1*(3), 145–172.

Victor, M., & Adams, R. D. (1953). The effect of alcohol on the nervous system. *Research Publications of the Association for Nervous and Mental Disease, 32*, 526–573.

Victor, M., Adams, R. D., & Collins, G. H. (1971). *The Wernicke–Korsakoff syndrome*. Philadelphia: F. A. Davis.

Wilkinson, D. A. (1982). Examination of alcoholics by computed tomographic (CT) scans: A critical review. *Alcoholism: Clinical and Experimental Research, 6*, 31–45.

13

Discussion

Neuropsychological Consequences of Alcohol Abuse: Questions, Hypotheses, and Models

MARLENE OSCAR-BERMAN

Introduction

Chapters 8, 9, and 10 of this volume have discussed neuropsychological changes that occur with long-term alcohol abuse. The chapter by Butters and Granholm, and that by Cermak, both center around Korsakoff's disease; Butters and Granholm concentrate on etiology and neuropathology, and Cermak explores current models of memory. The chapter by Parsons centers around alcoholics who do not show the severe amnesia characteristic of alcoholic Korsakoff's disease.

Parsons begins his chapter by asking a series of questions about research accomplishments in the neuropsychology of alcoholism, and devotes the rest of the chapter to answering them. Since these questions are broad-ranging, my discussion uses the gist of each of them to integrate and expand the themes of all three of the separate chapters. In this way, it becomes readily apparent that results of research from widely varying perspectives agree on the nature of significant progress that has evolved over the past 10–15 years. The first, fourth, and sixth questions of Parsons's are addressed directly in all three of the chapters, and the present discussion focuses principally upon them. These three questions are concerned, respectively, with the nature of the deficits; the degree of these assorted deficits within the different subgroups of alcoholics; and the models (anatomical and behavioral) that best describe the deficits within the different subgroups. By contrast, the second, third, and fifth questions, which are concerned, respectively, with parameters of alcohol consumption, alcoholics' self-perceptions. and premorbid functioning, are answered only indirectly in the chapters by

Marlene Oscar-Berman. Departments of Psychiatry and Neurology, Boston University School of Medicine, Boston, Massachusetts; Aphasia Research Center, Boston Veterans Administration Medical Center, Boston, Massachusetts.

Butters and Granholm and by Cermak, and receive less attention here. The very split in the emphasis among these chapters may itself be telling us that more progress has been made in defining existing subgroups, their deficits, and the presumed underlying bases of the deficits than has been made in defining antecedent conditions, including drinking history and personality traits.

1. What Are the Neuropsychological Deficits That Accompany Alcohol Abuse?

For Parsons, the answer to his first question is that problem-solving, abstracting, and perceptual–spatial abilities are impaired, with some depression of memory, new learning skills, and certain verbal–linguistic skills. Although Parsons's answer is applied mainly to the neuropsychological deficits of alcoholics who have no clinical signs of brain damage, he notes that it describes patients with known organic brain syndrome as well.

Cermak's answer to the first question is that the major neuropsychological deficit of patients with alcohol-based anterograde amnesia is in the realm of declarative memory of the episodic type. In other words, alcoholic Korsakoffs "know that" certain events have occurred, but they cannot identify the individual events because they do not efficiently encode incoming information. Their retrograde-memory loss (a gradient of increased impairment from disease onset to the present time) is described as reflecting an inability to search normally through an otherwise intact semantic-memory system (thus giving the appearance of an intact retrieval-processing mode). Cermak states further that alcoholics who do not develop Korsakoff's disease are in many ways qualitatively dissimilar to those who have the amnesia of alcohol-related etiology. Rather, non-Korsakoff alcoholics age prematurely and, like normal aging individuals, show an accelerated depression of *overall* performance, without the pattern of intact retrieval and impaired encoding seen in Korsakoffs.

In considering the memory impairments of alcoholic Korsakoffs, compared to those of patients suffering from progressive degenerative dementia (e.g., as in Alzheimer's disease), Butters and Granholm note that the latter have much more of a problem with semantic memory than do the former, but that both groups are severely impaired in the acquisition of episodic memories. In a number of studies from our laboratory (see Oscar-Berman, 1984, for a summary), we also have shown only mild impairments in semantic memory for alcoholic Korsakoff patients, compared to the severe impairments of patients with the progressive dementia accompanying Huntington's disease. For example, although Korsakoffs performed poorly on a series of difficult two-choice visual-discrimination problems (six individual two-choice problems presented concurrently in a single session), they evidenced significant within- and between-task improvement (Oscar-Berman &

Zola-Morgan, 1980). By contrast, Huntington patients, who also performed poorly, showed no evidence of within- or between-task improvement. In other words, on this difficult concurrent task, the Korsakoffs were more capable than the Huntington patients of forming the learning set "win–stay/lose–shift" (Harlow, 1959), which is helpful in the acquisition of new (episodic) information.

For Butters and Granholm, the anterograde and retrograde components of the amnesic syndrome are the foremost neuropsychological deficits, but visual–perceptual and problem-solving difficulties are also fundamental components of Korsakoff's syndrome. Our own work comes from a perspective that most closely resembles that of Butters and his research group, and so do our conclusions. However, we would add to the list of important "other" deficits the additional problems of (1) abnormal attention; (2) retarded perceptual-processing ability in several sensory modalities; and (3) reduced "motivation" (defined operationally in terms of sensitivity to reward parameters in our experiments). Deficits such as these have been documented in a series of studies from our laboratory (for summaries, see Oscar-Berman, 1980, 1984). The most recent demonstration was provided by results of an experiment designed specifically to tease apart the relative contributions of retarded visual-processing time, selective attention to visual cues, and memory for those cues (Oscar-Berman & Bonner, 1985).

We used a delayed matching-to-sample paradigm in which participants were required to match one of two laterally located response choices with a stimulus displayed in the center between them. Duration of the center sample stimulus varied between 20 and 500 milliseconds, and delay between sample offset and response-choice (match) onset varied between 0 and 30 seconds. Complexity of the sample stimulus also was varied, containing one or two dimensions (those of color and/or form). We compared performance by alcoholic Korsakoff patients to that of normals and of non-Korsakoff alcoholics, ranging from 35 to 70 years of age. Levels of performance for all groups improved with increased sample stimulus durations, and were negatively related to increased stimulus complexity and length of delay. Significant group differences in accuracy were evident with short stimulus exposures: The Korsakoff and older groups made more errors than the younger groups. Similarly, response times were influenced differentially by stimulus duration, stimulus complexity, and the delay between sample and matching stimuli, with young participants (alcoholics and controls) responding fastest.

In another recent study of Korsakoff patients (Oscar-Berman & Pulaski, 1984), we attempted to extend the generality of previous findings that alcohol abuse may lead to a deficiency in appreciating stimulus–reward associations (Mishkin, 1982; Oscar-Berman, 1984). To do this, we measured ability to learn and remember reward contingencies in a task that originated in animal laboratories (Gaffan, 1974) to test associative-learning functions after lesions of the fornix (a fiber tract with strong hippocampal connections). The task was a conditional discrimination that required subjects to learn to distinguish rewarded from equally familiar nonrewarded visual stimuli of controlled duration. By including "younger" (31–46 years) and "older" (55–68 years) subgroups of normal and non-Korsakoff alcoholic control subjects, the study also was able to explore the premature-aging hypothesis (Ryan, 1982; Wood & Elias, 1982) further.

There were two recurring phases inherent in the experimental design: an acquisition phase and a retention phase. The acquisition phase consisted of the successive presentation of 10 different stimuli, half of which were rewarded and half of which were not. The stimuli were colored picture slides of objects, back-projected onto the central key in an array of three response keys. On only half the acquisition trials (determined in advance by the experimenter), a press to the central stimulus delivered a reward (a penny); a brief tone followed responses to nonrewarded stimuli on the remaining half of the acquisition trials. Immediately after each set of 10 acquisition trials, 10 retention trials were presented. In the retention phase, subjects were required to choose between (1) the "positive" stimulus on the right-sided key (a picture that had been associated with reward), and (2) a constant alternative stimulus, a black disc on the left-sided key (if the picture on the right key had not been associated with reward). Thus, subjects could earn a penny on every trial for choosing the positive stimulus (the key on the right) or choosing the black disc (the key on the left) if they had learned to associate presence or absence of reward with each individual picture.

The Korsakoff patients were significantly impaired by comparison with all other groups. Older subjects, with and without a history of alcohol abuse, also showed some impairment when compared to younger groups of alcoholics and normals. These results, therefore, support the suggestion that the ability to associate stimulus information with reward is impaired in the amnesia of alcohol-related etiology, just as it is after hippocampal lesions in monkeys (Mahut, Zola-Morgan, & Moss, 1982). Furthermore, the results imply that aging and alcoholism are not compounded in their effects upon reward sensitivity. Thus, once again, the results emphasize the contribution of motivational, processing, and attentional deficits to other congitive impairments in aging and alcoholic individuals. However, the results also suggest that aging and alcoholism are not additive in their effects on our measures. (This aspect of the research comes up again in the discussion of the fourth and sixth questions, below.)

2. What Is the Relationship among Alcohol Intake, Duration of Alcoholism, and Associated Neuropsychological Impairments?

In regard to the second question, Parsons's data (obtained from middle-aged alcoholics abstinent for at least a month) indicate that frequent high levels of alcohol intake—not overall duration alone, nor a continual low level of consumption alone—correlate most significantly with degree of neuropsychological deficit. Cermak's chapter does not address the question of drinking patterns directly. However, it can be assumed from his discussion that neuropsychological symptoms develop gradually, and once they can be measured, there is a dichotomy between those who do and those who do not develop Korsakoff's disease. (Strictly speaking, for this conclusion to be valid, duration and amount of alcohol consumption must be matched in comparisons between Korsakoff and non-Korsakoff groups.) Butters and Granholm's chapter supports Cermak's logic with neuropathological information. Butters and Granholm attribute (1) the visual–perceptual and problem-solving deficits in Korsakoff and non-Korsakoff alcoholics to their shared regions of cortical damage, which probably result from the direct toxic effects of long duration and high doses of ethanol; and (2) the memory loss in Korsakoffs to hemorrhagic lesions in the medial diencephalic region, caused by thiamine deficiency. Early evidence for this latter assertion was presented by Blass and Gibson (1977), who demonstrated with *in vitro* cultures of dermal tissue that Korsakoffs show an abnormal use of thiamine as a cofactor in enzyme formation. However, additional studies are needed to confirm the genetic implications of these observations.

In a subsequent section of the chapter by Butters and Granholm, the anterograde and retrograde components of the amnesic syndrome are also tied to decreased cholinergic innervation of the cerebral cortex because of damage to basal forebrain structures. This point is discussed further below in connection with the sixth question.

3. Do Alcoholics Perceive Impairment in Their Everyday Cognitive and Perceptual–Motor Functioning?

Parsons notes, in response to his third question, that alcoholics tend to see themselves as less effective in certain skills than do nonalcoholics; that their reported symptoms are similar to those reported by patients with neurological disorders; and that the degree of self-perceived impairments in alcoholics correlates highly with reported alcohol intake. Depression and anxiety play a large part in subjective complaints, but not necessarily in objective measures of performance.

As with the preceding question, neither Cermak nor Butters and Granholm address the present question directly with respect to ecological validity. Both chapters stress the relative preservation of semantic as compared to episodic memories.

The following excerpts from two interviews at the Boston Veterans Administration Medical Center with a patient who had alcoholic Korsakoff's disease illustrate dramatically the degree and stability of perceived impairments in one patient over the course of 6 years (1970–1976). Both of the interviews were conducted by Dr. Butters. The excerpts are not meant to represent a formal study of Korsakoff's knowledge of their own deficiencies. They are presented in order to show in a single case that (1) the patient was cognizant of his memory problem; (2) he was not aware of the duration of his amnesia; and (3) he thought that the amnesia probably was due to attentional difficulties. The first excerpt dates from 1970.

DOCTOR: You seem to have some problems with your memory. Is that so?

PATIENT: I do have a problem, yeah.

DOCTOR: How come? What do you think it's due to?

PATIENT: I don't know. Probably not paying any attention . . . not paying any attention to it.

DOCTOR: Have you always had this problem?

PATIENT: To a degree, yeah.

DOCTOR: To a degree. Has it gotten any worse?

PATIENT: (*Pause*) It's stayed about the same, I guess.

DOCTOR: Stayed about the same, huh? Now you've been here in the hospital—actually for 2 weeks. Did you know that?

PATIENT: No, I wasn't aware of the length of time.

This next excerpt was conducted by Dr. Butters with the same patient 6 years later.

DOCTOR: Why do you think you're hospitalized?

PATIENT: Lack of memory, I guess.

DOCTOR: Lack of memory. What do you mean by "lack of memory"?

PATIENT: I don't remember. How else can you explain that?

DOCTOR: I see. And what sorts of things do you have trouble remembering?

PATIENT: I don't know why I came here, for instance. I don't know why I'm here, or I don't know what the background of it is.

DOCTOR: Why do you think you have problems with your memory? Have you had it all your life, this problem?

PATIENT: No, I used to have a pretty sharp memory at one time.

DOCTOR: Well, when was that? How long ago?

PATIENT: Oh, I don't know. A couple of years, maybe.

DOCTOR: How long ago?

PATIENT: A couple of years.

DOCTOR: A couple of years ago?

PATIENT: Yeah.

DOCTOR: Okay. Let me ask you a few things about current events. But first let me introduce you to these gentlemen. Do you know who these gentlemen are?

PATIENT: No.

DOCTOR: Okay. This is Dr. M.

PATIENT: Hi, Doctor!

DOCTOR: And this is Dr. A.

PATIENT: How do you do, Doctor!

DOCTOR: Me you know, right?

PATIENT: Yeah.

DOCTOR: Who am I?

PATIENT: Let's see, I don't know what your name is.

DOCTOR: Dr. Butters.

PATIENT: Dr. Butters, oh yeah.

DOCTOR: But these men you know, right? Dr. A., now, and Dr. . . .

PATIENT: Oh, I won't remember them 15 minutes later!

DOCTOR: You won't, really?

PATIENT: No, I got a memory like a pigeon!

DOCTOR: Well, we'll see.

This dramatic example graphically illustrates the degree of awareness of impairment that accompanies alcoholic Korsakoff's disease. The patient knew that his memory was impaired compared to an earlier time in his life, and he realized that he would not remember much of anything "15 minutes later." Unlike Parsons's non-Korsakoff alcoholics, the Korsakoff patient from Boston had no idea of the extent of the impairment, nor of its cause. At one time during the first interview, he was asked why he was in the hospital; his answer to the question was "Maybe something happened to my mother." Also, unlike Parsons's alcoholics, there was no apparent relationship in this patient between perceived impairment and depression or anxiety.

4. Are There Differences in Degree of Impairment Manifested by Subgroups of Alcoholics?

The answer to the fourth question depends upon the characteristics of different subgroups that are being compared, as well as the different neuropsychological assessment instruments that are employed in making the comparisons.

Parsons has described his work with male alcoholic veterans seen at the University of Oklahoma Health Sciences Center. Of the many individual differences that can characterize this relatively homogeneous population, Parsons concentrates on the subgroups he calls "Primary" and "Secondary." Primary alcoholics are those who are unable to identify precipitating causes for their excessive drinking, and have a number of other symptoms of excessive drinking; Secondary alcoholics do not meet these criteria. When education was covaried with performance of the two subgroups, they were found to differ in performance on Wechsler Memory Scale subtests and the Category Test, but not on performance on tests of perceptual–motor or verbal ability, or tests of attention. Parsons cautions that subgroups differing from his population in sex, race, and socioeconomic level need to be studied before one can generalize about the importance of his findings differentiating Primary from Secondary alcoholics.

The chapters by Cermak and by Butters and Granholm are concerned with the continuity hypothesis and thus, by definition, with the subgroups of Korsakoff versus non-Korsakoff alcoholics. Both chapters consider, and then dismiss, the idea that Korsakoff's syndrome is the end result of excessive long-term alcohol abuse. Rather, the amnesia that defines the salient symptom of Korsakoff's syndrome appears to be qualitatively different from the impairments observed in non-Korsakoff alcoholics. Cermak as well as Butters and Granholm attribute the amnesia to damage to some specific subcortical region—in particular, midline diencephalic structures and/or basal forebrain structures; they attribute other cognitive deficits characteristic of alcoholics (whether they have amnesia or not) to general diffuse deterioration of the CNS.

The similarities in symptomatology and in the diffuseness of damage that appear both in alcoholic and in normal aging individuals have prompted Cermak to consider subgroups based upon age differences. In the few studies that he has conducted, in which alcoholics were compared with normal aging individuals, the similarity was more apparent than not; and since both groups clearly differed from Korsakoffs, Cermak has entertained and supported speculations that alcoholism (without amnesia) leads to premature aging.

5. What Is the Likelihood That at Least Some of the Deficits in Alcoholics May Be Present Premorbidly?

The answer to the fifth question must be kept within the context of the first question asked—that is, what *are* the deficits? As we already have seen, not all investigators agree on the answer to the first question, although most do agree that deficits exist, and that they involve visual–spatial functions, problem-solving ability, and memory.

Most studies of alcohol abusers have been cross-sectional, yet the answer to this fifth question requires longitudinal studies including people who had no drinking history at the outset, but who eventually began to abuse alcohol. Vaillant's (1983) classic longitudinal research was conducted on 100 detoxified alcoholics followed over 8 years, and on 204 Harvard students and 456 Boston junior high school students followed over 40 years. Of the Harvard students, 13% became alcohol-dependent, compared to 24% of the core city students. Before they became alcoholics, there were no salient personality characteristics distinguishing the groups. Thus, Vaillant's findings support Parsons's results showing that traits such as anxiety and depression are not premorbid distinguishing characteristics (see the discussion of the third question, above). Alcoholics were found to be anxious and depressed, but these characteristics defined people with an ongoing and current drinking problem. The results of Vaillant's longitudinal observations also confirm Parsons's emphasis upon positive family history. Vaillant has pointed to the tolerance for drunkenness that exists in certain ethnic groups, the presence of alcoholic parents in the family who do not teach safe drinking practices, and the use of alcohol as a symptom of adolescent antisocial behavior. Parsons has shown that 63% of alcoholics with a positive family history, compared to 33% with a negative family history, were classified as primary alcoholics. Alcoholics with a positive family history also had significantly impaired neuropsychological functioning in comparison to alcoholics with a negative family history.

Parsons has gone on further to explore the possibility that neuropsychological impairments are related to premorbid symptoms of childhood hyperkinesis and/or minimal brain damage (Hk/MBD). However, he judges this explanation less satisfactory than others in accounting for a full range of alcohol-related problems (see the discussion of the sixth question, below). For example, only a third of Parsons's alcoholics had elevated scores on Hk/MBD dimensions reported for the premorbid years. Furthermore, Vaillant (1983) also reported that childhood hyperactivity was minimally correlated with subsequent alcohol abuse. A welcome control group for validating the relationship between neuropsychological impairments and alcoholism in a subgroup of Hk/MBD alcoholics would be a group of nondrinkers with an early history of Hk/MBD. As Parsons notes in his chapter, the existence and nature of premorbid neuropsychological deficits, and their implications for subtyping of alcoholics, remain fertile areas for future research.

6. What Neuropsychological Models Best Account for the Findings?

Three neuroanatomical models (areas of the CNS) are listed by Parsons to account for neuropsychological findings. These regions are, respectively, fronto-limbic areas, the right hemisphere, and the brain as a general, globally functioning organ. Butters and Granholm introduce a fourth area for consideration—the basal forebrain (in particular, the nucleus basalis of Meynert).

In addition to the proposed neuroanatomical models, Parsons also considers two neurobehavioral explanations, neither of which is tied directly to any specific neuroanatomical substrate: childhood Hk/MBD and premature aging. The former, which is touched upon in the preceding section of the present discussion, does not rest upon a large quantity of existing data. The latter has received considerable research attention (Ryan, 1982), and has been associated almost ubiquitously with generalized/diffuse brain damage (e.g., Cermak, Chapter 10, this volume; Wood & Elias, 1982) or with right-hemisphere involvement (Parsons & Leber, 1982). It should be noted here that recent reviews of childhood learning disabilities have associated many of the observed dysfunctions with right-hemisphere involvement (Denckla, 1978; Rourke, 1982; Weintraub & Mesulam, 1983) as follows: Right-hemisphere functions develop prior to left-hemisphere functions; left-hemisphere functions will not develop normally without prior right-hemisphere development; and diminished access to retarded right-hemisphere functions during development has serious consequences for acquisition and use of adaptive abilities. To my knowledge, the literature on childhood learning disabilities, *and* the literature on the neuropsychology of problem drinking, *have not been related or tied together in any direct way to a model of right-hemisphere dysfunction.* Perhaps, as Parsons suggests, there is a subset of alcoholics who do have Hk/MBD; if so, it would not be surprising that the right-hemisphere model has demanded so much attention in the alcoholism literature.

Additional consideration of the right-hemisphere model for explaining alcohol-related deficits has been given in several reviews (e.g., Oscar-Berman & Ellis, 1987; Parsons & Leber, 1982). Studies conducted in our laboratory over the past few years have investigated the right-hemisphere hypothesis in alcoholic and in aging individuals, in order to determine whether a parallel exists between changes resulting from alcohol abuse and those associated with normal aging. The tasks we used examined performance not only as a function of stimulus material (e.g., letters vs. spatial locations), but also as a function of task requirement (e.g., perceptual processing vs. memory; when the two cerebral hemispheres were challenged simultaneously vs. when they could work together; etc.). Our results have indicated that (1) visual processing and memory, and tactual discriminability, are more severely disrupted by aging than by alcoholism; (2) right-hemisphere function in aging and in alcoholic individuals may not be more selectively disrupted than left-hemisphere function; and (3) the combined effects of aging and alcoholism may result in additional subtle changes that are detectable only by sensitive behavioral measures (Ellis & Oscar-Berman, 1985; Oscar-Berman & Weinstein, 1985; Oscar-Berman, Weinstein, & Wysocki, 1983).

What about the model that suggests fronto-limbic involvement? In the 1950s and 1960s, animal research on brain mechanisms in memory placed considerable emphasis on prefrontal cortex and limbic system structures, and reviews of that literature are abundant (Fuster, 1980; Mahut & Moss, 1984; Mishkin, 1982; Oscar-Berman, 1984; Pribram, 1984). Although the frontal lobes and limbic system continue to receive attention in the 1980s, a model that stresses their role in human cognition does not adequately account for the many neuropsychological impairments observed in alcoholics. As an example, I shall describe one recent study (Freedman & Oscar-Berman, 1986) that was designed specifically to examine the role of frontal lobe functions in the memory problems of alcoholic Korsakoff patients and in patients with the dense anterograde amnesia that follows surgery for the treatment of a ruptured anterior communicating artery (Talland, Sweet, & Ballantine, 1967). We used tasks that are known to be sensitive to frontal lobe damage in nonhuman primates: delayed response (DR) and delayed alternation (DA). Performance of the two amnesic groups was compared to that of patients with CT-documented bilateral frontal lobe pathology, and non-Korsakoff alcoholics served as controls. Results showed that the patients with bilateral frontal lobe damage performed poorly on both of the tasks, relative to the alcoholic controls. The Korsakoffs were severely impaired on DA and mildly impaired on DR. By comparison, the amnesics with anterior communicating artery disease did not differ significantly from alcoholic controls on either DA or DR. The deficits of the frontal lobe patients and the Korsakoffs were not related to degree of clinically apparent memory loss. This was illustrated by the fact that among the frontal lobe patients, the most impaired subjects on both the DA and the DR tasks were those with the highest and lowest Wechsler Memory Scale scores, respectively. This was further supported by the lack of any significant correlation between performance on subtests of the Wechsler Memory Scale and error rate on DA and DR across all groups. The absence of any relationship within the frontal group between memory loss and impairment on DA and DR also suggested that those tasks were not sensitive to amnesia. These results were taken to support the view that certain of the deficits in alcoholic Korsakoffs (e.g., perseverative responding) can be attributed to associated frontal system pathology (see also Lhermitte & Signoret, 1976, and Oscar-Berman, 1980, 1984, for discussions of the frontal-like symptomatology in Korsakoff's disease). However, unlike destruction of medial temporal lobe structures (e.g., see Duyckaerts *et al.*, 1985), frontal damage does not appear to have any direct relationship to the amnesia, nor is it an outstanding calling card for other deficits of chronic alcoholics who do not have clinical signs of amnesia.

Parsons believes that the model that best fits most of the data on neuropsychological consequences in alcoholics is the one that suggests generalized/diffuse damage: "[A]lcohol abuse results in cortical and subcortical changes that give rise to different impairments, which may have different courses of recovery" (p. 172). Likewise, Cermak favors the same model explaining the similarity of neuropsychological effects of alcoholism and aging. For Cermak, however, the emphasis is upon diffuse *cortical* damage in aging and alcoholism; this contrasts sharply with the continuum theory, in which there is destruction of "'specific' midline diencephalic structures as seen in Korsakoff's syndrome" (p. 222). (Ideas about the relationship between alcoholism and aging have been published in numerous reports and reviews.) The generalized/diffuse model of brain damage as defined by Parsons encompasses the premature-aging explanation, as well as Butters and Granholm's model, which emphasizes (1) cortical abnormalities in Korsakoff and non-Korsakoff alcoholics; (2) mesial diencephalic structures in Korsakoffs and, to a lesser extent, in non-Korsakoff alcoholics; and (3) basal forebrain structures in Korsakoffs. Since the nucleus basalis of Meynert is a major source of cholinergic input to the neocortex and hippocampus, its destruction leaves both regions vulnerable (Arendt, Bigl, Arendt, & Tennstedt, 1983). Significant pathology in the nucleus basalis of Meynert was found in patients with Alzheimer's disease and paralysis agitans, as well as in Korsakoff patients, but not in Huntington patients, alcoholics without dementia, or patients with infantile brain damage (Arendt *et al.*, 1983). Therefore, the degeneration of that particular cholinergic system may very well be directly related to some of the neuropsychological changes in certain subgroups of alcoholics, but it seems inadequate to account for all.

Summary: Is There a Way to Integrate All of the Issues Touched Upon in These Three Chapters?

Perhaps the following answers have emerged from Chapters 8, 9, and 10:

1. There may be a subgroup of alcoholics whose right hemispheres develop abnormally and slowly, leaving them with Hk/MBD and/or learning disabilities.
2. Other alcoholics, with a (genetic?) predisposition to Korsakoff's disease, show signs of specific subcortical damage superimposed upon generalized cortical atrophy; perhaps this is related to cholinergic insufficiency, or to other forms of insult to amygdalo-hippocampal structures.
3. Still others develop generalized cortical atrophy (as do many aging nondrinkers), with minimal additional subcortical damage.
4. In some cases, the sequelae to alcoholism and aging may be additive.
5. Dietary influences and amount and duration of drinking play an important role in neuropsychological outcome.

Acknowledgments

Support for the writing of this chapter came from the Medical Research Service of the Veterans Administration and from the following grants: Grant No. AA05211 and Research Scientist Development Award No. AA00061 from the National Institute on Alcohol Abuse and Alcoholism, and Grant Nos. NS07615 and NS06209 from the National Institute of Neurological and Communicative Disorders and Stroke. I would like to thank Dr. Dorothy Weber for her helpful comments on an earlier draft.

References

Arendt, T., Bigl, V., Arendt, A., & Tennstedt, A. (1983). Loss of neurons in the nucleus basalis of Meynert in Alzheimer's disease. *Acta Neuropathologica, 61*, 101–108.

Blass, J. P., & Gibson, G. E. (1977). Abnormality of a thiamine-requiring enzyme in patients with Wernicke–Korsakoff syndrome. *New England Journal of Medicine, 297*, 1367–1370.

Denckla, M. B. (1978). Minimal brain dysfunction. In J. Chall & A. Mirsky (Eds.), *Education and the brain* (pp. 232–268). Washington, DC: National Society for the Study of Education.

Duyckaerts, C., Derouesne, C., Signoret, J. L., Gray, F., Escourolle, R., & Castaigne, P. (1985). Bilateral amygdalohippocampal lesions causing a pure amnesic syndrome. *Annals of Neurology, 18*, 314–319.

Ellis, R. J., & Oscar-Berman, M. (1985). *Effects of aging and alcoholism on recognition of dichhaptically presented stimuli.* Paper presented at the meeting of the International Neuropsychological Society, San Diego.

Freedman, M., & Oscar-Berman, M. (1986). Bilateral frontal lobe disease and selective delayed-response deficits in humans. *Behavioral Neuroscience, 100*, 337–342.

Fuster, J. M. (1980). *The prefrontal cortex.* New York: Raven Press.

Gaffan, D. (1974). Recognition impaired and association intact in the memory of monkeys after transection of the fornix. *Journal of Comparative and Physiological Psychology, 86*, 1100–1109.

Harlow, H. F. (1959). Learning set and error factor theory. In S. Koch (Ed.), *Psychology: A study of a science* (Vol. 2, pp. 492–537). New York: McGraw-Hill.

Lhermitte, F., & Signoret, J.-L. (1976). The amnesic syndrome and the hippocampal–mammillary system. In M. R. Rosenzweig & E. L. Bennett (Eds.), *Neural mechanisms of learning and memory* (pp. 49–56). Cambridge, MA: MIT Press.

Mahut, M., & Moss, M. (1984). Consolidation of memory: The hippocampus revisited. In L. R. Squire & N. Butters (Eds.), *Neuropsychology of memory* (pp. 297–315). New York: Guilford Press.

Mahut, M., Zola-Morgan, S. M., & Moss, M. (1982). Hippocampal resections impair associative learning and recognition memory in the monkey. *Journal of Neuroscience, 2*, 1214–1229.

Mishkin, M. (1982). A memory system in monkeys. *Philosophic Transactions of the Royal Society, B298*, 85–95.

Oscar-Berman, M. (1980). Neuropsychological consequences of long-term chronic alcoholism. *American Scientist, 68*, 410–419.

Oscar-Berman, M. (1984). Comparative neuropsychology and alcoholic Korsakoff's disease. In L. Squire & N. Butters (Eds.), *Neuropsychology of memory* (pp. 194–202). New York: Guilford Press.

Oscar-Berman, M., & Bonner, R. T. (1985). Matching- and delayed matching-to-sample performance in aging and alcoholic individuals. *Neuropsychologia, 23*, 639–651.

Oscar-Berman, M., & Ellis, R. J. (1987). Cognitive deficits related to memory impairments in alcoholism. In M. Galanter (Ed.), *Recent developments in alcoholism* (Vol. 5, pp. 59–80). New York: Plenum.

Oscar-Berman, M., & Pulaski, J. L. (1984). *Association memory in amnesia, alcoholism, and aging.* Paper presented at the meeting of the American Psychological Association, Toronto.

Oscar-Berman, M., & Weinstein, A. (1985). Visual processing, memory and lateralization in alcoholism and aging. *Developmental Neuropsychology, 1*, 99–112.

Oscar-Berman, M., Weinstein, A., & Wysocki, D. (1983). Bimanual tactual discrimination in aging alcoholics. *Alcoholism: Clinical and Experimental Research, 7*, 398–403.

Oscar-Berman, M., & Zola-Morgan, S. M. (1980). Comparative neuropsychology and alcoholic Korsakoff's syndrome: II. Two-choice visual discrimination learning. *Neuropsychologia, 18*, 513–526.

Parsons, O. A., & Leber, W. R. (1982). Alcohol, cognitive dysfunction and brain damage. In National Institute on Alcohol Abuse and Alcoholism (Ed.), *Biomedical processes and consequences of alcohol use* (Alcohol and Health Monograph 2, DHHS Publication No. ADM82-1191, pp. 213–253). Washington, DC: U.S. Government Printing Office.

Pribram, K. H. (1984). The organization of memory in nonhuman primate model systems. In L. R. Squire & N. Butters (Eds.), *Neuropsychology of memory* (pp. 340–363). New York: Guilford Press.

Rourke, B. P. (1982). Central processing deficiencies in children: Toward a developmental neuropsychological model. *Journal of Clinical Neuropsychology, 4*, 1–18.

Ryan, C. (1982). Alcoholism and premature aging: A neuropsychological perspective. *Alcoholism: Clinical and Experimental Research, 6*, 79–96.

Talland, G. A., Sweet, W. H., & Ballantine, H. T. (1967). Amnesic syndrome with anterior communicating artery aneurysm. *Journal of Nervous and Mental Disease, 145*, 179–192.

Vaillant, G. E. (1983). *The natural history of alcoholism.* Cambridge, MA: Harvard University Press.

Weintraub, S., & Mesulam, M.-M. (1983). Developmental learning disabilities of the right hemisphere. *Archives of Neurology, 40*, 463–468.

Wood, W. G., & Elias, M. F. (Eds.). (1982). *Alcoholism and aging: Advances in research.* Boca Raton, FL: CRC Press.

SECTION THREE

RECOVERY AND REMEDIATION OF NEUROPSYCHOLOGICAL FUNCTIONS

14

Do Neuropsychological Deficits Predict Alcoholics' Treatment Course and Posttreatment Recovery?

OSCAR A. PARSONS

Introduction

There is widespread evidence that many sober alcoholics in treatment programs manifest lowered performance in such important cognitive–perceptual functions as memory, new learning, abstracting, problem solving, and complex perceptual–motor performance (Parsons & Leber, 1982). If the deficits persist, they should be reflected in lessened effectiveness in the more complex behaviors that are necessary to meet life's demands, whether the latter are in the context of treatment programs of a psychotherapeutic nature or in posttreatment coping with life situations. This brings up the question of whether recovery from the deficits occurs, and, if it does, what its temporal course is.

Investigation of these questions has received increasing attention over the last decade. The problem area is of unusual interest to both clinicians and researchers in the alcoholism field. For example, if alcoholics recover over time to a "normal level" of neuropsychological functioning (i.e., cognitive and perceptual–motor functioning at levels that would be expected from age and education), there would be several implications. At the clinical level, such findings would imply that the former alcoholics should be able to meet the cognitive–perceptual and perceptual–motor demands of life tasks in a fashion typical of their peers. At the research level, such findings would suggest two conclusions: (1) The deficits found in alcoholics sober for several weeks are temporary and remediable, and (2) the hypothesized presence of premorbid deficits in alcoholics either is incorrect or holds for only a small minority of patients.

Oscar A. Parsons. Oklahoma Center for Alcohol and Drug-Related Studies, Department of Psychiatry and Behavioral Sciences, University of Oklahoma Health Sciences Center, Oklahoma City, Oklahoma.

In this chapter, four questions relevant to these issues are addressed:

1. What is the posttreatment course of recovery for impaired cognitive and perceptual–motor functions in treated alcoholics?
2. Do neuropsychological tests predict treatment benefits, recidivism, and recovery?
3. If sober alcoholics resume drinking, does it affect their neuropsychological test performance and life adaptation?
4. Will cognitive retraining speed the course of recovery?

Course of Recovery of Neuropsychological Functions in Alcoholics

In our reviews of the 21 studies that have appeared on this topic since 1975, we concluded that the evidence for significant improvement was impressive (Parsons & Leber, 1981, 1982). Seventeen of these studies (83%) reported improved performance by alcoholics on at least some aspect of neuropsychological functioning over periods ranging from 1 month to 4 years. Eleven of the 21 studies had control subjects who were either retested or served as a comparison group in an independent-groups design. Nineteen of these studies (91%) reported improvement on some aspects of cognitive and perceptual–motor functioning. Deficits in verbal abilities, such as verbal paired-associate learning, appeared to remit over a relatively short period of time—as early as 1 month (Goldman, 1983). However, areas of deficit behavior remained even in studies where alcoholics had been abstinent over a year.

Long and McLachlan (1974) retested alcoholics after 1 year of abstinence and compared them to nonalcoholic controls. They found at least partial recovery or better in visual–perceptual–motor skills, tactual performance, and abstracting ability, but not perceptual–motor speed. Schau, O'Leary and Chaney (1980) reported that visual–perceptual–motor skills and perceptual–motor speed improved in alcoholics after 14 months; however, compared to controls, alcoholics showed continued deficits in abstracting ability and tactual–motor performance. The latter two performance skills were also found by Hill, Reyes, Mikhael, and Ayre (1979) to be impaired in alcoholics after 12.5 months of sobriety. Visual retention, verbal paired-associate learning, and visual–perceptual–motor abilities were found to be improved in alcoholics tested after 3.7 years of abstinence, but an overall score reflecting "adaptive ability" remained significantly poorer than that of controls (Berglund, Leijonquist, & Horlen, 1977).

In our laboratories, using female subjects in an independent-groups design, we found that alcoholics sober for 4 years performed better than alcoholics sober for 1 month and not significantly differently from controls, except on one psychomotor test (the Digit Symbol subtest of the Wechsler Adult Intelligence Scale [WAIS]) and the Memory for Designs Test. Indeed, on the Halstead Cateogry Test, the long-term sober alcoholics were at the controls' mean (Fabian & Parsons, 1983). Nevertheless, when we tested the difference between the long-term sober alcoholics and the controls on an overall measure of impairment (Factor 1 score), they differed significantly ($t = 2.23$, $p < .05$). There was a mild but consistent trend for the long-term alcoholics to perform less efficiently (Figure 14-1).

Brandt, Butters, Ryan, and Bayog (1983) recently compared male alcoholics who had been abstinent for a short time (1–2 months at time of testing; $n = 159$), alcoholics who had been abstinent for a longer time (1–3 years; $n = 36$), and a prolonged-abstinence group (at least 5 years; $n = 30$). Significantly improved performance was found for the prolonged-abstinence group on short-term memory, delayed visual–spatial memory, and WAIS Digit Symbol tests, but not digit–symbol psychomotor performance, the Symbol–Digit Paired-Associate Learning Test, or the Embedded Figures Test.

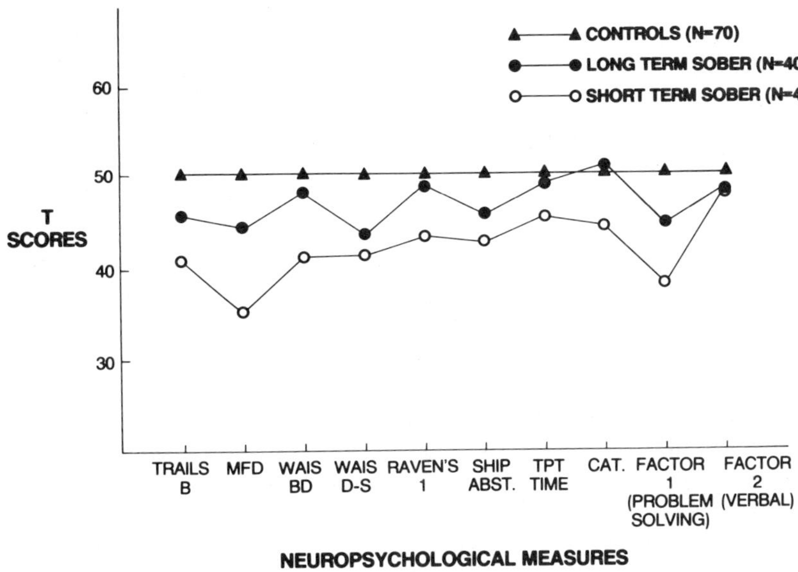

Figure 14-1. Comparison of nonalcoholic female controls, short-term sober alcoholic females, and long-term sober alcoholic females on neuropsychological tests (Trails B, Trail Making Test, Part B; MFD, Memory for Designs; WAIS BD, WAIS Block Design; WAIS D-S, WAIS Digit Symbol; Raven's 1, Raven's Progressive Matrices, Set 1; Ship. Abst., Shipley Abstracting Age; TPT Time, Tactual Performance Test Time; Cat., Halstead Category Test) and overall measures of impairment (Factor 1 and Factor 2).

Both of these studies suggest that the process of recovery in alcoholics is a long-term one and that there may be areas of functioning in which there are residual deficits. Both studies, however, used an independent-groups design—one in which investigators have the advantage of not contending with practice effects, but the disadvantage, inherent in that design, of not knowing whether the groups are equated on all other relevant variables.

The test–retest design is a more sensitive method for determining improvement, provided, of course that a control group is included to partial out practice effects. Such studies are difficult because of follow-up attrition and because of recidivism. We have conducted two follow-up studies using a test–retest design (Fabian & Parsons, 1983; Yohman, Parsons, & Leber, 1985). Both retested alcoholics over a year after treatment and gave rise to similar results.

In the first study (Fabian & Parsons, 1983), 25 alcoholic women and their matched controls were retested 22 months later on a battery of neuropsychological tests. Of the eight tests comprising the Factor 1 score previously described (Figure 14-1), the alcoholics differed from their controls on seven of them at both initial testing and retesting. On four of the seven tests, both groups improved significantly. However, there were no significant interactions between groups and testing. Thus, while alcoholics improved their performance on retest on most measures, so did controls; the net effect was that differences present on initial testing were also present on retesting.

In the second study (Yohman *et al.*, 1985), we compared 37 male alcoholics with 24 controls on different clusters of neuropsychological tests. Alcoholics were tested after an average of 7 weeks of sobriety and retested 13 months later. Nonalcoholic controls, equated on age and education, were also tested and retested with approximately the same time period intervening. The findings are presented in Figure 14-2. The straight horizontal line at $T = 50$ represents the performance of the control group. Comparing the alcoholics with the controls on initial testing resulted in significant differences between the groups on all clusters or indices. On retest, the same results were obtained: Alcoholics' performance remained significantly poorer than that of controls, although they improved on three of the four indices. Controls improved on all four indices. There is an inescapable methodological point evident here: Test–retest studies of recovery in alcoholics should always include a group of nonalcoholics as a comparison. Otherwise, it cannot be determined whether the effects obtained for alcoholics are the results of practice or of true recovery.

Resumption of Drinking and Recovery

While these findings from our test–retest studies would seem to imply a bleak future for recovery in cognitive functions in alcoholics, at least over 13

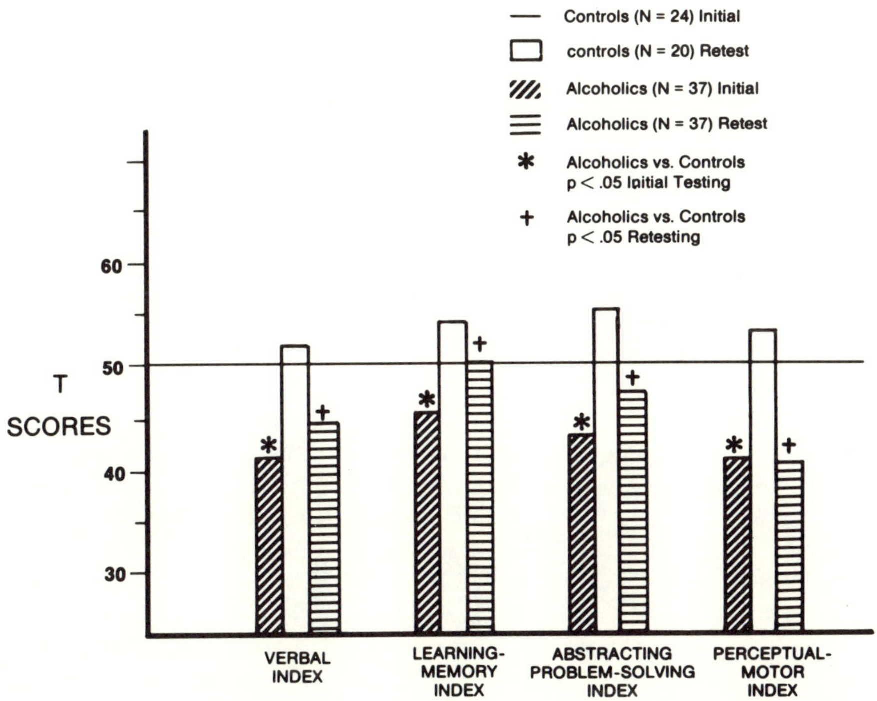

Figure 14-2. Test–retest differences between alcoholics and nonalcoholic controls on clusters of neuropsychological tests.

months, there is an important variable to be considered—that is, whether resumption of drinking plays a role in continued deficit.

In our first test–retest study of recoverability (Fabian & Parsons, 1983), we found that of the 25 alcoholic women retested 22 months after treatment, 9 had resumed drinking and 16 had remained abstinent or were infrequent drinkers. The "resumers" had reduced their pretreatment levels of ethanol consumption from 183.6 g per day to 37.5 g per day; the latter is equivalent to about 1.3 drinks per day, or the equivalent of moderate social drinking. The 16 abstainers did significantly worse than their 16 matched controls on only two of eight tests (recall that in the total group analyses, the 25 alcoholics did significantly worse than the controls on seven of eight tests). Comparing the 9 resumers with the 16 "abstainers" revealed that the former did significantly worse on five of eight tests than the latter, at both test and retest. These results are consistent with those reported for male Veterans Administration (VA) alcoholic patients by Eckardt, Parker, Paulter, Noble, and Gottschalk (1980) and with our recent study of similar VA patients (Yohman *et al.*, 1985).

We separated the 37 male alcoholics of the second recoverability study into resumers ($n = 17$) and abstainers ($n = 18$) (for two subjects, drinking status could not be ascertained). "Resumers" were defined as individuals who had drunk to the point of drunkenness at any time over the last year. None of the resumers had resumed drinking at their previous alcoholic level; most were at the level of moderate to heavy social drinking. Abstainers were those who at most may have had several drinks on a special occasion but were otherwise abstinent. Figure 14-3 shows the standings of resumers, abstainers, and controls on the indices. Abstainers at the 13-month retesting differed from controls only on the Perceptual–Motor index, although initially they were significantly poorer in performance on three of the four indices. Resumers on the other hand were significantly poorer than controls on all indices except Verbal on both testings. On initial testing, abstainers and resumers did not differ significantly, although abstainers performed better than resumers on three of four indices. However, on retesting (depicted by the wide diagonal stripes on top of the bars), abstainers improved significantly more than resumers on Abstracting/Problem Solving and Perceptual–Motor scores. These data correspond to what we found with our

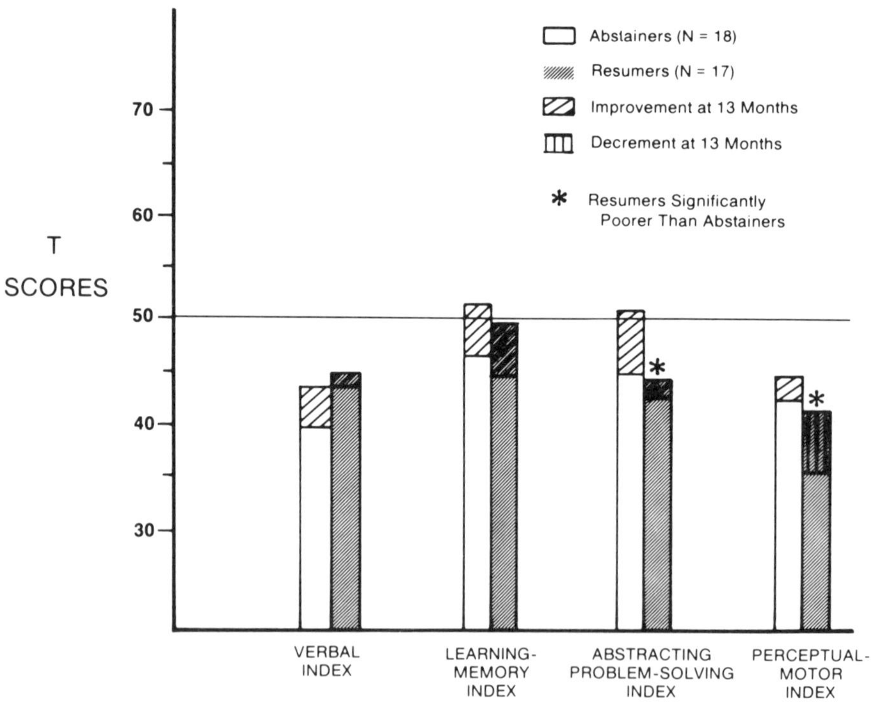

Figure 14-3. Test–retest differences between abstainer and resumer alcoholics on clusters of neuropsychological tests.

female alcoholics at the 22-month retesting (Fabian & Parsons, 1983)—that is, abstainers performed in the normal range, but resumers were impaired compared to controls on almost every test.

In both experiments, we found that the resumers tended to have lower scores on the neuropsychological tests at the initial testing and certainly at the retesting. These data suggest that studies of recovery must carefully elicit accurate drinking histories in the posttreatment period; otherwise, misleading conclusions may result. Abstainers appear to improve their performance to near-normal levels, although some areas of residual deficit remain. Whether these deficits are the result of premorbid deficiencies or are, in fact, the residual effects of alcohol abuse on the brain remains to be established. Finally, the data suggest that the resumers may have been somewhat more neuropsychologically impaired at initial testing. The hypothesis that this impairment contributes significantly to their recidivism needs to be tested.

The importance of investigating the consequences for former alcoholics of resuming drinking, even though the drinking may be markedly reduced over previous levels, is highlighted by another of our recent studies (Parsons, Leber, & Yohman, 1983–1984). In that report, we asked whether life adaptation of resumers and abstainers differed. The retested male alcoholics described above were interviewed as to level of functioning in a variety of life areas. Abstainers generally were functioning at a higher level than resumers. Significant differences between groups were found on a number of measures. More abstainers lived in their own houses, as opposed to living in some type of apartment, rooming house, or institution. They worked longer and had better incomes than resumers, and more were currently employed full-time than the resumers. Among abstainers, 61% had "no days" in which they were unable to carry out normal daily activities, in contrast to resumers' 18.7%. The two groups also tended to differ in other areas. Of the abstainers, 61% had improved relationships with family or close friends, compared to 42% of the resumers. In regard to sleep difficulties, 56% of the abstainers had no problems in the previous 6 months, compared to 31.2% of the resumers; similarly, for that period 82.4% of the abstainers had *no* memory lapses or blackouts, compared with 68.8% of the resumers. These results, coupled with those of the neuropsychological test differences between resumers and abstainers, give additional impetus to the need for considering this variable in recovery research with alcoholics.

Neuropsychological Test Performance and Treatment Course

Treatment course in relation to neuropsychological test performance has not received much attention in the literature. We have completed two studies in this area and have a third currently under way. In our initial study, we correlated neuropsychological test performance of alcoholics (n = 80) with ratings from their therapists on a 10-item scale of therapeutic behavior and improvement (Leber, Parsons, & Nichols, 1985). The subjects were volunteer middle-aged males from our VA alcohol treatment program. They were given our battery of neuropsychological tests over the third and fourth weeks of treatment and rated by their therapists at the end of the 9-week treatment program. Factor analysis of nine items (one item, Prognosis, was not included in the factor analyses) revealed three factors: Factor 1, Cognitive Functioning; Factor 2, Interpersonal Involvement; and Factor 3, Clinical Improvement; the items comprising these factors are given in Table 14-1. Correlations between the neuropsychological tests and the three factors are presented in Table 14-2. These correlations were modest, but were generally significant at the .01 or .001 level.

To turn to the relationship of neuropsychological test performance to Prognosis, we divided the group into those who were rated as having a good prognosis ($n = 22$) and those who were felt to have a poor prognosis ($n = 23$) (the groups constituted approximately the upper and lower 28% of the sample). The two groups were compared as to demographic variables. There were no differences between the groups on age and education. However, they did differ on duration of alcoholism, with the poor-prognosis group averaging about 6 more years of heavy drinking than the good-prognosis group. The number of years of drinking was therefore used as a covariate in the multivariate analysis of variance used to test for group differences. As expected, the poor-prognosis group had significantly poorer performance on the Abstracting/Problem Solving and Perceptual–Motor clusters than the good-prognosis group. As indicated by the differences in Table 14-3, the poor-prognosis group, compared to the good-prognosis group, had poorer verbal skills, short-term visual memory, visual–spatial

Table 14–1. Promax Rotated Factor Loadings of Rating Scale Items

Item	Factor 1 (Cognitive Functioning)	Factor 2 (Interpersonal Involvement)	Factor 3 (Clinical Improvement)
Ability to Generalize	.90	.11	−.07
Analogical Reasoning	.87	.21	−.07
Plans for Future	.61	−.21	.48
Approach toward Change	.56	−.13	.47
Participation in Group	.06	.90	−.04
Involvement in Therapy	.01	.67	.31
Therapeutic Benefit	−.11	.16	.88
Change in Psychological Functioning	.07	.06	.85
Insight	.31	.26	.47

Note. Loadings above .50 are considered significant.

Table 14-2. Correlations between Factor Scores and Neurological Tests or Demographic Variables for Combined Groups ($n = 80$)

Test/variable	Cognitive Functioning Factor	Interpersonal Involvement Factor	Clinical Improvement Factor
Verbal			
WAIS Comprehension	.24**	.29***	.16
Shipley Vocabulary Age	.45****	.27**	.30***
Shipley Mental Age	.44****	.23**	.28**
Shipley Conceptual Quotient	.33***	.19*	.25**
Learning/Memory			
Memory for Designs	−.54****	−.40****	−.45****
WAIS Digit Span	.24**	.03	.06
Verbal Paired-Associate Learning	−.13	−.11	−.11
Visual–Spatial Paired-Associate Learning	−.37****	−.19*	−.30***
Abstracting/Problem Solving			
WAIS Block Design	.32****	.30***	.27**
Wisconsin Card Sorting Test Categories Completed	.17	.07	.15
Wisconsin Card Sorting Test Perseverative Errors	−.37****	−.19*	−.32***
Raven's Progressive Matrices (Set 1)	.36***	.17	.22**
Shipley Abstracting Age	.39***	.19*	.24**
Perceptual–Motor			
Grooved Pegboard	−.28**	−.29***	−.28**
Trail Making Test, Part B	−.45****	−.33***	−.40****
WAIS Digit Symbol	.35***	.17	.26**
Digit Vigilance	−.25**	−.26**	−.10
Sentence Writing	−.33***	−.26**	−.34***
Halstead–Reitan Impairment Index	−.44****	−.22**	−.34***
Demographic			
Age	−.12	−.20	−.19
Chronicity	−.15	−.18	−.18

$p < .10$.

**$p < .05$.

***$p < .01$.

****$p < .001$.

paired-associate learning, visual–spatial analytical skills, and perceptual–motor set shifting, and greater perseveration. It seems clear that in this sample, neuropsychological test performance was predictive of therapists' ratings, particularly the ratings of Prognosis.

In a second study of the relationships between neuropsychological tests and therapists' ratings (Boon, 1982), we studied 60 patients from the Oklahoma City and the Dallas VA alcohol treatment programs. The therapists' rating scale was revised and expanded. Each patient was rated on a number of 5-point items by two therapists who were familiar with him. In general, these items were similar to those of the Leber *et al.* (1985) study. A battery

Table 14–3. Performance of Poor- and Good-Prognosis Groups

Test	Poor-prognosis group mean	Good-prognosis group mean	t
Verbal			
Comprehension	9.30	10.54	1.38
Shipley Vocabulary Age	15.12	16.75	2.31**
Shipley Mental Age	13.57	14.95	1.61
Shipley Conceptual Quotient	84.76	82.50	0.37
Learning/Memory			
Memory for Designs (errors)	5.17	2.36	2.35**
WAIS Digit Span	8.21	7.54	1.75*
Verbal Paired-Associate Learning (errors)	14.95	14.31	0.24
Visual–Spatial Paired-Associate Learning (errors)	17.95	13.32	1.76*
Abstracting/Problem Solving			
WAIS Block Design	7.60	9.04	2.00**
Wisconsin Card Sorting Test Categories Completed	3.43	4.00	1.02
Wisconsin Card Sorting Test Perseverative Errors	17.82	9.54	3.57****
Raven's Progressive Matrices (Set 1)	5.78	6.72	1.11
Shipley Abstracting Age	12.35	13.62	1.34
Perceptual–Motor			
Grooved Pegboard (sec)	94.91	84.77	.82
Trail Making Test, Part B (sec)	141.35	78.68	3.31***
WAIS Digit Symbol	7.82	8.72	1.56
Digit Vigilance (sec)	437.04	473.27	1.35
Sentence Writing (sec)	11.41	8.91	1.83*

Note. Hotelling's T^2 for each cluster was as follows: Verbal, $T^2 = 7.41$, n.s.; Learning/Memory, $T^2 = 7.45$, n.s.; Abstracting/Problem Solving, $T^2 = 17.94$, $p < .01$; and Perceptual–Motor, $T^2 = 26.30$, $p < .01$.

*$p < .10$.

**$p < .05$.

***$p < .01$.

****$p < .001$.

of neuropsychological tests was given to the alcoholics and matched non-alcoholic controls. Among these tests were three tests of problem-solving ability: Levine Hypothesis Testing (Levine, 1966); the Booklet Category Test (DeFillipis, McCampbell, & Rogers, 1979); and the Word Finding Test (Reitan, 1972). Using cluster analyses of the performance on these tests, we identified three groups of alcoholics: a high-problem-solving group, a moderate-problem-solving group, and a low-problem-solving group. The groups did not differ on education, socioeconomic status, anxiety, depression, or severity of alcohol dependence. The high-problem-solving group was significantly younger than the other two groups, but analyses of covariance between age and the neuropsychological measures revealed that the group differences could not be accounted for on that basis. Covariance for Shipley Vocabulary Age gave rise to similar conclusions.

Comparisons of the groups rated as high and low on the three problem-solving tests are presented in Table 14-4. In all significant comparisons, the high group was rated higher on the therapy rating scale. In the Treatment Behavior section of the scale, differences were obtained on Insight, Orientation toward Future, and Therapeutic Benefit, but not on Participation in Group, Involvement in Therapy, Motivation, and Approach toward Change. In the Cognitive Functioning during Treatment section, the differences on Ability to Learn and Analogical Reasoning were significant. On the Treatment Outcome at 1 Year (predictions) section, four of the six items were significantly different: Drinking Behavior, Vocational Status, Cognitive Functioning, and Quality of Life. Given these results, it would appear that the problem-solving behavior of alcoholics as measured by neuropsychological tests is certainly related to treatment behavior, cognitive functioning during therapy, and outcome as rated by therapists. It should be noted that there were approximately 20 different raters (therapists) used in this study, and that the items used for rating were only those on which there was satisfactory interrater agreement.

In an ongoing study, we are again examining relationships between neuropsychological tests and therapists' ratings. A preliminary analysis

Table 14-4. Comparison of High- and Low-Problem-Solving Alcoholics' Functioning on Items of Therapists' Rating Scale

	High scorers ($n = 16$)		Low scorers ($n = 22$)		
Rating item	*M*	(*SD*)	*M*	(*SD*)	*t*
Cognitive Functioning during Treatment					
Ability to Learn	4.14	(0.77)	3.23	(0.87)	3.22**
Memory	3.86	(0.95)	3.50	(0.86)	1.17
Analogical Reasoning	4.00	(0.78)	3.33	(0.97)	2.15*
Treatment Behavior					
Participation in Group	3.71	(1.38)	3.77	(1.02)	0.15
Involvement in Therapy	3.14	(1.51)	3.09	(1.15)	0.12
Motivation	3.32	(1.09)	2.95	(0.84)	1.79
Insight	4.14	(1.10)	3.32	(0.99)	2.33*
Approach toward Change	3.29	(1.33)	2.68	(1.05)	1.49
Orientation toward Future	3.86	(1.29)	2.95	(1.13)	2.21*
Therapeutic Benefit	3.86	(1.10)	2.55	(1.06)	3.57**
Treatment Outcome at 1 Year					
Drinking Behavior	3.79	(0.97)	3.05	(1.05)	2.21*
Length of Abstinence	3.21	(1.42)	2.64	(1.09)	1.37
Vocational Status	3.86	(1.17)	2.91	(1.38)	2.13*
Legal Status	4.29	(0.83)	4.00	(1.02)	0.88
Cognitive Functioning	4.36	(0.63)	3.45	(0.86)	3.39**
Quality of Life	3.43	(0.85)	3.20	(0.77)	2.33**

*$p < .05$.
**$p < .01$.

provides some interesting data. In Table 14.5, correlations between selected neuropsychological tests and therapists' ratings on the Cognitive Functioning during Treatment section of the scale are presented. The neuropsychological tests were given after 4 weeks of detoxification, and the therapists' ratings were made at the end of 9 weeks of treatment; therapists were blind to the neuropsychological test results. Aside from the Shipley Vocabulary Age, all the tests have been shown to discriminate between alcoholics and controls. Correlations with the Beck Depression Inventory (BDI; Beck, 1967) and the State Anxiety Inventory (AI; Spielberger, Gorsuch, & Lushene, 1970) are also included for comparative purposes. Correlations with the Face–Name Paired-Associate Learning Test were based on only 19 subjects; all others were based on 40 subjects.

When the individual correlations and the correlations with the overall measure of Cognitive Functioning during Treatment (last column) are considered, it is evident that the tests involving verbal and linguistic skills (Shipley Vocabulary Age, Shipley Abstracting Age, Wechsler Memory Scale [WMS] Semantic Memory, and the Conceptual Level Analogies Test) were the best predictors of therapists' ratings. Correlations with the remaining

Table 14-5. Correlations between Alcoholics' ($n = 40$) Performance on Neuropsychological Tests and Therapists' Ratings of Cognitive Functioning during Treatment

Test	Ability to Learn	Memory	Analogical Reasoning	Ability to Plan	Cognitive Functioning during Treatment
Shipley Vocabulary Age	.42**	.41**	.43**	.54***	.51***
WMS Semantic Memory—Delayed	.42**	.24	.13	.41**	.31*
WMS Figural Memory—Delayed	.33*	.28	.24	.17	.26
Shipley Abstracting Age	.48***	.43**	.31*	.22	.51***
Conceptual Level Analogies Test	.55***	.36*	.41**	.43	.36*
Symbol–Digit Paired-Associate Learning	.36	.19	.14	.23	.10
Face–Name Paired-Associate Learning ($n = 19$)	..25	.23	.22	.30	.41
BDI	−.22	−.15	−.12	−.07	−.10
AI	−.20	−.27	−.10	−.23	−.10

Note. Positive correlations mean that the better the cognitive test score, the higher the therapists' ratings (average of two therapists' ratings for each subject) on each item or section.

*$p < .05$.

**$p < .01$.

***$p < .001$.

performance tests were largely nonsignificant, and all involved nonverbal items (WMS Figural Memory, Symbol–Digit Paired-Associate Learning, and Face–Name Paired-Associate Learning). Neither BDI nor AI scores were significantly correlated with therapists' ratings. It seems clear that these therapists rated subjects with more intact verbal skills higher on Cognitive Functioning during Treatment.

The next question addressed was whether these tests were correlated with the Treatment Behavior and Treatment Outcome at 1 Year sections of the rating scale. The data are presented in Table 14-6. It is clear that there were fewer significant relationships with these therapist ratings than with those for Cognitive Functioning during Treatment. It is noteworthy that the test designed for ecological validity, the Face–Name Paired-Associate Learning Test (Becker, Butters, Hermann, & D'Angelo, 1983), correlated the highest with therapists' ratings on a number of dimensions, whereas the Symbol–Digit Paired-Associate Learning Test (Ryan & Butters, 1980) was not significantly correlated with any of the therapists' ratings. It is also

Table 14-6. Correlations between Alcoholics' ($n = 40$) Performance on Neuropsychological Tests and Ratings of Treatment Behavior, Likeability, and Treatment Outcome at 1 Year (Predicted)

		Treatment Outcome at 1 Year			
Test	Treatment Behavior	Abstracting	Cognitive Functioning	Quality of Life	Likeability
Shipley Vocabulary Age	.29	.15	.35*	.29	.36*
WMS Semantic Memory—Delayed	.08	.00	−.03	.09	.18
WMS Figural Memory—Delayed	.09	.12	.08	.18	.48**
Shipley Abstracting Age	.29	.15	.35*	.29	.36*
Conceptual Level Analogies Test	.05	−.04	.25	.18	.25
Symbol–Digit Paired-Associate Learning	.07	.07	.10	.17	.22
Face–Name Paired-Associate Learning ($n = 19$)	.45*	.51**	.04	.64**	.41
BDI	−.14	−.06	−.05	−.25	−.26
AI	.12	.22	−.07	−.13	−.10

Note. Positive correlations mean that the better the cognitive test scores, the higher the therapists' ratings (average of two therapists' ratings for each subject) on each item or section.

*$p < .05$.

**$p < .01$.

evident that the therapists responded to verbal intelligence, at least as related to predicted Cognitive Functioning and to likeability. Thus patients who were better at learning to associate names with to different pictures of persons of their general age were seen by the therapists as doing better in treatment and having a better prognosis for life adaptation than the patients who had more difficulty learning face–name pairings. Whether either the neuropsychological test performance or the therapists' ratings will predict actual outcome at 1 year remains to be seen.

There is considerable variability in certain aspects of the results of these three studies of relationships between neuropsychological test performance and therapists' ratings. In part, this appears to be a function of methodological variables. In our first study (Leber *et al.*, 1985), we had clinician/raters who had been on the service for a long period of time and shared a common treatment approach. In our second study (Boon, 1982) we used patients and therapist/raters from two different settings and greatly enlarged our rating scale (from 10 to 35 items). Finally, in our ongoing study, we have reduced the rating scale to 11 items (a more manageable task for our therapists), but our therapist teams have almost completely changed. Nevertheless, there are consistent findings that alcoholics who do more poorly on the neuropsychological tests are rated lower by therapists on Cognitive Functioning during Treatment. There is less predictability for Treatment Behavior and Treatment Outcome at 1 Year. Again, the final test of the role of the neuropsychological tests in predicting recovery will be in the follow-up studies of alcoholics' life adaptation in the years following treatment.

Cognitive Retraining and Recovery

The field of cognitive retraining for persons suffering from brain dysfunction has expanded enormously over the last several years. There have been only a handful of studies performed with alcoholic subjects. Hansen (1980) described a Danish program of retraining for alcoholics with mild to moderate impairment that focused upon visual–motor coordination, attention, concentration, abstracting, verbal functioning and memory. Unfortunately the program was evaluated only by patients' anecdotal self-reports (of increased memory and self-esteem), and not on the basis of a quantitative demonstration of improved functioning. Cermak (1980) demonstrated that alcoholic Korsakoff patients could improve their memory performance through the use of mnemonics, but that the Korsakoff patients rapidly forgot the mnemonics; presumably, the techniques might be of more lasting value in non-Korsakoff patients. Binder and Schreiber (1980) instructed alcoholics and nonalcoholics in the use of visual-imagery and verbal-mediation strategies. There was a significant main treatment effect on paired-associate learning, regardless of strategy. While this study presents data on only one measure of memory or learning, it does suggest that alcoholics may beneift from training. Finally, Goldman and his colleagues have conducted a series of studies demonstrating that with repeated trials over time, alcoholics improve their performance on perceptual–motor tests (Goldman, 1983 and Chapter 15, this volume). The question remains as to whether practice and training in other higher cognitive functions (i.e., memory, abstracting, and problem solving) can be demonstrated to have effects on a variety of measures of such abilities.

We are currently conducting such a study with three groups of VA treatment program alcoholics (eventually with *n*'s of 24 subjects each). One group is given 2 weeks of training and practice in problem-solving techniques. The second group has 2 weeks of training in memory strategies and mnemonic techniques. The third group receives no training during the 2 weeks. After the third week of sobriety, all subjects are given a 4-hour battery of neuropsychological (cognitive and perceptual–motor) tests, representing three areas of functioning: Learning/Memory (seven measures), Abstracting/Problem Solving (six measures), and Perceptual–Motor (five measures). After the 2 weeks of training or no training, all subjects retake the battery. This design will enable us to test for specific training effects by comparing the group given problem-solving training and the group given memory training individually with the no-training group. In addition, we can test for the more general effects of training by comparing training versus no-training groups.

The memory training has 10 sessions of 1¼ hours each, conducted over the 2-week period. Sessions focus on attention; chunking; visual imagery; peg words; AOEIU (attention, organization, elaboration, imagery, and understanding) as applied to stories; the key-word method; face–name learning by visual imagery; and verbal mediation. Practice with list-learning, paired-associates, and digit–symbol tests are given each day. For problem solving, the sessions are directed to attention, general problem-solving strategies (goal identification, determining relevant information needed); brainstorming (simplifying, paraphrasing, making list, drawing diagrams, learning from mistakes, identifying patterns); and the win–stay/lose–shift strategy. Each of the training sessions under both conditions emphasizes practice during the session, reviews basic principles, and encourages subjects to verbalize applications to their everyday life situations.

In a preliminary analysis, we compared 16 alcoholics with no training, 12 with memory training, and 10 with problem-solving training. While the *n*'s were too small to permit definitive analyses, the group with memory training performed significantly better at retest than the no-training group on WMS Semantic Memory ($t = 2.36$, $p = .03$) and manifested a similar trend on WMS Figural Memory ($t = 1.57$, $p = .12$). Also at retest, the group receiving problem-solving training did better than the no-training group at a level approaching significance ($t = 1.82, p = .08$) on the Conceptual Level Analogies Test. We should emphasize, however, that these groups were considered of a pilot nature, in that we were still changing our techniques in instruction. At this point, we are now running subjects in the final version of the training procedures. It is of interest to note that the reaction of our alcoholic patients to the training has been most rewarding. Our last group receiving problem-solving training, for example, was going to petition the director of the treatment program for more practice and time for instruction. In the memory training, some of the alcoholics expressed amazement at how well they could do in practice and gave feedback indicating increased self-esteem. Whether the subjective reports will be verified by our test data remains to be seen.

Summary and Implications

The course of recovery of functions in sober alcoholics is variable. Some functions appear to recover within months, others within years; however, even after 4 or 5 years some deficits are present. The possibility must be considered that such deficits may have been present before the persons became alcoholics. Neuropsychological tests predict therapists' ratings of cognitive functioning during treatment, and, to a lesser extent, of treatment behavior and predicted outcome. The extent and magnitude of these relationships depends on the neuropsychological tests employed, the therapists' rating scale utilized, and the experience and orientation of the therapists. Whether the neuropsychological tests predict alcoholics' adaptive behavior over several years after treatment remains to be investigated. In this connection, other treatment variables not investigated in our studies, such as posttreatment aftercare, also must be considered in outcome studies; this has been shown by Walker, Donovan, Kivlahan, and O'Leary (1983) and Donovan, Walker, and Kivlahan (Chapter 17, this volume).

Alcoholics who resume drinking (even though not at their earlier levels) tend to have more impaired initial neuropsychological test findings during treatment than eventual abstainers. However, at posttreatment examination, these resumers are decidedly more impaired than abstainers. Studies of recovery must obtain careful histories of posttreatment drinking behavior in assessing alcoholics' recovery from cognitive deficits. Cognitive retraining for alcoholics is in its infancy; whether such training procedures will result in significant improvement on measures of cognitive, intellectual, and perceptual–motor functioning remains to be demonstrated. However, there are indications from alcoholics' subjective reports that these training techniques may result in increased self-confidence and self-esteem.

In conclusion, it should be apparent that at this time we do not have a clear understanding of the recovery process in alcoholics. It is undoubtedly complexly determined, with many biological, psychological, and sociocultural variables playing both independent and interactive roles. Recovery from neuropsychological deficit may play a critical role in some alcoholics and an influential role in other alcoholics, but may be relatively unimportant in the remainder. Identifying the variables that distinguish these groups of patients and developing appropriate treatment strategies for them will remain a continuing challenge.

Acknowledgments

The research from my laboratory cited herein was supported in part by U.S. Public Health Service (National Institute on Alcohol Abuse and Alcoholism) Grant Nos. AA1434, AA01464, and AA06135. Thanks are due to the following members of our research team: Janice Boon, PhD; Ricardo DeObaldia, PhD; William Leber, PhD; Nancy Nichols, MA; Kim Walter Schaeffer, PhD; Melvin D. Shelton, PhD; and J. Robert Yohman, PhD. Their contributions have been invaluable in our research efforts.

References

Beck, A. T. (1967). *Depression: Clinical, experimental and theoretical aspects.* New York: Harper & Row.

Becker, J. T., Butters, N., Hermann, A., & D'Angelo, N. (1983). Learning to associate names and faces: Impaired acquisition on an ecologically relevant memory task by male alcoholics. *Journal of Nervous and Mental Disease*, *171*, 617–623.

Berglund, M., Leijonquist, H., & Horlen, M. (1977). Prognostic significance and reversibility of cerebral dysfunction in alcoholics. *Journal of Studies on Alcohol*, *38*, 1761–1769.

Binder, L. J., & Schreiber, J. (1980). Visual memory and memory aids. *Journal of Clinical Neuropsychology*, *2*, 71–74.

Boon, J. C. (1982). *Real life implications of problem-solving deficits in alcoholics.* Unpublished doctoral dissertation, Vanderbilt University.

Brandt, J., Butters, N., Ryan, C., & Bayog, R. (1983). Cognitive loss and recovery in long term alcohol abusers. *Archives of General Psychiatry*, *40*, 435–442.

Cermak, L. S. (1980). Improving retention in alcoholic Korsakoff patients. *Journal of Studies on Alcohol*, *41*, 159–169.

DeFillippis, N. A., McCampbell, E., & Rogers, P. (1979). Development of a booklet form of the Category Test: Normative and validity data. *Journal of Clinical Neuropsychology*, *1*, 339–342.

Fabian, M. S., & Parsons, O. A. (1983). Differential improvement of cognitive functions in recovering alcoholic women. *Journal of Abnormal Psychology*, *92*, 87–95.

Goldman, M. (1983). Cognitive impairment in chronic alcoholics: Some cause for optimism. *American Psychologist*, *38*, 1045–1054.

Hansen, L. (1980). Treatment of reduced intellectual functioning in alcoholics. *Journal of Studies on Alcohol*, *41*, 156–158.

Hill, S. Y., Reyes, R. B., Mikhael, M., & Ayre, F. (1979). Comparison of alcoholics and heroin abusers. Computerized transaxial tomography and neuropsychological functioning. In M. Galanter (Ed.), *Currents in alcoholism* (Vol. 5, pp. 187–205). New York: Grune & Stratton.

Leber, W. R., Parsons, O. A., & Nichols, N. (1985). Neuropsychological tests are related to ratings of alcoholics' therapeutic progress: A replicated study. *Journal of Studies on Alcohol, 46*, 116–121.

Levine, M. (1966). Hypothesis behavior by humans during discrimination learning. *Journal of Experimental Psychology, 71*, 331–338.

Long, J. A., & McLachlan, J. F. C. (1974). Abstract reasoning and perceptual–motor efficiency in alcoholics: Impairments and reversibility. *Quarterly Journal of Studies on Alcohol, 35*, 1220–1229.

Parsons, O. A., & Leber, W. R. (1981). The relationships between cognitive dysfunction and brain damage in alcoholics: Causal, interactive or epiphenomenal? *Alcoholism: Clinical and Experimental Research, 5*, 326–343.

Parsons, O. A., & Leber, W. R. (1982). Alcohol, cognitive dysfunction and brain damage. In National Institute on Alcohol Abuse and Alcoholism (Ed.), Biomedical processes and consequences of alcohol use (Alcohol and Health Monograph 2, DHHS Publication No. ADM 82-1191, pp. 213–253). Washington, DC: U.S. Government Printing Office.

Parsons, O. A., Leber, W. R., & Yohman, J. R. (1983–1984). Post-treatment adjustment of "resumer" and "abstainer" alcoholics. *Alcohol Technical Reports, 12–13*, 59–62.

Reitan, R. M. (1972). Verbal problem solving as related to cerebral damage. *Perceptual Motor Skills, 34*, 515–524.

Ryan, C., & Butters, N. (1980). Learning and memory impairments in young and old alcoholics: Evidence for the premature-aging hypothesis. *Alcoholism: Clinical and Experimental Research, 4*, 288–293.

Schau, E. J., O'Leary, M. R., & Chaney, E. F. (1980). Reversibility of cognitive deficits in alcoholics. *Journal of Studies on Alcohol, 41*, 733–740.

Spielberger, C. D., Gorsuch, R. L., & Lushene, R. E. (1970). *Test manual for the State–Trait Anxiety Inventory.* Palo Alto, CA: Consulting Psychologists Press.

Walker, R. D., Donovan, D. M., Kivlahan, D. R., & O'Leary, M. R. (1983). Length of stay, neuropsychological performance and aftercare: Influences on alcohol treatment outcome. *Journal of Consulting and Clinical Psychology, 51*, 900–911.

Yohman, J. R., Parsons, O. A., & Leber, W. R. (1985). Lack of recovery in alcoholics' neuropsychological performance one year after treatment. *Alcoholism: Clinical and Experimental Research, 9*, 114–117.

15

The Role of Time and Practice in Recovery of Function in Alcoholics

MARK S. GOLDMAN

Introduction

Two converging lines of research have recently demonstrated that the neurological and neuropsychological impairments seen in abstinent alcoholics are not static, but rather undergo dynamic changes in the weeks and months following the alcoholics' last drink, generally in the direction of improvement and recovery. Biologically oriented research has revealed a variety of such changes. Cerebrospinal fluid acidosis and ionic imbalances, which may be related to decreased cerebral blood flow (Begleiter, 1981), reverse in the first few days after drinking ceases (Carlen, 1982; Gross, Lewis, & Hastey, 1974). Alcohol-induced inhibition of brain protein synthesis reverses after approximately 2 weeks from the time that alcohol is removed in mice (Noble & Tewari, 1973). The cerebral atrophy of human alcoholics has been observed in recent computerized tomography (CT) studies to decrease over a few months following the last drink (Carlen, Wortzman, Holgate, Wilkinson, & Rankin, 1978). Carlen (1982) has speculated that an increase in dendritic arborization may be responsible for this change. EEG abnormalities reflecting hyperexcitability of the central nervous system (CNS) persist over weeks and even months after drinking ceases, but then normalize (Begleiter, 1981; Bennett, 1960). Sleep stage disturbances may take as long as 1–2 years to recover (Adamson & Burdick, 1973; Williams & Rundell, 1981).

In parallel with these biological changes, studies began to appear in the early 1970s that suggested that the cognitive and behavioral impairments observed early in the detoxification period in human alcoholics might also go through changes with continued abstinence. Since that time, methodological refinements and new data have sharpened our understanding of neuropsychological recovery following chronic alcohol abuse. In particular, we now appreciate the time course for recovery of different abilities and the

Mark S. Goldman. Department of Psychology, University of South Florida, Tampa, Florida. (Formerly, Department of Psychology, Wayne State University, Detroit, Michigan.)

relationship of subject characteristics, particularly age, to the course of recovery. To date, however, recovery of function research has been almost exclusively devoted to the study of spontaneous or "time-dependent" recovery. In this type of recovery, the functional improvement can be observed as time passes following the last drink, without the need for any special procedures or interventions. Presumably, the substrate for this functional recovery is one or more of the biological mechanisms noted earlier.

Animal researchers, however, are becoming increasingly familiar with functional recovery that depends in large measure on specific environmental stimulation for its occurrence (Finger, 1978a). That is, these investigations have shown that the reversal of behavioral impairments consequent to specific brain lesions can be accelerated by specific environmental manipulations. In fact, in some instances very little recovery would be seen without these environmental contingencies in place. An analogue to this work with laboratory animals can be found in clinical rehabilitation efforts with humans following certain types of brain damage (Diller & Gordon, 1981a, 1981b). Language retraining in aphasics after left-hemisphere stroke is an example of the importance of environmental events in functional recovery from brain damage.

Recent work in our laboratories at Wayne State University and the University of South Florida has forced us to consider whether these same "experience-dependent" processes might be relevant to the recovery of behavioral functioning in human alcoholics. However, because the cognitive deficits found in alcoholics are subtle and are far more obvious on sensitive neuropsychological tests than in the alcoholics' everyday functioning, the evaluation of this proposition in alcoholics is difficult. In fact, pursuing this line of inquiry necessitates some review of neuropsychological concepts in relation to alcohol-induced deficits. In this context, we must explore what is meant by a "neuropsychological function," and must come to some understanding of the neuropsychological implications of improvement on a neuropsychological test. For example, if we assume that a neuropsychological test measures a particular neuropsychological function, then does practice with this test constitute rehabilitation of the function? As we shall see, the answer to this question is not a simple one.

Addressing these issues is, however, an important task at this point in time. Evidence is accumulating that neuropsychological status is related, at least modestly, to treatment outcome (Abbott & Gregson, 1981; Berglund, Leijonquist, & Horlen, 1977; Gregson & Taylor, 1977; Walker, Donovan, Kivlahan, & O'Leary, 1983). If we can enhance neuropsychological status, we may thereby obtain a new handle on treatment.

The present chapter begins with an overview of the existing literature on time-dependent recovery on alcoholics, emphasizing the work performed in our laboratories at Wayne State over the past 10 years. Some of this work has been reviewed previously (Goldman, 1982, 1983). A discussion of the empirical findings and conceptual issues relating to experience-dependent recovery in alcoholics then constitutes the major portion of this chapter.

Time-Dependent Recovery

Once studies showing the reversibility of neuropsychological impairment in recovering alcoholics began to appear, it did not take long before a wide variety of psychological functions had been shown to improve once drinking ceased. Short-term memory (Allen, Faillace, & Reynolds, 1971; Allen, Faillace, & Wagman, 1971; Weingartner, Faillace, & Markley, 1971), general intellectual functioning (Clarke & Haughton, 1975; Page & Linden, 1974), and visual–motor performance (Farmer, 1973; Long & McLachlan, 1974; Tarter & Jones, 1971) were all observed to improve during the detoxification period subsequent to the cessation of drinking. These studies, however, enjoyed varying degrees of success in coping with the methodological demands of a clearly interpretable recovery study. As a result, we were left with some confusion as to the important parameters of functional recovery. For example, did improvement of intellectual functioning really require a year (Long & McLachlan, 1974), or could significant improvement be found in as little as a few weeks after drinking ceased (Page & Linden, 1974)? This confusion forced researchers to refine their methodology, and over the last decade there has been significant progress in our ability to specify recovery parameters.

Major methodological problems and some solutions that are exemplified in the studies to be presented next may be briefly summarized as follows: A recovery study requires at least two, and preferably more than two, assessments of neuropsychological functioning to demonstrate recovery and its associated time course. Multiple assessments within the same individual, however, register improvement due to repeated exposure to the test material as well as spontaneous improvement. A matched-groups, time-lag design, which compares different groups of subjects at each assessment point over the time period that is being studied, removes practice as a consideration. This design, unfortunately, also introduces the alternative problem of artifactual improvement due to unanticipated differences between the groups. Pretesting may help establish group equivalence, but may itself induce a practice effect. Repeated-measures, within-subjects designs can also be useful if the size of the practice effect is measured in control groups. Note that, as with most research design questions, there are trade-offs; the solution to one problem often introduces a second.

The study of long-term functional recovery by widely spaced test administrations presents problems that are extremely difficult to surmount. First, we cannot know whether the recovery observed really requires a lengthy time period to occur, or whether the bulk of the recovery takes place over a much more restricted period but goes unobserved. Failures to recover over the long term are obviously more significant. Second, the difficulties of longitudinal designs have caused researchers to study long-term recovery in whatever groups have been available with a lengthy history of abstinence. However, due to selection factors, it is unlikely that a sample of alcoholics studied during the first few weeks or months of abstinence would be directly comparable to a group of alcoholics with a lengthy period of abstinence taken from, for example, an Alcoholics Anonymous group.

It is evident that no single recovery study can deal with all these issues at the same time. However, there has by now been a sufficient accumulation of recovery studies using a variety of approaches to solving these methodological difficulties, so that a general pattern of spontaneous or "time-dependent" recovery has begun to emerge.

1 Month of Abstinence

The evidence is now strong that considerable functional recovery occurs during the first 2–3 weeks of abstinence. Page and Linden (1974) were the first to use a matched-groups, time-lag design in conjunction with a repeated-measures design to show that a number of subtests of the Halstead–Reitan Neuropsychological Test Battery are impaired in the first week after alcoholics cease drinking, but then recover considerably by the 2- to 3-week period. Since that time, others have used variations on this design to report similar results with the Halstead–Reitan Battery (Claiborne & Greene, 1981; Kish, Hagen, Woody, & Harvey, 1980). In none of these instances, however, did the alcoholics reach fully normal levels of performance, even up to as much as 6 months following their last drink (Page & Linden, 1974; Page & Schaub, 1974).

To broaden our understanding of the range of psychological abilities that might show deficits early in the recovery period, and to explore the potentially differential rates of recovery in these various abilities, we undertook a series of studies at Wayne State University beginning in 1974. A particular goal of these studies was to use tasks that not only would be sensitive to neuropsychological deficits, but would explore the learning ability of alcoholics who have ceased drinking. Since any behavioral change depends, in the broadest sense, upon an individual's ability to learn, knowledge of the differential rates of recovery of various learning abilities might suggest how to best structure the new learning involved in treatment of alcoholism. Our initial series of studies integrated the matched-groups, time-lag design with a repeated-measures design. This integrated design permitted an analysis of recovery effects independent of practice, while at the same time allowing a direct assessment of the size of the practice effect.

We begin with a relatively simple kind of learning—the ability to learn new vocabulary items. Learning new information in any technical field, including the learning by patients of new information about alcoholism, is often a question of acquiring new vocabulary. The graded vocabulary scale we used had the added advantage of equating the difficulty level of the new vocabulary items to be learned by each subject, regardless of the subjects' initial vocabulary levels. Assessment of initial vocabulary level also permitted an estimation of premorbid functioning, because vocabulary level generally does not deteriorate with most forms of brain damage. As predicted, existing vocabulary level was not deteriorated at any point in the initial month after drinking ceased, but the ability to learn new vocabulary was severely impaired during the first week of abstinence and then quickly recovered to normal levels (Sharp, Rosenbaum, Goldman, & Whitman, 1977).

Our second study (Ellenberg, Rosenbaum, Goldman, & Whitman, 1980) investigated paired-associate learning, using Stark's (1961) Verbal and Visuospatial (V-S) subtests, which had been equated for difficulty in normal subjects. In this way, any differential sensitivity of the tests to alcoholic dysfunction could not be attributed to the inherently greater difficulty of the V-S test. Since the results of this study have been discussed previously in relation to the question of lateralized brain damage in alcoholics (Ellenberg *et al.*, 1980), let me highlight two other findings that suggested further work we have since undertaken. First, we found that all alcoholics in their first week of abstinence were significantly impaired in their Verbal and V-S performance; as with our earlier study, the Verbal performance improved rapidly, but the V-S did not. The key finding, however, was that the V-S performance did not remain impaired in all alcoholics; rather, this impairment was confined to the older alcoholics with the longer drinking histories. In these older alcoholics, V-S performance remained impaired for up to 1 month of observation. Second, despite the sensitivity of the V-S test to alcoholic impairment, all alcoholics showed considerable improvement due to practice as they were repeatedly exposed to the V-S task. At the time, this strong practice effect was regarded as unimportant. In retrospect, it was this finding that served as the springboard for our work on experience-dependent recovery, which is discussed shortly.

To examine even more basic phenomena, we studied the 1-month recovery parameters of basic sensory and motor functioning (Goldman, Whitman, Rosenbaum, & VandeVusse, 1978). Cutaneous sensory functioning was examined using standard pressure thresholds, two-point thresholds, and palmar writing (graphesthesia). Results showed that cutaneous pressure threshold and form discrimination (as studied by palmar writing) were significantly impaired early in the abstinence period. Cutaneous form discrimination recovered by 2 weeks after drinking ceased, while no recovery was shown for cutaneous pressure threshold over 1 month. Two-point thresholds were not impaired at any point in the study sequence.

Three motor learning phenomena—reminiscence, bilateral transfer of training, and bilateral transfer of inhibition—were assessed using a backward digit-writing task (Goldman *et al.*, 1978). "Reminiscence" refers to the spontaneous increments in motor performance typically observed after rest periods on motor tasks. "Bilateral transfer" refers to the improvement in task performance by one extremity after practice with a contralateral extremity on the identical task. "Bilateral transfer of inhibition" refers to a decrement in task performance by one extremity that may be observed if rest is not permitted after practice with the contralateral extremity. Since bilateral transfer and bilateral transfer of inhibition would appear to require efficient communication of information across the cerebral hemispheres via the corpus callosum, measurement of these phenomena might offer a sensitive method of assessing the intactness of cerebral functioning. The findings for bilateral transfer of training repeated the general pattern observed earlier: Impairment was found during the first week, and full recovery was observed by 2 weeks after drinking ceased. Mean levels of reminiscence and bilateral transfer of inhibition remained below control levels throughout the 25-day period, but large intersubject variability precluded significant statistical findings. The fact that bilateral transfer of training did recover during the first month of abstinence shows that by approximately this point the corpus callosum can be expected to transfer information efficiently between the hemispheres.

In general, our 1-month recovery studies revealed severe neuropsychological impairment in the first week or two after drinking ceased, with considerable recovery occurring on most measures thereafter. Some tasks, however, showed little recovery over 1 month, and we had some suggestion that it was primarily older alcoholics with longer drinking histories who showed the most continuing impairment. To check whether these general observations had "ecological validity" (any relationship to real-world functioning), we conducted an investigation of alcoholics' ability to learn the informational content of an actual alcoholic treatment program (Binder, cited in Goldman & Rosenbaum, 1977). To this end, we constructed true–false tasks to be administered before and after actual training sessions administered by ward personnel on an alcohol treatment unit. Results showed little improvement from before to after a lecture at any of the three time delays studied following the cessation of drinking. While a number of methodological difficulties prevented us from regarding these results as conclusive, they certainly suggested that we should not be overly confident about our ability to impart very much to alcoholics during the first weeks of treatment.

2–6 Months

Short-term memory was measured in abstinent alcoholics over 8 weeks subsequent to their last drink, using a Peterson and Peterson (1959) short-term memory task with a delay of 12 seconds (VandeVusse, cited in Goldman, 1982). In this study, we also began to systematically evaluate the effect of the age of the alcoholics on their recovery of function. At the time we had no reason to use any specific age as a cutoff, so the alcoholic subjects were arbitrarily divided into those under 35 years of age and those 35 and above. The results showed that in the first week after drinking ceased, both the younger and older alcoholics were impaired relative to controls, with the older alcoholics performing worse than the younger alcoholics. At the 4-week point, both groups had improved significantly, but not to normal levels. No further improvement was observed up to the final testing at the 8-week point. The greater relative deficit of the older alcoholics was maintained throughout the sequence. The memory items in the Peterson and Peterson (1959) task were also systematically varied along a semantic or an acoustic dimension. The different associative relationships between the items had no effect on recovery. The differential recovery found in the young and old alcoholics replicated the results of a prior study by Cermak and Ryback (1976), although in that study full recovery was reported by 1 month.

We extended our studies of recovery to 3 months following the cessation of drinking, in an investigation of spatial generalization of voluntary reactions (Dwyer, Whitman, Rosenbaum, & Goldman, 1981). In this spatial-generalization paradigm, all subjects were trained to lift their index fingers as rapidly as possible when a light directly ahead in their visual field was illuminated. The visual field also included six lights placed peripherally to the central signal light, each uniformily spaced at 8° intervals on either side of the central light. Subjects were instructed *not* to respond to the peripheral lights, but only to the central signal light. Reaction times to the illumination of the central light and each peripheral light were recorded. Previous research had shown greater spatial generalization in a variety of pathological conditions in which subjects were thought to have impaired inhibitory control over their responses. Therefore, it was hypothesized that such a task might be sensitive to alcoholic dysfunction in the early stages of abstinence. This prediction was confirmed: Alcoholic subjects during the first week of abstinence more frequently produced generalized responses than did control subjects. The enhanced spatial-generalization effect disappeared by 6 weeks of abstinence and remained unexceptional at 12 weeks after drinking ceased. We inferred from these results that the normal balance between reactivity and inhibition of responses observed during normal performance was out of synchronization during the early abstinence phase, with the tendency to react overshadowing normal inhibitory controls.

Up to this point, all our studies had used a variation on the matched-groups, time-lag design. In a study designed from the outset to systematically evaluate the effects of age and drinking history on recovery of function, we switched to a repeated-measures design in which alcoholics grouped into three age categories—20–29, 30–39, and 40 and over—were repeatedly administered a neuropsychological test battery weekly over

3 months following their last drink (Goldman, Williams, & Klisz, 1983). To deal with potential practice effects, we selected the neuropsychological tests on the basis of their minimal reactivity to practice (Lewis & Rennick, 1979). Potential practice effects were directly assessed in nonalcoholic control groups. The results showed an important difference in the parameters of recovery in younger and older alcoholics. All alcoholics were impaired early in the recovery period, but the two younger alcoholic groups quickly recovered to normal levels. It is important to note that it was only the oldest group of alcoholics (age 40 and above), who began by showing severe impairment early in the recovery period and despite some improvement, continued to be impaired throughout the 3-month testing sequence. Partial correlational analysis confirmed that it was the age factor that was responsible for this differential recovery, not differences in drinking history. Note that age alone was not the key element; nonalcoholic individuals above age 40 showed no such deficit. Instead, age plus alcoholism seemed to be the culprit.

We recently began extending our investigations of the parameters of recovery to the 6-month point in a study of spatial probability learning (Dickey & Goldman, 1982). In spatial binary probability learning, the subject is asked to predict which of two events will occur on each trial of a long series of trials. Although the relative frequency of each event is predetermined, the specific occurrence of the particular event on each trial is randomized. The study of recoverability of probability learning in alcoholics is important, because most behaviors in which humans normally engage are reinforced on a probabilistic basis rather than with certainty. In addition, a number of experiments with animals suggest that probability-learning tasks are sufficiently sensitive to distinguish between normal responses to reward and responses altered by brain damage, especially damage to the limbic system (Douglas & Pribram, 1966; Nauta, 1972; Nonneman, Voigt, & Kolb, 1974; Stevens & Cowey, 1973).

The subjects used in this study were grouped into separate categories according to age (40 years of age or less, over 40 years) and duration of alcohol abuse (10 years or less, over 10 years). To assess recovery of function independently of practice with the measuring instruments, two separate samples of alcoholics were tested—one group who had been abstinent for 14–21 days ($n = 44$), and a second group who had been abstinent for at least 6 months ($n = 30$). A group of control subjects ($n = 36$) was also tested. All groups were matched for age, education, and socioeconomic status.

The apparatus consisted of a green, felt-covered, free-standing board upon which were mounted two white event lights located below a single red trial light. The task was presented to each subject as a betting game. Subjects were told to assume that the two event lights represented race horses upon which each subject was to gamble. For the current study, the probabilities of the two event lights were .70 and .30 (these were unknown to subjects), respectively. Subjects continued betting to a predefined criterion of success.

The results showed that alcoholics early in the recovery period took significantly longer to reach criterion-level performance than did alcoholics after 6 months of recovery. By the 6-month period, alcoholics did not differ significantly from normal control performance. Duration of drinking was not related to recovery, but the interaction between age and group (short vs. long abstinence) fell just short of significance, showing once again that older alcoholics tended to lag behind in their recovery of normal probability learning.

Long-Term Recovery

We have not as yet undertaken studies of recovery periods longer than 6 months in our laboratories at Wayne State, but other investigators have recently studied recovery periods of up to 5 years. As noted earlier, the methodological difficulties of these studies are even more monumental than those of the short-term recovery studies, and therefore the results of these studies must be treated cautiously. Despite these difficulties, however, the consistency of the deficits observed in the long-term studies with the continuing deficits noted in the shorter-term studies lends confidence to the results. There are suggestions in some of these studies that there is an intermediate recovery phase; that is, some of those neuropsychological capabilities that are not fully recovered by 6 months to 1 year after drinking ceases may show further improvement beyond that point. For example, Brandt, Butters, Ryan, and Bayog (1983) showed that short-term memory took a decided turn for the better during approximately a 3- to 5-year period after drinking ceased.

Overall Recovery Patterns

To reiterate the overall pattern of psychological recovery summarized in an earlier paper (Goldman, 1983),

> existing verbal abilities (vocabulary) are not impaired following drinking cessation. Most other abilities, especially when any new learning is involved, are impaired during the first week or two of abstinence. New verbal learning then recovers. Visual–spatial abilities, abstraction and problem solving, short-term memory, and perhaps simple sensory reception show persistent impairment, particularly in older alcoholics. It is possible that with prolonged abstinence, some of these abilities also recover. In general, the more novel, complex and rapid the information processing that a task requires, the longer it takes to recover. (pp. 1050–1051)

Two points from this earlier statement are worth elaborating: First, the observation of less recovery in older alcoholics is consistent with the neuropsychological studies of Cotman and his coworkers (Cotman & Nieto-Sampedro, 1982, p. 383), which showed the neural substrate to be less plastic in older organisms. Hence, decreased neural plasticity may be added to three other ideas advanced to explain reduced behavioral recovery in older alcoholics: the vulnerability of the aging brain (Jones & Parsons, 1971); the lengthy time period necessary for onset of clinically observable manifestation of an ongoing subclinical phenomenon (Grant, Reed, & Adams, 1980); and the decreased ability of older individuals to compensate for dysfunction (Goldman, 1983).

Second, recent work in information processing may offer the foundation for further clarification of the exact nature of the neuropsychological dysfunction that delays recovery in older alcoholics. Cooper and Regan (1982), in a review of the basic information-processing skills that underlie psychometric tests of ability, point to general processing speed (measured by reaction time), as well as speed of access to memory stores, as one possible common denominator. Also important may be the distinction between effortful processing (which demands attention) and automatic processing (Hasher & Zacks, 1979). Both of these information-processing parameters (and their attendant measures) may ultimately prove more useful in understanding the actual substrate for alcoholic dysfunction than are those mechanisms inferred from standard neuropsychological instruments.

Experience-Dependent Recovery

Up to this point, I have reviewed studies in which the researchers functioned as observers of spontaneously occurring events. Care was taken to use research methodologies that were minimally reactive with the phenomenon of interest, functional recovery. Hence, studies were designed to minimize the possibility that repeated exposure to the test instruments (i.e., practice) would have an effect on test scores as time passed. As summarized above, these designs ascertained that a good deal of functional recovery was indeed spontaneous. As time passed, some processes, presumably biological, were at work to improve the alcoholics' behavioral functioning.

We noticed, however, that in those of our studies in which practice was directly measured, the practice-induced performance improvements could be sizeable. Improvement occurred even in those tasks that were not recovering spontaneously over the same time period. An accumulating literature with animals was suggesting that generalized environmental enrichment might attenuate the behavioral effects of brain lesions (Finger, 1978a). Human clinical literature had also demonstrated the possibility of using environmental manipulations to improve initially impaired performance in individuals with established brain damage (Bach-y-Rita, 1980; Diller & Gordon, 1981a, 1981b). It occurred to us that the experience obtained by alcoholics during the repeated administration of the neuropsychological tasks might be analogous to environment enrichment, and thus might itself be a stimulant for functional recovery. We have recently begun to research the possibility of "experience-dependent" recovery, and have by now completed five studies addressing this issue. Some questions have been answered by these studies, but a number of methodological and theoretical questions have also been raised.

Empirical Investigations of Experience-Dependent Recovery

First, to establish whether the concept of experience-dependent recovery in alcoholics had any merit at all, we turned to an existing data pool collected during our large-scale "tracking" study (Goldman *et al.*, 1983). From this pool, we established two equivalent groups of alcoholics. The first group began, within the first week after they stopped drinking, a sequence of five testings over three weeks. The second group completed the identical five-testing sequence, but began the sequence *at least* 3 weeks after drinking ceased. This pattern of test administration produced a recovery design that was essentially a combination of the repeated-testing and multiple-group, time-lag designs. Comparisons between the first testing of each group gave an index of recovery due to spontaneous or "time-dependent" factors, whereas a comparison between the recovery rates within the repeated testings of each group gave an index of experience-dependent recovery. In this study (Goldman, Klisz, & Williams, 1981), we used only alcoholics below 40 years of age, because we knew this group would show some recovery and we were primarily interested in the type of recovery that would occur. The recovery patterns on three tasks—the Wechsler Adult Intelligence Scale (WAIS) Digit Symbol subtest, and the Halstead–Reitan Grooved Pegboard and Trail Making Test, Part B (TMT B)—were examined. We were not surprised to find that on the Digit Symbol and Grooved Pegboard tests, the typical time-dependent recovery pattern was observed: Performance at the initial testing of the second group (at least 3 weeks abstinent) was significantly better than the performance of the first group at their initial test (abstinent only a few days). The surprise was that improvement on the TMT B was *not* observed solely with the passage of time over the time span examined. However, despite the use of alternate forms of the TMT B, once repeated experience with the task began, both groups improved at equivalent rates. Hence, repeated experience with the TMT B did restore essentially normal levels of performance. These initial results encouraged us to look further for experience-dependent recovery in a series of prospectively designed studies.

The primary question that demanded attention at that point was whether a psychological function was being rehabilitated, or whether we were merely observing a performance increment that was limited to a specific set of stimuli. In the first prospective study in this series, we began addressing this question by examining the degree of generalization of performance improvement (Forsberg & Goldman, 1985). To this end, we used a study design that independently assessed time-dependent and experience-dependent recovery in two matched groups of alcoholics, as well as practice-induced performance improvement in a matched nonalcoholic control group. In this design (Table 15-1), each group received four sequential administrations of the training task; the alcoholic groups began this sequence at different time periods after drinking ceased (4 vs. 16 days of abstinence). In order to assess generalization of improvement at the end of the sequence, each group was administered an equivalent alternate form of the original training task with which they had no prior experience.

The tasks for both neuropsychological assessment and cognitive retraining used in this study were the Verbal and V-S subtests developed by Stark (1961). Our prior work (Ellenberg *et al.*, 1980) indicated that these tasks had the requisite sensitivity to alcohol-induced dysfunction, and showed a substantial practice effect. The alternate forms of these tasks had no stimulus or response elements in common with the original tasks, and were tested and refined until they were of equivalent difficulty level. The alcoholics used were all over 40 years of age and were taken from a treatment facility that included a high percentage of white-collar industrial workers and highly trained professionals. Since older alcoholics had shown the most initial impairment and the least recovery in prior investigations, this study represented a rigorous and clinically significant test of experience-dependent recovery.

The results showed no deficits in Verbal performance relative to controls at any point after the cessation of drinking. V-S performance was, however, significantly impaired at the alcoholics' initial testing, regardless of whether that initial testing came within 4 days or after 16 days of abstinence. Hence, no time-dependent recovery was observed on this task over 2–3 weeks. Once repeated task exposure began, however, performance improvement was rapid and dramatic. This improvement can be seen in

Table 15-1. Remediation Design of the Forsberg, Goldman, and Williams (1983) Study

	Days following drinking cessation						
Group	4	8	12	16	20	24	28
1	O_1	O_2	O_3	O_4, T			
2				O_1	O_2	O_3	O_4, T
Control	O_1	O_2	O_3	O_4, T			

Note. O_n, test number for the original task; T, transfer task.

Figure 15-1. Figure 15-2 contrasts the V-S scores of the alcoholic and control groups at their initial exposure to the original (training) V-S task with their errors on the alternate (transfer) V-S task. The lower error scores on the transfer task represent positive transfer of training. The controls also showed an advantage on the transfer task after repeated exposure to the original task.

However, the most clinically and conceptually significant index of the alcoholics' recovery after training was a comparison of the alcoholics' performance on the transfer task with the controls' performance at their initial administration of the original training task, prior to repetition of the training stimuli. This comparison provided a measure of how closely the remediated alcoholics' performance approached that of nonalcoholics' everyday functioning. Although the mean level of performance by the alcoholics on the V-S transfer task did not quite reach the normal control levels on the first administration of the original training task, the differences were in fact not statistically significant. Therefore, it could be concluded that the alcoholics' performance on the V-S transfer task fell within the

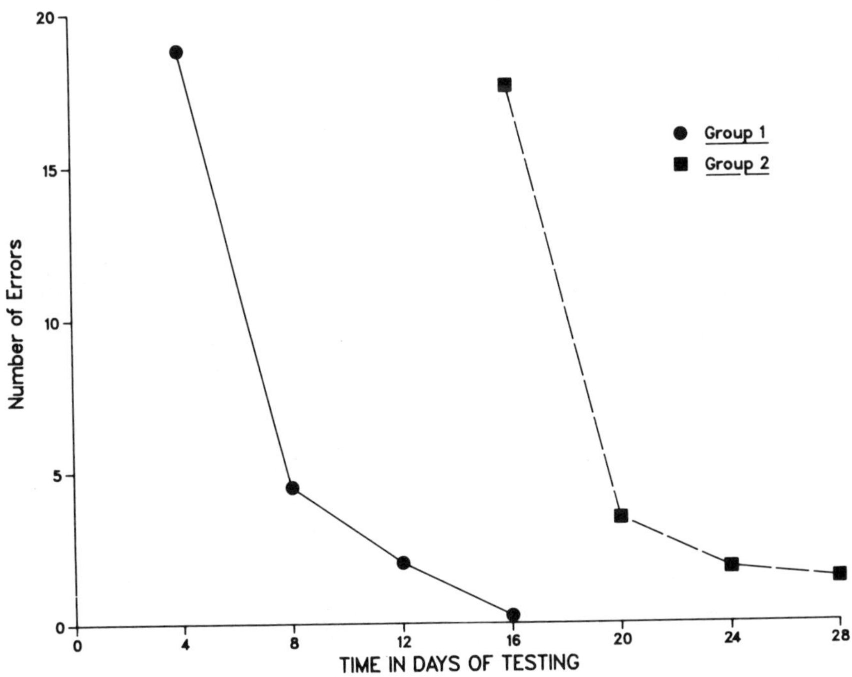

Figure 15-1. Mean error scores on each of the four sequential administrations of the original Stark V-S task, beginning in each alcoholic group at a different time period after drinking ceased (4 vs. 16 days).

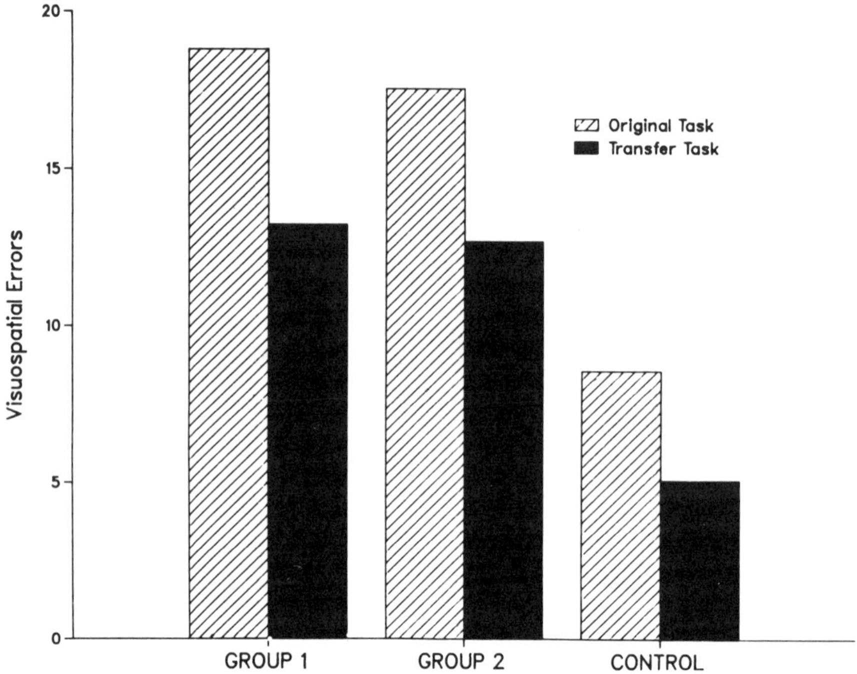

Figure 15-2. Comparison of mean error scores of Groups 1 and 2 and the control group on the original Stark V-S task and the transfer (alternate) version of the Stark V-S task.

normal range. The results reinforced the importance of experience-dependent recovery processes in alcoholics, and further showed that improvement due to repeated task practice was not just limited to the original training material, but could generalize to novel material.

An important question that needed to be addressed in connection with experience-dependent recovery was whether merely allowing neuropsychologically impaired individuals to practice with a task on which their deficits were manifest was the optimal strategy for inducing functional recovery. An alternative approach would be to rationally analyze a task into its component parts, then to train individuals to perform these parts, and then to integrate the parts into the final task product. Diller and Gordon (1981b) call this the "chemist" model and have used this method to advantage in the cognitive rehabilitation of other forms of brain damage. As an initial evaluation of the utility of the "chemist" or component-package approach with alcoholics, we attempted to remediate impairment on the TMT B by training individuals on skills presumed to underlie performance on the TMT B (R. S. Goldman & Goldman, 1984).

In order to compare time- versus experience-dependent recovery on this format, as well as the relative rates of experience-dependent recovery at two time periods following drinking cessation, the design illustrated in Table 15-2 was used. Four groups of alcoholics, all below 40 years of age, were tested. Each subject in Groups 1 and 2 received two identical remediation sessions on consecutive days at differing times after drinking ceased—Days 10–11 for Group 1, and Days 18–19 for Group 2. They were tested for transfer of training to the actual TMT B following the second remediation session. Groups 3 and 4 were not remediated, but were tested on the TMT B after the same amount of abstinence as the first two groups. Levels of impairment were established using standardized norms. The remediation package was designed by rationally analyzing the TMT B into its elementary skill components: speed and efficiency of visual scanning; integration of scanning and symbol manipulation; and alternation of verbal series. Three tasks, chosen to be representative of these components, were used as the remediation procedures. In visual-scanning training, subjects were asked to perform a series of 18 number- or letter-cancellation tasks of varying difficulty. In training for verbal-series alternation, subjects learned to alternate rapidly between pairs of verbal series. A digit–letter substitution task was used to train the alcoholics to successfully integrate visual scanning with symbol manipulation.

It can be seen from Figure 15-3 that the subjects who were remediated using the component-package remediation strategy were significantly faster at completing the TMT B than subjects in the two groups in which no remediation had occurred. There was, however, some variation in the degree to which training had been successful in the two remediated groups, probably due to some unintended differences in the initial characteristics of each group (despite matching). Note, though, that both remediated groups were at or below the cutoff for neuropsychologically impaired performance on the TMT B, whereas both nonremediated groups were clearly in the impaired range (Russell, Neuringer, & Goldstein, 1970). These findings again

Table 15-2. Remediation Design of the R. S. Goldman and Goldman (1984) Study

	Days following drinking cessation			
Group	10	11	18	20
1	R_1	R_2, T	—	—
2	—	—	R_1	R_2, T
3	—	T	—	—
4	—	—	—	T

Note. R_1, first remediation session; R_2, second remediation session; T, administration of TMT B and digit–symbol substitution task.

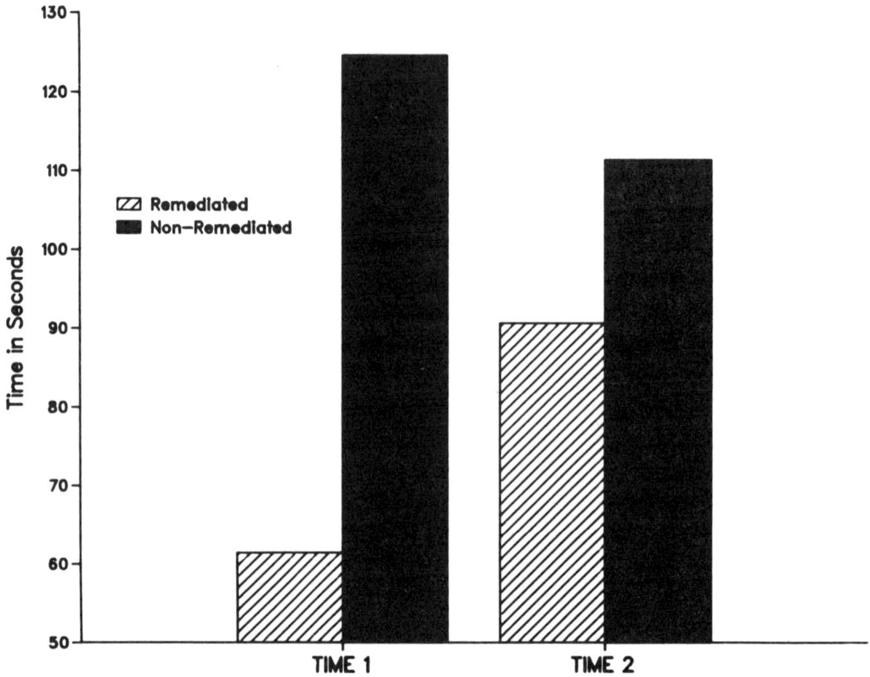

Figure 15-3. Times to complete the TMT B for the two remediated and two non-remediated alcoholic groups. Groups 1 and 2 were administered the TMT B on or about Day 11 of abstinence (Time 1); Groups 3 and 4 on or about Day 19 of abstinence (Time 2).

validated the concept of experience-dependent recovery. Furthermore, since the training tasks in this study were not the same as the tasks to be remediated (TMT B), it could be inferred that some degree of generalization of training had occurred.

Despite this initial success with a component-package approach, it remained possible that such an approach offered little advantage in alcoholics over a simple rehearsal (practice) strategy. Therefore, to determine whether any empirical differences existed between these two approaches, we compared these strategies with each other and with the spontaneous changes that occur as time passed since the last drink (Stringer & Goldman, 1984). The task to be remediated was the Block Design subtest from the WAIS, a test well known to be sensitive to alcohol-induced dysfunction (Parsons & Farr, 1981). Once again, a group of alcoholics between 40 and 65 years of age was used, because this group is known to have the least time-dependent functional recovery.

Examination of these differing approaches to the production of experience-dependent recovery required a slightly more complicated design than we had used earlier. This design is illustrated in Table 15-3. The first three groups in this design received both pretesting and posttesting on the WAIS Block Design subtest. In this way, equivalence among the first three groups could be examined, as could the change in performance consequent to the remediation procedures. Between pre- and posttesting, Group 1 received a component-package remediation procedure. Group 2 received only practice with WAIS-type block designs. Note that the practice block designs were not from the actual WAIS Block Design subtest; therefore, any improvement that might have been observed from pre- to posttesting in this group could not have been due to mere familiarity with the specific stimulus elements of the WAIS Block Design subtest. To assess any posttest improvement on block design that might have occurred merely as a function of experience with the block designs presented at pretesting, Group 3 received only the pretest and the posttest. To assess time-dependent recovery independent of any experience with block-design-type tests, Group 4 received only the posttesting. A nonalcoholic control group received a single administration of the WAIS Block Design as a comparison standard for matched normal performance on block designs.

Treatment Groups 1 and 2 received two remediation sessions lasting approximately 40 minutes between the pretesting (10–14 days aftrer admission) and posttesting (21–28 days following admission). The component-package treatment used in Group 1 consisted of 2×2, 3×3, and 4×4 block designs, each of which could be initially constructed with the help of a grid-and-number overlay placed upon the picture representation of the design. In this way, the borders between separate blocks were highlighted by lines in the grid, and an advantageous sequence for constructing the blocks was signaled by each block being given a number. This grid–number overlay was gradually faded during the course of the remediation session. Group 2 was to practice constructing the same designs, but had no training aids whatsoever.

Table 15-3. Remediation Design of the Stringer and Goldman (1984) Study

Group	Pretest	Remedial intervention	Posttest
T1	O_1	X_1	O_2
T2	O_1	X_2	O_2
T3	O_1	—	O_2
T4	—	—	O_2
Control	—	—	O_2

Note. O_1, administration of pretest; X_1, component-package remediation procedure; X_2, practice with WAIS-type block designs; O_2, administration of posttest.

Figure 15-4 depicts the results of this study. Unfortunately, Treatment Group 2 was slightly less impaired initially than the other treatment groups, and thus we could make only a limited comparison of the comparative success of the two training procedures. In any case, however, both Treatment Groups 1 and 2 showed definite improvement in WAIS Block Design performance to control levels as a consequence of remediation. Compare the slope of the change from pre- to posttesting in these two groups with that of Treatment Group 3, which received no intervening remediation. Treatment Group 3 showed very little improvement from pre- to posttesting. The impairment in Treatment Group 4 relative to controls, despite the longer period of abstention in Treatment Group 4, showed that time-dependent (spontaneous) recovery was not present on the WAIS Block Design over approximately 2–4 weeks following cessation of drinking. Clearly, experience-dependent recovery on the WAIS Block Design did occur. Although we cannot draw a final conclusion about the relative efficacy of the two remediation approaches, the results do suggest that simple practice might be as efficacious in producing experience-dependent recovery in

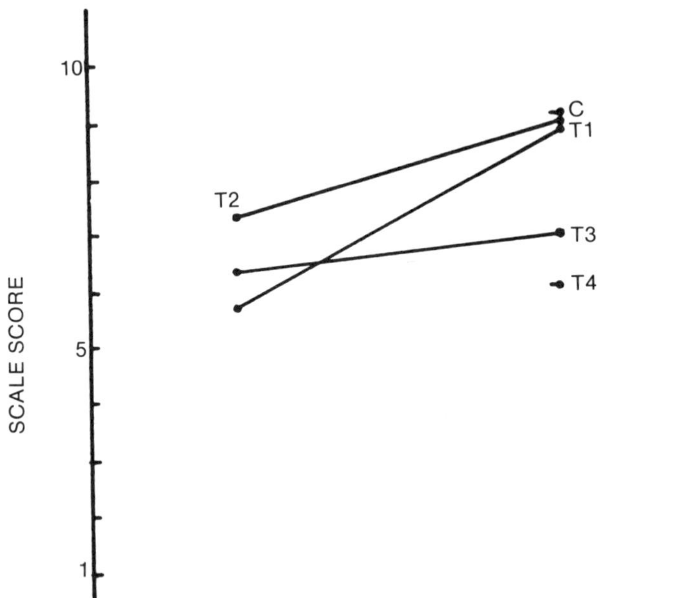

Figure 15-4. WAIS Block Design scores for the four alcoholic treatment groups and the control group. Treatment Groups 1–3 received pretesting and posttesting, Treatment Group 4 received only posttesting, and controls were tested once.

alcoholics as is the more complicated analysis-of-components remediation procedure.

The most extensive test of generalization of training from the remediation tasks to other neuropsychologically sensitive tasks of alcoholic dysfunction is now nearing completion in our laboratory by Forsberg. Final conclusions are precluded at this point because data collection is not complete; the sample size, however, is now sufficiently large to permit some preliminary statements. The design and the training task (Stark V-S task) were essentially the same as the study by Forsberg and Goldman (1985) reported earlier, but in this case we tested transfer of remediation to a number of neuropsychological tests known to be sensitive to alcoholism and to a relatively "pure" visual–spatial task. These tests included the alternate form of the Stark V-S task, the WAIS Digit Symbol subtest, the TMT B, the Benton Visual Retention Test, the Benton Line Orientation task (Benton, Hamsher, Varney, & Spreen, 1983), and the Halstead–Reitan Tactual Performance Test (TPT). Even though incomplete, the results already indicate some degree of transfer from the Stark V-S to all of the other tests except the TPT. Hence, despite the widely divergent demands of the visually presented tests, all improved consequent to training on only one. Not surprisingly, the sole failure of transfer was on the single test that was presented tactually rather than visually. It appears, therefore, that behavioral recovery is not task-specific, but generalizes to other tasks presented via the same sensory modality.

Experience-Dependent Recovery: Theoretical and Methodological Considerations

These studies immediately raise a number of important theoretical and methodological questions. How can mere practice with a test induce recovery from brain damage? How do we know that what appears to be functional improvement is anything more than simple task familiarity? Even if performance improvement can be induced on a series of neuropsychological tests, does this improvement bear any relation to any other aspect of the alcoholic's behavior? To address these questions, we must consider carefully what is meant by a "neuropsychological function" and "recovery of function," particularly in relation to the deficits produced by chronic, excessive alcohol consumption.

FUNCTION

In casual parlance, neuropsychologists speak of a test as but one measure of an underlying neuropsychological function, and further, often tend to conceive of neuropsychological functions as being carried out by particular parts of the brain. At first glance, therefore, it is difficult to understand how merely giving an individual practice with only one neuropsychological test could substantially affect the underlying neuropsychological function, and even less, how it could affect the neuropsychological substrate. Evidence that remediation procedures have done anything important would seem to require more than just improvement on a specific test. Instead, some demonstration that a neuropsychological function has been remediated would appear necessary.

Certainly a test is not a function, but when we consider how to demonstrate the remediation of a neuropsychological *function*, we encounter difficulties. While the term "neuropsychological function" conveys useful meaning in casual conversation, and impressive efforts to define the term can be found (Luria, 1966), it is far more difficult to compile a comprehensive list of neuropsychological functions, and virtually impossible to specify which tasks comprise the complete domain of any single function. As Lezak (1983) has indicated, "As more is learned about how the brain processes information, it becomes more difficult to make theoretically acceptable distinctions between the functions involved in human information processing" (p. 23). Neuropsychologists often tend to group tests together as measures of a function, either because of face or content validity (they appear to have psychological commonalities), and/or because they tend to show some statistically correlated sensitivity to particular kinds of brain lesions. But neuropsychologists have been aware for some time of the danger of using mere face validity and correlations between tests as a means of inferring underlying functions and neurological substrates (Walsh, 1978, pp. 21–24). Teuber (1955) introduced the notion of "double dissociation" to permit more careful analysis of this issue, but alcohol researchers are not at the point of being able to specify double dissociation for the typical deficits observed in connection with chronic alcoholics (assuming that we ever could be).[1]

Hence, we are not currently in a position to insist that, in alcoholics, functional recovery must be demonstrated by improvement in a specifiable domain of tasks that measure a particular function, or by a demonstration that we have induced a change in the neural substrate underlying this function. At the moment, all we can really ask is that the improved performance generalize beyond the task or tasks we have used for remediating the deficit. The extent of generalization thus becomes the criterion for successful remediation. If it should turn out that the tests to which remediation generalizes also correlate with each other in normals, we may gain support for inferring a common underlying mechanism (function). Hence, investigation of experience-dependent recovery may itself help us better understand neuropsychological functions.

1. "[D]ouble dissociation requires that symptom A appear in lesions in one structure but not with those in another, and the symptom B appear with lesions of the other but not of the one. Whenever such dissociation is lacking, specificity in the effects of lesions has not been demonstrated" (Teuber, 1959, p. 187).

When we consider the nature of alcohol-induced dysfunction, the problem becomes even more obvious. Except for the very severe cognitive deficits that are found in the Wernicke–Korsakoff syndrome, most alcohol-induced neuropsychological deficits are subtle. These deficits are most often not readily apparent from simple behavioral observation of the individual alcoholic, but rather manifest themselves primarily on sensitive neuropsychological tests. Therefore, in the case of alcoholism, the only deficits we have to work with are the low scores on neuropsychological tests. Hence, it is not improper to attempt to induce improved test performance as a means of assessing neuropsychological recovery. This is what Diller and Gordon (1981b) have called the "psychometrician" model of rehabilitation.

Examination of the neural substrate for the behavioral deficits observed in alcoholics also does not help us clarify the nature of the specific functions impaired by alcohol. Except in cases of the Wernicke–Korsakoff syndrome, there is little evidence that the morphological damage produced by alcohol is localized at the cortical level (e.g., Carlen *et al.*, 1978). From neuroanatomical evidence, we might expect that in alcoholics all functions would be impaired to a certain extent, rather than any single function or group of functions with discrete behavioral referents. Of course, we know that alcoholics do not show across-the-board behavioral deficiencies; however, as noted earlier, the types of tasks that are sensitive to alcohol-induced damage may have in common the dependence on rapid and efficient processing of new, complex information. Subsumed in this notion is the requirement that the brain efficiently *integrate* information from external input and from existing informational stores. When one considers the efficient integration of information within the nervous system, one immediately thinks about efficient synaptic transmission and neural conduction. There is good evidence that alcohol as a chemical agent has considerable effects upon these electrochemical processes (Goldstein, 1983). Hence, it may not be a specific function for which we are looking in relation to alcohol abuse, but rather the general capacity of the brain to effectively assemble the "working mosaic" discussed by Luria (1966) in his description of functional systems. There is probably no discrete group of tests that defines the full range of such a function. Once again, we are left with the conclusion that, in alcoholics, demonstration of experience-dependent recovery of function should not emphasize improvement in some specific and discrete group of tests, but rather should search for the widest possible generalization of performance improvement.

RECOVERY

One may initially hesitate to accept improved performance on a test as being equivalent to "recovery" from brain damage. Should not recovery from brain damage also include regrowth of neurons, collateral sprouting, and so on? It would certainly be exciting to see some neuropsychological indicator that demonstrates that a behavioral manipulation has produced fundamental changes in the neural substrate. Such a relationship might be examined in humans by looking at repeated CT scans in abstinent alcoholics or by examining such indices as auditory evoked potentials (Begleiter, 1984). These neuropsychological concomitants are, however, not necessary for the demonstration of behavioral recovery. At the behavioral level, what is important is to take individuals who are deficient in some aspect of behavior and make them adequate in this behavior, as demonstrated by comparisons with normal controls. We are incapable at this point of examining all the possible neuropsychological correlates of functional recovery. Not only would we have great difficulty measuring such changes in intact humans, but we remain ignorant of all the changes that may occur in the brain that are associated with behavioral improvement. Once again, therefore, we are forced to conclude that improved task performance, and generalization of that improvement to other tasks, are all we have when we consider functional recovery in alcoholics.

Furthermore, there are many ways in which functional recovery might occur that would not depend upon gross neuropsychological changes. There is considerable neural redundancy in the brain, and practice may induce other sets of neurons to "learn" the task, or to assume the information-processing load that had initially been performed by neurons which had been rendered less functional by alcohol. Smith (1981, p. 179) points out that destruction of 50% of the hearing appparatus in the CNS results in only a 2–3% reduction in measured auditory acuity. Also, in line with Luria's (1966) concept of functional systems, it is highly possible to perform most complex behavioral tasks in a variety of ways. Practice may afford an impaired individual the opportunity to develop an alternative strategy. Finally, it is well known that neuropsychologically impaired individuals frequently demonstrate negative emotional responses to their impairment. These emotional responses not only interfere with reacquisition of a behavior, but also take up the time that might be better spent on relearning the behavior. Practice may give individuals an opportunity to calm themselves emotionally and focus on the task at hand (Finger, 1978a).

We should not, however, rule out the possibility that practice induces actual neuropsychological change. The stimulation of the nervous system during practice on a demanding task may, in fact, induce increased dendritic arborization, collateral axon sprouting, or any of the other neuropsychological recovery mechanisms. Marshall (1984) has suggested that behavioral recovery is primarily based on alterations in transmitter synthesis, release, and postsynaptic sensitivity. As discussed earlier, it is very likely that these aspects of CNS functioning are highly affected by the chemical toxicity of alcohol. Hence, it is not difficult to speculate that practice-induced activation of the CNS would afford an opportunity to bring these mechanisms back toward normality.

It has been argued that one way of demonstrating that practice-induced improvement on a task corresponds to functional recovery of a more central or biological sort is to compare the rate of improvement in the impaired group (alcoholics) with the rate of improvement in normal controls. It is suggested that if the normals show the identical slope in their acquisition of the task at hand, then the performance improvement in the impaired group is less meaningful. This is not the case. Since we cannot know what the underlying substrate for the performance improvement is at a behavioral level, all we can hope for is to return initially impaired individuals to normal levels of functioning. Normal functioning is indicated by the performance of normal controls at their initial exposure to a task. Normal controls will, of course, improve with practice and may even reach levels of performance after an equivalent amount of practice than remain well above the performance of the initially impaired group. This observation would not reduce the significance of returning impaired individuals to normal levels of functioning. For example, normal individuals with memory training can acquire a digit span of 80 digits (Ericson & Chase, 1982); returning a brain-damaged individual with memory loss to normal levels of memory function (7 ± 2 digits) would still be remarkable. In fact, normals could improve faster than, as fast as, or slower than the impaired group without altering the significance of rehabilitating impaired individuals to normal levels. The differing rates of improvement would not contribute substantially to our understanding of the mechanism involved.

Up to this point, I have been discussing "practice" as a general term, without reference to the types of practice that might be employed. The different strategies of practice may be tentatively grouped as follows:

General Activation. In the general-activation strategy, increased cognitive activity is promoted in the hope that generalized "exercise" of cognitive functioning will result in increased levels of performance. There are suggestions in the animal literature that increased activity levels assist functional recovery (Wolgin & Teitelbaum, 1978). As long as the functional debility is not so severe that the individual is totally frustrated in the attempt to perform the behavior, encouraging increased cognitive activity can afford the opportunity for any of the varieties of psychological recovery and/or neuropsychological recovery. For example, the individual may increase the efficiency of integrating functional systems; may force the development of alternative modes of performing a complex behavior through trial and error; may overcome habitual cognitive "laziness" (the reluctance to work on demanding cognitive problems); or may even stimulate more efficient synaptic activity or even neuronal regrowth.

Stimulus-Specific Activation (Practice and Guided Rehearsal). General cognitive activation may not generalize to all of the behaviors that one might wish to remediate. If so, it would be necessary to give an individual experience with each of the specific types of tasks that were impaired and required improvement. For example, visual–spatial dysfunction might require repeated experience with visual–spatial tasks. If a task proved too complicated or difficult for an individual to perform with any degree of success at the beginning of the remediation process, it might be necessary to break down the task into component parts and provide experience with these components before shifting back to the original task. This approach is exemplified by two of the studies reported earlier (R. S. Goldman & Goldman, 1984; Stringer & Goldman, 1984). The underlying recovery mechanisms in this case are identical to those noted above in connection with the general-activation approach.

Behavioral Compensation. In the behavioral-compensation approach, a deliberate effort is made to train impaired individuals to use alternative strategies when performing tasks on which they have shown deficits. This approach is necessary if the individuals are neurologically incapable of performing the original behavior. As an analogue, we might think of a paraplegic individual who cannot locomote by walking, but is taught to locomote by using a wheelchair. In the compensation approach, the strategies are devised in advance by the experimenter, based either upon prior analyses of the ways in which a task may be performed, or upon knowledge of neurological systems. An example that relates to cognitive deficits in alcoholics is to help train visual–spatial performance with the use of verbal mediators. This is the most sophisticated rehabilitation approach, by may be unnecessary with certain human dysfunctions such as alcoholism, in that affected individuals might be able to devise their own compensatory schemes during the recovery process.

Implications for Treatment

Evidence has been accumulating that neuropsychological status has a significant relationship to treatment outcome (Abbott & Gregson, 1981; Berglund *et al.*, 1977; Gregson & Taylor, 1977; Walker *et al.*, 1983). This relationship has been characterized as "modest" (Walker *et al.*, 1983), but even such a modest relationship is noteworthy, given the many factors that contribute to successful treatment outcome in alcoholism (Wilkinson & Sanchez-Craig, 1981). In the context of this relationship, the data that have been accumulated on the phenomena of both time-dependent and experience-dependent recovery have substantial implications for changes that might be made in our current approaches to treatment; they even suggest new additions to the therapist's treatment armamentarium.

Time-Dependent Recovery and Treatment

A large percentage of treatment resources are concentrated in the first month after an alcoholic stops drinking, usually in the context of an inpatient alcoholism treatment program. The recovery parameters generated by the studies on time-dependent recovery in alcoholics indicate, however, that in the first week or two following the cessation of drinking, alcoholics' information-processing capabilities are not much better than those of severely brain-damaged individuals. Other than bedrest and medical aspects of treatment (nutritional supplements, medications, etc.), the vast majority of the components of an alcoholism treatment program consist of the presentation of new information. The new information comes in the form of material about alcohol and its effects on the body; alternative skills for coping with stress; learning how to integrate emotional states with ongoing behavior in a more efficacious manner; learning to increase interpersonal skills; and so on. Hence, it is highly likely that approximately half (if not more) of the primary treatment program is, to some degree, wasted. Data from the neuropsychological recovery studies suggest that the alcoholics at this point are just not capable of utilizing and integrating much of this new information. Hence, from the perspective of time-dependent recovery alone, it makes sense to delay the administration of major treatment components until 1–2 weeks after drinking ceases.

While a good deal of psychological recovery occurs during the first 2 weeks to 1 month following the cessation of drinking, we now know that the recovery process is an ongoing one. Hence, we cannot take for granted that at any single point in the recovery process the information-processing capacity of the alcoholic has improved sufficiently for the digestion of whatever information we are trying to convey. Repetition is the solution to this difficulty. All treatment components must be repeated numerous times over the weeks and months following cessation of drinking, if we are to insure that they have been absorbed. Alternative modes of presentation of essentially the same information must be used to prevent fatigue and boredom; nevertheless, repeated exposure to the same material is essential. This requirement must make it obvious that what is considered treatment cannot be limited to the abbreviated block of time that normally constitutes an inpatient program. Treatment must last for many months. This conclusion converges nicely with the observations of treatment researchers who have concluded that so-called "aftercare" or follow-up may be the most important part of the treatment program (Marlatt & Gordon, 1980).

We have seen that older alcoholics have the most severe cognitive deficits and the longest recovery times. In the older alcoholics, the ultimate level of recovery also may be limited. Therefore, even greater care must be taken with older alcoholics to repeat treatment components and to help the individuals return to everyday functioning, where they may experience greater frustrations in coping with job or family problems.

Experience-Dependent Recovery and Treatment

The implications of experience-dependent recovery for treatment of alcoholism are even more direct and potentially consequential than are those of the spontaneously occurring time-dependent processes. If neuropsychological status is related to treatment outcome, then it should not require too much of a leap to suggest that improving neuropsychological status may increase the success rates of alcoholism treatment. Clinicians working with alcoholics have long been familiar with the cognitive "haziness" the alcoholics experience after they stop drinking. Facilitating experience-dependent recovery may be analogous to lifting this cognitive haze. From the perspective of a clinician, it would certainly not seem far-fetched to speculate that lifting of this haze might have some beneficial impact on treatment; yet, to this point, direct interventions to achieve such a goal have been ignored. There are a number of potential benefits:

1. Increasing cognitive clarity may help alcoholics become better problem solvers. Increased problem-solving facility should have a positive effect on all aspects of day-to-day functioning.

2. Specifically, increased facility for information processing may help alcoholics to better absorb other components of an alcohol treatment program. Hence, experience-dependent cognitive recovery may have a generalized effect throughout treatment.

3. Increased cognitive clarity may better prepare alcoholics for coping with a variety of real-world problems in the aftercare portion of treatment. For example, any jobs that require some new learning, or jobs that are intrinsically more dependent on rapid information processing and problem solving, may be dealt with more successfully by alcoholics who have undergone cognitive remediation.

4. It is now reasonably well established that the likelihood of relapse relates directly to an alcoholic's experience of social and occupational stressors (Moos & Finney, 1983). Improved cognitive functioning may increase alcoholics' adaptability and thereby increase their resilience to the stressors.

5. Unlike most aspects of a typical alcoholism treatment program, to which alcoholics are exposed but in which they may not be actively engaged, cognitive remedial procedures require an active response. That is, built into the procedure is a requirement that the alcoholics engage in information processing. Not only is this engagement itself important, but the remediation task provides an ongoing measure of whether the patients are, in fact, progressing.

6. In addition to any actual increase in cognitive efficiency that alcoholics might obtain from these procedures, there is also a nonspecific aspect that should be considered. Most, if not all, alcoholics will improve on the remediation tasks to some degree. In fact, if the tasks are designed properly, we should be able to insure that improvement will occur. Hence, early in the recovery period, alcoholics will obtain a success experience. The perception that success can be obtained may give alcoholics more assurance when they have to face other problems in the future. Furthermore, many alcoholics

report worrying about whether they have lost some degree of mental facility. The observation of initial impairment on the remediation tasks, followed by later improvement, both reinforces their understanding of the negative effect of drinking and encourages them about the improving status of their mental facility. Alcoholic subjects in our studies have, in fact, reported pleasure at their improved performance.

Although at this point in time the issue is still being researched, we can make some informed guesses about the optimal strategy for incorporating cognitive remediation into an alcohol treatment program. Our data to this point indicate that the general activation approach is all that is necessary for optimal experience-dependent recovery in alcoholics. Therefore, in addition to sessions with a treatment program specifically devoted to the administration of cognitive remedial tasks, experience-dependent recovery should be integrated into all aspects of a treatment program for alcoholism. The cognitive demands of all aspects of the treatment program should be assessed. Less demanding content should be presented early, and as cognitive facility improves, the more difficult aspects should be presented. As much active responding to program content as possible should be encouraged. Lectures should not just be delivered or films presented; instead, explicit tests of the learning of such material should be administered in a structured learning format. These implications of the experience-dependent recovery research dovetail with the approaches that require learning of specific skills and active practice in these skills (Chaney, O'Leary, & Marlatt, 1978).

One final thought: Some of the recovery we have been attributing to time-dependent processes may actually be due to inadvertent experience-dependent recovery. That is, if cognitive stimulation and demands for cognitive processing are imposed (unintentionally) upon an individual alcoholic early in the detoxification period, some recovery that appears spontaneous may instead result from the effects of this stimulation. Such stimulation may derive from the active components of some treatment programs, or may even be self-induced by some alcoholics. In any case, the distinction between time- and experience-dependent recovery may not be as clear in actual clinical application as it would first appear.

Conclusions

In addition to increasing our understanding of neuropsychological recovery from alcoholism, the findings of the studies of time- and experience-dependent recovery also open up a new area in the pursuit of more efficacious alcoholism treatment. For the first time, neuropsychologists can shift from their role as assessors of cognitive dysfunction to an interventionist role that may help decrease the burden of this problem on society.

Acknowledgments

Portions of the work described in this chapter were supported by National Institute on Alcohol Abuse and Alcoholism Grant Nos. AA06123 and AA05946 to Mark S. Goldman. Appreciation is expressed to the staffs of the alcohol treatment units at Detroit Memorial Hospital, Harper Hospital, Henry Ford Hospital Maplegrove Treatment Center, Salvation Army Harbor Light, and the Veterans Administration Hospital.

References

Abbott, M. W., & Gregson, R. A. M. (1981). Cognitive dysfunction in the prediction of relapse in alcoholics. *Journal of Studies on Alcohol, 42*, 230–243.

Adamson, J., & Burdick, J. A. (1973). Sleep of dry alcoholics. *Archives of General Psychiatry, 28*, 146–149.

Allen, R. P., Faillace, L. A., & Reynolds, D. M. (1971). Recovery of memory functioning in alcoholics following prolonged alcohol intoxication. *Journal of Nervous and Mental Disease, 153*, 417–423.

Allen, R. P., Faillace, L. A., & Wagman, A. (1971). Recovery time for alcoholics after prolonged alcohol intoxication. *Johns Hopkins Medical Journal, 128*, 158–164.

Bach-y-Rita, P. (1980). *Recovery of function: Theoretical considerations for brain injury.* Baltimore: University Park Press.

Begleiter, H. (1981). Brain dysfunction and alcoholism: Problems and prospects. *Alcoholism: Clinical and Experimental Research, 5*, 264–266.

Begleiter, H. (1984, May). *Brain dysfunctions related to alcohol abuse.* Paper presented at the Conference on Clinical Implications of Recent Neuropsychological Findings, Boston.

Bennett, A. E. (1960). Diagnosis of intermediate stage of alcohol brain disease. *Journal of the American Medical Association, 172*, 1143–1146.

Benton, A. L., Hamsher, K. deS., Varney, N. R., & Spreen, O. (1983). *Contributions to neuropsychological assessment.* New York: Oxford University Press.

Berglund, M., Leijonquist, H., & Horlen, M. (1977). Prognostic significance and reversibility of cerebral dysfunction in alcoholics. *Journal of Studies on Alcohol, 38*, 1761–1769.

Brandt, J., Butters, N., Ryan, C., & Bayog, R. (1983). Cognitive loss and recovery in chronic alcohol abusers. *Archives of General Psychiatry, 40*, 435–442.

Carlen, P. L. (1982). Reversible effects of chronic alcoholism on the central nervous system: Possible biological mechanisms. In D. A. Wilkinson (Ed.), *Cerebral deficits in alcoholism* (pp. 107–122). Toronto: Addiction Research Foundation.

Carlen, P. L., Wortzman, G., Holgate, R. C., Wilkinson, D. A., & Rankin, J. G. (1978). Reversible cerebral atrophy in recently abstinent chronic alcoholics measured by computed tomography scans. *Science, 200*, 1076–1078.

Cermak, L. S., & Ryback, R. S. (1976). Recovery of verbal short-term memory in alcoholics. *Journal of Studies on Alcohol, 37*, 46–52.

Chaney, E. F., O'Leary, M. R., Marlatt, G. A. (1978). Skill training with alcoholics. *Journal of Consulting and Clinical Psychology, 46*, 1092–1104.

Claiborne, J. M., & Greene, R. L. (1981). Neuropsychological changes in recovering men alcoholics. *Journal of Studies on Alcohol, 42*, 757–765.

Clarke, J., & Haughton, H. (1975). A study of intellectual impairment and recovery rates in heavy drinkers in Ireland. *British Journal of Psychiatry, 126*, 178–184.

Cooper, L. A., & Regan, D. T. (1982). Attention, perception, and intelligence. In R. Sternberg (Ed.), *Handbook of human intelligence* (pp. 123–169). New York: Cambridge University Press.

Cotman, C. W., & Nieto-Sampedro, M. (1982). Brain function, synapse renewal, and plasticity. *Annual Review of Psychology, 33*, 371–401.

Dickey, J. H., & Goldman, M. S. (1982, August). *Probability learning indices of alcohol-related neuropsychological dysfunction and recovery.* Paper presented at the meeting of the Amercian Psychological Association, Washington, DC.

Diller, L., & Gordon, W. A. (1981a). Interventions for cognitive deficits in brain-injured adults. *Journal of Consulting and Clinical Psychology, 49,* 822–834.

Diller, L., & Gordon, W. A. (1981b). Rehabilitation and clinical neuropsychology. In S. Filskov & T. Boll (Eds.), *Handbook of clinical neuropsychology* (pp. 702–733). New York: Wiley.

Douglas, R., & Pribram, K. (1966). Learning and limbic lesions. *Neuropsychologia, 4,* 197–200.

Dwyer, P., Whitman, R. D., Rosenbaum, G., & Goldman, M. S. (1981, February). *Recoverability of psychological functioning following alcohol abuse: Spatial generalization effects.* Paper presented at the meeting of the International Neuropsychological Society, Atlanta.

Ellenberg, L., Rosenbaum, G., Goldman, M. S., & Whitman, R. D. (1980). Recoverability of psychological functioning following alcohol abuse: Lateralization effects. *Journal of Consulting and Clinical Psychology, 48,* 503–510.

Ericson, K. A., & Chase, W. G. (1982). Exceptional memory. *American Scientist, 70,* 607–615.

Farmer, R. H. (1973). Functional changes during early weeks of abstinence, measured by the Bender–Gestalt. *Quarterly Journal of Studies on Alcohol, 34*, 786–795.

Finger, S. (1978a). Environmental attenuation of brain-lesions symptoms. In S. Finger (Ed.), *Recovery from brain damage: Research and theory* (pp. 297–329). New York: Plenum Press.

Finger, S. (Ed.). (1978b). *Recovery from brain damage: Research and theory.* New York: Plenum Press.

Forsberg, L. K., & Goldman, M. S. (1985). Experience-dependent recovery of visuospatial functioning in older alcoholics. *Journal of Abnormal Psychology, 94*, 519–529.

Forsberg, L. K., Goldman, M. S., & Williams, D. L. (1983, August). *Experience-dependent recovery of visuospatial functioning in older alcoholics.* Paper presented at the meeting of the American Psychological Association, Anaheim, CA.

Goldman, M. S. (1982). Reversibility of psychological deficits in alcoholics: The interaction of aging with alcohol. In D. A. Wilkinson (Ed.), *Cerebral deficits in alcoholism* (pp. 79–105). Toronto: Addiction Research Foundation.

Goldman, M. S. (1983). Cognitive impairment in chronic alcoholics: Some cause for optimism. *American Psychologist, 10*, 1045–1054.

Goldman, M. S., Klisz, D. K., & Williams, D. L. (1981, February). *Active and passive recovery of neuropsychological deficits in chronic alcoholics.* Paper presented at the meeting of the International Neuropsychological Society, Atlanta.

Goldman, M. S., & Rosenbaum, G. (1977). Psychological recoverability following chronic alcohol abuse. In F. A. Seixas, (Ed.), *Currents in alcoholism* (Vol. 2, pp. 187–196). New York: Grune & Stratton.

Goldman, M. S., Whitman, R. D., Rosenbaum, G., & VandeVusse, D. (1978). Recoverability of motor and sensory function following chronic alcohol abuse. In F. A. Seixas (Ed.), *Currents in alcoholism* (Vol. 3, pp. 493–504). New York: Grune & Stratton.

Goldman, M. S., Williams, D. L., & Klisz, D. K. (1983). Recoverability of psychological functioning following alcohol abuse: Prolonged visual–spatial dysfunction in older alcoholics. *Journal of Consulting and Clinical Psychology, 51,* 370–378.

Goldman, R. S., & Goldman, M. S. (1984, August). *Remediation of problem-solving deficits in an alcoholic population.* Paper presented at the meeting of the American Psychological Association, Toronto.

Goldstein, D. B. (1983). *Pharmacology of alcohol.* New York: Oxford University Press.

Grant, I., Reed, R., & Adams, K. M. (1980). Natural history of alcohol and drug-related brain disorder: Implications for neuropsychological research. *Journal of Clinical Neuropsychology, 2,* 321–331.

Gregson, R. A. M., & Taylor, G. M. (1977). Prediction of relapse in men alcoholics. *Journal of Studies on Alcohol, 38,* 1749–1759.

Gross, M. M., Lewis, E., & Hastey, I. (1974). Acute alcohol withdrawal syndrome. In B. Kissin & H. Begleiter (Eds.), *The biology of alcoholism: Vol. 3. Clinical pathology* (pp. 191–263). New York: Plenum Press.

Hasher, L., & Zacks, R. T. (1979). Automatic and effortful processes in memory. *Journal of Experimental Psychology: General, 198,* 356–388.

Jones, B. M., & Parsons, O. A. (1971). Impaired abstracting ability in chronic alcoholics. *Archives of General Psychiatry, 24,* 71–75.

Kish, G. B., Hagen, J. M., Woody, M. M., & Harvey, H. M. (1980). Alcoholics' recovery from cerebral impairment as a function of duration of abstinence. *Journal of Clinical Psychology, 36,* 584–589.

Lewis, R., & Rennick, P. M. (1979). *Manual for the Repeatable Cognitive–Perceptual Battery.* Grosse Pointe, MI: Axon.

Lezak, M. (1983). *Neuropsychological assessments.* New York: Oxford University Press.

Long, J. A., & McLachlan, J. F. C. (1974). Abstract reasoning and perceptual motor efficiency in alcoholics. *Quarterly Journal of Studies on Alcohol, 35,* 1220–1229.

Luria, A. R. (1966). *Higher cortical functions in man.* New York: Basic Books.

Marlatt, G. A., & Gordon, J. R. (1980). Determinants of relapse: Implications for the maintenance of behavior. In P. Davidson (Ed.), *Behavioral medicine: Changing health lifestyles* (pp. 410–452). New York: Brunner/Mazel.

Marshall, J. F. (1984). Brain function: Neural adaptations and recovery from injury. *Annual Review of Psychology 35,* 277–308.

Moos, R. H., & Finney, J. W. (1983). The expanding scope of alcoholism treatment evaluation. *American Psychologist, 38,* 1036–1044.

Nauta, W. (1972). Neural associations of the frontal cortex. *Acta Neurobiologia Experimenta, 32,* 125–140.

Noble, E. P., & Tewari, S. (1973). Protein and ribonucleic acid metabolism in brains of mice following chronic alcohol consumption. *Annals of the New York Academy of Sciences, 215,* 333–345.

Nonneman, A., Voigt, J., & Kolb, B. (1974). Comparisons of behavioral effects of hippocampal and prefrontal cortex lesions in the rat. *Journal of Comparative and Physiological Psychology, 87,* 249–260.

Page, R. D., & Linden, J. D. (1974). Reversible organic brain syndrome in alcoholics. *Quarterly Journal of Studies on Alcohol, 35,* 98–107.

Page, R. D., & Schaub, L. H. (1974). Intellectual functioning in alcoholics during six months' abstinence. *Quarterly Journal of Studies on Alcohol, 38,* 1240–1246.

Parsons, O. A., & Farr, S. P. (1981). The neuropsychology of alcohol and drug use. In S. Filskov & T. Boll (Eds.), *Handbook of clinical neuropsychology* (pp. 320–365). New York: Wiley.

Peterson, L. R., & Peterson, M. J. (1959). Short-term retention of individual verbal items. *Journal of Experimental Psychology, 58,* 193–198.

Russell, A., Neuringer, C., & Goldstein, G. (1970). *Assessment of brain disease: A neuropsychological key approach.* New York: Wiley.

Sharp, J. R., Rosenbaum, G., Goldman, M. S., & Whitman, R. D. (1977). Recoverability of psychological functioning following alcohol abuse: Acquisition of meaningful synonyms. *Journal of Consulting and Clinical Psychology, 45,* 1023–1028.

Smith, A. (1981). Principles underlying human brain functions in neuropsychological sequelae of different neuropathological processes. In S. B. Filskov & T. J. Boll (Eds.), *Handbook of clinical neuropsychology* (pp. 175–226). New York: Wiley.

Stark, R. (1961). An investigation of unilateral cerebral pathology with equated verbal and visual–spatial tasks. *Journal of Abnormal and Social Psychology, 62*, 282–287.

Stevens, R., & Cowey, A. (1973). Effects of dorsal and ventral hippocampal lesions on spontaneous alternation, learned alternations, and probability learnig in rats. *Brain Research, 52,* 203–224.

Stringer, A. Y., & Goldman, M. S. (1984, August). *Remediation of spatial and problem solving deficits in male alcoholics.* Paper presented at the meeting of the American Psychological Association, Toronto.

Tarter, R. E., & Jones, B. M. (1971). Motor impairment in chronic alcoholics. *Diseases of the Nervous System, 32*, 632–636.

Teuber, H. L. (1955). Physiological psychology. *Annual Review of Psychology, 6,* 267–296.

Walker, R. D., Donovan, D. M., Kivlahan, D. R., & O'Leary, M. R. (1983). Length of stay, neuropsychological performance, and aftercare: Influences on alcohol treatment outcome. *Journalof Consulting and Clinical Psychology, 51*, 900–911.

Walsh, K. W. (1978). *Neuropsychology: A clinical approach.* New York: Churchill Livingstone.

Weingartner, H., Faillace, L. A., & Markley, H. G. (1971). Verbal information retention in alcoholics. *Quarterly Journal of Studies on Alcohol, 32,* 293–303.

Wilkinson, D. A., & Sanchez-Craig, M. (1981). Relevance of brain dysfunction to treatment objectives: Should alcohol-related cognitive deficits influence the way we think about treatment? *Addictive Behaviors, 6,* 253–260.

Williams, H. L., & Rundell, O. A., Jr. (1981). Altered sleep physiology in chronic alcoholics: Reversal with abstinence. *Alcoholism: Clinical and Experimental Research, 5,* 318–325.

Wolgin, D. L., & Teitelbaum, P. (1978). Role of activation and sensory stimuli in recovery from lateral hypothalamic damage in the cat. *Journal of Comparative and Physiological Psychology, 92*, 474–500.

16

Identification and Remediation of Everyday Problems in Memory-Impaired Patients

BARBARA WILSON

Introduction

The purpose of this chapter is to present findings from some recent neuropsychological studies at Rivermead Rehabilitation Centre in Oxford that have established procedures for identifying and remediating cognitive problems. Many of the studies focused upon adults whose problems resulted from either head injury, stroke, encephalitis, or tumor. Although alcoholics have a different etiology from these patients, the procedures involved in assessment and treatment should be equally applicable in cases where the cognitive problems encountered are similar. It is argued that the nature of the deficit is more important than etiology, which, after all, does not precisely specify the area of the brain damage or indicate what the resulting intellectual handicap will be (Baddeley & Wilson, 1983).

Identification of Everyday Memory Problems

The first neuropsychological study to be described is concerned with the identification or diagnosis of everyday problems resulting from organic memory deficit. Clinical memory testing is carried out by many neuropsychologists, but the results tell us little about the nature, frequency, or severity of the memory problems encountered in real life (Sunderland, Harris, & Baddeley, 1983). Conventional tests can answer such questions as these: How well does this person perform in comparison with the general population? Does this score fall in the abnormal range? Is the deficit more typical of organic or functional disturbance? Is there general intellectual

Barbara Wilson. Department of Psychology, Charing Cross Hospital, London, England. (Formerly, Department of Clinical Psychology, Rivermead Rehabilitation Centre, Oxford, England.)

impairment or a specific memory deficit? Is the deficit material- or modality-specific, or global? Such information is useful, of course, but it remains limited insofar as it fails to shed any light upon the difficulties experienced by the patient in everyday life.

It is suggested here that it is equally important to find answers to such questions as the following: Can this person find his or her way around the home environment? Will he or she be able to live alone? What is the best way to teach new information that will be applicable to the person in the management of daily living? The answers to these questions will require a different form of assessment. Interviews, checklists, and rating scales may provide helpful information. Observation in natural settings will be needed in order to identify a number of the problems that are manifested in real-life situations. Behavioral assessment will almost certainly be needed if the identification of problems is undertaken in order to plan treatment. A behavioral assessment attempts to (1) identify each particular problem precisely, clearly, and unambiguously; (2) determine the specific characteristics of a problem; and (3) evaluate the effectiveness of treatment.

The Rivermead Behavioural Memory Test[1]

The first neuropsychological study I describe here represents an attempt to combine the strengths of standardized tests with the strengths of behavioral assessment. The Rivermead Behavioural Memory Test (RBMT) is administered and scored in a standardized way, but it uses items analogous to real-life situations. Patients are required to carry out certain simple everyday tasks and to retain some information similar to that needed for adequate everyday functioning. There are several subtests, including remembering a short route, remembering an appointment, and learning a new skill. (The subtests are described in the Appendix to this chapter and in Wilson, 1987.) The test is still in the experimental stage, and research into its usage and effectiveness is being funded by the British Medical Research Council. However, pilot work has been carried out over the past several years, and the procedure looks promising (Wilson, Cockburn, & Baddeley, 1985). In particular, it appears to be helpful in identifying those particular problems that are likely to cause difficulties in normal living. It also suggests areas where therapists might concentrate treatment. For example, although a patient may have no difficulty in remembering a short route, that same patient may not be able to learn any of the steps involved in acquiring a new skill. A second patient might show the reverse by learning the new skill within a set period but failing to remember the short route. With the former patient, therapists would probably do better working out the best ways for

1. This test has recently been published. Details are obtainable from Thames Valley Test Company, 22 Bulmershe Road, Reading RG1 5 RJ, England.

the person to acquire new skills, and with the latter they would be advised to concentrate on the learning of routes. It is not always obvious which patterns are going to emerge. Severe amnesics usually fail on all subtests, but those with less severe memory difficulties show a wide variation. Results from the first 25 memory-impaired people tested can be seen in Table 16-1.

As a simple indication of whether a patient had everyday memory problems, we relied upon the occupational therapists treating the patients to

Table 16-1. Performance on the 12 Items of the RBMT of 25 Patients Categorized by Their Therapists as Having Memory Problems

	Items[a]												
Patient	1	2	3	4	5	6	7	8	9	10	11	12	Totals
1					*	*	*						3
2					*	*		*		*			4
3											*		1
4			*		*	*	*	*			*	*	7
5	*	*			*	*	*	*	*	*		*	9
6													0
7													0
8				*	*	*	*	*	*	*	*		8
9					*	*	*		*	*			5
10													0
11													0
12					*	*			*				3
13	*		*		*		*						4
14	*	*						*	*	*		*	6
15		*			*	*	*		*		*		6
16					*	*	*		*				4
17					*		*		*			*	4
18			*	*	*	*	*		*	*		*	8
19													0
20				*			*	*	*	**		*	6
21	*	*		*	*	*	*		*				0
22													0
23					*		*		*	*			4
24					*								1
25						*	*	*		*			4
Totals	4	4	3	4	15	12	14	7	12	9	4	6	

Note. An asterisk signifies that an item was successfully completed. From *Rehabilitation of Memory* by B. Wilson, 1987. New York: Guilford Press. Reprinted by permission.

[a]Items corresponding to numbers: 1, remembering a first name; 2, remembering a surname; 3, remembering a hidden belonging; 4, remembering an appointment; 5, immediate remembering of a short route; 6, delayed remembering of a short route; 7, remembering an errand; 8, learning a new skill; 9, orientation; 10, date; 11, face recognition; 12, picture recognition.

assess whether or not memory failures occurred during treatment. All the patients in Table 16-1 were judged by an occupational therapist to have memory problems. The mean number of correct responses was 3.76, with a range of 0–9 and a standard deviation of 2.84. A group of 16 people judged by an occupational therapist not to have memory problems scored a mean number of 10.12 correct responses, with a range of 9–12 and a standard deviation of 1.16. The test was also given to three Korsakoff patients, and their results can be seen in Table 16-2.

A small group of 20 non-brain-damaged people between the ages of 16 and 65 years has been tested, and all of them passed all the items. Therefore, any failure is likely to be abnormal, at least in the under-65 age group. (We do not yet know how severely depressed people would perform, but we plan to investigate this at a later date.)

A preliminary estimate of reliability was made by testing 11 patients on two occasions, 1 week apart, using alternative forms of the test. The correlation was .85. Interrater reliability was explored by requiring two raters to observe seven subjects on the same occasion. Agreement was 100%.

The RBMT would also appear to be sensitive to changes over time. (This is discussed further in "The Group Treatment," below.) Furthermore, it may prove to be a useful instrument in the assessment of dementia; a pilot study to determine this is currently under way with Zimmerman and his colleagues in Darmstadt, Germany, and with Alan Baddeley in Cambridge, England.

The Prices Test

The second study I wish to describe involves an instrument for measuring retrograde amnesia (RA). There are existing tests that attempt to determine the length of RA (e.g., Meudell, Northen, Snowden, & Neary, 1980; Squire & Cohen, 1982), but these tests are not always easy to obtain or update. Furthermore, although these tests can detect gaps of several years, they are insensitive to gaps of a few months. Another limitation is caused by the likelihood that young people may fail to remember events that happened

Table 16-2. Results of Three Korsakoff Patients on the RBMT Items

			Items												
Patient	Sex	Age	1	2	3	4	5	6	7	8	9	10	11	12	Totals
M. O.	F	52	0	0	0	0	0	0	0	0	0	0	0	0	0
A. B.	M	45	0	0	1	0	1	1	1	0	0	1	1	1	7
T. B.	M	46	0	0	0	0	0	0	0	0	0	1	1	1	3

Note. Item numbers are as in Table 16-1. 0, item was failed; 1, item was passed.

several years earlier, not because of amnesia but because they were previously too young to take much notice of what was going on around them. Thus, the RA tests can provide fairly useful information about elderly Korsakoff patients, but they may not be at all helpful in the testing of young alcoholics.

The Prices Test was triggered off in my mind in 1980 when I was treating Mr. B. (Wilson, 1982), an intelligent man who insisted (wrongly) that the Prime Minister of Great Britain at that time was Harold Wilson. In an attempt to determine whether Mr. B.'s RA extended back to the time of Harold Wilson's premiership for everything, or whether he was closer in time for some things, I asked him to estimate the cost of various common items (e.g., a pint of milk, a loaf of bread, etc.). Mr. B. underestimated the cost of every item, but by differing amounts. Following that preliminary study, a list of 25 items was drawn up and administered to 120 non-brain-damaged people aged from 16 to 65 years. The 10 items with the least variability were selected for the Prices Test.

The test is scored in the following manner:

1. The difference between the price estimated and the current price of the item is obtained.

2. The resultant figure is compared with the standard deviation. If the difference is equal to or less than one standard deviation, the subject scores 0 for that item.

3. If the difference between the estimated price and the current price is greater than one standard deviation, scoring is as follows: between one and two standard deviations, score 1; between two and three standard deviations, score 2; between three and four standard deviations, score 3; anything over four standard deviations, score 4.

4. Note for each item whether the difference is an overestimate or an underestimate. For overestimates use positive sign, and for underestimates use negative sign.

5. Sum the positive and negative scores separately.

T. B., a 46-year-old man with Korsakoff's syndrome, gave the answers shown in Table 16-3.

At the time of writing, the test has been given to 50 brain-damaged adults. Those without memory impairment have done slightly worse than the normal controls. Those with memory impairment (as measured by the RBMT) have done considerably worse. The results are shown in Table 16-4.

The Prices Test has several advantages. It is quick and easy to administer, and it is fairly easy to keep the items up to date. It is also more appropriate for many people than the "famous events" or "famous personalities" tests that are usually given to estimate RA. This is because more people are likely to remain ignorant about famous events and personalities than they are about the cost of items that enter into their daily lives; also, if people are famous they tend to remain so for considerable lengths of time,

Table 16-3. Performance of a 46-Year-Old Korsakoff Patient on the Prices Test

Item	Estimated price	Actual price	*SD*	Score
Loaf of bread	20 pence	43 pence	6 pence	−3
Pint of milk	15 pence	22 pence	2 pence	−3
New "Mini" car	2000 pounds	3000 pounds	900 pounds	−1
Pack of cigarettes	80 pence	1 pound, 7 pence	17 pence	−1
Guardian (newspaper)	12 pence	23 pence	5 pence	−2
Gallon of gasoline	1 pound	1 pound, 69 pence	17 pence	−4
1 lb. jar of jam	30 pence	38 pence	14 pence	0
Fish and chips	40 pence	64 pence	20 pence	−1
First-class stamp	5 pence	15.5 pence	0.5 pence	−4
Cup of coffee	30 pence	29 pence	8 pence	0

Note. Total score, −19.

so this means that such tests are insensitive to periods of RA lasting only a few months. Prices, on the other hand, change frequently (at least in Great Britain!). The test still needs considerable attention, and at present my colleague Janet Cockburn and I are collecting information about the cost of the items over the past 10 years. We hope to be able to provide a table whereby the scores obtained on the Prices Test can be converted into a mean number of months or years behind the current one. As some patients, particularly those with frontal lobe impairment, overestimate the prices, the

Table 16-4. The Mean Scores of 50 Brain-Damaged Patients on the Prices Test

Group	*n*[a]	Underestimates	Overestimates
All patients	50	8.17	2.42
Memory-impaired patients[b]	38	10.11	2.78
Non-memory-impaired patients	12	2.83	1.50
Korsakoffs	3	15.60	1.00
Postencephalitics	4	12.25	8.50
Patients with amnesic syndrome (not Korsakoff)	2	12.50	0.50
Patients with frontal lobe impairment	7	8.57	4.14
Patients with severe head injuries	18	8.00	3.00
Patients with right cerebrovascular accidents	8	4.60	2.00
Patients with tumors (left hemisphere)	1	15.00	3.00
Patients with tumors (right hemisphere)	2	3.00	0.50
Patients with multiple problems	5	13.40	0.60

[a]Some patients were in more than one category.

[b]Patients with more than three failures on the RBMT.

table will presumably have to allow for inflation and place the subjects at some point in the future!

I now propose to describe two treatment studies carried out at Rivermead, which I believe to be directly related to the treatment of alcoholic patients with memory deficits. The first is a single-case study, described in detail elsewhere (Wilson, 1982), and the second is a group study (Wilson, Cooper, & Kennerley, 1983).

The Single-Case Treatment

Single-case experimental designs are often more useful than group studies in evaluating treatment of individuals. The latter are more concerned with means or averages rather than with individual responses. Group studies do not usually report on how many people improved, how many remained unchanged, or how many deteriorated following any given treatment. In single-case studies, not only is the treatment tailored to the individual's particular needs, but responses to treatment are also continuously monitored and evaluated. Furthermore, effects of spontaneous recovery or improvements over time are subjected to controls set up within the design of the experiment. The several designs available are described more fully in Wilson and Baddeley (1986) and Wilson (1987).

The multiple-baseline designs are particularly useful in rehabilitation, as they are both flexible and adaptable to a wide range of problems and situations. The example I describe here is that of Mr. B., mentioned above (Wilson, 1982). Mr. B. had a bilateral cerebrovascular accident in April 1980, when he was 51 years old. He came to Rivermead 5 months after the stroke and was assessed in the clinical psychology department. Results indicated that he was a highly intelligent person with no physical or intellectual problems apart from a severe memory deficit. He was offered 6 weeks of memory training, and a program was designed for this purpose (see Table 16-5). Mr. B. followed this program for 4 days a week for the period of 6 weeks. From Friday to Sunday each week, he returned home.

A multiple-baseline procedure was used to evaluate the effectiveness of treatment. Baselines were taken on all four specific problems each day for 2 weeks. At the end of this time the baselines were stable, apart from remembering the timetable, which appeared to be improving without any special training. The second problem remembering the names of 12 members of the staff, was then tackled by means of visual imagery. The names were drawn for Mr. B. on cards. "Dr. Hunt," for example, was depicted as a hunting scene, and "Laurette" was drawn as a launderette. Improvement occurred only after the visual-imagery procedure was introduced. A week later, a strategy was introduced to help Mr. B. remember the shopping list: A first-letter mnemonic was introduced, and Mr. B. was told

Table 16-5. Daily Timetable for Mr. B.

Time	Department	Tasks
9–10:30 A.M.	Occupational Therapy	Write biography.
10:30–10:45 A.M.	Canteen	Coffee break.
10:45 A.M.–12 noon	Occupational Therapy	Verbal-memory tasks: Find day, date, etc.; write down. Read newspaper articles using PQRST strategy (Glasgow, Zeiss, Barrera, & Lewinsohn, 1977). Listen to tapes of stories, etc. Answer questions set by occupational therapist, etc.
12 noon–1:30 P.M.	Ward	Lunch break.
1:30–2:20 P.M.	Clinical Psychology	Nonverbal-memory tasks (e.g., Benton Visual Retention Test, Rey–Osterreith Figure, Rey–Davis Non-Verbal Learning, pursuit rotor, finger mazes, etc.).
2:30–3:15 P.M.	Clinical Psychology memory group	Work with other memory-impaired people at memory games, mnemonics, practice with notices, timers, diaries, etc.
3:15–3:30 P.M.	Canteen	Tea break.
3:30–4:45 P.M.	Clinical Psychology	Work on specific problem areas: remembering the daily timetable; remembering names of staff; remembering a shopping list; remembering short routes.
4:45 P.M.	Ward	

that the initial letters of the 10 items could be rearranged to spell the words "GO SHOPPING." The items were then written down and shown to him: grapes, oranges, sugar, ham, olives, paper, pears, ink, nails, and grass seed. For the next 2 days, Mr. B. needed reminding of the cue words. Once reminded, he remembered more words than in the baseline period. Thereafter he remembered the cue words too, and rapidly reached 100% success. The fourth and final problem to be tackled was the learning of eight short routes around the rehabilitation unit. Each day, prior to his treatment, all the signs in the unit were covered up. (Mr. B. usually found his way around the unit, with some difficulty, by first reading the signs and then reading instructions in his specially compiled notebook.) We wanted to see whether he could remember the routes without resorting to external aids. Four different methods were tried: extra rehearsal, fading out a chalk line, a letter-sequencing cue, and a letter–word mnemonic strategy. All of these failed to improve Mr. B.'s learning of the routes. However, Mr. B. had already demonstrated that he was able to circumvent the problem himself, by reading the signs and referring to his notebook. The most straightforward strategy was obviously the right one for him to use. The design and the results of this procedure can be seen in Figure 16-1.

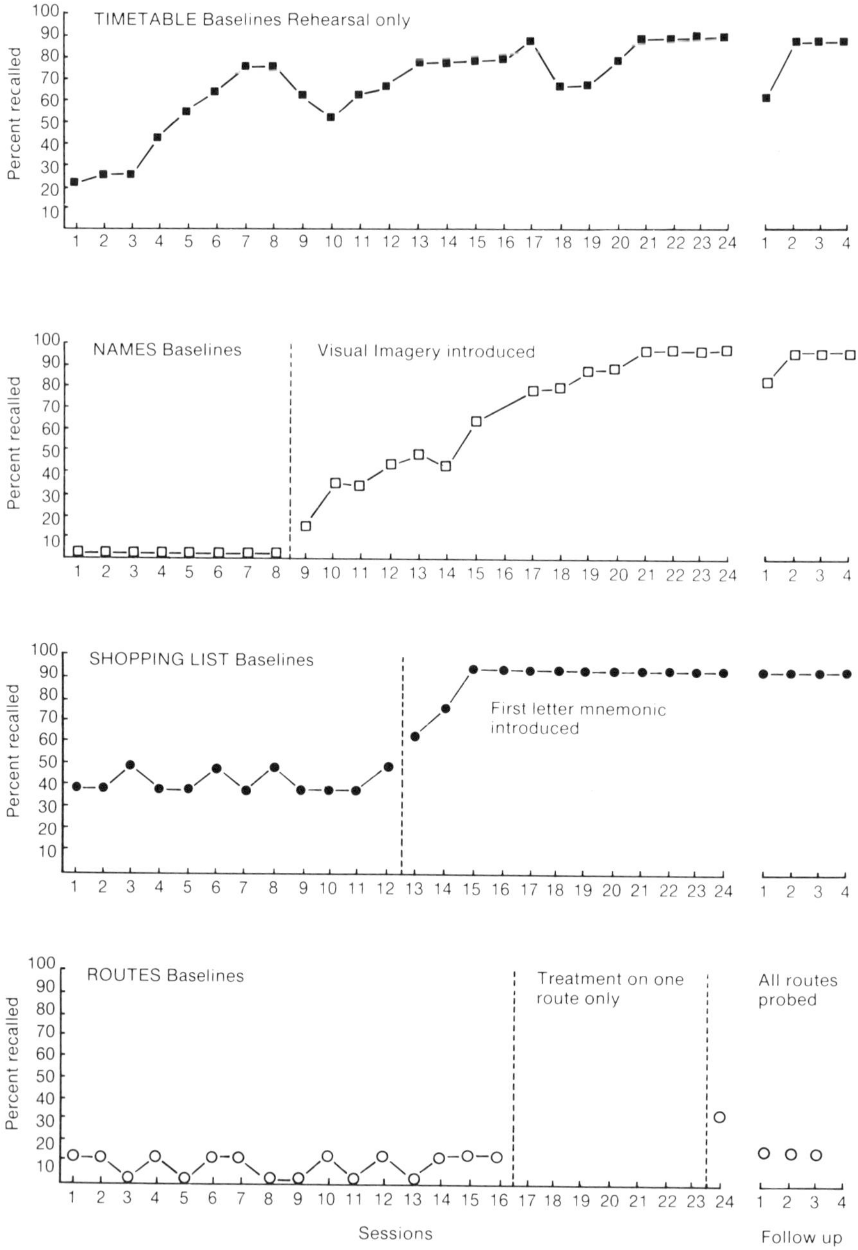

Figure 16-1. A multiple-baseline design to treat four specific memory problems, together with follow-up after a 3-month delay. (From "Success and Failure in Memory Training after a Cerebral Vascular Accident" by B. Wilson, 1982, *Cortex*, *18*, 581–594. Reprinted by permission.)

It can be seen that at a 3-month follow-up, Mr. B. retained most of the information he had previously learned. He has been seen in his own home twice since then. It was possible to reassess him on three of the problem areas: timetable, names, and shopping list. When last seen, 2½ years after his discharge from Rivermead, he recalled 90% of the shopping list accurately, including the cue words, and 55% of his timetable. When asked how many names of staff he could remember, he recalled only two (20%). However, when he was shown the original drawings (visual images), the recall was 80%. In addition, he has devised several strategies for overcoming some of his everyday difficulties. He also uses the first-letter mnemonic when he goes to the shops (although he takes a list in case the mnemonic fails). Furthermore, he asks his daughter to make pictures of the names of people he is trying to remember. He remains, nevertheless, severely amnesic, and is very dependent upon his wife. It is quite impossible, of course, for him to work. However, it has been possible to teach him new information, which he has retained well.

The information that Mr. B. has learned has been of some practical benefit, unlike that described in some studies, which have attempted to improve the memory functioning of brain-damaged adults by teaching them paired associates or lists of words that are unrelated to the patients' daily living. There is no convincing evidence to suggest that training on a laboratory task will generalize to everyday situations. Indeed, the evidence from Mr. B.'s case suggests that such carryover is unlikely to happen: His intensive general memory training resulted in very little improvement at all, apart from that on procedural-memory tasks. Such lack of support for generalizing from laboratory task training is in keeping with other findings (see, e.g., Brooks & Baddeley, 1976).

The multiple-baseline-across-behaviors design described above would be an effective method for assessing the effects of intervention with many alcoholic patients. The same would be true of a multiple-baseline-across-subjects design, should there be a small group of patients requiring treatment. Although this is not, strictly speaking, a single-case study design, the problems encountered with a small group of subjects are similar to those faced when dealing with individual subjects.

The Group Treatment

The final study to be described here is an investigation of the effectiveness of group training on memory functioning in patients with acquired brain damage (Wilson *et al.*, 1983). Memory groups are organized several times each year at Rivermead. Each course lasts for 3 weeks, and each session is held for 45 minutes a day, 5 days a week. There are usually between four and six people in a group, each of whom has a memory problem of one kind or another. The type and severity of these problems vary considerably: Some people have very specific problems, such as difficulty in remembering their way around the unit; others will have much more severe amnesia; and some will have general intellectual impairment in addition to memory deficits.

It became important to establish whether or not the memory groups really did improve memory functioning. There are no reports on the effectiveness of memory training carried out in groups, apart from those examining the effects of reality orientation (RO) with the elderly (e.g., Holden & Woods, 1982). The evidence suggests that RO can result in measurable but limited and often transient improvement. Furthermore, RO includes few specific strategies for improving memory. In contrast, work with younger patients using, for example, visual imagery (Jones, 1974; Wilson, 1981), external aids (Fowler, Hart, & Sheehan, 1972), and verbal techniques (Cermak, 1975; Wilson, 1982), has demonstrated improved performance on particular tasks. None of these studies, however, taught people in groups. So, on the one hand, we have group studies with the elderly, which tend not to use specific memory training; on the other hand, we have reports of specific strategies taught to younger individuals outside group situations. Although evidence suggests that neither practice nor training improves memory generally (Milner, Corkin, & Teuber, 1968; Wilson, 1982), the relevant studies were with patients who had severe global amnesia. There have been few investigations to discover whether those with less severe memory problems, such as head-injured patients or alcoholics without Korsakoff's syndrome, can benefit from such training. One such study (Jones, 1974) demonstrated that patients with left and right temporal lobectomies were able to benefit from visual imagery.

Early in 1982, Zafra Cooper and I designed a study that we hoped would answer the following question: Does memory training in groups improve general memory functioning in patients with acquired brain damage? The design of the study can be seen in Table 16-6.

Subjects were selected from patients at Rivermead. All patients referred to the clinical psychology department for memory treatment were considered potential candidates for the memory group, provided (1) that their scores on the preliminary assessment were in the impaired range and (2) that there was no evidence of spontaneous improvement prior to treatment. The first five suitable referrals were assigned to Treatment A, the second five to Treatment B, and so forth. There was no reason to believe that this procedure would introduce a systematic bias.

Of the 25 subjects referred, 22 were suitable for inclusion in the study. Of these 22, 2 were discharged before completion of treatment, leaving a total of 20 (8 of whom were female). Ages ranged from 13 to 59 years. Among the patients, 15 had received severe head injuries, 4 had suffered cerebrovascular accidents, and 1 was postencephalitic. Two Korsakoff pa-

Table 16-6. Design of the Memory Group Evaluation Study

Week	A (patients 1–5)	B (patients 6–10)	A (patients 11–15)	B (patients 16–20)
1	Pretreatment assessment	Pretreatment assessment	Pretreatment assessment	Pretreatment assessment
2	Pretreatment assessment	Pretreatment assessment	Pretreatment assessment	Pretreatment assessment
3, 4, 5	Memory group	Problem-solving group	Memory group	Problem-solving group
6	Intermediate assessment	Intermediate assessment	Intermediate assessment	Intermediate assessment
7, 8, 9	Problem-solving group	Memory group	Problem-solving group	Memory group
10	Posttreatment assessment	Posttreatment assessment	Posttreatment assessment	Posttreatment assessment

tients also attended the memory group on a part-time basis. Their results are not included here, but both improved their scores on the RBMT after treatment. For example, M. O., a 52-year-old woman, failed to score on two pretreatment assessments with the RBMT. Following treatment, she succeeded in passing five items on this test.

Assessment Procedures

At all four assessments, memory functioning was assessed using the following tests. (An asterisk after a test indicates that alternative versions of it are available.)

STANDARDIZED TESTS

1. Orientation (Wechsler, 1945).
2. Prose Recall—Immediate and Delayed (passages from the Wechsler Memory Scale; Wechsler, 1945).*
3. Digit Span (Wechsler, 1945).*
4. Paired-Associate Learning (Randt, Brown, & Osbourne, 1980).*

BEHAVIORAL MEASURES

1. The RBMT (described above).*
2. A questionnaire (Harris, 1980) regarding the use of external aids.
3. A rating scale (Kapur & Pearson, 1982) to assess the patients' own estimation of their memory difficulties.

Treatment Procedures

The memory group received the following six treatment stages:

1. Playing memory games and practicing various memory exercises.
2. Group discussion of problem-solving techniques.
3. Introduction to external memory aids (e.g., notebooks and electronic instruments).
4. Practice in the use of external aids.
5. Introduction to internal strategies (e.g., visual imagery, mnemonics).
6. Practice in the use of internal strategies.

The syllabus of the group may be found in Wilson and Moffat (1984).

The problem-solving group was designed to be as much like the memory group as possible, but no special techniques were introduced for improving or exercising memory. Obviously it was not possible to avoid memory tasks altogether, as memory is involved in all but the most reflexive activity. The tasks selected for the problem-solving group included both verbal and nonverbal tasks taken from a variety of sources, including the following:

1. *The Five Day Course in Thinking* (De Bono, 1979).
2. Raven's Progressive Matrices (Raven, 1960).
3. *Luria's Neuropsychological Investigation* (Christensen, 1975).
4. *Games of Logic* (Berloquin, 1980).
5. *Evans' Attainment Tests* (Wing & West, 1973).
6. A series of tests devised by the therapists at Rivermead (e.g., "How many words can you make from the word 'rehabilitation'?").

A comparison (*t* test) between Groups A and B at both pretreatment assessments yielded no significant differences on any of the measures of memory impairment.

A series of two-way analyses of variance was carried out. There was a significant improvement on the RBMT but not on any of the other measures, $F\ (2, 36) = 7.47$, $p < .01$. In order to determine the nature of this main effect, a series of Tukey's tests were performed. Results showed that improvement occurred both after the memory training and after the training in problem solving. This was slightly disappointing; however, if we look at the individual results, there were 11 people who improved more after being in the memory group; 5 people who improved more after being in the problem-solving group, and 4 who did not change after either group. Thus, even though the differences did not reach significance, there was a tendency for more people to improve after the memory group. It should be made clear, however, that changes in memory functioning were in most cases small. Dramatic improvement did not occur, so the results should be interpreted with caution.

One interesting finding was that only the RBMT showed changes. This test was designed to assess everyday memory problems, and as patients' scores on the first and second pretreatment assessment were stable, it appears that the test is more sensitive to change than the other measures.

It could be argued that the memory training included tasks similar to those in the RBMT, and this is why more improvement occurred after the memory group. However, this is unlikely to be true for two reasons. First, the memory group also included tasks similar to the standardized tests (e.g., prose recall and paired associates), yet improvement did not occur on these tests. Second, some people improved their RBMT scores after training in the problem-solving group, which did not include tasks similar to those on the RBMT. We might have achieved more significant results if the problem-solving group had been less similar to the memory group. The approach to memory training at Rivermead emphasizes that patients should attempt to find a way around their memory difficulties. In many ways this is a problem-solving activity, and, as such, is close to the activities carried out in the problem-solving group.

In summarizing the results of the group study, it should be pointed out that although improvement in memory functioning occurred after training in either of the groups, memory training tended to be better than training in the problem-solving group. The results can be regarded as encouraging, because more people improved after being in the memory group; it is possible that a larger study might have demonstrated a significant effect. The research continues, and a 1-year follow-up study of all the patients is currently under way.

Summary and General Conclusions

In this chapter, I have described some approaches to the assessment and treatment of everyday memory problems. Many of these problems are experienced by alcoholic and Korsakoff patients. The RBMT is an attempt to bridge the gap between standardized tests and naturalistic measures of memory. The relationship between performance on conventional tests and performance in everyday life is far from clear, and observations, questionnaires, and checklists may lead to unreliable, inaccurate, or subjectively biased information. The RBMT consists of items analogous to real-life situations; these are administered and scored in a standardized way. The test can be used (1) to indicate the severity of memory impairment; (2) to identify which aspects of memory functioning are likely to cause problems outside the test situation; (3) to indicate which skills in particular require treatment; and (4) to monitor change over time.

The Prices Test is a simple procedure that involves asking a patient the cost of 10 everyday items. The main purpose of the test is to estimate the length of RA but it has other uses as well. It can, for example, be used as an adjunct to "activities of daily living" assessment, and may be useful in measuring cognitive improvement during a detoxification or "drying-out" period in a treatment unit for alcoholics.

There are two treatment procedures described in the chapter: a single-case study using a multiple-baseline-across-behaviors design, and an evaluation of memory training in groups. The single-case experimental designs are powerful tools in the evaluation of individual treatments. Frequently used in behavior modification programs, these designs are also suitable for many other problems and are probably applicable to any diagnostic group. There are signs that neuropsychologists are beginning to recognize the value of single-case methodology, and some of them are already incorporating such an approach into their treatment programs.

The chapter concludes with an investigation of the effectiveness of group training on memory functioning in adults with acquired brain damage. The results are encouraging but not dramatic. My own view is that individual memory therapy is a preferable method of treatment, but the aim should not be to improve or retrain memory skills. Rather, therapy should attempt (1) to teach patients ways to bypass their memory deficits as far as possible and (2) to discover the most efficient way for individuals to retain new information. These ideas are expanded elsewhere (Wilson, 1984). However, even though individual training is preferred, memory groups are to be encouraged for two reasons. First, they provide additional therapy for those undergoing individual treatment. Second, groups may be of indirect therapeutic value in enabling patients to interact with others having similar difficulties. Such interaction may reduce the fears about madness and insanity that beset some amnesic people; it may lead to greater insight about the severity of memory impairment; and it may lead to improved confidence when group members realize they can succeed at some tasks. Perhaps the greatest indirect therapeutic advantage from such groups, though, is that they can be very enjoyable, giving pleasure that may otherwise rarely be available to many cognitively impaired people.

Appendix: The Rivermead Behavioural Memory Test

(All items are scored 1 or 0 unless otherwise specified. Total possible score is 12. A more sensitive scoring method is now available.)

1. *Remembering a name.* The patient is shown a photograph and told the person's first name and surname. Both names are tested after a delay, during which other tests are presented. One point is scored for correct recall of first name, and 1 point for correct recall of surname.

2. *Remembering a hidden belonging.* A possession of the patient (e.g., timetable, comb, or pen) is borrowed and secreted, and the patient is instructed to ask for it before leaving at the end of the test and to remember where it has been hidden.

3. *Remembering an appointment.* The patient is told to ask a particular question relating to the near future when he or she hears an alarm ring.

4. *Picture recognition.* Line drawings of 10 common objects are shown one at a time for 5 seconds each, and the patient is required to name each. He or she is later required to select the original 10 from a set of 20. (All need to be correct to score 1 point.)

5. *Prose recall.* The patient is read a short passage of prose and is asked to relate as much of it as he or she can remember, both immediately and after a delay.

6. *Remembering a short route.* The tester traces a short route within the test area comprising five sections. The patient is required to reproduce this route immediately and after a delay.

7. *Remembering an errand.* While demonstrating the route, the tester leaves an envelope at a specified location along the route. The patient is required to leave the envelope in the same location.

8. *Orientation.* The patient is asked the year, month, day of the week, place, and city. (All need to be correct to score 1 point.)

9. *Date.* This is scored separately from the other orientation questions, as the correlation between items 8 and 9 is not high.

10. *Face recognition.* The patient is shown photographs of 5 faces and later required to recognize them from a set of 10. (All need to be correct to score 1 point.)

11. *Learning a new skill.* The patient is given three trials to program a message into an electronic memory aid. There are six steps involved in programming the message. (All six steps must be correct by the third trial in order to score 1 point.)

Instructions for administering and scoring this test can be found in Wilson (1987).

References

Baddeley, A. D., & Wilson, B. (1983). *Differences among amnesias and between amnesics: the role of single case methodology in theoretical analysis and practical treatment.* Paper presented at the Princeton Amnesia Conference, Princeton, NJ.

Berloquin, P. (1980). *Games of logic.* London: Unwin.

Brooks, D. N., & Baddeley, A. D. (1976). What can amnesic patients learn? *Neuropsychologia, 14*, 111–122.

Cermak, L. S. (1975). Imagery as an aid to retrieval for Korsakoff patients. *Cortex, 11*, 163–169.

Christensen, A. L. (1975). *Luria's neuropsychological investigation.* New York: Spectrum.

De Bono, E. (1979). *The five day course in thinking.* Harmondsworth, England: Penguin.

Fowler, R., Hart, J., & Sheehan, M. (1972). A prosthetic memory: An application of the prosthetic environment concept. *Rehabilitation Counseling Bulletin, 15,* 80–85.

Glasgow, R. E., Zeiss, R. A., Barrera, M., & Lewinsohn, P. M. (1977). Case studies on remediating memory deficits in brain damaged individuals. *Journal of Clinical Psychology, 33,* 1049–1054.

Harris, J. E. (1980). Memory aids people use: Two interview studies. *Memory and Cognition, 8,* 753–758.

Holden, U. P., & Woods, R. T. (1982). *Reality orientation: Psychological approaches to the confused elderly.* London: Churchill Livingstone.

Jones, M. (1974). Imagery as a mnemonic aid after left temporal lobectomy: Contrast between material specific and general memory disorders. *Neuropsychologia, 12,* 21–30.

Kapur, N., & Pearson, D. (1982). *Memory symptoms and memory performance of neurological patients.* Paper presented at the Fifth European Conference of the International Neuropsychological Society, Deauville, France.

Meudell, P. R., Northern, B., Snowden, J. S., & Neary, D. (1980). Long term memory for famous voices in amnesic and normal subjects. *Neuropsychologia, 18,* 133–139.

Milner, B., Corkin, S., & Teuber, H. L. (1968). Further analysis of the hippocampal amnesic syndrome: A 14 year follow-up study of H. M. *Neuropsychologia, 6,* 215–234.

Randt, C. J., Brown, E. R., & Osbourne, D. P. (1980). A memory test for longitudinal measurement of mild to moderate deficits. *Clinical Neuropsychiatry, 6,* 184–194.

Raven, J. (1960). *Guide to the Standard Progressive Matrices.* London: H. K. Lewis.

Squire, L. R., & Cohen, N. J. (1982). Remote memory, retrograde amnesia and the neuropsychology of memory. In L. S. Cermak (Ed.), *Human memory and amnesia* (pp. 275–303). Hillsdale, NJ: Erlbaum.

Sunderland, A., Harris, J. E., & Baddeley, A. D. (1983). Do laboratory tests predict everyday memory? A neuropsychological study. *Journal of Verbal Learning and Verbal Behaviour, 22,* 341–357.

Wechsler, D. (1945). A standardized memory scale for clinical use. *Journal of Psychology, 19,* 87–95.

Wilson, B. (1981). Teaching a patient to remember people's names after removal of a left temporal lobe tumour. *Behavioural Psychotherapy, 9,* 338–344.

Wilson, B. (1982). Success and failure in memory training after a cerebral vascular accident. *Cortex, 18,* 581–594.

Wilson, B. (1984). Memory therapy in practice. In B. Wilson & N. Moffat (Eds), *Clinical management of memory problems* (pp. 84–111). London: Croom Helm.

Wilson, B. (1987). *Rehabilitation of memory.* New York: Guilford Press.

Wilson, B., & Baddeley, A. D. (1986). Single case methodology and the remediation of dyslexia. In G. Pavlides & D. Fisher (Eds.), *Dyslexia: Neuropsychology and treatment* (pp. 263–277). Hillsdale, NJ: Erlbaum.

Wilson, B., Cockburn, J., & Baddeley, A. D. (1985). *The Rivermead Behavioural Memory Test.* Reading, Berks, England: Thames Valley Test Company.

Wilson, B., Cooper, Z., & Kennerley, H. (1983). *An investigation into the effectiveness of group training on memory functioning in patients with acquired brain damage.* Paper presented at the meeting of the Society for Research in Rehabilitation, London.

Wilson, B., & Moffat, N. (1984). Running a memory group. In B. Wilson & N. Moffat (Eds.), *Clinical management of memory problems* (pp. 171–198). London: Croom Helm.

Wing, A., & West, G. (1973). *Evans' Attainment Tests.* London: Evans Brothers.

17

Discussion

Recovery and Remediation of Neuropsychological Functions: Implications for Alcoholism Rehabilitation Process and Outcome

DENNIS M. DONOVAN
R. DALE WALKER
DANIEL R. KIVLAHAN

Introduction

Alcohol ingestion to toxic levels is known to have acute, adverse effects upon cognitive function, particularly on memory tasks (Ryan & Butters, 1983). Furthermore, there is a substantial body of evidence, including much that is included in the present volume, that significant neuropsychological deficits are also associated with long-term abusive drinking and alcoholism (Chelune & Parker, 1981; Goldman, 1983; Miller & Saucedo, 1983; Parsons & Farr, 1981; Wilkinson & Carlen, 1981). The most commonly reported areas of impairment include abstract reasoning, utilization of feedback to help learn new concepts, attention and concentration span, cognitive flexibility, and both nonverbal-memory and subtle verbal-memory functions. Parsons (1977) proposed that the observed deficits in these neuropsychological areas represent important factors in the general adaptive functioning of alcoholics.

The extent and relative permanence of the deficits found among alcoholics would be expected to influence both the course and outcome of treatment. Goldman (1983) noted that in order to benefit from psychological treatment, one must be capable of receiving new information, integrating it with existing informational stores, and translating this input to more

Dennis M. Donovan, R. Dale Walker, and Daniel R. Kivlahan. Alcohol and Drug Dependence Treatment Programs, Veterans Administration Medical Center, Seattle, Washington; Department of Psychiatry and Behavioral Sciences, University of Washington School of Medicine, Seattle, Washington.

concrete behavioral change. The prerequisite cognitive competencies involved in the therapeutic process appear to be those in which alcoholics are often found to be impaired. Tarter (1976) suggested, for instance, that reduced abstracting abilities might minimize the utility of "insight" therapies in which individuals must use cognitive strategies in redirecting their lifestyles and gaining control over drinking behavior. The work of Parsons, Goldman, and Wilson presented in the present section provides a relatively new perspective on the relationship between such neuropsychological deficits and treatment.

Ecologically Relevant Assessment

Miller and Saucedo (1983) indicated that the incidence of cognitive deficits among alcoholics is sufficiently high that diagnostic and rehabilitation centers should screen patients for such impairment. Much of the assessment that has been conducted within both clinical and research contexts has emerged from traditional clinical-neuropsychological origins (Goldman, 1983), as exemplified by the work of Fitzhugh, Fitzhugh, and Reitan (1960, 1965). As Goldman has noted, such an approach employs tests with demonstrated sensitivity to the behavioral consequences of central nervous system damage. This assessment model has contributed significantly to our current knowledge base concerning the specific functional impairment and patterns of deficits associated with alcoholism. However, it is at times difficult to translate the meaning of specific tests to the ways in which the assessed function is manifested behaviorally.

As a result of such difficulties, an attempt has been made over the recent past to develop and validate "ecologically relevant" tests. Such measures are meant to match the behavioral requirements of the real world as closely as possible, while also being sensitive to alcohol-induced impairments (Goldman, 1983). Becker, Butters, Hermann, and D'Angelo (1983), for instance, investigated the ability of alcoholics and nonalcoholic control subjects to learn to associate names with faces. It was assumed that the memory and learning deficits associated with alcoholism would interfere with this task, which appears to represent the type of situation involved in their social function (e.g., learning to make new, nondrinking acquaintances). The alcoholics, as hypothesized, made significantly more errors while learning these associations than did controls.

Wilson's work (see Chapter 16, this volume) on the development of the Rivermead Behavioural Memory Test represents an attempt to standardize a battery of tasks within the framework of ecological relevance. It represents the use of behavioral assessment within natural settings to observe the nature and extent of memory problems manifested in real-life situations. The tasks involve abilities such as associating a name with a face, remembering to ask for a personal belonging at the end of the testing session, remembering to follow an instruction behaviorally after a delay, remembering a route, recognizing faces, orientation, and learning to program a message into an electronic memory aid. Such tasks represent ones that might be encountered within a rehabilitation center (e.g., remembering a counselor's name, being able to find a room within the hospital, being on time for appointments). The results presented by Wilson indicate that nonalcoholic patients of a general rehabilitation center who are judged by their occupational therapists as having a memory problem perform poorly on such tasks. No evidence is presented concerning the battery's sensitivity to alcohol-related impairment.

In Chapter 16, Wilson has also described an interesting measure of retrograde amnesia, the Prices Test. Subjects are asked to estimate the current market prices of 10 common items (e.g., a pint of milk, a cup of coffee, a gallon of gasoline, a newspaper). The score represents an index of the degree of error between a patient's estimates and the actual values. Wilson notes that the Prices Test has a number of advantages. An important one is that it may be a more appropriate measure of retrograde amnesia for younger patients than tests of "famous people" or "famous events," since younger people would be expected to maintain a greater awareness of the cost of everyday items.

While no data are provided concerning the direct utility of the Prices Test with alcoholics, it again represents an attempt to bridge the gap between standardized measures and naturalistic measures of memory. Recently, Sussman, Rychtarik, Muesser, Glynn, and Prue (1986) have developed a test based upon a similar rationale. The measure is called the Product Recall Test. It consists of the names of 20 relatively familiar products in five categories: alcohol, deodorants, cereals, soft drinks, and pickup trucks. In a study of the measure, alcoholics were tested after a minimum of 3 weeks of sobriety. Following brief (10-second) exposure to each of the 20 slides, subjects were asked to recall as many items as possible. Performance on the task was related to treatment outcome at a 3-month follow-up. Abstainers had significantly better recall than did drinkers. It is of interest to note that there was no difference between these groups on the Graham–Kendall Memory for Designs Test, a measure described by Sussman *et al.* (1986) as "ecologically irrelevant" and included for comparison purposes.

It appears that measures having some correspondence to situations encountered in everyday life have some promise in the assessment of alcoholics. Measures specific to the treatment setting are similarly important to consider. For instance, Becker and Jaffe (1984) presented a film dealing with a variety of aspects of alcoholism to inpatient alcoholics, members of Alcoholics Anonymous, and nonalcoholic patients from an orthopedic surgery ward. Following the film, subjects were given both recall and recognition tests. The inpatient alcoholics performed more poorly on both tests than either control group. The length of sobriety of the inpatient alcoholics moderated their performance. Those with less than 2 weeks of sobriety accounted for the observed differences; those with more than 2 weeks of sobriety performed comparably with the controls. Sanchez-Craig and Walker (1982) also assessed recall of treatment-relevant information. Alcoholics had been involved in a treatment program that focused on goal setting and interpersonal problem solving. One month after completion of the program, it was found that there were marked decrements in recall of the specific strategies the patients had previously learned. In each of these studies, the level of recall of treatment-relevant information was inversely related to the level of general cognitive deficits.

In summary, the approach to ecologically relevant assessment appears promising. A number of new measures, including those described by Wilson, are being developed. Tests should be available to assess information relevant both to general life function (e.g., Becker *et al.*, 1983; Sussman *et al.*, 1986) and to the treatment process (e.g., Becker & Jaffe, 1984; Sanchez-Craig & Walker, 1982). Further work is needed in this area. It is necessary to determine the extent to which skills assessed by ecologically relevant tests represent prerequisites for functioning well in the real world (Sussman *et al.*, 1986). Similarly, research is needed to determine the specificity of tests such as the Rivermead Behavioural Memory Test, the Prices Test, and the Product Recall Test to alcohol-related dysfunction. Finally, it would be important to determine the relationship between the loss of treatment-relevant information to the process and outcome of the rehabilitative endeavor.

Neuropsychology and the Process of Treatment

Work has been undertaken in an attempt to understand this latter relationship. As noted above, the level of neuropsychological impairment was found to be related to the deficits noted in the recall of alcohol-related and therapy-related information among alcoholics (Becker & Jaffe, 1984; Sanchez-Craig & Walker, 1982). O'Leary, Donovan, Chaney, and Walker (1979) similarly found that aspects of the treatment process were also related to such deficits. Alcoholics with higher levels of problem-solving and adaptive abilities were rated by clinicians as having functioned more adaptively during the course of treatment than were patients with impairments in these abilities. The former group of patients was also significantly more likely to complete the inpatient treatment program than were the more impaired patients.

In Chapter 14 of this volume, Parsons presents data from studies he and his colleagues have conducted in an attempt to explore further the relationship between neuropsychological deficits and the treatment process (Boon, 1982; Leber, Parsons, & Nichols, 1985). The general design involved administering a comprehensive battery of neuropsychological tests to alcoholics approximately 4 weeks following admission to inpatient treatment. At the end of the 9-week rehabilitation program, a patient's primary therapist, blind to the assessment results, rated the individual along a number of dimensions. Factor analysis of the clinical rating forms (Leber *et al.*, 1985) suggested three primary dimensions. The first represented cognitive functions assumed to be important to group psychotherapy. This factor was composed of ratings of the patients' ability to generalize, ability to reason by analogy, approach toward change in psychotherapy, and attitude toward planning change in their future lives. The second factor, representing interpersonal involvement in group therapy, was composed of ratings concerning personal level of involvement and participation in therapy. The third factor, composed of ratings of perceived change in psychological functioning and perceived therapeutic benefit, represented an index of clinical involvement and global progress in therapy. Therapists also rated patients with respect to their treatment prognosis or the anticipated outcome at 1 year following treatment.

The findings of this series of studies can be summarized in a general way. First, ratings across the three primary factors of the clinicians' ratings were significantly related to level of neuropsychological functioning. Patients evidencing greater levels of impairment were rated lower on these treatment-related factors. This finding is consistent with and extends that of O'Leary, Donovan, Chaney, and Walker (1979). Second, it appears that a measure assumed to have a high degree of ecological validity (e.g., associating names and faces) may be more predictive of therapist ratings than other less ecologically valid measures. Third, patients who, through cluster analysis of neuropsychological test results, were defined as having good problem-solving skills were rated higher on the therapists' rating scale than were those defined as having poor problem-solving skills. The latter individuals were rated as being less able to learn and as having fewer reasoning skills, as having less insight, and as deriving less benefit from therapy. Patients whose scores fell into the poor problem-solving subgroup were also predicted to have a poorer outcome at 1-year follow-up, with ratings that anticipated more drinking behavior and poorer cognitive functioning, vocational adjustment, and quality of life. Finally, as suggested by the latter results, alcoholic patients who were rated by therapists as having poorer prognoses had significantly greater impairment in neuropsychological function, particularly abstracting/problem solving and perceptual–motor skills, than those given good prognostic ratings.

These findings provide the most extensive data to date concerning the relationship between impairment and the treatment process. They also reflect both methodological and practical advances. While previous studies have attempted to develop ecologically valid measures (e.g., Becker *et al.*, 1983; Becker & Jaffe, 1984; Sussman *et al.*, 1986), there is still considerable distance between such measures and the ecological system in which they are expected to be anchored. For instance, it is clear that associating names with faces is a skill important to social interactions; however, deficits in such an ability are distant from other aspects of the treatment process. Evaluation of alcoholics' memory for treatment-relevant information, such as that presented in alcohol-related educational films (Becker & Jaffe, 1984) or lectures (Goldman & Rosenbaum, 1977), is less distant from treatment. The work of Parsons and his colleagues is an important step in attempting to define the salient features of the "ecosystem" of alcoholism treatment, against which the clinical and predictive utility of neuropsychological tests can be determined.

While the approach described above provides an advance in our conceptualization of the relationship between treatment and neuropsychological function, there remain limitations in it. First, the level of impairment is more highly related to rated cognitive behavior during therapy than to perceived therapeutic benefit or anticipated outcome. This suggests that a wide variety of patient factors other than or in addition to cognitive function may influence the therapeutic process (Wilkinson & Sanchez-Craig, 1981). Second, previous research has suggested that therapists' ratings of alcoholic patients, while having a significant impact on clinical decisions and therapeutic course, are influenced by a variety of implicit factors that may be relatively independent of patient characteristics (O'Leary, Donovan, Chaney, & O'Leary, 1979; O'Leary, Donovan, Chaney, & Speltz, 1979; O'Leary, Speltz, Donovan, & Walker, 1979). Thus, as Leber *et al.* (1985) noted, a wide variety of factors independent of neuropsychological status could have affected therapists' ratings of prognosis, and these other factors might have offset the level of cognitive impairment in the shaping of clinical judgments. Finally, no evidence yet exists concerning the predictive validity of such ratings. It would be of interest to determine the differential power of clinical judgments concerning prognosis versus assessed neuropsychological functioning in predicting actual outcome.

Neuropsychology and Treatment Outcome

The results presented in the preceding section suggest that the deficits found in many alcoholics may have a negative impact on the process of treatment. Inferences have similarly been drawn concerning the anticipated effects of neuropsychological deficits on the outcome of treatment. Neuropsychological impairment is usually associated with less effective adjustments to life tasks and demands (Parsons, 1977). The alcoholic is confronted by a wide array of such demands upon re-entry into the posthospital environment.

These demands have led Tarter (1976) and Chelune and Parker (1981) to suggest that difficulties in abstracting and problem solving make it less likely that alcoholics can successfully utilize those cognitive strategies involved in redirecting lifestyles and asserting control over drinking once they have left treatment.

Results from recent research provide some support for these assumptions. Guthrie and Elliot (1980), for example, found that impairment on a battery of tests assessing verbal learning, verbal memory, and visual–spatial memory was related to lower abstinence rates and reduced aftercare involvement at 6-month follow-up. Other investigators (Berglund, Leijonquist, & Horlen, 1977; Gregson & Taylor, 1977; O'Leary, Donovan, Chaney, & Walker, 1979) have also found poorer drinking outcomes for more impaired patients. Gregson and Taylor's (1977) findings suggest further that the level of impairment may be a more powerful predictor than measures of psychosocial or drinking-related variables.

Evidence suggests, then, that neuropsychological deficits associated with alcoholism are prognostic of subsequent outcome. However, the amount of variance accounted for in posttreatment functioning by measures of impairment is relatively small (Donovan, Kivlahan, & Walker, 1984). Neuropsychology's role in the prediction of treatment outcome continues to be undefined. The question thus remains concerning the centrality of neuropsychology in the prediction of treatment outcome.

In 1979, our research group (O'Leary & Donovan, 1979) began to investigate the interactive effects of neuropsychological impairment and length of inpatient hospitalization on treatment outcome among alcoholics. While posthospital environment was also assessed, the role of neuropsychology was assumed to be central and primary. It was hypothesized that alcoholics with a high degree of impairment would have poorer outcomes overall. This group was also expected to do more poorly following a 2-week hospitalization as compared to a 7-week hospitalization. On the other hand, patients with minimal or no impairment were expected to have a better overall outcome. The length of hospitalization was not expected to have a differential effect on outcome in this group.

The measure of function chosen was Reitan's (1973) Brain Age Quotient (BAQ), an age-adjusted index of current problem-solving abilities that had been found previously to discriminate alcoholics from matched controls (Schau & O'Leary, 1977). The six measures that comprise the BAQ are the Category Test, Tactual Performance Test (TPT) Time and Localization, and the Trail Making Test, Part B from the Halstead–Reitan Battery, and the Digit Symbol and Block Design subtests from the Wechsler Adult Intelligence Scale (WAIS). These represent six of the eight tests on which alcoholics have most consistently shown impairment compared to controls (Miller & Saucedo, 1983; Parsons & Farr, 1981). Subjects were assessed within their first week of hospitalization ($M = 6.3$ days $\pm$ 3.2) and reported an average of 23.7 days of sobriety (± 23.1) prior to the first day of testing. Analyses indicated that neither length of sobriety nor years of problem drinking was related to performance on the BAQ tests (Donovan *et al.*, 1984).

Subjects were randomly assigned to either a 2-week or a 7-week length of stay (LOS). A total of 245 male subjects completed their assigned treatments and entered into aftercare, consisting of once-weekly therapy meetings for a 9-month period. An overview of the general characteristics of the overall patient group is presented in Table 17-1. Subjects' drinking behavior and psychosocial function were assessed at 3-, 6-, and 9-month intervals following their completion of treatment. The findings from the study (Walker, Donovan, Kivlahan, & O'Leary, 1983) indicated that, overall, LOS had no bearing on subsequent outcome (Table 17-2). Furthermore, neuro-

Table 17-1. Demographic and Drinking Characteristics of Patient Sample

Demographic variables	
Age (mean ± *SD*)	45.7 ± 11.9
Education (mean ± *SD*)	12.4 ± 2.8
Social position index (mean ± *SD*)	55.1 ± 12.2
Social class (%)	
Upper/upper middle	4.9%
Middle	9.0%
Lower middle	42.9%
Lower	43.3%
Average monthly income (mean ± *SD*)	728 ± 658
Employment status[a] (%)	
Retired/disabled	20.4%
Unemployed	22.0%
Employed part-time	36.7%
Employed full-time	20.8%
Marital status (%)	
Single	20.0%
Married/remarried	31.5%
Divorced/separated/widowed	48.5%
Drinking-related variables	
Years of problem drinking (mean ± *SD*)	14.2 ± 10.6
Volume index[a] (mean ± *SD*)	3.1 ± 1.7
Heavy drinking days[a] (mean ± *SD*)	47.9 ± 32.0
Prior DWI arrest (%)	74.0%
Court-referred for treatment (%)	34.0%
Prior alcohol treatment (%)	62.0%

Note. From "Clinical Limitations of Neuropsychological Testing in Predicting Treatment Outcome among Alcoholics" by D. M. Donovan, D. R. Kivlahan, and R. D. Walker, 1984, *Alcoholism: Clinical and Experimental Research, 8,* 470–475. © by American Medical Society on Alcoholism and Other Drug Dependencies, Inc. The Research Society on Alcoholism. Reprinted by permission.

[a]Assessed over the 90 days prior to admission.

Table 17-2. Treatment Outcome by Levels of Neuropsychological Performance (NP) and LOS (in Percentages)

Performance	2 weeks	7 weeks	Total
Abstinence (n = 192)			
Low NP	38.5	39.5	39.1
Middle NP	44.8	33.3	39.0
High NP	48.6	57.6	52.9
Total	44.4	43.6	44.0
Treatment success (n = 218)			
Low NP	30.3	45.2	38.7
Middle NP	56.3	34.3	44.8
High NP	53.8	51.4	52.6
Total	47.1	43.9	45.4
Aftercare completion (n = 245)			
Low NP	22.2	43.2	33.7
Middle NP	38.5	22.0	30.0
High NP	46.5	40.5	43.5
Total	36.4	35.4	35.9
Full-time employment (n = 192)			
Low NP	22.2	34.2	29.2
Middle NP	41.4	30.0	35.6
High NP	57.1	57.6	57.4
Total	41.8	40.6	41.1

Note. From "Length of Stay, Neuropsychological Performance, and Aftercare: Influences on Alcohol Treatment Outcome" by R. D. Walker, D. M. Donovan, D. R. Kivlahan, and M. R. O'Leary, 1983, *Journal of Consulting and Clinical Psychology, 51*, 900–911. Copyright 1983 by the American Psychological Association. Reprinted by permission.

psychological status was found to have a significant but modest relationship to outcome (Table 17-2). Subjects with a better neuropsychological performance (BAQ > 97) were somewhat more likely to have remained continuously sober over the 9-month period, were significantly more likely to have been treatment successes (either continuous sobriety or only limited drinking over the 9-month period), and were significantly more likely to be employed full-time than the other groups. There was only marginal evidence for a neuropsychological status × LOS interaction. Subjects with the greatest level of impairment ("Low NP" in Table 17-2) were more likely to complete aftercare and to be employed full-time after a 7-week stay than a 2-week stay.

While the role of neuropsychological impairment in predicting treatment outcome was confirmed, the modest results implied that there might be other interactions that prevent a stronger predictive role. We (Donovan, Kivlahan, Walker, & Umlauf, 1985) began to question the role of a single summary score, expressed as the BAQ, to place subjects into groups defined by neuropsychological status. While previous research (Schau & O'Leary, 1977; Walker *et al.*, 1983) suggested that use of the BAQ provided sensitive results, it was possible that potentially useful information was lost by not including data from the larger set of neuropsychological measures collected on this sample.

We decided to expand the range of coverage of neuropsychological functioning and to allow an empirical, rather than arbitrary determination of group membership (Donovan *et al.*, 1985). This was done through the use of cluster-analytic methodology. Cluster analysis is a statistical methodology that groups subjects together based upon the degree of similarity between their profiles on a set of measures. The intent is to derive subgroups with maximum intragroup homogeneity and maximal difference from the other groups (i.e., intergroup heterogeneity). Other investigators have used cluster-analytic procedures to derive subtypes among alcoholics (e.g., Meyer, Babor, & Mirkin, 1983), including those based on neuropsychological functioning (Shelly & Goldstein, 1976).

Scores from 13 cognitive–neuropsychological measures were included in the cluster analysis. The measures involved in the analysis included the six components of the BAQ, the Group Embedded Figures Test, the Abstraction raw score from the Shipley–Hartford, the TPT Memory test, and the Arithmetic, Vocabulary, Picture Arrangement, and Picture Completion subtests from the WAIS. By using an average-linkage-clustering algorithm method, three primary clusters were derived, accounting for 225 of the original 245 subjects.

Scores for the three subtypes on the clustering variables are presented in Table 17-3. As can be seen, the clusters appear to fall along a continuum of increased impairment. Subtype 1 had mean scores on the WAIS and Halstead–Reitan measures that were in the average and unimpaired range. At the opposite end of this continuum was Subtype 3, which had WAIS scores ranging from average to below average and neuropsychological performances that fell within the impaired range. An examination of other variables indicated that the groups also differed on age, with Subtype 1 being the youngest ($M = 37.3$) and the remaining two groups being of comparable age ($M = 51.1$ for each). A difference was also found on years of problem drinking. Thus, age and years of problem drinking may have influenced the levels of performance found within each subtype, producing a possible confound.

The most crucial test of the validity of these clusters was the relationship of subtype membership to aspects of treatment outcome. Table 17-4 shows the percentage of subjects within each subtype with respect to outcome status. Overall, there were no differences across groups with respect to abstinence over the 9-month follow-up period. However, a significant difference was found when subjects in the 7-week program were considered. Within this condition, subjects in Subtype 3 (the older impaired group) were found to have the lowest incidence of abstinence, particularly in contrast to the higher rates of success among the comparably aged subjects

Table 17-3. Means on Neuropsychological Variables Used in Cluster Analysis

Variable	Cluster alcohol subtype 1 ($n = 95$)	2 ($n = 46$)	3 ($n = 85$)	Total accounted for ($n = 225$)
Group Embedded Figures	11.4	7.5	3.4	7.7
WAIS Arithmetic	11.1	12.3	8.9	10.4
WAIS Vocabulary	12.2	12.6	11.0	11.8
WAIS Digit Symbol	10.3	9.1	7.1	8.9
WAIS Picture Completion	11.7	11.3	9.3	10.8
WAIS Block Design	12.1	10.8	7.6	10.0
WAIS Picture Arrangement	10.8	9.2	7.6	9.3
Category Test	34.6	45.4	75.4	51.9
TPT Time	10.8	17.7	24.1	17.3
TPT Memory	8.4	7.2	6.9	7.6
TPT Localization	5.7	2.5	2.8	3.9
Trail Making Test, Part B	64.1	81.8	138.6	95.2
Shipley Abstraction raw score	26.4	16.4	13.6	19.8

Note. All univariate F tests significant at $p < .00001$. From "Derivation and Validation of Neuropsychological Clusters among Men Alcoholics" by D. M. Donovan, D. R. Kivlahan, R. D. Walker, and R. L. Umlauf, 1985, *Journal of Studies on Alcohol, 46,* 205–211. Copyright by Alcohol Research Documentation, Inc., Rutgers Center of Alcohol Studies, New Brunswick, New Jersey. Reprinted by permission.

of Subtype 2. An overall difference was found on aftercare completion, which appears to have been accounted for by the pattern found in the 2-week program. In each case, Subtype 2 subjects had a considerably higher rate of completion than those in either Subtype 1 or Subtype 3. A significant difference was found across groups with respect to the amount of time spent working during the last 3 months of the follow-up. This difference was maintained even when differences in age and self-reported retirement or disability status prior to treatment were accounted for. Subtype 3 members were working the least.

The results of the Donovan *et al.* (1985) study again represented a mixed blessing. On the one hand, the relevance of neuropsychological function to subsequent employment status was reinforced. Furthermore, differences began to emerge within a given LOS condition as a function of subtype membership. However, one of the findings was somewhat troubling. Subtype 1, having the best level of neuropsychological function, did not emerge on the measures of drinking behavior as having the best outcome. This was consistent with our repeated clinical observations that factors other than or in addition to neuropsychological impairment contribute to outcome. In attempting to interpret these results, it was assumed that a younger age may have contributed to Subtype 1's doing less well than

Table 17-4 Treatment Outcome as a Function of Cluster Group and LOS

Treatment outcome	LOS		
	2-week	7-week	Total
Abstinence (%)			
Cluster 1 (n = 69)	43.8	51.4	47.8
Cluster 2 (n = 39)	43.5	68.8	53.8
Cluster 3 (n = 67)	46.2	29.3	35.8
Total (n = 175)	44.4	44.7	44.6
χ^2	0.05	8.36*	3.73
Treatment success (%)			
Cluster 1 (n = 95)	42.9	37.7	40.0
Cluster 2 (n = 45)	50.0	55.0	52.2
Cluster 3 (n = 85)	34.2	37.0	35.7
Total (n = 225)	41.5	40.3	40.9
χ^2	1.79	2.84	3.76
Aftercare completion (%)			
Cluster 1 (n = 95)	26.2	30.2	28.4
Cluster 2 (n = 45)	57.7	45.0	52.2
Cluster 3 (n = 84)	30.8	37.0	34.1
Total (n = 224)	35.5	35.3	35.4
χ^2	7.56*	1.49	7.74*

Note. From "Derivation and Validation of Neuropsychological Clusters among Men Alcoholics" by D. M. Donovan, D. R. Kivlahan, R. D. Walker, and R. L. Umlauf, 1985, *Journal of Studies on Alcohol, 46*, 205–211. Copyright by Alcohol Research Documentation, Inc., Rutgers Center of Alcohol Studies, New Brunswick, New Jersey. Reprinted by permission.

*$p < .05$.

might have been expected on the basis of neuropsychological performance; however, level of impairment appeared to differentiate the older, comparably aged Subtypes 2 and 3.

Thus, we were left with compelling evidence that cognitive deficits may represent only one of a number of possible factors contributing to treatment outcome (Wilkinson & Sanchez-Craig, 1981). The findings suggest further that the continued focus on only the level or pattern of neuropsychological impairment, to the exclusion of other possible moderating variables, will continue to provide relatively limited predictive utility.

Recently, a multiple-domain approach to derivation of alcoholic subtypes has been advocated (Kivlahan, Donovan & Walker, 1983; Meyer *et al.*, 1983). The inclusion of measures from a large number of theoretically or empirically relevant variable classes allows the exploration of complex interactions among factors important to the development and maintenance of alcoholism. Following this approach, our most recent efforts (Kivlahan *et al.*, 1983; Donovan, Kivlahan, & Walker, 1986) have attempted to include measures of drinking behavior, social function, and emotional stability.

In our most recent analysis of this data base (Donovan *et al.*, 1986), two measures of neuropsychological status were included: the BAQ and a Verbal IQ prorated from the WAIS Vocabulary and Arithmetic scales. Three measures of demography and social function (age, social position, and hours worked per week), three measures of drinking behavior (number of days out of the 90 days prior to treatment in which five or more drinks were consumed, chronicity of drinking problem, and level of alcohol dependence), and five measures derived from an abbreviated Minnesota Multiphasic Personality Inventory (MMPI) were also utilized. The 13 variables were subjected to a sequential cluster-analytic process to eliminate outliers and to refine the resultant subtypes. The analysis yielded six subtypes, shown in Table 17-5. Means on all 13 clustering variables are presented.

Table 17-5. Means of the 13 Clustering Variables for the Six Empirically Derived *K*-Means Clusters

	Clusters					
Clustering variable	1 (n = 27)	2 (n = 37)	3 (n = 48)	4 (n = 51)	5 (n = 33)	6 (n = 38)
Age	31.3	39.1	42.2	49.9	54.2	54.7
Social position index[a]	58.5	59.7	58.1	50.8	46.0	61.3
Average hours worked per week[b]	29.2	12.5	9.9	20.2	12.9	14.2
Days of five or more drinks[b]	29.0	43.7	57.9	50.5	74.0	28.9
Chronicity (in years)	8.5	7.0	13.1	17.2	10.7	25.9
Alcohol Dependence Scale	19.2	11.4	20.9	13.5	15.3	20.1
Brain Age Quotient	88.1	82.7	86.9	99.7	93.5	82.8
WAIS Verbal IQ (prorated)	102.1	97.8	107.8	116.7	119.2	104.7
MMPI-168 Depression	66.0	60.6	87.2	58.2	79.2	69.9
MMPI-168 Psychopathic Deviate	76.4	58.6	80.5	59.3	68.6	64.1
MMPI-168 Psychasthenia	72.9	53.5	84.8	54.4	72.3	60.5
MMPI-168 Schizophrenia	73.7	51.6	85.6	54.4	66.0	57.3
MMPI-168 Social Desirability	9.2	11.3	7.5	11.4	8.9	9.6

Note. From "Alcoholic Subtypes Based on Multiple Assessment Domains: Validation against Treatment Outcome" by D. M. Donovan, D. R. Kivlahan, and R. D. Walker, 1986, in M. Galanter (Ed.), *Recent developments in alcoholism* (Vol. 4, pp. 207–222), New York: Plenum Press. Reprinted by permission.

[a]Hollingshead; lower values indicate higher social position.

[a]Based on the 90 days prior to admission.

Subtypes are shown from youngest (Cluster 1) to oldest (Cluster 6). Age was not the only discriminating variable; the profiles reflect considerable differences on demographic, alcohol-related, neuropsychological, and personality measures.

As can be seen, the results are quite complex and difficult to describe with brief summary statements. It is of interest to note the range of scores on the Verbal IQ and BAQ across groups and their pattern of integration with other variables. The complexity observed in the data may capture the underlying variability of our clinical population more accurately than a single index such as the BAQ or subtypes based solely on neuropsychological variables. Each of the subtypes also appears to correspond to types of individuals often seen within our clinical settings. These include individuals such as those in Cluster 1, who were relatively young, socially unstable men of average intelligence but with subtle deficits in problem-solving skills. Patients in this group evidenced considerable psychological distress coupled with high levels of alcohol dependence, despite a relatively short period of reported problem drinking. There were also individuals seen within our clinical setting who seemed to fit each of the remaining five derived subtypes.

The findings concerning the relationship of subtype membership to treatment outcome are similarly complex and are shown in Table 17-6. To summarize, cluster membership was significantly related to aftercare completion and employment status for the sample as a whole. A similar pattern of differences was found across subtypes in the 2-week LOS condition. However, no significant associations were found within the 7-week LOS condition. There was a marginal difference across subtypes within the 2-week LOS condition with respect to drinking disposition.

The results from this series of studies suggest that, consistent with previous research, neuropsychological deficits among alcoholics contribute to posthospital function and outcome. This relationship appears strongest in the prediction of subsequent employment status, but is considerably weaker in terms of predicting drinking-related behavior at outcome. The results challenge the position of primacy of neuropsychological impairment in determining treatment outcome (e.g., Gregson & Taylor, 1977). While an important component in the prediction process, the level of impairment may be less central than has often been suggested (Donovan *et al.*, 1984; Wilkinson & Sanchez-Craig, 1981). Future research in this area needs to consider a wide range of variables to include in either subtype derivation or prediction equations. Many of these are related to characteristics of clients entering treatment (e.g., Alterman & Tarter, 1985), as well as to aspects of the posthospital environment to which the patient returns (Billings & Moos, 1983) and of the type of aftercare treatment the individual enters as a means of support (Ito & Donovan, 1986). As Wilkinson and Sanchez-Craig (1981) note, the apparent influence of neuropsychological impairment will appear

Table 17-6. Predictive Validity of Clusters by LOS

Treatment outcome	LOS 2-week	LOS 7-week	LOS Total
Aftercare completion (%)			
Cluster 1 ($n = 27$)	5.9	40.0	18.5
Cluster 2 ($n = 37$)	29.4	30.0	29.7
Cluster 3 ($n = 48$)	30.0	32.1	31.3
Cluster 4 ($n = 51$)	46.4	26.1	37.3
Cluster 5 ($n = 33$)	69.2	50.0	57.6
Cluster 6 ($n = 38$)	40.0	39.1	39.5
Total ($n = 234$)	36.4	35.5	35.9
χ^2	14.9***	3.6**	11.6**
Treatment success (%)			
Cluster 1 ($n = 27$)	29.4	50.0	37.0
Cluster 2 ($n = 37$)	52.9	25.0	37.8
Cluster 3 ($n = 48$)	20.0	35.7	29.2
Cluster 4 ($n = 51$)	57.1	34.8	47.1
Cluster 5 ($n = 33$)	53.8	50.0	51.5
Cluster 6 ($n = 38$)	35.7	43.5	40.5
Total ($n = 234$)	42.2	38.7	40.3
χ^2	9.5*	3.7	5.4
Employment status (% working full-time)			
Cluster 1 ($n = 27$)	55.6	42.9	50.0
Cluster 2 ($n = 37$)	35.7	50.0	43.3
Cluster 3 ($n = 48$)	13.3	38.1	27.8
Cluster 4 ($n = 51$)	70.8	35.3	56.1
Cluster 5 ($n = 33$)	38.5	37.5	37.9
Cluster 6 ($n = 38$)	10.0	38.1	29.0
Total ($n = 234$)	41.2	39.8	40.4
χ^2	31.2***	9.39	24.2***

Note. From "Alcoholic Subtypes Based on Multiple Assessment Domains: Validation against Treatment Outcome" by D. M. Donovan, D. R. Kivlahan, and R. D. Walker, 1986, in M. Galanter (Ed.), *Recent developments in alcoholism* (Vol. 4, pp. 207–222), New York: Plenum Press. Reprinted by permission.

*$p < .10$.

**$p < .05$.

***$p < .01$.

minimal unless the amount of variance in treatment outcome accounted for by differences in such deficits is of at least the same order of magnitude as that produced by these other determining variables.

Recovery of Function as a Factor in Treatment

One variable that must also be taken into consideration as an influence on both treatment process and outcome is the relative permanence of or recovery from alcohol-related neuropsychological deficits. As Wilkinson and

Carlen (1981) indicate, evidence suggests that the behavioral, electrophysiological, and apparently even morphological deficits associated with impairment among alcoholics appear to diminish in some individuals after periods of abstinence. There appears to be considerable variability with respect to the rate and extent, as well as the nature, of the deficits in which change is seen (Parsons & Farr, 1981). The parameters involved in the recovery process must take into account such factors as individual-difference variables (e.g., age, years of problem drinking), the measures involved in the investigation, the type of alcoholic subjects studied, and the length of sobriety, as well as the extent and pattern of any drinking during the recovery period (Miller & Saucedo, 1983). This latter point was made by the results of Parsons, Leber, and Yohman (1983–1984), who found that in addition to having poorer psychosocial outcomes, those alcoholics who had resumed drinking over the course of 1-year follow-up also had lower levels of neuropsychological functioning at both admission to treatment and outcome than did abstainers.

The work of Goldman and colleagues, as reviewed in Chapter 15 of the present volume and elsewhere (Goldman, 1982, 1983), has been instrumental in attempting to clarify the recovery process. A major contribution provided by Goldman has been the development of a rigorous experimental design that simultaneously allows the assessment of the same individuals across time (within-subjects design), the comparison of alcoholic groups with differing degrees of sobriety (between-subjects design), and also the comparison of such groups to matched groups of nonalcoholic control subjects. This design provides the investigator the opportunity to examine the influence of practice effects, based upon repeated testing, on the apparent recovery of function. With this design, it was found that most tasks investigated were impaired during the first week of abstinence but showed nearly complete recovery from 2 weeks to 1 month after the last drinking episode (Goldman, 1983). Furthermore, it appeared that older alcoholics with longer drinking histories showed slower and less extensive recovery.

A second important feature of this research methodology involves the role of practice. It was found that much of the recovery of function occurred passively with the passage of time and increased sobriety; this process is what Goldman refers to as "time-dependent recovery." However, it was also found that practicing on cognitive tasks functionally similar to the target behaviors being assessed led to a more rapid recovery; this is what Goldman has described as "experience-dependent recovery" (Goldman, Klisz, & Williams, 1985). This finding—namely, that practice of certain cognitive tasks facilitates recovery—is the basis for a number of recent approaches on a more applied clinical level to develop cognitive retraining programs for impaired alcoholics. Hansen (1980), for instance, has provided such training, focusing on visual–motor coordination, attention and concentration, spatial functions, abstract thinking, and memory, for small groups of intellectually impaired alcoholics. Patients undergoing such training reported perceived improvement in memory and self-esteem. However, no actual follow-up measures of these dimensions were collected.

Both Wilson (Chapter 16, this volume) and Parsons (Chapter 14, this volume) have reported on similar retraining efforts. In a single-subject case study utilizing a multiple-baseline design, Wilson has presented strong evidence concerning the effectiveness of individually tailored and administered memory training in a brain-damaged nonalcoholic patient. Improved memory function was similarly found for cognitively impaired nonalcoholic patients following group involvement in either memory training or problem-solving training. The improvement in memory function was described as quite modest, was apparently of a lesser magnitude than that found in the previously noted single-subject case, and was not differentially influenced by training focused on memory versus that focusing on more general problem-solving skills. Preliminary data presented by Parsons and his colleagues provide support for such training groups in alcoholic patients with a minimum of 3 weeks of sobriety. Compared to control subjects receiving no such additional training, those who received the 10 special sessions have shown increased neuropsychological test performance. In a manner comparable to that reported by Hansen (1980), subjects of Parsons's study have also given anecdotal reports of increased memory and self-esteem.

The chapters in this section of the volume provide provocative results concerning direct therapeutic interventions into the area of impairment among alcoholics. These interventions are based, in part, upon Goldman's work on experience-dependent recovery. The subsequent studies have attempted to translate this work into clinically applicable strategies. This is an important step, given a concern expressed by Wilson that appears to have relevance to Goldman's work. Although it has been possible to demonstrate generalizability of performance across tasks having similar functional parameters, Wilson notes that there is not yet convincing evidence to suggest that training on such laboratory tasks will generalize to everyday situations.

A number of other issues need to be considered in both developing and testing the effectiveness of clinical remediation efforts. The first is related to assessment. It will be necessary to continue refining assessment techniques and targeting those deficits that are most pronounced and potentially most amenable to remediation. This undertaking may be made difficult, given the need for both breadth of assessment coverage and specificity of intervention targeting. A second issue concerns the nature of the remediation approach itself. It appears clear from Goldman's work and from Parsons's clinical trial that a minimum of 2–4 weeks of sobriety would be appropriate before attempting to intervene, thus allowing the acute effects of intoxication to dissipate. Beyond that, however, a decision must be made concerning individual versus group approaches. Wilson's work would suggest that an individual remediation approach might be more beneficial than group training. This would insure more specific focus on the patient's identified deficits than could be afforded in the more generalized training available in a group format. However, the results of both Parsons and Wilson suggest preliminarily that group involvement may result in improved cognitive function. Whether the resultant improvements reach both statistical and clinical significance is yet to be seen. If groups are to be the method of choice, decisions must be made concerning length of sessions and of the overall intervention. The groups for alcoholics described by Hansen (1980) met four times per week, each session lasting for 45 minutes, for 8 weeks. Parsons's subjects met for a total of 10 sessions of 75 minutes each over a 2-week period. On the basis of clinical impressions, Hansen (1980) advocated daily training sessions over a 6-month period.

Thus, future research must continue to address the relative effectiveness of cognitive remediation at an overall level, and then, if it is found to be both statistically and clinically significant, must explore parametric variations of such interventions. A final area to be considered is the impact of changes resulting from such training programs on the life adjustment of the alcoholic patients. There is an implicit assumption underlying such approaches (e.g., Goldman *et al.*, 1985) that improvement in neuropsychological functioning associated with remediation efforts may result in an increased likelihood of treatment success. This assumption needs to be tested through controlled clinical research exploring the relationship between improvement in neuropsychological function and treatment outcome.

Summary

The chapters in the present section of this volume provide an important perspective in understanding issues involved in the differential recovery of neuropsychological function among alcoholics, as well as the potential role neuropsychological impairment plays in the prediction of treatment outcome. It appears clear that such impairment influences the rehabilitative process and outcome. However, the role of neuropsychological functioning may be less central than once thought. The chapters in this section and the results of our group's current research suggest a much more complex process for predicting outcome than can be captured by an assessment of cognitive function alone. It appears that the measurement of such functions needs to be more firmly incorporated into a broader array of variables derived from a comprehensive assessment process. Other variables to consider fall within the broad categories of person variables brought into treatment by the individual (Alterman & Tarter, 1985; Gibbs & Flanagan, 1977; Meyer *et al.*, 1983); aspects of treatment itself, as well as the manner in which it interacts with these person variables (Donovan *et al.*, 1986); and aspects of the posttreatment environment, such as stressors, coping responses, social resources and supports, and therapeutic aftercare services (Billings & Moos, 1983; Ito & Donovan, 1986).

A number of authors (e.g., Chelune & Parker, 1981; Donovan & Chaney, 1985; Goldman, 1983 and Chapter 15, this volume) have discussed a number of ways in which treatment programs might be modified in order to deal with the problems associated with alcohol-related neuropsychological deficits. These represent both passive, time-dependent and active, experience-dependent strategies meant to help the individual overcome, accommodate, or compensate for the deficits. Again, further research is needed to evaluate the effectiveness of such program modifications. They also must be considered within the context of issues of cost containment, diagnostic related groups, and parameters involved in reimbursement for treatment.

A decade ago, Tarter (1976) indicated that a comprehensive assessment of the neuropsychological status of the alcoholic might have important therapeutic implications. However, at that point in our scientific evolution, Tarter felt that there was too little known about the intrinsic process of treatment and the manifestation of alcoholic cognitive deficits in real-life settings to indicate what factors contribute to successful rehabilitation. Although there appear to have been considerable advances in our understanding of the relationship between neuropsychological function and alcoholism rehabilitation since then, in part due to the work reviewed in the chapters of this section, many gaps remain in our knowledge. This contention is reinforced by the last sentence of Miller and Saucedo's (1983) extensive review of alcohol-related cognitive deficits, both providing a sense of the current state of the art and suggesting future direction: "Both future research and therapeutic endeavors with alcoholics need to address the relationships between cognitive dysfunction and treatment process and outcome" (p. 195). However, it has become increasingly clear that neither researchers nor clinicians can continue to focus exclusively on neuropsychological status in understanding these relationships. Cognitive deficits represent only one of a number of possible factors contributing to treatment and its outcome. As such, the continued focus on only the level of impairment, to the exclusion of other possible moderating variables, will continue to provide limited utility. Thus, neuropsychological functioning must be viewed as one component, albeit important, of a much more comprehensive assessment process that also involves measures of drinking behavior, social functioning, emotional stability, and environmental supports (Donovan *et al.*, 1984, 1985, 1986).

References

Alterman, A. I., & Tarter, R. E. (1985). Assessing the influence of confounding subject variables in neuropsychological research in alcoholism and related disorders. *International Journal of Neuroscience, 26*, 75–84.

Becker, J. T., Butters, N., Hermann, A., & D'Angelo, N. (1983). Learning to associate names and faces: Impaired acquisition on an ecologically relevant memory task by male alcoholics. *Journal of Nervous and Mental Disease, 171*, 617–623.

Becker, J. T., & Jaffe, J. H. (1984). Impaired memory for treatment-relevant information in inpatient men alcoholics. *Journal of Studies on Alcohol, 45*, 339–343.

Berglund, M., Leijonquist, H., & Horlen, M. (1977). Prognostic significance and reversibility of cerebral dysfunction in alcoholics. *Journal of Studies on Alcohol, 38*, 1761–1770.

Billings, A. G., & Moos, R. H. (1983). Psychosocial processes of recovery among alcoholics and their families: Implications for clinicians and program evaluators. *Addictive Behaviors, 8*, 205–218.

Boon, J. C. (1982). *Real life implications of problem-solving deficits in alcoholics.* Unpublished doctoral dissertation, Vanderbilt University.

Chelune, G. J., & Parker, J. B. (1981). Neuropsychological deficits associated with chronic alcohol abuse. *Clinical Psychology Review, 1*, 181–195.

Donovan, D. M., & Chaney, E. F. (1985). Alcoholic relapse prevention and intervention: Models and methods. In G. A. Marlatt & J. Gordon (Eds.), *Relapse prevention: Maintenance strategies in the treatment of addictive behaviors* (pp. 351–416). New York: Guilford Press.

Donovan, D. M., Kivlahan, D. R., & Walker, R. D. (1984). Clinical limitations of neuropsychological testing in predicting treatment outcome among alcoholics. *Alcoholism: Clinical and Experimental Research, 8*, 470–475.

Donovan, D. M., Kivlahan, D. R., & Walker, R. D. (1986). Alcoholic subtypes based on multiple assessment domains: Validation against treatment outcome. In M. Galanter (Ed.), *Recent developments in alcoholism* (Vol. 4, pp. 207–222). New York: Plenum Press.

Donovan, D. M., Kivlahan, D. R., Walker, R. D., & Umlauf, R. L. (1985). Derivation and validation of neuropsychological clusters among men alcoholics. *Journal of Studies on Alcohol, 46*, 205–211.

Fitzhugh, L. C., Fitzhugh, K. B., & Reitan, R. M. (1960). Adaptive abilities and intellectual functioning of hospitalized alcoholics. *Quarterly Journal of Studies on Alcohol, 21*, 414–423.

Fitzhugh, L. C., Fitzhugh, K. B., & Reitan, R. M. (1965). Adaptive abilities and intellectual functioning of hospitalized alcoholics: Further consideration. *Quarterly Journal of Studies on Alcohol, 26*, 402–411.

Gibbs, L., & Flanagan, J. (1977). Prognostic indicators of alcoholism treatment outcomes. *International Journal of the Addictions, 12*, 1097–1141.

Goldman, M. S. (1982). Reversibility of psychological deficits in alcoholics: The interaction of aging with alcohol. In D. A. Wilkinson (Ed.), *Cerebral deficits in alcoholism* (pp. 79–105). Toronto: Addiction Research Foundation.

Goldman, M. S. (1983). Cognitive impairment in chronic alcoholics: Some cause for optimism. *American Psychologist, 38*, 1045–1054.

Goldman, M. S., Klisz, D. K., & Williams, D. L. (1985). Experience-dependent recovery of cognitive functioning in young alcoholics. *Addictive Behaviors, 10*, 169–176.

Goldman, M. S., & Rosenbaum, G. (1977). Psychological recoverability following chronic alcohol abuse. In F. A. Seixas (Ed.), *Currents in alcoholism* (Vol. 2, pp. 187–196). New York: Grune & Stratton.

Gregson, R. A. M., & Taylor, G. M. (1977). Prediction of relapse in men alcoholics. *Journal of Studies on Alcohol, 34*, 1749–1760.

Guthrie, A., & Elliot, W. A. (1980). The nature and recoverability of cerebral impairment in alcoholism: Treatment implications. *Journal of Studies on Alcohol, 41*, 147–155.

Hansen, L. (1980). Treatment of reduced intellectual functioning in alcoholics. *Journal of Studies on Alcohol, 41*, 156–158.

Ito, J. R., & Donovan, D. M. (1986). Aftercare in alcoholism treatment: A review. In W. R. Miller & N. Heathers (Eds.), *The addictive behaviors: Processes of change* (pp. 435–456). New York: Plenum Press.

Kivlahan, D. R., Donovan, D. M., & Walker, R. D. (1983, August). *Alcoholic subtypes: Validity of clusters based on multiple assessment domains.* Paper presented at the meeting of the American Psychological Association, Anaheim, CA.

Leber, W. R., Parsons, O. A., & Nichols, N. (1985). Neuropsychological test results are related to ratings of men alcoholics' therapeutic progress: A replicated study. *Journal of Studies on Alcohol, 46*, 116–121.

Meyer, R. E., Babor, T. F., & Mirkin, P. M. (1983). Typologies in alcoholism: An overview. *International Journal of the Addictions, 18*, 235–249.

Miller, W. R., & Saucedo, C. F. (1983). Assessment of neuropsychological impairment and brain damage in problem drinkers. In C. J. Golden, J. A. Moses, Jr., J. A. Coffman, W. R. Miller, & F. D. Strider (Eds.), *Clinical neuropsychology: Interface with neurologic and psychiatric disorders* (pp. 141–195). New York: Grune & Stratton.

O'Leary, M. R., & Donovan, D. M. (1979). Male alcoholics: Treatment outcome as a function of length of treatment and level of current adaptive abilities. *Evaluation and the Health Professions, 2*, 373–384.

O'Leary, M. R., Donovan, D. M., Chaney, E. F., & O'Leary, D. E. (1979). Interpersonal attractiveness and clinical decisions in alcoholism treatment. *American Journal of Psychiatry, 136*, 618–622.

O'Leary, M. R., Donovan, D. M., Chaney, E. F., & Speltz, M. L. (1979). Correlates of clinicians' perceptions of clients in alcoholism treatment. *Journal of Clinical Psychiatry, 40*, 344–347.

O'Leary, M. R., Donovan, D. M., Chaney, E. F., & Walker, R. D. (1979). Cognitive impairment and treatment outcome with alcoholics: Preliminary findings. *Journal of Clinical Psychiatry, 40*, 397–398.

O'Leary, M. R., Speltz, M. L., Donovan, D. M., & Walker, R. D. (1979). Implicit preadmission screening criteria in an alcoholism treatment program. *American Journal of Psychiatry, 136*, 1190–1193.

Parsons, O. A. (1977). Neuropsychological deficits in alcoholics: Facts and fancies. *Alcoholism: Clinical and Experimental Research, 1*, 51–56.

Parsons, O. A., & Farr, S. P. (1981). The neuropsychology of alcohol and drug use. In S. B. Filskov & T. J. Boll (Eds.), *Handbook of clinical neuropsychology* (pp. 320–365). New York: Wiley.

Parsons, O. A., Leber, W. R., & Yohman, J. R. (1983–1984). Post-treatment adjustment of "resumer" and "abstainer" alcoholics. *Alcohol Technical Reports, 12–13*, 59–62.

Reitan, R. M. (1973, August). *Behavioral manifestations of impaired brain function in aging.* Paper presented at the meeting of the American Psychological Association, Montreal.

Ryan, C., & Butters, N. (1983). Cognitive deficits in alcoholics. In B. Kissin & H. Begleiter (Eds.), *The biology of alcoholism: Vol. 7. The pathogenesis of alcoholism: Biological factors* (pp. 485–538). New York: Plenum Press.

Sanchez-Craig, M., & Walker, K. (1982). Teaching coping skills to chronic alcoholics in a coeducational halfway house: I. Assessment of program effects. *British Journal of Addiction, 77*, 35–50.

Schau, E. J., & O'Leary, M. R. (1977). Adaptive abilities of hospitalized alcoholics and matched controls: The brain-age quotient. *Journal of Studies on Alcohol, 38*, 403–409.

Shelly, C. H., & Goldstein, G. (1976). An empirically derived typology of hospitalized alcoholics. In G. Goldstein & C. Neuringer (Eds.), *Empirical studies on alcoholism* (pp. 195–229). Cambridge, MA: Ballinger.

Sussman, S., Rychtarik, R. G., Muesser, K., Glynn, S., & Prue, D. M. (1986). Ecological relevance of memory tests and the prediction of relapse in alcoholics. *Journal of Studies on Alcohol, 47*, 305–310.

Tarter, R. E. (1976). Neuropsychological investigations of alcoholism. In G. Goldstein & C. Neuringer (Eds.), *Empirical studies of alcoholism* (pp. 231–256). Cambridge, MA: Ballinger.

Walker, R. D., Donovan, D. M., Kivlahan, D. R., & O'Leary, M. R. (1983). Length of stay, neuropsychological performance, and aftercare: Influences on alcohol treatment outcome. *Journal of Consulting and Clinical Psychology, 51*, 900–911.

Wilkinson, D. A., & Carlen, P. L. (1981). Chronic organic brain syndromes associated with alcoholism: Neuropsychological and other aspects. In Y. Israel, F. B. Glaser, H. Kalant, R. E. Popham, W. Schmidt, & R. G. Smart (Eds.), *Research advances in alcohol and drug problems* (Vol. 6, pp. 107–145). New York: Plenum Press.

Wilkinson, D. A., & Sanchez-Craig, M. (1981). Relevance of brain dysfunction to treatment objectives: Should alcohol-related cognitive deficits influence the way we think about treatment? *Addictive Behaviors, 6*, 253–260.

18

Discussion

Recovery, Treatment, and Rehabilitation in Chronic Alcoholics

GERALD GOLDSTEIN

Treatment of Alcoholism and Neuropsychology

A major question asked in this volume has been how the neuropsychologically oriented research accomplished during the past 25 years or so has affected clinical practice with alcoholic patients. Since clinical practice with most alcoholic patients relates to management and treatment, it would clearly be desirable to forge some relationships between this large body of neuropsychological research and the treatment area. As neuropsychologists interested in perceptual, motor, and cognitive function, we have been primarily interested in recovery and treatment of the abilities that constitute those three domains. Indeed, the chapters in this section by Parsons, Goldman, and Wilson all relate primarily to recovery of cognitive abilities. This choice of topic may appear strange to the non-neuropsychologist working with alcoholics, who may view treatment primarily as a variety of methods directed toward encouraging problem drinkers or alcoholics to discontinue drinking, or at least to reduce their intake of alcoholic beverages. Indeed, much alcoholism treatment is directed toward the prevention of those situations in which patients must meet neuropsychologists. As neuropsychologists in clinical practice, we generally come into contact with alcoholics in tertiary care facilities. That is, we deal mainly with patients whose alcoholism has become sufficiently severe to require hospitalization, generally for a fairly extended length of stay. When a physician makes a referral to a neuropsychologist to evaluate an alcoholic patient for suspected brain dysfunction, this generally connotes some concern that within the context of a general inpatient alcoholic population, the patient being referred may

Gerald Goldstein. Neuropsychology Research Program, Veterans Administration Medical Center, Pittsburgh, Pennsylvania; Departments of Psychiatry and Psychology, University of Pittsburgh, Pittsburgh, Pennsylvania.

have a clinically significant degree of reversible or irreversible brain dysfunction. Obviously, this consideration does not obtain in research programs in which all patients are routinely evaluated, but it would appear to be the case in most clinical settings. Aside from patients in time-limited inpatient treatment programs, neuropsychologists, of course, come into contact with long-term institutionalized patients with severe dementia associated with alcoholism, or with alcoholic Korsakoff's syndrome.

In initiating my discussion of the three chapters related to recovery and treatment, I would first like to point out that alcoholism remains among the most recalcitrant to treatment of the psychiatric disorders. The successes of psychiatry, particularly in the area of pharmacological treatment, with the anxiety disorders, the affective disorders, and even schizophrenia have not been accompanied by comparable successes in alcoholism treatment. Perhaps because of the absence of an established standard effective treatment for alcoholism, the field has become inundated by a plethora of treatment methods, as well as by abundant numbers of individuals and/or institutions claiming to have unusually effective methods of treating alcoholics. Thus, the field of alcohol treatment has had more than its share of "gurus," "Meccas," "Rebbes," "mayvens," "sages," and "cult leaders," all of whom seem to have the answers. The field has also become susceptible to perhaps excessive faddism, such that treatment methods greeted with great enthusiasm at one point in time may quickly go the way of the hula hoop. Since I have lived through an era during which these trends appeared to be at their height, it has given me great pleasure to read these three chapters, all of which make judicious and modest claims based on sound experimental and clinical investigation. If this work is representative, it seems likely that treatments and rehabilitation methods developed by neuropsychologists will not fall victim to the difficulties described above. Rather, the methods developed should ultimately become part of the repertoire of effective treatments when applied to appropriate patients.

Thus far, in brief outline, we appear to have the following information. There seems to be substantial recovery of cognitive function, in general, following cessation of drinking. Parsons points out that those who resume drinking do not do as well as abstainers. I might add parenthetically that some of the recovery effect may be in part attributable, not only to abstinence, but to resumption of a normal diet. This natural recovery process may in some cases be potentiated by special cognitive rehabilitation. There is a differentiated temporal course of recovery, such that certain cognitive functions come back quite rapidly, and some may take months if not years to return. Certain functions may not return at all. Brandt, Butters, Ryan, and Bayog (1983) have suggested that functions mediated by cerebral cortex may be recoverable, while subcortically mediated functions, such as certain aspects of memory, may not be recoverable. However, because of the work done in the area of antecedent neuropsychological deficit (described elsewhere in this volume), and in the absence of appropriate longitudinal research, some functions in some patients may never have been in the cognitive repertoire, and in these cases it would be inappropriate to speak of absence of recovery. To extrapolate from Wilson's chapter—in which the suggestion is made that treatment efforts should sometimes be directed toward aiding the patient in coping with a permanently impaired memory—as well as from the general research literature (Butters & Cermak, 1980), it would appear that there is no substantive recovery from alcoholic Korsakoff's syndrome once it has passed through its acute stage; that is, the amnesia is essentially irreversible.

Holding these findings in mind, one is struck in reading these chapters by the diversity of the patient populations. There are first of all Goldman's young alcoholics (those in their 20s and 30s). There are Goldman's older alcoholics and Parsons's male subjects, who, if they were Veterans Administration (VA) patients, are probably comparable in age to Goldman's older alcoholics (40+). Finally, there are Wilson's cases, all of whom were apparently clients of a rehabilitation hospital. This diversity creates difficulties for clinicians who scan the research literature with the intent of finding treatment methods that can be applied in their settings. Clearly, the 20- to 29-year-old alcoholics used as subjects in some of Goldman's studies must be quite different from the World War II veteran in his 50s or 60s being treated for alcoholism in a VA facility. Correspondingly, patients who find their ways to rehabilitation hospitals tend to be individuals with histories of severe brain damage. As Goldman points out, age alone does not appear to be the only consideration, since 40-year-old nonalcoholics typically perform quite normally on neuropsychological tests. There must be some interaction between age and the disease process. One way of conceptualizing this interaction may be to invoke Roth's (1980) idea concerning the "threshold phenomenon." Roth believes that following a particular point in quantitative aggregation of some form of pathological change, qualitative mental changes may appear in an abrupt manner. As an example, he cites some of his own research involving a study in which a mean plaque count of 11 at autopsy successfully separated patients who during life had been clearly demented from those free of signs of mental deterioration. In the case of alcoholism, the combination of alcohol abuse, age, and possibly alcohol- or age-associated disease processes pushes the alcoholic beyond the line, following which little recovery can be anticipated. Indeed, I have heard several highly experienced clinicians speak of a "line" in their alcoholic patients beyond which there is substantial deterioration and little hope of recovery. We may hope, as our work in this area becomes more refined, that efforts will be made to find "the right treatment for the right patient"—particularly since while alcoholism in some respects may be a single entity, alcoholics are a very diverse group from the point of view of level and pattern of cognitive abilities.

Granting this diversity, I would not go to the rather extreme position taken by Wilson involving essentially complete dependence upon single-subject designs. Surely, it may be possible, as has been demonstrated in Goldman's group-oriented studies, to develop treatment modules or packages amenable (with minimal modifications) to treatment of relatively large groups of patients. I would certainly concur with Wilson's view that any research reporting on treatment efficacy should provide data regarding how many patients got better, how many got worse, and how many stayed the same; it is not necessary to do single-subject research, however, to provide this kind of data. The case presented in Wilson's chapter does provide an excellent example of when single-subject research is highly appropriate. It would be my view that it is the method of choice when one is dealing with a very unusual patient of particular theoretical interest. Wilson's patient Mr. B. exemplified a rare combination—an isolated memory deficit resulting from bilateral stroke in an individual of exceptionally high intelligence.

In the case of alcoholism, one can rough out the subpopulations that might be considered when doing treatment planning. There are, first of all, the more complicated cases in which there is clear antecedent neuropsychological deficit and/or concurrent psychopathology. In cases of antecedent deficit, it is particularly important not to pitch the retraining at a level that would have exceeded the patients' capacity even before acquisition of the alcoholism. In cases of concurrent psychopathology, it is often advisable to develop a combined program, possibly involving some mixture of behavioral and pharmacological treatment, in order to minimize the interfering effects of the concurrent psychopathology (e.g., severe depression) on cognitive retraining. Indeed, I am somewhat surprised that none of the three chapters in this section mentions the matter of pharmacological intervention.

A second subpopulation to be considered is that of the less complex cases, such as Goldman's young alcoholics. Here, I think what we do is help these patients recover more rapidly from the effects of toxicity. As Goldman puts it, we help "lift the cognitive haze." Thus, tasks that increase alertness, involve exercise of cognitive abilities, and demand attention may all have haze-lifting effects. If they do, then these patients may be more capable of benefiting from conventional treatments such as group psychotherapy or alcoholism counseling.

Older, long-term chronic alcoholics are a somewhat different matter, since they may have permanent cognitive deficits that persist beyond detoxication. In all frankness, it is not yet well established that the cognitive rehabilitation programs now available are genuinely helpful to these patients. Nevertheless, we should applaud the work of Goldman and Parsons with such patients, because without their beginning efforts, it would not be possible to make any progress in this difficult area. As some clinicians are aware, there is an aura of pessimism concerning any hope of recovery for the middle-aged long-term alcoholic. While these individuals may sometimes become abstinent, or substantially reduce the amount they drink, they often do not return to independent life in the community. They may not return to work, or may take jobs far less demanding than they held in the past. Perhaps some of these new methods, as they develop, can provide some hope for such patients.

I think we take another quantum leap when we consider the frankly demented alcoholic, or the patient with alcoholic Korsakoff's syndrome. These patients are frequently more or less permanently institutionalized, or in any event do not live independent lives. Here, I think Wilson's work comes to the fore, and two mutually compatible treatment strategies emerge. One of them, in Wilson's terminology, relates to teaching the patient to "bypass" the memory deficit, perhaps through the use of various prosthetics. The other involves developing methods to help the caretaker help the patient. In essence, the treatment of the demented or amnesic alcoholic becomes much like the treatment of non-alcoholism-related dementia or amnesia. It may be noted that patients with these disorders are often not active drinkers. Either the addiction "burns out," or the patient lacks the resources necessary to acquire alcoholic beverages. Indeed, in these cases, without a good medical and social history, it is sometimes difficult to determine whether the dementia or amnesia is alcoholism-related. The reasons for optimism with regard to rehabilitation of these kinds of patients have largely to do with the development of new training methods and prosthetics, and possibly of new drugs. There remains little hope of recovery from the underlying neuropathology in these cases, and the issues usually salient in conventional alcoholism treatment, such as maintenance of abstinence, are usually not pertinent here. However, these patients may benefit from the renewed hope offered chronically brain-damaged patients by the cognitive rehabilitation movement (Diller & Gordon, 1981; Goldstein & Ruthven, 1983; Wilson & Moffat, 1984).

In summary, it would appear that neuropsychology has something to offer in the area of treatment of alcoholism. In the case of the young alcoholic, it may provide methods of dispelling the "cognitive haze" more rapidly than through the usual natural recovery or pharmacologically assisted methods. New methods under development in the area of cognitive rehabilitation may aid in working with severely amnesic and demented alcoholics, and with their caretakers. It would be my view that the major problems remain with the long-term chronic alcoholic, who is typically middle-aged and who may still be an active alcoholic. As Goldman nicely points out, these patients have complex but subtle deficits not readily amenable to intervention through established rehabilitation methods. Workers in this area may be envious of the speech/language, physical, or occupational therapist, for whom there are typically identifiable symptoms and outcomes; the patient can or cannot talk, walk, or perform activities of daily living following treatment. I may be oversimplifying to make the point here, but it is clear that the outcome of alcoholism treatment in the area of cognitive function is quite a bit more difficult to assess than it is in the case of disorders in which there are clear symptoms or symptom patterns. Remediating impairment of function noted on such complex measures as the Halstead Category or Trail Making Tests remains a formidable problem.

Types of Rehabilitation

I would now like to touch briefly on a number of points and then go on to discuss some broader issues. A great deal of work in the cognitive rehabilitation area relates to choice of methodology and level of technology. As we know, some therapists have developed "package" programs that are used in conjunction with microcomputers. Unfortunately, it has often been the case that those developing the computer programs have not always demonstrated the efficacy of those programs in controlled studies with well-documented cases. On the other hand, several investigations of efficacy, such as those described in these three chapters, have not taken full advantage of the computer technology available. It would seem to be worthwhile for the efficacy people to get together somehow with the computer people, so that we may ultimately be able to develop computer-assisted "packages" *of demonstrated value*. Without this collaboration, I fear the proliferation of these rather attractive and convenient "packages" without crucial demonstrations of efficacy.

With regard to methodology, particularly in the area of memory training, there has been some debate regarding the relative efficacy of "strategy training" (often using visual imagery and related mnemonics), as opposed to straightforward practice and rehearsal. I am pleased to see Goldman's endorsement of straight rehearsal methods, since our research group's own limited experience goes along well with that notion. In a recent study (Goldstein *et al.*, 1985), we were able to demonstrate satisfactory learning of specific materials in densely amnesic patients through three different methods of training, all of which involved some form of simple practice or rehearsal. Previous efforts with these patients indicated that while they were very good at performing mnemonic-device-related tasks, such as forming visual images or producing verbal elaborations, these skills were of absolutely no assistance to them in improving their memories. However, through extended practice, they were generally quite capable of learning the material we attempted to teach them. At the other end of the spectrum of impairment, more intact individuals may develop their own compensatory strategies, as Goldman has pointed out.

It would appear that the educational methodology used in rehabilitation is a crucial consideration, and is dependent to a large extent on the neuropsychology of the individual patient. Reading Luria's (1948/1963) book on restoration of function, one obtains a very detailed view of how precisely the educational method used may be fitted to the patient's pattern of impaired and preserved abilities. Thus, strategy training is not always good and rote rehearsal always bad, and vice versa. It depends upon the specifics of the patient's cognitive dysfunction. Thus, the patient who is as likely to forget a mnemonic device as the material one is attempting to teach would not appear to be a good candidate for strategy training. On the other hand, there seems little point in teaching a patient with a mild memory deficit limited amounts of information through slavish repetition, when the patient really requires information about how to learn and recall material more effectively. Indeed, even some of the methods developed for normal adults (e.g., Lorayne & Lucas, 1974) might be helpful with such patients.

With regard to the above-described considerations, it has always been a source of puzzlement to me why memory training has been chosen as a promising treatment modality for chronic alcoholics. The recent literature suggests that while these individuals have mild memory and learning deficits, their deficits in other areas, notably abstraction and complex problem solving, may be outstandingly severe. I am not denying the reality of chronic alcoholics' memory deficit, but rather am suggesting, as has been pointed out by Butters and Cermak (1980), that it might be quite subtle. On the other hand, the ability to solve problems requiring conceptual reasoning or the ability to shift or maintain sets during problem solving may be blatantly impaired. Perhaps part of the difficulty may be attributed to the emphasis DSM-III placed on memory impairment in the diagnosis of dementia, and in part to the residual confusion between chronic alcoholism and alcoholic Korsakoff's syndrome. While memory training might be quite appropriate as the treatment of choice for Korsakoff patients, its value appears to be questionable in the case of chronic alcoholism. There may be greener pastures in some of the areas of cognitive rehabilitation described in Goldman's chapter (e.g., visual–spatial learning). Indeed, Goldman's discussion of the nature of the neuropsychological deficits commonly found among chronic alcoholics suggests—correctly, I believe—that we are not dealing with a domain-specific function, but rather with a general deficit in the brain's capacity to process information. When an alcoholic fails a memory test, it may be because information is not being integrated specifically within the memory domain, but this processing failure may manifest itself in essentially any domain of cognitive function. This formulation would also appear to be consistent with the premature-aging hypothesis, since elderly people may share the same essential difficulty.

If these considerations are correct, it seems crucial that we conceptualize rehabilitation programs for chronic alcoholics in terms of attempting to achieve improved capacity to integrate information, rather than in terms of improvement in terms of some specific domain or instrumentality, such as memory, language, or perceptual–motor skills. In this way, the cognitive situation with the chronic alcoholic may be quite different from the case of the Korsakoff patient, or the patient with focal brain damage of other types. These considerations, in addition to their compatibility with the recently formulated premature-aging hypothesis, would also comport well with the older holistic concepts of brain function developed by Luria (1948/1963), K. Goldstein and Scheerer (1941), and their intellectual relatives. Indeed, K. Goldstein's concept of "impairment of the abstract attitude" may be another way of putting what Goldman describes as "efficient integration of information." After all, abstraction is the major tool by means of which we impose order on what might otherwise be a chaotic universe. The practical import of this is that cognitive rehabilitation of chronic alcoholics may achieve more pertinence (and, we may hope, success) through working with problem-solving activities of as complex a nature as the patients can absorb, rather than through working in some limited, domain-specific area. The problem-solving techniques training described briefly by Parsons in Chapter 14 seems promising in that regard.

Efficacy of Treatment and the Role of Motivation

When one is a discussant, it sometimes seems useful to attempt to view the scene from the perspective of someone not directly involved in the specifics of the area under consideration. From that stance, I think that the non-neuropsychologist might raise two major questions about the chapters in this section:

1. What benefits actually accrue from these training efforts when alcoholic patients following active treatment frequently resume drinking? Shouldn't the treatment focus be largely on eliminating or reducing the addiction to alcohol?

2. How does one expect alcoholics, or any other patient group for that matter, to sustain their rehabilitation efforts, particularly after leaving the inpatient phase of their treatment, if they are not sufficiently motivated to do so? Indeed, aren't some of the impairments noted on neuropsychological tests determined to some unknown extent by failures of motivation?

The first question may be answered in a simple and in a more complex manner. The simple answer is that many of the patients seen by clinical neuropsychologists are no longer active alcoholics. This situation is mainly the case for patients with frank dementia or Korsakoff's syndrome. As Parsons has indicated, patients who undergo cognitive rehabilitation therapy, or conventional inpatient therapy associated with lengthy periods of abstinence, and who resume drinking following treatment do not do as well as patients who remain abstinent. A more complex set of considerations relates to the notion that a smooth integration of cognitive retraining with conventional, abstinence-oriented treatment might in fact promote abstinence. Goldman's report that patients are provided with lectures and discussions and are asked to participate in verbal therapies during the point in treatment when they are least able to process information is not an isolated instance. It is a commonplace occurrence in time-limited inpatient programs. The stimulation provided by the cognitive training sessions might provide improved capacities for such patients to participate in treatment, without the lengthening of hospital stay that would be necessitated by waiting until natural recovery occurs. A related consideration is that the neuropsychological assessment might provide clinicians with information concerning the level of intellectual complexity the patients can absorb in verbal therapy. Surely, one does not help alcoholic patients alter their lifestyles in support of abstinence or reduction in consumption of alcohol when the information provided to support these changes is not comprehended or remembered. Without the need for resorting to an elaborate neuropsychological assessment, even a brief mental status examination would often suggest that newly admitted alcoholic inpatients are often not in a condition to absorb much new information, particularly if they are intoxicated at the time of admission. One strategy used in some settings is to do detoxification prior to admission to a formal alcoholism treatment program. However, even in these cases, one needs to be assured that the patient is sufficiently detoxified to integrate the content of the program.

With regard to the matter of motivation, two findings reported in this volume provide reasons for optimism. First, Parsons (see Chapter 8) has shown through the use of the Patient's Assessment of Own Functioning Inventory (PAOFI) that alcoholics do recognize their functional incapacities; they view themselves as less effective than nonalcoholics. Second, Parsons points out in Chapter 14 that his patients have enjoyed and appreciated their cognitive rehabilitation sessions, even petitioning the hospital director to provide more time for them. Thus, it would appear that chronic alcoholics appear to appreciate the realities of their cognitive impairments, and can accept remediation-oriented treatment.

The matter of motivation in the cognitive rehabilitation of brain-damaged patients has not received widespread attention (see Mello, Chapter 12, this volume), although the neuropsychological aspects of emotion and motivation have recently become matters of great interest (Heilman, Bowers, & Valenstein, 1985; Heilman & Satz, 1983). With regard to cognitive rehabilitation, most brain-damaged patients taken into treatment have some degree of awareness of their impairment, and the hope of recovery is sufficient to sustain them through a sometimes long and arduous rehabilitation program. These patients are in many respects not unlike patients with physical injuries, who will undergo many sessions of often uncomfortable if not painful exercise in order to recover the use of an arm or a leg. If it is the case that alcoholics are aware of their deficits and appreciate treatments offered to remediate them, then one might anticipate that their motives will be similar to those of most brain-damaged patients in the sense that they want to recover.

The first major exception here would appear to involve patients with severe concurrent psychopathology that has implications for motivation, such as major depression or schizophrenia, or dementia or amnesia that is sufficiently advanced to deprive the patients of their capacity to appreciate the presence of significant cognitive deficit. The other exception would involve those cases in which a neurological disorder has direct implications for the emotional–motivational system. Patients with right-hemisphere brain damage (Etcoff, 1986), limbic system lesions, and frontal lobe lesions often fall into that category. In the case of alcoholism-related disorders, the patient with Korsakoff's syndrome might be the clearest example of an individual whose neurological disorder has direct implications for the emotional–motivational system. In the case of chronic alcoholism, it would appear that this direct involvement is not a major consideration, except in those cases in which there is frank dementia.

There is, of course, the broader issue of the role of motivation in the general neuropsychology of alcoholism, and the implications of that role for treatment and rehabilitation. I think that we can dispense with the naive notion that alcoholics do poorly on neuropsychological tests because of some general apathy or failure of motivation. If that were the case, one would expect to find generalized impairment on tests, rather than the patterned impairment that is almost universally found. Even the Korsakoff patient can come up with an average Wechsler Adult Intelligence Scale IQ, despite devastating memory impairment. At a more sophisticated level, I think we are discovering that the attempt to separate motivational from cognitive determinants of task performance is a pseudoissue, because, in a manner of speaking, the brain does not make that separation. To borrow again from the research on Korsakoff patients, Butters (1981) mentions George Talland's belief that the Korsakoff patient's failure to code new information thoroughly and inability to organize a search for old information are both related to motivational and arousal deficits. This view makes perfectly good sense when one considers that the diencephalic lesions generally thought to be the basis for Korsakoff's syndrome are likely to interrupt the reticular activating system, as well as to be related to the memory impairment. Similarly, Luria's (1973) conceptualization of frontal lobe function clearly blurs artificial distinctions between motivation and cognition. For example, consider the following quotation: "The frontal lobes participate in the regulation of the activation processes lying at the basis of voluntary attention" (Luria, 1973, p. 189). Clearly, Luria is speaking in favor of a unity between arousal (motivational-level) and cognitive (attentional) processes. Many years ago, the cognitive psychologist Leeper (1948) made a remark to the effect that there is no cognition without emotion and no emotion without cognition.

These considerations suggest that chronic alcoholics may have a motivational difficulty, in the sense that the neurological consequences of the disorder may have implications for the arousal system as well as for cognitive processes. Such combinations are not at all unusual across a wide variety of neurological disorders. However, we have no evidence that alcoholics typically fail tests because of some motivational deficiency that exists at a high level of awareness (i.e., they are not faking). If such were the case, we would most likely see global rather than patterned deficit. The fact that alcoholics may be able to improve test performance under conditions of provision of external incentives is not inconsistent with these views, since salient external incentives could raise arousal levels and associated attentional processes. Thus, the clinician doing work of a rehabilitative nature with chronic alcoholics may wish to remain aware that these patients are likely to have limited arousal levels and that it may be necessary to take special precautions to maintain their attention during training. However, as Parsons has pointed out, these patients are typically aware of their deficits, and if Goldman's and Parsons's findings hold up, it would appear that they accept, appreciate, and enjoy cognitive retraining.

Interdisciplinary Integration of Treatment

The next general issue I would like to raise relates to integration of treatment efforts. The material presented in the three chapters under discussion does not make much mention of the context in which the cognitive treatment takes place. Obviously, these patients are receiving other treatments, but they are not described in detail. Parsons has interacted with therapists in the sense of relating neuropsychological test results to therapists' ratings, but nowhere else do we learn what the nature of the interaction is between the cognitive therapy and other treatments. For example, were the inpatients in Goldman's studies medication-free? It is not uncommon for alcoholic patients who have been in treatment for only 1 month to still be taking diazepam or a related compound, and in some settings lithium is commonly used with alcoholics. Was this the case in Goldman's studies, and, if so, what influence might it have had?

An area in which neuropsychologists might appropriately interact with other clinicians relates to the developing field of medical management of alcoholism. For example, there is a wide and growing variety of treatments for liver disorders, ranging from dietary control to transplantation. There have been some productive interactions between neuropsychologists and gastroenterologists, with sharing of information leading to establishment of potentially important connections between cerebral function and liver status. The endocrinological consequences of chronic alcoholism would appear to be a particularly fertile field to pursue, particularly in view of what is known about the relationships between endocrine function and the neurotransmitters. There are also numerous unfortunate interactions between alcohol consumption and various physical illnesses, notably cardiovascular disease and diabetes. These relationships produce crucial treatment and management consequences in certain patients. For example, the alcoholism therapist should have a thorough awareness of the possible consequences of alcohol use in diabetic patients.

In a more general sense, alcoholism would appear to represent a major interface between neuropsychology and health psychology or behavioral medicine. The health maintenance programs developed by practitioners in health psychology and behavioral medicine would appear to represent an exciting new approach to alcoholism treatment. The area of diet and nutrition would appear to be a particularly promising one. Another potentially important health-related consideration is that there is evidence that smoking increases during periods of alcohol consumption (Griffiths, Bigelow, & Liebson, 1976), and so alcohol use may potentiate the development of smoking-related diseases. Obviously, interactions with psychopharmacologists attempting to develop compounds effective in the treatment of alcoholism could potentially be quite productive.

The Future of Neuropsychology in Alcoholism Treatment

My last discussion point relates to the matter of obstacles to neuropsychology's impact on alcoholism treatment, and I make some suggestions here concerning how some of them may be circumvented. At this writing, it has only been a little over 25 years since Fitzhugh, Fitzhugh, and Reitan (1960) published their pioneering paper on adaptive abilities in hospitalized alcoholics. I have therefore found it interesting to review the chapter on alcoholism written by Zwerling and Rosenbaum (1959), published 1 year earlier, for the first edition of the *American Handbook of Psychiatry* (Arieti, 1959). The review of the work done with psychological tests mentions the Rorschach, the Thematic Apperception Test, and the field independence–dependence tests developed by Witkin and collaborators. Zwerling and Rosenbaum also cite a study in which human figure drawings, the Blacky Picture Test, the Wechsler–Bellevue, the Minnesota Multiphasic Personality Inventory, and several other brief tests were used. There is no mention whatsoever of neuropsychological tests in this review, nor of any implications the tests administered might have for brain function. There is another chapter in the *Handbook* largely devoted to acute and chronic alcohol-related brain disorders (Thompson, 1959), but here again, no neuropsychological research is cited. The situation reflected here apparently had two major implications. First, alcoholism was viewed in 1959 as a psychosocial or personality disorder, with psychoanalytic theory playing a major role in its conceptualization. Second, the role of the psychologist in alcoholism-related clinical practice was traditional in nature, involving diagnostic and personality evaluations that utilized standard tests, and providing traditional individual and group psychotherapy.

To the best of my knowledge, clinical neuropsychological assessment was invited into a limited number of alcoholism treatment programs as a research endeavor. The clinical aspects of those programs were generally psychosocially oriented, and appeared to involve the adoption of some combination of Alcoholics Anonymous and psychoanalytic philosophies. Later on, some behavioral and some pharmacologically oriented programs began to develop. Thus, when the neuropsychologists began reporting their findings concerning impaired cognitive function in alcoholics and to comment on the implications of these findings for brain function and for treatment, the clinical audience taking in these materials may not have been predisposed to view their alcoholic patients in the manner presented. Some of the interactions between neuropsychologists and other clinicians at that time therefore tended to be nonproductive in nature. The reasons for this appeared to be largely related to differing philosophies of alcoholism, or, as noted above in the discussion of neuropsychological consequences, there may have been different "images" of the alcoholic. It was also noted by some observers that the postulation of the presence of "brain damage" in middle-aged, clinically undemented alcoholics may have been threatening to some individuals.

The replications of the neuropsychological findings in many settings, and their widespread promulgation and acceptance, appear to have alleviated this problem to a great extent. As reported by Parsons and Goldman, their cognitive rehabilitation programs are taking place within the context of what are apparently relatively traditional alcoholism treatment programs. It would be highly instructive to find out how Parsons and Goldman accomplished that task, and what the reactions of their treatment teams were to the initiation of those programs. In any event, one suggestion for the field would involve establishment of model programs in major centers in which the capacity is available not only to do the treatment, but to evaluate efficacy and report findings.

In this very new area of cognitive rehabilitation of chronic alcoholism, it is probably not sufficient to do a neuropsychological assessment containing recommendations for rehabilitation, with the expectation that trained rehabilitation specialists, perhaps in some other facility, will read the report and carry out the recommendations. We do not have trained rehabilitation specialists in this area. The traditionally trained alcoholism counselor typically has no expertise in cognitive retraining, or in implementing, for example, any of the programs described in Goldman's chapter. At the moment, we as neuropsychologists have to do our own training, and will have to do so until a rehabilitation specialty is developed that has the expertise to manage the kinds of treatments discussed here. Thus, a second suggestion I would offer is that if the centers described above are established, they should contain training programs for rehabilitation specialists who wish to work with alcoholic patients.

When one considers the wide range of cognitive capacity seen in patients with alcoholism, ranging from essentially intact function to severe dementia or amnesia, it seems apparent that not all alcoholics can be treated within a single program or setting. Some of the difficulties I have experienced in putting together Wilson's chapter with the chapters by Goldman and Parsons seem to be related to the fact that very different kinds of patients are considered in these chapters. It is understood that the cognitive rehabilitation research coming out of rehabilitation hospitals may have significant implications for work with chronic alcoholics. However, that does not imply that patients who appropriately belong in rehabilitation hospitals should be sent to time-limited alcoholism treatment programs, nor is the reverse suggested. A related dilemma is that patients who are in primary need of cognitive rehabilitation and who are admitted to traditional alcoholism treatment programs may not find such treatment available. Even when neuropsychologists are present in such settings, they often are not in positions permitting them to make major decisions regarding the nature and orientation of the treatment program. Ideally, two conditions should obtain. First, when an alcoholic patient is being taken into treatment, some sort of triage procedure should be initiated so that the patient is sent to the appropriate setting. In our group's observation, there are three major possibilities. Patients with severe dementia or amnesia would probably benefit most from placement in a rehabilitation facility where remediation of cognitive dysfunction is the major consideration. Patients with major concurrent psychopathology should, at least initially, be sent to psychiatric programs designed to treat those conditions. The remaining patients would probably benefit most from the traditional short-term alcoholism treatment programs. Sometimes there are also patients who, on admission to a hospital for alcoholism treatment, demonstrate such severe and acute medical pathology that they may benefit most from immediate admission to a medical ward, following which they may go to some appropriate treatment or rehabilitation program for their alcoholism.

Second, I would hope that ultimately neuropsychologists begin to plan, organize, and implement rehabilitation programs of their own, based on their own research findings and theoretical frameworks. There are certainly models for such program development, notably that provided by Leonard Diller and his associates at the Rusk Institute and that established by Barbara Wilson at Rivermead Rehabilitation Centre. Outside of neuropsychology but within psychology as a whole, we have seen models of this kind of program building in the development of token economies (Kazdin, 1977) and in the extensive psychosocial program for schizophrenic patients developed by Paul and Lentz (1977). Such programs would be specifically designed for alcoholic and nonalcoholic patients whose primary treatment needs are in the cognitive rehabilitation area. I am not at all suggesting that cognitive rehabilitation is typically the treatment of choice for all chronic alcoholics; rather, for those chronic alcoholics whose major treatment need is cognitive rehabilitation, there should be available some specialized facility that is designed to meet that need. Neither am I suggesting that cognitive rehabilitation should move away entirely from the traditional alcoholism treatment program. As Goldman has indicated, this form of treatment can be effective in dispelling the cognitive dysfunction associated with toxicity, thereby possibly enhancing the efficacy of conventional treatment, and may be useful in other applications as well. What is to be avoided, however, is the not uncommon situation in which substantially demented or amnesic alcoholic patients are placed in a conventional alcoholism treatment program and gain little or no benefit from it because of their cognitive limitations. I am suggesting that such patients may be better served in neuropsychologically oriented rehabilitation settings in which their specific treatment needs may be met.

Summary

Neuropsychologists working in several centers have begun rehabilitation efforts aimed at direct remediation of the cognitive deficits often noted among alcoholic patients. Some of these deficits are transitory, but cognitive rehabilitation methods may have the potential of reducing them sooner than would happen by means of natural recovery processes. These methods can therefore be productively used in conjunction with traditional methods of inpatient treatment that address themselves to issues related to attaining abstinence or reduction in alcohol consumption. At the other end of the alcoholism continuum, methods have been devised to assist patients with severe and permanent memory and other cognitive disorders and to help them cope with their deficits. Some of this work has taken place in short-term inpatient treatment programs, while other aspects of it have been accomplished in rehabilitation hospitals. A problem for growth in this area of cognitive rehabilitation of alcoholics is seen as the diversity in patient populations that comes as a result of working in these diverse clinical settings. A second, related problem has to do with the necessity of developing interdisciplinary and interideological cooperation among those who work with alcoholic patients. It is recommended that the health care systems involved in the treatment of alcoholics develop some form of assessment system by means of which it will become possible to place patients in the appropriate clinical settings, in consideration of the pattern of directly alcohol-related, psychopathological, medical, and neuropsychological symptoms displayed by individual patients. Neuropsychologists should be prepared to take a leadership role in those cases in which cognitive dysfunction is a major treatment issue.

Acknowledgment

Indebtedness is expressed to the Veterans Administration for support of this work.

References

Arieti, S. (Ed.). (1959). *American handbook of psychiatry*. New York: Basic Books.

Brandt, J., Butters, N., Ryan, C., & Bayog, R. (1983). Cognitive loss and recovery in long term alcohol abusers. *Archives of General Psychiatry, 40*, 435–442.

Butters, N. (1981). The Wernicke–Korsakoff syndrome: A review of psychological, neuropsychological and etiological factors. In M. Galanter (Ed.), *Currents in alcoholism* (pp. 205–232). New York: Grune & Stratton.

Butters, N., & Cermak, L. S. (1980). *Alcoholic Korsakoff's syndrome: An information processing approach to amnesia*. New York: Academic Press.

Diller, L., & Gordon, W. A. (1981). Rehabilitation and clinical neuropsychology. In S. B. Filskov & T. J. Boll (Eds.), *Handbook of clinical neuropsychology* (pp. 702–733). New York: Wiley.

Etcoff, N. L. (1986). The neuropsychology of emotional expression. In G. Goldstein & R. E. Tarter (Eds.), *Advances in clinical neuropsychology* (Vol. 3, pp. 127–179). New York: Plenum.

Fitzhugh, L. C., Fitzhugh, K. B., & Reitan, R. M. (1960). Adaptive abilities and intellectual functioning in hospitalized alcoholics. *Quarterly Journal of Studies on Alcohol, 21*, 414–423.

Goldstein, G., & Ruthven, L. (1983). *Rehabilitation of the brain damaged adult*. New York: Plenum.

Goldstein, G., Ryan, C., Turner, S. M., Kanagy, M., Barry, K., & Kelly, L. (1985). Three methods of memory training for severely amnesic patients. *Behavior Modification, 9*, 357–374.

Goldstein, K., & Scheerer, M. (1941). Abstract and concrete behavior: An experimental study with special tests. *Psychological Monographs, 2* (Whole No. 239).

Griffiths, R. R., Bigelow, G. E., & Liebson, I. (1976). Facilitation of human tobacco self-administration by ethanol: A behavioral analysis. *Journal of the Experimental Analysis of Behavior, 25*, 279–292.

Heilman, K. M., Bowers, D., & Valenstein, E. (1985). Emotional disorders associated with neurological diseases. In K. M. Heilman & E. Valenstein (Eds.), *Clinical neuropsychology* (pp. 377–402). New York: Oxford University Press.

Heilman, K. M., & Satz, P. (Eds.). (1983). *Neuropsychology of human emotion*. New York: Guilford Press.

Kazdin, A. E. (1977). *The token economy: A review and evaluation*. New York: Plenum Press.

Leeper, R. A. (1948). A motivational theory of emotion to replace "emotion as disorganized response." *Psychological Review, 55*, 5–21.

Lorayne, H., & Lucas, J. (1974). *The memory book*. New York: Stein & Day.

Luria, A. R. (1963). *Restoration of function after brain injury* (B. Haigh, Trans.). New York: Macmillan. (Original work published 1948)

Luria, A. R. (1973). *The working brain*. New York: Basic Books.

Paul, G. L., & Lentz, R. J. (1977). *Psychosocial treatment of chronic mental patients: Milieu versus social-learning programs*. Cambridge, MA: Harvard University Press.

Roth, M. (1980). Senile dementia and its borderlands. In J. O. Cole & J. E. Barrett (Eds.), *Psychopathology in the aged* (pp. 205–232). New York: Raven Press.

Thompson, G. N. (1959). Acute and chronic alcoholic conditions. In S. Arieti (Ed.), *American handbook of psychiatry* (pp. 1203–1221). New York: Basic Books.

Wilson, B. A., & Moffat, N. (1984). *Clinical management of memory problems*. Rockville, MD: Aspen.

Zwerling, I., & Rosenbaum, M. (1959). Alcoholic addiction and personality (nonpsychotic conditions). In S. Arieti (Ed.), *American handbook of psychiatry* (pp. 623–644). New York: Basic Books.

SECTION FOUR

IMPLICATIONS FOR TREATMENT AND FUTURE RESEARCH DIRECTIONS

19

Discussion

Implications of Neuropsychological Research Findings for the Treatment and Rehabilitation of Alcoholics

BARBARA S. McCRADY

Introduction

This chapter addresses the interface between the findings on neuropsychological impairment in alcoholics and the delivery of treatment. To date, the vast wealth of neuropsychological literature on alcoholics has had virtually no effect on the ways in which treatment for alcoholics is planned, either on a programmatic or on an individual level. Researchers and clinicians who work in the area of neuropsychology and those who work in the treatment area have had little contact, and few researchers work in the areas of both neuropsychology and treatment of alcoholism. This chapter addresses practical issues related to assessment, treatment, and program planning for alcoholic patients, based on recent neuropsychological findings. The chapter briefly summarizes recent neuropsychological findings about alcoholism, then addresses the implications of these findings for the alcoholism health care delivery system and for individual treatment planning. The implications of the findings for treatment outcome research designs are also addressed.

Recent Neuropsychological Findings

Research on morphological changes in the brains of alcoholics, neuropsychological changes, and changes in performance on neuropsychological measures are covered in this section. Much of this work is addressed in detail in other chapters in this book, and is reviewed only briefly here.

Barbara S. McCrady. Rutgers Center of Alcohol Studies, Rutgers—The State University of New Jersey, Piscataway, New Jersey.

A number of recent studies using computerized tomography (CT) scans have reported clear differences between detoxified alcoholics and normals. For example, Bergman (Chapter 2, this volume) found cortical changes in 61% of male alcoholics and 52% of female alcoholics in his sample; changes in the lateral ventricles of 34% of male and 19% of female alcoholics; and changes in the third ventricles of 55% of male and 31% of female alcoholics. All subjects were detoxified, and were not drinking at the time of the assessment.

In studies of neuropsychological functioning, Porjesz and Begleiter (1985; see also Chapter 3, this volume) have studied evoked potential responses in alcoholics. Their work suggests that alcoholics, and the nonalcoholic preadolescent sons of alcoholic men, have abnormalities in certain components of the evoked potential response. Their work, along with that of Bergman and others, illustrates that there are clear changes in the brain structure and brain functioning of alcoholics. It is important to note that these differences have not been found for all subjects in their samples; this suggests that some alcoholics do not have brain damage, even after many years of heavy drinking.

Neuropsychological data also demonstrate deficiencies in some alcoholics. Alcoholics consistently perform more poorly than normal controls on the Block Design, Digit Symbol, and Object Assembly subtests of the Wechsler Adult Intelligence Scale (WAIS) (Parsons & Farr, 1981). When using standardized neuropsychological test batteries such as the Halstead–Reitan Neuropsychological Test Battery, alcoholics perform in the impaired range on the Category Test, Part B of the Trail Making Test, and the Tactual Performance Test (Parsons & Farr, 1981). When these deficits are examined more closely to determine the reasons for the poor performance, it appears that alcoholics may use inefficient problem-solving strategies, shift problem-solving sets too soon, or persist in using the same problem-solving set long after it is clearly ineffective. They also may use weak or inappropriate encoding strategies to learn new information, which makes later recall of the information extremely difficult (Goldman, 1983).

Other researchers have also pointed to problems in visual–motor coordination, as well as attention and concentration difficulties (Hansen, 1980). Inspection of the animal literature reveals that animals who have been maintained on nutritionally balanced diets, but who have consumed alcohol heavily, show impairment on avoidance and maze learning (Bauer, 1984). Bauer has suggested that these results imply that chronic alcoholics will show deficits on learning tasks, and may not respond to contingencies of reinforcement in ways that would be predicted by the usual laws of learning. It is important to emphasize that these impairments are noted not only by neuropsychological researchers, but also by alcoholics themselves. Parsons (Chapter 8, this volume) has reported that alcoholics perceive themselves as impaired in memory, language, perceptual–motor skills, and cognitive–intellectual tasks.

Important questions related to these observed deficits include when they occur, whether they recover over time, what the time course is for recovery, and whether there is a pattern of recovered and nonrecovered functions. In reviewing this literature, Goldman (1983; see also Chapter 15, this volume) notes that alcoholics show impairment in most areas during the first 1–2 weeks after stopping drinking. New verbal learning appears to recover fairly soon thereafter. Other areas show continued improvement, but deficits in short-term memory and paired-associates learning have been assessed as long as 5 years after treatment (Brandt, Butters, Ryan, & Bayog, 1983). In general, alcoholics will show the most impairment on tasks that require the processing of novel or complex information (Goldman, 1983). Porjesz and Begleiter's (1985) work suggests that recovery in brain stem evoked potentials occurs by approximately 3–4 months after drinking stops, but that deficits in cortical evoked potentials persist, and can even be detected in alcoholics who have been abstinent for 2–5 years.

As noted above, not all alcoholics in these studies show impairment on neuropsychological, neurophysiological, or morphological measures. Those subjects that show the most impairment on neuropsychological measures tend to be over 40 years of age (Goldman, 1983). Primary alcoholics (those who experience withdrawal symptoms, demonstrate tolerance to alcohol, have an early onset of heavy drinking and drinking problems, experience positive psychic effects from drinking, and were never social drinkers; see DeObaldia & Parsons, 1984) also show more severe impairment on these measures (Parsons, Chapter 8, this volume), are lower on educational achievements, and report more symptoms associated with childhood hyperkinesis and/or minimal brain damage. These findings, and the findings of Porjesz and Begleiter on the sons of alcoholics, raise questions about the etiology of the neuropsychological and physiological findings that are beyond the scope of this chapter. However, it should be noted that alcoholics who show deficits may have been impaired in some ways before ever drinking, and may also have brains that are more susceptible to the effects of alcohol.

It would be expected that if some alcoholics have poorly functioning brains while in treatment, the poor functioning should have some relationship to the outcomes of treatment. Data about the relationship between neuropsychological impairment and treatment outcome are scant. Two recent studies demonstrate a lack of consistency in the findings. Abbott and Gregson (1981) studied 106 alcoholic inpatients, assessing them after 6–14 days of abstinence. They found that their measure of cognitive dysfunction, the Patterned Cognitive Impairment Test, was one of the strongest predictors of time to first drink. In contrast, Walker and his colleagues (Walker, Donovan, Kivlahan, & O'Leary, 1983; see also Chapter 17, this volume) found that time to first drink was unrelated to neuropsychological functioning. They found a trend ($p < .06$) for patients high in neuropsychological functioning to be most likely to be abstinent 9 months after inpatient treatment in a Veterans Administration hospital, and also found that the highest-functioning patients had the best employment status at follow-up. They also postulated that neuropsychologically impaired alcoholics would have better outcomes if kept in a longer treatment program (7 weeks vs. 2 weeks), but this hypothesis was not supported by the results.

Both studies suggest a relationship between neuropsychological functioning at the start of treatment and ultimate treatment outcome, despite differences in the measures used and the timing of the testing. Abbott and Gregson's (1981) findings are stronger, and the reasons for the difference in the degree of relationship between neuropsychological status and treatment outcome are unclear.

In summary, it is clear that some alcoholics suffer either short-term or long-term cognitive deficits. Some of these deficits improve substantially over time, and some do not. Those persons who are most vulnerable to cognitive deficits appear to be over 40, and also appear, in terms of Parsons's classification, to be Primary rather than Secondary alcoholics.

The Alcoholism Health Care Delivery System

The alcoholism health care delivery system contains several components, including detoxification centers, residential rehabilitation programs (which are either free-standing or associated with hospitals), halfway houses, partial hospital programs, and outpatient programs. Employee assistance programs (EAPs) and programs for those convicted of driving while intoxicated (DWI) are newer additions to the complement of services. In addition, Alcoholics Anonymous (AA) should be included, although it is a self-help group and is not properly described as "treatment." The most visible and rapidly growing parts of this treatment system are the residential rehabilitation programs and EAPs.

Most residential rehabilitation programs use a fairly standardized treatment program, which is applied to all persons who come to the program. While the programs vary, they usually have several features in common. Most programs are 28–30 days in length, and have a fairly low staff-to-patient ratio. Most of the staff are paraprofessional alcoholism counselors. The programs usually begin with a physical examination and psychological assessment, and a short detoxification period (2–3 days for most patients). The backbone of these programs includes a large alcohol education component (as much as 10 hours per week or more of lectures), films about alcoholism, group therapy, use of confrontational techniques, and introduction to and involvement in AA. Most clients have an individual counselor, but counselors may have 10–12 patients assigned to them, and may run the group sessions and alcohol education programs as well as doing individual counseling. Insurance regulations support this treatment model, as many insurance policies cover a 28- to 30-day rehabilitation, and the many state laws that mandate insurance coverage for the treatment of alcoholism require 28–30 days of inpatient coverage per year (usually with a lifetime limit allowed).

These programs can be effective for some alcoholics (Alford, 1980). However, many alcoholics who participate in inpatient rehabilitation programs relapse after discharge. One of the reasons for the lack of success with some patients may be due to cognitive deficits that they exhibit in the early weeks of abstinence; these may make it difficult for them to absorb the information presented in the treatment program.

To alter the structure of rehabilitation programs would require several steps. First, since many alcoholics are fairly cognitively impaired in the first few weeks after they stop drinking, involving them in intensive treatment that requires the acquisition of a large amount of new knowledge is inappropriate. Programs that have a set length of stay should carefully screen clients for appropriateness for such a program; they should exclude those patients who show clear evidence of mild brain damage, and should take special care to evaluate patients who are over 40 and who are Primary alcoholics. Second, programs should allow for a longer detoxification period, because of the acute effects of alcohol on the brain and the acute changes in brain function in the first week after the initiation of abstinence. If any information is provided during that first week, it should be repeated later in the treatment to insure that it is presented at a time when the patient is likely to be able to learn and retain it.

For programs that are going to provide treatment to older alcoholics, who are likely to have significant cognitive impairments in the first few weeks after abstinence is initiated, several changes should probably be made in their structure. First, there is a need for a higher staff-to-patient ratio in such programs, since material may have to be presented differently, more often, and with more attention to the individual learning rate of each patient in the program. Second, such programs may have to develop a preprogram setting for patients who have slow cognitive recovery. A small group of patients can be placed in an environment in which they are well cared for in terms of physical needs, are prohibited from using alcohol, and are provided a congenial living arrangement. Beyond that, however, no treatment is provided. The cognitive functioning of patients who remain in this setting can be assessed and when they are functioning well enough to be able to benefit from a more structured program, they can then be transferred to the more intensive rehabilitation program. This model, of course, is exactly opposite to that of most rehabilitation programs, which provide intensive treatment first, followed by outpatient or halfway house treatment.

If such variability is to be introduced into the treatment system, both clinicians and insurance underwriters will have to be convinced of its wisdom. Such programs will become more costly, because of the longer length of stay and the higher staff-to-patient ratio. If it can be demonstrated, however, that such programs have a significantly greater success rate than traditional rehabilitation programs for this subgroup of alcoholics, then the savings in health care dollars over time should make the greater initial expenditures justifiable.

EAPs are another major component of the current alcoholism treatment system. EAPs usually have several components, including training supervisory staff in the identification of troubled employees; development of policies for handling employees with poor job performance; on-site or off-site presence of a counselor to work with troubled employees; referral to treatment programs; and posttreatment monitoring. Such programs have proliferated in recent years, in the hope that employees who are performing poorly on the job can get appropriate help and be able to return to work instead of being subjected to disciplinary action or dismissal. Such programs have been helpful to many employees, and many have found that their alcoholic employees can return to full job functioning after involvement in an EAP (Schramm, 1980). However, like their inpatient rehabilitative counterparts, EAPs have given little attention to the variability in their client population. In general, groups that market EAPs to companies sell them as ways to decrease costs and provide a humanitarian service at the same time. Rarely do such marketing campaigns address the issue of treatment failures. Since older employees who are alcoholics may have poorer outcomes, programs should address this issue, both in the marketing of the program and in planning services for such employees. If this is not done, the failures of EAPs could undermine the positive contributions they make.

Individual Treatment Planning

The preceding section addresses programmatic issues related to neuropsychological deficits in alcoholics. This section considers possible alterations in treatment that can be made by the individual practitioner.

The first implication is that a careful assessment must be made of each client who presents for treatment for a drinking problem. A careful diagnostic assessment should be made, in order to evaluate several areas. First, the issue of alcohol dependence versus alcohol abuse should be assessed. If the client is alcohol-dependent and requires supervised alcohol withdrawal, not only should this be arranged, but the clinician should also then be aware of the implications of alcohol dependence for the client's cognitive functioning. The client will be experiencing acute withdrawal symptoms for the first several days, and then subacute withdrawal symptoms for several weeks or months thereafter (Goldman, 1983). The nutritional and health status of the client should also be assessed, as nutritional deficits may also contribute to cognitive deficits (Porjesz & Begleiter, 1985). Third, the presence of Primary versus Secondary alcoholism should be assessed (DeObaldia & Parsons, 1984, give criteria with which to make this distinction), in order to assess the degree of risk for cognitive impairment. Finally, the clinician should assess whether the client has a past history of learning disabilities, which may interfere with the treatment. These areas should be assessed in addition to the usual areas that a clinician would assess when planning treatment for an alcoholic client (McCrady, 1985).

The second phase of treatment relevant to cognitive functioning should be an assessment of recovery-relevant skills. In the neuropsychological field, there has been a recent cry for ecologically relevant measures, and this is especially pertinent here. In the area of recovery from alcoholism, several skills that may be affected by neuropsychological functioning are probably necessary. There are currently virtually no good measures of any of these skill areas, and development of good measures for each skill would be a significant contribution. The skills include (1) the ability to remember information presented in treatment; (2) the ability to remember why drinking is a problem and why abstinence is necessary; (3) the ability to find the treatment program, find one's way around the treatment facility, and find AA meetings in the community; (4) the ability to associate names with faces of people met at AA or in group therapy; (5) the ability to listen to discussions and sort relevant from irrelevant information in therapy and group discussions; (6) the ability to identify situations that could provide difficulties in terms of maintaining abstinence; (7) the ability to generate ideas about how to handle drinking-related situations and to generate ideas about how to handle life problems that have arisen because of or independent of drinking; (8) the ability to select possible solutions to problems, try them out, evaluate their effectiveness as solutions, and assess other solutions if the first ones prove ineffective; (9) the ability to converse with people; and (10) the ability to recognize consequences of continued drinking and act accordingly. The possible list of such skills is long, and the ones given here represent only a sampling of recovery-relevant skills that may be affected by neuropsychological deficits.

My own clinical experience suggests that neuropsychologically impaired alcoholics have more difficulty with each of these skills. Treatment often becomes very redundant, with a clinician going over material repeatedly, while a patient reacts each time to the repeated information as if it were new. Such clients have extraordinary trouble applying treatment-acquired knowledge to new problems, and a clinician often has to show a client how to apply a skill to a new situation. Verbal behavior (e.g., "I'll do such-and-such") and situational behavior are often divergent, making the clinician's task difficult. Clinicians are often aware that these clients are different (e.g., Leber, Parsons, & Nichols, 1985), but it is tempting for a clinician to frame these problems as motivational deficits. Reframing the problems as learning deficits may make it easier for the clinician to work with such patients, and suggests a modified approach to treatment.

The individual clinician can assess a client's skill level in each of the above-listed areas, and then develop treatment interventions to teach the client those skills that the client is lacking. Treatment should not be a set length, but instead should continue until the client demonstrates mastery of the skill being taught. Once mastery is demonstrated in the treatment environment, then generalization to the natural environment will have to be carefully programmed, to assure generalization to actual relevant situations. Existing training procedures to teach drink-refusal skills (Foy, Miller, Eisler, & O'Toole, 1976), problem-solving skills (Marlatt, 1980), and drinking-related social skills (Chaney, O'Leary, & Marlatt, 1978) can be used and modified as appropriate for a population that has difficulty in learning new skills. The clinician, to be maximally effective, will probably do well to plan clear rewards for behavior change and for implementation of the new behaviors learned in treatment. Finally, the clinician should plan ways to maximize retention and utilization of the new skills after formal treatment is completed (Marlatt & Gordon, 1985).

Several ethical issues must be considered in the individual treatment of alcoholics. First, clinicians should provide accurate information to patients and their families when there is evidence of brain damage or cognitive impairment. That information should include the extent of the impairment, the probable course of recovery, the likelihood of continued impairment if drinking is resumed (Fabian & Parsons, 1983), and ideas about how to compensate for specific deficits. A clinician also has to make difficult ethical decisions if a client is found to have significant cognitive or visual–spatial impairment, even if the clinician believes that most of the impairment will abate with long-term abstinence. For example, if a client has a job in which visual–spatial impairment would seriously affect job performance, the clinician must decide what recommendations to make. A recommendation might be made that the client should not return to work for an extended period of time, or should seek alternative work in the same company or occupation. However, if a school bus driver or surgeon has serious visual–spatial deficits and refuses to delay returning to employment, then the clinician must decide what his or her responsibility is at that time. Detailed assessments lead to difficult choices for clinicians, but ones that must be made rather than ignored.

Research Issues

In addition to the many ways in which treatment should be altered to take neuropsychological findings into account, treatment research should also be altered in light of what is known. A difficult decision to be made in any treatment outcome research project concerns the timing of the initial data collection. Most good projects collect data after detoxification is complete, but early in treatment (up to 14 days after initiation of abstinence). For patients whose memory is still impaired in the first few weeks of abstinence, however, this early data collection could lead to data of poor validity. However, collecting data later could lead to the information's being contaminated by the treatment experience. Thus, early data collection is important, but the research team should attempt to insure that clients have adequate memory functioning before beginning baseline assessment. Whenever possible, the researchers should also obtain baseline data from collateral sources and should resolve any discrepancies, rather than merely retaining two different sets of baseline data.

Treatment outcome designs should also allow for the assessment of the impact of specific intervention strategies on specific cognitive or abstinence skills. Single-case experimental designs (Hersen & Barlow, 1976) are ideally suited to such assessments. A clinician might assess several deficit areas, and begin training in one area, while continuing to assess functioning in each of the skills areas of interest. A multiple-baseline design allows for the assessment of whether the specific intervention is affecting the skill targeted for intervention, and also allows for assessment of the overall rate of recovery in skills over time.

Finally, studies of recovery of neuropsychological function should use state-of-the-art treatment outcome research strategies. Emrick and Hansen (1985) have carefully detailed the elements of a good treatment research study in the alcoholism field. They recommend frequent collection of follow-up data, use of neutral interviewers, validation of client self-reports through use of multiple data sources, use of biological tests to assess outcomes (such as liver function tests), and other procedures. These standards should be applied to studies of the recovery of cognitive functioning in alcoholics, to assure that there is adequate information abut whether the subjects are drinking, abstinent, or drinking in a limited fashion during the follow-up period. Without such information, it is impossible to make reasonable inferences about recovery of neuropsychological functioning with abstinence.

Research Implications

This chapter has attempted to address the implications of neuropsychological findings for the actual treatment of alcoholics who are seeking help. Many ideas have been proposed, but all are untested. Research questions abound. First, it is still unclear whether the observed neuropsychological deficits have anything to do with the success or failure of treatment. The literature is mixed in this area, because of the varied measures used, the varied times of measurement, and the deficits measured. If the observed deficits are correlated with poorer treatment outcome, the mechanisms underlying these correlations will have to be isolated. In this chapter, I have proposed that the deficits are directly associated with skills required to maintain abstinence from alcohol, but the relationship between neuropsychological deficits and recovery-relevant skills has not been established. If these skills are associated with neuropsychological deficits, it is still not known whether these skills can be taught, and, if so, what training techniques would be most appropriate. If these skills are necessary to maintaining abstinence, it is an important practical issue to determine how best to get clients to stay abstinent while they are learning such skills. Perhaps use of sheltered environments, such as suggested earlier in the chapter, or the use of chemical agents such as disulfiram, would be appropriate. If these skills can be successfully taught, a next research question is whether or not teaching such recovery skills affects long-term treatment outcome. Finally, research is needed to develop better ways to identify for what clients these altered treatment methods are most important and most effective.

Summary

This chapter has argued that the findings of recent neuropsychological research have profound implications for the treatment of alcoholism. There are implications at several levels, including policy making, restructuring of the alcoholism health care delivery system, the planning of treatment for the individual alcoholic, and the designing of treatment outcome research in the alcoholism field. All of the ideas presented are just that—ideas, awaiting empirical tests.

References

Abbott, M. W., & Gregson, R. A. M. (1981). Cognitive dysfunction in the prediction of relapse in alcoholics. *Journal of Studies on Alcohol, 42,* 230–243.

Alford, G. S. (1980). Alcoholics Anonymous: An empirical outcome study. *Addictive Behaviors, 5,* 359–370.

Bauer, R. M. (1984). Alcohol-related memory and operant learning deficits: Current status and implications for alcohol research. *Bulletin of the Society of Psychologists in Substance Abuse, 3,* 11–19.

Brandt, J., Butters, N., Ryan, C., & Bayog, R. (1983). Cognitive loss and recovery in long-term alcohol abusers. *Archives of General Psychiatry, 40,* 435–442.

Chaney, E. F., O'Leary, M. R., & Marlatt, G. A. (1978). Skill training with alcoholics. *Journal of Consulting and Clinical Psychology, 46,* 1092–1104.

DeObaldia, R. D., & Parsons, O. A. (1984). Reliability and validity of the Primary/Secondary Alcoholism Classification Questionnaire and the HK/MBD Childhood Symptoms Checklist. *Journal of Clinical Psychology, 40,* 1257–1263.

Emrick, C. D., & Hansen, J. (1985). Thoughts on treatment evaluation methodology. In B. S. McCrady, N. E. Noel & T. D. Nirenberg (Eds.), *Future directions in alcoholism treatment research* (NIAAA Research Monograph 16, DHHS Publ. No. ADM 85-1322, pp. 137–172). Washington DC: U.S. Government Printing Office.

Fabian, M. S., & Parsons, O. A. (1983). Differential improvement of cognitive functions in recovering alcoholic women. *Journal of Abnormal Psychology, 92,* 87–95.

Foy, D. W., Miller, P. M., Eisler, R. M., & O'Toole, D. H. (1976). Social skills training to teach alcoholics to refuse drinks effectively. *Journal of Studies on Alcohol, 37,* 1340-1345.

Goldman, M. S. (1983). Cognitive impairment in chronic alcoholics: Some cause for optimism. *American Psychologist, 38,* 1045–1054.

Hansen, L. (1980). Treatment of reduced intellectual functioning of alcoholics. *Journal of Studies on Alcohol, 41,* 156–158.

Hersen, M., & Barlow, D. H. (1976). *Single case experimental designs.* Oxford: Pergamon Press.

Leber, W. R., Parsons, O. A., & Nichols, N. (1985). Neuropsychological test results are related to ratings of men alcoholics' therapeutic progress: A replicated study. *Journal of Studies on Alcohol, 46,* 116–121.

Marlatt, G. A. (1980). *Relapse prevention: A self-control program for the treatment of addictive behaviors.* Unpublished manuscript.

Marlatt, G. A., & Gordon, J. (Eds.) (1985). *Relapse prevention: Maintenance strategies in the treatment of addictive behaviors.* New York: Guilford Press.

McCrady, B. S. (1985). Alcoholism. In D. H. Barlow (Ed.), *Clinical handbook of psychological disorders: A step-by-step treatment manual* (pp. 245–298). New York: Guilford Press.

Parsons, O. A., & Farr, S. P. (1981). The neuropsychology of alcohol and drug use. In S. Filskov & T. Boll (Eds.), *Handbook of clinical neuropsychology* (pp. 320–365). New York: Wiley.

Porjesz, B., & Begleiter, H. (1985). Human brain electrophysiology and alcoholism. In R. Tarter & D. van Thiel (Eds.), *Alcohol and the brain* (pp. 139–182). New York: Plenum.

Schramm, C. J. (1980). Evaluating industrial alcoholism programs: A human-capital approach. *Journal of Studies on Alcohol, 41,* 702–713.

Walker, R. D., Donovan, D. M., Kivlahan, D. R., & O'Leary, M. R. (1983). Length of stay, neuropsychological performance, and aftercare: Influences on alcohol treatment outcome. *Journal of Consulting and Clinical Psychology, 51,* 900–911.

20

Research Directions: The Next Decade

NELSON BUTTERS
OSCAR A. PARSONS
PETER E. NATHAN

This volume has focused upon the neuropsychological impairment of alcoholics and the implications such cognitive disabilities may have for the diagnosis and treatment of alcoholism. The approaches assumed by the contributors to this volume have mirrored their varied, yet interconnected, research interests. The alcoholics' cognitive, neurological, and neurophysiological anomalies have been thoroughly described in a number of chapters. Although all contributors have recognized the potential neurotoxic effects of alcohol, many have also presented compelling evidence that genetic (i.e., family history of alcoholism), metabolic, and environmental variables may also play a major role in the cognitive status of a given alcoholic (for review, see Tarter & Alterman, 1984). Since these various factors affecting the alcoholics' cognitive–neurological disabilities have great import for our definition and treatment of alcoholism and for recovery of function with prolonged abstinence, it seems imperative that the final chapter of this volume be dedicated to clarifying and discussing these implications. If our didactic exercise is successful, this final chapter should serve as an excellent prognosticator of the next decade's research in the neuropsychology of alcoholism.

Nelson Butters. Psychology Service, San Diego Veterans Administration Medical Center, San Diego, California; Department of Psychiatry, University of California at San Diego School of Medicine, La Jolla, California.

Oscar A. Parsons. Oklahoma Center for Alcohol and Drug-Related Studies, Department of Psychiatry and Behavioral Sciences, University of Oklahoma Health Sciences Center, Oklahoma City, Oklahoma.

Peter E. Nathan. Rutgers Center of Alcohol Studies, Rutgers—The State University of New Jersey, Piscataway, New Jersey; Graduate School of Applied and Professional Psychology, Rutgers—The State University of New Jersey, New Brunswick, New Jersey.

Changes in Brain Structure and Cognitive Functions in Alcoholics

Since the availability of CT scans became widespread in the early 1970s, there have been numerous investigations of the extent of neurological damage associated with long-term alcoholism (Bergman, Chapter 2, this volume; Wilkinson, Chapter 5, this volume; Ron, Chapter 1, this volume). In general, there are a number of findings about which there is little disagreement. First, the CT scans of recently detoxified long-term alcoholics are characterized by a widening of frontal and parietal cortical sulci, and often of the lateral and third ventricles of the brain. Second, while these long-term alcoholics are impaired on problem-solving tasks, visuoperceptual tasks, and some memory tasks (especially those using nonverbal visual stimuli), correlations between specific tests (or functions) and anatomical structures seen on CT scans have been generally low and sometimes absent. In fact, in many investigations age, rather than alcoholism, has been shown to correlate best with linear measurements and/or computer-generated indices derived from CT scans. Third, despite some controversy about the reliability of early reports, it is now evident that extended abstinence leads to recovery of some behavioral functions and a significant reduction in brain abnormalities seen on CT scans. In some cases, significant correlations have been reported between these positive neuroradiological and cognitive changes.

Given these findings, what issues should dominate the next 10 years of research on the relationship of brain structure and cognitive function? Certainly, extensive attention will be paid to the recent evidence that individuals with a positive family history for alcoholism (FH+) are more likely to be impaired on neuropsychological (Parsons, Chapter 8, this volume; Schaeffer, Parsons, & Yohman, 1984) and electrophysiological (Begleiter, Porjesz, Bihari, & Kissin, 1984; Porjesz & Begleiter, Chapter 3, this volume) measures than are subjects with a negative family history for alcoholism (FH−). It is possible that FH+ and FH− alcoholics (and their nonalcoholic offspring) will evidence quantitative as well as qualitative differences both in their pattern of cognitive impairments and in brain morphology. The separation of alcoholics along this genetic dimension may reduce some of the "noise" that has contributed to the unimpressive brain–behavior correlations in alcoholics. The importance of family history for recovery also must be emphasized. If, as suggested by Parsons (Chapter 8, this volume) and by Porjesz and Begleiter (Chapter 3, this volume), the FH+ alcoholics have some subtle brain abnormalities prior to the commencement of their drinking history, their brains may be not only more vulnerable to the detrimental effects of ethanol, but also less likely to recover with abstinence. Such a finding would force us to reconsider treatment and rehabilitation plans when faced with long-term FH+ alcoholics.

In addition to family history, the role of numerous medical risk factors should receive close scrutiny in future studies. The degree to which abuse of multiple drugs, liver disease, affective illness, poor nutrition, and a prior history of hyperactivity and/or minimal brain damage have influenced the findings of neuropsychological and CT scan studies has not been determined (Tarter & Alterman, 1984). Although it is unlikely that all of the cognitive and brain changes noted by Bergman (Chapter 2, this volume), Ron (Chapter 1, this volume), Wilkinson (Chapter 5, this volume), and Risberg and Berglund (Chapter 4, this volume) can be attributed to these medical factors, we need to know for practical clinical purposes how these variables interact with the neurotoxicity of ethanol. The possibility that even mild intermittant liver dysfunction may increase the severity of cognitive impairment (and CT scan abnormalities) and reduce the rate of cognitive recovery is critical, for both scientific and clinical reasons.

One additional point concerning the measurement of brain function should be made. Although we have been discussing CT scans in these predictions of future research directions, it is evident that recent advances in neuroradiological technology will soon result in the adoption of magnetic resonance imaging (MRI) for studies of brain–behavior relationships. Besides eliminating possible health hazards associated with radiation, MRI will provide pictures with greatly improved resolution and demarcation of specific neuroanatomical structures. There will be increased certainty that measures of tissue density emanate from the specific structures being studied, and investigators will be able to identify structural abnormalities (e.g., small strokes) not visible with even the most recent generation of CT scanners. Paralleling the shift from CT to MRI technology will be the increased utilization of blood flow and positron emission tomography (PET) scan techniques to provide a "dynamic" view of the alcoholic's brain (Risberg & Berglund, Chapter 4, this volume). When sophisticated neuropsychological and MRI measures are combined with dynamic images of brain functioning, much will be learned about structural abnormalities and about compensatory brain mechanisms that develop with recovery of functions. The use of PET and blood flow techniques to evaluate the brain functioning of individuals with FH+ and FH− backgrounds is yet another unattempted but fascinating venture.

Brain–Behavior Relationships in Alcoholics with Korsakoff's Syndrome

The inclusion of research on alcoholic Korsakoff's syndrome in a volume dedicated to the clinical implications of neuropsychological studies of alcoholism may seem inappropriate to some readers. Such prejudice has its origins in the traditional view that alcoholism and Korsakoff's syndrome represent two separate, unrelated disorders. To some clinicians and investigators, Korsakoff's syndrome is etiologically related to the acute, adverse effects of thiamine deficiency, not to the neurotoxic effects of alcohol (Victor, Adams, & Collins, 1971). However, as Butters and Granholm (Chapter 9, this volume) have noted, the demonstrations that alcohol is neurotoxic and that long-term alcoholics and alcoholic Korsakoff patients have similar problem solving and visuoperceptual impairments question the generality of this traditional teaching. Furthermore, the CT scan findings reported in several chapters of this book (Bergman, Chapter 2; Wilkinson, Chapter 5; Ron, Chapter 1) raise questions about Victor *et al.*'s (1971) claim that the Korsakoff patients' severe amnesia is due to a series of acute hemorrhages in the medial diencephalon. The consistent findings that long-term (non-Korsakoff) alcoholics have significant dilation of the third ventricle and low computer-generated density measures in the diencephalic tissue surrounding this ventricle (Gebhardt, Naeser, & Butters, 1984) suggest that hemorrhagic lesions within the diencephalon may be more pervasive than neuropathological examinations limited to the brains of Korsakoff patients have led us to believe.

To compare the brains of long-term alcoholics and of Korsakoff patients will require a major neuropathological investigation. Arendt, Bigl, Arendt, and Tennstedt's (1983) report that Korsakoff patients, but not alcoholics, have significant neuronal loss in the basal forebrain represents an intriguing first step. However, since Arendt *et al.* limited their examination to the basal forebrain and globus pallidus, there is still no indication whether long-term (non-Korsakoff) alcoholics with mild memory deficits have the hemorrhagic diencephalic lesions that many assume are the hallmark of the alcoholic Korsakoff population. Needless to say, a convincing demonstration that long-term alcoholics and alcoholics with Korsakoff's syndrome have similar cortical and diencephalic neuropathology will force us to re-examine our conceptions about the development of alcoholics' cognitive deficits, as well as many of the conclusions about brain–behavior (e.g., medial diencephalon–amnesia) relationships drawn from studies limited to Korsakoff patients. The suggestion made by Butters and Granholm (Chapter 9, this volume) that the critical lesion in alcoholic Korsakoff's syndrome may involve several basal forebrain structures (and consequently the cholinergic system) may prove to be more than idle speculation.

By stressing the need for large-scale neuropathological studies of the brains of alcoholics, we do not wish to imply that future neuropsychological studies of the memory, visuoperceptual, and problem-solving deficits of alcoholic Korsakoff patients are unnecessary. Quite the contrary: Despite the multitude of investigations that have appeared since Talland's (1965) classic volume, there are numerous issues left to be determined (Cermak, Chapter 10, this volume; Oscar-Berman, Chapter 13, this volume). For example, how do the patients' encoding and episodic-memory deficits (Cermak, 1984 and Chapter 10, this volume) interact with their attentional–motivational deficiencies (Oscar-Berman, Chapter 13, this volume)? Also, how do the information-processing deficits underlying the Korsakoff patients' amnesia differ from those responsible for the severe memory disorders of patients with other neurological disorders (e.g., Alzheimer's disease, herpes encephalitis, Huntington's disease)?

Subtypes of Alcoholics and Neuropsychological Deficits

The studies covered in preceding chapters give ample indication of the presence of neuropsychological deficits in alcoholics. In country after country, laboratory after laboratory, groups of alcoholics have proved to be significantly impaired when compared with nonalcoholics. However, it is important to note that neuropsychological impairment is not found in all alcoholics. It has been estimated that from 30% to 50% of the alcoholics will perform within the normal range for controls (Parsons, in press). This raises the problem of specifying individual-difference variables that may be predictive of impairment in alcoholics—a research area that will receive much attention during the next decade.

Data set forth in the preceding chapters suggest that the amount and kinds of neuropsychological deficits manifested by alcoholics are dependent upon a number of patient characteristics. As Bergman, Ron, and Wilkinson have pointed out in their chapters, two major types of neuropsychological deficits, each associated with its own pattern of neuropathological findings, have been tentatively identified in alcoholics. One pattern is characterized by memory deficits and CT scan evidence of subcortical changes. The other pattern involves primarily visuoperceptual, abstracting, and problem-solving behaviors and is associated with cortical changes. Investigation of the reliability and validity of the identification of these two types of patients on the basis of their neuropsychological performance, across laboratories, could result in a subclassification of alcoholics that might be useful in diagnosis and treatment.

Another approach that has potential for subclassification is that of family history for alcoholism. As noted by Parsons in Chapter 8, there is evidence for a variety of differences, including performance on neuropsychological tests, between FH+ and FH− male alcoholics and nonalcoholics. A recent study conducted by Turner (1985) in Parsons's laboratory suggests that the family history variable gives rise to similar neuropsychological differences in female alcoholics. Indeed, the difference between alcoholics and nonalcoholics in Turner's study were almost completely attributable to the FH+ group; FH− alcoholics did not differ from controls. Given these findings, many questions arise. Are the FH+ and FH− alcoholics differentially distributed with regard to the two types of neuropsychological deficits mentioned earlier? If so, does the sex of the patient make any difference? Are FH+ females more susceptible to one or the other type of deficit, compared to FH+ males? If the work of Cloninger and his colleagues, referred to by Williams (Chapter 6, this volume), is any criterion, we can expect to find complex interactions among family history, gender, and neuropsychological deficit that will take time and patience to resolve.

Research questions similar to those proposed for the family history variable can also be asked about the subtypes of alcoholics that are based on the Primary–Secondary Scale (Tarter, McBride, Buopane, & Schneider, 1976). In addition, one of the consistent findings with this scale in alcoholics is that Primaries have significantly higher self-reported childhood symptoms of hyperkinesis and minimal brain dysfunction. These symptoms strongly suggest that many alcoholics have an attention deficit disorder as children. Furthermore, there is a positive relationship between Primary–Secondary alcoholism and a positive family history of alcoholism. In light of the report that one-third of the male alcoholics in several treatment units were found to have residual attention deficit disorders (Wood, Wender, & Reimherr, 1983), the unraveling of the determinants of the relationships among Primary–Secondary alcoholism, family history of alcoholism, and the presence of attention deficit disorders should contribute to our theoretical and empirical understanding of subgroup heterogeneity in alcoholics. In this regard, Oscar-Berman's suggestions in Chapter 13 of this volume concerning the possible relationship among childhood learning disabilities, right-hemisphere dysfunction, and the neuropsychological findings in alcoholics are particularly worthy of investigation.

The final "subtype" of alcoholics that remains to be investigated in the future is based on possible differences between alcoholics who differ in motivational patterns as a function of personality or psychopathological states. Goldstein (Chapter 11, this volume) has presented a lucid account of how such dimensions and their correlated motivational patterns might be related to neuropsychological deficits. Both Goldstein and Mello (Chapter 12, this volume) emphasize that the relationship of motivation to performance in neuropsychological experiments has not received the attention it deserves. Indeed, except for Oscar-Berman's studies of Korsakoff patients (where alcoholics are used mainly as a reference group), we have been unable to find any studies that have directly addressed this issue by experimentally manipulating motivation in detoxified alcoholics. Such studies would be of decided importance. Suppose alcoholics were to improve their performance under incentive conditions to a greater extent than controls; this would certainly suggest that the performance deficit is, in part, attributable to altered motivational patterns, as opposed to cognitive deficits per se. If, on the other hand, alcoholics under incentive conditions were to improve less than controls, or parallel increments in performance were to be found in the two groups, motivational variables could not account for the neuropsychological impairments.

DSM-III Diagnoses and Neuropsychological Deficits

One tangible example of the potential importance of neuropsychological findings for improvements in the reliability and utility of diagnosis can be found in current plans for the revision of the "substance use disorders" section of the *Diagnostic and Statistical Manual of Mental Disorders*, third edition (DSM-III; American Psychiatric Association, 1980). The group charged with revising this section of the taxonomy for DSM-III-R, the forthcoming revision of DSM-III, recommended elimination of the distinction DSM-III makes between "alcohol abuse" and "alcohol dependence." The DSM-III diagnosis of "alcohol dependence" is made when patients report having experienced either withdrawal symptoms or tolerance phenomena, in addition to the pathological combination of alcohol use and adverse interpersonal, vocational, or personal consequences that together define DSM-III's "alcohol abuse."

This basic change in the "substance use disorders" nomenclature stems from the inability of clinicians using the DSM-III criteria for "alcohol dependence" and "alcohol abuse" to differentiate one reliably from the other. Tolerance and withdrawal symptoms, it seems, are the principal culprits; it turns out to be extremely difficult to differentiate these phenomena from other alcohol-related behaviors they resemble (including hangover and non-tolerance-related increases in alcohol consumption or changes in drinking pattern).

It seems reasonable to anticipate, based in part on data already reviewed in this volume, that neuropsychological changes specific to the alcohol dependence syndrome, and hence not a part of the alcohol abuse syndrome, might ultimately be identified. Accordingly, it also seems reasonable to anticipate the development of assessment measures during the next decade that will permit more reliable differentiation of alcohol abuse syndromes from more serious alcohol dependence syndromes on the basis, in part, of identification of characteristic differences between the two syndromes in neuropsychological functioning. Such nosological distinctions should ultimately lead to the development of differentially effective approaches to treatment for the two groups of patients.

The advances in understanding of neuropsychological correlates and effects of alcohol dependence suggested by findings discussed elsewhere in this volume have another important consequence for diagnosis that is at variance with the scenario envisioned above. This consequence derives from the potential these findings might have for confirmation or disconfirmation of the so-called "alcohol dependence syndrome" described by Edwards and his colleagues (Edwards & Gross, 1976; Stockwell, Hodgson, & Edwards, 1979). In their explication of the alcohol dependence syndrome, Edwards and his coworkers explicitly reject the decision of the drafters of DSM-III to dichotomize "alcohol abuse" and "alcohol dependence," and, by so doing, to act as though there were not great overlap between the two syndromes. By contrast, Edwards and his colleagues believe that the process of dependence lies along a continuum of severity, with mild dependence corresponding to what some have called "problem drinking" and severe dependence corresponding to what is called "alcoholism." Those who are more severely dependent experience more symptoms of dependence, have experienced them for longer periods of time, and experience them as more troublesome and more debilitating.

If, as seems entirely possible, points along the continuum of alcohol dependence correspond to constellations of neuropsychological dysfunction associated with abusive drinking, then it ought to be possible to link the behavioral and neuropsychological consequences of abusive drinking, in order to enable a more precise and replicable placement of patients along the continuum of alcohol dependence. If such greater precision in placement along the continuum then proves to be useful in treatment planning, the utility of this linkage would be enhanced. It is also likely that the data-based dimensionalization of the alcohol dependence syndrome permitted by this anticipated linkage of neuropsychological and behavioral findings would terminate the unreliable distinction between problem drinkers and alcoholics that the drafters of DSM-III attempted to operationalize and the drafters of DSM-III-R have subsequently rejected.

Recovery of Cognitive Functions

The importance of investigating the natural course of recovery from neuropsychological deficits in alcoholics cannot be overemphasized. If it could be demonstrated that abstinent alcoholics ultimately recover to normal age- and education-appropriate levels of cognitive functioning, and if the time course were known for each type of cognitive function involved, many obvious clinical and theoretical problems would be resolved (Parsons, Chapter 14, this volume). As reviewed earlier, alcoholics do manifest recovery of certain functions, especially if one institutes practice on relevant tasks early in the recovery process (Goldman, 1983 and Chapter 15, this volume). However, cross-sectional studies of alcoholics indicate that even after 4 or 5 years of abstinence, they continue to manifest deficits in some areas of cognitive functioning (Brandt, Butters, Ryan, & Bayog, 1983; Fabian & Parsons, 1983). These findings have recently received support in a cross-sectional study of recovering alcoholics in Alcoholics Anonymous (DeSoto, O'Donnell, Allred, & Lopes, 1985). In this study, a symptom checklist was given to groups of male and female alcoholics who varied as to years of abstinence. After 2, 5, and even 10 years of abstinence, the percentage of alcoholics claiming symptoms of cognitive dysfunction (memory problems, concentration difficulties, and mind "going blank") was quite significantly higher than that reported in the general population. This finding occurred despite the demonstration that in the group abstinent for 10 years or more, scores on nine primary symptom dimensions (e.g., depression, anxiety, psychoticism, etc.) were in the normal range.

However, the conclusion that residual impairments in abstinent alcoholics are present 5 or 10 years later is open to the criticism that some alcoholics may have premorbid cognitive deficits, especially if they come from FH+ families (Schaeffer *et al.*, 1984). In other words, these FH+ alcoholics may have had some mild deficits in cognitive abilities (e.g., memory, abstracting, or problem-solving abilities) before they developed their alcoholism. After 4–5 years of abstinence, they may have recovered from the effects of alcohol abuse and returned to their premorbid level of mild cognitive deficits. This question could be addressed by a long-term longitudinal study. A large random sample of the population could be administered neuropsychological tests at adolescence and repeat tests at intervals over several decades. Those who developed alcoholism could then be compared with those who did not, and the possibility of premorbid cognitive deficits in alcoholics as a function of family history could be tested. Obviously, this would be a long-term and very costly project. However, there is a precedent. The current Rutgers Health and Human Development Project (Pandina, Labouvie, & White, 1984), investigating alcohol and drug use patterns in a large random sample of New Jersey adolescents ($n = 1381$), could provide this type of information if continued for several decades.

Alternatively, a large-scale cross-sectional study could be designed and modeled after the studies of Brandt *et al.* (1983) and DeSoto *et al.* (1985). FH+ and FH− recovering alcoholics, placed into groups according to their years of abstinence, would be administered cognitive neuropsychological tests. If the differences between the FH− alcoholics and peer nonalcoholic controls on cognitive tests were to decrease and disappear as years of abstinence increased, while in the FH+ alcoholics the differences with respect to the controls were to remain stable over years of abstinence, the possibility of mild premorbid cognitive impairment in a substantial subgroup of alcoholics would be enhanced.

Neuropsychological Findings and the Treatment of Alcoholism

By now, considerable data have accumulated that make the telling point that kind, content, locus, and intensity of treatment for alcoholism are generally unrelated to outcome of treatment for alcoholism (Nathan & Skinstad, in press; Saxe, Dougherty, & Esty, 1985; Vaillant, 1983). Such treatment factors as theoretical orientation of therapist and therapy, locus of treatment (whether the patient is treated as an inpatient or outpatient), and identity and training of primary therapist (whether treatment is provided by paraprofessionals who have had little formal education in alcoholism or by doctoral-level psychologists or psychiatrists) all turn out to be less important to treatment outcome than the resources the patient brings to treatment. These resources include degree of motivation, social and interpersonal competence, vocational and family status, and concurrent psychopathology (Pattison, 1985; Polich, Armor, & Braiker, 1981; Vaillant, 1983).

When these data on the relative unpredictability of treatment outcome from factors specific to treatment are considered in conjunction with data demonstrating that neuropsychological deficit is an even more frequent consequence of abusive drinking than many have believed, the situation appears serious indeed. As emphasized in part by Donovan, Walker, and Kivlahan (Chapter 17, this volume), the neuropsychological deficits that accompany alcoholism seem to exert their major impact on the very factors that seem to affect treatment outcome most significantly (e.g., vocational functioning, continued involvement with family and friends, ability to function independently, psychopathological status), even while having little or no impact on factors that do not seem to affect treatment outcome so strongly (e.g., kind, duration, or intensity of the intervention).

Is there something that research during the coming decade might do to confront this curious problem? One research focus that comes to mind is a detailed evaluation of the extent to which mild and moderate neuropsychological deficits, in contrast to severe deficits, affect the ability to maintain intact those behaviors of positive prognostic value. As elaborated in this volume by Goldstein (Chapter 18), McCrady (Chapter 19), and Wilson (Chapter 16), the development of skills training programs designed specifically to help the neuropsychologically impaired alcoholic maintain or return to adequate functioning in those areas with positive recovery potential may prove to be vital.

Vaillant (1983) has written extensively and influentially about "the natural healing process" that he believes is central to the process of recovery from alcoholism. His view is that treatment administered by others is generally ineffective in inducing abstinence from alcohol. Instead, Vaillant affirms, the alcoholic himself or herself must provide the healing—and Vaillant specifies the factors he feels are associated with this healing.

There is a clear need to test the validity of Vaillant's conclusions and to evaluate the means by which many alcoholic patients heal themselves, without intervention by others. Finally, we should try to determine the extent to which neuropsychological impairments associated with long-term alcohol abuse interfere with the natural healing process, just as we must assess the extent to which cognitive deficits interfere with treatment by others. To this end, a number of the elements of natural healing Vaillant identifies could be vulnerable to interference by neuropsychological impairment. Such proposed natural healing elements as the development of a new, alcohol-free social system, capacity to seek out and utilize long-term social and psychological support, and ability to adhere to a positive addiction all seem vulnerable to the effects of moderate to severe cognitive dysfunction.

References

American Psychiatric Association. (1980). *Diagnostic and statistical manual of mental disorders* (3rd ed.). Washington, DC: Author.

Arendt, T., Bigl, V., Arendt, A., & Tennstedt, A. (1983). Loss of neurons in the nucleus basalis of Meynert in Alzheimer's disease, paralysis agitans and Korsakoff's disease. *Acta Neuropathologica, 61*, 101–108.

Begleiter, H., Porjesz, B., Bihari, B., & Kissin, B. (1984). Event–related brain potentials in boys at risk for alcoholism. *Science, 225*, 1493–1496.

Brandt, J., Butters, N., Ryan, C., & Bayog, R. (1983). Cognitive loss and recovery in long-term alcohol abusers. *Archives of General Psychiatry, 40*, 435–442.

Cermak, L. S. (1984). The episodic–semantic distinction in amnesia. In L. R. Squire & N. Butters (Eds.), *Neuropsychology of memory* (pp. 55–62). New York: Guilford Press.

DeSoto, C. B., O'Donnell, W. E., Allred, L. J., & Lopes, C. E. (1985). Symptomatology in alcoholics at various stages of abstinence. *Alcoholism: Clinical and Experimental Research, 9*, 505–512.

Edwards, G., & Gross, M. (1976). Alcohol dependence: Provisional description of a clinical syndrome. *British Medical Journal, 1*, 1058–1061.

Fabian, M. S., & Parsons, O. A. (1983). Differential improvement of cognitive functions in recovering alcoholic women. *Journal of Abnormal Psychology, 92*, 87–95.

Gebhardt, C. A., Naeser, M. A., & Butters, N. (1984). Computerized measures of CT scans of alcoholics: Thalamic region related to memory. *Alcohol, 1*, 133–140.

Goldman, M. (1983). Cognitive impairment in chronic alcoholics: Some cause for optimism. *American Psychologist, 38*, 1045–1054.

Nathan, P. E., & Skinstad, A. H. (in press). Alcoholism treatment outcome: Current methods, problems and results. A survey and methodologic critique. *Journal of Consulting and Clinical Psychology*.

Pandina, R. J., Labouvie, E. W., & White, H. R. (1984). Potential contributions of the life span developmental approach to the study of adolescent alcohol and drug use: The Rutgers Health and Human Development Project, a working model. *Journal of Drug Issues*, 253–268.

Parsons, O. A. (in press). Intellectual impairment in alcoholics: Persistent issues. *Acta Psychiatrica Scandinavica.*

Pattison, E. M. (1985). The selection of treatment modalities for the alcoholic patient. In J. H. Mendelson & N. K. Mello (Eds.), *The diagnosis and treatment of alcoholism* (pp. 189–294). New York: McGraw-Hill.

Polich, J. M., Armor, D. J., & Braiker, H. B. (1981). *The course of treatment: Four years after treatment.* New York: Wiley-Interscience.

Saxe, L., Dougherty, D., & Esty, K. (1985). The effectiveness and cost of alcoholism treatment: A public policy perspective. In J. H. Mendelson & N. K. Mello (Eds.), *The diagnosis and treatment of alcoholism* (pp. 485–539). New York: McGraw-Hill.

Schaeffer, K. W., Parsons, O. A., & Yohman, J. R. (1984). Neuropsychological differences between male familial and nonfamilial alcoholics and nonalcoholics. *Alcoholism: Clinical and Experimental Research, 8*, 347–351.

Stockwell, R., Hodgson, R., & Edwards, G. (1979). The development of a questionnaire. *British Journal of Addiction, 74*, 79–87.

Talland, G. A. (1965). *Deranged memory*. New York: Academic Press.

Tarter, R. E., & Alterman, A. I. (1984). Neuropsychological deficits in alcoholics: Etiological considerations. *Journal of Studies on Alcohol, 45*, 1–9.

Tarter, R. E., McBride, H., Buopane, N., & Schneider, D. U. (1977). Differentiation of alcoholics: Childhood history of minimal brain dysfunction, family history, and drinking pattern. *Archives of General Psychiatry, 34*, 761–768.

Turner, J. R. (1985). *Verbal and nonverbal abstracting and problem-solving abilities, familial alcoholism and primary and secondary alcoholism in female alcoholics*. Unpublished master's thesis, University of Oklahoma Health Sciences Center.

Vaillant, G. E. (1983). *The natural history of alcoholism*. Cambridge, MA: Harvard University Press.

Victor, M., Adams, R. D., & Collins, G. H. (1971). *The Wernicke–Korsakoff syndrome*. Philadelphia: F. A. Davis.

Wood, D., Wender, P. H., & Reimherr, R. W. (1983). The prevalence of attention deficit disorder, residual type, or minimal brain dysfunction, in a population of male alcoholic patients. *American Journal of Psychiatry, 140*, 95–98.

INDEX